Dear Student:

You have chosen to begin a career as a business professional by majoring in a business discipline. If your experience is anything like mine, you will not regret your choice. Working in business leads to fulfilling and enjoyable experiences and relationships with interesting, quality people. Working in a company you admire that sells products or services in which you believe will enable you to feel positive about yourself, your contributions, and your professional life.

The overall purpose of this book is to help you prepare for success in your business career. In writing the book, I kept in mind three goals:

1. To explain how you can use information systems to solve problems and make better decisions in business.
2. To show you how to increase your utility (and marketability) in business by applying knowledge of information systems.
3. To describe, in the context of management information systems (MIS), how you can become a better business professional.

Notice the emphasis is on *you*. It's up to you to prepare yourself. No particular book, no course, no professor, no TA can do it for you. However, many people have worked hard to structure this book so that you can maximize the benefit from your study time.

To help you achieve your goals, we have included three unique features in this book. First, every chapter and every chapter extension is organized around a set of questions. Use these questions to manage your study time. Read until you can answer the questions. Second, every part and every chapter begins with a real-life scenario of a business professional who needs knowledge of information systems. Use those scenarios to understand how you can apply the knowledge of information systems to gain a personal competitive advantage. Finally, read the two-page boxed inserts, called "Guides." If possible, discuss the questions in these guides with other students. Such discussions will give you a chance to practice your listening skills and to learn to assert your own opinions in an effective manner.

Like all worthwhile endeavors, this course is work. That's just the way it is. No one succeeds in business without sustained focus, attention, desire, motivation, and hard work. It won't always be easy, it won't always be fun. On the other hand, you will learn concepts, skills, and behaviors that will serve you well throughout your business career.

I wish you, as an emerging business professional, the ve

D1444893

Seattle, Washington

THE GUIDES

Each chapter includes two *unique* guides focused on the issues in information systems that are currently most relevant. In each chapter, one deals with ethics, and the other deals with an issue related in some other way to the chapter topic. (Some of the chapter extensions contain one or more guides as well.) In business, you'll deal with issues similar to those presented and discussed in the guides, and you may be asked to recommend solutions to these problems. Each guide includes questions intended to stimulate thought, discussion, and active participation to help you develop your problem-solving skills.

Ethical issues abound in business, and as recent news stories indicate, some businesspeople are better than others at sorting through ethical conflicts. The "Ethics Guides" stimulate debate on how ethics apply to information systems issues. These guides will help you respond to future ethical dilemmas authentically and in a way that is consistent with your own values.

The other guides tackle topics that will help improve the quality of your thinking, which will improve any information system that you use and your ability to use MIS in your career.

Some present ideas from cognitive science and apply them to MIS. Others introduce you to someone who disagrees with one of the main ideas or methods in the chapter. In almost any business situation, you will find people with opinions contrary to the generally accepted wisdom. Having some practice managing opposing opinions will help you respond to them effectively. Finally, other guides state some strong personal opinions of the author. In business, people will differ in their opinions and then "agree to disagree"—they will back off, reflect, and sometimes alter their viewpoints. These guides will help you practice your reflection skills as you evaluate and discuss others' opinions.

All of the guides in the book will bring into your study thoughts and issues that will deepen your experience of MIS, both in the classroom and in preparation for helping you become a better business professional.

A listing of the guides follows, along with a page reference for its location in the book. The "Ethics Guide" in each chapter is indicated. (Twenty additional guides are available for instructional use at *www.prenhall.com/kroenke.*)

LEARNING AIDS FOR STUDENTS

We have structured this book so you can maximize the benefit from the time you spend reading it. As shown in the table below, each chapter includes a series of learning aids to help you succeed in this course.

RESOURCE	DESCRIPTION	BENEFIT	EXAMPLE
"This Could Happen to You" (located at the start of each part and each chapter)	Parts and chapters open with a running business scenario, the likes of which could entwine you in just a few years.	Sets up the chapter content and provides an obvious example of why the chapter is relevant to you.	Dee's blog at Emerson Pharmaceuticals, pp. 2 and 4 Internship at DSI, p. 156
Question-Driven Chapter Learning Objectives	These queries, and the subsequent chapter sections written around them, focus your attention and make your reading more efficient.	Identifies the main point of the section. When you can answer each question, you've learned the main point of the section.	pp. 37, 38, 39, 40
Guides	Each chapter includes two guides that focus on current issues relating to information systems. One of the two deals with an ethical issue.	Stimulates thought and discussion. Helps develop your problem solving skills. Helps you learn to respond to ethical dilemmas in business.	pp. 99a, 105a
"MIS in Use" Cases	Each chapter includes an "MIS in Use" case study of the experiences of an actual company. In some chapters, an "MIS in Use" case continues in a "Case Study" in the homework material.	Provides you with an inside look at real companies in action and how they are embracing information technology.	pp. 121, 132
"How Does Knowledge in This Chapter Help . . . You?" (near the end of each chapter)	This section revisits the opening scenario and discusses what the chapter taught you about it.	Summarizes the "takeaway" points from the chapter as they apply to the person in the story, and to you.	p. 49
Active Review	Each chapter concludes with a summary-and-review section, organized around the chapter's study questions.	Offers a review of important points in the chapter. If you can answer the questions posed, you will understand the material	p. 50
Key Terms	Highlights the major terms and concepts with their appropriate page reference.	Provides a summary of key terms for for review before exams.	p. 50
"Applying Your Knowledge"	These exercises ask you to take your new knowledge to the next step by applying it to a practice problem.	Tests your critical thinking skills and keeps reminding you that you are learning material that applies to the real world.	pp. 50–52
Case Study	A case study closes each chapter. You will reflect on the use in real organizations of the technology or systems presented in the chapter and recommend solutions to business problems.	Requires you to apply newly acquired knowledge to real situations.	p. 52
"International Dimension" (follows the final chapter in each part)	Each of the book's four parts closes with a module on the international aspects of the part topic.	Helps you understand international applications and issues relating to MIS.	pp. 138–141

RESOURCE	DESCRIPTION	BENEFIT	EXAMPLE
"Reflection on Your Net Worth" (in the review section at the end of each part)	These exercises ask you to think about how you can use the text material in your career.	Helps you see ways that the knowledge from your study of the text can give you a competitive advantage in the marketplace.	p. 142
"Career Assignments" (in the review section at the end of each part)	These exercises require you to do online research for information about career opportunities. You will analyze what knowledge you need and what real-world experiences (such as internships) might be beneficial.	Presents strategies and tactics for exploring ways to use MIS in careers and for finding the right job for you.	pp. 143–144
"Application Exercises" (in the review section at the end of each part)	These exercises ask you to solve business situations using spread-sheet (Excel) or database (Access) applications.	Helps develop your computer skills.	pp. 145–147
"Part Cases" (at the end of each part)	Two case studies, similar to the case studies at the end of each chapter, demonstrate how real organizations use the tech-nology or systems presented in the part.	Requires you to apply knowledge gained from several chapters to real business situations.	pp. 148, 151
Glossary (end of book)	A comprehensive list includes def-initions of the key terms.	Provides one place for your quick review of terms and concepts.	p. 603
Video programs available	(1) All chapter and part opening scenarios are depicted in a series of short dramatizations that emphasize the importance of the chapter content.	(1) Bring to life the opening sce-narios and put you right in the action.	These accompany each part opening and chapter opening
	(2) Author David Kroenke gives tutorial discussions of key topics throughout the textbook.	(2) Further discuss chapter mate-rial and help you develop better study skills.	An icon in the margin of the book (e.g., see p. 7) indicates related CD clips of the author.
Companion Website	Includes self-study quizzes for each chapter, plus PowerPoint presentations and a glossary. You will receive automatic feedback upon submitting each quiz.	Helps you cement your under-standing of the material in the text.	**www.prenhall.com/ kroenke**
Online Testing	An online test bank is available for each chapter and "International Dimension," organized by the list of numbered study questions within the chapter.	Helps you increase the productivity-of your study. Answers are scored according to study ques-tions in the chapter. Use the results to prioritize your study.	**www.prenhall.com/ kroenke/**
VangoNotes	These are study notes you can download to any MP3 player. Each chapter's notes contain the following: the "big ideas" you need to know for each chapter; a practice test; audio "flashcards" of key terms; and a "rapid review" quick drill session.	VangoNotes are flexible and efficient: You can download all material directly to your player, or download only the chapter(s) you need. With notes on your MP3 player, you can study or review "on the go"—wherever you are.	**www.vangonotes.com**; click on "Computing" for more information

Experiencing MIS

David M. Kroenke
University of Washington

Pearson Prentice Hall
Upper Saddle River, New Jersey 07458

Library of Congress Cataloging-in-Publication Data
Kroenke, David.
    Experiencing MIS / David M. Kroenke
        p. cm.
    ISBN 0-13-233777-0
1. Management information systems. 2. Business—Data processing. I. Title.
T58.6.K767 2006
658.4'038011—dc22

AVP/Executive Editor: Bob Horan
VP/Editorial Director: Jeff Shelstad
Editorial Assistant: Kelly Loftus
VP/Director of Development: Steve Deitmer
Development Editor: Ann Torbert
Senior Media Project Manager: Peter Snell
AVP/Director of Marketing: Eric Frank
Marketing Assistant: Laura Cirigliano
Associate Director, Production Editorial: Judy Leale
Production Editor: Suzanne Grappi
Permissions Coordinator: Charles Morris
Associate Director, Manufacturing: Vinnie Scelta
Manufacturing Buyer: Arnold Vila
Creative Director: Maria Lange
Design/Composition Manager: Christy Mahon
Composition Liaison: Suzanne Duda
Cover Illustration/Photo: Amanda Duffy
Illustration (Interior): Amanda Duffy
Director, Image Resource Center: Melinda Patelli
Manager, Rights and Permissions: Zina Arabia
Manager: Visual Research: Beth Brenzel
Image Permission Coordinator: Annette Linder
Photo Researcher: Rachel Lucas
Composition: GGS Book Services
Full-Service Project Management: GGS Book Services
Printer/Binder: Quebecor World Color/Versailles
Typeface:10/13 Utopia

Credits and acknowledgments borrowed from other sources and reproduced, with
permission, in this textbook appear on appropriate page within text (or on page XX).

Microsoft® and Windows® are registered trademarks of the Microsoft Corporation
in the U.S.A. and other countries. Screen shots and icons reprinted with permission
from the Microsoft Corporation. This book is not sponsored or endorsed by or
affiliated with the Microsoft Corporation.

Copyright © 2008 by Pearson Education, Inc., Upper Saddle River, New Jersey, 07458.
Pearson Prentice Hall. All rights reserved. Printed in the United States of America.
This publication is protected by Copyright and permission should be obtained
from the publisher prior to any prohibited reproduction, storage in a retrieval
system, or transmission in any form or by any means, electronic, mechanical,
photocopying, recording, or likewise. For information regarding permission(s),
write to: Rights and Permissions Department.

Pearson Prentice Hall™ is a trademark of Pearson Education, Inc.
Pearson® is a registered trademark of Pearson plc
Prentice Hall® is a registered trademark of Pearson Education, Inc.

Pearson Education LTD.   Pearson Education Australia PTY, Limited
Pearson Education Singapore, Pte. Ltd   Pearson Education North Asia Ltd
Pearson Education, Canada, Ltd   Pearson Educación de Mexico, S.A. de C.V.
Pearson Education–Japan   Pearson Education Malaysia, Pte. Ltd.

This work is protected by United States copyright laws and is provided solely for the use of instructors in teaching their courses and assessing student learning. Dissemination or sale of any part of this work (including on the World Wide Web) will destroy the integrity of the work and is not permitted. The work and materials from it should never be made available to students except by instructors using the accompanying text in their classes. All recipients of this work are expected to abide by these restrictions and to honor the intended pedagogical purposes and the needs of other instructors who rely on these materials. Anywhere.

ALL RIGHTS RESERVED.

10 9 8 7 6 5 4 3 2 1
ISBN: 0-13-241099-0

To C.J. and Carter

CONTENTS OVERVIEW

Experiencing MIS offers basic topic coverage of MIS in its 12 chapters and more in-depth, expanded coverage in its chapter extensions. This modular organization allows you to pick and choose among those topics. Here, chapter extensions are shown below the chapters to which they are related. You will preserve continuity if you use each of the 12 chapters in sequence. In most cases, a chapter extension can be covered *any time* in the course after its related chapter. You need not use any of the chapter extensions if time is short.

Part 1 introduces MIS and explains why and how it is important for business students. Its three chapters address basic MIS definitions and the five-component framework, show how information and information relates to business processes, and explain the role of IS in supporting organizational strategy and competitive advantage.

Chapter extensions for Part 1 concern collaboration, decision making, and knowledge management and expert systems.

Part 2 addresses fundamental IT concepts. Its three chapters cover hardware and software, database processing, and data communications.

Chapter extension 4 covers preparation of a computer budget. Extensions 5 and 6 address database design and using Microsoft Access. Extensions 7 and 8 provide technical detail on how the Internet works and setting up a SOHO network.

Part 3 focuses on how organizations use IS for competitive strategy. Its three chapters consider use of information systems within the organization, across organizations, and for decision making.

Extensions related to Chapter 7 address functional information systems, and cross-functional systems (CRM, ERP, and EAI). Extensions related to use of IS across organizations are e-commerce, supply chain management, and IT for data exchange. Extensions on database marketing, reporting systems and OLAP, and use of IS for counterterrorism purposes extend the Chapter 9 coverage.

Part 4 addresses managing information systems, with chapters on systems development, IS management, and IS security.

Extensions for Chapter 10 consider development of both small-scale and large-scale systems, and alternative development techniques. Extensions related to Chapter 11 address outsourcing issues and the financing and accounting for IT projects. Extensions related to the security chapter cover managing computer security risk, SSL/TLS and https, and computer crime and forensics.

CONTENTS

Chapter Extensions

PREFACE TO INSTRUCTORS

This text was conceived in the classroom. In the autumn of 2005, I was teaching a section of typical Intro to MIS students. Some were interested, and some were not. Some would attend class regularly, and some came only sporadically. Some had relevant work experience and were confident, and some greatly feared the class.

That term I was conducting an optional, evening review session a few days before the mid-term, and the students were awake, motivated, listening, asking good questions—all the behaviors I'd been hoping for (in vain) during regular class. They were interested and motivated because they were preparing for *the test*. But the format of the review also had something to do with it.

My agreement with students for review sessions is that I will answer any question they ask, but I will not spoon-feed the exam to them. So, they would pose a question, and I would answer it. Then, they would pose another question, and I would answer. If they couldn't understand the answer, they'd ask more. They were attentive and interested.

As I drove home that night, I pondered this experience. Why not structure my lectures using questions? Why not set out five to seven questions per lecture and tell the students that the final exam would be taken from that list of questions? Hence, every class session would become a mini-review session. If the students came to class, paid attention, and could answer each question, then they would be ready for the final. They wouldn't have to guess what questions I'd ask; they would know from the lecture questions. And, assuming I structured the questions correctly, they would be learning the important material.

About that time I attended a seminar on modern teaching techniques taught by Professor Marilla Svinicki. Professor Svinicki conducts educational research in the psychology department at the University of Texas, Austin. I took a number of important ideas away from that seminar, one of which was her statement, "Never give a reading assignment like, 'Read pages 120 to 133.'" Instead, she said, "Give the students a list of questions to answer and tell them to use pages 120 to 133 as background material for answering those questions."

She went on to explain that asking the students first to read pages is too vague. Students can't know when they are done. So, they give themselves goals like, "I'll read for an hour," but such goals have nothing to do with understanding the material. She recommended that we tell our students to use the questions as their study criteria: "When you can answer the questions, you're done. Quit reading."

That idea fit nicely with what I wanted to do with the question format, so I added it to my class. I revised all the reading assignments to start with a list of questions and gave page numbers for material that pertained to the questions in that list.

It worked. It wasn't a miracle, but it worked. My students, who are so pragmatic in their learning, used the questions as a guide. And, I told them, "When you can answer the questions, you're done." Truthfully, not much that I do matters to the best learners. They're going to get the material, no matter what. And, it didn't do much for the students who are so distracted by personal issues or uninterested in their education for other reasons that they make little of their college experience. But I think it did help the students in the middle. And that's the group that can benefit from my efforts, anyway.

I learned other important ideas from Professor Svinicki, who graciously allowed me to post her PowerPoint slides on the blog, *http://teachingMIS.com*. (Look for two different presentations on that blog under her name.) Before discussing some of her additional ideas, though, I want to describe the learning characteristics of the students I have and for whom this book was designed.

Characteristics of MIS Students Today

The students whom I teach today learn differently than students learned when I began teaching, many years ago. First, as mentioned previously, my students are *very pragmatic learners*. Although there are occasional exceptions, most of them are not in the College of Business to explore intellectual ideas. Most of them want to learn skills that will enable them to succeed in business. Some want to make a fortune in finance, some want to run dentist offices, some want to create the world's next great marketing campaign. Whatever their goals, they are very focused on learning skills that will help them.

Most of us professional educators became professional educators because we *do* like to explore intellectual ideas. So, we differ from our students. I don't think that makes us right and them wrong; it just creates a gap. That gap doesn't mean we have to fold our intellectual tents. I can offer up interesting and intriguing ideas to them (see for example, the Ethics Guide, "Egocentric Versus Empathetic Thinking" on page 31a) but I shouldn't be too surprised or disappointed if they yawn. It's just not who they are, at least right now.

In additional to pragmatism, I think today's students *expect action*. They expect action movies, action commercials, and action education—including my classroom. They were reared on *Sesame Street* and similar programs. When I write a *2* on the board, they wait for it to explode into ribbons and stars. Alas, my *2* is just a *2*. They sit in their chairs watching for the alphabet to come marching into the room as three-dimensional, animated characters, and for some famous movie star or singer to jump out of the letter *B*. Alas, they watch in vain.

A third characteristic of my students is that they're *quick to change channels*. They'll listen to me for a short while, but if they judge that what I'm saying is not worth listening to, they're gone. They do not have a TV remote to switch channels, but they'll use their PCs to do email and IM, just the same. So, I'll have their bodies, but not their minds. That is, I'll have their bodies until break time.

Furthermore, most of my students come to class with *serious misconceptions* of the topic. They think it's the computer class; they think it's the advanced Excel or Access class; or they don't know quite what to think of the class. Every term I have one or two techie students who want to test out of the class, but few of them pass the test. They are surprised that there is something to learn besides the definitions of RAM and IP addresses.

I don't think it's all negative, however. Once the students understand that MIS concerns something that can give them a personal competitive advantage—once they understand how MIS relates to marketing, sales, operations, management, and other business functions, they are *willing to work*, sometimes hard. The challenge is to keep reminding the students of the importance of IS to their future.

Helping Students Learn

Svinicki states that students need four different types of help with their learning:

- Decreasing their focus on *memorization*
- Increasing their *self-regulation strategies*
- Increasing and focusing their own *motivation*
- Recognizing the need to *transfer* learning from the classroom to the real world

I believe we can deal with the first two items in her list by carefully choosing the questions for the students to answer. If I ask a question like, "What is ERP?" I will increase their focus on memorization, which is the opposite of what I want. On the other hand, if I ask a question like, "How does ERP relate to the primary activities in Porter's value chain model?" the students will apply the definitions of *ERP* and *value chain model*, which will require them to learn the meaning of those terms, *but they will learn them in a context*.

Organizing the reading around questions helps with *self-regulation* because the questions enable the students to know when they're done. They need read only to the point at which they can provide good answers. They can check the quality of the answers using the activities in the Active Review at the end of each chapter and chapter extension. If they cannot answer the questions, then *they* know they need to read more.

Svinicki suggested another way to decrease memorization by using conceptual grids to organize their knowledge. I use many such grids in my class (and in this book), but two that appear repeatedly are the five-component model of an information system (first shown in Figure 1-1, page 6) and Porter's value-chain model (first shown in Figure 3-5, page 41).

According to recent educational research, there are numerous techniques we can use to help students increase and foster motivation.[1] One, termed *hot cognition*, refers to the role of emotion in learning. Simply stated, students are motivated to learn more if they are emotionally involved.[2] If we can cause the students to care about something, they will try harder and longer.

In related research, Bandura found that self-efficacy, the belief in one's ability to learn something, was the single most important characteristic of success in the classroom.[3] He cited four elements of increasing self-efficacy, one of which is *vicarious learning*. The idea is that students see someone to whom they can relate succeeding, and they begin to believe that they, too, can succeed.

We can bring hot cognition and vicarious learning together if we can create role models for students to emulate. Hence, to address the issue of student motivation, I have added stories (cases, if you will) of young professionals needing MIS knowledge. Prentice Hall has developed a video series of those stories to increase the students' emotional involvement. See the next section for further explanation.

Vicarious learning also addresses the need for *transfer* of what students are learning in the classroom to skills they will need in the "real world" and more importantly, in the workplace. I need to remember to remind the students they are not learning this material in a vacuum. It relates to what they're doing today (for example, unprotected email in a coffee shop hotspot), and, even more, will relate to what they will be doing in their careers. Students quickly forget this point; they lapse back into passive acceptance of the topic, and I must continually remind them to think about transferring the knowledge they're gaining into their major field of study and their future career.

How Do the Elements of This Text Relate to Modern Learning Theory?

I altered my course and wrote this text to address the learning styles of the students I have today and to utilize new ideas from learning research. I planned specific features and elements of this book to relate to learning theory, as described next.

Question Format

First, every section of this text is driven by questions. Every chapter, every chapter extension, every International Dimension section begins with questions. Then, every top-level heading is a question, and every chapter concludes with a review based on those same questions.

Why use this approach? I found that it makes the job easier for the student to identify the main point of the section, and to know when he or she has "got the point." Thus, the

---

[1]See for example, M. Svinicki, *Learning and Motivation in Postsecondary Classrooms* (Bolton, MA: Anker Press, 2004).
[2]Paul R. Pintrich, R. Marx, and R. Boyle, "Beyond Cold Conceptual Change: The Role of Motivational Beliefs and Classroom Contextual Factors in the Process of Conceptual Change," *Review of Educational Research*, 63:2 (1993), pp. 167–199.
[3]A. Bandura, *Self-Efficacy, the Exercise of Control* (New York: W.H. Freeman, 1997).

question format addresses the learning issues of motivation and memorization. Coincidentally, I found that it also has made me a more "honest" author: As I wrote the book, I could tell when I was pontificating; it was easy to tell when I was on a topic not directly related to the question that I was supposed to be addressing, which helped me get "off the stump" and back on topic.

Question-Oriented Online Tests

We also used the text questions to structure the online test bank at www.prenhall.com/ kroenke. The online test bank that accompanies this book is keyed to the numbered text questions. Thus, the results of the online test will point students to the questions they need to study further.

Key AACSB Assessment

Finally, Prentice Hall asked William Wagner of Villanova University to correlate the chapter questions to the key AACSB guidelines. Using our testing system, you can assess how your students are doing with regard to those guidelines by correlating the students scores on each question back to the AACSB guide.

Active Review

Each element of this text concludes with a summary-and-review section titled "Active Review." This review presents a set of questions that relate to each of the top-level questions in the text portion of the chapter. If the student performs those activities, he or she will understand the text material. See, for example, the "Active Review" for Chapter 1 on page 17.

Applying Your Knowledge/Your Net Worth

Each element of this text concludes with activities that ask the student to *transfer* the knowledge he or she has gained from the chapter into a business setting. Titled "Applying Your Knowledge," these activities are formatted as questions, in which the goal is to keep reminding students that they are learning this material *for a purpose*. The nature of the questions should appeal to the pragmatic nature of today's students.

Each of the book's four parts concludes with a section of activities entitled "Consider Your Net Worth." Like the "Applying Your Knowledge" activities at the end of each chapter, these exercises also address *knowledge transfer*, and do so in a very in-your-face manner. Students are asked to explain how the knowledge from the part will increase their *personal* net worth by giving them a competitive advantage in the job marketplace or by some other means. Besides promoting knowledge transfer, "Net Worth" activities also engage students' motivation through hot cognition—the thought that the learning from this class can pay off later in an ability to present oneself successfully in the job market.

Modular Design

For some reason, two-thirds of my most recent MIS class were marketing majors. I think it was just a random event, or perhaps a conflict with a required marketing class in another time slot, that caused me to have so many marketing students. In any case, the primary interest for most of the students in the class was marketing. So, considering the goals of helping the students to *increase their motivation* as well as helping them to *transfer their knowledge* to their business careers, I decided to devote considerable time to marketing information systems. We addressed CRM, database marketing, and other marketing-oriented IS in some detail.

In writing this text, I decided that I needed to use an organization that would help other instructors support specializations like that. Courses differ from university to university not just because of student interests, but also because of the local employment environment, the grade level at which the class is taught, the background and educational maturity of the students, and other factors.

To support such specialization, the text is organized into four parts with three chapters each. The chapters are short and describe the minimum essentials of each topic. Additional material on each chapter topic can then be found in optional Chapter Extensions. Thus, for example, Chapter 10 addresses the basic ideas and purpose of the systems development life cycle (SDLC). Chapter 10, then, is supported by three chapter extensions: one on small-scale systems development, one on large-scale systems development, and one on alternative development techniques. You can pick the extensions that relate to your class's interests and needs, or you can use just the chapter itself and devote class time to other extensions that might be of greater interest.

The chapter extensions reflect the nature of the part in which they appear. Some are technical, like those in Part 2, and some are more managerial, like those in Part 4. For a more specific description of how the book is organized, see the section below titled "How Is This Text Organized?"

International Dimension

Each of the book's four parts concludes with a module that relates the material of that part to international aspects of MIS. In my own class, I've found it too distracting to attempt to address international issues in every lecture. But having a single section that addresses international issues for the entire term seems too isolating. Placing the "International Dimension" in each part allows me to consider international aspects four times in the term, which seems about right. The "International Dimension" discussions are driven by questions and include an "Active Review." The "International Dimension" helps students transfer their knowledge from the textbook to future international business experience.

Opening Scenarios for Parts and Chapters

Each part and each chapter open with a scenario intended to get the students involved. I want students to mentally place themselves in the situation and to realize that this situation—or something like it—could happen to them! The scenarios set up the chapter's content and provide an obvious example of why the chapter is relevant to the students. These scenarios help support the goals of student motivation and learning transfer.

At the end of the chapter, we return to the situation set up in the opening scenario. The section titled "How Does the Knowledge in This Chapter Help . . . You?" summarizes the main takeaway points from the chapter as they apply to the protagonist in the scenario and to student learners. The next two sections describe the companies used in these opening and closing scenarios.

Emerson Pharmaceuticals

Parts 1 and 2 are tied together using a case of a company called Emerson Pharmaceuticals. This case concerns a young, aggressive business professional who wants to improve her communication with a large sales force by creating a blog. The case is based on a company that I observed and in which I played a role. Unfortunately, after the case had been written, that company declined to allow its name to be published. To avoid possible embarrassment to that company, I changed the industry. However, every aspect of that case occurred, and the actors in the case exist and said and did what they are reputed to have done. As you will see in the annotations for the case, the marketing communications manager suffered for lack of IS knowledge. In the video (see description below), she is not particularly likable, nor is her behavior always fair or appropriate, but most students will relate to her frustration. Again, the pedagogical goal is to create motivation and knowledge transfer vicariously. In her enthusiasm, she ultimately used her boss's boss to bludgeon the IT department into opening its doors in a way that created vulnerability to a serious security threat.

No harm was done, but it could have been. Emerson is used primarily in Parts 1 and 2, and again in Part 4 when the security aspects of this case are addressed.

Dorset-Stratford Interiors

Parts 3 and 4 focus on a company called Dorset-Stratford Interiors (DSI), which illustrates the ways in which information systems support an organization's competitive advantage. DSI is an actual company—a custom manufacturing company with roughly $60 million in sales. Unfortunately, after I had written the case, the CEO of the company on which DSI is based requested that I not publish information about his company, for fear that it would give away proprietary information and possibly give competitors an advantage. Also, as you can read in the case, the real company behind DSI strives to achieve a competitive advantage through high labor-force productivity. It is a nonunion shop, and the CEO feared that publishing his goal of high labor productivity would pose a red flag to union organizers. So, as with Emerson, I changed the name of the company and the industry. Again, everything related in that case happened. There is a real company that has the problems and opportunities described for DSI.

Video Programs

This text is accompanied by two different video programs. In order to increase the students' emotional involvement ("hot cognition") and also to provide an experience that relates to our media-reared students, Prentice Hall produced a series of videos that illustrate some of the events in both the Emerson and DSI cases. The script for those videos was written by Chris Cole and Shanga Parker. I believe both you and your students will be pleased with the quality of those videos, and we hope they will add another dimension of interest to your class.

In addition to the Emerson and DSI videos, the text is accompanied by a set of videos of me addressing some aspect of the text. The availability of such a video is indicated in the text by the video icon in the margin.   **Video**

Guides

This book, like my earlier book *Using MIS*, contains boxed essays called "Guides" that amplify each chapter's core material. These inserts are intended to encourage students to grapple with some intriguing aspect of the core material, to think about its relevance to them and their future needs as business people, and to discuss that material in small groups or in class.

Each chapter contains two guides—one that addresses ethics and one on some other topic. Guides appear in some of the chapter extensions as well. Use of the "Ethics Guides" will expose students to some of the fundamental principles of law and ethics as they relate to information systems and their use in business. The other guides present a variety of ideas: some from cognitive science that will help students become better problem solvers; some that show "contrarian" opinions that have been commonly voiced in business settings; and some that state my own personal opinions. All of the guides encourage students to grapple with an idea and how it applies to them either now or as future business professionals. Working with the guides should help students transfer knowledge from their MIS class to other classes and eventually to their business careers.

Guideline answers for the guides' discussion questions are included in the "Teaching Guidelines" inserts (pale green pages) in the *Annotated Instructor's Edition*, and also in the "Supplementary Materials for Instructors" section of the text's Web site. For more on the "Teaching Guidelines," see the description on page xxxvii of this Preface.

How Is This Text Organized?

The text is organized into four parts. See the graphic outline, titled "Chapter Overview," on page x and xi of the front matter for a visual presentation of the parts and chapters and of the relationship of the chapter extensions to the parts and chapters.

Part 1, "MIS and You," introduces MIS and explains why and how it is important for business students. The three chapters in Part 1 address basic MIS definitions and the five-component framework, show how information relates to business processes, and explain the role of IS in support organizational strategy and competitive advantage. Chapter extensions for Part 1 concern collaboration, decision making, and knowledge management and expert systems. The Part 1 International Dimension considers the global economy and its impact on MIS.

Part 2, "Using IT," addresses fundamental IT concepts. The three chapters in Part 2 are hardware and software, database processing, and data communications. Part 2 chapter extensions address preparing a computer budget, database design, using Microsoft Access, how the Internet works, and setting up a SOHO network. The localization of software and databases and the impact of global communications are the subjects of Part 2's "International Dimension."

We use the vignette of Dee Clarke at Emerson Pharmaceuticals and her desire to create a blog to increase student motivation for Parts 1 and 2. Dee is considerably hampered by her lack of knowledge of IS and IT, and were it not for her consultant, her project would have failed. Even still, her actions exposed Emerson to a serious security risk.

Part 3, "IS and Competitive Strategy," and the three chapters in this part consider information systems within the organization, information systems across organizations, and information systems for decision making. Part 3 chapter extensions discuss functional information systems, CRM, ERP, and EAI cross-functional systems, e-commerce, supply chain management, information technology for data exchange (EDI and XML), database marketing, reporting systems and OLAP, and information systems and counterterrorism. Part 3's "International Dimension" considers the impact of global IS and the value chain.

Student motivation for Part 3 is increased by placing the student in the role of a summer intern at DSI. The intern is competing, somewhat unfairly as you will see, against two other interns for a single full-time job. Knowledge of how IS can enhance competitive advantage is crucial to the success of the intern-protagonist.

Part 4, "Information Systems Management," concludes the text with three chapters that address systems development, IS management, and information security management. Part 4 chapter extensions consider small-scale systems development, large-scale systems development, alternative development techniques, outsourcing, financing and accounting for IT projects, managing computer security risk, SSL/TLS and https, and computer crime and forensics.

The motivational scenarios in Part 4 compare and contrast Emerson's IS management, which has an IT department of several hundred, to DSI's IS management, which has an IT department of one (yes, that is true, one) employee. The scenarios contrast development, IS management, and security between the two companies. Furthermore, the scenarios ask students to consider and contemplate the risk that Dee forced on Emerson with her actions.

Again, the goal of the modular organization of this text is to allow you to pick and choose among those topics that best fit your needs. You will preserve continuity if you use each of the 12 chapters in sequence, but you need not use any of the chapter extensions if time is short.

Supplements

The following supplements are available to ease and improve your experience teaching the MIS course:

Instructor's Resource Center Online and CD-ROM

Both the online resource center (accessible through *www/prenhall.com/kroenke*) and CD-ROM include all the supplements: Instructor's Manual, Test Item File, TestGen, TestGen conversions in WebCT and Blackboard-ready files, PowerPoint Presentations, and Image Library (text art). Through either medium, you have easy access to the entire supplements package.

Instructor's Manual

Prepared by Roberta Roth of the University of Northern Iowa, the manual includes answers to review and discussion questions, exercises, and case questions, plus teaching tips and lecture notes.

Test Item File, TestGen, and TestGen Conversions

Prepared by William Wagner of Villanova University, the test items include a large selection of questions in various formats. The test file is a convenient source of questions for class quizzes and exams, delivered in MS Word as well as in the form of TestGen and the TestGen conversions for WebCT, Blackboard, and Course Compass.

PowerPoint Presentations

Prepared by Linda Fried of the University of Colorado at Denver, the PowerPoints highlight text chapter objectives and key topics. An excellent aid for classroom presentations and lectures, they are also available on the Web at *www.prenhall.com/kroenke*.

Image Library

This collection of the figures and tables from the text offers another aid for classroom presentations and PowerPoint slides.

Online Courses

Available in WebCT (*www.prenhall.com/webct*), Blackboard (*www.prenhall.com/blackboard*), and CourseCompass (*www.prenhall.com/coursecompass*) formats, these resources are all that you need to plan and administer the course. They also are all that students need for anywhere-anytime access to your course materials conveniently organized by text chapter. For various levels of content and support, contact your Prentice Hall sales representative.

Using MIS Tutorial Videos

These videos feature author David Kroenke giving insights into key topics. They provide an out-of-class supplement to instructor lectures as well as a visual study tool.

My MIS Lab

My MIS Lab provides students with pretests, a testing system correlated to study objectives and AACSB guidelines. It also contains tutor videos and video dramatizations of each chapter-opening scenario.

VangoNotes

This resource enables students to download chapter reviews onto any MP3 player, for study anywhere, anytime. Study notes include the "big ideas" they need to know for each chapter, a practice test, audio "flashcards" of key terms, and a quick "rapid review" drill session.

Acknowledgments

I wish to thank Bob Grauer of the University of Miami for many interesting conversations about the content of this book and of the goals and objectives of the MIS class. I also thank Elota Patton of the University of Texas, Austin, for the ideas she's given me on teaching the MIS class. Additionally, I thank the many contributors to *http://teachingMIS.com* with whom I have shared ideas about challenges of teaching this class.

This past spring I met with many dedicated teaching professionals during a seminar series, and I thank all of them for the ideas and encouragement they offered. This book also greatly benefited from comments and ideas provided by the reviewers listed on the next page.

I owe special thanks to Professor Marilla Savincki for many of the teaching ideas and techniques that form the core of this book. Thanks, too, to Don Nilson of the Microsoft Corporation for numerous informative conversations on emerging technologies. Also, a special thanks to Rick Leenstra and Admiral Bruce Harlow of Applied Technical Systems for reviewing the chapter extension on data mining and counterterrorism.

This project would not have occurred without the untiring work of its development editor, Ann Torbert. Ann provided thoughtful guidance and wise counsel throughout the project and was always cheerfully available to serve as a helpful sounding board for developing emerging ideas. More than anyone else, Ann made this book happen. Thanks also to Cassie Schulenburg who provided assistance to Ann during the development process.

Prentice Hall continues to provide talented and creative people who ably translate the manuscript into the actual product you are holding. Thanks to Suzanne Grappi and Judy Leale, who organized the process and kept it moving; to Rachel Lucas and Cypress Integrated Systems for the remarkably efficient photo research process; to Maria Lange and Pat Smythe for the book's superb design and artwork, particularly the art that supports the guides; to Charles Morris for his persistence in tracking down permissions. Thanks, too, to the staff at GGS Books who guided the composition and production processes.

As always, I owe tremendous thanks to Bob Horan, my editor. Bob believed in this project and was willing to support it in the face of challenging schedule constraints and other risks. Bob's wise guidance provided a solid foundation for bringing the disparate components of this project together. Thanks also to Jeff Shelstad for helping develop the initial ideas of the manuscript and for backing all the dimensions of this project, including the innovative video series. Finally, thanks to my wife Lynda, for her untiring love and support.

David Kroenke
Seattle, Washington

Reviewers

Thank you to the following reviewers whose comments on various chapters and aspects of the entire project helped us to understand the needs of both instructors and students.

Hans-Joachim Adler, *The University of Texas at Dallas*

Ihssan Alkadi, *University of Louisiana at Lafayette*

Michel Avital, *Case Western Reserve University*

Nick Ball, *Brigham Young University*

Hellene Bankowski, *Philadelphia University*

Hooshang M. Beheshti, *Radford University*

Ernst Bekkering, *Northeastern State University*

Carolyn Borne, *Louisiana State University, Baton Rouge*

Charles Butler, *Colorado State University*

Joni M. Catanzaro, *Louisiana State University, Baton Rouge*

Joseph Cazier, *Appalachian State University*

Nettie M. Chaffee, *Kent State University*

Nancy Chase, *Gonzaga University*

Robert Chi, *California State University, Long Beach*

Izic Chon, *University of Washington*

Anne Cohen, *University of St. Thomas, Minneapolis*

John Cole, *Portland State University*

Charles Cowell, *Tyler Junior College*

Martin B. Dumas, *Baruch College—The City University of New York*

Al Fundaburk, *Bloomsburg University*

Jeffrey Gaines, *San Jose State University*

Russell Ginnings, *East Tennessee State University*

Bonnie C. Glassberg, *Miami University*

Sam Goh, *The University of Tennessee at Chattanooga*

Richard Grenci, *John Carroll University*

Kenneth Griggs, *California Polytechnic State University, San Luis Obispo*

Sandra Gustavson, *Kent State University*

Albert L. Harris, *Appalachian State University*

Rosie Hauck, *Illinois State University*

Bonnie Homan, *San Francisco State University*

Mark Hwang, *Central Michigan University*

Abdou Illia, *Eastern Illinois University*

Ken Jones, *Northeastern State University*

Karthik Kannan, *Purdue University*

Pairin Katerattanakul, *Western Michigan University*

Bob Keim, *Arizona State University*

George Kelley, *Erie Community College—City Campus*

Mark Kesh, *The University of Texas at El Paso*

Sang Hyun Kim, *Kyungpook National University*

Ronald J. Kizior, *Loyola University Chicago*

Michael Knight, *Appalachian State University*

Parag Kosalge, *Grand Valley State University*

Brian Kovar, *Kansas State University*

Ram Kumar, *The University of North Carolina at Charlotte*

Subodha Kumar, *University of Washington*

Terry F. Landry, *Louisiana State University, Baton Rouge*

David Lewis, *University of Massachusetts, Lowell*

Paul Licker, *Oakland University School of Business Administration*

Maurie Lockley, *The University of North Carolina at Greensboro*

Steve Loy, *Eastern Kentucky University*

Mary Malliaris, *Loyola University Chicago*

Byron Marshall, *Oregon State University*

Sue A. McCrory, *Missouri State University*

Don McCubbrey, *University of Denver*

Earl McKinney, *Bowling Green State University*

Patricia McQuaid, *California Polytechnic State University, San Luis Obispo*

Rayman Meservy, *Brigham Young University*

Richard Mickool, *Northeastern University*

Michael Pangburn, *University of Oregon*

Manimoy Paul, *Siena College*

Sharma Pillutla, *Towson University*

Taner Pirim, *The University of Mississippi*

Jim Quan, *Salisbury University*

R. A. Rademacher, *Colorado State University*

Madhav Raghunathan, *Bowling Green State University*

Betsy Ratchford, *University of Northern Iowa*

Muhammad Razi, *Western Michigan University*

Roberta M. Roth, *University of Northern Iowa*

Werner Schenk, *University of Rochester*

Andrew Schwarz, *Louisiana State University, Baton Rouge*

Jaymeen Shah, *Texas State University*

Ganesan Shankaranarayanan, *Boston University School of Management*

Mahmudul Sheikh, *The University of Mississippi*

Rod Sink, *Northern Illinois University*

Elliot Sloane, *Villanova University*

Robert St. Louis, *Arizona State University*

John Storck, *Boston University*

Lou Thompson, *The University of Texas at Dallas*

Michael W. Totaro, *University of Louisiana at Lafayette*

Cherie Trumbach, *The University of New Orleans*

Emmanuelle Vaast, *Long Island University*

Barbara Warner, *University of South Florida*

Dwayne Whitten, *Texas A&M University*

Rosemary Wild, *California Polytechnic State University, San Luis Obispo*

Elaine Winston, *Hofstra University*

Michael Zack, *Northeastern University*

John A. Zarb, *The University of Toledo*

Guoying Zhang, *University of Washington*

Zhiwei Zhu, *University of Louisiana at Lafayette*

INTRODUCTION TO THE TEACHING SUGGESTIONS

*T*he textbook you have in your hands is an annotated instructor's version of *Experiencing MIS*. It differs from the student version in that it contains suggested teaching ideas for the introductory scenarios for each chapter and for each of the "Guides" in the chapters and chapter extensions. These suggestions are printed on pale green pages, easily identifiable from the regular text pages.

I wrote these annotations in the hope that they will provide you with useful background, save you time, and possibly make the class more fun to teach. Consider the material in the annotations as fodder for your class preparation, to be used in any way that meets your needs. You may decide to use them as is, or you might combine them with your own stories, or adapt them to companies in your local area, or use them as examples with which you disagree. Or, if they do not fit your teaching style, just ignore them. The text will work just fine without the annotations.

TeachingMIS.com

Nearly 2,000 people teach an introduction to MIS class in the United States alone, and yet we seldom have a chance to talk with one another and compare notes. I've set up a blog, at *http://teachingMIS.com*, which is intended to help reduce this sense of isolation. It addresses contemporary issues for teaching the MIS class. The goal with the blog is to provide a place where our community of MIS teachers can openly discuss challenges and opportunities for teaching this class. You can leave comments at the blog, send an email to *ideas@teachingMIS.com*, or email me there at *DavidKroenke@teachingMIS.com*.

Notation

The teaching guidelines have two types of information: information for you, and also information for you to give to your students. Thus, we needed to introduce some notation to separate one category from the other. Comments and questions that you can address *directly to students* are typeset in boldface type and appear as follows:

- **What are some of the major limitations of data mining?**
- **If you are interested in learning more about data-mining techniques, you should take the department's database processing class. Drop me an email if you want to know more.**

Because these statements are intended for the instructor's use, the *me* in the above statement refers to you, the professor (and not me, the author). These are just thoughts for statements you might want to make.

General statements and conceptual points *addressed to you, the instructor,* are set in regular type, as follows:

> I like to start the class even before the class begins. I arrive five minutes or so early and talk with the students. I ask the students their names, where they are from, what their majors are, what they know about computers, etc., as a way of breaking the ice.

I hope at least some of this will be useful to you. Have fun!

David Kroenke

PART 1

MIS and You

This could happen to you

Knowledge of information systems will be critical to your success in business. If you are majoring in accounting, marketing, or management, or if you have selected some other nontechnical major, you may not yet know how important such knowledge will be to you. The purpose of Part 1 of this textbook is to demonstrate why this subject is so important to every business professional today. We begin with a real-life case.

Dee Clark is the Hospital Sales Marketing Director for the Academic and Hospital Division of Emerson Pharmaceuticals, a $4 billion pharmaceutical company.[1] Emerson employs a team of 450 salespeople to present its drugs and information about their effectiveness and use to doctors in many different settings. Dee's division focuses on doctors and pharmacists in medical schools and in hospitals. Emerson introduces dozens of new drugs each year, and it is both difficult and very important for the salespeople to learn the characteristics, efficacy, dosage recommendations, and relevant research for each of these drugs.

The pharmaceutical industry is competitive. Many other companies compete for medical professionals' attention and business. The competitors, too, employ large professional sales forces. Dee's job is to ensure that all of her reps have the information they need to succeed in this very competitive environment. As one rep develops a technique that successfully presents a product, overcomes a doctor's or pharmacist's reluctance, or causes the professional to choose Emerson's drugs over those of the competition, Dee wants to disseminate that technique to as many other salespeople as possible.

[1]The people and the events in this case are real. Everything related here actually happened. However, to protect the innocent, the guilty, and the publisher of this text, the name of the company and the company's industry have been changed. Dee does exist, and she does work with a 450-person sales force.

Thus, a big part of Dee's job is to inform the salespeople about the drugs she markets and to make sure the salespeople have all the information they need to succeed. Dee sometimes invites doctors and other professionals to seminars conducted by leading medical researchers, and sometimes she herself makes presentations to hospitals. She wants the sales force to know about these events and the sales that result from them.

In the fall of 2006, Dee was looking for better ways to connect with her salespeople. She was discussing this need with some of her friends, who suggested that she use a blog to disseminate the latest product news, the latest competitive threats and responses, recent successes, and other information. A **blog**, or **weblog**, is an online journal. Blogs use information technology to publish information over the Internet. One of the first and most famous blogs is *www.DrudgeReport.com*. (If you are not familiar with blogs, visit that site now.)

Dee liked the idea of a blog, but time was pressing. Her friend suggested the blog in November 2006, and she needed the blog to be up and running by the company's national sales meeting in January 2007. As she pondered this idea, she asked herself questions like these:

- **Is this possible? Can I have it done on time?**

- **What will I need to learn? How hard will it be to post my thoughts and pictures of other resources on the blog?**

- **How can I keep the competition from reading my blog?**

- **Will the salespeople use the blog? What can I do to make it easy for them to do so?**

- **What kind of computer do I need to support the blog?**

- **Where do I begin?**

Dee's situation illustrates why the knowledge in this class is so vitally important to business professionals today. Dee is a *marketing manager*. In college, she majored in marketing. She is not an information systems professional, and she never thought she'd need to know how to manage the construction of an information system. Yet that is exactly what her job now requires her to do.

Keep thinking about Dee as you read this text. This exact scenario could happen to you!

1 IS in the Life of Business Professionals

This could happen to you

Dee Clark does not know it, but she needs to build an information system (IS). As a marketing manager, she will not build the system herself. She won't buy the computer hardware and hook it up. She won't acquire or write any computer programs. She will, however, hire and manage the people who will do exactly that. As you will see, she will also be confronted along the way with the need for knowledge that she does not possess.

Dee's lack of knowledge will cost her company, and it will impede her progress. Her ignorance about MIS (management information systems) will leave her at a disadvantage in conversations with technical people and frustrate her ability to get the job done. Her uncertainty about what to do will delay the project and keep her from doing her other job tasks. Because of her lack of IS knowledge, she will work many extra hours and spend sleepless nights worrying about the success of her project. What's especially sad is that it didn't need to be this way. She just needed the knowledge that you are about to obtain.

For example, consider this question: What is an information system made of? When people say they want to build a new garage, you have some idea of what they're going to do. But when people say they're going to build a new information system, what are they going to build? We begin with that question.

An optional Extension for this chapter is CE1, "Information Systems for Collaboration."

Study Questions

Q1 What is an information system?

Q2 What is MIS?

Q3 How does IS differ from IT?

Q4 How do successful business professionals use IS?

Q5 What new opportunities for IS are developing today?

Q6 How can you create a strong password?

Q7 What is this class about?

How does the knowledge in this chapter help Dee and you?

Q1 What Is an Information System?

A **system** is a group of components that interact to achieve some purpose. As you might guess, an **information system (IS)** is a group of components that interact to produce information. That sentence, although true, raises another question: What are these components that interact to produce information?

Figure 1-1 shows the **five-component framework** of **computer hardware**, **software**,[1] **data**, **procedures**, and **people**. These five components are present in every information system—from the simplest to the most complex. For example, when you use a computer to write a class report, you are using hardware (the computer, storage disk, keyboard, and monitor), software (Word, WordPerfect, or some other word-processing program), data (the words, sentences, and paragraphs in your report), procedures (the methods you use to start the program, enter your report, print it, and save and back up your file), and people (you).

Consider a more complex example, say an airline reservation system. It, too, consists of these five components, even though each one is far more complicated. The hardware consists of dozens or more computers linked together by telecommunications hardware. Further, hundreds of different programs coordinate communications among the computers, and still other programs perform the reservations and related services. Additionally, the system must store millions upon millions of characters of data about flights, customers, reservations, and other facts. Hundreds of different procedures are followed by airline personnel, travel agents, and customers. Finally, the information system includes people, not only the users of the system, but also those who operate and service the computers, those who maintain the data, and those who support the networks of computers.

The five components in Figure 1-1 are common to all information systems. Dee will need these five components for the information system that will support her blog. Note especially the *people* and *procedures* components of her system. Dee and her product managers will contribute to the blog. They will need training and procedures for doing so. The salespeople will need procedures for accessing the blog, and someone will need to support the hardware and software as well as administer the data contained in the blog.

Before we move forward, note that we have defined an information system to include a computer. Some people would say that such a system is a **computer-based information system**. They would note that there are information systems that do not include computers, such as a calendar hanging on the wall outside of a conference room that is used to schedule the room's use. Such systems have been used by businesses for centuries. Although this point is true, in this book we focus on computer-based information systems. To simplify and shorten the book, we will use the term *information system* as a synonym for *computer-based information system*.

Figure 1-1
Five Components of an
Information System

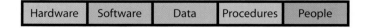

---

[1]In the past, the term *software* was used to refer to computer components that were not hardware (e.g., programs, procedures, user manuals, etc.). Today, the term *software* is used more specifically to refer only to programs, and that is how we use the term throughout this book.

Q2 What Is MIS?

There are thousands, even millions, of information systems in this world. Not all relate to business. In this textbook, we are concerned with **MIS**, or **management information systems**. MIS is *the development and use of information systems that help businesses achieve their goals and objectives*. This definition has three key elements: *development and use*, *information systems*, and *business goals and objectives*. We just discussed *information systems*. Now consider *development and use*, and *business goals and objectives*.

Development and Use of Information Systems

Information systems do not pop up like mushrooms after a hard rain; they must be constructed. You may be saying, "Wait a minute. I'm a finance (or accounting, or management) major, not an information-systems major. I don't need to know how to build information systems."

If you are saying that, you are like a lamb headed for fleecing. Like Dee, throughout your career, in whatever field you choose, you will need new information systems. To have an information system that meets your needs, you need to take an *active role* in that system's development. Even if you are not a programmer or a database designer or some other IS professional, you must take an active role in specifying the system's requirements and in helping manage the development project. Without active involvement on your part, it will only be good luck that causes the new system to meet your needs.

To that end, throughout this text we will discuss your role in the development of information systems. In addition, we devote all of Chapter 7 to this important topic. As you read this text and think about information systems, you should ask yourself questions like, "How was that system constructed?" and "What roles did the users play during its development?" If you start asking yourself these questions now, you will be better prepared to answer them once you start a job, when financial, career, and other consequences will depend on your answers.

In addition to development tasks, you will also have important roles to play in the *use* of information systems. Of course, you will need to learn how to employ the system to accomplish your goals. But you will also have important ancillary functions as well. For example, when using an information system, you will have responsibilities for protecting the security of the system and its data. You may also have tasks for backing up data. When the system fails (most do, at some point), you will have tasks to perform while the system is down as well as tasks to accomplish to help recover the system correctly and quickly.

Finally, throughout your career, you may from time to time be faced with ethical issues involving your use of information systems. To help you prepare for those challenges, in every chapter of this book, we have included an *Ethics Guide*. These Guides will get you to start thinking about ethical dilemmas, which will help you clarify your values and make you ready to respond authentically to future ethical challenges. The first *Ethics Guide*, on pages 7a–7b, considers how to use information that comes your way but was not intended for you.

Ethics of Misdirected Information Use

Consider the following situations:

Situation A: Suppose you are buying a condo and you know that at least one other party is bidding against you. While agonizing over your best strategy, you stop at a local Starbucks. As you sip your latte, you overhear a conversation at the table next to yours. Three people are talking so loudly that it is difficult to ignore them, and you soon realize that they are the real estate agent and the couple who is competing for the condo you want.

They are preparing their offer. Should you listen to their conversation? If you do, do you use the information you hear to your advantage?

Situation B: Consider the same situation from a different perspective—instead of overhearing the conversation, suppose you receive that same information in an email. Perhaps an administrative assistant at the agent's office confuses you and the other customer and mistakenly sends you the terms of the other party's offer. Do you read that email? If so, do you use the information that you read to your advantage?

Situation C: Suppose that you sell computer software. In the midst of a sensitive price negotiation, your customer accidentally sends you an internal email that contains the maximum amount that the customer can pay for your software. Do you read that email? Do you use that information to guide your negotiating strategy? What do you do if your customer discovers that the email may have reached you and asks, "Did you read my email?" How do you answer?

Situation D: Suppose a friend mistakenly sends you an email that contains sensitive personal medical data. Further, suppose you read the email before you know what you're reading and you're embarrassed to learn something very personal that truly is none of your business. Your friend asks you, "Did you read that email?" How do you respond?

Situation E: Finally, suppose that you work as a network administrator and your position allows you unrestricted access to the mailing lists for your company. Assume that you have the skill to insert your email address into any company mailing list without anyone knowing about it. You insert your address into several lists and, consequently, begin to receive confidential email that no one intended for you to see. One of those emails indicates that your best friend's department is about to be eliminated and all of its personnel fired. Do you forewarn your friend?

DISCUSSION QUESTIONS

1. Answer the questions in situations A and B. Do your answers differ? Does the medium by which the information is obtained make a difference? Is it easier to avoid reading an email than it is to avoid hearing a conversation? If so, does that difference matter?

2. Answer the questions in situations B and C. Do your answers differ? In situation B, the information is for your personal gain; in C, the information is for both your personal and your organization's gain. Does this difference matter? How do you respond when asked if you have read the email?

3. Answer the questions in situations C and D. Do your answers differ? Would you lie in one case and not in the other? Why or why not?

4. Answer the question in situation E. What is the essential difference between situations A through D and situation E? Suppose you had to justify your behavior in situation E. How would you argue? Do you believe your own argument?

5. In situations A through D, if you access the information you have done nothing illegal. You were the passive recipient. Even for item E, although you undoubtedly violated your company's employment policies, you most likely did not violate the law. So for this discussion, assume that all of these actions are legal.

   a. What is the difference between legal and ethical? Look up both terms in a dictionary, and explain how they differ.

   b. Make the argument that business is competitive and that if something is legal, then it is acceptable to do it if it helps to further your goals.

   c. Make the argument that it is never appropriate to do something unethical.

6. Summarize your beliefs about proper conduct when you receive misdirected information.

Achieving Business Goals and Objectives

The last part of the definition of MIS is that information systems exist to help businesses achieve their *goals and objectives*. First, realize that this statement hides an important fact: Businesses themselves do not "do" anything. A business is not alive, and it cannot act. It is the people within a business who sell, buy, design, produce, finance, market, account, and manage. So information systems exist to help people who work in a business to achieve the goals and objectives of that business.

Information systems are not created for the sheer joy of exploring technology. They are not created so that the company can be "modern" or so that the company can claim to be a "new-economy company." They are not created because the information systems department thinks it needs to be created or because the company is "falling behind the technology curve."

This point may seem so obvious that you wonder why we mention it. Every day, however, some business somewhere is developing an information system for the wrong reasons. Right now, somewhere in the world, a company is deciding to create a Web site for the sole reason that "every other business has one." This company is not asking questions like, "What is the purpose of the Web site?" or, "What is it going to do for us?" or, "Are the costs of the Web site sufficiently offset by the benefits?"—but it should be!

Even more serious, somewhere right now, an IS manager has been convinced by some vendor's sales team or by an article in a business magazine that his or her company must upgrade to the latest, greatest high-tech gizmo. This IS manager is attempting to convince his or her manager that this expensive upgrade is a good idea. We hope that someone somewhere in the company is asking questions like, "What business goal or objective will be served by the investment in the gizmo?"

Throughout this text, we will consider many different information system types and underlying technologies. We will show the benefits of those systems and technologies, and we will illustrate successful implementations of them. *MIS in Use* cases, such as the one about the Internal Revenue Service in *MIS in Use 1*, discuss IS implementations in specific real-world organizations. As a future business professional, you need to learn to look at information systems and technologies only through the lens of *business need*. Learn to ask, "All of this technology may be great, in and of itself, but what will it do for us? What will it do for our business and our particular goals?"

Again, MIS is the development and use of information systems that help businesses achieve their goals and objectives. Already you should be realizing that there is much more to this class than buying a computer, writing a program, or working with a spreadsheet.

Q3 How Does IS Differ from IT?

Information technology and *information system* are two closely related terms, but they are different. **Information technology (IT)** refers to methods, inventions, standards, and products. As the term implies, it refers to raw technology, and it concerns only the hardware, software, and data components of an information system. In contrast, an information system is a system of hardware, software, data, procedures, and people that produce information.

MIS in use 1

Requirements Creep at the IRS

The United States Internal Revenue Service (IRS) serves more people in the United States than any other public or private institution. Each year, it processes over 200 million tax returns from more than 180 million individuals and more than 45 million businesses. The IRS itself employs more than 100,000 people in over 1,000 different sites. In a typical year, it adapts to more than 200 tax law changes and services more than 23 million telephone calls.

Amazingly, the IRS accomplishes this work using information systems that were designed and developed in the 1960s. In fact, some of the computer programs that process tax returns were first written in 1962. In the mid-1990s, the IRS set out on a Business System Modernization (BSM) project that would replace this antiquated system with modern technology and capabilities. However, by 2003, it was clear that this project was a disaster. Billions of dollars had been spent on the project, and all major components of the new system were months or years behind schedule.

In 2003, newly appointed IRS commissioner Mark W. Everson called for an independent review of all BSM projects. Systems development experts from the Software Engineering Institute at Carnegie Mellon University and the Mitre Corporation, as well as managers from the IRS, examined the project and made a

list of factors that contributed to the failure as well as recommendations for solutions. In their report, the first two causes of failure cited were:

- "There was inadequate business unit ownership and sponsorship of projects. This resulted in unrealistic business cases and continuous project scope 'creep' (gradual expansion of the original scope of the project)."
- "The much desired environment of trust, confidence, and teamwork between the IRS business units, the BSM organization (the team of IRS employees established to manage the BSM project), the Information Technology Services (ITS, the internal IRS organization that operates and maintains the current information systems), and the Prime (the prime contractor, Computer Sciences Corporation) did not exist. In fact, the opposite was true, resulting in an inefficient working environment and, at times, finger pointing when problems arose."

The BSM team developed the new system in a vacuum. Neither the existing IRS business units (the future users of the system) nor the existing ITS staff accepted, understood, or supported the new system that had been engineered by the BSM team. Consequently, the BSM team poorly understood the system needs, and that misunderstanding resulted in continual changes in project requirements, changes that occurred after systems components had been designed and developed. Such requirements creep is a sure sign of a mismanaged project and always results in schedule delays and wasted money. In this case, the delays were measured in years and the waste in billions of dollars. The bottom line: Users must be involved in both the *development* and *use* of information systems.

Sources: "Independent Analysis of IRS Business Systems Modernization, Special Report," IRS Oversight Board, 2003, *www.treas.gov/irsob/index.html*; "For the IRS, There's No EZ Fix," *CIO Magazine,* April 1, 2004.

IT, by itself, will not help an organization achieve its goals and objectives. It is only when IT is embedded into an IS—only when the technology within the hardware, software, and data is combined with the people and procedure components—that IT becomes useful.

Think about these statements from the standpoint of the information systems at your university. Do you care that the university network uses the latest, greatest technology to send messages across campus? Do you care that the university's Web site uses the latest, fastest hardware to show you available classes? Not really. It is only when the humans at the university (including you) use procedures to do something—to enroll in a class, for example—that the IT becomes useful to you.

Consider Dee and her blog. She will use IT, but that isn't her primary interest. Her goal is to combine the IT in hardware, software, and data with procedures to enable herself, Emerson's product managers, and her sales reps to accomplish their own goals and objectives.

Successful business people understand this crucial difference between IT and IS, and they take advantage of it, as we show next.

Q4 How Do Successful Business Professionals Use IS?

Today, every business professional uses numerous information systems. Some people do little more than write email, access Web pages, and do instant messaging. While the ability to use such basic information systems is essential, that level of knowledge and use does not give anyone a competitive advantage in the workplace.

To gain a competitive advantage, you need to do more. You need to learn to think about IT and IS when you consider the problems and opportunities that confront your department or organization. Dee Clark, the marketing manager at the start of this chapter, is an excellent example. She needs to rapidly and conveniently transmit the latest news, advice, and opportunities to the sales reps with whom she deals. She considered this need creatively and realized she could use a blog to disseminate that information. Doing so gave both her and her sales reps a competitive advantage.

Recent research supports this claim. The RAND Corporation (a famous technology institution that invented dozens of new technologies, including the design of the Internet) published a study on trends in the world workforce in the twenty-first century.[2] That study predicted strong demand for business professionals who have the ability to create innovative applications using emerging technology. Further, that demand will continue for the next 50 years.

To take advantage of this trend, you need not be a developer of technology. Rather, you need to think creatively about problems, challenges, and opportunities in your business and organization, and then you need to be able to apply new technology to your business needs.

Amazon.com is a perfect example. Jeff Bezos, founder and CEO of Amazon.com, did not invent any technology. He was one of the first to see, however, that the emerging technology of the Internet, combined with existing database technology, enabled a new business model. He developed an organization that became one of the world's largest users of information systems. In fact, on December 14, 2005, the information systems at Amazon processed an average of 41 items per second for 24 hours. Truly, Amazon represents an innovative application of the technology that was emerging when Bezos founded the company.

---

[2]Lynn A. Karoly and Constantijn W. A. Points, *The 21st Century at Work* (Santa Monica, CA: RAND Corporation, 2004), xvii–xviii.

Q5 What New Opportunities for IS Are Developing Today?

"That's fine," you might be saying. "That was then, and this is now. The Internet is old news. All the good opportunities are gone." If you think this way, you are wrong. In fact, there are great opportunities right now.

For example, read the news item in Figure 1-2. On October 9, 2006, Google bought YouTube for $1.62 billion in stock. Amazingly, this company was founded in the summer of 2005, and in August 2006, it had attracted 19.1 million customers. All 67 YouTube employees shared in the $1.62 billion buyout price! Consider two other such opportunities as well, which are discussed in the section that follows.

Two Opportunities, Right Now

Information technology has developed in such a way that, for all practical purposes, data storage and data communication are free. Of course, no business resource is free, but the costs of storage and data transmission are so low that, when compared to other business expenses, they are essentially zero.

Whenever an important business resource becomes free, new opportunities for using that resource abound. In the case of free data storage and free data transmission, consider Getty Images (*www.GettyImages.com*; see also *Part Case 1-1*, page 6). Getty Images sells pictures over the Internet. The pictures are electronic; they are made of binary digits (see Chapter 4). Because the cost of both data storage and data transmission is essentially zero, the variable cost of production of a new image to Getty is zero. (See The Getty image in Figure 1-3 on page 12.)

Reflect on that statement: "The cost of production is zero." Any revenue that Getty makes on an image goes straight to the bottom line. Truly, this is a business that has found an innovative application of IT.

Figure 1-2
A Great IS Opportunity—Google's Purchase of YouTube for $1.62 Billion.

Figure 1-3
Another IS Opportunity—Getty Images Supplies Photographic Images Electronically

For another example, consider Media Partners (*www.MediaPartners.com*), a partnership that produces video training and sells it to commercial organizations and the government. Recently, Media Partners has developed an online training program to teach principles of customer service. In this program, the trainee takes a short exam, watches a video, and then takes another exam. Results of the tests are sent via email to the employee's supervisor.

This entire system is automated. Because the cost of data storage and data transmission is essentially zero, the variable cost of producing the program is essentially zero. All of the revenue from these programs goes straight to the bottom line. Media Partners harnessed IT to produce a veritable money machine.

These opportunities are real, right now, but the best news is that there is no sign that technology development is slowing down. New opportunities like this will continue to emerge, as predicted by Moore's Law.

Moore's Law

Gordon Moore is the cofounder of Intel Corporation, the world's leading manufacturer of computer chips and other computer-related components. In 1965, he said that because of technology improvements in electronic chip design and manufacturing, "The number of transistors per square inch on an integrated chip doubles every 18 months." This observation is known as **Moore's Law**. Moore's prediction has proved generally accurate in the more than 40 years since it was made.

The density of transistors on a computer chip relates to the speed of the chip, and so you will sometimes hear Moore's Law expressed as, "The speed of a computer chip doubles every 18 months." This is not exactly what Moore said, but it comes close to the essence of his idea.

Dramatic Reduction in Price/Performance Ratio

As a result of Moore's Law, the price/performance ratio of computers has fallen dramatically for years (see Figure 1-4). As a result, computers have shrunk from multimillion dollar, room-filling machines in 1968 to $300 small desktop devices in 2006. Along the way, the availability of increased computing power has enabled developments such as laser printers, graphical user interfaces like Windows, high-speed communications, cell phones, PDAs, email, and the Internet.

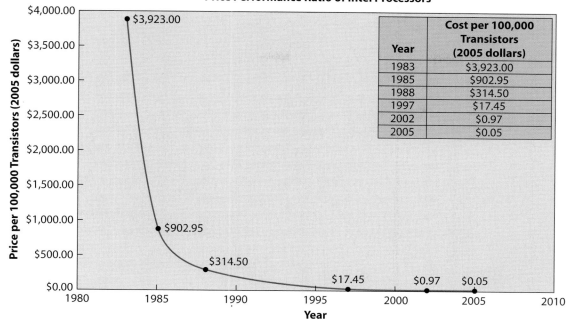

Figure 1-4
Computer
Price/Performance
Ratio Decreases

Moore's Law is the principal reason why data storage and data transmission are essentially free today. All indications are that the price/performance ratio of IT products will continue to fall. New opportunities for applying new technology will continue to emerge; you just need to learn to look for them!

Q6 How Can You Create a Strong Password?

Whatever opportunities you find for using information systems in your career and your life, one issue that will remain constant is security of those systems. Security is vitally important. As a user of information systems in a business organization, you will be given a user name and password. You will be instructed to create a strong password, and it is vitally important for you to do so. (In fact, you should now be using such passwords at your university.) So what is a strong password, and how do you create one?

Strong Passwords

Microsoft, a company that has many reasons to promote effective security, defines a **strong password** as one with the following characteristics:

- Has seven or more characters
- Does not contain your user name, real name, or company name
- Does not contain a complete dictionary word in any language
- Is different from previous passwords you have used
- Contains both upper- and lowercase letters, numbers, and special characters (such as ~ ! @; # $ % ^ &; * ( ) _ +; – =; { } | [ ] \ : " ; ' <; >; ?, . /)

Examples of good passwords are:

- Qw37^T1bb?at
- 3B47qq<3>5!7b

The problem with such passwords is that they are nearly impossible to remember. And the last thing you want to do is write your password on a piece of paper and keep it near the workstation where you use it. Never do that!

One technique for creating memorable, strong passwords is to base them on the first letter of the words in a phrase. The phrase could be the title of a song or the first line of a poem or one based on some fact about your life. For example, you might take the phrase, "I was born in Rome, New York, before 1990." Using the first letters from that phrase and substituting the character < for the word *before*, you create the password IwbiR,NY<1990. That's an acceptable password, but it would be better if all of the numbers were not placed on the end. So, you might try the phrase, "I was born at 3:00 A.M in Rome, New York." That phrase yields the password Iwba3:00AMiR,NY which is a strong password that is easily remembered.

Password Etiquette

Once you have created a strong password, you need to protect it with proper behavior. Proper password etiquette is one of the marks of a business professional. Never write down your password, and do not share it with others. Never ask others for their passwords, and never give your password to someone else.

But what if you need someone else's password? Suppose, for example, you ask someone to help you with a problem on your computer. You sign on to an information system, and for some reason, you need to enter that other person's password. In this case, say to the other person, "We need your password," and then get out of your chair, offer your keyboard to the other person, and look away while he or she enters the password. Among professionals working in organizations that take security seriously, this little "do-si-do" move—one person getting out of the way so that another person can enter a password—is common and accepted.

If someone asks for your password, do not give it out. Instead, get up, go over to that person's machine, and enter your own password yourself. Stay present while your password is in use, and ensure that your account is logged out at the end of the activity. No one should mind or be offended in any way when you do this. It is the mark of a professional.

Q7 What Is This Class About?

Many students enter this class with an erroneous idea of what they will study. Often, students think of it as a computer class—or at least a class that has something to do with computers and business. Many students think this class is about learning how to use Excel or Access or FrontPage. Figure 1-5 lists a number of reasons that students have given me when explaining why they

- "I already know how to use Excel and Word. I can build a Web site with FrontPage. OK, it's a simple Web site, but I can do it. And when I need to learn more, I can. So let me out of this class!"
- "We're going to learn how to work with information systems? That's like practicing the stomach flu. If and when the time comes, I'll know how to do it."
- "I'm terrified of computers. I'm a people-person, and I don't do well with engineering-like things. I've put this class off until the last quarter of my senior year. I hope it's not as bad as I fear; I just wish they didn't make me take it."
- "There's really no content in this class. I mean, I've been programming since high school, I can write in C++, though PERL is my favorite language. I know computer technology. This class is just a bunch of management-babble mixed up with some computer terms. At least, it's an easy class though."
- "Well, I'm sure there is some merit to this class, but consider the opportunity cost. I really need to be taking more microeconomics and international business. The time that I spend on this class could be better spent on those subjects."
- "The only thing I need to know is how to surf the Web and how to use email. I know how to do those, so I just don't need this class."
- "What, you mean this class is not about learning Excel and FrontPage? That's what I thought we were going to learn. That's what I need to know. Why all this information systems stuff? How do I make a Web site? That's what I need to know."

Figure 1-5
Student Thoughts About Why
"I Don't Need This Class"

don't need to take this class. As you can see, opinions vary on what the class is about.

By now, you should have an idea that this class is much broader than just learning how to use Excel or Access. You may, in fact, use those programs in this class, but the focus will not be on learning what keys to push to make the program work as you want. Instead, the focus will be on *learning to use* those tools to accomplish a business purpose.

Consider the definition of MIS again: the development and use of information systems that help organizations (and the people who work in them) accomplish their goals and objectives. Thus, to understand MIS, you need to understand both business and technology, and you need to be able to relate one to the other.

The table of contents of the chapters in this book will give you an idea of how we will proceed. In the next two chapters, we will discuss the relationship of business processes and information systems, and we will show how information systems can be used to gain competitive advantages. Then in Chapters 4–6, you will learn about hardware, software, database, and data communications technology. With that foundation, in Chapters 7–9, we will show how that technology can be used to gain a competitive advantage in three different ways. Finally, you will learn about the management of systems development, IS resources, and security in Chapters 10–12. The *Guide* on pages 15a–15b shares my personal opinion about why these chapters—and this book—matter to you.

Duller Than Dirt?

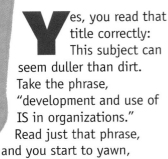

Yes, you read that title correctly: This subject can seem duller than dirt. Take the phrase, "development and use of IS in organizations." Read just that phrase, and you start to yawn, wondering, "How am I going to absorb 600+ pages of this?"

Stop and think: Why are you reading this book? Right now in the Sea of Cortez, the water is clear and warm, and the swimming and diving are wonderful. You could be kayaking to Isla San Francisco this minute. Or somewhere in the world, people are skiing. Whether in Aspen, Colorado, or Portillo, Chile, people are blasting through the powder somewhere. You could be one of them, living in a small house with a group of friends, having good times at night. Or whatever it is that you like to do, you could be doing it right now. So why are you here, where you are, reading this book? Why aren't you there?

Waking up should be one of your goals while in college. I mean waking up to your life. Ceasing to live according to someone else's plan and beginning to live your own plan. Doing that requires you to become conscious of the choices you make and the consequences they have.

Suppose you take an hour to read your assignment in this book tonight. For a typical person, that is 4,320 heartbeats (72 beats times 60 minutes) that

you have used to read this book—heartbeats that you will never have again. Despite the evidence of your current budget, the critical resource for humans is not money; it is time. No matter what we do, we cannot get more of it. Was your reading today worth those 4,320 heartbeats?

For some reason, you chose to major in business. For some reason, you are taking this class, and for some reason, you have been instructed to read this textbook. Now, given that you made a good decision to major in business (and not to kayak in Baja), and given that someone is requiring you to read this text, the question then becomes, "How can you maximize the return on the 4,320 heartbeats you are investing per hour?"

The secret is to personalize the material. At every page, learn to ask yourself, "How does this pertain to me?" and "How can I use this material to further my goals?" If you find some topic irrelevant, ask your professor or your classmates what they think. What's this topic for? Why are we reading this? What am I going to do with it later in my career? Why is this worth 1,000 (or whatever) heartbeats?

MIS is all-encompassing. To me, that's one of its beauties. Consider the components: hardware, software, data, procedures, and people. Do you want to be an engineer? Then work the hardware component. Do you want to be a programmer? Write software. Do you want to be a practicing philosopher, an applied epistemologist? Learn data modeling. Do you like social systems and sociology? Learn how to design effective group and organizational procedures.

Do you like people? Become an IS trainer or a computer systems salesperson. Do you enjoy management? Learn how to bring all of those disparate elements together.

I've worked in this industry for almost 40 years. The breadth of MIS and the rapid change of technology have kept me fascinated for every one of those years. Further, the beauty of working with intellectual property is that it doesn't weigh very much; moving symbols around won't wear you out. And you do it indoors in a temperature-controlled office. They may even put your name on the door.

So wake up. Why are you reading this? How can you make it relevant? Jump onto Google, and search for MIS careers or use some other phrase from this chapter and see what you get. Challenge yourself to find something that is important to you personally in every chapter.

You just invested 780 heartbeats in reading this editorial. Was it worth it? Keep asking!

DISCUSSION QUESTIONS

1. Explain what it means to "wake up to your life."

2. Are you awake to your life? How do you know? What can you do once a week to ensure that you are awake to your life?

3. What are your professional goals? Are they yours, or are they someone else's? How do you know?

4. How does this class pertain to your professional goals?

5. How are you going to make the material in this class interesting?

How does the knowledge in this chapter help Dee and you?

This chapter should encourage Dee. She's on the right track: She's looking for innovative applications of emerging technology. She wants to use an information system (her blog) to find ways to give her sales force a competitive advantage.

Dee's work can be guided by the five components. She will need a computer with software and data to store and process her blog. She doesn't know yet how that will be done, but she knows that they need to exist. She also knows that someone will need to follow procedures to set up and administer her blog. She herself will need a computer with software to post entries to her blog, and she will need procedures (and training) for doing so. Finally, she knows that the salespeople will need procedures for accessing the blog and for sending her comments about various blog entries.

She also knows that using the blog is not the end of the story. Technology will continue to develop and improve, and she'll need to think constantly about how she can use other technology in other systems to help her accomplish her goals and objectives.

Finally, Dee knows how to create a strong password. She will need one to control access to her blog—she certainly wouldn't want someone from the competition, for example, to post entries to her blog. But she also wants to block well-intentioned people from making unauthorized entries to the blog. She wants to control the timing, for example, of important news, and using security with a strong password will help her do that.

Dee's blog is one type of collaboration information system. If you wish to learn about other types of information systems used for collaboration, see Chapter Extension 1.

Active ? Review

Use this Active Review to verify that you understand the material in the chapter. You can read the entire chapter and then perform the tasks in this review, or you can read the material for just one question and perform the tasks in this review for that question before moving on to the next one.

Q1 What is an information system?

List the components of an information system. Explain how knowledge of these components will guide Dee's work as she builds her information system.

Q2 What is MIS?

List the three elements of MIS. Why does a nontechnical business professional need to understand all three? Why are information systems developed? Why is part of this definition misleading?

Q3 How does IS differ from IT?

Define *IS*. Define *IT*. Does IT include IS or does IS include IT? Why does technology, by itself, not constitute an information system?

Q4 How do successful business professionals use IS?

How will developing the blog help Dee? Explain the employment trend involving emerging technology. How does this trend pertain to Jeff Bezos, CEO of Amazon.com?

Q5 What new opportunities for IS are developing today?

Explain what IT resources are essentially free today. Describe two opportunities for taking advantage of those free resources.

Q6 How can you create a strong password?

Define *strong password*. Explain an easy way to create and remember a strong password. Under what circumstances should you give someone else your password?

Q7 What is this class about?

In your own words, tell what this class is about. Look at the table of contents of this book. What major themes does it address? How will those themes relate to you as a business professional? If you were (or are) employed and if you had to justify the expense of this class to your boss, how would you do it?

How does the knowledge in this chapter help Dee and you?

How can Dee's plan for her blog be guided by the five components of information systems? Why does Dee need a strong password to control access to her blog?

Key Terms and Concepts

Using Your Knowledge

1. Using your own knowledge and opinions as well as those listed in Figure 1-5 (page 15), describe three misconceptions of the purpose of this class. In your own words, describe what you think the purpose of this class is.

2. Describe three to five personal goals for this class. None of these goals should include anything about your GPA. Be as specific as possible, and make the goals personal to your major, interests, and career aspirations. Assume that you are going to evaluate yourself on these goals at the end of the quarter or semester. The more specific you make these goals, the easier it will be to perform the evaluation.

3. Consider costs of a system in light of the five components: costs to buy and maintain the hardware; costs to develop or acquire licenses to the software programs and costs to maintain them; costs to design databases and fill them with data; costs of developing procedures and keeping them current; and finally, human costs both to develop and use the system.
   a. Over the lifetime of a system, many experts believe that the single most expensive component is people. Does this belief seem logical to you? Explain why you agree or disagree.
   b. Consider a poorly developed system that does not meet its defined requirements. The needs of the business do not go away, but they do not conform themselves to the characteristics of the poorly built system. Therefore, something must give. Which component picks up the slack when the hardware and software programs do not work correctly? What does this say about the cost of a poorly designed system? Consider both direct money costs as well as intangible personnel costs.
   c. What implications do you, as a future business manager, recognize after answering questions (a) and (b)? What does this say about the need for your involvement in requirements and other aspects of systems development? Who eventually will pay the costs of a poorly developed system? Against which budget will those costs accrue?

Case Study 1

IRS Requirements Creep, Revisited

Read the "Requirements Creep at the IRS" case on page 9. In response to the problems that it identified, the IRS Oversight Board recommended the following two actions:[3]

- "The IRS business units must take direct leadership and ownership of the Modernization program and each of its projects. In particular, this must include defining the scope of each project, preparing realistic and attainable business cases, and controlling scope changes throughout each project's life cycle . . . "
- "Create an environment of trust, confidence, and teamwork between the business units, the BSM and ITS organizations, and the Prime. . . . "

[3]The report identified more than two problems and made more than two recommendations. See the "Independent Analysis of IRS Business Systems Modernization Special Report" at *www.irsoversightboard.treas.gov*.

Questions

1. Why did the Oversight Board place leadership and ownership of the Modernization program on the business units? Why did it not place these responsibilities on the Information Technology Services (ITS) organization?

2. Why did the Oversight Board place the responsibility for controlling scope changes on the business units? Why was this responsibility not given to the BSM? To ITS? To Computer Sciences Corporation?

3. The second recommendation is a difficult assignment, especially considering the size of the IRS and the complexity of the project. How does one go about creating "an environment of trust, confidence, and teamwork"?

   To make this recommendation more comprehensible, translate it to your local university. Suppose, for example, that your College of Business embarked on a program to modernize its computing facilities, including computer labs, and the computer network facilities used for teaching, including Internet-based distance learning. Suppose that the Business School dean created a committee like the BSM that hired a vendor to create the new computing facilities for the college. Suppose further that the committee proceeded without any involvement of the faculty, staff, students, or the existing computer support department. Finally, suppose that the project was one year late, had spent $400,000, was not nearly finished—and that the vendor complained that the requirements kept changing.

   Now assume that you have been given the responsibility of creating "an environment of trust, confidence, and teamwork" among the faculty, staff, other users, the computer support department, and the vendor. How would you proceed?

4. The problem in question 3 involves at most a few hundred people and a few sites. The IRS problem involves 100,000 people and over 1,000 sites. How would you modify your answer to question 3 for a project as large as the IRS's?

5. If the existing system works (which apparently it does), why is the BSM needed? Why fix a system that works?

Teaching Suggestions

Emerson Pharmaceuticals, Part 1 and Chapter 1

GOALS

Use Dee's blog[1] to:

* Convince the students that knowledge of MIS will be critical to their success in business.

* Create cognitive dissonance for students who think this will be the "computer" class or the class on Excel or Access.

* Use the students' cognitive dissonance to motivate learning definitions of IS, MIS, IT, and the five-component model.

BACKGROUND

1. This case is real. I helped Dee formulate the idea for her blog. When she ran into trouble, I introduced her to Don Gray (who really exists and who does provide such consulting services). Dee does not work in the pharmaceutical industry, but the dynamics of her actual industry are nearly identical. She does provide marketing communications to a 450-person sales force.

2. Dee was able to get her blog up and running in time for the sales meeting, and she used it very successfully throughout the sales season. Given her lack of knowledge about information systems, she would never have succeeded without Don. She was completely dependent on Don's knowledge and professionalism. Had he been less able or a scoundrel, Dee's project would have failed.

3. At no time did Dee have any idea of what she was doing. She had read blogs, and she knew she could write one. She also understood that she needed to restrict the blog to her own salespeople, but she had no idea how to do that. As the project developed, she was like a ping-pong ball between her IT department and Don. The IT department would raise an objection, and she would take it to Don. She had no idea what the objection meant, so she would report it

verbatim. Don would tell her how to respond, and she would respond, *verbatim*. It drove her nuts to be so ignorant about what they were saying, and she became incredibly frustrated. She was also lucky that it all worked out.

4. *Atlantic Monthly* published an excellent background article on pharmaceutical sales, "The Drug Pushers," by Carl Elliott, *Atlantic Monthly*, April 2006, pp. 82–93. It is great reading and very useful for this case.

5. Students don't know what MIS is, nor do they know the importance of information systems in business. *We must teach the students what MIS is and why it matters to today's business professionals.* Again and again I remind myself to do that. I know that MIS is important, and I'm surprised that they don't respond. Their lack of response becomes more understandable when I remember that they haven't worked in business and they don't know how important information systems are. Dee's blog is a small, but understandable, example of how MIS knowledge will be useful to the business graduates.

HOW TO GET THE STUDENTS INVOLVED

1. Do everything possible to get the students to identify with Dee. Ask questions like:

   a. Is anyone here majoring in marketing?

   b. What do you think of using a blog to provide information to salespeople?

   c. Can you imagine wanting to do this?

   d. Even if you don't major in marketing, can you see the need for this sort of information and blog delivery?

2. Develop the business case: The blog worked. Sales people loved it because Dee gave them the latest news on what sales strategies were working, what the competition was doing, where the competition was vulnerable, and she told stories of superior efforts of particular salespeople.

   a. How could Dee's blog give Emerson a competitive advantage over the competition?

   b. What information might Dee provide during the sales season?

   c. How did having the blog enhance Dee's position vis-à-vis the sales force?

   d. How did the blog save Dee time?

   e. How did the blog save the time of the sales force?

[1]Note: The goals in these annotations refer only to the use of Emerson Pharmaceuticals or Dorset-Stratford Interiors (DSI). Each chapter has additional goals as indicated by the chapter's introductory questions. In general, the goals of all the Emerson and DSI scenarios are to increase motivation by engaging the students' emotions. See the discussion of *hot cognition* in the Instructor's Preface. The videos are also designed to engage emotions; you might consider showing them in class.

3. Show the introductory video about Dee.

4. Having established the business case, now ask the students the clincher:

   a. **What would you do?**

   b. **How would you set up the blog?**

   c. **What is a blog made of? How could you build one if you don't know?**

   d. **What is an information system made of?**

   e. **How could Dee use the five components to guide her project?**

   f. **What are the five components of a blog system?**

   g. **Will Dee build the system herself? Will she write any programs? Will she build any databases? Just what will she do?**

   h. **What do you think Dee needs to learn from this class?**

5. Assign the *Atlantic Monthly* reading (background item 4) to two or three students and ask them to report to the class on the nature of the pharmaceutical industry. Have the students in the class comment on the utility of a blog in this situation.

BOTTOM LINE

* Business professionals need knowledge of information systems—not computer programming, not just the use of Excel or Access, and not IT in isolation. They need to know how information systems, with the five components, contribute to businesses' successes.

Using the Ethics Guide: Ethics of Misdirected Information Use
(page 7a)

GOALS

* Teach students about the problem of unintentionally revealing sensitive information in public places.

* Explore ethical issues concerning the use of misdirected information.

* Differentiate between *unethical* and *illegal*.

BACKGROUND AND PRESENTATION STRATEGIES

I begin by asking the students what are the only two questions that a business professional can ask in an elevator. Usually someone will have worked in a law or CPA office and they'll know. The standard answer is:

➤ **What floor?**

➤ **How is the weather?**

That's it. *No other question is allowed in an elevator.* Airplanes and public places, like Starbucks in this story, are other places to avoid conversations about sensitive matters.

The first scenario happened to me. Fortunately, I was relieved of my ethical dilemma when a third party purchased the property from underneath all of us.

The people were loud and boorish. I wasn't sneaking around picking up newspapers by their table. I was passively sitting while they talked, very loudly. They were speaking loudly on cell phones to their inspector and their bank! I suppose I'm confounding my dislike for loud, public, cell phone users with my ethical principles. What difference does it make, ethically, if they were rude?

Did I have a responsibility to move to another table where I couldn't hear them? Or to warn them that I could hear them and that I was bidding on the same property? Or, did fate just drop something in my lap, like winning the lottery? I asked our agent about it, and she said by all means use the information. But do I want the realtor to be the guardian of my ethical principles? If so, I am avoiding my personal responsibility.

Usually, my students say they would use the information and never look back. I don't think I agree.

When evaluating behavior in business, we can consider three sets of criteria: *ethics, corporate policy,* and *laws.* Behaviors concerning the latter two categories are easy to define: Is the behavior against a law or corporate policy?

Ethical behavior is harder to define. Microsoft Encarta defines ethical as *"conforming to accepted standards"* or *"consistent with agreed principles of correct moral conduct"* and ethics as *"a system of moral principles governing the appropriate conduct for an individual or group."*

So, the question becomes, *"What system of moral principles governs conduct for business professionals?"* This is the core of the matter that we will address in all of the "Ethics Guides" in the text.

The legal community makes this issue clear, at least among lawyers and in the courts. Use of any misdirected information is unethical, and court judgments can be lost by a party that uses such information. Legal ethics state that if a lawyer mistakenly receives a document intended for the other side, the lawyer is forbidden to use the contents of that document and is supposed to direct the document to its proper source, or at least return it to the sender with an appropriate notice. Often, law firms place a notice reminding the receiver of that obligation at the bottom of every email or other correspondence. (You also will find it at the bottom of some corporate emails.)

➤ **If we apply the lawyer's criteria to the scenarios in A–D, they are all unethical.**

➤ **Should professional business people have a lower standard than lawyers?**

❓ SUGGESTED RESPONSES FOR DISCUSSION QUESTIONS

1. I don't think the medium should make a difference. Using the lawyer's criteria mentioned earlier, the use of information in either case is unethical. Also, there's a difference in that the email server at the real estate office has a record that it sent that email to you. In scenario A, no one could prove you heard. That difference doesn't change the ethics—it just changes the chance that you might be discovered.

   Also, in scenario B there is another possibility: If you received the terms of their offer, there's a good chance the addresses were switched and they received the terms of your offer. From a practical per-spective, setting aside the ethical issues, it's probably best to let your agent know what happened.

2. Scenario C is more complicated. For one, what if the customer wants you to have that information? Or, what if that information is false, the real number is higher, but the customer wants you to think that's their top number? This could be a mistake or a negotiating ploy. I think notifying the customer is not only ethical, it's also smart.

   ➤ **Nothing is more serviceable than the truth. Maybe it's not the most convenient, but it's the easiest in the long run.**

   ➤ **I don't think whether the information gives you or your company an advantage is relevant. By the way, your company may have a written ethical policy that governs your behavior here. You could lose your job by not following those guidelines.**

3. I think a person could make an argument that it is more ethical to lie to your friend about having received the email. The purpose of your lie would be to save your friend from embarrassment. However, lying to friends is not a great way to build relationships. It might be better to tell your friend that you did receive the email; that you're available to talk about it if he or she wants; and that, as a good friend, you can also forget all about it.

4. I think the actions of the person in scenario E are most unethical and undoubtedly against corporate policy. This is *"You're fired!"* territory. Were I that person's employer, I would not provide a reference. I don't think the person should have received the email, and I don't think the person should notify his or her friend. Anyone who abused his job authorities in this way is unlikely to care about the ethical principles of telling his or her friend, however. They'd probably tell. To me, the whole scenario stinks!

   ➤ **By the way, we'll talk about this in Chapters 6 and 12, but corporate email is not secure. Even if someone has not invaded the corporate system, as this person did, emails you send at work are not private.**

5. **a.** For definitions, see "Background and Presentations Strategies."

   b. I suppose one could argue that business is competitive; it's dog eat dog, and you'll take any advantage that falls in your lap. (There is the possibility that the emails are setups, and you could be playing into someone's plan.) Or, it might be that in some industries, such behaviors are normal. If they are truly normal, if everyone accepts them, then according to the definition of ethical, these behaviors are ethical.

   c. One argument, a pragmatic one, centers on the idea that "nothing is more serviceable than the truth." Once you start taking advantage of information under the table, you've placed yourself in a spot to be manipulated (if, for example, the top number in scenario C is not really the top number). Another argument is a personal one: "I strive to act ethically, and I know I won't be happy engaging in unethical behavior. I want to work around people and industries in which ethical behavior is expected." A third argument takes the moral high ground. It doesn't matter if ethical behavior is pragmatic or personally preferred, unethical behavior is just wrong.

6. Answer is up to the students. See the Wrap Up.

WRAP UP

Some questions to summarize the discussion:

➤ **How do you define the difference between legal and ethical?**

➤ **Can something be against corporate policy and still be legal?**

➤ **What is your personal policy about dealing with information that is misdirected to you?**

➤ **Did your thoughts about this matter change as a result of this discussion? If so, how?**

Using the Guide: Duller Than Dirt? *(page 15a)*

GOALS

* Share our excitement about MIS with our students.

* Establish the fact that this class is work. Some topics take time and effort to learn. That's OK.

* Discuss strategies for making the subject interesting.

* Introduce students to the idea of "waking up to your life."

BACKGROUND AND PRESENTATION STRATEGIES

I use the "waking up to your life" theme as a wrap up for this lecture. See the "Wrap Up" (next page).

I take the students' goal of being a business professional very seriously—occasionally more seriously than some of them do. Given that goal, I'm here to help those who want to learn how to use IS and related topics to help them strengthen their personal competitiveness.

I love this field, and you probably do too. Tell the students why! They will be very interested to know why you picked this discipline, what you like about it, what the challenges are, what you find interesting. Few students will want to be professors, but they will want to know what aspects of your interests will apply to them.

This class can be *fun and incredibly interesting.* Especially if students learn to *personalize the topics*; that is, to constantly to ask themselves, how can I use this knowledge to get a job? To get a better job? To gain a competitive advantage? To be a better professional? Examples:

➤ **How will I, as a future public relations agent, use this material? What do I need to know to get a public relations job in technology? How can I use data communications technology to make me more productive?**

➤ **What do I, as a future general manager, need to know about this subject? What do I need to know about developing information systems? What do I need to know about using IT to advance corporate strategy?**

➤ **Should I think about an IS career? Although hardware and software jobs exist, not every IS professional writes computer programs or installs network gear. It's all about the innovative application of IT and IS for the solution of business problems. That could be interesting!**

Having said all of that, at times this topic is duller than dirt. No getting around it. So, sometimes a person just has to buckle down and do the work. *Ignorance is curable, but it doesn't cure itself.* Not every topic will be exciting and interesting to every student all the time. That doesn't mean the topics aren't important.

Depending on the students' age and maturity, sometimes I leave it at that. But, if they are young and need coaching, I'll go on with something like:

➤ **Like any challenging course, you cannot succeed by channel surfing. You can't switch channels when the going gets hard. You have to stay with it.**

➤ **If you're a CFO and the financial statements have to be filed, they have to be filed, and you make that happen. It's all part of being a business professional.**

➤ **If you're a manager, and the computer budget needs to be submitted, you do what you have to do. If you don't know what something is or does, you find out. It doesn't matter how tired you are, how many other things you have to do, you just keep working; it must be done. At least, you do that *if you're a professional.***

➤ **So, learn not to quit when the going gets rough. Learn that behavior now, before you start your career!**

Students are students, and undergraduates are undergraduates. Many are young. They get busy with other classes; they get distracted with their friends; they get involved in campus activities that consume their study time. As the class proceeds, I have to keep stoking the fires of their interest by showing them my excitement about the material. Ultimately, however, *it's not my excitement about the class that motivates them; it's their excitement.* Mine just gets them going.

Every lecture, I need to do something to build that excitement. If I can do that, this class is a joy to teach. When I don't do that, it's like dragging a 500-pound sack of potatoes across campus. Again, it's the excitement of the students that moves the class along.

SUGGESTED RESPONSES FOR DISCUSSION QUESTIONS

1. To realize that every morning I'm a day older. That my life is going by and whether or not I'm aware of it, decisions I make each day impact the quality of my life. Here's a question that is sometimes revealing to students:

   ➤ **Have you ever heard the statement, "You need to take responsibility for your life"?**

   ➤ **I'm curious, how can any of us *not* take responsibility for our lives?**

   If we choose not to think about our lives, that's taking responsibility by default. It's taking responsibility by not taking responsibility. We cannot avoid taking responsibility for our lives. We're condemned to it.

2. You might ask the class the following questions:

   ➤ **Do you think about your goals? About how well you're accomplishing your goals? Do you think about what you want to accomplish in "this awkward time between birth and death"?**

   ➤ **Write a note to remind yourself that you cannot avoid responsibility for your life. Make goals; see how you're doing. Once a week may be too often. How about once a month?**

3. The purpose of this question is to ask the students to ask themselves whether they're living their lives by someone else's criteria. I think that's such an important task for undergraduates—especially for the traditional 20-year-old junior. Why do they attend college? Why are they business majors? What to they want to do? Are these their goals or their parents' goals? Are they an interpretation of what it means to be successful?

   If the answers to these questions indicate they chose these goals for themselves, then the students can rededicate themselves to the goals. But if not, now's the time to find out. If you'd rather be a painter, an engineer, or a biochemist, now's the time to figure that out.

4. Because it will help you learn to use IS to solve problems, make better decisions, and become a more complete business professional.

5. The text suggests personalizing it—making the material relevant to the students' goals.

WRAP UP

Sometimes I wrap up the first lecture with the following:

➤ **You and I, all of us, have just invested 3,600 heartbeats in the last 50 minutes. That's 3,600 heartbeats we'll never have again. Was it worth it? If not, what can *we* (that is *all of us—you and me*) do to make it worth it next time?**

➤ **Over the years, I've come to view a class like a woven tapestry. Each of us contributes one string of yarn, one string of the warp or one of the weft. We weave this experience together. I bring my excitement for the topic, my knowledge, my experiences, and I frame the experience. What happens, next, however, is up to you. Did you do the homework? Did you read the assignment? Are you surfing the Web or sending emails or are you listening? Are you relating this material to your goals?**

➤ **We make this experience together. I hope we will weave a beautiful tapestry, and to that end, I will do all I can. I hope you will, too. See you next time!**

2 Business Processes, Information, and Information Systems

This could happen to you

Before Dee could go very far with her project to create a blog for the sales force, she needed a budget. For that, she needed the approval of her boss. When Dee explained the idea to him, he was pleased that she was thinking innovatively, and he was positively inclined to support the project. However, he wanted more specifics and told her that before he'd approve spending any money, he wanted answers to three questions:

- **"How will this blog impact the sales process?"**
- **"How will the salespeople use it?"**
- **"How will it help us gain sales?"**

Dee began her career as a salesperson, and she is intimately acquainted with the sales process. Consequently, it was easy for her to answer these questions. Before we consider her responses, however, you need to learn more about business processes and how they relate to information systems.

An optional Extension for this chapter is CE2, "Information Systems and Decision Making."

Study Questions

Q1 "How did this stuff get here?"

Q2 What is a business process?

Q3 What are the components of a business process?

Q4 What is information?

Q5 What is the role of information in business processes?

Q6 How do information systems support business processes?

How does the knowledge in this chapter help Dee and you?

Q1 "How Did This Stuff Get Here?"

Suppose you've graduated, attained just the job you'd hoped to get, and have a year or two of experience. Maybe you're an auditor, a financial analyst, or a salesperson. . . . You can be whatever you want to be. One April day, your company asks you to travel to New York City for a meeting in Manhattan. Like any responsible business professional, you've arrived a bit early, so you decide to have a cup of coffee and a scone at the Europa Café on 53rd Street and 3rd Avenue.

Sitting down with your coffee and scone, you let your mind wander. As you look around the room, the question occurs to you, "How did this stuff get here? The milk? The coffee? The scone? How did it get here?"

You know that somewhere there must be a cow that produced the milk that's in your coffee. Where is that cow? Who owns that cow? Who milked that cow? Who decided to ship that particular milk to the Europa that morning? Who delivered the milk? On what truck? How was the truck routed to customers? Who trained the truck driver?

For that matter, how did the coffee get here? It was grown in Kenya, shipped to the United States, roasted in New Jersey, packaged by a vendor, and delivered to the Europa. How did all of that happen? Or the scone? Who baked it? When? How many scones did they bake? How did they make that decision?

What about the chair you're sitting on? The wood was grown in Brazil and shipped to China, where the chair was manufactured, and then it was delivered to an import/export business in San Francisco. How did it get here? Who bought it? For whom did they work? Who paid them? How?

The more you think about it, the more you realize that a near miracle occurred just to bring you to this experience. Hundreds, if not thousands, of different processes had successfully interacted just to bring together your scone and coffee and you. (Wait! How did you get here? You flew up from your office in Atlanta. . . . Think about the processes in that, too!)

It's truly amazing. And those processes had to do more than just work. They had to work in such a way that all of the economic entities involved obtained a payment to cover their costs and make a profit. How did that occur? Who set the prices? Who computed the quantity of nonfat milk to be shipped through the Lincoln Tunnel the night before? How does all of this come about? The more you think about this, the more amazing it is.

In truth, all of this activity comes about through the interaction of business processes. The Europa has a process for ordering, receiving, storing, and paying for ingredients like milk and coffee. The coffee roaster has a process for assessing demand, ordering its raw materials, and making deliveries. All of the other businesses have processes for conducting their affairs as well.

Q2 What Is a Business Process?

A **business process** is a network of activities, resources, facilities, and information that interact to achieve some business function. A business process is a system, and sometimes business processes are also referred to as **business systems**. In this text, we will use the term *business process*.

Examples of business processes are inventory management processes, manufacturing processes, sales and support processes, and so forth. Figure 2-1 shows a model of a portion of an inventory management business process that might be used at the Europa Café.

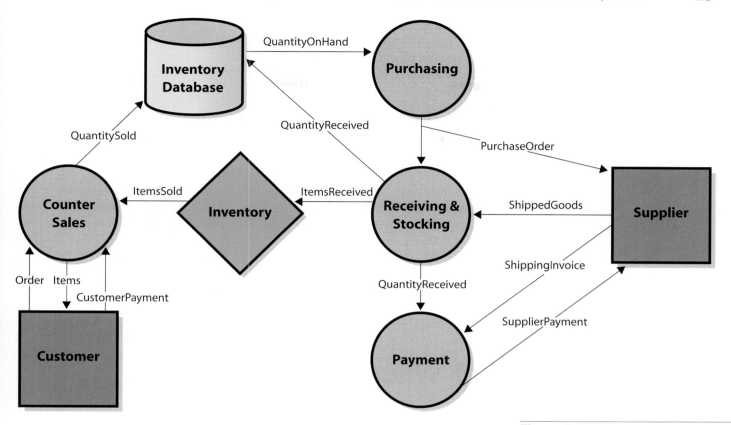

Figure 2-1
Portion of Inventory Management Business Process

Purchasing (an activity) queries the Inventory Database (a facility) and obtains *QuantityOnHand* (information) for a particular product. If the quantity is below the reorder quantity, Purchasing generates and sends a *PurchaseOrder* (information) to a Supplier (a resource). Purchasing sends a copy of the *PurchaseOrder* to Receiving and Stocking (an activity). When the goods arrive, Receiving and Stocking places them in Inventory (a facility), and it then sends a record of the *QuantityReceived* to both the Inventory Database and to Payment (an activity). When the Supplier sends a *ShippingInvoice* (information) to Payment, the payment process compares the *ShippingInvoice* to the *PurchaseOrder*, and it generates a *SupplierPayment* (a resource), as appropriate. *CounterSales* (an activity) interacts with the Customer (resource), Inventory, and the Inventory Database as shown in Figure 2-1.

Consider the diagram in Figure 2-1 as a snapshot of the system. It does not show logic; it does not show what causes what. It is just a picture of the elements of the business process and how they interact. Also, there are many different ways of representing a business process. Many vendors of business process software have their own documentation standards. Any clear and consistent representation will do.

Q3 What Are the Components of a Business Process?

As stated, a business process consists of activities, resources, facilities, and information. **Activities** transform resources and information of one type into resources and information of another type. The Payment activity transforms *QuantityReceived* and *ShippingInvoice* information into a *SupplierPayment* (resource). The Payment activity has rules and procedures that it follows for doing this.

An activity can be manual (people following procedures), it can be automated (hardware directed by software), or it can be a combination of manual and automated.

Resources are items of value. A case of milk is a resource, a check is a resource, and the customer's cash is a resource. In Figure 2-1, both Supplier and Customer are also considered resources because they have value to this process. They are not considered activities because they are external to Europa and hence are not under the Europa's direction and control.

In business processes, **facilities** are structures used within the business process. Typical facilities are inventories and databases (as in Figure 2-1). Other examples of facilities are factories, pieces of equipment, trucks, file cabinets, and the like.

Information is the fourth element of a business process. Activities use information to determine how to transform the inputs they receive into the outputs they produce. Because this book is about *information* systems, understanding the nature of information and ways of defining it are crucial.

Q4 What Is Information?

Information is one of those fundamental terms that we use every day but that turns out to be surprisingly difficult to define. Defining *information* is like defining words such as *alive* and *truth*. We know what those words mean, we use them with each other without confusion, but they are nonetheless difficult to define.

In this text, we will avoid the technical issues of defining *information* and will use common, intuitive definitions instead. Probably the most common definition is that **information** is *knowledge derived from data*, where *data* is defined as recorded facts or figures. Thus, the facts that employee James Smith earns $17.50 per hour and that Mary Jones earns $25.00 per hour are *data*. The statement that the average hourly wage of all employees in the Garden Department is $22.37 per hour is *information*. *Average wage* is knowledge that is derived from the data of individual wages.

Another common definition is that *information is data presented in a meaningful context*. The fact that Jeff Parks earns $10.00 per hour is data.[1] The statement that Jeff Parks earns less than half the average hourly wage of the Garden Department, however, is information. It is data presented in a meaningful context.

Another definition of *information* that you will hear is that *information is processed data*, or sometimes, *information is data processed by summing, ordering, averaging, grouping, comparing, or other similar operations*. The fundamental idea of this definition is that we do something to data to produce information.

There is yet a fourth definition of information, presented in the *Guide* on pages 25a–25b. There, information is defined as a *difference that makes a difference*.

---

[1]Actually, the word *data* is plural; to be correct, we should use the singular form *datum* and say, "The fact that Jeff Parks earns $10.00 per hour is a datum." The word *datum*, however, sounds pedantic and fussy, and we will avoid it in this text.

- Accurate
- Timely
- Relevant
  - To context
  - To subject
- Just sufficient
- Worth its cost

Figure 2-2
Characteristics of Good
Information

For the purposes of this text, any of these definitions of information will do. Choose the definition of information that makes sense to you. The important point is that you discriminate between data and information. You also may find that different definitions work better in different situations.

Characteristics of Good Information

All information is not equal: Some information is better than other information. Figure 2-2 lists the characteristics of good information.

Accurate

First, good information is **accurate information**. Good information is based on correct and complete data, and it has been processed correctly as expected. Accuracy is crucial; managers must be able to rely on the results of their information systems. The IS function can develop a bad reputation in the organization if a system is known to produce inaccurate information. In such a case, the information system becomes a waste of time and money as users develop work-arounds to avoid the inaccurate data.

A corollary to this discussion is that you, a future user of information systems, ought not to rely on information just because it appears in the context of a Web page, a well-formatted report, or a fancy query. It is sometimes hard to be skeptical of information delivered with beautiful, active graphics. Do not be misled. When you begin to use an information system, be skeptical. Cross-check the information you are receiving. After weeks or months of using a system, you may relax. Begin, however, with skepticism.

Timely

Good information is **timely information**—produced in time for its intended use. A monthly report that arrives six weeks late is most likely useless. The information arrives long after the decisions have been made that needed that information. An information system that tells you not to extend credit to a customer after you have shipped the goods is unhelpful and frustrating. Notice that timeliness can be measured against a calendar (six weeks late) or against events (before we ship).

When you participate in the development of an IS, timeliness will be part of the requirements you will request. You need to give appropriate and realistic timeliness needs. In some cases, developing systems that provide information in near real time is much more difficult and expensive than producing information a few hours later. If you can get by with information that is a few hours old, say so during the requirements specification phase.

Consider an example. Suppose you work in marketing and you need to be able to assess the effectiveness of new online ad programs. You want an information system that will not only deliver ads over the Web, but will also enable you to determine how frequently customers click on those ads. Determining click ratios in near real time will be very expensive; saving the data in a batch and processing

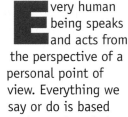

Understanding Perspectives and Points of View

Every human being speaks and acts from the perspective of a personal point of view. Everything we say or do is based on—or equivalently, is biased by—that point of view. Thus, everything you read in any textbook, including this one, is biased by the author's point of view. Authors may think that they are writing unbiased accounts of neutral subject material. But no one can write an unbiased account of anything, because we all write from a perspective.

Similarly, your professors speak to you from their points of view. They have experience, goals, objectives, hopes, and fears, and, like all of us, they use those elements to provide a framework from which they think and speak.

Sometimes, when you read or hear an editorial or opinion-oriented material, it is easy to recognize a strongly held point of view. It does not surprise you to think that such opinions might contain personal biases. But what about statements that are less apparently opinions? For example, consider the following definition of *information*: "Information is a difference that makes a difference." By this definition, there are many differences, but only those that make a difference qualify as information.

This definition is obviously not an opinion, but it nevertheless was written from a biased perspective. The perspective is just less evident because the statement appears as a definition, not an opinion.

But, in fact, it is the definition of information in the opinion of the well-known psychologist Gregory Bateson.

I find his definition informative and useful. It is imprecise, but it is a pretty good guideline, and I have used it to advantage when designing reports and queries for end users. I ask myself, "Does this report show people a difference that makes a difference to them?" So I find it to be a useful and helpful definition.

My colleagues who specialize in quantitative methods, however, find Bateson's definition vapid and useless. They ask, "What does it say?" or "How could I possibly use that definition to formalize anything?" or "A difference that makes a difference to what or whom?" Or they say, "I couldn't quantify anything about that definition; it's a waste of time."

And they are right, but so am I, and so was Gregory Bateson. The difference is a matter of perspective, and surprisingly, conflicting perspectives can all be true at the same time.

One last point: Whether it is apparent or not, authors write and professors teach not only from personal

perspectives, but also with personal goals. I write this textbook in the hope that you will find the material useful and important and that you will tell your professor that it is a great book so that he or she will use it again. Whether you (or I) are aware of that fact, it and my other hopes and goals bias every sentence in this book.

Similarly, your professors have hopes and goals that influence what and how they teach. Your professors may want to see light bulbs of recognition on your face, they may want to win the Professor of the Year award, or they may want to gain tenure status in order to be able to do some advanced research in the field. Whatever the case, they, too, have hopes and goals that bias everything they say.

So as you read this book and as you listen to your professor, ask yourself, "What is her perspective?" and "What are his goals?" Then compare those perspectives and goals to yours. Learn to do this not just with your textbooks and your professors, but with your colleagues as well. When you enter the business world, being able to discern and adapt to the perspectives and goals of those with whom you work will make you much more effective.

DISCUSSION QUESTIONS

1. Consider the following statement: "The quality of your thinking is the most important component of an information system." Do you agree with this statement? Do you think it is even possible to say that one component is the most important one?

2. Though it does not appear to be so, the statement "There are five components of an information system: hardware, software, data, procedures, and people" is an opinion based on a perspective. Suppose you stated this opinion to a computer engineer who said, "Rubbish. That's not true at all. The only components that count are hardware and maybe software." Contrast the perspective of the engineer with that of your MIS professor. How do those perspectives influence their opinions about the five-component framework? Which is correct?

3. Consider Bateson's definition: "Information is a difference that makes a difference." How can this definition be used to advantage when designing a Web page? Explain why someone who specializes in quantitative methods might consider this definition to be useless. How can the same definition be both useful and useless?

4. Some students hate open-ended questions. They want questions that have one correct answer, like "7.3 miles per hour." When given a question like that in question 3, a question that has multiple, equally valid answers, some students get angry or frustrated. They want the book or the professor to give them the answer. How do you feel about this matter?

5. Do you think individuals can improve the quality of their thinking by learning to hold multiple, contradictory ideas in their minds at the same time? Or do you think that doing so just leads to indecisive and ineffective thinking? Discuss this question with some of your friends. What do they think? What are their perspectives?

it some hours later will be much easier and cheaper. If you can live with information that is a day or two old, the system will be easier and cheaper to implement.

Relevant

Information should be **relevant** both to the context and to the subject. Considering context, you, the CEO, need information that is summarized to an appropriate level for your job. A list of the hourly wage of every employee in the company is unlikely to be useful. More likely, you need average wage information by department or division. A list of all employee wages is irrelevant in your context.

Information should also be relevant to the subject at hand. If you want information about short-term interest rates for a possible line of credit, then a report that shows 15-year mortgage interest rates is irrelevant. Similarly, a report that buries the information you need in pages and pages of results is also irrelevant to your purposes.

Just Barely Sufficient

Information needs to be **sufficient** for the purpose for which it is generated, but **just barely so**. We live in an information age; one of the critical decisions that each of us has to make each day is what information to ignore. The higher you rise into management, the more information you will be given, and because there is only so much time, the more information you will need to ignore. So information should be sufficient, but just barely.

Worth Its Cost

Information is not free. There are costs for developing an information system, costs of operating and maintaining that system, and costs of your time and salary for reading and processing the information the system produces. For information to be **worth its cost**, there must be an appropriate relationship between the cost of information and its value.

Consider an example. What is the value of a daily report of the names of the occupants of a full graveyard? Zero, unless grave robbery is a problem for the cemetery. The report is not worth the time required to read it. It is easy to see the importance of information economics for this silly example. It will be more difficult, however, when someone proposes some new system to you. You need to be ready to ask, "What's the value of the information?" or "What is the cost?" or "Is there an appropriate relationship between value and cost?" Information systems should be subject to the same financial analyses to which other assets are subjected.

Q5 What Is the Role of Information in Business Processes?

The discussion about information may seem overly theoretical. What does it have to do with realistic business processes? How can Dee use the definitions of *information* to build a better blog?

Look again at the inventory management process in Figure 2-1. Consider the Payment process, which compares the *QuantityReceived* (from Receiving and Stocking) to the *ShippingInvoice* (from the Supplier). If the goods received match the goods billed, then Payment generates a *SupplierPayment*.

Now let's apply some of the definitions from the last section. Is *QuantityReceived* an example of *data*, or is it *information*? By itself, it is just data, a recorded fact or figure: "We, Europa, received these items from that supplier on this date." Similarly, the *ShippingInvoice* could also be considered to be just data: "We, Supplier X, delivered these items to Europa on this date."

When we bring these two items together, however, we generate information. Consider Bateson's definition of *information*: "Information is a difference that makes a difference." If the *QuantityReceived* says we received five cases of milk but the *ShippingInvoice* is billing us for eight cases (or three), we have a difference that makes a difference. By comparing records of the amount we received to records of the amount we were billed, we are presenting data in a meaningful context, which is another definition of information.

Thus, the business process generates information by bringing together important items of data in a context. However, it also generates information at an even higher level. Over time, this process will generate information that will be useful for management and strategy decisions. For example, we could use the information produced by the process in Figure 2-1 to determine which are the cheapest, or fastest, or most reliable suppliers. We could use the information in the Inventory Database to assess our inventory ordering strategy. We could also use it to estimate pilferage and theft losses. For more discussion of this topic, see Chapter Extension 2, "Information Systems and Decision Making," on page 329.

Q6 How Do Information Systems Support Business Processes?

Information systems are used by the activities in a business process, but the particular relationship varies among business processes. In some processes, several activities use one information system. In other processes, each activity has its own information system, and in still other processes, some activities use several different information systems.

During systems development, the systems designers determine the relationship of activities to information systems. You will learn more about this topic in Chapters 7, 8, and 10.

What Does It Mean to Automate a Process Activity?

We will consider the role of information systems for several of the activities in Figure 2-1, but before we do that, think about the five components of an information system. In Figure 2-3 on page xx, notice the symmetry of components. The outermost components, hardware and people, are both *actors*; they can take actions. The software and procedure components are both sets of *instructions*: Software is instructions for hardware, and procedures are instructions for people. Finally, data is the bridge between the computer side on the left and the human side on the right.

When an activity in a business process is handled by an **automated system**, it means that work formerly done by people following procedures has been moved so that computers now do that work by following instructions in software. Thus, the automation of a process activity consists of moving work from the right-hand side of Figure 2-3 to the left.

Figure 2-3
Characteristics of the Five
Components

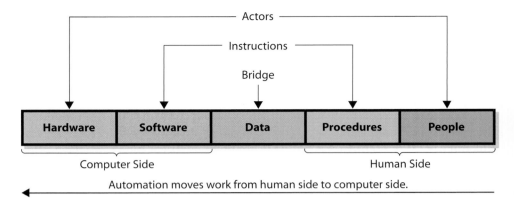

An Information System to Support Counter Sales

According to Figure 2-1, the Counter Sales activity interacts with the customer. It receives the customer's order, takes the items from inventory, and receives the customer's payment. This is just a model of the familiar process of ordering coffee and a scone at a café.

Counter Sales uses the information system shown in Figure 2-4. This system is automated, however, and the cashiers do not even know they are using an information system. The cash registers contain a computer that communicates with another computer that hosts the inventory database. Programs in the cash register record sales and make appropriate changes to the inventory database whenever the cashier rings up a sale. The cashiers need to be trained only in how to use the cash register; they never need to work directly with the sales-recording programs on the computer.

The designers of this system decided to fully automate it because the cashier's job is a low-skill-level position with high turnover. The designers did not want the cashiers to obtain training beyond learning to use the cash registers.

An Information System to Support Payment

Now consider the Payment activity in Figure 2-1. Payment receives the *QuantityReceived* and the *ShippingInvoice*, and it produces *SupplierPayment*. (In actuality, Payment does not generate the check to the supplier. Because of

Figure 2-4
Sales Recording
Information
System, Used by
Counter Sales in
Figure 2-1

Hardware	Software	Data	Procedures	People
– Cash register computer – Database host computer	– Sales-recording program on cash register	– Sales data – Inventory database	– Operate cash register	– Cashier

Mostly an automated system.
Almost all work is done by computers and software.

Hardware	Software	Data	Procedures	People
– Personal computer	– Adobe Acrobat Reader – Email	– *QuantityReceived* – *ShippingInvoice*	– Reconcile receipt document with invoice. – Issue payment authorization, if appropriate. – Process exceptions.	– Accounts payable

Mostly a manual system.
Little work is done by computers and software.
Most work is done by Accounts Payable clerk.

Figure 2-5
Payment System, Used by Payment Activity in Figure 2-1

accounting controls, no single person should approve a payment and generate the check. Instead, Payment generates an authorization and sends it to someone else to cut the check. These details are omitted here for simplicity–they are important, however!)

As you can see in Figure 2-5, the information system that supports the Payment activity is a mostly **manual system**. The Accounts Payable clerk receives both the *QuantityReceived* and the *ShippingInvoice* as Adobe Acrobat pdf files (the same sort of pdf files that you receive over the Internet). He or she then reads those documents, compares the quantities, and issues the payment authorization as appropriate. If there is a discrepancy, the Accounts Payable clerk investigates and takes action as appropriate.

The designers of this system chose to leave it as a manual system because processing the exceptions is complicated. There are many different exceptions, and each requires a different response. The designers thought that programming all of those exceptions would be expensive and probably not very effective. The designers decided it would be better to let humans deal with such varied situations. This means, by the way, that the Accounts Payable clerks will need much more training than the cashiers. Accounting management will need to ensure that Accounts Payable clerk turnover is low.

An Information System to Support Purchasing

Now consider the information system that supports the Purchasing activity in Figure 2-1. This system, shown in Figure 2-6, balances the work between automation and manual activity. The Purchasing clerk has a personal computer that is connected to the computer that hosts the database. Her computer runs an Inventory application program that queries the database and identifies items that are low in stock and need to be ordered. That application produces a report that the Purchasing clerk reads.

The clerk decides which items to order and from which suppliers. In making this decision, she is guided by Europa's inventory management practices. When she does decide to order, she runs a Purchasing program on her computer. It is that program that generates the *PurchaseOrder* shown in Figure 2-1.

The designers of this information system decided to balance the work between the computer and the human. Searching the Inventory Database for items that are low in stock is a perfect application for a computer. It is a repetitive

Figure 2-6
Purchasing
Information
System, Used by
Purchasing
Activity in
Figure 2-1

Hardware	Software	Data	Procedures	People
– Personal computer – Database host computer	– Inventory application program – Purchasing program	– Inventory database	– Issue *PurchaseOrder* according to inventory management practices and guidelines.	– Purchasing clerk

Balance between computer and human work.

process that humans find tedious. On the other hand, selecting which supplier to use is a process that can require human judgment. The clerk needs to balance a number of factors: quality of supplier, recent supplier experience, the need to have a variety of suppliers, and so forth. Such complicated balancing is better done by a human. Again, this means that the Purchasing clerks will need much more training than the cashiers.

The three different information systems at the café support the needs of users in the company's various business processes—counter sales, payments, and purchasing. As *MIS in Use 2* discusses, though, some companies choose to *integrate* their information systems into a single system. We will discuss such integration in more detail later in the book.

Before we leave these five components, it is important for you to understand how YOU will relate to information systems. We consider that next.

What Is Your Role?

You are part of every information system that you use. When you consider the five components of an information system, the last component, *people*, includes you. Your mind and your thinking are not merely *a* component of the information systems you use; they are *the most important* component.

Consider an example. Suppose you have the perfect information system, one that can predict the future. No such information system exists, but assume that it does for this example. Now suppose that on December 14, 1966, your perfect information system tells you that the next day, Walt Disney will die. Say you have $50,000 to invest; you can either buy Disney stock or you can short it (an investment technique that will net you a positive return if the stock value decreases). Given your perfect information system, how do you invest?

Before you read on, think about this question. If Walt Disney is going to die the next day, will the stock go up or down? Most students assume that the stock will go down, so they short it, on the theory that the loss of a company's founder will mean a dramatic drop in the share price.

In fact, the next day, the value of Disney stock increased substantially. Why? The market viewed Walt Disney as an artist; once he died, he would no longer be able to create more art. Thus, the value of the existing art would increase because of scarcity, and the value of the corporation that owned that art would increase as well.

The Brose Group Integrates Its Systems—One Site at a Time

The Brose Group supplies windows, doors, seat adjusters, and related products for more than 40 auto brands. Major customers include General Motors, Ford, DaimlerChrysler, BMW, Porsche, Volkswagen, Toyota, and Honda. Founded as an auto and aircraft parts manufacturer in Berlin in 1908, the company today has facilities at more than 30 locations in 20 different countries. Revenue for 2004 exceeded 2 billion euros.

In the 1990s, Brose enjoyed rapid growth but found that existing information systems were unable to support the company's emerging needs. Too many different information systems meant a lack of standardization and hampered communication among suppliers, plants, and customers. Brose decided to standardize operations using software that integrates different business processes. Rather than attempt to implement those processes on its own, Brose hired SAP Consulting to lead the project.

The SAP team provided process consulting and implementation support, and it trained end users. According to Christof Lutz, SAP project manager, "Our consultants and the Brose experts worked openly, flexibly, and constructively together. In this atmosphere of trust, we created an implementation module that the customer can use as a basis for the long term."

The Brose/SAP consulting team decided on a pilot approach. The first installation was conducted at a new plant in Curitiba, Brazil. The team constructed the implementation to be used as a prototype for installations at additional plants. Developing the first implementation was no small feat, because it involved information systems for sales and distribution, materials management, production planning, quality management, and financial accounting and control.

Once the initial system was operational at the Curitiba plant, the prototype was rolled out to additional facilities. The second implementation, in Puebla, Mexico, required just 6 months for first operational capability, and the next implementation in Meerane, Germany, was operational in just 19 weeks.

The conversion to the integrated system has contributed to dramatically increased productivity. In 1994, Brose achieved sales of 541 million euros with 2,900 employees, or 186,000 euros per employee. Ten years later, in 2004, Brose attained sales of 2 billion euros with 8,200 employees, or 240,000 euros per employee.

Sources: brose.de/en/pub/company (accessed November 2004); sap.com/industries/automotive/pdf/CS[lowline]Brose_Group.pdf (accessed November 2004).

Here's the point: Even if you have the perfect information system, if you do not know what to do with the information that it produces, you are wasting your time and money. The *quality of your thinking* is a large part of the quality of the information system. Substantial cognitive research has shown that although you cannot increase your basic IQ, you can dramatically improve the quality of your thinking. You cannot change the computer in your brain, so to speak, but you can change the way you have programmed your brain to work. The *Guide* on pages 31a–31b discusses one way of improving the quality of your thinking—that is, actively working to learn how others think in an activity called empathic thinking.

ETHICS
GUIDE

Egocentric vs. Empathetic Thinking

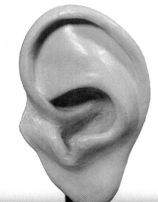

According to one definition of the term, a *problem* is a perceived difference between what is and what ought to be. When developing information systems, it is critical for the development team to have a common definition and understanding of the problem. This common understanding, however, can be difficult to achieve.

Cognitive scientists distinguish between egocentric and empathetic thinking. Egocentric thinking centers on the self; someone who engages in egocentric thinking considers his or her view as "the real view" or "what really is." In contrast, those who engage in empathetic thinking consider their view as one possible interpretation of the situation and actively work to learn what other people are thinking.

Different experts recommend empathetic thinking for different reasons. Religious leaders say that such thinking is morally superior; psychologists say that empathetic thinking leads to richer, more fulfilling relationships. In business, empathetic thinking is recommended because it's smart. Business is a social endeavor, and those who can understand others' points of view are always more

effective. Even if you do not agree with others' perspectives, you will be much better able to work with them if you understand their views.

Consider an example. Suppose you say to your MIS professor, "Professor Jones, I couldn't come to class last Monday. Did we do anything important?" Such a statement is a prime example of egocentric thinking. It takes no account of your professor's point of view and implies that your professor talked about nothing important. As a professor, it's tempting to say, "No, when I noticed you weren't there, I took out all the important material."

To engage in empathetic thinking, consider this situation from the professor's point of view. Students who do not come to class cause extra work for their professors. It doesn't matter how valid your reason for not coming to class was; you may actually have been contagious with a fever of 102. But no matter what, your absence is more work for your professor. He or she must do something extra to help you recover from the lost class time.

Using empathetic thinking, you would do all you can to minimize the impact of your absence on your professor. For example, you could say, "I couldn't come to class, but I got the class notes from Mary. I read through them, and I have a question about establishing alliances as competitive advantage. . . . Oh, by the way, I'm sorry to trouble you with my problem."

Before we go on, let's consider a corollary to this scenario: Never, ever, send an email to your boss that says, "I couldn't come to the staff meeting on Wednesday. Did we do anything important?" Avoid this for the same reasons as those for missing class. Instead, find a way to minimize the impact of your absence on your boss.

Now what does all of this have to do with MIS? Suppose that you buy a new laptop computer and within a few days, it fails. Repeated calls to customer support produce short-term fixes, but no one remembers who you are or what has been suggested to you in the past. Assume the keyboard continues to lock up every few days. In that scenario, there are a few views of the problem: (1) Customer support reps do not have data about prior customer contacts; (2) the customer support rep recommended a solution that did not work; and (3) the company is shipping too many defective laptops. The solution to each of these problem definitions requires a different IS.

Now imagine yourself in a meeting about this situation, and suppose that different people in the meeting hold the three problem views. If everyone engages in egocentric thinking, what will happen? The meeting will be argumentative and likely will end with nothing accomplished.

Suppose, instead, that the attendees think empathetically. In this case, people will make a concerted effort to understand the different points of view, and the outcome will be much more positive—possibly a definition of all three problems ranked in order of priority. In both scenarios, the attendees have the same information; the difference in outcomes results from the thinking style of the attendees.

Empathetic thinking is an important skill in all business activities. Skilled negotiators always know what the other side wants; effective salespeople understand their customers' needs. Buyers who understand the problems of their vendors get better service. And students who understand the perspective of their professors get better. . . .

DISCUSSION QUESTIONS

1. In your own words, explain the difference between egocentric and empathetic thinking.

2. Suppose you and another person differ substantially on a problem definition. Suppose she says to you, "No, the real problem is that . . . ," followed by her definition of the problem. How do you respond?

3. Again, suppose you and another person differ substantially on a problem definition. Assume you understand his definition. How can you make that fact clear?

4. Explain the statement, "In business, empathetic thinking is smart." Do you agree?

How does the knowledge in this chapter help Dee and you?

Dee needs to obtain a budget from her boss for her blog. When she asked him about the project, he wanted answers to the following three questions:

- "How will this blog impact the sales process?"
- "How will the salespeople use it?"
- "How will it help us gain sales?"

Dee can use the knowledge from this chapter to craft her responses. To answer the first question, she needs to diagram the sales *process* in a format like that in Figure 2-1. The diagram will show the sales reps, the doctors and pharmacists, and the various stages of the sales process. It also needs to show information that the sales reps need during this process.

To answer the second question, Dee can add the blog as a *facility* that the sales reps can access. She would then amend the first diagram to show how the *information* would be accessed from the Web.

Dee can structure her answer to the third question using the Bateson definition of information: a difference that makes a difference. For example, she can use the blog to publish successful sales strategies. When she does that, she will be publishing a difference (a new sales strategy) that makes a difference (it worked!). She can also publish other information (differences that make a difference) from herself, from sales management, and from doctors and pharmacists.

Her boss didn't ask for it, and it probably is beyond what Dee wants to do at this point, but she could also create diagrams like Figures 2-4, 2-5, and 2-6. In one figure, she could summarize the five components of the information system that the reps will use when they access the blog. In another figure, she could summarize the five components of the information system she will use when she (or others) publishes and creates blog entries.

If you want to know more about the use of blogs and other similar facilities, read Chapter Extension 3, "Knowledge Management and Expert Systems," on page 335.

Active ? Review

Use this Active Review to verify that you understand the material in the chapter. You can read the entire chapter and then perform the tasks in this review, or you can read the material for just one question and perform the tasks in this review for that question before moving on to the next one.

Q1 "How did this stuff get here?"

Imagine yourself at a baseball or football game, or at some other athletic event. What business processes are involved in producing that event? How did you buy a ticket? What processes were involved in that activity? What processes are needed to print the ticket? Who cleaned the stadium? What processes are involved in hiring, managing, and paying the cleaning staff? What processes must exist to support the coaches and athletes? What about the referees? Look up in the publicity booth. What processes exist to support the newscasters and their crews?

Q2 What is a business process?

What is the definition of a business process? Consider one of the processes in your answer to Q1, and make a diagram similar to the one in Figure 2-1.

Q3 What are the components of a business process?

List the components of a business process. Define each component. Identify each type of component on your diagram in your answer to Q2.

Q4 What is information?

Give four definitions of information. Rank those definitions in order of usefulness in business. Justify your ranking.

Q5 What is the role of information in business processes?

Explain how information is created in the Payment activity in Figure 2-1. Describe three different types of information that could be produced from the data in the Inventory Database.

Q6 How do information systems support business processes?

Explain the meaning of each cell in Figures 2-4, 2-5, and 2-6. Explain the differences in the balance between automated and manual systems in these three information systems. Summarize the justification that the systems' designers used for constructing systems with the balance shown.

How does the knowledge in this chapter help Dee and you?

Summarize the ways in which Dee will use the knowledge in this chapter to answer the three questions her boss asked her. What do you think of this strategy? Is it likely to satisfy her boss? Can you think of other ways of responding to these questions that would be more effective?

Key Terms and Concepts

Using Your Knowledge

1. Consider the four definitions of information presented in this chapter. The problem with the first definition, "knowledge derived from data," is that it merely substitutes one word we don't know the meaning of (*information*) for

a second word we don't know the meaning of (*knowledge*). The problem with the second definition, "data presented in a meaningful context," is that it is too subjective. Whose context? What makes a context meaningful? The third definition, "data processed by summing, ordering, averaging, etc.," is too mechanical. It tells us what to do, but it doesn't tell us what information is. The fourth definition, "a difference that makes a difference," is vague and unhelpful.

Also, none of these definitions helps us to quantify the amount of information we receive. What is the information content of the statement that every human being has a navel? Zero—you already know that. On the other hand, the statement that someone has just deposited $50,000 into your checking account is chock-full of information. So good information has an element of surprise.

Considering all of these points, answer the following questions:
a. What is information made of?
b. If you have more information, do you weigh more? Why or why not?
c. If you give a copy of your transcript to a prospective employer, is that information? If you show that same transcript to your dog, is it still information? Where is the information?
d. Give your own best definition of information.
e. Explain how you think it is possible that we have an industry called the *information technology industry*, but we have great difficulty defining the word *information*.

2. The text states that information should be worth its cost. Both cost and value can be broken into tangible and intangible factors. *Tangible* factors can be directly measured; *intangible* ones arise indirectly and are difficult to measure. For example, a tangible cost is the cost of a computer monitor; an intangible cost is the lost productivity of a poorly trained employee.

Give five important tangible and five important intangible costs of an information system. Give five important tangible and five important intangible measures of the value of an information system. If it helps to focus your thinking, use the example of the class scheduling system at your university or some other university information system. When determining whether an information system is worth its cost, how do you think the tangible and intangible factors should be considered?

3. Suppose you manage the Purchasing department for a chain of coffee shops like Europa Café. Assume that your company is in the process of developing the requirements for a new purchasing application. As you think about those requirements, you wonder how much autonomy you want your employees to have in selecting the supplier for each purchase. You can develop a system that will make the supplier selection automatically, or you can build one that allows employees to make that selection. Explain how this characteristic will impact:
a. The skill level required for your employees.
b. The number of employees you'll need.
c. Your employee hiring criteria.
d. Your management practices.
e. The degree of autonomy for your employees.
f. Your flexibility in managing your department.

Suppose management has left you out of the requirements definition process. Explain how you could use the knowledge you developed in answering this question to justify your need to be involved in the requirements definition.

Case Study 2

Customer Support and Knowledge Management at Microsoft

Many companies believe that "the best customer service is no service at all": The product works, the customer never calls, and there's never a need for service. The next best customer service is that in which someone else pays—for example, when users support one another. To this end, Microsoft and other software vendors create and administer "user communities" of newsgroups, user groups, and most valuable professionals (MVPs). See *microsoft.com/communities* for examples.

In a *newsgroup*, users post questions about errors, problems, and product use. Other customers who have experience and expertise with the relevant product answer the posted questions. Microsoft employees can also post answers to questions. A side benefit to Microsoft is that it learns about product and documentation problems from the questions that are posted to the newsgroups.

A *user group* consists of product users who meet periodically in a particular geographic location. For example, a Microsoft Office user group in Washington, D.C., meets periodically to discuss best practices, new developments, problems, and other issues related to the use of Microsoft Office. User groups not only save Microsoft support dollars, but they also promulgate Microsoft products in a more intimate, local setting. Microsoft employees attend user groups as speakers, advisers, and observers.

Microsoft designates 1,900 individuals as MVPs. These users possess expert-level knowledge of Microsoft products that they share with peers and other Microsoft product users. Microsoft selects these people "for their outstanding efforts to help people around the world do amazing things with technology." These people, who are not Microsoft employees, serve as Microsoft product and technology ambassadors. Microsoft hosts them in an annual MVP Conference at which they meet senior executives like Bill Gates and Steve Ballmer.

Source: Microsoft, microsoft.com (accessed May 2005).

Questions

1. Explain why the best customer support is none at all.

2. List the benefits and costs to Microsoft of supporting newsgroups.

3. Why do users bother to answer other users' questions? What's in it for them? Suppose you manage a group of technical personnel. How much time do you want them to spend each day solving other peoples' problems? How can you control such activities?

4. What are the dangers to Microsoft in supporting a newsgroup? A user group? How can each group backfire on Microsoft? Do you think Microsoft edits or censors a newsgroup's postings? Should it be able to do so? What control can Microsoft exert over user groups?

5. What are the benefits and costs to Microsoft of supporting user groups? The MVP program? Consider both customer support and marketing benefits.

6. How does an individual benefit from joining a user group?

7. Why, besides the chance to meet Bill Gates, would someone want to become an MVP? What benefits accrue with that status?

8. Summarize the information systems that Microsoft uses to support these programs.

Teaching Suggestions

Emerson Pharmaceuticals, Chapter 2

GOALS

Use Dee's blog to:

* Demonstrate the creation of a business process diagram for the sales process.

* Apply definitions of information.

* Illustrate the relationship of information systems and business processes.

* Understand how information systems support business processes.

BACKGROUND

1. Dee's boss wants to know whether or not to fund her blog. He wants to know the benefits of the blog, and he asks that question by asking how it will impact the sales process. His bottom line is the third question, "How will it help us gain sales?"

2. His questions are perfectly legitimate. Dee's task is to find a credible way to answer them. She could blather on and on about how cool the blog will be, how her reps will love it, how it will make Emerson look modern, etc., but he isn't interested in that. He wants to know how the blog *will generate more sales.* Maybe introduce *tangible and intangible benefits* here. Looking cool and modern is an intangible benefit; generating more sales is a tangible benefit. He wants to know the tangible benefit.

3. Realistically, Dee is unlikely to draw a process diagram like that in Figure 2-1. She might, however, draw part of one—showing how the salespeople would access the blog before making sales calls. Drawing even part of such a diagram will show her boss that she understands his questions and concerns and can place them in the context of a business process.

4. Part 4 contains Chapter Extension 21, "Financing and Accounting for IT Projects," which considers the use of net present value and similar types of analysis. Such an analysis is unlikely to be used here for two reasons: the short time frame and low development cost (around $5,000 for software and Don's services). Dee's boss just wants a back-of-the-envelope understanding of the benefits of the blog. Were the project larger and more costly, Emerson would use a more formalized procedure.

HOW TO GET THE STUDENTS INVOLVED

1. At this point in the class, I want to move the responsibility for the learning from my shoulders to the students' shoulders. I want them to take responsibility for what they do or do not learn. Given that goal, I would start this chapter by playing devil's advocate. I'd ask questions and make statements like the following:

   a. **What makes you think more information increases sales?**

   b. **I don't believe it. Tell me why.**

   c. **Dee is just trying to impress her boss. Is there any real value in providing sales people more information?**

   d. **Why is a blog necessary? Why not just use email?**

2. Somewhere in the middle of the questions in 1, I'd probably ask for the four definitions of information provided in the text. Then, I'd ask the class to tell me how each definition applies to Dee's blog. Some definitions are more pertinent than others. Does that make those definitions better? Why or why not?

3. If you haven't used the "Duller than Dirt" Guide in Chapter 1, this might be a good place to use it. Ask the students: **Who is responsible for their applying the ideas of this chapter to this problem?**

4. Ask the students to help you make a process diagram of the sales process. They can use Figure 2-1 as an example.

   a. **What are the elements of a process diagram?**

   b. **How are those elements related for a diagram of the sales process to a hospital or pharmacy?**

   The trick is to keep the process diagram to a reasonable level of detail. One way to do that is to first make a short list of the major activities, such as prepare for call, make sales call, take order, receive order, write prescription, fill prescription, pay. Given that list, then show their relationship to resources, facilities, and information flow.

   I don't think creating an accurate process diagram is the goal here, and we have too little information to build one or to know if we have built one. Here I just want to illustrate the components of such a process and give examples of their interactions.

5. The process diagram in Figure 2-1 and the sales process just diagrammed show different ways information systems *produce* information. To illustrate, use the Bateson definition: "Information is a difference that makes a difference." In the reconciliation of amount received and amount billed, the system is producing, potentially, differences that make a difference.

6. Dee's blog produces information differently. Dee learns of differences that make a difference (for example, she learns of one salesperson's innovative strategy for selling more of a particular drug), and she uses her blog to broadcast that information to the sales force. In Figure 2-1, the system produces the information. In the sales process, Dee produces the information and uses the blog as a delivery mechanism.

7. Items 5 and 6 suggest two different ways that information systems support business processes. Ask the students for other examples.

   a. How does a general ledger information systems support the budgeting process?

   b. How does an organization's Web site support business processes?

   (Possibly use your university's, college's, or department's Web site as an example.)

   c. How does an inventory management system support the in-bound logistics process?

   d. How does an inventory management system support the university libraries' business processes?

BOTTOM LINE

* Information systems exist to support business processes. To answer questions like, "How will your blog generate more sales?" we need to understand how the blog relates to the sales process. When considering the purpose, functions, or benefits of any information system, ask first, "What business process(es) does this system support?"

Using the Guide: Understanding Perspectives and Points of View
(page 25a)

GOALS

✱ Reinforce the text's statement that, although none of us can change our IQ, we can improve the way we think, and thus improve our effective "smarts."

✱ Teach the importance of perspective in thinking and communication—everyone interprets the world in the context of their perspective.

✱ Encourage the students to think critically about the text, about your presentations, and about comments made by their fellow students.

BACKGROUND AND PRESENTATION STRATEGIES

I begin the discussion of this guide with the text's story (on page 30) about Walt Disney's death and the impact it had on Disney's stock price. (By the way, this story was told to me many years ago by an investor whose girlfriend worked at the hospital where they admitted Walt Disney. She told him she doubted that Disney would live through the night. He shorted Disney for the next day and lost his shirt. He told me, "That was the last time I traded on insider information. Not only is it illegal, it seldom works.")

Considerable academic research supports the notion that one can improve the quality of one's thinking. If the students Google "critical-thinking skills" or "problem-solving skills," they will find hundreds of references.

If the students learn nothing else from this class except how to improve their thinking skills, even a little bit, it will be worth hundreds of hours of labor and thousands of dollars. (And, they're going to learn a lot more than that!)

Here's an example of perspective:

➤ **If I say that our MIS class is more important than Intro to Accounting and if your accounting professor says that Intro to Accounting is more important than MIS, is either of us wrong?**

➤ **Is one of us lying? Is one of us being insincere?**

➤ **Is it possible to prove that one of us is right and one of us is wrong?**

➤ **In fact, each of us is right. So, here's the million-dollar question:**

➤ **What do you, as a student, do about that? Whom do you believe?**

➤ **How does the concept of perspective—mine and the accounting prof's—relate to this?**

No one can make any statement except from a perspective. Just as one must have a physical location (one has to be standing, sitting, or reclining somewhere), so, too, one's statements arise from a mental location, from a perspective. We cannot speak about anything except from some perspective. Usually, when two people disagree strongly, it is because they have different perspectives. Which leads to:

➤ **If I have a different perspective from someone, and if we're arguing about something, will any discussion about the facts of the matter have any impact on the outcome?**

(No. We have to come to the same perspective.)

➤ **How likely is it that the other person will change his or her perspective?**

(Not very.)

➤ **So what can I do?**

(Understand what's going on and adapt.)

It's very difficult for people to change their perspective. Most people will resist, and strongly. However, successful businesspeople seem to have mastered the skill, or at least are better at it than most people.

There's a story about Bill Gates in the early days of the computer profession, when he was meeting with another company, and the meeting was going nowhere. Finally, Gates is supposed to have said, "Wait. I see the problem. We think we're the customer, and you think you're the customer. Actually, you're right—you are the customer. We need to go back and rethink our position. We'll get back to you in a couple of weeks." There are so many apocryphal stories about Bill Gates, but I think this one is true. It was told to me by someone who was in the meeting.

A key skill: Being able to perceive that difference in perspective is the root of a problem, and being able to alter one's perspective to achieve a solution, or to at least be able to communicate about a solution.

➤ **The key difference between animals and humans isn't that humans can think. Animals can think. The key difference is that humans can think about thinking. We can examine how we think, evaluate how our techniques are working for us, and choose to change how we think. Try it!**

SUGGESTED RESPONSES FOR DISCUSSION QUESTIONS

1. I wrote that statement based on my perspective. I wrote it because I've watched end users misuse the outputs of well-designed information systems or not use them at all. But, another author, one with a different perspective, might say something else.

   The students don't have enough experience to know if they agree or not. They might decide provisionally to believe that statement until they know more. At this stage, the biggest impact on what they believe is you, their professor!

   From one perspective: If a system is like a chain, then every link is equally important. The third link is not more important than the fifth one. So all five components are the same. From a different perspective: How one thinks about the information people receive has the greatest impact on what they will do with that information. So, from that perspective, the statement is true.

2. There's a lot of research to back it up. Usually the students will agree, too, or at least they'll **want** to believe that it's true.

   The point of this question is to compel the students to think about different kinds and quality of thinking. Here are three examples of three different qualities:

   "I'm taking this class because it's required."

   "I'm not sure about this class. In fact, I'm not sure I'm in the right major. I always thought I'd be a business major, but that was because my Dad so loved accounting. I'm starting to wonder about my goals."

   "My expectations are modest. If I can get three or four useful skills or ideas out of a class, and if it's more or less interesting and enjoyable, then I'm content. I hope this will be one of those classes."

3. The engineer will have spent his or her career thinking about computer design. All the "interesting" problems will lie there. The MIS professor will have spent his or her career thinking about information systems; that is, what they are, how they are built, and how they do or do not facilitate the goals of organizations. The "important" problems arise when groups of people try to work together to accomplish something.

   Both are correct, from their own perspectives.

4. Design the Web page so that the critical information, the differences that are important to that person, are obvious and easily perceived. But, in quantitative methods, where's the equation? What can I compute? That definition is given from a perspective—it's useful for problems that are within the scope of its perspective.

5. Most classes have students who are at different levels of thinking. Some students will feel most comfortable when the answer is concrete. Others will have advanced to understand that thinking occurs within a particular context. I like to address this issue head on. Often students with higher cognitive skills can help those with less-developed skills. This exercise works well in groups—especially if the students have varying ages and life experiences. William Perry wrote several articles on this topic that had a profound impact on my teaching.[1]

6. The discussion, especially involving students of different levels of cognitive maturity, is the critical part of this exercise. Multifaceted thinking can seem (and be) indecisive. However, it can be wise. There is no answer. It depends. Some students will be squirming at this point, and that's OK. I just want to keep them talking about why they're squirming.

WRAP UP

➤ **The quality of your thinking can be improved.**

➤ **One way to improve your thinking is to consider perspectives—yours and others.**

➤ **Suppose you ask two people how far it is to the business school library. Suppose one of them is sitting next to you in class and the other is sitting at the nearest airport.**

➤ **Will they give different answers to the same question? Of course! Is either wrong? No. Are you surprised?**

➤ **Suppose you ask two people if college tuition is too high. Suppose one works two jobs to pay for school and the other is dying of cancer. Will they give different answers?**

➤ **Bottom line: Consider perspectives when understanding yourself and anyone else!**

---

[1]William A. Perry, "Different Worlds in the Same Classroom," *On Teaching and Learning,* Harvard Danforth Center (May 1985), pp. 1–17; and William A. Perry, "Cognitive and Ethical Growth," in Arthur W. Chickering (Ed.), *The Modern American College* (San Francisco: Jossey-Bass, 1981), pp. 76–115. The first is available at *www.bokcenter.harvard.edu/docs/perry.html.*

Using the Ethics Guide: Egocentric Versus Empathetic Thinking *(page 31a)*

GOALS

* Raise the level of professionalism in the class.

* Explore empathetic thinking and discuss why it's smart.

* Discuss two applications of empathetic thinking.

* Emphasize that a problem is a perception and that perceptions differ among people. Different problem perceptions require different information systems.

* Investigate if (or when) empathetic thinking can be manipulative. Discuss whether manipulation is ethical.

BACKGROUND AND PRESENTATION STRATEGIES

How many times have we all been asked, "I couldn't come to class. Did we do anything important?" I'm always tempted to say, "No, when I saw you weren't here, I took all the important material out." Another rejoinder, more mature on my part is, "Well, first tell me what you think important material is." If they say, "Is it going to be on the test . . . ?" then we have some talking to do.

You might want to underline the corollary about not asking your boss, when you've missed a meeting, "Did we do anything important?"

Part of the reason for this guide is to raise the level of professionalism in the class. I find students' maturity rises to meet expectations. By asking them to engage in empathetic thinking with regard to not coming to class, I'm also asking them to step up in their maturity:

➤ **If you choose not to come to class, that's your choice. But, realize there's a cost to me and our teaching assistants, and do what you can to minimize that cost.**

Empathetic thinking does result in better relationships, but this guide says that businesspeople should engage in it because it's smart. Negotiators, for example, need to know what the other side wants, what's important to it, what issues they can give on, and what ones are nonnegotiable.

Here's a simple example:

➤ **Suppose you have an employee who wants more recognition in the group. You know the employee is doing a good job, and you want to reward her. Not engaging in empathic thinking, you give her a pay raise. What have you done?**

➤ **How could empathetic thinking have helped you in this situation?**

So, using this example, just what is empathetic thinking?

* Understanding the other person's perspective (See the "Guide" earlier in the chapter, on page 25a)

* Realizing that people who hold a perspective different from yours are not necessarily WRONG (but you don't have to be wrong, either)

* Not attempting to convince the other person that his or her perspective should be changed to match yours

* Adapting your behavior in accordance with the other person's perspective

➤ **Does thinking empathically mean that you change your way of thinking to match the other person's?**

(No.)

➤ **Does it mean always giving the other person what he or she wants?**

(No.)

➤ **What are different ways you could adapt your behavior in accordance with another person's perspective?**

All of us have been in meetings that are going nowhere. Whenever we find ourselves in such a meeting, is the problem due to different perspectives? If so, one can sometimes find the root cause by engaging in empathetic thinking.

The scenario at the end of the guide is right on point. If three factions hold three different problem definitions, and if they don't realize they hold those different definitions, then the meeting will go nowhere. And it doesn't matter what the "facts" are. The facts aren't the problem; the different problem definitions are.

Ethical issues can arise from empathetic thinking, however, by using empathetic thinking, it is entirely possible to leave someone with the impression that you agree with them. It is also possible to manipulate someone by causing them to think you agree with them.

➤ **In what ways can empathetic thinking be manipulative?**

➤ **As a manager, is it ever unethical to manipulate an employee into doing what you want him or her to do? If you direct that employee, how is manipulation into doing what you want ever wrong?**

 ## SUGGESTED RESPONSES FOR DISCUSSION QUESTIONS

1. Considering the other person's perspective.

   ➤ **What are some examples of egocentric thinking?**

   ➤ **What are some examples of empathetic thinking?**

2. First, based on her words, the *real problem* is that you know she is not engaged in empathetic thinking. Notice that you are in a much stronger position than she is. You know that there are two (yours and hers), and possibly more, different problem definitions. Unlike her, your thinking is broad and flexible enough to understand that multiple perceptions, and hence multiple problem definitions, can exist at the same time.

   You have at least four different strategies: (1) Change your definition to match hers. (2) Try to teach her about empathetic thinking. (3) Without saying anything about her thinking skills, and without needlessly repeating your understanding of the problem, use your understanding of her and her definition to arrive at a solution that is mutually acceptable. (4) Say something polite and close the conversation because you're just wasting your time.

   ➤ **Under what circumstances would you use each of these strategies?**

3. Restate his position to him. "You perceive the problem as . . . ," and do the best possible job of restating his position. This does not mean you agree with his position, but it will let him know that you understand his words. He'll know, if you continue to disagree with him, that it's not because you don't understand him.

   Having convinced him that you understand his position, you should attempt to express your view of the problem. His knowing that you understand his position may allow him to be able to understand yours. However, he may not be able to, in which case there may be no possibility of good communication with him on this issue.

4. This is tough. If you immediately attempt to explain how your point of view differs, you will take away from your empathetic answer. The person will feel as if you're trying to trick them. On the other hand, if you don't say that you disagree, you may leave a false impression that can be harmful in the long run. One approach is to paraphrase what the person said and then see if there is someone else in the group who will express the view that you hold.

WRAP UP

Sometimes I end with a little practice:

➤ **Anybody learn anything today? What?**

➤ **All right, let's practice. Using empathetic thinking, tell me why you think I included this exercise in today's presentation.**

3 Organizational Strategy, Information Systems, and Competitive Advantage

This could happen to you

When Dee asked her boss for a budget to create her blog, he responded by asking the questions at the start of Chapter 2 (page 20). Using the knowledge in that chapter, she was able to respond, and he tentatively approved her budget request. Before he did so, however, he said that he wanted a memo from her on how her blog would provide a competitive advantage. He wanted that memo so that he could include it in the documentation he would use to justify the expense to his manager. The knowledge presented in this chapter will help her write that memo.

An optional Extension for this chapter is CE3, "Knowledge Management and Expert Systems."

Study Questions

Q1 How does organizational strategy determine information systems structure?

Q2 What five forces determine industry structure?

Q3 What is competitive strategy?

Q4 What is a value chain?

Q5 How do value chains determine business processes and information systems?

Q6 How do information systems provide competitive advantages?

How does the knowledge in this chapter help Dee and you?

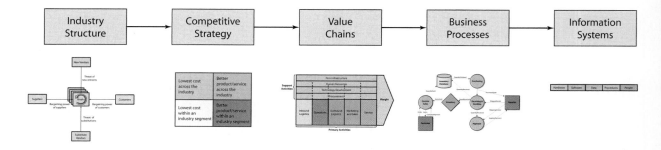

Figure 3-1
Organizational Strategy
Determines Information Systems

Q1 How Does Organizational Strategy Determine Information Systems Structure?

Recall from the definition of MIS that information systems exist to help organizations achieve their goals and objectives. As you will learn in your business strategy class, an organization's goals and objectives are determined by its *competitive strategy*. Thus, ultimately, competitive strategy determines the structure, features, and functions of every information system.

Figure 3-1 summarizes this situation. In short, organizations examine the structure of their industry and determine a competitive strategy. That strategy determines value chains, which in turn determine business processes like those we discussed in Chapter 2. As you saw in that chapter, the nature of business processes determines the structure of an information system.

Michael Porter, one of the key researchers and thinkers in competitive analysis, developed three different models that help one understand the elements of Figure 3-1. We begin with his five forces model.

Q2 What Five Forces Determine Industry Structure?

Organizational strategy begins with an assessment of the fundamental characteristics and structure of an industry. One model used to assess an industry structure is Porter's **five forces model**,[1] shown in Figure 3-2. According to this model, five competitive forces determine industry profitability: bargaining power of customers, threat of substitutions, bargaining power of suppliers, threat of new entrants, and rivalry among existing firms. The intensity of each of the five forces determines the characteristics of the industry, how profitable it is, and how sustainable that profitability will be.

To understand this model, consider the strong and weak examples for each of the forces in Figure 3-3. A good check on your understanding is to see if you can think of different forces of each category in Figure 3-3. Also, take a particular industry—say, auto repair—and consider how these five forces determine the competitive landscape of that industry.

Organizations examine these five forces and determine how they intend to respond to them. That examination leads to competitive strategy.

[1]Michael Porter, *Competitive Strategy: Techniques for Analyzing Industries and Competitors* (New York: Free Press, 1980).

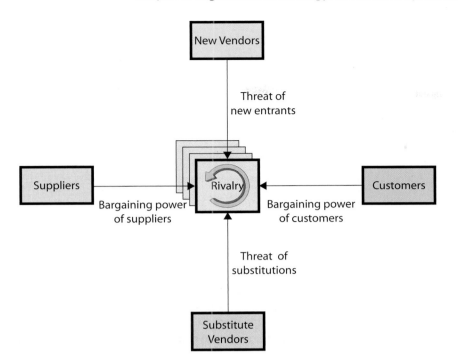

Figure 3-2
Porter's Model of Industry
Structure

Source: Adapted with the permission of The Free Press,
a Division of Simon & Schuster Adult Publishing Group,
from *Competitive Advantage: Creating and Sustaining
Superior Performance* by Michael E. Porter. Copyright
© 1985, 1998 by Michael E. Porter. All rights
reserved.

Force	Example of Strong Force	Example of Weak Force
Bargaining power of customers	Toyota's purchase of auto paint	Your power over the procedures and policies of your university
Threat of substitutions	Frequent-traveler's choice of auto rental	Patients using the only drug effective for their type of cancer
Bargaining power of suppliers	Students purchasing gasoline	Grain farmers in a surplus year
Threat of new entrants	Corner latte stand	Professional football team
Rivalry	Used car dealers	Internal Revenue Service

Figure 3-3
Examples of Five Forces

Q3 What Is Competitive Strategy?

An organization responds to the structure of its industry by choosing a **competitive strategy**. Porter followed his five forces model with the model of four competitive strategies shown in Figure 3-4.[2] According to Porter, a firm can engage in one of these four fundamental competitive strategies. An organization can focus on being the cost leader, or it can focus on differentiating its products from those of the competition. Further, the organization can employ the cost or differentiation strategy across an industry, or it can focus its strategy on a particular industry segment.

[2]Michael Porter, *Competitive Strategy* (New York: Free Press, 1985).

Figure 3-4
Porter's Four Competitive
Strategies

	Cost	**Differentiation**
Industry-wide	Lowest cost across the industry	Better product/service across the industry
Focus	Lowest cost within an industry segment	Better product/service within an industry segment

Consider the car rental industry, for example. According to the first column of Figure 3-4, a car rental company can strive to provide the lowest-cost car rentals across the industry, or it can seek to provide the lowest-cost car rentals to an industry segment—say, U.S. domestic business travelers.

As shown in the second column, a car rental company can seek to differentiate its products from the competition. It can do so in various ways—for example, by providing a wide range of high-quality cars, by providing the best reservations system, by having the cleanest cars or the fastest check-in, or by some other means. The company can strive to provide product differentiation across the industry or within particular segments of the industry, such as U.S. domestic business travelers.

According to Porter, to be effective, the organization's goals, objectives, culture, and activities must be consistent with the organization's strategy. To those in the MIS field, this means that all information systems in the organization must facilitate the organization's competitive strategy.

Q4 What Is a Value Chain?

Organizations analyze the structure of their industry, and using that analysis, they then formulate a competitive strategy. They then need to organize and structure the organization to implement that strategy. If, for example, the competitive strategy is to be *cost leader*, then business activities need to be developed to be as economically advantageous as possible.

On the other hand, a business that selects a *differentiation* strategy would not necessarily structure itself around least-cost activities. Instead, such a business might choose to develop more costly systems, but it would do so only if those systems provided a net benefit, or **margin**, to the differentiation strategy. This line of thinking leads to Porter's definition of a third model, that of value chains.

A **value chain** is a network of value-creating activities. Figure 3-5 shows the generic value chain model as developed by Porter. That generic chain consists of five **primary activities** and four **support activities**.

Primary Activities in the Value Chain

To understand the essence of the value chain, consider a small manufacturer—say, a bicycle maker. First, the manufacturer acquires raw materials using the in-bound logistics activity. This activity concerns the receiving and handling of raw materials and other inputs. The accumulation of those materials adds value in the sense that even a pile of unassembled parts is worth something to some customer. A collection of the parts needed to build a bicycle is worth more than

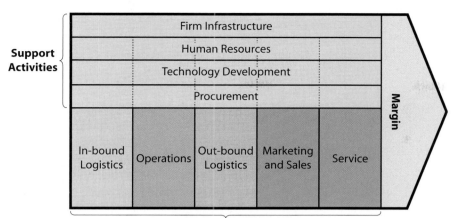

Figure 3-5
Porter's Value Chain Model

Source: Adapted with the permission of The Free Press, a Division of Simon & Schuster Adult Publishing Group, from *Competitive Advantage: Creating and Sustaining Superior Performance* by Michael E. Porter. Copyright © 1985, 1998 by Michael E. Porter. All rights reserved.

an empty space on a shelf. The value is not only the parts themselves, but also the time required to contact vendors for those parts, to maintain business relationships with those vendors, to order the parts, to receive the shipment, and so forth.

In the operations activity, the bicycle maker transforms raw materials into a finished bicycle, a process that adds more value. Next, the company uses the outbound logistics activity to deliver the finished bicycle to a customer. Of course, there is no customer to send the bicycle to without the marketing and sales value activity. Finally, the service activity provides customer support to the bicycle users.

Each stage of this generic chain accumulates costs and adds value to the product. The net result is the total margin of the chain, which is the difference between the total value added and the total costs incurred. Figure 3-6 summarizes the primary activities of the value chain.

Support Activities in the Value Chain

The support activities in the generic value chain contribute indirectly to the production, sale, and service of the product. They include procurement, which consists of the processes of finding vendors, setting up contractual arrangements, and negotiating prices. (This differs from in-bound logistics, which is concerned with ordering and receiving in accordance with agreements set up by procurement.)

Porter defined technology broadly. It includes research and development, but it also includes other activities within the firm for developing new techniques, methods, and procedures. He defined human resources as recruiting, compensation, evaluation, and training of full-time and part-time employees.

Primary Activity	Description
In-bound logistics	Receiving, storing, and disseminating inputs to the product
Operations	Transforming inputs into the final product
Out-bound logistics	Collecting, storing, and physically distributing the product to buyers
Marketing and sales	Inducing buyers to purchase the product and providing a means for them to do so
Service	Assisting customer's use of the product and thus maintaining and enhancing the product's value

Figure 3-6
Task Descriptions for Primary Activities of the Value Chain

Source: Adapted with the permission of The Free Press, a Division of Simon & Schuster Adult Publishing Group, from *Competitive Advantage: Creating and Sustaining Superior Performance* by Michael E. Porter. Copyright © 1985, 1998 by Michael E. Porter. All rights reserved.

MIS in use 3

Horizon Healthcare Services

Horizon Healthcare Services is New Jersey's largest health insurer, providing coverage to more than 2.9 million people throughout the state. Although Horizon employs 1,200 people in its customer service call center, service quality suffered because the service representatives were hampered by cumbersome and difficult-to-use information systems. In fact, Horizon used five separate customer and claim systems, and the service representatives had no unified record of customer interactions. Customers had to call multiple phone numbers, were frequently transferred from one representative to another, and often had to reexplain their needs several times.

To solve this problem, Horizon launched a new IT strategy to integrate the information from these disparate systems into a single display that provided a comprehensive view of the customer. To implement this strategy, Horizon licensed a call center application from Siebel Systems, a division of the Oracle Corporation, a San Mateo, California, enterprise software vender. The new system reduced customer service times by 20 percent and increased customer service productivity by 15 percent. Additionally, the new system reduced the training time for new customer service hires from 20 weeks to 4 weeks. Also, it allowed Horizon to balance workload and handle call overflow by moving people between service teams. Horizon experienced a $2.1 million reduction in expenses in the first year; it expects to save a total of $21 million in the first 5 years of use.

Source: © 2005 Siebel Systems, Inc., 2207 Bridgepointe Parkway, San Mateo, California 94404. All rights reserved.

Finally, firm infrastructure includes general management, finance, accounting, legal, and government affairs.

Supporting functions add value, albeit indirectly, and they also have costs. Hence, as shown in Figure 3-5, supporting activities contibute to a margin. In the case of supporting activities, it would be difficult to calculate the margin because the specific value added of, say, the manufacturer's lobbyists in Washington, D.C., is difficult to know. But there is a value added, there are costs, and there is a margin, even if it is only in concept.

Linkages in the Value Chain

Porter's model of business activities includes **linkages**, which are interactions across value activities. Linkages are important sources of efficiencies and are readily supported by information systems. For example, manufacturing systems use linkages to reduce inventory costs. Such a system uses sales forecasts to plan production; it then uses the production plan to determine raw materials needs and then uses the material needs to schedule purchases. The end result is just-in-time inventory, which reduces inventory sizes and costs.

By describing value chains and their linkages, Porter started a movement to create integrated, cross-departmental business systems. Over time, Porter's work led to the creation of a new discipline called *business process design*. The central idea is that organizations should not automate or improve existing functional systems. Rather, they should create new, more efficient business processes that integrate the activities of all departments involved in a value chain. *MIS in Use 3* demonstrates some of the benefits of systems integration.

Q5 How Do Value Chains Determine Business Processes and Information Systems?

As you learned in the last chapter, a business process is a network of activities, resources, facilities, and information that accomplish a business function. Now we can be more specific and say that business processes implement value chains or portions of value chains. Thus, each value chain consists of one or more business processes.

For example, Figure 3-7 shows a portion of the Operations value chain for a bicycle rental company. The top part of this figure shows how a company having a

Figure 3-7
Operations Value Chains for Bicycle Rental Companies

	Value Chain Activity	Greet Customer	Determine Needs	Rent Bike	Return Bike & Pay
Low-Cost Rental to Students	**Message that implements competitive strategy**	"You wanna bike?"	"Bikes are over there. Help yourself."	"Fill out this form, and bring it to me over here when you're done."	"Show me the bike." "OK, you owe $23.50. Pay up."
	Supporting business process	None.	Physical controls and procedures to prevent bike theft.	Printed forms and a shoe box to store them in.	Shoebox with rental form. Minimal credit card and cash receipt system.
High-Service Rental to Business Executives at Conference Resort	**Message that implements competitive strategy**	"Hello, Ms. Henry. Wonderful to see you again. Would you like to rent the WonderBike 4.5 that you rented last time?"	"You know, I think the WonderBike Supreme would be a better choice for you. It has..."	"Let me just scan the bike's number into our system, and then I'll adjust the seat for you."	"How was your ride?" "Here, let me help you. I'll just scan the bike's tag again and have your paperwork in just a second." "Would you like a beverage?" "Would you like me to put this on your hotel bill, or would you prefer to pay now?"
	Supporting business process	Customer tracking and past sales activity system.	Employee training and information system to match customer and bikes, biased to "up-sell" customer.	Automated inventory system to check bike out of inventory.	Automated inventory system to place bike back in inventory. Prepare payment documents. Integrate with resort's billing system.

competitive strategy of providing low-cost rentals to college students might implement this portion of its operations value chain. The bottom part shows how a company with a competitive strategy of providing high-quality rentals to business executives at a conference resort might implement this portion of that same value chain.

Note the value chain activities are they same for both companies. Both greet the customer, determine the customers' needs, rent a bike, and return the bike. However, each company implements these activities in ways that are consistent with its competitive strategy.

The low-cost vendor has created bare-bones, minimum processes to support its value chain. The high-service customer service vendor has created more elaborate business processes (supported by information systems) that are necessary to differentiate its service from that of other vendors. As Porter says, however, these processes and systems must create sufficient value that they will more than cover their costs. If not, the margin of those systems will be negative.

Before we continue, review Figure 3-1 again. The material in these first three chapters is presented from the right to the left in this figure. We began with the components of an information system in Chapter 1. We then considered business processes in Chapter 2. In this chapter, we have considered value chains, competitive strategy, and industry structure.

Q6 How Do Information Systems Provide Competitive Advantages?

In your business strategy class, you will study the Porter models in greater detail than we have discussed here. When you do so, you will learn numerous ways that organizations respond to the five competitive forces. For our purposes, we can distill those ways into the list of principles shown in Figure 3-8. Keep in mind that we are applying these principles in the context of the organization's competitive strategy. (You can also apply these principles to a personal competitive advantage, as the *Guide* on pages 45a–45b discusses.)

Some of these competitive techniques are created via products and services, and some are created via the development of business processes. Consider each.

Competitive Advantage via Products

The first three principles in Figure 3-8 concern products or services. Organizations gain a competitive advantage by creating *new* products or services, by *enhancing* existing products or services, and by *differentiating* their

Figure 3-8
Principles of Competitive
Advantage

Product Implementations
1. Create a new product or service
2. Enhance products or services
3. Differentiate products or services

System Implementations
4. Lock in customers and buyers
5. Lock in suppliers
6. Raise barriers to market entry
7. Establish alliances
8. Reduce costs

products and services from those of their competitors. As you think about these three principles, realize that an information system can be part of a product or it can provide support for a product or service.

Consider, for example, a car rental agency like Hertz or Avis. An information system that produces information about the car's location and provides driving instructions to destinations is part of the car rental and thus is part of the product itself (see Figure 3-9a). In contrast, an information system that schedules car maintenance is not part of the product, but instead supports the product (Figure 3-9b). Either way, information systems can achieve the first three objectives in Figure 3-8.

The remaining five principles in Figure 3-8 concern competitive advantage created by the implementation of business processes.

Competitive Advantage via Business Processes

Organizations can *lock in customers* by making it difficult or expensive for customers to switch to another product. This strategy is sometimes called establishing high **switching costs**. Organizations can *lock in suppliers* by making it difficult to switch to another organization, or, stated positively, by making it easy to connect to and work with the organization. Finally, competitive advantage can be gained by *creating entry barriers* that make it difficult and expensive for new competition to enter the market.

Another means to gain competitive advantage is to *establish alliances* with other organizations. Such alliances establish standards, promote product awareness and needs, develop market size, reduce purchasing costs, and provide other benefits. Finally, organizations can gain competitive advantage by *reducing costs*. Such reductions enable the organization to reduce prices and/or to increase profitability. Increased profitability means not just greater shareholder value, but also more cash, which can fund further infrastructure development for even greater competitive advantage.

a. Information System as Part of a Car Rental Product

b. Information System That Supports a Car Rental Product

Figure 3-9
Two Roles for Information Systems Regarding Products

Daily Service Schedule — November 17, 2005

StationID	22						
StationName	Lubrication						
	ServiceDate	ServiceTime	VehicleID	Make	Model	Mileage	ServiceDescription
	11/17/2005	12:00 AM	155890	Ford	Explorer	2244	Std. Lube
	11/17/2005	11:00 AM	12448	Toyota	Tacoma	7558	Std. Lube
StationID	26						
StationName	Alignment						
	ServiceDate	ServiceTime	VehicleID	Make	Model	Mileage	ServiceDescription
	11/17/2005	9:00 AM	12448	Toyota	Tacoma	7558	Front end alignment inspect
StationID	28						
StationName	Transmission						
	ServiceDate	ServiceTime	VehicleID	Make	Model	Mileage	ServiceDescription
	11/17/2005	11:00 AM	155890	Ford	Explorer	2244	Transmission oil change

Your Personal Competitive Advantage

Consider the following possibility: You work hard, earning your degree in business, and you graduate, only to discover that you cannot find a job in your area of study. You look for six weeks or so, but then you run out of money. In desperation, you take a job waiting tables at a local restaurant. Two years go by, the economy picks up, and the jobs you had been looking for become available. Unfortunately, your degree is now two years old; you are competing with students who have just graduated with fresh degrees (and fresh knowledge). Two years of waiting tables, good as you are at it, does not appear to be good experience for the job you want. You're stuck in a nightmare—one that will be hard to get out of, and one that you cannot allow to happen.

Examine Figure 3-8 again, but this time consider those elements of competitive advantage as they apply to you personally. As an employee, the skills and abilities you offer are your personal product. Examine the first three items in the list, and ask yourself, "How can I use my time in school—and in this MIS class, in particular—to create new skills, to enhance those I already have, and to differentiate my skills from the competition?" (By the way, you will enter a national/international market. Your competition is not just the students in your class; it's also students in classes in Ohio, California, British Columbia, Florida, New York, and every place else they're teaching MIS today.)

Suppose you are interested in a sales job. Perhaps, like Dee, you want to sell in the pharmaceutical industry. What skills can you learn from your MIS class that will make you more competitive as a future salesperson? Ask yourself, "How does the pharmaceutical industry use MIS to gain competitive advantage?" Get on the Internet and find examples of the use of information systems in the pharmaceutical industry. How does Parke-Davis, for example, use a customer information system to sell to doctors? How can your knowledge of such systems differentiate you from your competition for a job there? How does Parke-Davis use a knowledge management system? How does the firm keep track of drugs that have an adverse effect on each other?

The fourth and fifth items in Figure 3-8 concern locking in customers, buyers, and suppliers. How can you interpret those elements in terms of your personal competitive advantage? Well, to lock in, you first have to have a relationship to lock in. So do you have an internship? If not, can you get one? And once you have an internship, how can you use your knowledge of MIS to lock in your job so that you get a job offer? Does the company you are interning for have a CRM system (or any other information system that is important to the company)? If users are happy with the system, what characteristics make it worthwhile? Can you lock in a job by becoming an expert user of this system? Becoming an expert user not only locks you into your job, but it also raises barriers to entry for others who might be competing for the job. Also, can you suggest ways to improve the system, thus using your knowledge of the company and the system to lock in an extension of your job?

Human resources personnel say that networking is one of the most effective ways of finding a job. How can you use this class to establish alliances with other students? Does your class have a Web site? Is there an email list server for the students in your class? How can you use those facilities to develop job-seeking alliances with other students? Who in your class already has a job or an internship? Can any of those people provide hints or opportunities for finding a job?

Don't restrict your job search to your local area. Are there regions of your country where jobs are more plentiful? How can you find out about student organizations in those regions? Search the Web for MIS classes in other cities, and make contact with students there. Find out what the hot opportunities are in other cities.

Finally, as you study MIS, think about how the knowledge you gain can help you save costs for your employers. Even more, see if you can build a case that an employer would actually save money by hiring you. The line of reasoning might be that because of your knowledge of IS, you will be able to facilitate cost savings that more than compensate for your salary.

In truth, few of the ideas that you generate for a potential employer will be feasible or pragmatically useful. The fact that you are thinking creatively, however, will indicate to a potential employer that you have initiative and are grappling with the problems that real businesses have. As this course progresses, keep thinking about competitive advantage, and strive to understand how the topics you study can help you to accomplish, personally, one or more of the principles in Figure 3-8.

DISCUSSION QUESTIONS

1. Summarize the efforts you have taken thus far to build an employment record that will lead to job offers after graduation.

2. Considering the first three principles in Figure 3-8, describe one way in which you have a competitive advantage over your classmates. If you do not have such competitive advantage, describe actions you can take to obtain one.

3. In order to build your network, you can use your status as a student to approach business professionals. Namely, you can contact them for help with an assignment or for career guidance. For example, suppose you want to work in banking and you know that your local bank has a customer information system. You could call the manager of that bank and ask him or her how that system creates a competitive advantage for the bank. You also could ask to interview other employees and go armed with the list in Figure 3-8. Describe two specific ways in which you can use your status as a student and the list in Figure 3-8 to build your network in this way.

4. Describe two ways that you can use student alliances to obtain a job. How can you use information systems to build, maintain, and operate such alliances?

All of these principles of competitive advantage make sense, but the question you may be asking is, "How do information systems help to create competitive advantage?" To answer that question, consider a sample information system.

How Does an Actual Company Use IS to Create Competitive Advantages?

ABC, Inc.[3] is a worldwide shipper with sales well in excess of $1 billion. From its inception, ABC invested heavily in information technology and led the shipping industry in the application of information systems for competitive advantage. Here we consider one example of an information system that illustrates how ABC successfully uses information technology to gain competitive advantage.

ABC maintains customer account data that include not only the customer's name, address, and billing information, but also data about the identity of that customer and the locations to which the customer ships. Figure 3-10 shows a Web form that an ABC customer is using to schedule a shipment. When the ABC system creates the form, it fills the Company name drop-down list with the names of companies that the customer has shipped to in the past. Here, the user is selecting Prentice Hall.

When the user clicks on the Company name, the underlying ABC information system reads the customer's contact data from a database. The data consist of names, addresses, and phone numbers of recipients from past shipments. The user then selects a Contact name, and the system inserts that contact's address and other data into the form using data from the database, as shown in Figure 3-11. Thus, the system saves customers from having to reenter data for people to whom they have shipped in the past. Providing the data in this way also reduces data-entry errors.

Figure 3-12 shows another feature of this system. On the right-hand side of this form, the customer can request that ABC send email messages to the sender (the customer), the recipient, and others as well. The customer can choose for ABC

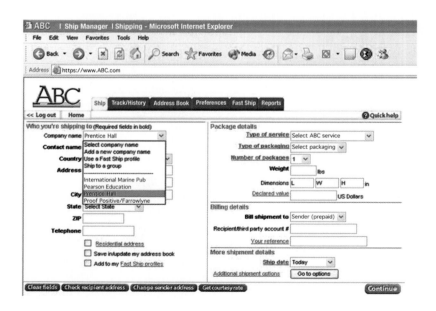

Figure 3-10
ABC, Inc. Web Page to Select a Recipient from the Customer's Records

---

[3]The information system described here is actually used by a major transportation company.

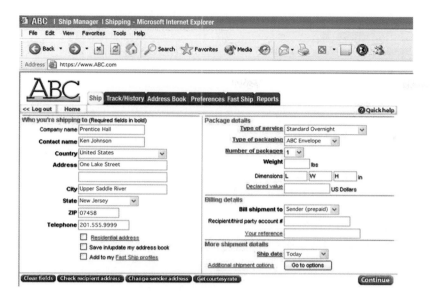

Figure 3-11
ABC, Inc. Web Page to Select a Contact from the Customer's Records

to send an email when the shipment is created and when it has been delivered. In Figure 3-12, the user has provided three email addresses. The customer wants all three addresses to receive delivery notification, but only the sender will receive shipment notification. The customer can add a personal message as well. By adding this capability to the shipment scheduling system, ABC has extended its product from a package-delivery service to a package- *and* information-delivery service.

Figure 3-13 shows one other capability of this information system. It has generated a shipping label, complete with bar code, for the user to print. By doing this, the company not only reduces errors in the preparation of shipping labels, but it also causes the customer to provide the paper and ink for document printing! Millions of such documents are printed every day, resulting in a considerable savings to the company.

Note that only customers who have access to the Internet can use this shipping system. Do organizations have an ethical obligation to provide equivalent services to those who do not have access? The *Ethics Guide* on pages 47a–47b explores this question.

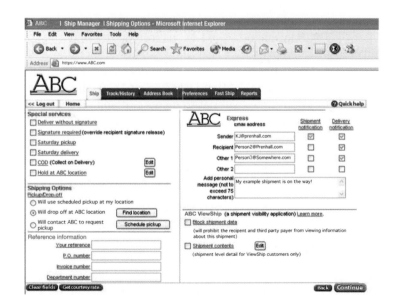

Figure 3-12
ABC, Inc. Web Page to Specify Email Notification

Limiting Access to Those Who Have Access

An adage of investing is that it's easier for the rich to get richer. Someone who has $10 million invested at 5 percent earns $500,000 per year. Another investor with $10,000 invested at that same 5 percent earns $500 per year. Every year, the disparity increases as the first investor pulls farther and farther ahead of the second.

This same adage applies to intellectual wealth as well. It's easier for those with considerable knowledge and expertise to gain even more knowledge and expertise. Someone who knows how to search the Internet can learn more readily than someone who does not. And every year, the person with greater knowledge pulls farther and farther ahead. Intellectual capital grows in just the same way that financial capital grows.

Searching the Internet is not just a matter of knowledge, however. It's also a matter of access. The increasing reliance on the Web for information and commerce has created a digital divide between those who have Internet access and those who do not. This divide continues to deepen as those who are connected pull farther ahead of those who are not.

Various groups have addressed this problem by making Internet access available in public places, such as libraries, community centers, and retirement homes. The Bill and Melinda Gates Foundation has given more than $262 million to public libraries for the purchase

of personal computers and Internet access for them. Such gifts help, but not everyone can be served this way, and even with such access, there's a big convenience difference between going to the library and walking across your bedroom to access the Internet—and you don't have to stand in line.

The advantages accrue to everyone with access, every day. Do you want directions to your friend's house? Want to know when a movie is playing at a local theater? Want to buy music, books, or tools? Want convenient access to your checking account? Want to decide whether to refinance your condo? Want to know what TCP/IP means? Use the Internet.

All of this intellectual capital resides on the Internet because businesses benefit by putting it there. It's much cheaper to provide product support information over the Internet than on printed documents. The savings include not only the costs of printing, but also the costs of warehousing and mailing. Further, when product specifications change, the organization just changes the Web site. There is no obsolete material to dispose of and no costs for printing and distributing the revised material. Those who have Internet access gain current information faster than those who do not.

What happens to those who do not have Internet access? They fall farther and farther behind. The digital divide segregates the haves from the have-nots, creating new class structures. Such segregation is subtle, but it is segregation, nonetheless.

Do organizations have a responsibility to address this matter? If 98 percent of our market segment has Internet access, do we have a responsibility to provide

DISCUSSION QUESTIONS

1. Do you see evidence of a digital divide on your campus? In your hometown? Among your relatives? Describe personal experiences you've had regarding the digital divide.

2. Do organizations have a legal responsibility to provide the same information for nonconnected customers that they do for connected customers? If not, should laws be passed requiring organizations to do so?

3. Even if there is no current legal requirement for organizations to provide equal information to nonconnected customers, do they have an ethical responsibility to do so?

4. Are your answers to questions 2 and 3 different for government agencies than they are for commercial organizations?

5. Because it may be impossible to provide equal information, another approach for reducing the digital divide is for the government to enable nonconnected citizens to acquire Internet access via subsidies and tax incentives. Do you favor such a program? Why or why not?

6. Suppose that nothing is done to reduce the digital divide and that it is allowed to grow wider and wider. What are the consequences? How will society change?

non-Internet materials to that other 2 percent? On what basis does that responsibility lie? Does a government agency have a responsibility to provide equal information to those who have Internet access and those who do not? When those who are connected can obtain information nearly instantaneously, 24/7, is it even possible to provide equal information to the connected and the unconnected?

It's a worldwide problem. Connected societies and countries pull farther and farther ahead. How can any economy that relies on traditional mail compete with an Internet-based economy?

If you're taking MIS, you're already connected; you're already one of the haves, and you're already pulling ahead of the have-nots. The more you learn about information systems and their use in commerce, the faster you'll pull ahead. The digital divide increases.

Figure 3-13
ABC, Inc. Web Page to Print a
Shipping Label

Shipping Label: Your shipment is complete

How Does This System Create a Competitive Advantage?

Now consider the ABC shipping information system in light of the competitive advantage factors in Figure 3-8. This information system *enhances* an existing product because it eases the effort of creating a shipment to the customer while reducing errors. The information system also helps to *differentiate* the ABC package delivery product from competitors that do not have a similar system. Further, the generation of email messages when ABC picks up and delivers a package could be considered to be a *new* product.

Because this information system captures and stores data about recipients, it reduces the amount of customer work when scheduling a shipment. Customers will be *locked in* by this system: If a customer wants to change to a different shipper, he or she will need to rekey recipient data for that new shipper. The disadvantage of rekeying data may well outweigh any advantage of switching to another shipper.

This system achieves a competitive advantage in two other ways as well: First, it raises the barriers to market entry. If another company wants to develop a shipping service, it will not only have to be able to ship packages, but it will also need to have a similar information system. In addition, the system reduces costs. It reduces errors in shipping documents, and it saves ABC paper, ink, and printing costs. (Of course, to determine if this system delivers a *net savings* in costs, the cost of developing and operating the information system will need to be offset against the gains in reduced errors and paper, ink, and printing costs. It may be that the system costs more than the savings. Even still, it may be a sound investment if the value of intangible benefits, such as locking in customers and raising entry barriers, exceeds the net cost.)

Before continuing, review Figure 3-8. Make sure that you understand each of the principles of competitive advantage and how information systems can help achieve them. In fact, the list in Figure 3-8 probably is important enough to memorize, because you can also use it for non-IS applications. You can consider any business project or initiative in light of competitive advantage.

How does the knowledge in this chapter help Dee and you?

Knowledge of industry structure gives Dee background and perspective that will make it easier for her to communicate with her senior management. At her level of management, she is unlikely to perform an analysis of industry structure and of the five competitive forces. Managers at a level much higher than Dee's perform that analysis. Years ago, George Emerson (long deceased) must have considered these factors when he started the company. Today, Emerson is a multinational company, headquartered in London. Someone at Dee's level is unlikely to be deciding how to position the company within the worldwide pharmaceutical industry.

This knowledge does enable her, however, to understand the company's competitive strategy and to translate that strategy into her project. For example, suppose that Emerson's competitive strategy is quality differentiation across the entire pharmaceutical market. Furthermore, suppose that Emerson defines quality as meaning that it produces and sells drugs based on the very latest medical research.

If this is the case, then all business systems in Emerson must facilitate that strategy. Drug developers must seek out the most current, leading-edge researchers, production must create processes that enable the drugs to flow through their medical-testing process as quickly as possible, and the sales team must be trained, reinforced, and financially rewarded for effectively presenting the "products based on the most current research" message to customers.

Here is where Dee can directly apply knowledge from this chapter. She can build her blog to provide the latest messages, examples, techniques, and success stories for delivering that message. When one sales person succeeds with a technique, Dee can publish and broadcast that technique on the blog. With these features, she can state that her blog supports the competitive strategy by providing a cost-effective way of disseminating accurate and up-to-the-minute information to salespeople on how best to communicate the "most current" message. For more on the use of IS to manage knowledge and expertise, see Chapter Extension 3 "Knowledge Management and Expert Systems," on page 335.

Dee would document these ideas in the memo that her boss asked her to write. While she's writing that memo, she can also use the list of competitive advantage factors in Figure 3-8. In particular, her blog will help the sales team to differentiate its drugs from those of competitors and lock in their customers (help the sales force convince medical professionals they are getting products based on the most current research), and it will also help to raise barriers to market entry for new drugs or pharmaceutical companies (the need for other companies to commit resources to researching and producing the most current drugs).

Active ? Review

Use this Active Review to verify that you understand the material in the chapter. You can read the entire chapter and then perform the tasks in this review, or you can read the material for just one question and perform the tasks in this review for that question before moving on to the next one.

Q1 How does organizational strategy determine information systems structure?

Diagram and explain the relationship of industry structure, competitive strategy, value chains, business systems, and information systems. Working from the bottom up, explain how the knowledge you've gained in these first three chapters pertains to that diagram

Q2 What five forces determine industry structure?

Name and briefly describe the five forces. Give your own examples of both strong and weak forces of each type similar to those in Figure 3-3.

Q3 What is competitive strategy?

Describe four different strategies as defined by Porter. Give an example of four different companies that have implemented each of the strategies.

Q4 What is a value chain?

How does the structure of a value chain relate to competitive strategy? Name and describe five primary value chain activities. Name and describe four support value chain activities. Explain value chain linkages.

Q5 How do value chains determine business processes and information systems?

What is the relationship between a value chain and a business process? How do business processes relate to competitive strategy? How do information systems relate to competitive strategy? Justify the comments in the row labeled "Supporting business process" in Figure 3-7.

Q6 How do information systems provide competitive advantages?

List and briefly describe eight principles of competitive advantage. Consider your college bookstore. List one application of each of the eight principles. Strive to include examples that involve information systems.

How does the knowledge in this chapter help Dee and you?

Is Dee herself likely to perform an analysis of industry structure for Emerson? If not, how can Dee use knowledge of the five competitive forces in building her blog? How can she use knowledge of the competitive forces in writing the memo to her boss justifying the budget for her blog?

Key Terms and Concepts

Competitive strategy 39	Margin 40	Switching costs 45
Five forces model 38	Primary activities 40	Value chain 40
Linkages 42	Support activities 40	

Using Your Knowledge

1. Apply the value chain model to a retailer such as Target (*target.com*). What is its competitive strategy? Describe the tasks Target must accomplish for each of the primary value chain activities. How does Target's competitive strategy

and the nature of its business influence the general characteristics of Target's information systems?

2. Apply the value chain model to a mail-order company such as L.L Bean (*llbean.com*). What is its competitive strategy? Describe the tasks L.L. Bean must accomplish for each of the primary value chain activities. How does L.L. Bean's competitive strategy and the nature of its business influence the general characteristics of its information systems?

3. Suppose you decide to start a business that recruits students for summer jobs. You will match available students with available jobs. You need to learn what positions are available and what students are available for filling those positions. In starting your business, you know you will be competing with local newspapers, "Craig's List" (*www.craigslist.org*), and with your college. You will probably have other local competitors as well.
   a. Analyze the structure of this industry according to Porter's five forces model.
   b. Given your analysis in a, recommend a competitive strategy.
   c. Describe the primary value chain activities as they apply to this business.
   d. Describe a business process for recruiting students.
   e. Describe information systems that could be used to support the business process in d.
   f. Explain how the process you describe in d and the system you describe in e reflect your competitive strategy.

4. Consider the two different bike rental companies in Figure 3-7. Think about the bikes that they rent. Clearly, the student bikes will be just about anything that can be ridden out of the shop. The bikes for the business executives, on the other hand, must be new, shiny, clean, and in tip-top shape.
   a. Compare and contrast the operations value chains of these two businesses as they pertain to the management of bicycles.
   b. Describe a business process for maintaining bicycles for both businesses.
   c. Describe a business process for acquiring bicycles for both businesses.
   d. Describe a business process for disposing of bicycles for both businesses.
   e. What roles do you see for information systems in your answers to the earlier questions? The information systems can be those you develop within your company or they can be those developed by others, such as "Craig's List."

5. Samantha Green owns and operates Twigs Tree Trimming Service. Samantha graduated from the forestry program of a nearby university and worked for a large landscape design firm, performing tree trimming and removal. After several years of experience, she bought her own truck, stump grinder, and other equipment and opened her own business in St. Louis, Missouri.

   Although many of her jobs are one-time operations to remove a tree or stump, others are recurring, such as trimming a tree or groups of trees every year or every other year. When business is slow, she calls former clients to remind them of her services and of the need to trim their trees on a regular basis.

   Samantha has never heard of Michael Porter nor any of his theories. She operates her business "by the seat of her pants."
   a. Explain how an analysis of the five competitive forces could help Samantha.

    b. Do you think Samantha has a competitive strategy? What competitive strategy would seem to make sense for her?

    c. How would knowledge of her competitive strategy help her sales and marketing efforts?

    d. Describe, in general terms, the kind of information system that she needs to support sales and marketing efforts.

6. FiredUp, Inc., is a small business owned by Curt and Julie Robards. Based in Brisbane, Australia, FiredUp manufactures and sells a lightweight camping stove called the FiredNow. Curt, who previously worked as an aerospace engineer, invented and patented a burning nozzle that enables the stove to stay lit in very high winds—up to 90 miles per hour. Julie, an industrial designer by training, developed an elegant folding design that is small, lightweight, easy to set up, and very stable. Curt and Julie manufacture the stove in their garage, and they sell it directly to their customers over the Internet and via phone.

    a. Explain how an analysis of the five competitive forces could help FiredUp.

    b. What does FiredUp's competitive strategy seem to be?

    c. Briefly summarize how the primary value chain activities pertain to FiredUp. How should the company design these value chains to conform to its competitive strategy?

    d. Describe business processes that FiredUp needs in order to implement its marketing and sales and also its service value chain activities.

    e. Describe, in general terms, information systems to support your answer to question d.

Case Study 3

Bosu Balance Trainer

The Bosu balance trainer is a device for developing balance, strength, and aerobic conditioning. Invented in 1999, Bosu has become popular in leading health clubs, in athletic departments, and in homes. Bosu stands for "both sides up," because either side of the equipment can be used for training.

    Bosu is not only a new training device, but it also reflects a new philosophy in athletic conditioning that focuses on balance. According to the Bosu inventor, David Weck, "The Bosu Balance Trainer was born of passion to improve my balance. In my lifelong pursuit of enhanced athleticism, I have come to understand that balance is the foundation on which all other performance components are built." Bosu devices are sold by Bosu.com.

    Bosu devices have been successful enough that copycat products are undoubtedly on the way. For Bosu to be successful over the long term, it must transform its early market lead into a sustainable and durable market share. This means that Bosu must be used and recommended by coaches, personal trainers, and other significant purchase influencers. Bosu must develop a reputation among these market leaders as delivering significant benefits without risk of injury.

Source: Bosu, *bosu.com* (accessed May 2005).

Questions

1. Review the principles of competitive advantage in Figure 3-8. What information systems can Bosu create to enhance its product or differentiate it from existing and emerging competition?

2. What information systems can Bosu develop to create barriers to entry to the competition and to lock in customers?

3. What information systems can Bosu develop to establish alliances?

4. Read Case Study 2, "Customer Support and Knowledge Management at Microsoft," on page 35. (You need not answer the questions in this case; just understand how Microsoft uses newsgroups, focus groups, and MVPs.) How can Bosu develop programs similar to those used by Microsoft to provide customer support and create a competitive advantage?

5. What information systems will Bosu need to develop to support the programs identified in your answer to question 4?

Teaching Suggestions

Emerson Pharmaceuticals, Chapter 3

GOALS

Use Dee's blog to:

* Illustrate a practical application of business strategy for someone who works at a relatively junior level in an organization.

* Understand how some competitive advantages are relevant to organizational strategy and some are not.

* Emphasize the relationship of information systems and competitive advantage.

BACKGROUND

1. In the first years of their careers, few students will participate in establishing organizational strategy. As stated in Q7, Dee is unlikely to perform an analysis of industry structure and the five competitive forces for Emerson. She is much too junior for that. So, why do our students need to know this material? Beyond general business knowledge, I believe there is a practical reason for understanding organizational strategy: It guides the specification of relevant competitive advantages.

2. Dee's boss asked her to tell her how the proposed blog would create a competitive advantage. He didn't mean just *any* competitive advantage. He meant (though he didn't say it), competitive advantages that relate to Emerson's organizational strategy. If we just start thinking of competitive advantages using the items in Figure 3-8 as a guide, we'll end up with many competitive advantages that have nothing to do with Emerson. Hence, we need to start further up the thought-chain, understanding Emerson's strategy before addressing competitive advantages.

3. Figure 3-1 is a very important conceptual grid. An analysis of industry structure gives rise to a competitive strategy. Business people use that strategy to structure value chains, which in turn lead to business processes, which, as demonstrated in Chapter 2, give rise to information systems.

4. As presumed in Q7, Emerson's competitive strategy is *quality differentiation*, across the entire pharmaceutical market. Furthermore, quality is defined as producing and selling leading-edge drugs—those based on the very latest medical research. A discussion

around the items in Figure 3-8 will be more meaningful if it is constrained by that competitive strategy.

5. By the way, notice that Dee's boss wants the memo on the competitive advantage of the blog so he can give it to his boss. This proposed idea, even if it is not approved, has already given Dee a boost within the organization. She will be perceived by her boss and her boss's boss as an innovative thinker. Career-wise, having Dee's boss mention her name and proposal to his boss is a *very good thing*. Given this, I ask the students if they can see how having a knowledge of IS will give them a career boost, even if they never work in IS.

HOW TO GET THE STUDENTS INVOLVED

1. I try first to get their emotions involved with a series of questions like:

   a. **So, what do you think about your boss asking for a memo for his boss? Is that a good thing?**

   b. **What if you do a poor job with the memo? What will happen?**

   c. **You'll get a lot of questions from your boss; some are more important than others. How important is this one?**

   d. **Would you be out of line to ask your boss if you can present your memo (with him in the meeting)?**

   e. **How does the quality of your answer to his question relate to the likelihood and desirability of presenting the memo yourself?**

   f. **How is this project giving Dee a competitive advantage within Emerson?**

   g. **In what ways could this project backfire on Dee? How can she prevent that?**

   h. **What should Dee do if her boss takes the idea and memo and presents it to his boss as *his* idea?**

2. One way to start this is to ask the students to answer Dee's boss's question: How could Dee's blog give a competitive advantage? My goal is to get a lot of ideas—maybe 20 or so. I don't evaluate them, I just get a long list. If the discussion runs down, point the students to Figure 3-8.

3. I want to move the discussion into an understanding of Figure 3-1. To do that, I'll say something like the following:

   a. **Dee's boss wants a memo, not a term paper. A list of 20 or so competitive advantages is too long. How can we prioritize this list?**

b. What criteria should we use in evaluating items on this list?

c. What parts of Figure 3-1 can help us understand how to prioritize this list?

d. What is Emerson's competitive strategy?

e. In light of that strategy, which are the top five items on this list?

4. Figure 3-1 provides a guide to the knowledge presented in Chapters 1-3. Does anyone see how?

(Chapters 1, 2, and 3 work from right to left in Figure 3-1. Chapter 1 defined information systems and their components. Chapter 2 showed the relevance of IS and business processes. Chapter 3 discusses the three Porter models for industry structure, competitive strategy, and value chains.)

5. *Heads-up:*

a. Value chains will be addressed many times in Part 3. This is just the introduction to them.

b. You'll see them again and again!

BOTTOM LINE

* Information systems can provide competitive advantages. However, they ought not to support just *any* competitive advantage. They should support the competitive advantages that are relevant to the organization's competitive strategy.

Using the Guide: Your Personal Competitive Advantage *(page 45a)*

GOALS

* Raise students' awareness that they should be engaged in job planning/searching right now.

* Show the application of the principles of competitive advantage to career planning.

* Suggest innovative tasks for job searching.

BACKGROUND AND PRESENTATION STRATEGIES

Students seldom understand how their status as students gives them access to businesspeople that they will lose after they graduate. Ask the students if they understand the difference in the response they will receive to the following two statements:

➤ **Hi, my name is XXX, and I'm a student at YYY University. We're studying information systems and competitive advantage. I see that your company, ZZZ, is using a CRM application. I'm wondering if you would have a few minutes to talk with me about how your CRM system gives ZZZ a competitive advantage.**

➤ **Hi, my name is XXX, and I'm looking for a job. I see that your company, ZZZ, is using a CRM application. I'm wondering if you would have a few minutes to talk with me about how your CRM system gives you a competitive advantage.**

What will be the difference in response? Huge. In the first, the person will feel like they're helping some bright, ambitious person. Most will say, sure, and maybe offer to buy the student a cup of coffee. In the second, the person will feel like they're being manipulated to find a job. Most will say, "Contact our HR department."

Why should students talk with businesspeople, and now? To build their networks.

➤ **Have the conversation. Make a list of great questions to ask; be appreciative that the businessperson took the time. Then, toward the end of the interview, ask if the person has any advice for finding a job in that industry. Not, *do they have a job*, but rather, *do they have any advice for finding a job*. If they have a job, they'll tell you. If not, they may give you some good advice. Even if you get no good advice,**
you have another point in your network. Take Figure 3-8 along and ask the person how you can use it to gain a competitive advantage.

See question 3.

Why do students not use their special student status in this way? I don't know, but I try to ensure that they at least know about these strategies.

Some students may be too shy. If this is the case, sometimes I make it an assignment, possibly an extra credit assignment.

Similarly, students should be availing themselves of every resource the university provides for outreach to businesspeople.

➤ **If there is a mentor program, get a mentor. If there is a chance to visit a business, go visit the business. If someone from industry speaks on a topic of interest, by all means go. Talk to the speaker afterwards, make one or two positive comments, and ask a good question. Ask for the person's business card. In a day or two, send them an email thanking them. See if you can get an interview to discuss some topic of mutual interest.**

Sometimes I lead them carefully through the disaster scenario. I tell them I had this horrible dream last night. And my dream was that they graduated, couldn't get a job, took a dead-end job for two years, and then couldn't get out of that track. To avoid this nightmare, they have to start thinking about their jobs, now! (I'm assuming mostly junior-level students.)

By the way, every part ending in the text has a section of questions called "Career Assignments" that will ask them to look for information about jobs in the IS field. I ask my students to answer these questions in at least two of the chapters sometime during the class.

 SUGGESTED RESPONSES FOR DISCUSSION QUESTIONS

1. Answer depends on the student. Sometimes I say, "If your list is short, tell me what you plan to do in the next quarter."

2. Again, the answer depends on the student. I also encourage them to realize that they aren't competing just with the students they see on our campus. They're competing with students all over the world. (More on this topic in Chapter 4.)

3. There are many ways to build networks. Here are two types of answers:

- Read trade magazines, relevant Web sites (e.g., *www.cio.com*), and other sources. Find an article on a topic of interest and think of ways the ideas in that article apply to you and one or more items in the list in Figure 3-8. Contact the author of the article. Make a few complimentary comments; ask questions that pertain to the article, you, and the list.

- Approach businesspeople working in your major field of study and ask them how you can use knowledge of information systems to gain a competitive advantage in that field. Tell them of your interest in both your major and in IS. Use this situation to generate further introductions, perhaps to specialists in your field.

4. Get active. Join clubs. Meet with lots of students. Participate in campus life both in and beyond the business school. As we'll discuss in the Ethics Guide in Chapter 6, you add more connections to your network by meeting students that are outside of your major or even outside of the business school. As you meet people, tell them of your career interests. Ask if they know anyone working in that field. Ask if they know someone you could meet with, as described in question 3.

    Join a business-specific club, for example, the Accounting Club or the Marketing Club. Get involved, especially with activities that engage local businesspeople. Arrange for speakers and host speakers on campus. As you meet businesspeople on campus, query them about their careers. How did they get where they are?

    Use an IS to keep track of the people whom you've met. Put contacts in a spreadsheet or database. Keep track of contacts you've had, emails you've sent, meetings you've attended. At an interview, when appropriate, show off your database. Use the Web and email to contact people who are doing interesting things.

WRAP UP

➤ You don't want to find just any job. You want to find a *great* job! You want to find one with appropriate responsibilities, with a growing company, with job growth potential, and where you work with interesting people. You also want one that pays well.

➤ Finding that great job may not be easy. Start now! Start thinking about what kind of job you want, and start preparing yourself to find that job. The last semester of your senior year will be too late.

➤ If you're not an IS major, combining IS knowledge with your other major can make for a great combination. Think about taking some more IS classes.

Using the Ethics Guide: Limiting Access to Those Who Have Access *(page 47a)*

GOALS

* Teach students that knowledge grows exponentially—just like capital.

* Sensitize students to the social problem of the digital divide.

* Explore the responsibilities for business and government with respect to the digital divide.

BACKGROUND AND PRESENTATION STRATEGIES

The more money you have, the easier it is to make more money. **And the more knowledge you have, the easier it is to acquire more knowledge.** Knowledge and capital both grow exponentially.

Thus, learning the *strategies for learning* is critical. Learning how to learn efficiently using the Web and other contemporary resources should be one of the students' primary goals while in college.

Being connected, by the way, means being able to send emails, use ftp, engage in instant messaging and texting, etc. All these are also important ways of learning. (IM as a tool for learning? It could be.)

But what about those who are on the nonconnected side of the digital divide? What happens to them? They fall farther and farther behind. Actually, they stay right where they are, and the rest of the world moves farther and farther ahead, accelerating. The gap grows exponentially.

The Bill and Melinda Gates Foundation donated over $262 million for libraries to buy computers to provide Internet access for the public. See *www.gatesfoundation.org/libraries* for more information about the Foundation's library program, including a state map that describes library donations.

To the surprise of many (including, I believe, the Gates Foundation), the most popular activity on those library computers was finding a job!

The Gates's donation was a generous and appropriate action for the world's richest couple. But what about businesses? What about government?

➤ Today, in the United States, what groups of people are not connected to the Internet? (Examples include those living in poverty, the elderly, the poorly educated, and those who've stuck their heads in the sand.)

➤ Does it make sense for benefactors or government agencies to provide access to those in poverty?

➤ What keeps the elderly from accessing the Internet?

➤ Should the government help the elderly?

➤ What could be done to provide Internet access for the poorly educated? Does government have a role?

Most MIS classes have a number of foreign students. If yours does, you might want to consider this guide from a world perspective.

➤ Some of you are from outside the United States. What is the connectivity situation in your country?

➤ Is there a digital divide?

➤ Are some countries more behind the connectivity trend than others?

➤ What does this mean for those countries' ability to compete? For the citizens of those countries?

Today, two trends are underway that complicate the situation: ubiquitous high-speed data communications and the merger of computers and entertainment devices.

➤ How do these changes alter the situation for the nonconnected?

I think these questions lead to an optimistic note. Once televisions are merged with Internet access devices, then anyone who can afford and operate a TV will have some kind of computer. And, with cheaper and cheaper data communications, they will have at least some access to the Internet.

❓ SUGGESTED RESPONSES FOR DISCUSSION QUESTIONS

1. Answers will depend on students' experiences. Are there students on campus who are disadvantaged by a lack of computer equipment? How do they cope? Do they have access at home or through relatives?

   What about foreign students? Is their situation different from students in the United States? See comments in the Background section about bringing in the perspective of different countries.

2. No, there is no law that requires organizations to provide equal access to the nonconnected. *Should there be?*

   Laws imply enforcement, and enforcement implies lawsuits. This all gets very expensive for society. Some would say it would be better to focus resources on programs like the Gates's library donation.

   Another argument uses the Declaration of Independence. Citizens have an equal right to life, liberty, and the pursuit of happiness. If being non-connected threatens any of these, then laws should be passed to protect the disconnected.

   But, is going to a movie one aspect of the pursuit of happiness? So, if movie theaters have a Web site, do they have a responsibility to provide access for the nonconnected? This seems silly.

3. Whether organizations have an ethical obligation to provide equal access depends on the organization. A religious organization would seem to have an ethical responsibility to ensure equal access to information for its members. What about a yacht club? What about an athletic league?

4. I think most would agree that government agencies have greater responsibilities than do commercial entities. Public health information, for example, should be equally available to the connected and the nonconnected. But, how is this possible? With instantaneous 24/7 connectivity, there is no way that a nonconnected person can have the same access to late-breaking disease information as the connected person. However, what government will buy comput-ers for its citizens just for that reason?

5. What groups are nonconnected? Would those groups be helped by subsidies or tax incentives? Is the answer in education? Or, is the problem of Internet access so low on the list of priorities of these groups that any available tax dollars should be spent on other programs? Obviously, there is no clear answer.

6. The following are several questions to explore this:

   ➤ **Is the gap between the connected and the nonconnected the same gap as that between the educated and the noneducated?**

   ➤ **In the future, will there be just three kinds of employees: techies, flunkies, and managers?**

   ➤ **What sort of world will that be? Will it be stable?**

   ➤ **Those of us on an academic campus will have opportunities that those on the wrong side of the digital divide will not have. What responsibilities do we have to help those nonconnected people?**

WRAP UP

➤ **Knowledge grows exponentially. Those with more knowledge will be able to obtain new knowledge at a faster rate. Not being connected reduces the rate at which people can obtain knowledge.**

➤ **In school, it is important to focus on ways to use the Web and other resources to learn, and to do so efficiently.**

➤ **People who are not connected are at a serious disadvantage. It's not an easy disadvantage to fix. Equal access through traditional means is impossible. A brochure cannot provide the latest information, 24/7.**

➤ **Possibly the best hope, the great equalizer, will be the blending of televisions and Internet devices. Then, everyone with a TV (almost every person) can have Internet access. Cheap data communications will make it easy to connect as well.**

PART 1 The International Dimension

The Global Economy

Study Questions

Q1 Why is the global economy important today?

Q2 How does the global economy change the competitive environment?

Q3 How does the global economy change competitive strategy?

Q4 How does the global economy change value chains and business processes?

Q5 How does the global economy change information systems?

The International Dimension

Q1   Why Is the Global Economy Important Today?

Businesses compete today in a global market. International business has been sharply increasing since the middle of the twentieth century. After World War II, the Japanese and other Asian economies exploded when those countries began to manufacture and sell goods to the West. The rise of the Japanese auto industry and the rise of the semiconductor industry in southern Asia greatly expanded international trade. At the same time, the economies of North America and Europe became more closely integrated.

Since then, a number of other factors have caused international business to explode. The fall of the Soviet Union opened the economies of Russia and also Eastern Europe to the world market. Even more important, the telecommunications boom during the dot-com heyday caused the world to be encircled many times over by optical fiber that can be used for data and voice communications.

After the dot-com bust, this fiber was largely underutilized and could be purchased for pennies on the dollar. Plentiful, cheap telecommunications enabled people worldwide to participate in the global economy. Prior to the advent of the Internet, for a young Indian professional to participate in the western economy, he or she had to migrate to the West—a process that was politicized and limited. Today, that same young Indian professional can sell his or her

goods or services over the Internet without leaving home. During this same period, the Chinese economy became more open to the world, and it too benefits from plentiful, cheap telecommunications.

Thomas Friedman estimates that from 1991 until now, some 3 billion people have been added to the world economy.[1] Not all of those people speak English, and not all are well enough educated (or equipped) to participate in the world economy. But even if just 10 percent are, then 300 million people have been added to the world economy in the last 15 years!

Q2 How Does the Global Economy Change the Competitive Environment?

To understand the impact of globalization, consider each of the elements in Figure 3-1 (page 38), starting with industry structure. The changes have been so dramatic that the structure of seemingly every industry has changed. The enlarged and Internet-equipped world economy has altered every one of the five competitive forces. Suppliers have to reach a wider range of customers, and customers have to consider a wider range of vendors. As you will learn when we address e-commerce in Chapter 8, suppliers and customers benefit not just from the greater size of the economy, but also by the ease with which businesses can learn of each other using infrastructure like Google.

Because of the information available on the Internet, customers can more easily learn of substitutions. The Internet has made it easier for new market entrants, although not in all cases. Amazon.com, Yahoo!, and Google, for example, have garnered such a large market share that it would be difficult for any new entrant to challenge them. Still, in other industries, the global economy facilitates new entrants. Finally, the global economy has intensified rivalry by increasing product and vendor choices and by accelerating the flow of information about price, product, availability, and service.

Q3 How Does the Global Economy Change Competitive Strategy?

Today's global economy changes thinking about competitive strategies in two major ways. First, the sheer size and complexity of the global economy means that any organization that chooses a strategy allowing it to compete industrywide is tak-

ing a very big bite! Competing in many different countries, with products localized to the language and culture of those countries, is an enormous and expensive task.

For example, to promote its Windows monopoly, Microsoft must produce a version of Windows in dozens of different languages. Even in English, there are U.K. versions, U.S. versions, Australian versions, and so forth. The problem for

Microsoft is even greater because different countries use different character sets. In some languages, one writes left to right. In other languages, one writes right to left. When Microsoft set out to sell Windows worldwide, it embarked on an enormous project.

The second major way today's world economy changes competitive strategies is that its size, combined with the Internet, enables unprecedented product differentiation. If you choose to produce the world's highest quality and most exotic oatmeal—and if your production costs require you to sell that oatmeal for $350 a pound—your target market may contain only 200 people worldwide. The Internet allows you to find them—and them to find you.

The decision involving a global competitive strategy requires the consideration of these two changing factors.

[1]Thomas L. Friedman, *The World Is Flat: A Brief History of the Twenty-First Century* (New York: Farrar, Strauss, and Giroux, 2005).

Q4 How Does the Global Economy Change Value Chains and Business Processes?

The growth in the world economy has major impacts on all activities in the value chain. An excellent example concerns the manufacture of the Boeing 787. Every primary activity for this airplane has an international component. Companies all over the world produce its parts and subassemblies. Major components of the airplane are constructed in worldwide locations and shipped for final assembly to Boeing's plant in Everett, Washington. *Outbound logistics* for Boeing refers not just to the delivery of an airplane, but also to the delivery of spare parts and supporting maintenance equipment. All of those items are produced at factories worldwide and delivered to customers worldwide. The global sales also change the marketing, sales, and service activities for the 787.

As you learned in Chapter 3, each value chain activity is supported by one or more business processes. Those processes span the globe and need to address differences in language, culture, and economic environments. A process for servicing 787 customers in Egypt will be very different from the same service process in China, the United States, or India. For example, a business process organized around a central leader with strong authority may be expected in one culture and resisted in another. Global companies must design their business processes with these differences in mind.

Q5 How Does the Global Economy Change Information Systems?

To understand the impact of internationalization on information systems, consider the five components. Computer hardware is sold worldwide, and most vendors provide documentation in at least the major languages, so internationalization has little impact on that component. The remaining components of an information system, however, are markedly affected.

To begin, consider the user interface for an international information system. Does it include a localized version of Windows? What about the software application itself? Does an inventory system used worldwide by Boeing suppose that each user speaks English? If so, at what level of proficiency? If not, what languages must the user interface support? Most computer programs are written in computer languages that have an English base, but not all. Can an information system use a localized programming language?

Next, consider the data component. Suppose that the inventory database has a table for parts data and that table contains a column named Remarks. Suppose Boeing needs to integrate parts data from three different

vendors: one in China, one in India, and one in Canada. What language is to be used for recording Remarks? Does someone need to translate all of the Remarks into one language? Into three languages?

The human components—procedures and people—are obviously affected by language and culture. As with business processes, information systems procedures need to reflect local cultural values and norms. For systems users, job descriptions and reporting relationships must be appropriate for the setting in which the system is used. We will say more about this in Part IV, when we discuss the development and management of information systems.

Active ❓ Review

Use this Active Review to verify that you understand the material in the International Dimension. You can read the entire minichapter and then perform the tasks in this review, or you can read the material for just one question and perform the tasks in this review for that question before moving on to the next one.

Q1 Why is the global economy important today?

Describe how the global economy has changed since the mid-twentieth century. Explain how the dot-com bust influenced the global economy and changed the number of workers worldwide.

Q2 How does the global economy change the competitive environment?

Summarize the ways in which today's global economy influences the five competitive forces. Explain how the global economy changes the way organizations assess industry structure.

Q3 How does the global economy change competitive strategy?

Explain how size and complexity change the costs of a competitive strategy. Describe what the size of the global economy means to differentiation.

Q4 How does the global economy change value chains and business processes?

Describe, in general terms, how international business impacts value chains and business processes. Use the example of the Boeing 787 in your answer.

Q5 How does the global economy change information systems?

Describe how international business impacts each of the five components of an information system. Identify the components that are most impacted by the need to support multiple cultures and languages.

Consider Your Net Worth

The ideas presented in the three chapters in this part can contribute substantially to your net worth as an employee as well as to your personal net worth. The key is to understand how to apply what you have learned here to your career goals. Here is one way to do that:

1. Write a description of what you want to do. Consider the following questions: Why do you want to work in business? What, specifically, do you want to do? Why did you choose your major? What would be the ideal first job for you?

2. Read the lists of questions that start each chapter. Think about each question in light of your answer in 1. Select seven questions that seem particularly relevant to your career. Explain why each of them seems important to you.

3. Write a single paragraph answer to each one of the questions you selected in 2 above.

4. Considering your answer to question 1, reflect on the experience of Dee, the marketing manager who wants to construct a blog. Even if you do not plan to work in marketing and even though you're unlikely to start a blog, what can you learn from Dee's experiences that might help you in your own career?

5. Assume you are about to be interviewed for the job you described in question 1. Using your answers to questions 3 and 4, prepare a list of notes that you could use to describe, in 5 minutes or so, how this knowledge you've gained from these three chapters will enable you to perform well in your new job.

Career Assignments

1. Using Google (*google.com*) or your favorite Web search tool, search for job opportunities that relate to information systems. Some terms that you might use in your search are:

- Information systems job opportunities.

- Computer sales job opportunities.

- Computer support job opportunities.

- Computer training job opportunities.

- Systems analyst job opportunities.

- Business computer programmer job opportunities.

- Software testing job opportunities.

- Computer software product manager job opportunities.

- Computer-based marketing job opportunities.

2. Using your favorite Web search engine, search for one topic from the following list:

- Accounting information systems

- Marketing information systems

- Sales information systems

- Manufacturing information systems

- Financial information systems

- Information systems in another functional business area in which you have an interest

3. Using the results from your search in Career Assignment 2, search for job opportunities. Consider sales, marketing, support, or management of companies that sell or support the systems you found in 2.

4. Select two of the job types in your answers to questions 1 and 2 in which you might be interested. From the descriptions, describe the general educational requirements of these two jobs. Describe the general experience requirements of these two jobs.

5. For each of your two job types in your answers to questions 1 and 2, search the Web for internship possibilities. For example, if you were interested in software testing, search for "software testing internship jobs." Identify two or three different possibilities.

6. Summarize actions you can take to prepare for these two jobs. Consider not just what courses you should take, but also part-time work, internships, volunteer work, and other activities.

Application Exercises

 1. Suppose that you are seeking employment and you want to keep track of companies and the contacts you've had with those companies.

    a. Create a spreadsheet with the following headings: CompanyName, WebSite, City, State, ContactDate, PersonContacted, EmailAddress, Phone, ContactRemarks.

b. Place sample data in your spreadsheet. Your data should have multiple companies and multiple contacts per company.

c. Describe how the five components of an information system can be used with a spreadsheet to obtain a job.

d. Suppose you share this spreadsheet with a group of other students— perhaps roommates or classmates or members of a student club. Describe how your group could use the five components of an information system with this spreadsheet.

e. How does your answer differ between questions c and d above? What general conclusions can you draw from this example?

 2. Suppose that you are seeking employment and you want to keep track of companies and the contacts you've had with those companies.

a. Create an Access database with two tables: COMPANY, having the columns CompanyName, WebSite, City, State; and CONTACT, having the columns ContactDate, PersonContacted, EmailAddress, Phone, ContactRemarks, and CompanyName. Assume that CompanyName in CONTACT relates to CompanyName in COMPANY.

b. Place sample data in both tables. Your data should have multiple companies and multiple contacts per company.

c. Create a data entry form for both tables. The type of form you create depends on your knowledge of Access. If you are a novice, just open the tables and add the data.

d. Create a simple report that lists companies and the contacts you've made with those companies. Use the Access Report wizard. (*Hint:* First define the relationship between COMPANY and CONTACT. In Access, click on Tools/Relationships. Right-click in the design space, and select Show Table. Add tables COMPANY and CONTACT. In the design space, drag CompanyName from COMPANY and drop on CompanyName in CONTACT. Click Create. Close the design space and save your changes. Now run the Report Wizard to create your report.)

e. Describe how the five components of an information system can be used with this database to obtain a job.

f. Suppose you share this database with a group of other students— perhaps roommates or classmates or members of a student club. Describe how your group could use the five components of an information system with this database.

g. How does your answer differ between questions e and f above? What general conclusions can you draw from this example?

Getty Images Serves Up Profit

Getty Images was founded in 1995 with the goal of consolidating the fragmented photography market by acquiring many small companies, applying business discipline to the merged entity, and developing modern information systems. The advent of the Web drove the company to e-commerce and in the process enabled Getty to change the workflow and business practices of the professional visual content industry. Getty Images has grown from a startup to become, by 2004, a global, $600 million plus, publicly traded (NYSE: GYI), very profitable company.

Getty Images obtains its imagery (both still and movie) from photographers under contract, and it owns the world's largest private archive of imagery. Getty also employs staff photographers to shoot the world's news, sport, and entertainment events. In the case of photography and film that it does not own, it provides a share of the revenue generated to the content owner. Getty Images is both a producer and a distributor of imagery, and all of its products are sold via e-commerce on the Web.

Getty Images employs three licensing models: The first is *subscription*, by which customers contract to use as many images as they want as often as they want (this applies to the news, sport, and entertainment imagery). The second model is *royalty-free*. In this model, customers pay a fee based on the file size of the image and can use the image any way they want and as many times as they want. However, under this model, customers have no exclusivity or ability to prevent a competitor from using the same image at the same time.

The third model, *rights managed*, also licenses creative imagery. In this model, which is the largest in revenue terms, users pay fees according to the rights that they wish to use—size, industry, geography, prominence, frequency, exclusivity, and so forth.

According to its Web site:

> Getty Images has been credited with the introduction of royalty-free photography and was the first company to license imagery via the Web, subsequently moving the entire industry online. The company was also the first to employ creative researchers to anticipate the visual content needs of the world's communicators, and Getty Images remains the first and only publicly traded imagery company in the world. (*corporate.gettyimages.com/ source/company*, accessed December 2004)

In 2003, Getty Images' Web site, *gettyimages.com*, received more than 51 million visits and served over 1.3 billion pages. Visitors to the site viewed more than 6.7 billion thumbnail-sized photos in the third quarter of 2004 alone.

Because Getty Images licenses photos in digital format, its variable cost of production is essentially zero. Once the company has obtained a photo and placed it in the commerce server database, the cost of sending it to a customer is zero. Getty Images does have the overhead costs of setting up and operating the e-commerce site, and it does pay some costs for its images—either the costs of employing the photographer or the cost of setting up and maintaining the relationship with out-of-house photographers. For some images, it also pays a royalty to the owner. Once

these costs are paid, however, the cost of producing a photo is nil. This means that Getty Images' profitability increases substantially with increased volume.

Figure 1 shows a page that the Getty Images commerce server produced when the user selected creative, royalty-free photography and searched on the term *Boston*.

When the user clicked "Calculate price" for the image named Photodisc Green, the commerce server produced the page shown in Figure 2. This Web page shows a default price. Users in different countries may have a different price depending on agreements, taxes, and local policies.

Source: gettyimages.com (accessed December 2004).

Questions

1. Visit *GettyImages.com*, and select "Creative/Search royalty-free." Search for an image of a city close to your campus. Select a photo and determine its default prices.

2. Explain how Getty Images' business model takes advantage of the opportunities described in Chapter 1.

3. Evaluate the photography market using Porter's five forces. Do you think Getty Images' marginal cost is sustainable? Are its prices sustainable? What is the key to its continued success?

4. What seems to be Getty Images' competitive strategy?

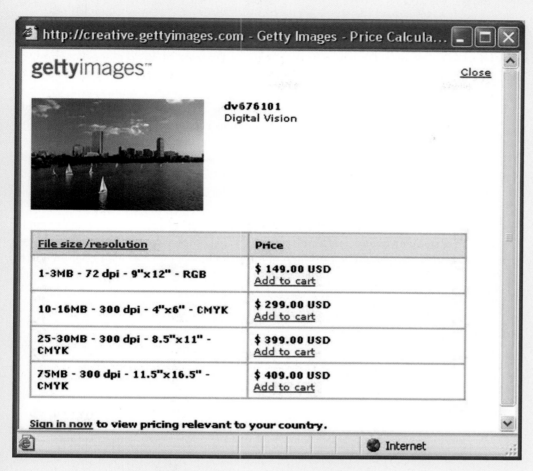

5. Explain how Getty Images has used information systems to gain a competitive advantage.

6. Based on your answers to the previous questions, would you choose to buy Getty Images stock?

7. Getty Images has the enviable position of a near-zero variable cost of production. Describe two other businesses that could use emerging IT to attain the same advantage.

CASE 1-2

Knoll Inc.

Knoll, Inc. (*knoll.com*) is a leading manufacturer of office equipment. Founded in 1938, Knoll has always been known for its groundbreaking, innovative, and fashionable designs. Today, such innovation includes not only modern, contemporary designs, but also designs that recognize changes in the nature of the work environment. Knoll understood early on that new information systems would drive the redesign of value chains and business processes. Knoll realized that these changes would, in turn, impact the physical design of the workers' environments and alter the requirements for office furniture.

According to Christine Barber, who is Director of Workplace Research at Knoll, "The explosion of information technology has caused a fundamental shift in company offices away from clerical and toward professional, managerial, and creative work. . . . Whereas white-collar labor in the nineteenth and most of the twentieth century involved an army of clerical workers performing rote tasks under the supervision of an elite corps of managers, most of the grunt work has now been turned over to computers. . . . Two-thirds [of office workers] describe themselves as 'problem solvers,' 'information analyzers,' and 'idea generators'. . . . Half of those working in midsize to large companies characterize their work as 'collaborative' in nature" (Barber and Yee, 2004).

Because of the importance of workplace changes to its market, Knoll commissioned a study involving 1,500 interviews of 350 office workers. Researchers asked those workers to rate the importance of office factors in terms of their contribution to productivity. The following are the top five factors, rated in decreasing order of productivity impact:

- State-of-the-art computer technology

- Ample storage space for work items

- Control over temperature

- Quiet workspace

- Space that can be personalized

In this study, Knoll also found a curious paradox in workers' attitudes toward privacy. Most workers want it both ways: They want their own office or private space in which to concentrate, perform uninterrupted work, and hold private meetings, but they also want open space for collaboration, a feeling of teamwork, and a sense of family. Modern workers, according to Knoll's study, "crave both privacy and intimacy." They want an open space design rather than a cubicle configuration. In fact, according to the research study, "the cubicle is the symbol of everything 'old economy' in workplace design, evoking images of 'prison,' conformity, being a number or stamped with a barcode" (Barber and DYG, Inc., 2004).

According to Barber, "As the workforce of the new economy performs increasingly cerebral, self-directed, and multidisciplinary tasks, the gap between managers and [those who are] managed narrows dramatically in terms of skills, experience, and responsibility. But the flattening of the organizational pyramid has not inspired any real change in office space" (Barber and DYG, Inc., 2004).

These are intriguing statements. We know that information systems improve communication and that they foster cross-departmental, process thinking. Do they also change the shape of the workplace? They should, at least according to Barber: "Businesses feel compelled to invest in cutting-edge information technology to stay competitive; but they persist in seeing offices as assembly lines, rather than as think tanks, for producing knowledge-based products and services" (Barber and Yee, 2004).

Sources: Christine Barber and DYG, Inc., "The 21st Century Workplace"; Christine Barber and Roger Yee, "Brave New Workplace," 2004, knoll.com/research/index.htm (accessed March 2005).

Questions

1. Given the fact that Knoll sponsored the research described here, is Knoll more likely to be engaging in a cost leader or differentiator competitive strategy? Explain your answer.

2. How will the change from hierarchical to cross-departmental process thinking affect the design of office furniture and equipment? Do you think there will be sufficient impact to justify Knoll's concern and research? What are the dangers to a company like Knoll of not considering these trends?

3. Describe two nontechnology-related industries, other than the office furniture industry, that are likely to be changed by cross-departmental, enterprise-wide information systems and related organizational changes. Explain the nature of the impact on those industries.

4. Suppose you are a product manager in Knoll's marketing group. Describe three ways you could use the five productivity factors listed in this case to design new products, product features, or product enhancements.

5. Suppose you manage a sales department with two types of salespeople: those who call on prospects to obtain new customers and those who sell to existing customers. Assume that each salesperson works in a personal cubicle and that salespeople are assigned to cubicles regardless of the type of sales they perform. Suppose your department is converting to a new sales support system, and you take that opportunity to propose an improvement to your sales team's workplace.

a. Given the information in this case, what changes would you make?

b. Suppose you ask the manager of the new sales support project for funds to purchase new office furniture and equipment. Suppose she rejects your request saying, "New furniture has absolutely nothing to do with the success of our new system." How do you respond?

c. Rank the importance of the workspace arrangement for the users of a new information system. Is the environment as important as the system's features? More important? Less important? Explain your answer.

PART 2
Using Information Technology

This could happen to you

Dee knows that she needs an information system to support her blog. She knows that it has five components; she has justified it by explaining how it will positively impact the sales process and how it will give Emerson a competitive advantage. She's presented all of this to her boss, and he's endorsed the idea, but he wants to know how much it will cost before he'll give final approval.

How much will it cost? It depends. The cheapest solution would be to use one of the commercial sites that sponsor blogs, like MSN and Yahoo. She can't do that, however, because she needs to restrict access to Emerson employees. A public blog would be accessible by the competition.

So she needs to set up her own blog. But how? What's involved? She knows she has to think about hardware, software, data, procedures, and people. The people will be both the sales force and herself. The sales force will need procedures for accessing the blog and leaving comments; Dee will need procedures for posting entries to the blog. Although she's never done that before, she's confident that she can learn the procedures required.

The hardware, software, and data components, however, have her flummoxed. When she talked with her IT staff, she met a barrage of questions that she didn't understand, let alone know how to answer them. Questions included, "Are you going to run on a Windows or Linux server? What blog software will you use? Are you going to put it on the Emerson network? If so, how are you going to get the software set up? Emerson uses Oracle, but what does your blog software require? Will you run it within the VPN, or will you use some private set of accounts and passwords?"

And finally: "You want it WHEN? By early January!?? You've got to be kidding! This is early December, and the holidays are coming up. There's no way."

Dee, however, is not easily put off. As a salesperson, she believes that the sale starts when the customer says, "No." She brought that same attitude to this project, and she wasn't about to quit. Through professional acquaintances, she learned about Don Gray, a consultant who specializes in setting up blogs and similar sites.

When she contacted him, Don responded more positively. Even he, however, asked her questions that she couldn't understand.

Dee needed the knowledge in the three chapters in this part. She needed a basic understanding of hardware; she needed to know the basics of database processing; and she needed to know about computer networks, firewalls, and something called a VPN. Had she possessed this knowledge, it would have taken her half as much time as it did—or even less time than that. She also would have had much less worry, anxiety, and stress.

4 Hardware and Software

Because of the short time available, Dee decided to hire Don Gray, a consultant who specializes in setting up systems like blogs. Don has many years of experience working with people like Dee, and he knew not to throw a barrage of technical questions at her. However, before he could help her develop a cost estimate, he needed answers to a few basic questions:

- **"Will you run your blog on an internal Emerson site or contract with an outside hosting service?"**
- **"Either way, will your site use a Windows or Linux server?"**
- **"What blog software do you want to use?"**
- **"How do you want to code your entries? Are you going to use FrontPage, or do you want me to build in an html editor in your blog software?"**
- **"What browsers do you want to support? IE? Firefox? Netscape? Others?"**
- **"Do you care if your blog doesn't render perfectly in all browsers?"**

Dee was in a bind. She didn't know the answers to these questions (she didn't even know what some of them meant—such as "render perfectly in all browsers"). She really had nowhere to turn. The people in her internal IT department had told her there was no way the project could be done on time, and they were dismissive of her requests for help—even just to answer the questions above. She could ask Don to help her with the answers, but he had a potential conflict of interest: As a consultant, he might want to pad his bill with features she didn't need. While Don's references indicated that this was unlikely, she was reluctant to ask him to answer the very questions he was asking. In short, Dee needed the knowledge in this chapter.

As a future business professional, you may find yourself in the same spot. You may not be creating a blog, but you may be creating some other information system and need to answer questions similar to those Don posed. As you read this chapter, think about these kinds of questions, and focus on gaining a foundation in hardware and software terms and concepts. The discussion is not technical; it focuses on knowledge that a future manager will need.

An optional Extension for this chapter is CE4, "Preparing a Computer Budget."

Study Questions

Q1 What does a manager need to know about computer hardware?

Q2 What's the difference between a client and a server?

Q3 What does a manager need to know about software?

Q4 What buying decisions do you make?

Q5 What are viruses, Trojan horses, and worms?

How does the knowledge in this chapter help Dee and you?

Q1 What Does a Manager Need to Know about Computer Hardware?

As discussed in the five-component framework, **hardware** consists of electronic components and related gadgetry that input, process, output, and store data according to instructions encoded in computer programs or software. The essential knowledge that you need in order to be an effective manager and consumer of computer hardware is summarized in Figure 4-1.

Students vary in the hardware knowledge they bring to this class. If you already know the terms in this grid, skip to the next question on page 63: "What's the difference between a client and a server?"

Input, Processing, Output, and Storage Hardware

Figure 4-1
What a Manager Needs to Know
About Hardware

To make sense of the rows in Figure 4-1, consider Figure 4-2, which shows the components of a generic computer. Notice that basic hardware categories are input, process, output, and storage.

Component	Performance Factors	Beneficial for:	Example Application
CPU and data bus	• CPU speed • Cache memory • Data bus speed • Data bus width	• Fast processing of data once the data reside in main memory	• Repetitive calculations of formulas in a complicated spreadsheet • Manipulation of large picture images
Main memory	• Size • Speed	• Holding multiple programs at one time • Processing very large amounts of data	• Running Excel, Word, Paint Shop Pro, Adobe Acrobat, several Web sites, and email while processing large files in memory and viewing video clips • 3D games
Magnetic disk	• Size • Channel type and speed • Rotational speed • Seek time	• Storing many large programs • Storing many large files • Swapping files in and out of memory	• Store detailed maps of countries in the United States • Large data downloads from organizational servers • Partly compensate for too little main memory
Optical disk—CD	• Up to 700 MB • CD-ROM • CD-R (recordable) • CD-RW (rewritable)	• Reading CDs • Writable media can be used to back up files	• Install new programs • Play and record music • CD being replaced by DVD • Back up data
Optical disk—DVD	• Up to 4.7 GB • DVD-ROM • DVD-R (recordable) • DVD-RW (rewritable)	• Process both DVDs and CDs • Writable media can be used to back up files	• Install new programs • Play and record music • Play and record movies • Back up data
Monitor—CRT	• Viewing size • Dot pitch • Optimal resolution • Special memory?	• Limited budgets	• Nongraphic applications, such as word processing • Less-used computers
Monitor—LCD	• Viewing size • Pixel pitch • Optimal resolution • Special memory?	• Crowded workspaces • When brighter, sharper images are needed	• More than one monitor in use • Lots of graphics to be processed • Continual use

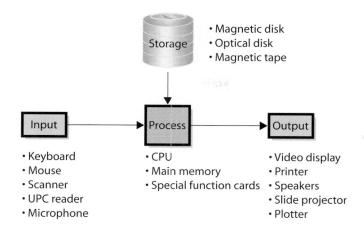

- Magnetic disk
- Optical disk
- Magnetic tape

Storage

Input → Process → Output

- Keyboard
- Mouse
- Scanner
- UPC reader
- Microphone

- CPU
- Main memory
- Special function cards

- Video display
- Printer
- Speakers
- Slide projector
- Plotter

Figure 4-2
Input, Process, Output, and Storage Hardware

As shown in Figure 4-2, typical **input hardware** devices are the keyboard, mouse, document scanners, and bar-code (Universal Product Code) scanners like those used in grocery stores. Microphones also are input devices; with tablet PCs, human handwriting can be input as well. Older input devices include magnetic ink readers (used for reading the ink on the bottom of checks) and scanners like the Scantron test scanner shown in Figure 4-3.

Processing devices include the **central processing unit (CPU)**, which is sometimes called "the brain" of the computer. Although the design of the CPU has nothing in common with the anatomy of animal brains, this description is helpful because the CPU does have the "smarts" of the machine. The CPU selects instructions, processes them, performs arithmetic and logical comparisons, and stores results of operations in memory.

CPUs vary in speed, function, and cost. Hardware vendors such as Intel, Advanced Micro Devices, and National Semiconductor continually improve CPU speed and capabilities while reducing CPU costs (as discussed under Moore's Law in Chapter 1). Whether you or your department needs the latest, greatest CPU depends on the nature of your work.

The CPU works in conjunction with **main memory**. The CPU reads data and instructions from memory, and it stores results of computations in main memory. We will describe the relationship between the CPU and main memory later in the chapter.

Finally, computers also can have **special function cards** (see Figure 4-4 on page 72) that can be added to the computer to augment the computer's basic capabilities. A common example is a card that provides enhanced clarity and refresh speed for the computer's video display.

Output hardware consists of video displays, printers, audio speakers, overhead projectors, and other special-purpose devices, such as large flatbed plotters.

Storage hardware saves data and programs. Magnetic disk is by far the most common storage device, although optical disks such as CDs and DVDs are

Figure 4-3
Scantron Scanner

Figure 4-4
Special Function Card

also popular. In large corporate data centers, data are sometimes stored on magnetic tape.

Computer Data

Before we can further describe hardware, we need to define several important terms. We begin with binary digits.

Binary Digits

Computers represent data using **binary digits**, called **bits**. A bit is either a zero or a one. Bits are used for computer data because they are easy to represent physically, as illustrated in Figure 4-5. A switch can be either closed or open. A computer can be designed so that an open switch represents zero and a closed switch represents one. Or the orientation of a magnetic field can represent a bit; magnetism in one direction represents a zero, magnetism in the opposite direction represents a one. Or for optical media, small pits are burned onto the surface of the disk so that they will reflect light. In a given spot, a reflection means a one; no reflection means a zero.

Sizing Computer Data

All computer data are represented by bits. The data can be numbers, characters, currency amounts, photos, recordings, or whatever. All are simply a string of bits.

For reasons that interest many but are irrelevant for future managers, bits are grouped into 8-bit chunks called **bytes**. For character data, such as the letters in a person's name, one character will fit into one byte. Thus, when you read a specification that a computing device has 100 million bytes of memory, you know that the device could hold up to 100 million characters.

Figure 4-5
Bits Are Easy to Represent
Physically

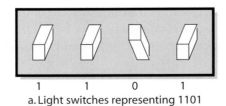

a. Light switches representing 1101

b. Direction of magnetism representing 1101

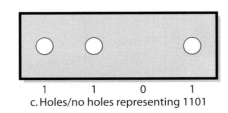

c. Holes/no holes representing 1101

Term	Definition	Abbreviation
Byte	Number of bits to represent one character	
Kilobyte	1,024 bytes	K
Megabyte	1,024 K = 1,048,576 bytes	MB
Gigabyte	1,024 MB = 1,073,741,824 bytes	GB
Terabyte	1,024 GB = 1,099,511,627,776 bytes	TB

Figure 4-6
Important Storage-Capacity Terminology

Bytes are used to measure sizes of noncharacter data as well. Someone might say, for example, that a given picture is 100,000 bytes in size. This statement means the length of the bit string that represents the picture is 100,000 bytes or 800,000 bits (because there are 8 bits per byte). The specifications for the size of main memory, disk, and other computer devices are expressed in bytes. Figure 4-6 shows the set of abbreviations that are used to represent data-storage capacity. A **kilobyte**, abbreviated **K**, is a collection of 1,024 bytes. A **megabyte**, or **MB**, is 1,024K bytes. A **gigabyte**, or **GB**, is 1,024MB bytes, and a **terabyte**, or **TB**, is 1,024GB.

Sometimes you will see these definitions simplified as 1K equals 1,000 bytes and 1MB equals 1,000K. Such simplifications are incorrect, but they do ease the math. Also, disk and computer manufacturers have an incentive to propagate this misconception. If a disk maker defines 1MB to be 1 million bytes—and not the correct 1,024K—the manufacturer can use its own definition of MB when specifying drive capacities. A buyer may think that a disk advertised as 100MB has space for 100 × 1,024K bytes, but in truth the drive will have space for only 100 × 1,000,000 bytes. Normally, the distinction is not too important, but be aware of the two possible interpretations of these abbreviations.

In 293 Words, How Does a Computer Work?

Figure 4-7 shows a snapshot of a computer in use. The CPU (central processing unit) is the major actor. To run a program or process data, the CPU must first transfer the program or data from disk to *main memory*. Then, to execute an

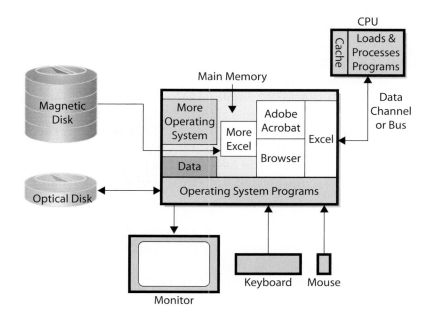

Figure 4-7
Computer Components

instruction, it moves the instruction from main memory into the CPU via the **data channel** or **bus**. The CPU has a small amount of very fast memory called a **cache**. The CPU keeps frequently used instructions in the cache. Having a large cache makes the computer faster, but cache is expensive.

Main memory of the computer in Figure 4-7 contains program instructions for Excel, Acrobat, and a browser (Internet Explorer or Firefox). It also contains instructions for the **operating system (OS)**, which is a program that controls the computer's resources as well as a block of data.

Main memory is too small to hold all of the programs and data that a user may want to process. For example, no personal computer has enough memory to hold all of the code in Microsoft Word, Excel, and Access. Consequently, the CPU loads programs into memory in chunks. In Figure 4-7, one portion of Excel was loaded into memory. When the user requested additional processing (say, to sort the spreadsheet), the CPU loaded another piece of Excel.

If the user opens another program (say, Word) or needs to load more data (say, a picture), the operating system will direct the CPU to attempt to place the new program or data into unused memory. If there is not enough memory, it will remove something, perhaps the block of memory labeled More Excel, and then it will place the just-requested program or data into the vacated space. This process is called **memory swapping**.

Why Does a Manager Care How a Computer Works?

You can order computers with varying sizes of main memory. An employee who only runs one program at a time and who processes small amounts of data requires very little memory—256K would be just fine. On the other hand, a employee who processes many programs at the same time (say, Word, Excel, Firefox, Access, Acrobat, and other programs) or an employee who processes very large files (pictures, movies, or sound files) needs lots of main memory, perhaps a megabyte or more. If that employee's computer has too little memory, then the computer will constantly be swapping memory, and it will be slow. (This means, by the way, that if your computer is slow and if you have many programs open, you likely can improve performance by closing one or more programs. Depending on your computer and the amount of memory it has, you might also be able to add more memory to it.)

You can also order computers with CPUs of different speeds. CPU speed is expressed in cycles called *hertz*. In 2006, the CPU of a fast personal computer had a speed of 3.0 Gigahertz; a slow computer has a speed of less than 1 Gigahertz. As predicted by Moore's Law, CPU speeds continually increase.

An employee who does only simple tasks such as word processing does not need a fast CPU; less than 1 Gigahertz will be fine. On the other hand, an employee who processes large, complicated spreadsheets or who manipulates large database files or edits large picture, sound, or movie files needs a very fast CPU—say, 3 Gigahertz or more. The *Ethics Guide* on pages 75a–75b poses questions about computer hardware and software that offer *more* than many users need.

One last comment: The cache and main memory are **volatile**, meaning their contents are lost when power is off. Magnetic disk and optical disk are **nonvolatile**, meaning their contents survive when power is off. If you suddenly lose power, the contents of unsaved memory—say, documents that have been altered—will be lost. Therefore, get into the habit of frequently (every few minutes or so) saving documents or files that you are changing. Save your documents before your roommate trips over the power cord.

Q2 What's the Difference Between a Client and a Server?

Before we can discuss computer software, you need to understand the difference between a client and a server. Figure 4-8 shows the environment of the typical computer user. Users employ **client** computers for word processing, spreadsheets, database access, and so forth. Most client computers also have software that enables them to connect to a network. It could be a private network at their company or school, or it could be the Internet, a public network. (We will discuss networks and related matters in Chapter 6. Just wait!)

Servers, as their name implies, provide some service. Dee will use a server to run her blog. Other servers publish Web sites, sell goods, host databases, and provide other functions.

As you might expect, server computers need to be faster, larger, and more powerful than client computers. Servers usually have very simple video displays, and some servers have no display at all because they are only accessed from another computer via the network. For large commerce sites such as Amazon.com, the server is actually a large collection of computers (called a **server farm**) that coordinate all activities.

(By the way, the phrase *coordinate all activities* hides an incredibly sophisticated and fascinating technology dance: hundreds, possibly thousands, of transactions coming and going per minute as well as dozens of computers

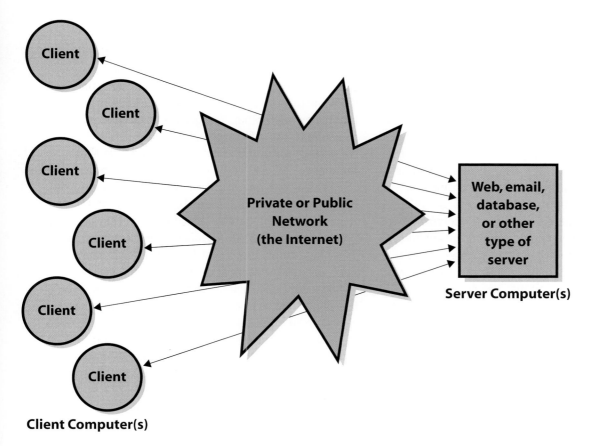

Figure 4-8
Client and Server Computers

Churn and Burn

An anonymous source, whom we'll call Mark, made the following statements about computing devices:

"I never upgrade my system. At least, I try not to. Look, I don't do anything at work but write memos and access email. I use Microsoft Word, but I don't use any features that weren't available in Word 3.0, 10 years ago. This whole industry is based on 'churn and burn': They churn their products so we'll burn our cash.

"All this hype about 3.0GHz processors and 120GB disks—who needs them? I'm sure I don't. And if Microsoft hadn't put so much junk into Windows, we could all be happy on an Intel 486 processor like the one I had in 1993. We're suckers for falling into the 'you gotta have this' trap.

"Frankly, I think there's a conspiracy between hardware and software vendors. They both want to sell new products, so the hardware people come up with these incredibly fast and huge computers. Then, given all that power, the software types develop monster products bloated with features and functions that nobody uses. It would take me months to learn all of the features in Word, only to find out that I don't need those features.

"To see what I mean, open Microsoft Word, click on View, then select Toolbars. In my version of Word, there are 19 toolbars to select, plus one more to customize my own toolbar. Now what in the world do I need with 19 toolbars? I write all the time, and I have two selected: Standard and Formatting. Two out of 19! Could I pay Microsoft 2/19 of the price of Word, because that's all I want or use?

"Here's how they get you, though. Because we live in a connected world, they don't have to get all of us to use those 19 toolbars, just one of us. Take Bridgette, over in legal, for example. Bridgette likes to use the redlining features, and she likes me to use them when I change draft contracts she sends me. So if I want to work on her documents, I have to turn on the Reviewing toolbar. You get the idea; just get someone to use a feature and, because it is a connected world, then all of us have to have that feature.

"Viruses are one of their best ploys. They say you better buy the latest and greatest in software—and then apply all the patches that follow so that you'll be protected from the latest zinger from the computer 'bad guys.' Think about that for a minute. If vendors had built the products correctly the first time, then there would be no holes for the baddies to find, would there? So they have a defect in their products that they turn to a sales advantage. You see, they get us to focus on the virus and not on the hole in their product. In truth, they should be saying, 'Buy our latest product to protect yourself from the defective junk we sold you last year.' But truth in advertising hasn't come that far.

"Besides that, users are their own worst enemies as far as viruses are concerned. If I'm down on 17th Street at 4 in the morning, half drunk and with a bundle of cash hanging out of my pocket, what's likely to happen to me? I'm gonna get mugged. So if I'm out in some weirdo chat room—you know, out where you get pictures of weird sex acts and whatnot—and download and run a file, then of course I'm gonna get a virus. Viruses are brought on by user stupidity, that's all.

"One of these days, users are going to rise up and say, 'That's enough. I don't need any more. I'll stay with what I have, thank you very much.' In fact, maybe that's happening right now. Maybe that's why software sales aren't growing like they were. Maybe people have finally said, 'No more toolbars!'"

DISCUSSION QUESTIONS

1. Summarize Mark's view of the computer industry. Is there merit to his argument? Why or why not?

2. What holes do you see in the logic of his argument?

3. Someone could take the position that these statements are just empty rantings—that Mark can say all he wants, but the computer industry is going to keep on doing as it has been. Is there any point in Mark sharing his criticisms?

4. Read the section on viruses, trojan horses, and worms that appears later in this chapter (pages 82–85). Comment on Mark's statement— "Viruses are brought on by user stupidity, that's all."

5. All software products ship with known problems. Microsoft, Adobe, and Apple all ship software that they know has failures. Is it unethical for them to do so? Do software vendors have an ethical responsibility to openly publish the problems in their software? How do these organizations protect themselves from lawsuits for damages caused by known problems in software?

6. Suppose a vendor licenses and ships a software product that has both known and unknown failures. As the vendor learns of the unknown failures, does it have an ethical responsibility to inform the users about them? Does the vendor have an ethical responsibility to fix the problems? Is it ethical for the vendor to require users to pay an upgrade fee for a new version of software that fixes problems in an existing version?

Server Farm.

handing off partially completed transactions to one another, keeping track of data that has been partially changed, picking up the pieces when one computer fails—all in an eye-blink, with the user never needing to know any part of the miracle underway. It's absolutely gorgeous engineering!)

Q3 What Does a Manager Need to Know About Software?

The essential knowledge that you need to know about computer software is summarized in Figure 4-9. If you already possess this knowledge, skip to the next question—"What buying decisions do you make?"—on page 81.

Consider the two fundamental types of software. We have already spoken briefly about the *operating system*, which is a large and complicated program that controls the computer's resources, but there is also *application software*, which are programs that perform specific user tasks. An example of an operating system is Windows, and examples of applications are Microsoft Word and Oracle Customer Relationship Management.

Also, you need to understand two important software constraints. First, a particular version of an operating system is written for a particular type of hardware. In some cases, such as Windows, there is only one commercially important version. Windows works only on processors from Intel and companies that make processors that conform to the Intel **instruction set** (the commands that a CPU can process). In other cases, such as Linux, many versions exist for many different instructions sets.

Second, application programs are written to use a particular operating system. Microsoft Access, for example, will run only on the Windows operating system. Some applications come in multiple versions. There are, for example, Windows and Macintosh versions of Microsoft Word. But unless informed otherwise, assume that a particular application runs on just one operating system.

Category	Operating System (OS)	Instruction Set	Common Applications	Typical User
Client	Windows	Intel	Microsoft Office: Word, Excel, Access, PowerPoint, many other applications	Business. Home.
	Mac OS (pre-2006)	Power PC	Macintosh applications plus Word and Excel	Graphic artists. Arts community.
	Mac OS (post-2006)	Intel	Macintosh applications plus Word and Excel. Can also run Windows on Macintosh hardware.	Graphic artists. Arts community.
	Unix	Sun and others	Engineering, computer-assisted design, architecture	Difficult for the typical client, but popular with some engineers and computer scientists.
	Linux	Just about anything	Open Office (Microsoft Office look-alike)	Rare—used where budget is very limited.
Server	Windows	Intel	Windows server applications	Business with commitment to Microsoft.
	Unix	Sun and others	Unix server applications	Fading…Linux taking its market.
	Linux	Just about anything	Linux & Unix server applications	Very popular—promulgated by IBM.

Figure 4-9
What a Manager Needs to Know About Software

What Are the Four Major Operating Systems?

The four major operating systems listed in Figure 4-9—Windows, Mac OS, Unix, and Linux—are very important. We describe them in the following sections.

Windows

For business users, the most important operating system is Microsoft **Windows**. Some version of Windows resides on more than 85 percent of the world's desktops, and considering just business users, the figure is more than 95 percent. There are many different versions of Windows; some versions run on user computers and some support server computers for Web sites, email, and other processes (discussed in Chapter 6). Windows runs the Intel instruction set.[1]

Mac OS

Apple Computer, Inc. developed its own operating system for the Macintosh, **Mac OS**. The current version is Mac OS X. Macintosh computers are used primarily by graphic artists and workers in the arts community. Mac OS was designed originally to run the line of CPU processors from Motorola. In 1994, Mac OS switched to the PowerPC processor line from IBM. As of 2006, Macintosh computers are available for both PowerPC and Intel CPUs. A Macintosh with an Intel processor is able to run both Windows and the Mac OS.

Most people would agree that Apple has led the way in developing easy-to-use interfaces. Certainly, many innovative ideas have first appeared in a Macintosh and then later been added, in one form or another, to Windows.

---

[1]There are versions of Windows for other instruction sets, but they are unimportant for our purposes here.

Unix

Unix is an operating system that was developed at Bell Labs in the 1970s. It has been the workhorse of the scientific and engineering communities since then. Unix is generally regarded as being more difficult to use than either Windows or the Macintosh. Many Unix users know and employ an arcane language for manipulating files and data. However, once they surmount the rather steep learning curve, most Unix users swear by the system. Sun Microsystems and other vendors of computers for scientific and engineering applications are the major proponents of Unix. In general, Unix is not for the business user.

Linux

Linux is a version of Unix that was developed by the **open-source community**. This community is a loosely coupled group of programmers who mostly volunteer their time to contribute code to develop and maintain Linux. The open-source community owns Linux, and there is no fee to use it. Linux can run on client computers, but it is most frequently used for servers, particularly Web servers.

IBM is the primary proponent of Linux. Although IBM does not own Linux, IBM has developed many business systems solutions that use Linux. By using Linux, IBM does not have to pay a license fee to Microsoft or another vendor.

Own Versus License

When you buy a computer program, you are not actually buying that program. Instead, you are buying a **license** to use that program. For example, when you buy Windows, Microsoft is selling you the right to use Windows. Microsoft continues to own the Windows program.

In the case of Linux, no company can sell you a license to use it. It is owned by the open-source community, which states that Linux has no license fee (with certain reasonable restrictions). Companies such as IBM and smaller companies such as RedHat can make money by supporting Linux, but no company makes money selling Linux licenses.

Video

What Types of Applications Exist, and How Do Organizations Obtain Them?

Application software consists of programs that perform a business function. Some application programs are general purpose, such as Excel or Word. Other application programs are specific. QuickBooks, for example, is an application program that provides general ledger and other accounting functions. We begin by describing categories of application programs and then move on to describe sources for them.

What Categories of Application Programs Exist?

Horizontal-market application software provides capabilities common across all organizations and industries. Word processors, graphics programs, spreadsheets, and presentation programs are all horizontal-market application software.

Examples of such software are Microsoft Word, Excel, and PowerPoint. Examples from other vendors are Adobe Acrobat, Photoshop, and PageMaker and Jasc Corporation's Paint Shop Pro. These applications are used in a wide variety of businesses, across all industries. They are purchased off-the-shelf, and little customization of features is necessary (or possible).

Vertical-market application software serves the needs of a specific industry. Examples of such programs are those used by dental offices to schedule appointments and bill patients, those used by auto mechanics to keep track of customer data and customers' automobile repairs, and those used by parts warehouses to track inventory, purchases, and sales.

Vertical applications usually can be altered or customized. Typically, the company that sold the application software will provide such services or offer referrals to qualified consultants who can provide this service.

One-of-a-kind application software is developed for a specific, unique need. The IRS develops such software, for example, because it has needs that no other organization has.

Some application software does not neatly fit into the horizontal or vertical category. For example, customer relationship management (CRM) software is a horizontal application because every business has customers. But it usually needs to be customized to the requirements of businesses in a particular industry, and so it is also akin to vertical market software.

You will learn about other examples of such dual-category software in Chapter 7 when we discuss materials requirements planning (MRP), enterprise resource planning (ERP), and other such applications. In this text, we will consider such applications to be vertical market applications, even though they do not fit perfectly into this category.

How Do Organizations Acquire Application Software?

You can acquire application software in exactly the same ways that you can buy a new suit. The quickest and least risky option is to buy your suit off-the-rack. With this method, you get your suit immediately, and you know exactly what it will cost. You may not, however, get a good fit. Alternately, you can buy your suit off-the-rack and have it altered. This will take more time, it may cost more, and there's some possibility that the alteration will result in a poor fit. Most likely, however, an altered suit will fit better than an off-the-rack one.

Finally, you can hire a tailor to make a custom suit. In this case, you'll have to describe what you want, be available for multiple fittings, and be willing to pay considerably more. Although there is an excellent chance of a great fit, there is also the possibility of a disaster. Still, if you want a yellow and orange polka-dot silk suit with a hissing rattlesnake on the back, tailor-made is the only way to go. You can buy computer software in exactly the same ways: **off-the-shelf, off-the-shelf with alterations**, or tailor-made. Tailor-made software is called **custom-developed software**.

Organizations develop custom application software themselves or hire a development vendor. Like buying the yellow and orange polka-dot suit, such development is done in situations in which the needs of the organization are so unique that no horizontal or vertical applications are available. By developing custom software, the organization can tailor its application to fit its requirements.

Custom development is difficult and risky. Staffing and managing teams of software developers is challenging. Managing software projects can be daunting. Many organizations have embarked on application development projects only to find that the projects take twice as long—or longer—to finish as planned. Cost overruns of 200 and 300 percent are not uncommon.

Software Source

Figure 4-10
Software Sources and Types

	Off-the-shelf	Off-the-shelf and then customized	Custom-developed
Horizontal applications	░░░		
Vertical applications	▓▓▓	▓▓▓	
One-of-a-kind applications			░░░

(Software Type)

In addition, every application program needs to be adapted to changing needs and changing technologies. The adaptation costs of horizontal and vertical software are amortized over all of the users of that software, perhaps thousands or millions of customers. For custom software developed in-house, however, the developing company must pay all of the adaptation costs itself. Over time, this can be a heavy burden.

Because of the risk and expense, in-house development is the last-choice alternative and is used only when there is no other option. Figure 4-10 summarizes software sources and types.

Over the course of your career, application software, hardware, and firmware will change, sometimes rapidly. The *Guide* on pages 81a–81b challenges you to *choose* a strategy for addressing this change.

What Is Firmware?

Firmware is computer software that is installed into devices like printers, print servers, and various types of communication devices. The software is coded just like other software, but it is installed into special, read-only memory of the printer or other device. In this way, the program becomes part of the device's memory; it is as if the program's logic is designed into the device's circuitry. Users do not need to load firmware into the device's memory.

Firmware can be changed or upgraded, but this is normally a task for IS professionals. The task is easy, but it requires knowledge of special programs and techniques that most business users choose not to learn.

What Is the Difference Between a Thin and Thick Client?

When you use applications such as Word, Excel, or Acrobat, those programs run only on your computer. You need not be connected to the Internet or any other network for them to run.

Other applications, however, require code on both the client and the server. Email is a good example. When you send email, you run a client program such as Microsoft Outlook on your computer, and it connects over the Internet or a private network to mail server software on a server. Similarly, when you access a Web site, you run a browser (client software) on your computer that connects over a network to Web server software on a server.

An application that requires nothing more than a browser is called a **thin client**. An application such as Microsoft Outlook that requires programs other than a browser on the user's computer is called a **thick client**. The terms *thin* and *thick* refer to the amount of code that must run on the client computer. All other things being equal, thin client applications are preferred to thick client applications because they do not require the installation and administration of client

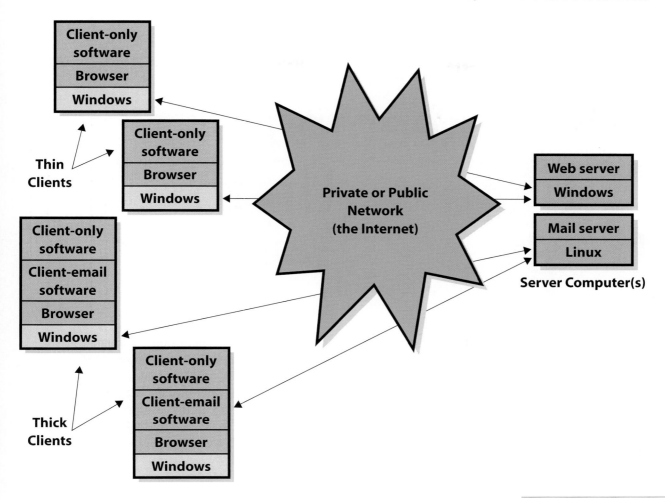

Figure 4-11
Thin and Thick Clients

software. On the other hand, the thick client application may provide features and functions that more than compensate for the expense and administration of their installation.

Client and server computers can run different operating systems. Many organizations have standardized on Windows for their clients and Linux for their servers. Figure 4-11 shows an example. Two thin clients are connecting via browsers to a Web server that is running Windows. Two thick clients are connecting via an email client to an email server that is running Linux. Those two clients are thick because they have client email software installed.

Q4 What Buying Decisions Do You Make?

In general, most business professionals have some role in the specification of the client hardware and software they use. Business managers also play a role in the specification of client hardware and software for employees whom they manage. The particular role depends on the policy manager's organization. Large organizations will have an IS department that is likely to set standards for client hardware and software. You will learn more about such standards in Chapter 11.

In medium to small organizations, policies are often less formal, and managers will need to take an active role in setting the specifications for their own

Keeping Up to Speed

Have you ever been to a cafeteria where you put your lunch tray on a conveyor belt that carries the dirty dishes into the kitchen? That conveyor belt reminds me of technology. Like the conveyor, technology just moves along, and all of us run on top of the technology conveyor, trying to keep up. We hope to keep up with the relentless change of technology for an entire career without ending up in the techno-trash.

Technology change is a fact, and the only appropriate question is, "What am I going to do about it?" One strategy you can take is to bury your head in the sand: "Look, I'm not a technology person. I'll leave it to the pros. As long as I can send email and use the Internet, I'm happy. If I have a problem, I'll call someone to fix it."

That strategy is fine, as far as it goes, and many business people use it. Following that strategy won't give you a competitive advantage over anyone, and it will give someone else a competitive advantage over you, but as long as you develop your advantage elsewhere, you'll be OK—at least for yourself.

What about your department, though? If an expert says, "Every computer needs a 120GB disk," are you going to nod your head and say, "Great. Sell 'em to me!" Or are you going to know enough to realize that's a big disk (by 2006 standards, anyway) and ask why

everyone needs such a large amount of storage? Maybe then you'll be told, "Well, it's only another $150 per machine from the 30GB disk." At that point, you can make a decision, using your own decision-making skills, and not rely solely on the IS expert. The prudent business professional in the twenty-first century has a number of reasons not to bury his or her head in the technology sand.

At the other end of the spectrum are those who love technology. You'll find them everywhere—they may be accountants, marketing professionals, or production-line supervisors who not only know their field, but also enjoy information technology. Maybe they were IS majors or had double majors that combined IS with another area of expertise (e.g., IS with accounting). These people read CNET News and ZDNet most days, and they can tell you the latest on IPv6 addresses (Chapter 6—just wait!). Those people are sprinting along the technology conveyor belt; they will never end up in the techno-trash, and they will use their knowledge of IT to gain competitive advantage throughout their careers.

Many business professionals are in between these extremes. They don't want to bury their heads, but they don't have the desire or interest to become technophiles (lovers of technology) either. What to do? There are a couple of strategies. For one, don't allow yourself to ignore technology. When you see a technology article in the *Wall Street Journal,* read it. Don't just skip it because it's about technology. Read the technology ads, too. Many vendors invest heavily in ads that instruct without seeming to. Another option is to take a seminar or pay attention to

professional events that combine your specialty with technology. For example, when you go to the banker's convention, attend a session or two on "Technology Trends for Bankers." There are always sessions like that, and you might make a contact in another company with similar problems and concerns.

Probably the best option, if you have the time for it, is to get involved as a user representative in technology committees in your organization. If your company is doing a review of its CRM system, for instance, see if you can get on the review committee. When there's a need for a representative from your department to discuss needs for the next-generation help-line system, sign up. Or later in your career, become a member of the business practice technology committee, or whatever they call it at your organization.

Just working with such groups will add to your knowledge of technology. Presentations made to such groups, discussions about uses of technology, and ideas about using IT for competitive advantage will all add to your IT knowledge. You'll gain important contacts and exposure to leaders in your organization as well.

It's up to you. You get to choose how you relate to technology. But be sure you choose; don't let your head fall into the sand without thinking about it.

DISCUSSION QUESTIONS

1. Do you agree that the change of technology is relentless? What do you think that means to most business professionals? To most organizations?

2. Think about the three postures toward technology presented here. Which camp will you join? Why?

3. Write a two-paragraph memo to yourself justifying your choice in question 2. If you chose to ignore technology, explain how you will compensate for the loss of competitive advantage. If you're going to join one of the other two groups, explain why, and describe how you're going to accomplish your goal.

4. Given your answer to question 2, assume that you're in a job interview and the interviewer asks about your knowledge of technology. Write a three-sentence response to the interviewer's question.

Category	Hardware	Software
Client	Specify: • CPU speed • Size of main memory • Size of magnetic disk • CD or DVD and type • Monitor type and size	Specify: • Windows, Mac, or Linux OS. May be dictated by organizational standard. • PC applications such as Microsoft Office Adobe Acrobat, Photoshop, Paint Shop Pro. may be dictated by organizational standard. • Browser such as Internet Explorer, FireFox, or Netscape Navigator. • Requirements for the client side of client-server applications. • Need for thin or thick client.
Server	In most cases, a business manager has no role in the specification of server hardware (except possibly a budgetary one).	• Specify requirements for the server side of client-server applications. • Work with technical personnel to test and accept software.

and their employees' computers. Figure 4-12 lists the major criteria for both hardware and software.

Except in rare circumstances, medium-to-small organizations will usually standardize on a single client operating system because the costs of supporting more than one are unjustifiable. Most organizations choose Windows clients. Some arts and design businesses standardize on the Macintosh, and some engineering firms standardize on Unix. Organizations that have limited budgets might choose to use Linux on the clients, but this is rare.

Managers and their employees may have a role in specifying horizontal application software such as Microsoft Office or other software appropriate for their operating systems. They will also have an important role in specifying requirements for vertical market or custom applications. We will say more about this role in Chapter 10.

Concerning the server, a business manager typically has no role in the specification of server hardware, other than possibly approving the budget. Instead, technical personnel make such decisions. A business manager and those who will be the clients of a client-server application specify the requirements for vertical and custom-server software. They will also work with technical personnel to test and accept that software.

In addition, business managers may be called on to provide unusual support involving IS, as *MIS in Use 4* describes.

Q5 What Are Viruses, Trojan Horses, and Worms?

A **virus** is a computer program that replicates itself. Unchecked replication is like computer cancer; ultimately, the virus consumes the computer's resources. Furthermore, many viruses also take unwanted and harmful actions.

The program code that causes unwanted activity is called the **payload**. The payload can delete programs or data—or, even worse, modify data in undetected ways. Imagine the impact of a virus that changed the credit rating of all customers. Some viruses publish data in harmful ways—for example, sending out files of credit card data to unauthorized sites.

4

Using IS in Hurricane Katrina Recovery

Information systems—both hardware and software—played a vital role in rescue and recovery operations following Hurricane Katrina. During rescue operations, normal street addresses had little meaning to helicopter pilots flying over flooded streets and neighborhoods. To help pilots locate those in need, the U.S. Geological Survey provided computer-based information and maps that converted street addresses to GPS (latitude and longitude) coordinates.

Many U.S. businesses used information systems to provide support for disaster victims. For example, the hurricane displaced more than 34,000 Wal-Mart employees, severely damaged 17 of the company's stores and distribution centers, and damaged a total of 89 Wal-Mart facilities. Despite these disruptions, Wal-Mart responded rapidly. Using the sophisticated information systems that support its supply chain, Wal-Mart located and shipped needed items from distribution centers, warehouses, and suppliers across the United States. The company was able to ship to hurricane victims 1,900 truckloads of merchandise and food for 100,000 meals. Even before the hurricane made landfall, Wal-Mart had stocked 45 trucks with goods specific to the needs of survivors.

Other companies also provided assistance using information systems. IBM and Lenovo donated 1,500 laptop computers for use by agencies tracking air and water quality tests and by relief agencies reg-istering evacuees for food stamps, Medicaid, and other social services. The donations included database management software (see Chapter 5), which is especially useful for tracking purposes.

After the hurricane, businesses faced the huge challenge of recovering from the disaster and resuming operations. Northrop Grumman, a $30 billion shipbuilder and defense contractor, employs thousands of people in facilities at New Orleans and at Gulfport and Pascagoula, Mississippi. Northrop used its Web site to inform employees of policies and directives during the hurricane recovery. Immediately after the hurricane, it published contact phone numbers for employees to use and disseminated information about employee payment policy. In the following weeks, Northrop used the Web to inform employees where and when they should report to work. This use of the Web saved days and weeks of administrative chaos for both the company and its employees.

Larger companies like Wal-Mart and Northrop Grumman had established backup and recovery facilities for their information systems in sites well away from the hurricane's damage. Such companies were able to quickly resume information systems operations in those remote sites.

Some medium- and many small-sized organizations were less fortunate. For them, restoring their customer, sales, human resources, and accounting systems was time-consuming and difficult. To help these small businesses, the Louisiana Technology Park in Baton Rouge offered free use of office space, computers, and Internet connections to New Orleans businesses having 25 or fewer employees. Such facilities enabled businesses to reconnect with their employees, customers, and suppliers, and to plan for restarting their businesses.

Sources: Michael Barbaro and Justin Gillis, "Wal-Mart at Forefront of Hurricane Relief," *Washington Post,* September 6, 2005, p. D01; IBM, "IBM Response Gains Ground in Aftermath of Katrina," *www.ibm.com* (accessed September 2005); Joseph F. Kovar, "Technology Park Open for New Orleans Small Businesses," CRN, September 6, 2005, *www.crn.com* (accessed September 2005); *www.northropgrumman.com/katrina/index.html* (accessed September 2005); and U.S. Geological Survey Web site, *www.usgs.gov/katrina/* (accessd September 2005).

There are many different virus types. **Trojan horses** are viruses that masquerade as useful programs or files. The name refers to the gigantic mock-up of a horse that was filled with soldiers and moved into Troy during the Trojan War. A typical Trojan horse appears to be a computer game, an MP3 music file, or some other useful, innocuous program.

Macro viruses attach themselves to Word, Excel, or other types of documents. When the infected document is opened, the virus places itself in the startup files of the application. After that, the virus infects every file that the application creates or processes.

A **worm** is a virus that propagates using the Internet or other computer network. Worms spread faster than other virus types because they are specifically programmed to spread. Unlike nonworm viruses, which must wait for the user to share a file with a second computer, worms actively use the network to spread. Sometimes, worms so choke a network that it becomes unusable.

In 2003, the Slammer worm clogged the Internet and caused Bank of America ATM machines and the information systems of hundreds of other organizations to fail. Slammer operated so fast that 90 percent of the vulnerable machines were infected within 10 minutes.

You can take several measures to prevent viruses. First, most viruses take advantage of security holes in computer programs. As vendors find these holes, they create program modifications, called **patches**, that fix the problem. To keep from getting a virus, check Microsoft and other vendor sites for patches, and apply them immediately. A patch for the Slammer worm was available from Microsoft several months before Slammer occurred. The worm did not infect any site that had applied the patch.

When you think about it, it is not surprising that the problem occurred some time after the patch appeared. As soon as a vendor publishes the problem and the patch, every computer criminal in the world can learn about the hole. Virus developers can then write code to exploit the hole, and any machine that does not apply the patch is then doubly vulnerable. Therefore, the first rule in preventing viruses is to find and apply patches to the operating system and to applications.

Other prevention steps are:

- Never download files, programs, or attachments from unknown Web sites.
- Do not open attachments to emails from strangers.
- Do not open unexpected attachments to emails, even from known sources.
- Do not rely on file extensions. A file marked *MyPicture.jpg* is normally a picture (because of the *jpg* file extension). For a variety of reasons, however, this file may be something else—a virus.
- Companies such as Symantec, Sophos, McAfee, Norton, and others license products that detect and possibly eliminate viruses. Such products can operate in proactive mode by checking attachments as you receive them. They can also operate retroactively by checking memory and disk drives for the presence of viral code. You should run a retroactive antivirus program at regular intervals—at least once a week.

Such **antivirus programs** search the computer's memory and disk for known viruses. Obviously, if a virus is unknown to the antivirus software, then that virus will remain undetected. You should periodically obtain updates for the latest virus patterns from the vendor who produces the antivirus product. Additionally, realize that even though you use antivirus software, you are still vulnerable to viruses that are unknown to the virus detection company.

Now for the ugly news: What do you do if you have a virus? Most antivirus products include programs for removing viruses. If you have a virus, you can follow the instructions provided by that software to remove it. However, it is possible that the virus may have mutated into a different form. If so, then the antivirus product will not see the mutated version, and it will remain on your computer.

Unfortunately, the only sure way to eliminate a virus is to delete everything on your magnetic disk by reformatting it. Then you must reinstall the operating system and all applications from known, clean sources (e.g., the original CD from the vendor). Finally, one by one, you must reload data files that you know are free of the virus. This is a laborious and time-consuming process, and it assumes that you have all of your data files backed up. Because of the time and expense involved, few organizations go through this process. However, reformatting the disk is the only sure way of removing a virus.

Viruses are expensive. C/Net estimated that the Slammer worm caused between $950 million and $1.2 billion in lost productivity during the first five days of its existence. To protect your organization, you should ensure that procedures exist to install patches as soon as possible. Also, every computer should have and use a copy of an antivirus program. You and your organization cannot afford not to take these precautions. We will discuss other problematic programs, such as spyware, in more detail in Chapter 12.

How does the knowledge in this chapter help Dee and you?

While this chapter does not help Dee answer all of the questions her consultant asked, the knowledge in this chapter would have helped her answer some of them. It also would have given Dee more confidence as she dealt with her IT department and with her consultant. If her consultant had drawn a schematic like the one in Figure 4-13, Dee would have been able to understand the relationship of clients and servers, and she would be able at least to understand the questions.

Also, with the knowledge in this chapter, she would have reduced the work (and fee) of her consultant by stating:

1. "No new client hardware. The sales reps need to use the hardware they have."
2. "Only a thin client on the sales reps computers. Sales reps must not be required to install any special software on their computers.
3. "I would prefer a thin client on my computer, but I would install software for creating blog entries on my computer if I have to."
4. "Blog server software must be installed on an Emerson server."
5. "I don't care whether the server runs Linux or Windows—the IT department should decide."
6. "The IT department must tell me what operating system it wants to use, and Don, I expect you to select blog server software that runs on that operating system."
7. "Either the IT department or you, Don, must set up and install the blog software."
8. "I need a program on my computer with which I can author html. I need help on this decision."

You need more knowledge from later chapters of this text to fully appreciate this list. For example, the reason Dee would specify item 4 is that she wants access to the blog to be secure within the Emerson network. You will learn more about that in Chapter 6. After you read Chapter 11, you'll know that item 7 is going to be a problem: The IT department has not endorsed her project because its staff thinks her timeline is unrealistic. The consultant says he can complete the project on time, but the IT department is going to resist letting an outsider install software on its servers. Dee is going to have a battle here, and she does not yet know it. Finally, after you read Chapter Extension 11, you'll know what html is and what kind of an editor Dee needs.

Even still, you are well on your way to having the knowledge you need to sponsor a project like Dee's.

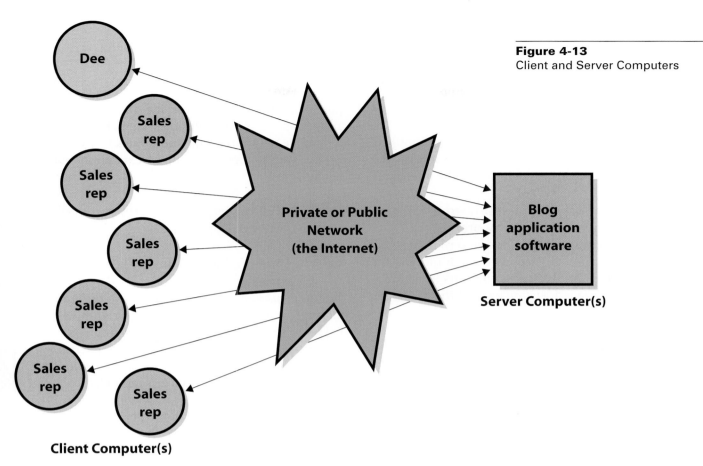

Figure 4-13
Client and Server Computers

Key Terms and Concepts

Antivirus programs 84

Application software 78

Binary digit 72

Bit 72

Bus 74

Byte 72

Cache memory 74

Central processing unit (CPU) 71

Client 75

Custom-developed software 79

Data channel 74

Firmware 80

Gigabyte (GB) 73

Hardware 70

Horizontal-market application 78

Input hardware 71

Instruction set 76

Kilobyte (K) 73

License 78

Linux 78

Mac OS 77

Macro virus 84

Main memory 71

Megabyte (MB) 73

Memory swapping 74

Nonvolatile 74

Off-the-shelf software 79

One-of-a-kind application 79

Open-source community 78

Operating system (OS) 74

Output hardware 71

Patch 84

Payload 82

Server 75

Server farm 75

Special function cards 71

Storage hardware 71

Terabyte (TB) 73

Trojan horse 84

Thick client 80

Thin client 80

Unix 78

Vertical-market application 79

Virus 82

Volatile 74

Windows 77

Worm 84

Active ? Review

Use this Active Review to verify that you understand the material in the chapter. You can read the entire chapter and then perform the tasks in this review, or you can read the material for just one question and perform the tasks in this review for that question before moving on to the next one.

Q1 What does a manager need to know about computer hardware?

List the categories of hardware. Describe memory swapping. Explain situations in which more main memory is needed. Explain situations in which a faster CPU is needed. Define each of the hardware terms in Figure 4-1.

Q2 What's the difference between a client and a server?

Explain the difference between a client and a server. Describe the differences in hardware requirements for clients and servers. Describe a server farm.

Q3 What does a manager need to know about software?

Explain the difference between an operating system and an application program. Describe the con-straint on an operating system imposed by a computer's instruction set. Describe the constraint on applications and an operating system. Describe the difference between a thin and a thick client. When would you use one or the other? Explain the terms in Figure 4-9.

Q4 What buying decisions do you make?

Explain the terms in Figure 4-12.

Q5 What are viruses, Trojan horses, and worms?

Define *virus* and *payload*. Explain the differences among Trojan horses, macro viruses, and worms. Explain the importance of applying patches promptly. Describe other prevention steps. Explain the use of anti-virus software. Describe actions to take to eradicate a virus from a computer.

How does the knowledge in this chapter help Dee and you?

Describe how Dee can use the knowledge from this chapter. Explain how you can use the knowledge from this chapter in your future career.

Using Your Knowledge

1. Assume that you have been asked to prepare a computer hardware budget. Your company has identified three classes of computer user. Class-A employees use the computer for email, Web browsing, Internet connectivity, and limited document writing. Class-B employees use the computer for all of the activities of class A, plus they need to be able to read and create complicated documents. They also need to be able to create and process large spreadsheets and process small graphics files. Class-C employees are data analysts who perform all of the tasks that class-A and class-B employees do; they also analyze data using programs that make extensive computations and produce large and complicated graphics.
   a. Using the Internet, determine two appropriate alternatives for each class of employee. Search *dell.com, lenovo.com, hewlett-packard.com,* and any other sites you think appropriate.
   b. Justify each of the selections in your answer to part a.
   c. Specify the cost of each of the selections in part a.

2. Search the Internet for the term *OpenOffice*. Explain what OpenOffice is. How do users obtain it? How much does it cost? Given this information, why do you think companies use Microsoft Office rather than OpenOffice? Why do you?

3. Describe the three categories of applications software. Give an example of each. Explain Figure 4-10. Search the Internet for an example of horizontal and vertical market software, other than those mentioned in this chapter. Search the Internet for the product QuickBooks. Briefly describe the functions of that product. What operating system(s) does it require? Suppose you wish to install and use QuickBooks, but you need some functions to be altered. Search the Internet for vendors or consultants who could help you. List two or three such vendors or consultants.

Case Study 4

Dell Leverages the Internet, Directly

When Michael Dell started Dell Computer in 1984, personal computers were sold only in retail stores. Manufacturers shipped to wholesalers, who shipped to retail stores, which sold to end users. Companies maintained expensive inventories at each stage of this supply chain. Dell thought that if he could eliminate the retail channel by selling computers directly to consumers, he could dramatically reduce the machines' prices. In 2004, while speaking to a group of students in New York City, he recalled,

> I was inspired by how I saw computers being sold. It seemed to me that it was very expensive and it was inefficient. A computer cost at the time about $3,000 but there were only about $600 worth of parts inside the computer. And so I figured, hey, what if you sold the computer for $800? You don't need to sell it for $3,000. And so we changed the whole way computers were being sold by lowering the cost of distribution and sales and taking out this extra cost that was inefficient.
>
> Now, what I didn't know was that the Internet would come along and now people can go on the Internet and they can go to *Dell.com* and buy a computer and that makes it a lot easier.
>
> I'd say the most important thing we did was listen very carefully to our customers. We asked, what do they want, what do they need and how can we meet their needs and provide something that's really valuable to them? Because if we could take care of our customers, they'll want to buy more products from us, and they have.[2]

Indeed they have. In 2006, Dell's revenue topped $56 billion, representing over 18 percent of the computer hardware market. Dell employs over 50,000 people worldwide, and its investors have benefited as well. A share of Dell purchased for $8.50 in the initial public offering would be worth over $2,400 in 2006 (allowing for multiple stock splits over the years).

Eliminating retail stores not only reduced costs, but it also brought Dell closer to the customer, enabling it to listen better than the competition. It also eliminated sales channel inventories, which allowed Dell to rapidly bring new

---

[2]Michael Dell, speech before the Miami Springs Middle School, September 1, 2004. Retrieved from *dell.com*, under Michael/Speeches (accessed January 2005).

computers with new technology to the customer. This eliminates the need to recycle or sell off existing pipeline inventory whenever a new model is announced. In fact, today Dell builds every computer system to customer order. Every computer in Dell's finished goods inventory has already been sold!

Additionally, Dell focused on its suppliers and has one of the most efficient supply chains in the industry. Dell pays close attention to its suppliers and shares information with them on product quality, inventory, and related subjects via its secure Web site *valuechain.dell.com*. According to its Web site, the first two qualities Dell looks for in suppliers are (1) cost competitiveness and (2) an understanding of Dell's business. Dell listens to its customers, and it expects its suppliers to do the same in return.

In addition to computer hardware, Dell provides a variety of services. It provides basic technical support with every computer, and customers can upgrade this basic support by purchasing one of four higher levels of support. Additionally, Dell offers deployment services to organizations to configure and deploy Dell systems, both hardware and preinstalled software, into customers' user environments. Dell offers additional services to maintain and manage Dell systems once they have been deployed.

Questions

1. Explain how selling direct has given Dell a competitive advantage. Use the factors listed in Figure 3-8 (page 44) in your answer.

2. What information systems does Dell need to have to sell directly to the consumer? Visit *dell.com* for inspiration and ideas.

3. Besides selling direct, what other programs has Dell created that give it a competitive advantage?

4. Hewlett-Packard, Toshiba, Sony, and other computer manufacturers sell both directly and through Internet stores. Visit *www.cnet.com* and search for the term *notebook*. The site will return laptop computers from several manufacturers. If you look at notebooks from Hewlett-Packard, Toshiba, or Sony, you will see that they must be purchased from Internet vendors. (Click **Check Prices** to see vendor sources.) In contrast, Dell computers can be purchased only from Dell, as you will see when you check for prices for one of its computers.

   In order to use an intermediary, Hewlett-Packard and others must sell their computers to the supplier at a price below the consumer's price; otherwise the supplier has no incentive to sell the product. But those vendors cannot offer the supplier's price to the public without losing its suppliers. Does this situation mean that Dell computers will be cheaper than Hewlett-Packard and other computers? Why or why not?

5. Assume that, because of the need to sell through a channel, Hewlett-Packard's computers will always be more expensive than Dell's. How can Hewlett-Packard successfully compete with Dell?

6. What information systems can Hewlett-Packard set up that will better enable it to compete with Dell? Visit *hp.com* for inspiration and ideas.

7. Do you think Dell would have been successful if the Internet had not been invented? Why or why not?

Source: © 2005 Dell Inc. All Rights Reserved.

Teaching Suggestions

Emerson Pharmaceuticals, Part 2 and Chapter 4

GOALS

Use Dee's blog to:

* Illustrate a realistic and practical use for knowledge of IT concepts.

* Show how IT knowledge is needed by *all* business professionals, not just techies.

* Use a simple business system to demonstrate the nature of each of the five components of an information system.

BACKGROUND

1. Dee sold her boss and her boss's boss on the idea of a blog without any idea of how to create one. She had no knowledge of what needed to be done. Dee got the idea for this blog by watching me set up *www.TeachingMIS.com*. She saw that it didn't take me too long to do that, so she assumed she could do the same. "It can't be that hard."

2. One important difference between Dee's blog and TeachingMIS is that TeachingMIS is public—the more the merrier. Dee, on the other hand, had to restrict access to her blog to Emerson salespeople. She had no idea how to do that—or whether it would be easy or hard to do.

3. Dee was a lamb heading for fleecing. Her IT department said, "No way," and blew her off after they heard her schedule. Being a very determined person, however, Dee wasn't going to take no for an answer. So, she pressed on with Don. What she didn't realize was that he had a potential conflict of interest: He could pad her systems with features she didn't need or pad her project with unneeded expense items. He didn't. He's been in the business for a long time, and he knows that good service provided on a fair and honest basis will serve him well over time.

4. *Late-breaking news:* I don't know if you want to mention this to your class, but Dee left Emerson for a more senior position with another "pharmaceutical" company. Guess what was one of the first things she did in her new job? She set up several blogs. And guess whom she hired? Don. And I suppose she's still creating security risks (see the next point).

5. *Warning:* Ultimately, at Emerson, Dee was able to bludgeon her IT department to allow Don to install software within the Emerson server network. This is a serious security breach, and it exposed Emerson to risks that far outweigh any benefit Emerson might obtain by having Dee's blog ready for the sales meeting. We will address this matter in Part 4. You might forewarn your students, however, that Emerson assumed huge risk in allowing Don to install software within its network.

HOW TO GET THE STUDENTS INVOLVED

This discussion is fun! Dee so clearly needs some knowledge of IT, and, she would never have guessed that she would.

1. Some questions to start your class discussion:

   a. **If someone had asked Dee in October 2005, if she needed knowledge of Linux and Windows servers, what would she have said? (Yet here she is, a sheep headed for fleecing.)**

   b. **Why is the IT department not helping her?**

   c. **Why is Don willing to help?**

   d. **What is Don's potential conflict of interest?**

   e. **How can Dee deal with that conflict?**

2. One way to get the class involved is to take Don's questions at the start of Chapter 4 and assign them to the class (or groups within the class). Not all these questions are addressed in Chapter 4, but many of them are. Also, there is usually enough prior knowledge among the students in the class for the students to be able to answer these questions. Ask them to assume they are Dee and that they don't have you to rely upon. How are they going to answer the following?

   a. **Are you going to run your blog on an internal Emerson site, or will you contract with an outside hosting service?**

   b. **Either way, will your site use a Windows or Linux server?**

   c. **What blog software do you want to use?**

   d. **How do you want to code your entries? Are you going to use FrontPage, or do you want me to build in an html editor in your blog software?**

   e. **What browsers do you want to support? IE? Firefox? Netscape? Others?**

   f. **Do you care if your blog doesn't render perfectly in all browsers?**

3. Another idea is to take Dee's statements in Q6 and ask the class to explain to each other why she said what she said. The statements are:

   a. No new client hardware. The sales reps need to use the hardware they have.

   b. Only a thin client on the sales reps' computers. They must be able to access the site with browsers only.

   c. She would prefer a thin client on her computer, but would install software for creating blog entries on her computer if she had to.

   d. Blog server software must be installed on an Emerson server.

   e. She doesn't care whether the server runs Linux or Windows—the IT department should decide.

   f. However, they must tell her what operating system they want to use, and her consultant must select blog server software that runs on that operating system.

   g. Either the IT department or the consultant must set up and install the blog software.

   h. She needs a program on her computer with which she can author html. She needs help from the consultant on this decision.

4. In the questions in item 2 (and to a lesser extent 3), if the students don't know the answer, ask them to provide a strategy for getting an answer.

5. I find it helpful to resist the temptation to jump in and answer any of these questions. I also try to get them to evaluate the quality of their answer:

   a. How satisfied are you with that answer?

   b. Have you completely answered that question?

   c. Would you bet the success of the blog on the quality of your answer?

   d. What will happen if you're wrong?

6. This is a good place to ask the students to transfer their knowledge:

   a. Is this situation rare?

   b. Does this knowledge pertain only to developing blogs?

   c. Do you think the need for knowledge like this is likely to increase or decrease in the future?

   d. What are you going to do about your answers to a through c?

BOTTOM LINE

* As a business professional, you may need to answer questions that require a basic knowledge of IT. Even if you don't know the answer, you need to know how to obtain the answer. Dee's situation is not rare; it could very well happen to you!

Using the Ethics Guide: Churn and Burn (page 75a)

GOALS

✳ Think critically about software products.

✳ Assess the responsibilities of users and software vendors.

✳ Be a better consumer of software products by learning when to hold software vendors accountable.

BACKGROUND AND PRESENTATION STRATEGIES

You can use this guide not only to engage the students via the opinions of the contrarian, but also to extend the discussion beyond basic definitions to consider software as a product, the nature of the software industry, and the financial needs of software vendors. Questions 4 through 6 work well for this purpose.

Products like Microsoft Office are developed from market feedback. Microsoft and others convene hundreds of focus groups that tell them what features to add. They invite groups of typical users, show them various possibilities, and ask for opinions. They also ask typical users what else they want. The favorite feature of every one of these focus groups gets put "into the pot," for possible inclusion in the product. This is feature design by committee—and it leads to bloated products with little conceptual integrity.

Taking items out of the pot is the job of product managers. But it's difficult for product managers to say, "No, that's just too much, we won't add that feature." The design strategy has been to hide the extra complexity behind not-visible toolbars. As long as the semiconductor industry keeps churning out faster computers with bigger memories, this strategy will probably continue to work.

Software vendors should be *held accountable for security holes* in their products. They allowed the problem to be there in the first place, and they should bear some consequences. In some ways, computer users are too polite; they should object more to security holes than they do.

To avoid continuing PR problems, vendors like Microsoft and Adobe are making it easier and easier to obtain and install updates to their products. This easy installation *hides the fact that they are fixing glitches* in their products. Microsoft is now making such installations automatic, as AOL has done for years.

SUGGESTED RESPONSES FOR DISCUSSION QUESTIONS

These questions are all open-ended and subject to judgment and interpretation. Thus, this section provides questions to ask the students to stimulate the conversation.

1. One way to answer this question is to ask:

   ➤ **What can we learn from Mark's contrarian position? Describe some of the points he makes.**

   Write the list on the board and then ask the class to rank the items in order of importance. At each point, ask the class if they agree with the point, and how important it is. You might also ask them what the software vendors could do differently to eliminate the problem.

   ➤ **Do you agree with Mark's point about software patches and security holes?**

   Vendors want to manage this patch process so as to make it as invisible as possible and avoid close scrutiny and the attendant bad PR. In truth, the vendors did leave the holes in the product in the first place, and they did leave their customers vulnerable to attack. They should be accountable in some way. However, read the license agreements—according to the agreements, the vendors are liable for the cost of the CD, at most $1.50. They may not be liable even for that much, if the product was shipped electronically.

   Another line of questions relates to the analogy of being mugged in a bad neighborhood. You might ask:

   ➤ **Are viruses brought on by user stupidity?**

   ➤ **Is the analogy of being mugged in a bad neighborhood a good one?**

   ➤ **How can a student find out which cyber-neighborhoods are bad?**

2. You may have answered this question if you asked the students to prioritize the list in question 1. If not, here are some questions to ask to stimulate the discussion:

   ➤ **Are software products bloated?**

   ➤ **Isn't it an advantage to have features that you don't need now, but might need in the future?**

   ➤ **Would Mark really be happy with his old computer? It might take him hours just to read his email.**

> What is the relationship between hardware and software vendors? How do they depend on one another? What will happen to software if Moore's Law stops?

3. This is a fun question that we ask for many of the contrarians.

> Is there any point in Mark sharing his opinions?

> Does it do any good for him to say what he says?

> Is there a way that Mark could change his questions and behavior to accomplish more good?

4. One way to answer this question is to consider the process software vendors use to create products. Explain the use of focus groups. Some useful follow-up questions are:

> If you were the product manager for Word, would you behave any differently in responding to focus groups?

> How would you go about deciding what features to put in and which to take out?

> How does the idea of "highest common denominator" help you as a product manager for products like Word?

> Suppose you are in charge of cash management at Microsoft or Adobe. What happens if you don't bring out a new version of the company's products every year or every other year? How might these factors influence you as a product manager at Microsoft?

5. The easy part of this question is that software vendors protect themselves via end-user license agreements that limit their liability to the cost of a CD (if the product was shipped on a CD). Whether or not shipping a product with known failures is ethical or not, or whether vendors have an ethical responsibility to reveal known failures, is more difficult to answer. The vendors never claim their products are failure-free, so they are not truly deceiving anyone. On the other hand, most people would tend to believe that a product from Microsoft or Apple would be bug-free, or nearly so. I think it's a tough call, but one that vendors ignore. Regarding publishing lists of known failures, many failures are published, and many fixes are documented on the vendor's Web sites. Vendors are in a bind regarding publishing security holes. They certainly do not want to publish them before they have a fix. To me, there are no clear answers here, and this should make a good class discussion.

6. When a vendor finds a serious problem in a software product, most people would agree that it has a responsibility to tell customers about it. Using the definition of ethical as in accordance with accepted norms, the vendor does have such an ethical responsibility. However, in practice, few vendors go out of their way to inform their customers about new failures. And, of course, security holes cannot be divulged until the fix is available. Does the vendor have an ethical responsibility to fix known problems? Usually, there are so many of them that the vendor cannot afford to fix all of them. Certainly, it would seem to me that vendors have an ethical responsibility to fix serious problems. Whether or not customers should have to pay for fixes is not really an ethical question, it's a pricing question. If the vendors can get away with it, they will. Customers should revolt on this one, though, at least in my opinion.

WRAP UP

Most students will agree that people like Mark do exist. I tell the class:

> Contrarians are like hot-pepper flakes: They make a great contribution to the stew, but too much ruins the dinner. The question is how to manage someone like Mark without letting him ruin the group.

Chances are there's a Mark in the class. It's very interesting to see how such students respond to these contrarians' comments. Often, their responses are insightful.

Using the Guide: Keeping Up to Speed (page 81a)

GOALS

* Raise students' awareness of the unrelenting change of technology.

* Encourage students to take a stand about how they will react to technological change—in the words of the guide, to "choose a posture."

* Emphasize that this issue is inescapable in modern business. If students ignore it, they are unknowingly and by default choosing a personal competitive *disadvantage*.

* Teach the students the benefits of this class and of IS education, in general.

BACKGROUND AND PRESENTATION STRATEGIES

Technological change is a factor in every businessperson's life. Many of the hardware facts described in this chapter are susceptible to change. It's *perishable content*. Just like produce at the market, it has a short shelf life.

So what's a professional to do? One response is to recognize the problem and to *choose a response*. Business professionals must decide how to respond. They may choose to stick their heads in the sand, but if so, they'd better find other ways to gain a competitive advantage over their peers.

I tell my students:

➤ **Please, after taking the MIS class, don't let random happenstance determine your technology posture. Instead, consciously choose a posture.**

Students who don't want to stick their heads in the sand and ignore technology need to learn coping strategies. First, *they need to learn how to learn about technology*, and they need to learn *how to learn it efficiently*.

The best strategy, I think, is to combine learning about technology with some other activity. This essay recommends volunteering to sit on technology review committees, volunteering to work with systems development professionals as user representatives, going to conferences, and sitting in on at least one or two technology sessions.

The advantage of such a strategy is that it's a "three-fer":

1. As a business professional, you are serving the business, while at the same time making a deposit in your knowledge bank.

2. You also are networking, so the next time you need an answer to a difficult technology question, you'll know whom to ask.

3. It's also a way of being noticed in a positive way while learning and extending—a great way to obtain a competitive advantage.

Encourage students who are currently employed to *volunteer for projects* now, even as interns. I had a student who, as an intern, volunteered to sit on a CRM review committee to provide end-user feedback. He made his section of the report, and the manager of the review committee was impressed and asked him why he volunteered for the committee. He said he learned about it in his MIS class. The manager said, "Be sure our company picks up the cost of that class."

All this is just creating strategies to turn a problem—the rapid change of technology—into a *competitive advantage*. If you are comfortable confronting your class, ask them to look around and see who is bored and not paying attention and who isn't. Those who are actively participating are creating a competitive advantage. I ask my students just to think about it. This is also a good time to promote additional IS classes—maybe a database class or a systems development class—for the non-IS major.

Another perspective concerns the *off-shore outsourcing* of jobs. According to a recent RAND study, jobs that are unlikely to be off-shored are those that involve creative ways of applying new technology to solve business problems in innovative ways.

Example: In spite of Wal-Mart's pronouncement that every vendor must supply *RFID tags* on their goods, nobody (not even Wal-Mart) has quite figured out how best to use RFID in retailing. But you can bet that the person who does won't find his or her job off-shored to the Far East.

Taken to the next step, rapidly changing technology creates opportunities for *entrepreneurship*. When technology stagnates, products become commodities, and opportunities for new products are rare. With rapidly changing technology, opportunities for new products and companies abound.

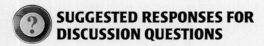

SUGGESTED RESPONSES FOR DISCUSSION QUESTIONS

1. Technology change is a good news/bad news situation.

   ➤ **How does technology change impact you in positive ways?**

   - It continuously creates new opportunities.
   - You'll never get bored; there will always be something new to learn and do.
   - Technology change will relevel the playing field frequently. People who have dominant expertise in some technology domain will lose that expertise—creating an opportunity for you.

   ➤ **How does technology change impact you in negative ways?**

   - You constantly need to learn.
   - Your expertise is perishable. Without renewal or without knowledge of new technology, you'll fall behind.

   ➤ **How does technology change impact organizations in positive ways?**

   - It continuously creates new opportunities for competitive advantage.
   - It will relevel the playing field frequently. Organizations that have dominant expertise in some technology domain will lose that expertise—creating an opportunity for your organization.

   ➤ **How does technology change impact organizations in negative ways?**

   - The cost of adapting to new technology can be high.
   - Competitive advantages may not be sustainable.

2. The three choices are:

   - Head-in-the-sand
   - Technophile
   - Technology-informed professional Ask sample students:

   ➤ **Which posture do you choose? Why?**

   If students choose head-in-the-sand, they'd better develop a competitive advantage in another field or discipline.

   ➤ **Does choosing technophile or technology-informed mean writing computer programs or designing electronic circuits?**

   No, definitely not! It means knowing about *technology and how to use it* to solve business problems in innovative ways.

3. The purpose of this question is to *compel* the students to choose a posture. They must not kid themselves—which posture will they choose and why?

   You might ask the students to read their memos to the class.

4. This is another question to *compel* the students to choose a posture. There can be good reasons for the head-in-the-sand posture, but again, does the student truly want to choose that posture? But rather than focus on that posture, I like to ask:

   ➤ **For those of you who have chosen to be IS technology-informed professionals, how do you respond?**

   Then I help them hone and improve their answers. I know, all this discussion is advertising for IS education, but, hey, this is an IS class!

WRAP UP

➤ **Wake up to the opportunities that the conveyor belt of technology change offers.**

➤ **Because you cannot ignore this issue, choose a strategy. Otherwise, fate will choose a strategy for you.**

➤ **Learning about IS does not mean, necessarily, becoming a computer programmer or a communications technician. It means helping businesses to use information technology and information systems to accomplish their goals and objectives. (This is the definition of MIS given in Chapter 1.)**

➤ **If you want to know about other IS classes we offer that you should be taking, drop me an email or come by my office.**

5 Database Processing

This could happen to you

Working with her consultant, Dee selected an application program called Moveable Type for her blog. While that program was a bit more difficult to use than other programs, it had certain advanced features that gave her greater control over the look and feel of the blog. Her consultant said it was a professional-grade product.

Shortly after selecting the product, Don, the consultant, mentioned that she would need to install MySQL as well. "You need a DBMS to store your blog entries," he explained. "A what?" asked Dee. "Oh, right," explained Don, "a database management system—a DBMS."

Dee had decided that her blog needed to run within the Emerson network (you'll learn why in the next chapter), and Don told her to check with her IT department to see if they already had MySQL. When she asked her IT department, she was told, "No, we've standardized on Oracle. We don't run any other DBMS products."

When Dee reported this news to Don, he said that this would be a problem. He told her that Oracle is difficult to work with, even though it generates terrific performance on large databases. He would have to revise his labor estimates for the project if they were going to use Oracle. Also, he said he'd have to determine if there was an Oracle version of Moveable Type. If not, they'd have to pick another application. That meant backing up to reconsider the decisions they'd already made.

Meanwhile, time was ticking away. It was now the second week in December, and Dee needed the blog up and running by the first week in January.

"Look," Don advised, "talk to them again. Installing MySQL isn't that hard. We're not talking about running the business on it, we're just going to run your blog. I can install it, and you can work out the license issues yourself. It won't be that expensive or hard."

When Dee called the IT department back, she was met with strong resistance and a barrage of terminology that she didn't understand. She needed the knowledge in this chapter.

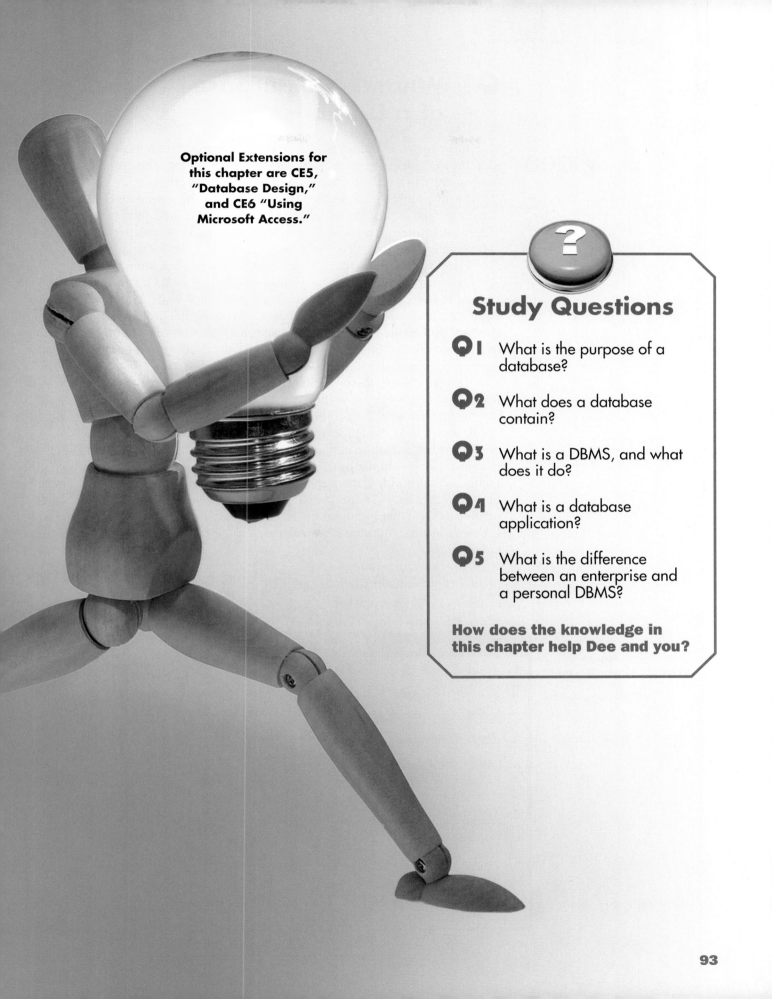

Optional Extensions for this chapter are CE5, "Database Design," and CE6 "Using Microsoft Access."

Study Questions

Q1 What is the purpose of a database?

Q2 What does a database contain?

Q3 What is a DBMS, and what does it do?

Q4 What is a database application?

Q5 What is the difference between an enterprise and a personal DBMS?

How does the knowledge in this chapter help Dee and you?

Q1 What Is the Purpose of a Database?

The purpose of a database is to keep track of things. When most students learn that, they wonder why we need a special technology for such a simple task. Why not just use a list? If the list is long, put it into a spreadsheet.

Many professionals do keep track of things using spreadsheets. If the structure of the list is simple enough, there is no need to use database technology. The list of student grades in Figure 5-1, for example, works perfectly well in a spreadsheet.

Suppose, however, that the professor wants to track more than just grades. The professor may want to record email messages as well. Or perhaps the professor wants to record both email messages and office visits. There is no place in Figure 5-1 to record that additional data. Of course, the professor could set up a separate spreadsheet for email messages and another one for office visits, but that awkward solution would be difficult to use because it does not provide all of the data in one place.

Instead, the professor wants a form like that in Figure 5-2. With it, the professor can record student grades, emails, and office visits all in one place. A form like the one in Figure 5-2 is difficult, if not impossible, to produce from a spreadsheet. Such a form is easily produced, however, from a database.

The key distinction between Figures 5-1 and 5-2 is that the list in Figure 5-1 is about a single theme or concept. It is about student grades only. The list in Figure 5-2 has multiple themes; it shows student grades, student emails, and student office visits. We can make a general rule from these examples: Lists that involve a single theme can be stored in a spreadsheet; lists that involve multiple themes require a database. We will learn more about this general rule as this chapter proceeds.

To summarize, the purpose of a database is to keep track of things that involve more than one theme.

Figure 5-1
A List of Student Grades

	A	B	C	D	E
1	**Student Name**	**Student Number**	**HW1**	**HW2**	**MidTerm**
2					
3	BAKER, ANDREA	1325	88	100	78
4	FISCHER, MAYAN	3007	95	100	74
5	LAU, SWEE	1644	75	90	90
6	NELSON, STUART	2881	100	90	98
7	ROGERS, SHELLY	8009	95	100	98
8	TAM, JEFFREY	3559		100	88
9	VALDEZ, MARIE	5265	80	90	85
10	VERBERRA, ADAM	4867	70	90	92

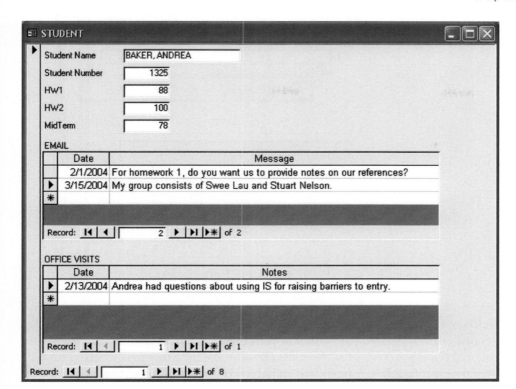

Figure 5-2
Student Data Shown in
Form from a Database

Q2 What Does a Database Contain?

A **database** is a self-describing collection of integrated records. To understand this definition, you first need to understand the terms illustrated in Figure 5-3. As you learned in Chapter 4, a **byte** is a character of data. Bytes are grouped into **columns**, such as *Student Number* and *Student Name*. Columns are also called

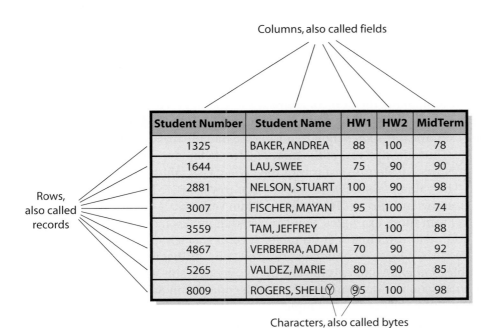

Figure 5-3
Student Table (also called file)

Columns, also called fields

Student Number	Student Name	HW1	HW2	MidTerm
1325	BAKER, ANDREA	88	100	78
1644	LAU, SWEE	75	90	90
2881	NELSON, STUART	100	90	98
3007	FISCHER, MAYAN	95	100	74
3559	TAM, JEFFREY		100	88
4867	VERBERRA, ADAM	70	90	92
5265	VALDEZ, MARIE	80	90	85
8009	ROGERS, SHELLY	95	100	98

Rows, also called records

Characters, also called bytes

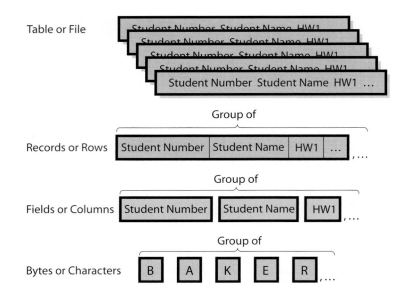

Table or File

Figure 5-4
Hierarchy of Data Elements

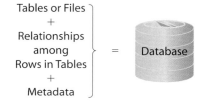

Figure 5-5
Components of a Database

fields. Columns or fields, in turn, are grouped into **rows**, which are also called **records**. In Figure 5-3, the collection of data for all columns (*Student Name, Student Number, HW1, HW2,* and *MidTerm*) is called a row or a record. Finally, a group of similar rows or records is called a **table** or a **file**. From these definitions, you can see that there is a hierarchy of data elements, as shown in Figure 5-4.

It is tempting to continue this grouping process by saying that a database is a group of tables or files. This statement, although true, does not go far enough. As shown in Figure 5-5, a database is a collection of tables *plus* relationships among the rows in those tables, *plus* special data, called *metadata*, that describes the structure of the database. By the way, the cylindrical symbol 🗄 represents a computer disk drive. It is used in diagrams like that in Figure 5-5 because databases are normally stored on magnetic disks.

Relationships Among Records

Consider the terms on the left-hand side of Figure 5-5. You know what tables are. To understand what is meant by *relationships among rows in tables*, examine Figure 5-6. It shows sample data from the three tables *Email, Student,* and *Office_Visit*. Notice the column named *Student Number* in the *Email* table. That column indicates the row in *Student* to which a row of *Email* is connected. In the first row of *Email*, the *Student Number* value is 1325. This indicates that this particular email was received from the student whose *Student Number* is 1325. If you examine the *Student* table, you will see that the row for Andrea Baker has this value. Thus, the first row of the *Email* table is related to Andrea Baker.

Now consider the last row of the *Office_Visit* table at the bottom of the figure. The value of *Student Number* in that row is 4867. This value indicates that the last row in *Office_Visit* belongs to Adam Verberra.

From these examples, you can see that values in one table relate rows of that table to rows in a second table. Several special terms are used to express these ideas. A **key** is a column or group of columns that identifies a unique row in a table. *Student Number* is the key of the *Student* table. Given a value of *Student Number*, you can determine one and only one row in *Student*. Only one student has the number 1325, for example.

Every table must have a key. The key of the *Email* table is *EmailNum*, and the key of the *Student_Visit* table is *VisitID*. Sometimes more than one column is needed to form a unique identifier. In a table called *City*, for example, the key would consist of the combination of columns (*City, State*), because a given city name can appear in more than one state.

Student Number is not the key of the *Email* or the *Office_Visit* tables. We know that about *Email* because there are two rows in *Email* that have the *Student Number* value 1325. The value 1325 does not identify a unique row; therefore, *Student Number* is not the key of *Email*.

Nor is *Student Number* a key of *Office_Visit*, although you cannot tell that from the data in Figure 5-6. If you think about it, however, there is nothing to prevent a student from visiting a professor more than once. If that were to happen, there would be two rows in *Office_Visit* with the same value of *Student Number*. It just happens that no student has visited twice in the limited data in Figure 5-6.

Columns that fulfill a role like that of *Student Number* in the *Email* and *Office_Visit* tables are called **foreign keys**. This term is used because such columns are keys, but they are keys of a different (foreign) table than the one in which they reside.

Before we go on, databases that carry their data in the form of tables and that represent relationships using foreign keys are called **relational databases**. (The term *relational* is used because another, more formal name for a table is **relation**.) In the past, there were databases that were not relational in format, but such databases have nearly disappeared. Chances are you will never encounter one, and we will not consider them further.[1]

Figure 5-6
Example of Relationships Among Rows

Email Table

EmailNum	Date	Message	Student Number
1	2/1/2004	For homework 1, do you want us to provide notes on our references?	1325
2	3/15/2004	My group consists of Swee Lau and Stuart Nelson.	1325
3	3/15/2004	Could you please assign me to a group?	1644

Student Table

Student Number	Student Name	HW1	HW2	MidTerm
1325	BAKER, ANDREA	88	100	78
1644	LAU, SWEE	75	90	90
2881	NELSON, STUART	100	90	98
3007	FISCHER, MAYAN	95	100	74
3559	TAM, JEFFREY		100	88
4867	VERBERRA, ADAM	70	90	92
5265	VALDEZ, MARIE	80	90	85
8009	ROGERS, SHELLY	95	100	98

Office_Visit Table

VisitID	Date	Notes	Student Number
2	2/13/2004	Andrea had questions about using IS for raising barriers to entry.	1325
3	2/17/2004	Jeffrey is considering an IS major. Wanted to talk about career opportunities.	3559
4	2/17/2004	Will miss class Friday due to job conflict.	4867

[1]Another type of database, the **object-relational database**, is rarely used in commercial applications. Search the Web if you are interested in learning more about object-relational databases. In this book, we will consider only relational databases.

Metadata

Recall the definition of database again: A database is a self-describing collection of integrated records. The records are integrated because, as you just learned, relationships among rows are represented in the database. But what does *self-describing* mean?

It means that a database contains, within itself, a description of its contents. Think of a library. A library is a self-describing collection of books and other materials. It is self-describing because the library contains a catalog that describes the library's contents. The same idea also pertains to a database. Databases are self-describing because they contain not only data, but also data about the data in the database.

Metadata are data that describe data. Figure 5-7 shows metadata for the *Email* table. The format of metadata depends on the software product that is processing the database. Figure 5-7 shows the metadata as they appear in Microsoft Access. Each row of the top part of this form describes a column of the *Email* table. The columns of these descriptions are *Field Name, Data Type*, and *Description. Field Name* contains the name of the column, *Data Type* shows the type of data the column may hold, and *Description* contains notes that explain the source or use of the column. As you can see, there is one row of metadata for each of the four columns of the *Email* table: *EmailNum, Date, Message*, and *Student Number*.

The bottom part of this form provides more metadata, which Access calls *Field Properties*, for each column. In Figure 5-7, the focus is on the *Date* column (note the filled-in right-face pointer next to its name, like the one shown here ▶). Because the focus is on *Date* in the top pane, the details in the bottom pane pertain to the *Date* column. The *Field Properties* describe formats, a default value for Access to supply when a new row is created, and the constraint that a value is required for this column. It is not important for you to remember these details. Instead, just understand that metadata are data about data and that such metadata are always a part of a database.

Figure 5-7
Example of Metadata
(in Access)

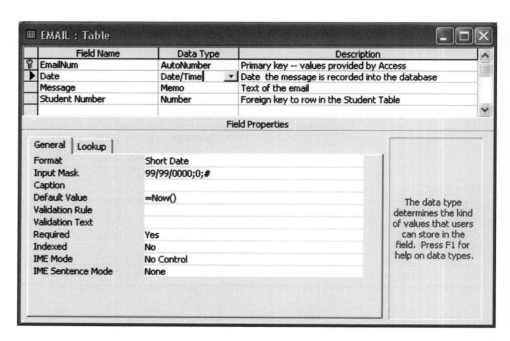

The presence of metadata makes databases much more useful than spreadsheets or data in other lists. Because of metadata, no one needs to guess, remember, or even record what is in the database. To find out what a database contains, we just look at the metadata inside the database. Metadata make databases easy to use—for both authorized and unauthorized purposes, as described in the *Ethics Guide* on pages 99a–99b.

Q3 What Is a DBMS, and What Does It Do?

A database, all by itself, is not very useful. The tables in Figure 5-6 have all of the data the professor wants, but the format is unwieldy. The professor wants to see the data in a form like that in Figure 5-2 and also as a formatted report. Pure database data are correct, but in raw form they are not pertinent or useful.

Figure 5-8 shows the components of a **database application system**. Such applications make database data more accessible and useful. Users employ a database application that consists of forms (like that in Figure 5-2), formatted reports, queries, and application programs. Each of these, in turn, calls on the database management system (DBMS) to process the database tables. We will first describe DBMSs and then discuss database application components.

The Database Management System

A **database management system (DBMS)** is a program used to create, process, and administer a database. As with operating systems, almost no organization develops its own DBMS. Instead, companies license DBMS products from vendors like IBM, Microsoft, Oracle, and others. Popular DBMS products are **DB2** from IBM, **Access** and **SQL Server** from Microsoft, and **Oracle** from the Oracle Corporation. Another popular DBMS is **MySQL**, an open-source DBMS product that is free for most applications. Other DBMS products are available, but these five process the great bulk of databases today.

Note that a DBMS and a database are two different things. For some reason, the trade press and even some books confuse the two. A DBMS is a software program; a database is a collection of tables, relationships, and metadata. The two are very different concepts.

Creating the Database and Its Structures

Database developers use the DBMS to create tables, relationships, and other structures in the database. The form in Figure 5-7 can be used to define a new table or to modify an existing one. To create a new table, the developer just fills out a new form like the one in Figure 5-7.

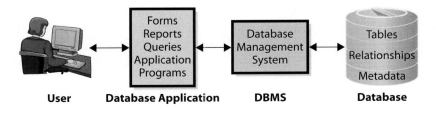

Figure 5-8
Components of a Database Application System

Nobody
Said I
Shouldn't

"**M**y name is Kelly, and I do systems support for our group. I configure the new computers, set up the network, make sure the servers are operating, and so forth. I also do all of the database backups. I've always liked computers. After high school, I worked odd jobs to make some money, then I got an associate degree in information technology from our local community college.

"Anyway, as I said, I make backup copies of our databases. One weekend, I didn't have much going on, so I copied one of the database backups to a CD and took it home. I had taken a class on database processing as part of my associate degree, and we used SQL Server (our database management system) in my class. In fact, I suppose that's part of the reason I got the job. Anyway, it was easy to restore the database on my computer at home, and I did.

"Of course, as they'll tell you in your database class, one of the big advantages of database processing is that databases have metadata, or data that describe the content of the database. So, although I didn't know what tables were in our database, I did know how to access the SQL Server metadata. I just queried a table called sysTables to

learn the names of our tables. From there it was easy to find out what columns each table had.

"I found tables with data about orders, customers, salespeople, and so forth, and just to amuse myself and to see how much of the query language SQL that I could remember, I started playing around with the data. I was curious to know which order entry clerk was the best, so I started querying each clerk's order data, the total number of orders, total order amounts, things like that. It was easy to do and fun.

"I know one of the order-entry clerks, Jason, pretty well, so I started looking at the data for his orders. I was just curious, and it was very simple SQL. I was just playing around with the data when I noticed something odd. All of his biggest orders were with one company, Valley Appliances, and even stranger, every one of its orders had a huge discount. I thought, well, maybe that's typical. Out of curiosity, I started looking at data for the other clerks, and very few of them had an order with Valley Appliances. But, when they did, Valley didn't get a big discount. Then I looked at the rest of Jason's orders, and none of them had much in the way of discounts, either.

"The next Friday, a bunch of us went out for a beer after work. I happened to see Jason, so I asked him about Valley Appliances and made a joke about the discounts. He asked me what I meant, and then I told him that I'd been looking at the data for fun and that I saw this odd pattern. He just laughed, said he just 'did his job,' and then changed the subject.

"Well, to make a long story short, when I got to work on Monday morning, my office was cleaned out. There was nothing there except a note telling me to go see my boss. The bottom line was, I was fired. The company also threatened that if I didn't return all of its data, I'd be in court for the next five years . . . things like that. I was so mad I didn't even tell them about Jason. Now my problem is that I'm out of a job, and I can't exactly use my last company for a reference."

DISCUSSION QUESTIONS

1. Where did Kelly go wrong?

2. Do you think it was illegal, unethical, or neither for Kelly to take the database home and query the data?

3. Does the company share culpability with Kelly?

4. What do you think Kelly should have done upon discovering the odd pattern in Jason's orders?

5. What should the company have done before firing Kelly?

6. Is it possible that someone other than Jason is involved in the arrangement with Valley Appliances? What should Kelly have done in light of that possibility?

7. What should Kelly do now?

8. "Metadata make databases easy to use—for both authorized and unauthorized purposes." Explain what organizations should do in light of this fact.

Figure 5-9
Adding a New Column
to a Table (in Access)

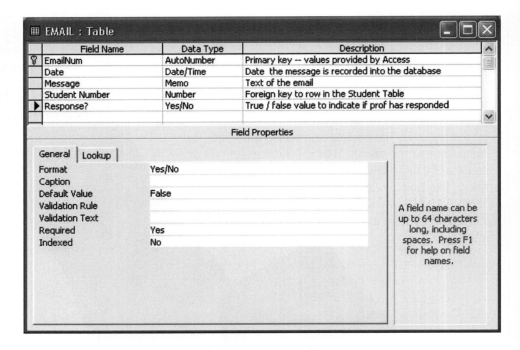

To modify an existing table—for example, to add a new column—the developer opens the metadata form for that table and adds a new row of metadata. For example, in Figure 5-9 the developer has added a new column called *Response?* This new column has the data type *Yes/No*, which means that the column can contain only one of the values—Yes or No. The professor will use this column to indicate whether he has responded to the student's email. Other database structures are defined in similar ways.

Processing the Database

The second function of the DBMS is to process the database. Applications use the DBMS for four operations: to *read, insert, modify,* or *delete* data. The applications call upon the DBMS in different ways. From a form, when the user enters new or changed data, a computer program that processes the form calls the DBMS to make the necessary database changes. From an application program, the program calls the DBMS directly to make the change.

Structured Query Language (SQL) is an international standard language for processing a database. All five of the DBMS products mentioned earlier accept and process SQL (pronounced "see-quell") statements. As an example, the following SQL statement inserts a new row into the *Student* table:

```
INSERT INTO Student
   ([Student Number], [Student Name], HW1, HW2, MidTerm)
   VALUES
   (1000, 'Franklin, Benjamin', 90, 95, 100)
```

Statements like this one are issued "behind the scenes" by programs that process forms. Alternatively, they can also be issued directly to the DBMS by an application program.

You do not need to understand or remember SQL language syntax. Instead, just realize that SQL is an international standard for processing a database. Also, SQL can be used to create databases and database structures. You will learn more about SQL if you take a database management class.

Dealing with Database Growth

Tektronix Corporation of Beaverton, Oregon, is a world leader in test, measurement, and monitoring electronic equipment. Founded in 1946, Tektronix operates in more than 25 countries, and its revenue in 2004 exceeded $920 million. Tektronix focuses on products that support the convergence of computers and communications. According to its Web site, "Almost any time you view a Web site, you touch the work of Tektronix."

Tektronix uses an Oracle database to store and process all of its financial data. The financial database applications average 800 concurrent users throughout the day, and with so much activity, the database grows rapidly. Unfortunately, such growth has a negative impact on performance. "Despite tuning exercises and hardware upgrades, a growth rate of 1.25GB per month caused performance to decline," said Lois Hughes, a senior systems analyst with Tektronix.

Database administration personnel examined data usage and determined that the system was storing large amounts of seldom-used data. The database contained considerable historical data, but almost all database activity involved recently created data. The unused, older data were causing unacceptable response times for the financial application users.

Database growth is not just a Tektronix problem. According to *Computerworld*, many organizations suffer the same fate. The database at Kennametal, Inc., of Latrobe, Pennsylvania, was growing at 27GB per month when the company decided to do something about it. "Our overweight database was months away from crashing due to exceeding our production disk-space capacity," says Larry Cuda, global data archiving and migration project leader. "Management determined that we could no longer just keep throwing more disks at the problem."

The obvious answer to these problems is to remove some database data. Unfortunately, that solution can be difficult to implement. Determining which data are still needed is not easy. For example, data that are still needed to close open transactions cannot be removed. Also, even data that are not needed to close transactions may still be needed for reporting about them.

The problem is compounded by a host of government data-retention laws and regulations. Section 302 of The Sarbanes-Oxley Act of 2002 requires the CEO and CFO of a company to certify the accuracy of annual and quarterly reports. Data necessary to support this certification must be kept. Also, organizations engaged in securities trading must comply with SEC Rule 17-A, which sets out very specific data-retention rules and requirements. Similarly, the Final Rule adopting HIPAA standards specifies a series of administrative, technical, and physical security procedures for data in hospitals, doctors' offices, and other health-provider organizations.

These three examples are just for the United States. Organizations that operate in foreign countries have even greater problems. Considering just accounts receivable data, for example, China requires data retention for 15 years, Brazil for 10, Italy for 7, and the United States for 3.

Clearly, data archiving is not just a problem for IS technicians. Users and user management must be actively involved with the database administration staff in order to define data-archiving requirements, policies, and procedures. Most experts agree with the following guidelines:

1. Convince senior management and end-users of the importance of data archiving and of the need for an approved data-archiving policy.
2. Ensure the policy addresses legal requirements for each country in which the organization operates.
3. Create a plan for implementing the archiving policy—ensure the plan prioritizes business requirements ahead of disk space reduction requirements.
4. Structure the plan to never archive data about open transactions
5. Implement the data-archiving plan before data volumes cause performance problems.
6. Secure and back up the data archive.

Adapted from: *Computerworld*, March 8, 2004, *www.computerworld.com*, accessed December 2004.

Administering the Database

A third DBMS function is to provide tools to assist in the administration of the database. Database administration involves a wide variety of activities. For example, the DBMS can be used to set up a security system involving user accounts, passwords, permissions, and limits for processing the database. To provide database security, a user must sign on using a valid user account before she can process the database.

Permissions can be limited in very specific ways. In the *Student* database example, it is possible to limit a particular user to reading only *Student Name* from the *Student* table. A different user could be given permission to read all of the *Student* table, but limited to update only the *HW1, HW2,* and *MidTerm* columns. Other users can be given still other permissions.

In addition to security, DBMS administrative functions include backing up database data, adding structures to improve the performance of database applications, removing data that are no longer wanted or needed, and similar tasks. One of these tasks involves setting up a system for dealing with database growth, as discussed in *MIS in Use 5.*

Q4 What Is a Database Application?

A **database application** is a collection of forms, reports, queries, and application programs that process a database. A database may have one or more applications, and each application may have one or more users. Figure 5-10 shows three applications; the top two have multiple users. These applications have different purposes, features, and functions, but they all process the same inventory data stored in a common database.

Forms, Reports, and Queries

Figure 5-2 (page 95) shows a typical database application data entry **form**, and Figure 5-11 shows a typical **report**. Data entry forms are used to read, insert, modify, and delete data. Reports show data in a structured context.

Some reports, like the one in Figure 5-11, also compute values as they present the data. An example is the computation of *Total weighted points* in Figure 5-11.

Figure 5-10
Use of Multiple Database
Applications

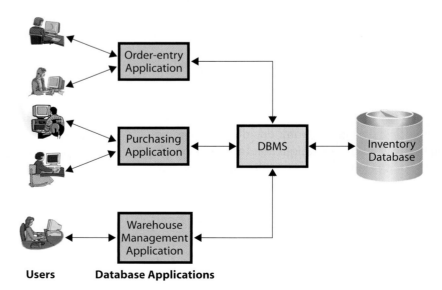

Users　　**Database Applications**

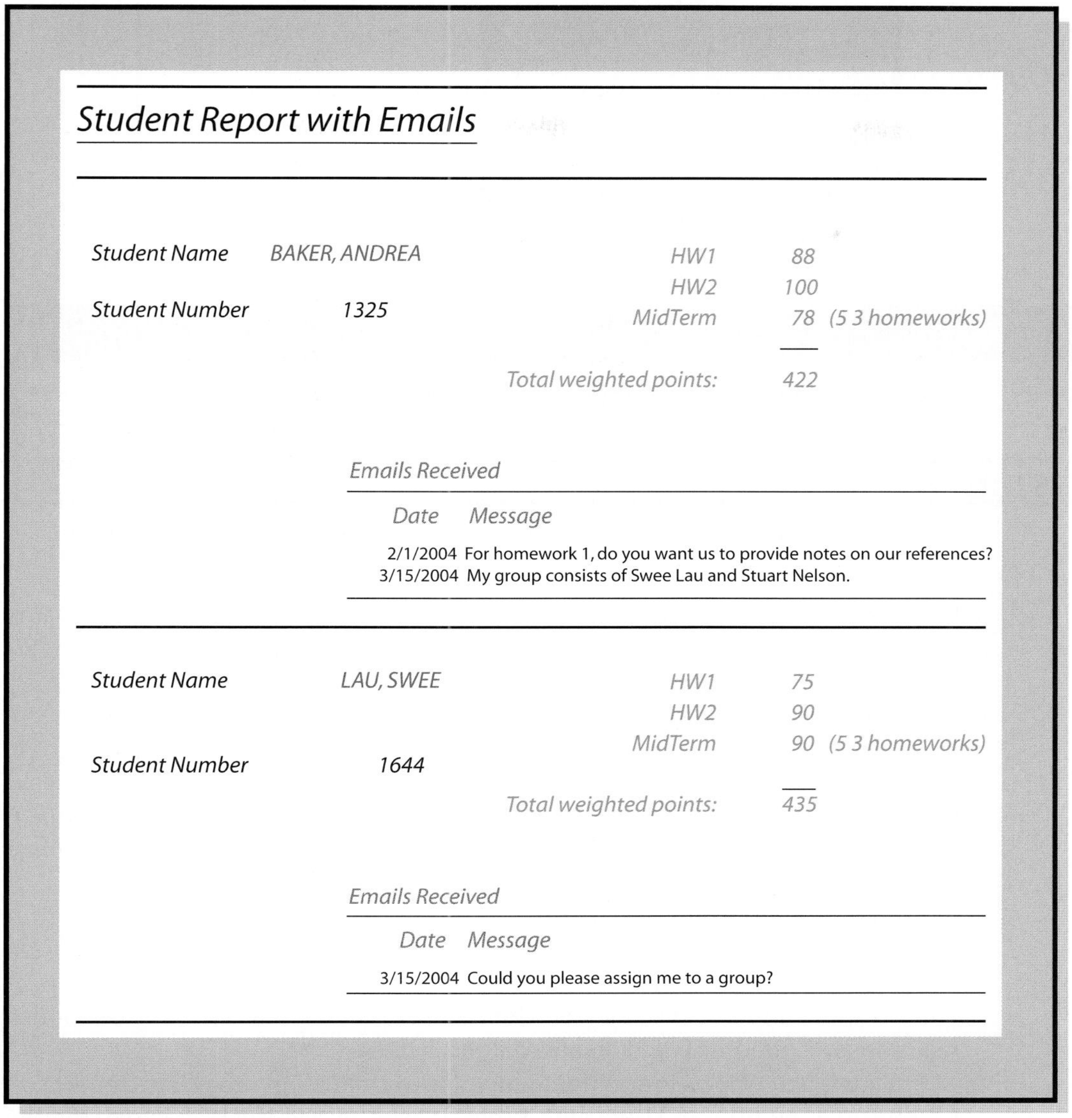

Student Report with Emails

Student Name	BAKER, ANDREA	HW1	88
		HW2	100
Student Number	1325	MidTerm	78 (5 3 homeworks)
			—
	Total weighted points:		422

Emails Received

Date   Message

2/1/2004 For homework 1, do you want us to provide notes on our references?
3/15/2004 My group consists of Swee Lau and Stuart Nelson.

Student Name	LAU, SWEE	HW1	75
		HW2	90
		MidTerm	90 (5 3 homeworks)
Student Number	1644		—
	Total weighted points:		435

Emails Received

Date   Message

3/15/2004 Could you please assign me to a group?

Figure 5-11
Example of a Student Report

Recall from Chapter 1 that one of the definitions of information is "data presented in a meaningful context." The structure of this report creates information because it shows the student data in a context that will be meaningful to the professor.

DBMS programs provide comprehensive and robust features for querying database data. For example, suppose the professor who uses the Student database remembers that one of the students referred to the topic *barriers to entry* in an office visit, but cannot remember which student or when. If there are hundreds of students and visits recorded in the database, it will take some effort and time for the professor to search through all office visit records to find that event. The DBMS, however, can find any such record quickly. Figure 5-12(a) (page 104) shows a **query** form in which the professor types in the keyword for which she is looking. Figure 5-12(b) shows the results of the query.

Database Application Programs

Forms, reports, and queries work well for standard functions. However, most applications have unique requirements that a simple form, report, or query cannot meet. For example, in the order entry application in Figure 5-10, what should

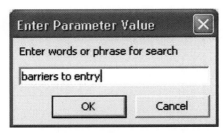

a. Form used to enter phrase for search

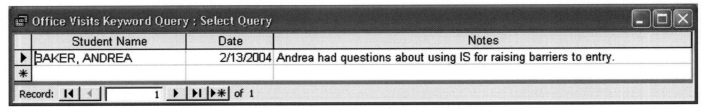

b. Results of query operation

Figure 5-12
Example of a Query

be done if only a portion of a customer's request can be met? If someone wants 10 widgets and we only have 3 in stock, should a backorder for 7 more be generated automatically? Or should some other action be taken?

Application programs process logic that is specific to a given business need. In the Student database, an example application is one that assigns grades at the end of the term. If the professor grades on a curve, the application reads the breakpoints for each grade from a form, and then processes each row in the *Student* table, allocating a grade based on the break points and the total number of points earned.

Another important use of application programs is to enable database processing over the Internet. For this use, the application program serves as an intermediary between the Web server and the database. The application program responds to events, such as when a user presses a submit button; it also reads, inserts, modifies, and deletes database data.

Figure 5-13 shows four different database application programs running on a Web server computer. Users with browsers connect to the Web server via the Internet. The Web server directs user requests to the appropriate application program. Each program then processes the database as necessary. You will learn more about Web-enabled databases in Chapter Extension 11.

Multiuser Processing

Figures 5-10 and 5-13 show multiple users processing the database. Such **multiuser processing** is common, but it does pose unique problems that you, as a future manager, should know about. To understand the nature of those problems, consider the following scenario.

Two users, Andrea and Jeffrey, are clerks using the order entry application in Figure 5-10. Andrea is on the phone with her customer, who wants to purchase 5 widgets. At the same time, Jeffrey is talking with his customer, who wants to purchase 3 widgets. Andrea reads the database to determine how many widgets are in inventory. (She unknowingly invokes the order entry application when she types in her data entry form.) The DBMS returns a row showing 10 widgets in inventory.

Meanwhile, just after Andrea accesses the database, Jeffrey's customer says she wants widgets, and so he also reads the database (via the order entry appli-

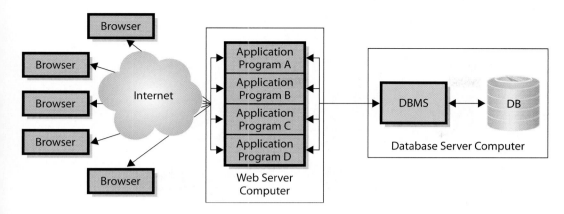

Figure 5-13
Four Application
Programs on a Web
Server Computer

cation program) to determine how many widgets are in inventory. The DBMS returns the same row to him, indicating that 10 widgets are available.

Andrea's customer now says that he'll take 5 widgets, and Andrea records this fact in her form. The application rewrites the widget row back to the database, indicating that there are 5 widgets in inventory.

Meanwhile, Jeffrey's customer says that he'll take 3 widgets. Jeffrey records this fact in his form, and the application rewrites the widget row back to the database. However, Jeffrey's application knows nothing about Andrea's work and subtracts 3 from the original count of 10, thus storing an incorrect count of 7 widgets in inventory. Clearly, there is a problem. We began with 10 widgets, Andrea took 5 and Jeffrey took 3, but the database says there are 7 widgets in inventory. It should show 2, not 7.

This problem, known as the **lost-update problem**, exemplifies one of the special characteristics of multiuser database processing. To prevent this problem, some type of locking must be used to coordinate the activities of users who know nothing about one another. Locking brings its own set of problems, however, and those problems must be addressed as well. We will not delve further into this topic here, however.

Realize from this example that converting a single-user database to a multiuser database requires more than simply connecting another user's computer. The logic of the underlying application processing needs to be adjusted as well.

Be aware of possible data conflicts when you manage business activities that involve multiuser processing. If you find inaccurate results that seem not to have a cause, you may be experiencing multiuser data conflicts. Contact your MIS department for assistance.

For a contrarian's view of databases, see the *Guide* on pages 105a–105b.

Q5 What Is the Difference Between an Enterprise and a Personal DBMS?

DBMS products fall into two broad categories. **Enterprise DBMS** products process large organizational and workgroup databases. These products support many (perhaps thousands) of users and many different database applications. Such DBMS products support 24/7 operations and can manage databases that span dozens of different magnetic disks with hundreds of gigabytes or more of data. IBM's DB2, Microsoft's SQL Server, and Oracle's Oracle are examples of enterprise DBMS products.

No, Thanks, I'll Use a Spreadsheet

"I'm not buying all this stuff about databases. I've tried them and they're a pain—way too complicated to set up, and most of the time, a spreadsheet works just as well. We had one project at the car dealership that seemed pretty simple to me: We wanted to keep track of customers and the models of used cars they were interested in. Then, when we got a car on the lot, we could query the database to see who wanted a car of that type and generate a letter to them.

"It took forever to build that system, and it never did work right. We hired three different consultants, and the last one finally did get it to work. But it was so complicated to produce the letters. You had to query the data in Access to generate some kind of file, then open Word, then go through some mumbo jumbo using mail/merge to cause Word to find the letter and put all the Access data in the right spot. I once printed over 200 letters and had the name in the address spot and the address in the name spot and no date. And it took me over an hour to do even that. I just wanted to do the query and push a button to get my letters generated. I gave up. Some of the salespeople are still trying to use it, but not me.

"No, unless you are General Motors or Toyota, I wouldn't mess with a database. You have to have professional IS people to create it and keep it running. Besides, I don't really want to share my data with anyone. I work pretty hard to develop my client list. Why would I want to give it away?

"My motto is, 'Keep it simple.' I use an Excel spreadsheet with four columns: Name, Phone Number, Car Interests, and Notes. When I get a new customer, I enter the name and phone number, and then I put the make and model of cars they like in the Car Interests column. Anything else that I think is important I put in the Notes column—extra phone numbers, address data if I have it, email addresses, spouse names, last time I called them, etc. The system isn't fancy, but it works fine.

"When I want to find something, I use Excel's Data Filter. I can usually get what I need. Of course, I still can't send form letters, but it really doesn't matter. I get most of my sales using the phone, anyway."

DISCUSSION QUESTIONS

1. To what extent do you agree with the opinions presented here? To what extent are the concerns expressed here justified? To what extent might they be due to other factors?

2. What problems do you see with the way that the car salesperson stores address data? What will he have to do if he ever does want to send a letter or an email to all of his customers?

3. From his comments, how many different themes are there in his data? What does this imply about his ability to keep his data in a spreadsheet?

4. Does the concern about not sharing data relate to whether or not he uses a database?

5. Apparently, management at the car dealership allows the salespeople to keep their contact data in whatever format they want. If you were management, how would you justify this policy? What disadvantages are there to this policy?

6. Suppose you manage the sales representatives, and you decide to require all of them to use a database to keep track of customers and customer car interest data. How would you sell your decision to this salesperson?

7. Given the limited information in this scenario, do you think a database or a spreadsheet is a better solution?

Figure 5-14
Personal Database System

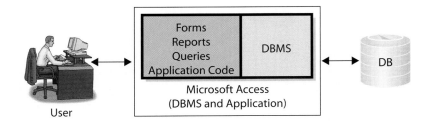

Personal DBMS products are designed for smaller, simpler database applications. Such products are used for personal or small workgroup applications that involve fewer than a 100 users, and normally fewer than 15. In fact, the great bulk of databases in this category have only a single user. The professor's Student database is an example of a database that is processed by a personal DBMS product.

In the past, there were many personal DBMS products—Paradox, dBase, R:base, and FoxPro. Microsoft put these products out of business when it developed Access and included it in the Microsoft Office suite. Today, the only remaining personal DBMS is Microsoft Access.

To avoid one point of confusion for you in the future, the separation of application programs and the DBMS shown in Figure 5-10 is true only for enterprise DBMS products. Microsoft Access includes features and functions for application processing along with the DBMS itself. For example, Access has a form generator and a report generator. Thus, as shown in Figure 5-14, Access is both a DBMS and an application development product.

Figure 5-15
Role of DBMS for Dee's Blog

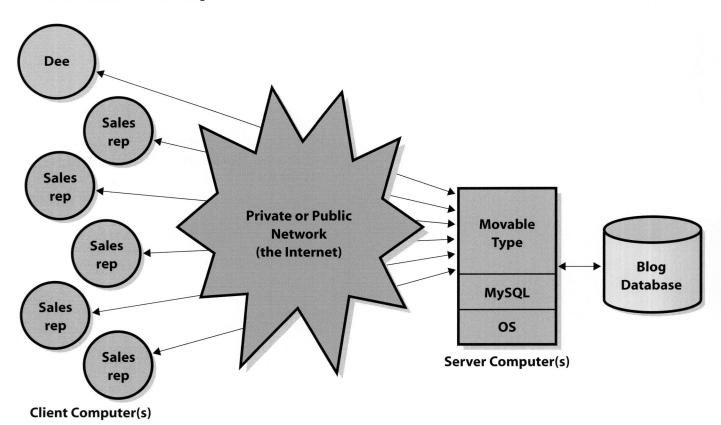

How does the knowledge in this chapter help Dee and you?

The knowledge in this chapter would have helped Dee to know what a DBMS is and what role it plays. She would have been able to understand the diagram in Figure 5-15 on the previous page (and perhaps even draw it herself). This is the same diagram as you saw in Figure 4-13, page 85, except now we have filled in the software that runs on the server computer. The application is Moveable Type, and it calls the DBMS MySQL, which processes the database. Of course, like every computer, the server also has an operating system like Windows or Linux.

While this system does run a DBMS, it is completely isolated from the rest of the Emerson databases and really should not be of concern to the IT department. Dee is not proposing to replace Oracle with MySQL for the processing of orders or the paying of salespeople. She just wants to include MySQL, as part of the functionality of her application, on the server.

With this knowledge, Dee could explain what she wants to do and that her project is no threat or exception to the Oracle standard. It is an isolated system that needs MySQL to run.

Ultimately, Don made that exact argument to the IT department. Once the department understood Dee's plan, they had no problem with Dee's use of MySQL—as long as she paid any required license fees for it out of her own budget. Unfortunately, without knowledge of database concepts, Dee was unable to make that argument herself, so she was forced to hire her consultant to make that argument for her. Doing this meant a delay of another few days as well as an additional expense. Still, she had passed another hurdle on the way to developing her system.

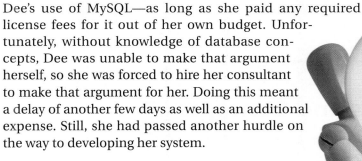

Active ? Review

Use this Active Review to verify that you understand the material in the chapter. You can read the entire chapter and then perform the tasks in this review, or you can read the material for just one question and perform the tasks in this review for that question before moving on to the next one.

Q1 What is the purpose of a database?
Describe the purpose of a database. Explain when to use a spreadsheet and when to use a database.

Q2 What does a database contain?
Explain the hierarchy of data from bytes to tables. Show how a database stores the relationships among rows. Define *key* and *foreign key*. Define *metadata*, and explain how metadata makes databases more useful.

Q3 What is a DBMS, and what does it do?
Describe a database application system. Define *DBMS*. Name three prominent DBMS products. Describe the difference between a database and a DBMS. Explain the three major functions of a DBMS. What is SQL used for?

Q4 What is a database application?
Name and describe the components of a database application. Describe the circumstances that require a special logic for database applications. Describe the lost-update problem. Explain, in general terms, how this problem is prevented.

Q5 What is the difference between an enterprise and a personal DBMS?
Explain the function of an enterprise DBMS and describe its characteristics. Explain the function of a personal DBMS and describe its characteristics. Name the only surviving personal DBMS. Explain the differences between Figure 5-10 and Figure 5-15.

How does the knowledge in this chapter help Dee and you? Explain the diagram in Figure 5-15. Decide whether Dee's blog is a threat or exception to Emerson's Oracle standard. Explain what knowledge Dee needed in order to explain to the IT department her need for MySQL.

Key Terms and Concepts

Access 99
Byte 95
Column 95
Database 95
Database application 102
Database application system 99
Database management system (DBMS) 99
DB2 99
Enterprise DBMS 105
Field 96

File 96
Foreign key 97
Form 102
Key 96
Lost-update problem 105
Metadata 98
Multiuser processing 104
MySQL 99
Object-relational database 97
Oracle 99
Query 103

Personal DBMS 106
Record 96
Relation 97
Relational database 97
Report 102
Row 96
SQL Server 99
Structured Query Language (SQL) 100
Table 96

Using Your Knowledge

1. Suppose you are a marketing assistant for a consumer electronics company and are in charge of setting up your company's booth at trade shows. Weeks before the shows, you meet with the marketing managers and

determine what displays and equipment they want to display. Then, you identify each of the components that need to be shipped and schedule a shipper to deliver them to the trade-show site. You then supervise convention personnel as they set up the booths and equipment. Once the show is over, you supervise the packing of the booth and all equipment as well as schedule its shipment back to your home office. Once the equipment arrives, you check it into your warehouse to ensure that all pieces of the booth and all equipment are returned. If there are problems due to shipping damage or loss, you handle those problems. Your job is important; at a typical show, you are responsible for more than a quarter of a million dollars of equipment.

   a. You will need to track data about booth components, equipment, shippers, and shipments. List typical fields for each type of data.

   b. Could you use a spreadsheet to keep track of this data? What would be the advantages and disadvantages of doing so?

   c. Using your answer to question a, give an example of two relationships that you need to track. Show the keys and foreign keys for each.

   d. Which of the following components of a database application are you likely to need: data entry forms, reports, queries, or application program? Explain one use for each that you will need.

   e. Will your application be single-user or multiuser? Will you need a personal DBMS or an enterprise DBMS? If a personal DBMS, which product will you use?

2. Samantha Green (the same Samantha we met at the end of Chapter 3, p. 51) owns and operates Twigs Tree Trimming Service. Recall that Samantha has a degree from a forestry program, and recently opened her business in St. Louis, Missouri. Her business consists of many one-time operations (e.g., remove a tree or stump), as well as recurring services (e.g., trimming customers' trees every year or two). When business is slow, Samantha calls former clients to remind them of her services and of the need to trim their trees on a regular basis.

   a. Name and describe tables of data that Samantha will need to run her business. Indicate possible fields for each table.

   b. Could Samantha use a spreadsheet to keep track of this data? What would be the advantages and disadvantages of doing so?

   c. Using your answer to question a, give an example of two relationships that Samantha needs to track. Show the keys and foreign keys for each.

   d. Which of the following components of a database application is Samantha likely to need: data entry forms, reports, queries, or application program? Explain one use for each that she needs.

   e. Will this application be single-user or multiuser? Will she need a personal DBMS or an enterprise DBMS? If a personal DBMS, which product will she use?

3. FiredUp, Inc., (the same FiredUp we met at the end of Chapter 3, p. 52) is a small business owned by Curt and Julie Robards. Based in Brisbane, Australia, FiredUp manufacturers and sells FiredNow, a lightweight camping stove. Recall that Curt used his previous experience as an aerospace engineer to invent a burning nozzle that enables the stove to stay lit in very high winds. Using her industrial design training, Julie designed the stove so that it is small, lightweight, easy to set up, and very stable. Curt and Julie sell the stove directly to their customers over the Internet and via phone. The warranty on

the stove covers five years of cost-free repair for stoves used for recreational purposes.

FiredUp wants to track every stove and the customer who purchased it. They want to know which customers own which stoves, in case they need to notify customers of safety problems or need to order a stove recall. Curt and Julie also want to keep track of any repairs they have performed.

a. Name and describe tables of data that FiredUp will need. Indicate possible fields for each table.

b. Could FiredUp use a spreadsheet to keep track of this data? What would be the advantages and disadvantages of doing so?

c. Using your answer to question a, give an example of two relationships that FiredUp needs to track. Show the keys and foreign keys for each.

d. Which of the following components of a database application is FiredUp likely to need: data entry forms, reports, queries, or application program? Explain one use for each needed component.

e. Will this application be single-user or multiuser? Will FiredUp need a personal DBMS or an enterprise DBMS? If a personal DBMS, which product will it use? If an enterprise DBMS, which product can they obtain license-free?

Case Study 5

Benchmarking, Bench Marketing, or Bench Baloney?

Which DBMS product is the fastest? Which product yields the lowest price/performance ratio? What computer equipment works best for each DBMS product? These reasonable questions should be easy to answer. They are not.

In fact, the deeper you dig, the more problems you find. To begin with, which product is fastest doing what? To have a valid comparison, all compared products must do the same work. So, vendors and third parties have defined *benchmarks*, which are descriptions of work to be done along with the data to be processed. To compare performance, analysts run competing DBMS products on the same benchmark and measure the results. Typical measures are number of transactions processed per second, number of Web pages served per second, and average response time per user.

At first, DBMS vendors set up their own benchmark tests and published those results. Of course, when vendor A used its own benchmark to claim that its product was superior to all others, no one believed the results. Clearly, vendor A had an incentive to set up the benchmark to play to its product strengths. So, third parties defined standard benchmarks. Even that led to problems, however. According to *The Benchmark Handbook* (at *benchmarkresources.com/handbook*):

> When comparative numbers were published by third parties or competitors, the losers generally cried foul and tried to discredit the benchmark. Such events often caused benchmark wars. Benchmark wars start if someone loses an important or visible benchmark evaluation. The loser reruns it using regional specialists and gets new and winning numbers. Then the opponent reruns it using his regional specialists, and of course gets even better numbers. The loser then reruns it using some one-star gurus. This progression can continue all the way to five-star gurus.

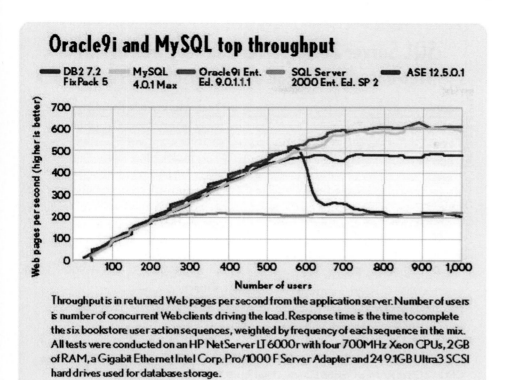

Figure C5-1
Results of First Nile
Benchmark Test

For example, in July 2002, *PC Magazine* ran a benchmark using a standard benchmark called the *Nile benchmark*. This particular test has a mixture of database tasks that are processed via Web pages. The faster the DBMS, the more pages that can be served. The results of the test were as shown in Figure C5-1.

The test compared five DBMS products: DB2 (from IBM), MySQL (a free, open-source DBMS product from MySQL.com), Oracle (from Oracle Corporation), SQL Server (from Microsoft), and ASE (from Sybase Corporation). The vertical axis in the graph shows the number of pages processed per second; as the label says, higher is better.

From this graph, you can see that SQL Server's performance was the worst. In the magazine review, the authors stated that they believed SQL Server scored poorly because the test used a new version of a non-Microsoft driver (a program that sends requests and returns results to and from the DBMS).

As you might imagine, no sooner was this test published than the phones and email server at *PC Magazine* were inundated by objections from Microsoft. *PC Magazine* reran the tests, replacing the suspect driver with a full panoply of Microsoft products. The article doesn't say, but one can imagine the five-star Microsoft gurus who chartered the next airplane to PC Labs, where the testing was done. (You can read about both phases of the benchmark at *eweek.com/article2/0,4149,293,00.asp.*)

Rerunning the test with the Microsoft-supporting software, the SQL Server results were as shown in Figure C5-2 (on p. 112).

In the second test, SQL Server performed better than all of the other products in the first test. But now we're comparing apples and oranges. The first test used standard software, and the second test used Microsoft-specific software.

Figure C5-2
Results of Second Nile
Benchmark Test

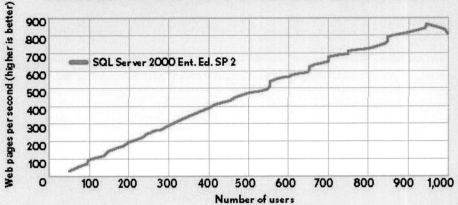

Throughput is in returned Web pages per second from the application server. Number of users is number of concurrent Web clients driving the load. Response time is the time to complete the six bookstore user action sequences, weighted by frequency of each sequence in the mix. All tests were conducted on an HP NetServer LT 6000r with four 700MHz Xeon CPUs, 2 GB of RAM, a Gigabit Ethernet Intel Pro/1000 F Server Adapter and 24 9.1GB Ultra3 SCSI hard drives used for database storage.

When the five-star gurus from Oracle or MySQL use *their* favorite supporting products and "tune" to this particular benchmark, their re-rerun results will be superior to those for SQL Server. And round and round it will go.

Questions

1. Suppose you manage a business activity that needs a new IS with a database. The development team is divided on which DBMS you should use. One faction wants to use Oracle, a second wants to use MySQL, and a third wants to use SQL Server. They cannot decide among themselves, and so they schedule a meeting with you. The team presents all of the benchmarks shown here. How do you respond?

2. Performance is just one criterion for selecting a DBMS. Other criteria are the cost of the DBMS, hardware costs, staff knowledge, ease of use, ability to tune for extra performance, and backup and recovery capabilities. How does consideration of these other factors change your answer to question 1?

3. The Transaction Processing Council (TPC) is a not-for-profit corporation that defines transaction processing and database benchmarks and publishes vendor-neutral, verifiable performance data. Visit its Web site at *tpc.org*.
   a. What are TPC-C, TPC-R, and TPC-W?
   b. Suppose you work in the marketing department at Oracle Corporation. How would you use the TPC results in the TPC-C benchmark?
   c. What are the dangers to Oracle in your answer to part b?
   d. Suppose you work in the marketing department for DB2 at IBM. How would you use the TPC results in the TPC-C benchmark?

    e. Do the results for TPC-C change your answer to question 1?

    f. If you are a DBMS vendor, can you ignore benchmarks?

4. Reflect on your answers to questions 1 through 3. On balance, what good are benchmarks? Are they just footballs to be kicked around by vendors? Are advertisers and publishers the only true beneficiaries? Do DBMS customers benefit from the efforts of TPC and like groups? How should customers use benchmarks?

Teaching Suggestions

Emerson Pharmaceuticals, Chapter 5

GOALS

Use Dee's blog to:

* Understand how information systems support business processes.

* Motivate the need for knowledge of database terms like DBMS, Oracle, and MySQL, even among non-IT business professionals.

* Understand the reason for the IT department's reluctance to allow a non-standard DBMS and why this situation is a justifiable exception.

BACKGROUND

1. Emerson has standardized on Oracle. The Emerson IT department has a default policy that there will be no other server DBMSs. Users and user departments can have their own Access databases, but no Emerson server is to run a DBMS other than Oracle.

2. Dee is becoming a problem to the IT department. She's been assigned to work with a very junior systems analyst whose principal concern is not to miss any of his upcoming vacation. He thinks Dee's schedule is ridiculous, and he's not ambitious. It's possible (even likely) that he's using the Oracle standard to block Dee's project.

3. Moveable Type (MT) uses MySQL to manage the blog's data; MySQL is never visible either to Dee or the salespeople. It's just a behind-the-scenes data manager. Dee has no intention of developing any other application using MySQL.

4. There are two real issues about MySQL:

   a. Who will install and support it? This is a real issue; Dee intends to contract with Don for support, but that will mean that Don be given access to programs within the Emerson network. Dee forces Emerson to let Don in the network—an action that exposes Emerson to serious security risks, as stated in the annotations for Chapter 4.

   b. What sort of license does Emerson need? Because Emerson is using it for commercial purposes, it may need to obtain a commercial license. However, MySQL is distributed under the GPL, so if Moveable Type is open-source, then MySQL would be license-free. Even if Emerson needs

a commercial license, such a license will be relatively inexpensive ($600 or so per year).

   c. Chapter Extension 21, on accounting for and financing information systems, discusses total cost of ownership. I don't think I'd complicate the discussion here, however, with licensing issues. Just explain that Don or the Emerson IT department has to find out what is required.

5. Dee needed enough knowledge to explain to the IT department that she wasn't doing anything other than using MySQL to support Moveable Type. She needed to point out that there are hundreds of Moveable Type installations that successfully run MySQL. The MySQL installation would pose no burden on the IT department. Furthermore, if there were problems, only Dee's blog would be affected.

6. The big picture here is not so much to teach students about Oracle versus MySQL, but rather to help them become better consumers of the IT department's services. This problem is only a sample of many issues that can arise between users and IT professionals. From this situation, students should strive to gain ideas on ways of working with IT departments in the future.

HOW TO GET THE STUDENTS INVOLVED

1. Before getting started, the students need to understand the purposes of a DBMS. They also need to know the differences in nature, maintenance, and application of server DBMS products like Oracle (and MySQL) and single-user DBMS products like Microsoft Access.

2. There are at least three possible explanations of this situation:

   a. The IT department's objection is legitimate; it wants only Oracle used on its network. It will not support any other server DBMS.

   b. This issue is bogus, and the IT person is using it to avoid work. In this case, he's taking advantage of Dee's lack of knowledge.

   c. The IT person is inexperienced and is blindly enforcing a corporate data standard. He does not understand Dee's proposed use of MySQL and why it might qualify as an exception.

3. Dee's best response depends on whether 2a, 2b, or 2c are true.

   a. **How can she find out?**

   b. **What questions can she ask Don?**

   c. **What questions can she ask the IT person?**

4. If she thinks explanation 2a is true, what can Dee do?

   a. First, why would the IT department have such a limitation?

   b. Using empathic thinking, how could Dee approach that department?

   c. If there is no way that MySQL will be installed, what can Dee do?

   d. Dee might be wrong. Explanation 2b or 2c might be true. What are the consequences if she acts as if 2a is true?

5. If Dee thinks explanation 2b is true, what can she do?

   a. Call the person lazy and say she's going to report him to her manager?

   b. Get permission to have Don install and support MySQL?

   c. If Dee admits that she has no idea what a DBMS is or does, how does that weaken her position in this case?

   d. Other?

   e. Dee might be wrong. Explanation 2a or 2c might be true. What are the consequences if she acts as if 2b is true?

6. If she thinks explanation 2c is true, what can she do?

   a. Tell the IT person he doesn't know what he's doing?

   b. Ask the IT person to contact someone else in IT and find out if there are ever exceptions to the Oracle-only policy?

   c. Ask Don to call the IT person and talk through the issue?

   d. Other?

   e. Dee might be wrong. Explanation 2a or 2b might be true. What are the consequences if she acts as if 2c is true?

7. Wrap up: What should Dee do, and why?

BOTTOM LINE

* Lack of IT knowledge can place you at a disadvantage. If Dee does not know what a DBMS is, if she does not know how to learn or how to bring in expertise to help her, her project may fail needlessly. Learn what you can during this class, but even more important, *learn that you can (and should) learn IT concepts.*

* How does Dee's willingness to deal with this issue give her a competitive advantage vis-à-vis Emerson's competition? How does it give her a competitive advantage vis-à-vis other marketing communications managers within Emerson?

Using the Ethics Guide: Nobody Said I Shouldn't (page 99a)

GOALS

* Illustrate the utility of metadata and SQL, even for nonauthorized purposes.

* Investigate what constitutes unauthorized data access.

* Discuss the ethics of unauthorized data access.

* Consider the need for organizational data policies.

BACKGROUND AND PRESENTATION STRATEGIES

SQL was designed to be powerful and easy to use. Here's a SQL statement Kelly used to display the average order total and average discount for each combination of company and salesperson:

```
SELECT      AVG(Total),  AVG(Discount),
            CompanyName,  SPName
FROM        SALES_ORDER
GROUP BY    CompanyName,  SPName;
```

That's all Kelly needed! No programs, no special interfaces, just those few lines of SQL entered into the DBMS. It could be done in 5 minutes or less.

➤ **As a future business manager or owner, what does the ease with which this can be done tell you?**

In order for Kelly to write the SQL statement above, he needed to know the names of the tables and columns to query. The names were easy for him to obtain because every database contains metadata that describes its content. Kelly used the DBMS to query the metadata to learn there was a table named Sales_Order that contained the columns *Total, Discount, CompanyName,* and *SPName.*

Nothing that Kelly did was illegal; it's even questionable that what he did was unethical. Suppose he stumbled upon an internal criminal conspiracy, one unknown to the company's management or ownership. By discovering it, he would be a hero, if the discovery was reported to someone not involved in the conspiracy.

If the company has a policy that no employee is to remove company data from the company premises, then he violated that policy. Can any company enforce such a policy today? If a sales manager sends an email with proprietary company product information to a

salesperson working at a customer site, that action would be a violation of the policy not to remove data from company premises. But if the salesperson needs the data to support a crucial sale, who would want to prohibit that data access? Still, removing an entire database is on a different scale from sending an attachment in an email.

Data is an asset. Data is just as much an asset as buildings, trucks, and equipment. It has value and needs to be protected.

➤ **What is a reasonable policy for an organization to have regarding employees taking data home?**

This question is not easy to answer. The policy needs to be loose enough to allow employees to do their work, while providing appropriate protection to data assets. Most employment contracts use statements like "protect the company's data assets as directed by management" or other general language.

Bottom line: Companies need to have policies with regard to the data asset. We'll discuss this further when we discuss security management in Chapter 12.

We could view Kelly as the victim of bad luck: His curiosity, knowledge of database technology, ambition, and friendships caused him to lose his job.

Kelly probably should hire an attorney who might advise him to contact law enforcement as well. He may not get his job back, he may not want his job back, but he's probably entitled to some compensation. He also deserves a decent job referral—assuming he was otherwise a desirable employee.

 SUGGESTED RESPONSES FOR DISCUSSION QUESTIONS

1. Kelly went wrong by taking the data home. Had he processed the data at work, it would be hard to fault him.

   ➤ **Was he in error about mentioning to his friend what he'd found?**

   ➤ **Once he saw the odd pattern, what should he have done?**

   This is a tough one. Either forget about it or do a careful analysis and then take the results to the most senior manager he can meet. But what if this is an innocuous coincidence? Then he'll look like he betrayed his friend. Maybe Kelly hasn't done anything wrong, yet. *Maybe the story isn't over.* One possible continuation of the story is that he goes to an attorney who advises him to contact senior management and law enforcement.

2. It was not illegal. Taking the data home may have been against corporate policy. He may have been overly curious, but is that unethical? I think taking the data home might be construed as poor judgment on the part of a smart and ambitious employee, but I wouldn't say it was unethical. Recall Encarta's definition of ethical: "Consistent with agreed principles of correct moral conduct."

➤ **Do his intentions matter? If he had gone home with the intention of using the customer data to sell his own home-care products, would your answer be different?**

➤ **If he had gone home with the hope of gathering dirt on fellow employees, would your answer be different?**

➤ **Why should his intentions matter?**

It goes back to "agreed principles." Most would find it hard to fault improving one's job skills, even if there is an element of unbridled curiosity.

3. Culpability for what? For allowing him to take home the data? If there is no clear company policy, if he had not been instructed not to remove data, then the company probably does share culpability. If he violated a clearly stated company policy of which he had been made aware, then probably not. Culpability for firing him? It depends on how high up the organization the conspiracy reaches. If it goes all the way to the top, then they do. If not, then firing him was the protective action of guilty employees. Company culpability depends on what happens next.

4. First, I ask the class to vote:

➤ **How many of you think that Kelly should:**

   • **Ignore the whole thing?**

   • **Confirm his analysis, gather even stronger evidence, if possible, and then take the information he has to the CFO?**

   • **Never have learned SQL? (This is a joke!)**

   • **Done what he did, and now go see an attorney?**

Now ask the students why they voted the way they did.

My vote: probably go to the CFO. If he then is fired, definitely go to the attorney.

5. If there is no criminal conspiracy, then I believe the company's actions were precipitous. He ought not to be fired for his ambition and knowledge, even if he did show poor judgment in taking the data home.

First, the company should determine if the information he created reveals employee wrongdoing. If not, then he should be instructed not to take data home, or maybe put on probation, but firing him seems overly harsh. This also depends on whether he violated a clear corporate policy on which he had been trained.

If there is a criminal conspiracy, then the company has major problems. They need to consult their attorneys and law enforcement. They also possibly should hire investigators to identify members of the conspiracy and then clean up the organization.

6. I think there's little doubt that someone else is involved. Jason is not in a position to force Kelly's firing. In that case, he should have not spoken with Jason. He should have gone as high in the organization as he could. But, see question 4.

7. Say nothing to anyone. Hire an attorney with expertise in labor law.

➤ **Do you think he should "sue the pants off" this company?**

8. Understand their vulnerability. Treat organizational data as an important asset. Establish data policies and train employees on those policies. (More on this in Chapter 12.)

WRAP UP

➤ **This is a rather weird case. Should we conclude:**

   • **A little knowledge is a dangerous thing?**

   • **Curiosity got the cat?**

   • **Don't stick your nose in other people's business?**

   • **Don't socialize with fellow employees after work?**

➤ **Two sure conclusions:**

   • **Data is an important asset that needs to be protected.**

   • **Metadata and SQL are powerful.**

➤ **We're in the middle of the story. What happened next? Did he hire an attorney? Or, did he slink off and take an entry-level job in another industry?**

➤ **Assume he hired an attorney, and you finish the story. Think about it tonight and next class, after which two or three of you can tell us how the story ends.**

Using the Guide: No Thanks, I'll Use a Spreadsheet *(page 105a)*

GOALS

✳ Explore the differences between a spreadsheet and a database.

✳ Understand one way that users respond to technology challenges.

✳ Discuss ways of managing a difficult employee (or perhaps just a difficult situation).

BACKGROUND AND PRESENTATION STRATEGIES

The story of the failed database project is, unfortunately, quite common. Often it involves small businesses or workgroups that have attempted to develop a database on their own. On the basis of my experience, the cause of such failures is usually either incompetent database developers or underfunding of the project. (This, by the way, differs from the causes of failure for information systems in general. Based on a review of all systems development projects and not just database projects at small businesses, the most likely causes of failure are poor communication between users and systems developers, a lack of clear requirements, and an inability to manage requirements.)

It took this company three consultants to obtain a database that works. *But the one that "works" doesn't meet the requirements*—or at least it doesn't meet the requirements of this salesperson.

➤ **Organizations smaller than General Motors or Toyota can develop their own databases, but developing a database and its applications in house does take time, money, and management attention. You, as a future manager, need to know what should be happening.**

➤ **We'll talk about systems development techniques in Chapter 10 and Chapter Extension 19, but to build a database correctly, here's a quick summary of the work that needs to be done:**

- **Determine and document requirements.**
- **Construct a data model and have users validate it.**
- **Design the database.**
- **Implement the database and fill it with data (imported from other sources?).**

- **Design, build, and test database applications.**
- **Write procedures.**
- **Train the users.**
- **Maintain the system.**

➤ **Notice I said *management attention*. Suppose you manage the dealership. What role do you see for yourself when a customer database is being developed for your sales staff?**

In light of the amount of work, the dealership might be better off to look for appropriate off-the-shelf software, such as Act! or GoldMine. These products, which do use databases, already exist and have interfaces that are built just for sales. Many small business salespeople use and recommend such products.

The issue of whether salespeople should share data is independent of the technology that the salesperson uses. Sharing data is a management policy. If management decides that salespersons' data should be private, there are ways to implement that policy with a database just as well as with a spreadsheet.

It's possible this person is using the failure of the database application to avoid sharing his data. He can hide his spreadsheet from management; they don't know that he's got his own customer data. It could be that he wants to keep his customer data private so that he can take it with him if he decides to work for another dealership. He might be using his disgust with the database project to cover his intentions.

Or, maybe not, but something doesn't fit: He doesn't want to use the database because it's difficult for him to send form letters or email. Yet, he says that he can't send them with his spreadsheet either and that sending letters is not that important to his sales activity.

Another possibility: His data are actually not his. He may have been stealing customers from other salespeople, and he doesn't want them to know that. Putting his data in a centralized database will reveal his actions.

Scrambling all of his data into the *Car Interests* and *Notes* columns will cause enormous problems if he ever wants to import his data to a database. Those problems will also be expensive to fix, because the work of separating the data into proper columns must be done manually. See pages 112–113 of the tenth edition of *Database Processing*[1] for a discussion of these issues.

[1]David Kroenke, *Database Processing*, 10th ed. (Upper Saddle River, NJ: Prentice Hall, 2006).

"Keep it simple" is a great motto, but it shouldn't be simpler than it needs to be. What happens when his customers stop answering their phones because they prefer to use email? He can still send emails one at a time, but without some kind of database application, it will be impossible to send bulk emails announcing the arrival of new cars, and so on. This person is condemning himself to the old-world style of business.

 ## SUGGESTED RESPONSES FOR DISCUSSION QUESTIONS

1. Ask the students their opinions. I believe users have a right to information systems that allow them to do their jobs. Something doesn't fit here, though. He objects to the database application because it's difficult to send form letters, but then he says they're not that important to the way he sells. What else is going on? (See earlier comments.)

2. He's creating a nightmare for himself. How will he ever disentangle the addresses from the *Notes* column? What a mess!

3. I think some likely themes are *Customer, Auto_Interest, Contact*, and possibly others.

   ➤ *Multiple themes mean: Use a database!*

4. I suspect the concern does relate to using a database, but it ought not. Databases can be private and secure; accounts and roles can be set up so that salespeople do not share each other's data. However, I think he's hiding his desire not to share his data by complaining about the database. He's using frustration with technology to hide from the management policy of sharing data.

   ➤ **If you were a manager, how would you deal with this possibility?**

5. First, management may not be allowing each salesperson to have his or her own format. They may be trying to discourage it by building the shared database. The question is, who owns the contact data—the salespeople or the dealership? If the salespeople own it, then they can do what they want with it. If the dealership owns the data, then they can specify whatever format they want. The disadvantages to allowing different ways of keeping the data are inconsistent quality, missing data, difficulty of accessing common data, duplicated data, and so on.

6. Well, there's the soft approach and there's the tough one. The soft approach is to explain the need for the database—how it will make everyone more efficient, and how it will help salespeople not lose control of their customers to other salespeople. Also, explain that the database offers better security and control, including better protection, because it will be backed up and stored off-premises. Finally, explain that the database can integrate customer sales data with customer service data, and so forth.

   The tough approach is to mandate it: "We need centralized customer data to beat the competition and, ultimately, to survive. This may require you to make some changes, and it may be difficult for a while, but it's the way we're going to go. Get with it!" Then, provide support to ease the conversion efforts.

   ➤ **Or, as I once heard between a partner in a law firm and a reluctant junior associate: "What possible incentive do I have to use this new system?" asked the junior associate. "Continued employment," responded the partner.**

7. A database is a better solution. Whether it's a database developed in house or one that is embedded in a product like Act! or GoldMine is another question. But this type of problem begs for a database solution.

WRAP UP

➤ **No doubt about it, databases can involve a lot of work and involve management challenges. That's one reason you should read this chapter carefully.**

➤ **Given that databases can be expensive to develop in house (not to mention expensive to maintain), for a common need like customer management for sales, look first to off-the-shelf applications.**

➤ **Sometimes people are frustrated with new systems and technology for justifiable reasons. Other times, they use that frustration for a cover for some other reason. That may have happened here. As a manager, keep that possibility in mind.**

6 Data Communications

When Dee first proposed the idea of her blog, one of the first questions she was asked was, "Are you going to run it inside the Emerson network?" This question was crucial to the development of her blog, and she did not understand why. She wanted to say, "I don't know. What difference does it make?" but sensed that it would be unwise to reveal that much lack of knowledge.

In order to provide a competitive advantage, the information on Dee's blog needs to be kept private. She wants the sales reps to have easy access to the blog, but she wants to keep it from the competition. Many sales reps work from home, and many travel extensively, using their computers from hotels. She knows that they can access the Internet from either home or hotel, but if she makes her blog publicly available on the Internet, the competition could access it too.

An alternative is for Dee to require that the salespeople provide a user ID and password to access the blog. That, however, is just one more thing for them to remember to do, and, in the busy sales season, they are likely to forget their ID or password or leave it at home. Still, it could be done.

Emerson supports a private network that is protected from outside access by a firewall (discussed in this chapter). Employees can access that network from the Internet using a VPN (discussed in this chapter). So, if she places the blog server within the Emerson network, it will be protected from unauthorized access, and the salespeople can access it using the same password they use to access the VPN. Placing the blog within the network requires the permission and support of the internal IT department. As you will see, Dee could have used the knowledge from this chapter to enlist (or leverage) the support of that department.

Optional Extensions for this chapter are CE7, "How the Internet Works," and CE8, "Understanding SOHO Networks."

Study Questions

Q1 What is a computer network?

Q2 What are the components of a LAN?

Q3 What are the alternatives for a WAN?

Q4 How does encryption work?

Q5 What is the purpose of a firewall?

Q6 What is a VPN, and why is it important?

How does the knowledge in this chapter help Dee and you?

Q1   What Is a Computer Network?

A computer **network** is a collection of computers that communicate with one another over transmission lines. As shown in Figure 6-1, the three basic types of networks are local area networks, wide area networks, and internets.

A **local area network (LAN)** connects computers that reside in a single geographic location on the premises of the company that operates the LAN. The number of connected computers can range from two to several hundred. The distinguishing characteristic of a LAN is *a single location.* **Wide area networks (WANs)** connect computers at different geographic locations. The computers in two separated company sites must be connected using a WAN. To illustrate, the computers for a College of Business located on a single campus can be connected via a LAN. The computers for a College of Business located on multiple campuses must be connected via a WAN.

The single versus multiple-site distinction is important. With a LAN, an organization can place communications lines wherever it wants, because all lines reside on its premises. The same is not true for a WAN. A company with offices in Chicago and Atlanta cannot run a wire to connect computers in the two cities. Instead, the company must contract with a communications vendor that is licensed by the government and already has lines or has the authority to run new lines between the two cities.

An **internet** is a network of networks. Internets connect LANs, WANs, and other internets. The most famous internet is "**the Internet**" (with an upper-case letter *I*), the collection of networks that you use when you send email or access a Web site. In addition to the Internet, private networks of networks, called internets, also exist.

The networks that comprise an internet use a large variety of communication methods and conventions, and data must flow seamlessly across them. To provide seamless flow, an elaborate scheme called a *layered protocol* is used. You can learn more about them in Chapter Extension 7 "How the Internet Works." For now, understand that a **protocol** is a set of rules that two communicating devices follow. There are many different protocols; some are used for LANs, some are used for WANs, some are used for internets and the Internet, and some are used for all of these. The important point is that for two devices to communicate, they must both use the same protocol.

Q2   What Are the Components of a LAN?

A local area network (LAN) is a group of computers connected together on a single company site. Usually the computers are located within a half mile or so of each other, although longer distances are possible. The key distinction, however,

Figure 6-1
Major Network Types

Type	Characteristic
Local Area Network (LAN)	Computers connected at a single physical site
Wide Area Network (WAN)	Computers connected between two or more separated sites
The Internet and internets	Networks of networks

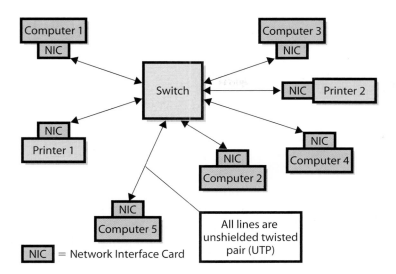

Figure 6-2
Local Area Network (LAN)

is that all of the computers are located on property controlled by the company that operates the LAN. This means that the company can run cables wherever needed to connect the computers.

Consider the LAN in Figure 6-2. Here, five computers and two printers connect via a **switch**, which is a special-purpose computer that receives and transmits messages on the LAN. In Figure 6-2, when Computer 1 accesses Printer 1, it does so by sending the print job to the switch, which then redirects that data to Printer 1.

Each device on a LAN (computer, printer, etc.) has a hardware component called a **network interface card (NIC)** that connects the device's circuitry to the cable. The NIC works with programs in each device to implement the protocols necessary for communication. On older machines, the NIC is a card that fits into an expansion slot. Newer machines have an **onboard NIC**, which is an NIC built into the computer.

Figure 6-3 shows a typical NIC device. Each NIC has a unique identifier, which is called the **MAC (media access control) address**. The computers, printers, switches, and other devices on a LAN are connected using one of two media. Most connections are made using **unshielded twisted pair (UTP) cable**. Figure 6-4 (page 118) shows a section of UTP cable that contains four pairs of twisted wire. A device called an RJ-45 connector is used to connect the UTP cable into NIC devices on the LAN.

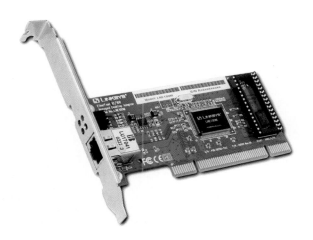

Figure 6-3
Network Interface Card (NIC)

Figure 6-4.
Unshielded Twisted Pair (UTP)
Cable

By the way, wires are twisted for reasons beyond aesthetics and style. Twisting the wires substantially reduces the cross-wire signal interference that occurs when wires run parallel for long distances.

Some LANs, usually those larger than the one in Figure 6-2, use more than one switch. Typically, in a building with several floors, a switch is placed on each floor, and the computers on that floor are connected to the switch with UTP cable. The switches on each floor are connected together by a main switch, which is often located in the basement.

The connections between switches can use UTP cable, but if they carry a lot of traffic or are far apart, UTP cable may be replaced by **optical fiber cables**. The signals on such cables are light rays, and they are reflected inside the glass core of the optical fiber cable. The core is surrounded by a *cladding* to contain the light signals, and the cladding, in turn, is wrapped with an outer layer to protect it. Optical fiber cable uses special connectors called ST and SC connectors, which are shown as the blue plugs in Figure 6-5. The meaning of the abbreviations ST and SC are unimportant; they are just the two most common optical connectors.

Figure 6-5
Optical Fiber Cable

The IEEE 802.3, or Ethernet, Protocol

For a LAN to work, all devices on the LAN must use the same protocol. The Institute for Electrical and Electronics Engineers (IEEE, pronounced "I triple E") sponsors committees that create and publish protocols and other standards. The committee that addresses LAN standards is called the *IEEE 802 Committee*. Thus, IEEE LAN protocols always start with the numbers 802.

Today, the world's most popular protocol for LANs is the **IEEE 802.3 protocol**. This protocol standard, also called **Ethernet**, specifies hardware characteristics, such as which wire carries which signals. It also describes how messages are to be packaged and processed for transmission over the LAN.

Most personal computers today are equipped with an onboard NIC that supports what is called **10/100/1000 Ethernet**. These products conform to the 802.3 specification and allow for transmission at a rate of 10, 100, or 1,000 Mbps (megabits per second). Switches detect the speed that a given device can handle and communicate with it at that speed. If you check computer listings at Dell, Hewlett-Packard, Toshiba, and other manufacturers, you will see PCs advertised as having 10/100/1000 Ethernet.

By the way, the abbreviations used for communication speeds differ from those used for computer memory. For communications equipment, *k* stands for 1,000, not 1,024 as it does for memory. Similarly, *M* stands for 1,000,000, not 1,024 × 1,024; *G* stands for 1,000,000,000, not 1,024 × 1,024 × 1,024. Thus, 100 Mbps is 100,000,000 bits per second. Also note that communications speeds are expressed in *bits*, whereas memory sizes are expressed in *bytes*.

LANs with Wireless Connections

In recent years, wireless connections have become popular with LANs. Figure 6-6 shows a LAN in which two of the computers and one printer have wireless connections. Notice that the NIC for the wireless devices have been replaced by a **wireless NIC (WNIC)**. For laptop computers, such devices can be cards that slide into an expansion slot or they can be built-in, onboard devices.

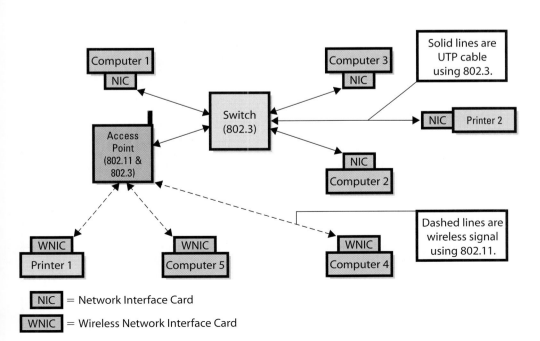

Figure 6-6
Local Area Network with Wireless

Several different wireless protocols exist. As of 2006, the most popular is IEEE 802.11g. The differences among the variations are beyond the scope of this discussion. Just note that the current standard, 802.11g, allows speeds of up to 54 Mbps.

Observe that the LAN in Figure 6-6 uses both the 802.3 and 802.11 protocols. The NICs operate according to the 802.3 protocol and connect directly to the switch, which also operates on the 802.3 standard. The WNICs operate according to the 802.11 protocol and connect to an **access point (AP)**. The AP must be able to process messages according to both the 802.3 and 802.11 standards, because it sends and receives wireless traffic using the 802.11 protocol and then communicates with the switch using the 802.3 protocol. Characteristics of LANs are summarized in the top part of Figure 6-7.

Figure 6-7
Summary of LAN and WAN Networks

Type	Topology	Transmission Line	Transmission Speed	Equipment Used	Protocol Commonly Used	Remarks
Local Area Network	Local area network	UTP or optical fiber	10, 100, or 1,000 Mbps	Switch NIC UTP or optical	IEEE 802.3 (Ethernet)	Switches connect devices, multiple switches on all but small LANs.
	Local area network with wireless	UTP or optical for non-wireless connections	Up to 54 Mbps	Wireless access point Wireless NIC	IEEE 802.11g	Access point transforms wired LAN (802.3) to wireless LAN (802.11).
Wide Area Network	Dial-up modem to Internet service provider (ISP)	Regular telephone	Up to 55 kbps	Modem Telephone line	Modulation standards (V.32, V90, V92), PPP	Modulation required for first part of telephone line. Computer use blocks telephone use.
	DSL modem to ISP	DSL telephone	Personal: Upstream to 256 kbps, downstream to 768 kbps Business: to 1.544 Mbps	DSL modem DSL-capable telephone line	DSL	Can have computer and phone use simultaneously. Always connected.
	Cable modem to ISP	Cable TV lines to optical cable	Upstream to 256 kbps Downstream 300–600 kbps (10 Mbps in theory)	Cable modem Cable TV cable	Cable	Capacity is shared with other sites; performance varies depending on others' use.
	Point to point lines	Network of leased lines	T1–1.5 Mbps T3– 44.7Mbps OC48–2.5Gbps OC768–40 Gbps	Access devices Optical cable Satellite	PPP	Span geographically distributed sites using lines provided by licensed communications vendors. Expensive to set up and manage.
	PSDN	Lease usage of private network	56 Kbps–40 Mbps+	Leased line to PSDN POP	Frame-relay ATM 10 Gbps and 40 Gbps Ethernet	Lease time on a public switched data network–operated by independent party. Ineffective for inter-company communication.
	Virtual private network (VPN)	Use the Internet to provide private network	Varies with speed of connection to Internet	VPN client software VPN server hardware and software	PPTP IPSec	Secure, private connection provides a tunnel through the Internet. Can support intercompany communication.

Knowledge of local area networks and wireless technology enabled one student to start a successful and profitable business, while still in college. Read the *MIS in Use 6* feature on page 122 to see how.

Q3 What Are the Alternatives for a WAN?

Video

A wide area network (WAN) connects computers located at physically separated sites. A company with offices in Detroit and Atlanta must use a WAN to connect the computers together. Because the sites are physically separated, the company cannot string wire from one site to another. Rather, it must obtain connection capabilities from another company (or companies) licensed by the government to provide communications.

Although you may not have realized it, when you connect your personal computer to the Internet, you are using a WAN. You are connecting to computers owned and operated by your **Internet service provider (ISP)** that are not located physically at your site.

An ISP has three important functions. First, it provides you with a legitimate Internet address. Second, it serves as your gateway to the Internet. The ISP receives the communications from your computer and passes them on to the Internet, and it receives communications from the Internet and passes them on to you. Finally, ISPs pay for the Internet. They collect money from their customers and pay access fees and other charges on your behalf.

We begin our discussion of WANs by considering modem connections to ISPs.

Connecting the Personal Computer to an ISP: Modems

Home computers and those of small businesses are commonly connected to an ISP in one of three ways: using a regular telephone line, using a special telephone line called a DSL line, or using a cable TV line.

All three of these alternatives require that the *digital data* in the computer be converted to an **analog**, or wavy, signal. A device called a **modem**, or modulator/demodulator, performs this conversion. Figure 6-8 shows one way of converting the digital byte 01000001 to an analog signal.

As shown in Figure 6-9, once the modem converts your computer's digital data to analog, that analog signal is then sent over the telephone line or TV cable. If sent by telephone line, the first telephone switch that your signal reaches converts the signal into the form used by the international telephone system.

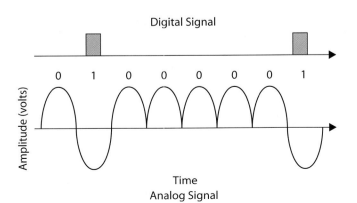

Figure 6-8
Analog Versus Digital Signals

MIS in use 6

Larry Jones (Student) Network Services

In 2003, Larry Jones was an entering freshman at Big State University. (This case is real; however, to protect privacy, the student and university names are fictional.) Larry had always been interested in technology and as a high school student had won a scholarship from Cisco Corporation (a maker of communications hardware). As part of his scholarship, Larry had attended several Cisco training classes on setting up LANs, switches, and other devices.

Larry pledged a fraternity at Big State, and when the fraternity leadership learned of his expertise, they asked him to set up a LAN with an Internet connection for the fraternity house. It was a simple job for Larry, and his fraternity brothers were quite satisfied with his solution. He did it for free, as a volunteer, and

appreciated the introductions the project gave him to senior leaders of the fraternity. The project enabled him to build his network of personal contacts.

Over the summer of 2003, however, it dawned on Larry that his fraternity was not the only one on the Big State campus that had the need for a LAN with access to the Internet. Accordingly, that summer he developed marketing materials describing the need and the services he could provide. That fall he called on fraternities and sororities and made presentations of his skills and of the network he had built for the fraternity. Within a year, he had a dozen or so fraternities and sororities as customers.

Larry quickly realized that he couldn't just set up a LAN and Internet connection, charge his fee, and walk away. His customers had continuing problems that required him to return to resolve problems, add new computers, add printer servers, and so forth. At first, he provided such support as part of his installation package price. He soon learned that he could charge a support fee for regular support, and even add extra charges for support beyond normal wear and tear. By the end of 2004, the support fees were meeting all of Larry's college expenses, and then some.

When I last saw him, Larry had formed a partnership with several other students to expand his services to local apartment houses and condominiums.

This case is continued as Case Study 6 at the end of this chapter (page 136).

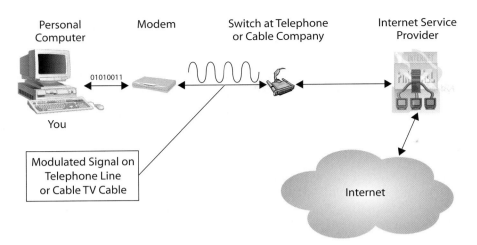

Figure 6-9
Personal Computer (PC) Internet Access

Dial-Up Modems

A **dial-up modem** performs the conversion between analog and digital in such a way that the signal can be carried on a regular telephone line. As the name implies, you dial the phone number for your ISP and connect. The maximum transmission speed for a switch is 56 kbps (in practice, the limit is 53 kbps). By the way, when two devices connected by modems use different speeds, the slower speed is the one at which they operate.

Modulation is governed by one of three standards: V.34, V.90, and V.92. These standards specify how digital signals will be transformed into analog. The way in which messages are packaged and handled between your modem and the ISP is governed by a protocol known as the **Point-to-Point Protocol (PPP)**.

DSL Modems

A **DSL modem** is the second modem type. DSL stands for **digital subscriber line**. DSL modems operate on the same lines as voice telephones and dial-up modems, but they operate so that their signals do not interfere with voice telephone service. DSL modems provide much faster data transmission speeds than dial-up modems. Additionally, DSL modems always maintain a connection, so there is no need to dial up; the Internet connection is available immediately.

Because DSL signals do not interfere with telephone signals, DSL data transmission and telephone conversations can occur simultaneously. A device at the telephone company separates the phone signals from the computer signals and sends the latter signal to the ISP. DSL modems use their own protocols for data transmission.

There are gradations of DSL service and speed. Most home DSL lines can download data at speeds ranging from 256 kbps to 768 kbps and can upload data at slower speeds—for example, 256 kbps. DSL lines that have different upload and download speeds are called **asymmetric digital subscriber lines (ADSL)**. Most homes and small businesses can use ADSL because they receive more data than they transmit (e.g., pictures in news stories), and hence. they do not need to transmit as fast as they receive.

Some users and larger businesses, however, need DSL lines that have the same receiving and transmitting speeds. They also need performance-level guarantees. **Symmetrical digital subscriber lines (SDSL)** meet this need by offering the same fast speed in both directions. As much as 1.544 Mbps can be guaranteed.

Cable Modems

A **cable modem** is the third modem type. Cable modems provide high-speed data transmission using cable television lines. The cable company installs a fast, high-capacity optical fiber cable to a distribution center in each neighborhood that it serves. At the distribution center, the optical fiber cable connects to regular cable-television cables that run to subscribers' homes or businesses. Cable modems modulate in such a way that their signals do not interfere with TV signals. Like DSL lines, they are always on.

Because up to 500 user sites can share these facilities, performance varies depending on how many other users are sending and receiving data. At the maximum, users can download data up to 10 Mbps and can upload data at 256 kbps. Typically, performance is much lower than this. In most cases, the speed of cable modems and DSL modems is about the same. Cable modems use their own protocols. Figure 6-7 (page 120) summarizes these alternatives.

You will sometimes hear the terms *narrowband* and *broadband* with regard to communications speeds. **Narrowband** lines typically have transmissions speeds less than 56 kbps. **Broadband** lines have speeds in excess of 256 kbps. Thus, a dial-up modem provides narrowband access, and DSL and cable modems provide broadband access.

The variety of LAN and WAN connections have resulted in the almost unbelievable growth of personal and business computing in the past 10 years. The *Guide* on pages 125a–125b discusses possible responses to such exponential growth.

Networks of Leased Lines

As shown in Figure 6-7, a second WAN alternative is to create a **network of leased lines** between company sites. Figure 6-10 shows a WAN that connects computers located at three geographically distributed company sites. The lines that connect these sites are leased from telecommunications companies that are licensed to provide them.

A variety of **access devices** connect each site to the transmission lines. These devices are typically special-purpose computers; the particular devices required depend on the line used and other factors. Sometimes switches are used, and in other cases, a device called a router is used. A **router** is a special-purpose computer that moves network traffic from one node on a network to another. See Chapter Extension 7 "How the Internet Works" (p. 395) for more information.

Figure 6-10
WAN Using Leased Lines

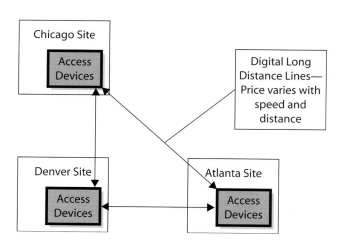

Line Type	Use	Maximum Speed
Telephone line (twisted pair copper lines)	Dial-up modem	56 Kbps
	DSL modem	1.544 Mbps
	WAN—T1—using a pair of telephone lines	1.544 Mbps
Coaxial cable	Cable modem	Upstream to 256 Kbps Downstream to 10 Mbps (usually much less, however)
Unshielded twisted pair (UTP)	LAN	100 Mbps
Optical fiber cable	LAN and WAN—T3, OC-768, etc.	40 Gbps or more
Satellite	WAN—OC-768, etc.	40 Gbps or more

Figure 6-11
Transmission Line Types, Uses, and Speeds

Several leased-line alternatives exist. As shown in Figure 6-11, lines are classified by their use and speed. A T1 line can support up to 1.544 Mbps; a T3 line can support up to 44.736 Mbps. Using optical fiber cable, even faster lines are possible; an OC-768 line supports 40 Gbps. Except for T1 speeds, faster lines require either optical fiber cable or satellite communication. T1 speeds can be supported by regular telephone wires as well as by optical fiber cable and satellite communication.

Setting up a point-to-point line, once it has been leased, requires considerable work by highly trained, expensive specialists. Connecting the company's LANs and other facilities is a challenging task, and maintaining those connections is expensive. In some cases, organizations contract with third parties to set up and support the lines they have leased.

Notice, too, that with point-to-point lines, as the number of sites increases, the number of lines required increases dramatically. If another site is added to the network in Figure 6-11, up to three new leased lines will be needed. In general, if a network has *n* sites, as many as *n* additional lines need to be leased, set up, and supported to connect a new site to all the other sites.

Furthermore, only predefined sites can use the leased lines. It is not possible for an employee working at a temporary, remote location, such as a hotel, to use this network. Similarly, customers or vendors cannot use such a network, either.

However, if an organization has substantial traffic between fixed sites, leased lines can provide a low cost per bit transmitted. A company like Boeing, for example, with major facilities in Seattle, St. Louis, and Los Angeles, could benefit by using leased lines to connect these sites. The operations of such a company require transmitting huge amounts of data between those fixed sites. Further, such a company knows how to hire and manage the technical personnel required to support such a network.

Public Switched Data Network

Yet another WAN alternative is a **public switched data network (PSDN)**, a network of computers and leased lines that is developed and maintained by a vendor that leases time on the network to other organizations. A PSDN is a utility that supplies

Thinking Exponentially Is Not Possible, but . . .

Nathan Myhrvold, the chief scientist at Microsoft Corporation during the 1990s, once said that humans are incapable of thinking exponentially. Instead, when something changes exponentially, we think of the fastest linear change we can imagine and extrapolate from there, as illustrated in the figure on the next page. Myhrvold was writing about the exponential growth of magnetic storage. His point was that no one could then imagine how much growth there would be in magnetic storage, and what we would do with it.

This limitation pertains equally well to the growth of computer network phenomena. We have witnessed exponential growth in a number of areas: the number of Internet connections, the number of Web pages, and the amount of data accessible on the Internet. And, all signs are that this exponential growth isn't over.

What, you might ask, does this have to do with me? Well, suppose you are a product manager for home appliances. When most homes have a wireless network, it will be cheap and easy for appliances to talk to one another. When that day arrives, what happens to your existing product line? Will the competition's talking appliances take away your market share? On the other hand, talking appliances may not satisfy a real need. If a toaster and a coffee pot have nothing to say to each other, you'll be wasting money to create them.

Every business, every organization, needs to be thinking about the ubiquitous and cheap connectivity that is growing exponentially. What are the new opportunities? What are the new threats? How will our competition react? How should we position ourselves? How should we respond? As you consider these questions, keep in mind that because humans cannot think exponentially, we're all just guessing.

So what can we do to better anticipate changes brought by exponential phenomena? For one, understand that technology does not drive people to do things they've never done before, no matter how much the technologists suggest it might. (Just because we *can* do something does not mean anyone will *want* to do that something.)

Social progress occurs in small, evolutionary, adaptive steps. Right now, for example, thousands of people are driving to stores to rent a movie. When they get there, they may not find the movie they want, they may wait in a long line, or they may never find a parking spot. Is it likely that someone would want to rent a movie online, over the Internet, if they could? Probably so; online rental is an extension of what people are already doing. It solves a problem that people already have. So, when network capacities support online movie rental, it's likely to be a success.

On the other hand, emerging network technology enables my dry cleaner to notify me the minute my clothes are ready. Do I want to know? How much do I care to know that my clothes are ready Monday at 1:45 rather than sometime after 4:00 on Tuesday? In truth, I don't care. Such technology does not solve a problem that I have.

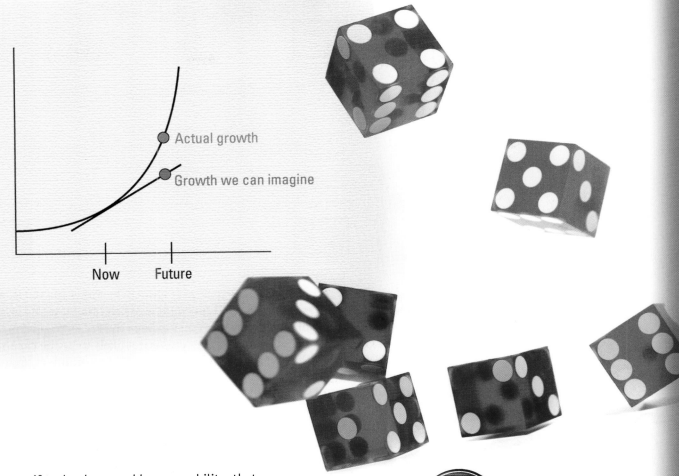

Actual growth

Growth we can imagine

Now   Future

So even if technology enables a capability, that possibility doesn't mean anyone wants that capability. People want to do what they're already doing, but more easily; they want to solve problems that they already have.

Another response to exponential growth is to hedge your bets. If you can't know the outcome of an exponential phenomenon, don't commit to one direction. Position yourself to move as soon as the direction is clear. Develop a few talking appliances, position your organization to develop more, but wait for a clear sign of market acceptance before going all out.

Finally, notice in the exponential curve that the larger the distance between Now and the Future, the larger the error. In fact, the error increases exponentially with the length of the prediction. So if you read in this textbook that wireless LANs will replace wired LANs in one year, assign that statement a certain level of doubt. On the other hand, if you read in this text that they will replace wired LANs in three years, assign that statement an exponentially greater level of doubt.

Discussion Questions

1. In your own words, explain the meaning of the claim that no one can think exponentially. Do you agree with this claim?

2. Describe a phenomenon besides connectivity or magnetic memory that you believe is increasing exponentially. Explain why it is difficult to predict the consequences of this phenomenon in five years.

3. To what extent do you think technology is responsible for the growth in the number of news sources? On balance, do you think having many news sources of varying quality is better than having a few with high quality control?

4. List three products or services, like movie rental, that could dramatically change because of increased connectivity. Do not include movie rental.

5. Rate your answers to question 3 in terms of how closely they fit with problems that people have today.

Figure 6-12
WAN Using PSDN

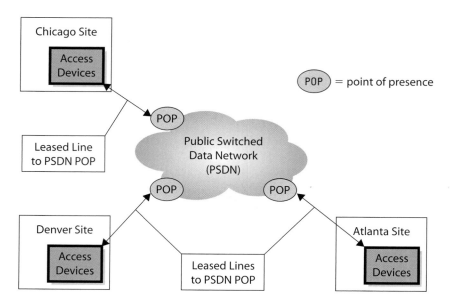

a network for other companies to lease. Figure 6-12 shows the PSDN as a cloud of capability. What happens within that cloud is of no concern to the lessees. As long as they get the availability and speed they expect, the PSDN could consist of strings of spaghetti connected by meatballs. (This is not likely to be the case, however.)

When using a PSDN, each site must lease a line to connect to the PSDN network. The location at which this occurs is called a **point of presence (POP)**; it is the access point into the PSDN. Think of the POP as the phone number that one dials to connect to the PSDN. Once a site has connected to the PSDN POP, the site obtains access to all other sites connected to the PSDN.

PSDNs save the setup and maintenance activities required when using leased lines. They also save costs because a company does not have to pay for the entire network; the company can pay just for the traffic that it sends. Further, using a PSDN requires much less management involvement than using leased lines. Another advantage of PSDNs is that only one line is required to connect a new site to all other sites.

Three protocols are used with PSDNs: Frame Relay, ATM (asynchronous transfer mode), and Ethernet. **Frame Relay** can process traffic in the range of 56 kbps to 40 Mbps. **Asynchronous transfer mode (ATM)** can process speeds from 1 to 156 Mbps. Frame Relay, although slower, is simpler and easier to support than ATM, and PSDNs can offer it at lower cost than ATM. On the other hand, some organizations need ATM's faster speed. Also, ATM can support both voice and data communication.

Often, PSDNs offer both Frame Relay and ATM on their network. Customers can choose whichever technique best fits their needs. Some companies use a PSDN network in lieu of a long-distance telephone carrier.

Ethernet, the protocol developed for LANs, also is used as a PSDN protocol. Newer versions of Ethernet can operate at speeds of 10 and 40 Gpbs.

Criteria for Comparing WANs

As you have learned, many different computer networking alternatives are available, each with different characteristics. Choosing among them can be a complicated task. Figure 6-13 lists three categories of criteria you can use to compare alternatives.

Criteria Category	Criteria	Description
Cost	Initial setup	Transmission line; equipment setup fees, including labor and training costs
	Operational	Fees for leases of lines and equipment; ISP and other service fees; ongoing training
	Maintenance	Periodic maintenance costs; problem diagnosis and repair costs; mandatory upgrade costs
Performance	Speed	Line and equipment speed
	Latency	Delays during busy periods
	Availability	Frequency of service outage
	Loss rate	Frequency retransmission required
	Transparency	User involvement in operation
	Performance guarantees?	Vendors agree to cost penalties if levels of service not met
Other	Growth potential	How difficult to upgrade when service needs or capacity increase?
	Commitment periods	Length of leases and other agreements
	Management time	How much management activity is required?
	Risk, financial	How much is at stake if system not effective?
	Technical	If using new technology, what is the likelihood of failure?

Figure 6-13
Criteria for Comparing
Networking Alternatives

As shown, managers need to consider three types of costs. *Setup costs* include the costs of acquiring transmission lines and equipment, such as switches, routers, and access devices. If lines or equipment are leased, setup fees also may be involved. Additionally, if your company is performing some of the setup work itself, labor costs need to be included. Finally, there are training costs. *Operational costs* include lease fees for lines and equipment, charges of the ISP, and the cost of ongoing training. *Maintenance costs* include those for periodic maintenance, for problem diagnosis and repair, and for mandatory upgrades.

Figure 6-13 shows six considerations with regard to performance: Line and equipment *speed* are self-explanatory. *Latency* is the transmission delay that occurs due to network congestion during busy periods. *Availability* refers to the frequency and length of service outages. *Loss rate* is the frequency of problems in the communications network that necessitate data retransmission. *Transparency* is the degree to which the user is unaware of the underlying communications system. For example, a DSL modem that is always connected is more transparent than a dial-up modem, which must find a phone line that is not in use and then dial the ISP number. The greater the transparency, the greater the ease of network use. Finally, many vendors of communications equipment and services are willing to make *performance guarantees* that commit them to levels of service quality. When a performance guarantee is in place, the vendor agrees to cost penalties if agreed-upon levels are not met.

Other criteria to consider when comparing network alternatives include the growth potential (greater capacity) and the length of contract commitment periods. Shorter periods allow for greater flexibility and usually are preferred. Also, how much management time is required? An alternative that requires in-house technical staff will require more management time than one that does not. The final two criteria consider financial and technical risk.

Q4 How Does Encryption Work?

Encryption is the process of transforming clear text into coded, unintelligible text for secure storage or communication. Considerable research has gone into developing **encryption algorithms** that are difficult to break. Commonly used methods are DES, 3DES, and AES; search the Internet for these terms if you want to know more about them.

A **key** is a number used to encrypt the data. The encryption algorithm applies the key to the original message to produce the coded message. Decoding (decrypting) a message is similar; a key is applied to the coded message to recover the original text. In **symmetric encryption**, the same key is used to encode and to decode. With **asymmetric encryption**, different keys are used; one key encodes the message, and the other key decodes the message. Symmetric encryption is simpler and much faster than asymmetric encryption.

A special version of asymmetric encryption, **public key/private key**, is popular on the Internet. With this method, each site has a public key for encoding messages and a private key for decoding them. (For now, suppose we have two generic computers, A and B.) To exchange secure messages, A and B send each other their public keys as uncoded text. Thus, A receives B's public key and B receives A's public key, all as uncoded text. Now, when A sends a message to B, it encrypts the message using B's public key and sends the encrypted message to B. Computer B receives the encrypted message from A and decodes it using its private key. Similarly, when B wants to send an encrypted message to A, it encodes its message with A's public key and sends the encrypted message to A. Computer A then decodes B's message with its own private key. The private keys are never communicated. Encryption can be used only for short messages.

Most secure communication over the Internet uses a protocol called **HTTPS**. With HTTPS, data are encrypted using a protocol called the **Secure Socket Layer (SSL)**, also known as **Transport Layer Security (TLS)**. SSL/TLS uses a combination of public key/private key and symmetric encryption. It works as follows: First, your computer obtains the public key of the Web server to which it will connect. Your computer then generates a key for symmetric encryption and encodes that key using the Web site's public key. It sends the encrypted symmetric key to the Web site. The Web site then decodes the symmetric key using its private key.

From that point forward, your computer and the Web site communicate using symmetric encryption. At the end of the session, your computer and the secure site discard the keys. Using this strategy, the bulk of the secure communication occurs using the faster symmetric encryption. Also, because keys are used for short intervals, there is less likelihood they can be discovered.

Use of SSL/TLS makes it safe to send sensitive data like credit card numbers and bank balances. Just be certain that you see https//: in your browser and not just http://. If you wish to learn more about SSL/TLS, https, and public/private keys, read Chapter Extension 23.

Warning: Under normal circumstances, neither email nor instant messaging (IM) uses encryption. It would be quite easy for one of your classmates or your professor to read any email or IM that you send over a wireless network in your classroom, in the student lounge, at a coffee shop, or in any other wireless setting. Let the sender beware! If you wish to learn more about SSL/TLS, https, and public/private keys, read Chapter Extension 23.

Q5 What Is the Purpose of a Firewall?

A **firewall** is a computing device that prevents unauthorized network access. A firewall can be a special-purpose computer, or it can be a program on a general-purpose computer or on a router.

Organizations normally use multiple firewalls. A **perimeter firewall** sits outside the organizational network; it is the first device that Internet traffic encounters. In addition to perimeter firewalls, some organizations employ **internal firewalls** inside the organizational network. Figure 6-14 shows the use of a perimeter firewall that protects all of an organization's computers and a second internal firewall that protects a LAN.

A **packet-filtering firewall** examines each part of a message and determines whether to let that part pass. To make this decision, it examines the source address, the destination address(es), and other data.

Packet-filtering firewalls can prohibit outsiders from starting a session with any user behind the firewall. They can also disallow traffic from particular sites, such as known hacker addresses. They also can prohibit traffic from legitimate, but unwanted addresses, such as competitors' computers. Firewalls can filter outbound traffic as well. They can keep employees from accessing specific sites, such as competitors' sites, sites with pornographic material, or popular news sites.

A firewall has an **access control list (ACL)**, which encodes the rules stating which addresses are to be allowed and which are to be prohibited. As a future manager, if you have particular sites with which you do not want your employees to communicate, you can ask your IS department to enforce that limit via the ACL in one or more routers. Most likely, your IS organization has a procedure for making such requests.

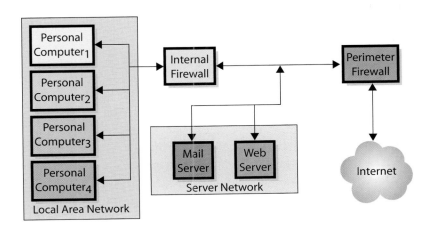

Figure 6-14
Use of Multiple Firewalls

Packet-filtering firewalls are the simplest type of firewall. Other firewalls filter on a more sophisticated basis. If you take a data communications class, you will learn about them. For now, just understand that firewalls help to protect organizational computers from unauthorized network access.

No computer should connect to the Internet without firewall protection. Many ISPs provide firewalls for their customers. By nature, these firewalls are generic. Large organizations supplement such generic firewalls with their own. Most home routers include firewalls, and Windows XP has a built-in firewall as well. Third parties also license firewall products.

Q6 What Is a VPN, and Why Is It Important?

The **virtual private network (VPN)** is the fourth WAN alternative shown in Figure 6-7 (page 120). A VPN uses the Internet or a private internet to create the appearance of private point-to-point connections. In the IT world, the term *virtual* means something that appears to exist that does not in fact exist. Here, a VPN uses the public Internet to create the appearance of a private connection.

A Typical VPN

Figure 6-15 shows one way to create a VPN to connect a remote computer, perhaps an employee working at a hotel in Miami, to a LAN at the Chicago site. The remote user is the VPN client. That client first establishes a connection to the Internet. The connection can be obtained by accessing a local ISP as shown in the figure; or, in some hotels, the hotel itself provides a direct Internet connection.

In either case, once the Internet connection is made, VPN software on the remote user's computer establishes a connection with the VPN server in Chicago. The VPN client and VPN server then have a point-to-point connection. That connection, called a **tunnel**, is a virtual, private pathway over a public or shared network from the VPN client to the VPN server. Figure 6-16 illustrates the connection as it appears to the remote user.

VPN communications are secure, even though they are transmitted over the public Internet. To ensure security, VPN client software *encrypts*, or codes, the original message so that its contents are hidden. Then the VPN client appends the Internet address of the VPN server to the message and sends that

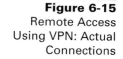

Figure 6-15
Remote Access
Using VPN: Actual
Connections

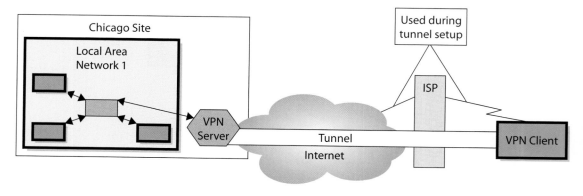

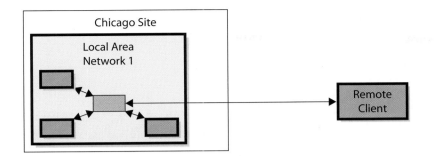

Figure 6-16
Remote Access Using VPN:
Apparent Connection

package over the Internet to the VPN server. When the VPN server receives the message, it strips its address off the front of the message, *decrypts* the coded message, and sends the plain text message to the original address on the LAN. In this way, secure private messages are delivered over the public Internet.

VPNs offer the benefit of point-to-point leased lines, and they enable remote access, both by employees and by any others who have been registered with the VPN server. For example, if customers or vendors are registered with the VPN server, they can use the VPN from their own sites. Figure 6-17 shows three tunnels; one supports a point-to-point connection between the Atlanta and Chicago sites, and the other two support remote connections.

Microsoft has fostered the popularity of VPNs by including VPN support in Windows. All versions of Microsoft Windows have the capability of working as VPN clients. Windows server products can operate as VPN servers.

In this chapter, you've learned (a lot, we hope) about computer networks. Read the *Ethics Guide* on pages 131a–131b for insights into the importance of your *human* networks as well.

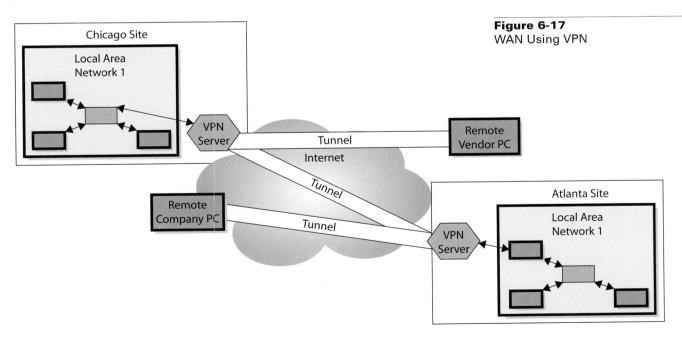

Figure 6-17
WAN Using VPN

ETHICS
GUIDE

Human Networks Matter More

In case you missed it, *Six Degrees of Separation* is a play by John Guare that was made into a movie starring Stockard Channing and Donald Sutherland. The title is related to the idea, originated by the Hungarian writer Frigyes Karinthy, that everyone on earth is connected to everyone else by five (Karinthy) or six (Guare) people.[1] For example, according to the theory, you are connected to Eminem by no more than five or six people, because you know someone who knows someone, who knows someone, etc. By the same theory, you are also connected to a Siberian seal hunter. Today, in fact, with the Internet, the number may be closer to three people than to five or six, but in any case, the theory points out the importance of human networks.

Suppose you want to meet your university's president. The president has a secretary who acts as a gatekeeper. If you walk up to that secretary and say, "I'd like a half an hour with President Jones," you're likely to be palmed off to some other university administrator. What else can you do?

If you are connected to everyone on the planet by no more than six degrees, then surely you are connected to your president in fewer steps. Perhaps you play on the tennis team, and you know that the president plays tennis. In that case, it is likely that the tennis coach knows the president. So arrange a tennis match with your coach and the president. Voilà! You have your meeting. It may even be better to have the meeting on the tennis court than in the president's office.

[1]See "The Third Link" in Albert Laszlo Barabasi's book *Linked* (New York: Perseus Publishing, 2002) for background on this theory.

The problem with the six-degree theory, as Stockard Channing said so eloquently, is that even though those six people do exist, we don't know who they are. Even worse, we often don't know who the person is with whom we want to connect. For example, there is someone, right now who knows someone who has a job for which you are perfectly suited. Unfortunately, you don't know the name of that person.

It doesn't stop when you get your job, either. When you have a problem at work, like setting up a blog within the corporate network, there is someone who knows exactly how to help you. You, however, don't know who that is.

Accordingly, most successful professionals consistently build personal human networks. They keep building them because they know that somewhere there is someone whom they need to know or will need to know. They meet people at professional and social situations, collect and pass out cards, and engage in pleasant conversation (all part of a social protocol) to expand their networks.

You can apply some of the ideas about computer networks to make this process more efficient. Consider the network diagram here.

Assume that each line represents a relationship between two people. Notice that the people in your department tend to know each other, and the people in the accounting department also tend to know each other. That's typical.

Now suppose you are at the weekly employee after-hours party and you have an opportunity to introduce yourself either to Linda or Eileen. Setting aside personal considerations, thinking just about network building, which person should you meet?

131a

If you introduce yourself to Linda, you shorten your pathway to her from two steps to one and your pathway to Shawna from three to two. You do not open up any new channels because you already have them to the people in your floor.

However, if you introduce yourself to Eileen, you open up an entirely new network of acquaintances. So, considering just network building, you use your time better by meeting Eileen and other people who are not part of your current circle. It opens up many more possibilities.

The connection from you to Eileen is called a *weak tie* in social network theory,[2] and such links are crucial in connecting you to everyone in six degrees. *In general, the people you know the least contribute the most to your network.*

This concept is simple, but you'd be surprised by how few people pay attention to it. At most company events, everyone talks with the people they know, and if the purpose of the function is to have fun, then that behavior makes sense. In truth, however, no business social function exists for having fun, regardless of what people say. Business functions exist for business reasons, and you can use them to create and expand networks. Given that time is always limited, you may as well use such functions efficiently.

[2]See Terry Granovetter, "The Strength of Weak Ties," *American Journal of Sociology*, May 1973.

DISCUSSION QUESTIONS

1. Determine the shortest path from you to your university's president. How many links does it have?

2. Give an example of a network to which you belong that is like your floor in the figure on the preceding page. Sketch a diagram of who knows whom for six or so members of that group.

3. Recall a recent social situation and identify two people, one of whom could have played the role of Linda (someone in your group whom you do not know) and one of whom could have played the role of Eileen (someone in a different group whom you do not know). How could you have introduced yourself to either person?

4. Does it seem too contrived and calculating to think about your social relationships in this way? Even if you do not approach relationships like this, are you surprised to think that others do? Under what circumstances does this kind of analysis seem appropriate, and when does it seem inappropriate? Are you using people?

5. Consider the phrase, "It's not what you know, it's whom you know that matters." Relate this phrase to the diagram. Under what circumstances is this likely to be true? When is it false? When is it ethical?

6. Describe how you can apply the principle, "The people you know the least contribute the most to your network" to the process of a job search. Are you abusing your relationships for personal gain?

How does the knowledge in this chapter help Dee and you?

The knowledge in this and the prior two chapters enables Dee to understand a diagram of the IS that supports her blog, like the one shown in Figure 6-18. On the left are two types of client computers: Dee's and the computers used by the salespeople. Both types are thin clients; Dee uses a page provided by Moveable Type that enables her to create blog entries, and the salespeople use pages of blog content that are also served by Moveable Type.

The client computers contain VPN client software. That software interacts with the VPN server via the Internet. By using the VPN, both Dee and the salespeople have a secure, private connection over the Internet. On the server side, a firewall stops any traffic that is not addressed to the VPN server; only snoopers or viruses would attempt to access this network without using the VPN. Once authenticated by user ID and password, the VPN server will allow access to the servers within the network, including the blog server.

Figure 6-18
Using a Firewall and the VPN for the Blog

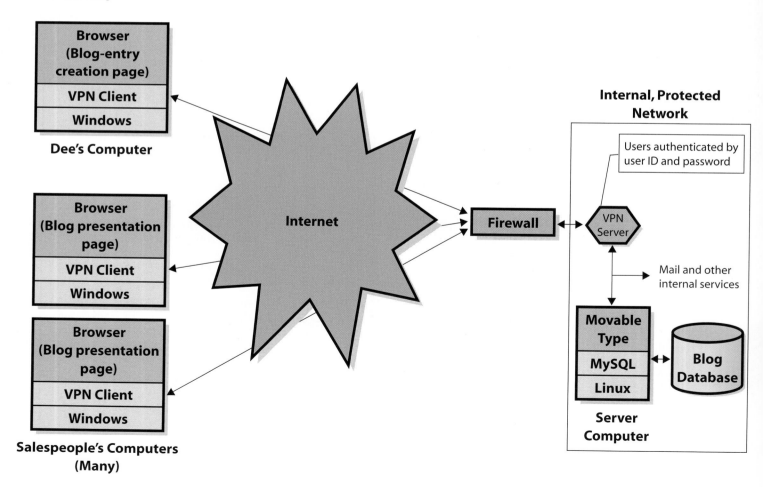

The salespeople already know how to access the VPN, so Dee wants them to use this system. Because of the short time frame, however, the Emerson IT department says that they are unable to schedule the resources necessary to set up the blog server. Dee's consultant Don has the time and skill to set up that server, but the Emerson IT department will not allow an outside person to access their network. Once inside, anyone with technical skills and a desire to cause mischief could easily do so.

Dee is at an impasse. She understands why Emerson doesn't want a stranger installing programs on her computer. Meanwhile, her boss is asking her daily whether her blog will be ready for the national sales meeting.

In desperation, she calls Don, who suggests the following compromise: If Emerson will make an unprotected, test server available to him, one that is outside its network, he can set up all of the blog software exactly as it will need to exist on the operational server. He, Dee, and the IT department can test that server. Once it is working, he can write instructions for the IT personnel to copy the test-server software onto a server within the network, and the production blog will be up and running.

This is not a perfect solution. It does require some internal IT department labor. Also, were Don a criminal, it would be possible for him to include a Trojan horse virus in his code. To avoid this possibility, Don creates the instructions so that the IT department will be installing only public software from known sources; they can obtain Moveable Type from its vendor, MySQL from its vendor, and Linux from its vendor. Then they copy the blog database from the test server. In this way, the IT department will be installing software from known sources, and none of Don's code will ever reside on any production server.

Ultimately, this is exactly what happened. However, it was not easy for Dee. She had to get an email from her boss's boss to a high-level IT manager in order to get the approval. Also, she used the knowledge she'd gained from Don and her negotiating skills to force the IT department's hand. She threatened that if they didn't cooperate, she would set up her own system of user IDs and passwords and place her blog on a public server on which she would rent time. She hoped it would not come to that, but she knew that the IT department knew that such a duplicate set of user IDs and passwords would confuse the salespeople. Ultimately, it would be the IT department who would have to straighten out the mess. She wanted them to view her proposal as the lesser of two evils. That's not exactly fair play, as we learn when we view this situation from the IT department's perspective in Chapter 11, but it worked for Dee in this instance.

You are the ultimate beneficiary of this story, however. Dee had to pay in blood, sweat, tears, lost sleep, and money to learn what she needed to know. All you had to do was read six chapters.

Active ? Review

Use this Active Review to verify that you understand the material in the chapter. You can read the entire chapter and then perform the tasks in this review, or you can read the material for just one question and perform the tasks in this review for that question before moving on to the next one.

Q1   What is a computer network?

Define *computer network*. Explain the differences among LANs, WANs, internets, and the Internet. Describe the purpose of a protocol.

Q2   What are the components of a LAN?

Explain the key distinction of a LAN. Describe the purpose of each of the components of Figure 6-2. Define MAC and UTP. Describe the placement of switches on a building with many floors. Explain when optical fiber cables are used for a LAN. Explain Ethernet. Describe the purpose of each of the wireless components in Figure 6-6.

Q3   What are the alternatives for a WAN?

Explain why your connection to an ISP is a WAN and not a LAN. Describe the purpose of a modem. Explain three ways you can connect to the Internet. Describe the difference between DSL and cable modems. Explain the advantages and disadvantages of leased lines. Explain each cell of Figure 6-7. Explain each cell of Figure 6-11. Explain each cell of Figure 6-13.

Q4   How does encryption work?

Define the terms *encryption* and *key*. Distinguish between an encryption key and a key of a database table (Chapter 5). Explain the difference between symmetric and asymmetric encryption. Describe the advantages of each. Explain how public key/ private key encryption works. Explain why SSL/TLS is important. Explain why you should be careful with what you write in emails and instant messages.

Q5   What is the purpose of a firewall?

Define *firewall*. Explain the role for each firewall in Figure 6-14. Describe how a manager might ask to shut off access to or from a particular site.

Q6   What is a VPN, and why is it important?

Describe the problem that a VPN solves. Use Figure 6-15 to explain one way that a VPN is set up and used. Define *tunnel*. Describe how encryption is used in a VPN. Explain why a Windows user need not license nor install other software to use a VPN.

How does the knowledge in this chapter help Dee and you?

Explain why, in Figure 6-18, the client computers in Dee's blog can be thin clients. Describe what kind of software will be used on the client computers for the blog. Explain the benefit of the VPN to Dee's blog.

Key Terms and Concepts

Access control list (ACL) 129
Access device 124
Access point (AP) 120
Analog signal 122
Asymmetric digital subscriber line (ADSL) 123
Asymmetric encryption 128

Asynchronous transfer mode (ATM) 126
Broadband 124
Cable modem 124
Dial-up modem 123
DSL (digital subscriber line) modem 123

Encryption 128
Encryption algorithms 128
Ethernet 119
Firewall 129
Frame relay 126
HTTPS 128
IEEE 802.3 protocol 119

Using Your Knowledge

1. Suppose you manage a group of seven employees in a small business. Each of your employees wants to be connected to the Internet. Consider two alternatives:
   - Alternative A: Each employee has his own modem and connects individually to the Internet
   - Alternative B: The employees' computers are connected using a LAN and the network uses a single modem to connect.
   a. Sketch the equipment and lines required for each alternative.
   b. Explain the actions you need to take to create each alternative.
   c. Compare the alternatives using the criteria in Figure 6-13.
   d. Which of these two alternatives do you recommend?

2. Consider the situation of a company that has two offices at physically separated sites. Suppose each office has a group of 15 computers.
   a. If the two offices are retail art galleries, what is likely to be the most common type of interoffice communication? Given your answer, what type of WAN do you think is most appropriate?
   b. Suppose the two offices are manufacturing sites that communicate via email and that regularly exchange large drawings and plans. What are the advantages and disadvantages of each of the four WAN types for these offices? Under what circumstances would you recommend a leased-line WAN?
   c. Suppose the two offices are the same as described in part b, but that in addition, each has salespeople on the road who need to connect to the office computers. How would your answer to part b change?
   d. Would you change your answer to part c if both offices are located in the same building? Why or why not?
   e. What additional factors would you need to consider if one of the offices in part c was in Los Angeles and the other was located in Singapore?

Case Study 6

Larry Jones Network Services

Small office–home office (SOHO) networks are increasing in popularity. Today, many homes have multiple computers, and although they have a need to share resources like printers, the major drive for networking home computers is to share an Internet connection. Each home user must have Internet access, but no one wants (or needs) to pay for a separate connection for each.

The situation is likely to become more complex in the future as computer networks are used for entertainment as well as for information. We can see the start of that movement in Internet games, but those games require little networking compared to what will be needed when TV, radio, movies, and music are downloaded over the Internet. At that point, every computing device in the home will need to be networked.

Reread the case concerning Larry Jones on page 121 and then answer the following questions.

Questions

1. Consider the first fraternity house that Larry equipped. Explain how a LAN could be used to connect all of the computers in the house. Would you recommend an Ethernet LAN, an 802.11 LAN, or a combination? Justify your answer.

2. This chapter did not provide enough information for you to determine how many switches the fraternity house might need. However, in general terms, describe how the fraternity could use a multiple-switch system.

3. Considering the connection to the Internet, would you recommend that the fraternity house use a dial-up, a DSL, or a cable modem? Although you can rule out at least one of these alternatives with the knowledge you already have, what additional information do you need in order to make a specific recommendation?

4. Should Larry develop a standard package solution for each of his customers? What advantages accrue from a standard solution? What are the disadvantages?

5. Do you perceive an opportunity at your campus for a service like Larry's? If you do not have fraternities and sororities, are there apartments and condos for which you could provide such services?

6. Using Larry Jones's experience as a guide, what opportunities will exist for small, local consulting companies for setting up SOHO networks?

7. Few home entertainment consumers will want to learn the technical details of network setup. In response, vendors will attempt to ease the setup of home entertainment networks by hiding the technology. Ultimately, they will be successful, but in the near-term, customer support will be a burden to them. Although some of that support can be outsourced and sent overseas, the installation and setup of equipment must be done locally. Describe business opportunities that exist for you to provide customer support for vendors.

8. Are there local retailers selling home entertainment equipment that might be interested in a home network setup service? If so, describe their needs and the services you could provide.

Teaching Suggestions

Emerson Pharmaceuticals, Chapter 6

GOALS

Use Dee's blog to:

* Continue to emphasize the importance of IT and IS knowledge for business professionals.

* Illustrate a practical application of VPNs.

* Appreciate the security risk of allowing an unknown consultant to install and modify programs inside the corporate network.

* Demonstrate how knowledge of IT and IS can increase power.

BACKGROUND

1. Dee must find a way to restrict blog access to Emerson employees. She can either use a public server and restrict access with a system of user IDs and passwords, or she can place the blog within the Emerson network, where it will be protected by Emerson's firewalls and access will be allowed using the Emerson VPN.

2. Don told Dee that using the VPN is a much better alternative, for two reasons: One, Dee would have to pay Don more to set up a security system on a public blog. Second, such a system would require Emerson salespeople to have separate credentials just to access the blog. Many salespeople would forget their blog ID or password, and this would create an administrative problem for them and Dee. Most likely the salespeople would stop using the blog.

3. The IT department did not want to allow Don to have access inside their network. They compromised by allowing him to install software on the test server. This compromise allowed Don to gain entry to a portion of the Emerson network, but not all of it. Hence, it was better than unrestricted access, but it still exposed Emerson to risk.

4. As I watched the progress of this project, it seemed to me that the IT department either had too junior of a person working on Dee's project or that person simply didn't want to do this task. When Don finally got access to the test server, he had been told that the IT person had already installed MySQL and Moveable Type. In fact, the directory was empty. Nothing had been done.

5. When presenting this case, I worry about leaving the impression with the students that IT departments are always resistant and uncooperative. *This is certainly not the case.* I believe the fundamental problem was that, from the IT department's perspective, Dee had an unrealistic schedule. That department simply wasn't going to move as fast as Dee wanted. So, she pushed, and they resisted. Dee finally went to a very high level to force them to allow Don access. She won, but in the process, she exposed Emerson to a serious security risk.

6. In the final analysis, I think the wrong decision was made. Even though the IT department was represented by a lazy or incompetent worker, Don should not have been given access to the internal network. Dee's project was not important enough to justify that risk. Given more time, the IT department could have assigned other personnel or taken other action to create the blog and support her needs. I think Dee's schedule expectations were unrealistic.

7. I use Figure 6-18 to summarize Chapters 4, 5, and 6. I expect my students to know the meaning of all the terms on that figure and to be able to explain how they work together. If there is any student left who thinks this material is irrelevant, they should think about Dee. She needed that knowledge to succeed; had Don been less professional, she could have been fleeced.

HOW TO GET THE STUDENTS INVOLVED

1. I introduce this scenario with the following questions:

   a. **Why should access to Dee's blog be restricted? What would happen if the blog were hosted on a public site?**

   b. **What are the two alternatives for protecting her site?** (See Background comment 1)

   c. **What are the advantages and disadvantages of each alternative?**

   d. **Which did she choose?**

   e. **Was her decision the correct one?**

2. As a way of checking the class's understanding of the material in Chapters 4 through 6, I go around the room asking the students to explain the elements in Figure 6-18. For each element (computer, software, Web page), I ask:

   a. **What is the component?** (e.g., hardware, software, data)

    b. What is the component's function?

    c. How does the component interface with other components?

3. Dee played hardball with the IT department. She knew they didn't want her to create a separate site with separate user IDs and passwords, so she threatened to do so in order to get access for Don.

    a. Was her action ethical?

    b. Was is smart?

    c. Was it beneficial for Emerson?

    d. Was it beneficial for the sales force?

4. Let's recap and evaluate the results:

    a. What was Dee's goal?

    b. How did she accomplish that goal?

    c. How did she use knowledge of IT to increase her power?

    d. Do you think situations like this are common or rare in business today?

5. Were some alternatives not addressed?

    a. What actions might Dee or Emerson have taken to reduce the risk of allowing Don access?

    b. Were there alternatives other than allowing Don to access to the network? What?

    c. What do you think Emerson should have done?

BOTTOM LINE

＊ Business professionals can increase their own and their organization's competitive strength by finding innovative applications of IS and IT.

＊ Doing so requires business professionals to have basic knowledge of hardware, software, data, and communications technologies.

＊ Knowledge creates power.

＊ Dee's actions caused the blog to be implemented, but exposed Emerson to a significant security risk.

＊ Was it worth it?

Using the Guide: Thinking Exponentially Is Not Possible, But . . . *(page 125a)*

GOALS

* Sensitize students to the difficulty (impossibility?) of thinking exponentially.

* Describe strategies that students can use to deal with exponential phenomena in their professional lives.

BACKGROUND AND PRESENTATION STRATEGIES

When Nathan Myhrvold was the chief technology officer at Microsoft, he wrote a paper entitled "Road Kill on the Information Superhighway," a classic that contained the statement, "No one can think exponentially." He was a graduate student of Stephen Hawking, later started his own company, and became a Microsoft employee when his company was acquired by Microsoft. Working at a very senior level at Microsoft during its glory years of the 1990s, he amassed vast wealth (and no longer works for Microsoft).

The graph in this guide shows it all. When told something grows exponentially, we think fast growth, but we do so *linearly*. We just cannot image the changes posed by exponential growth; it is even more difficult to understand the consequences. The exponential growth in the number of Internet users is a case in point. Who would have imagined the changes in politics and the news media that the bloggers have brought forward? So fast that the word *blog* doesn't appear in the current (2005) standard Microsoft Word dictionary.

I underline the words of caution regarding the talking appliances. Although we have the technology for the alarm clock to signal the coffee pot and for the coffee pot to signal the toaster, does anybody really want that capability?

I find it helps to discuss a contemporary example of a possibly exponential phenomenon. RFID could be one example. Another one that has begun to emerge since the text was written is *podcasting*, which is the preparation and distribution of MP3 audio files for playback on iPods and similar devices. Podcasts can be registered with aggregators like podcasting.net for inclusion in podcast directories.

The following sequences of questions use podcasting as the example. They could use RFID or IPv6 instead, if you prefer.

➤ **Podcasting is so recent that the text doesn't address it. What is podcasting?**

➤ **What are potential commercial uses of podcasting? In public relations? In advertising? For employee education and training? Other?**

➤ **How could a company use podcasting to increase the productivity of its sales force while traveling on the road?**

➤ **How can we apply the principles of this guide to podcasting?**

➤ **The guide recommends hedging one's bets when addressing new technology. Put a little money on one or more possibilities; be positioned to move in the direction that the market takes. Watch and wait; move when the direction is clear.**

➤ **How could we hedge our bets with regard to podcasting?**

Notice the impact of time on the size of the disparity between linear and exponential thinking. What will podcasting do in one year? Five years? Ten years?

➤ **Learn to read technology articles critically. Where exponential phenomena are concerned, any statement that begins, "XXX (the phenomenon) will double in five years," is so full of uncertainty as to be nearly meaningless.**

Here are two cases in point in our business: RFID and IPv6. For the first, organizations are still trying to figure out how to use it. Everyone seems to say that it will be important, but no one (including Wal-Mart) knows how, when, or why. The impetus for IPv6 was that the world was going to run out of IP addresses. With DHCP and NAT, however, the utility of the existing IPv4 address space has expanded dramatically. IPv6 still has advantages over IPv4, but the pressure to convert is much less than most would have thought just three years ago.

? SUGGESTED RESPONSES FOR DISCUSSION QUESTIONS

1. I think it's hard to disagree with this statement, but it will be interesting to see what the students think. The goal of the question is to make sure the students understand the point of the remark.

2. See the earlier discussion of podcasting. RFID adoption is another. It hasn't yet caught on, but once RFID becomes a standard in the supply chain, watch out! Everyone will begin to use it. Overnight it will become a true (as opposed to today's Wal-Mart-dictated) requirement. Another example: What will be the demand for HDTV in three years?

3. It's having a huge impact. Not just the 500 channels of TV, but the blogs and podcasters. Also consider video podcasting (by whatever name it will have). Look at how the blogs influenced the 2004 election; blogs claim they played a key role in the early retirement of Dan Rather at CBS.

   Quality is interesting; a debate is underway right now. Mainstream media (MSM) claims that political blogs are of poor quality. The bloggers respond, "No, way—if I publish junk, other bloggers will be all over it in a matter of hours. It's much easier to publish rubbish in a newspaper than in a blog."

4. Three possibilities are:

   • How-to magazines could supplement or replace how-to articles with video clips. (*www.FineWoodworking.com* is doing this now.)

   • Parents could use GPS and embedded-under-the-skin RFID chips to keep track of their children.

   • Insurance companies could use onboard auto video recordings to determine who did what during an accident.

These examples all fit closely with problems that people have today. We know that how-to magazines are meeting a market need because they currently sell well. Parents always need to know where their kids are, and insurance companies could use the video to reduce litigation and other accident expenses. In terms of *closeness to real problems*, I'd rank the three ideas as 2, 1, and 3. Child-embedded RFID is probably socially infeasible, however.

WRAP UP

➤ The *terrific news in this guide is that technology constantly creates new opportunities* for products and services. Your future career can be just as exciting as Steve Jobs's has been. The opportunities will be there.

➤ Don't automatically suppose people will want to do what technology enables them to do. People want to do what they are already doing, but better, faster, or cheaper.

➤ Be careful with exponential phenomena. We don't *know* what all the ubiquitous, nearly free, ever-faster connectivity means. It will mean something—it will mean substantial change—but we don't know what.

➤ Stay tuned!!! Lots of opportunities will come your way during your career!

Using the Ethics Guide: Human Networks Matter More (page 131a)

GOALS

* Teach students the importance of networking.

* Emphasize that business social functions are always business functions.

* Teach a useful skill for increasing one's network at business social functions.

BACKGROUND AND PRESENTATION STRATEGIES

Successful businesspeople are constantly networking. They constantly add to their set of acquaintances. This is true even at the highest levels: Every summer Microsoft has a meeting of the CEOs of the world's 100 largest corporations. Almost all attend, not so much because of the presentations, but because they have so few opportunities to meet each other informally. When the CEO of 3M bumps into the CEO of Citibank at the coffee pot, who knows what transpires? The start of a new board seat for someone?

Business is nothing but relationships. People do business *with people.* Meeting the right people in an informal context makes it possible to better accomplish work in formal contexts. At the weekly softball game, when Brenda makes (or doesn't make) a double play with Don and Bill, a bond is formed that makes it more likely that Brenda and Bill will come to Don's network requirements meeting. It may not make sense, but that's just the way people are. In business, relationships are everything.

So, even though it may seem contrived and awkward, students should learn to attend business social events and to use those events for network building. Sometimes people go to events because they want to meet someone in particular, and sometimes they go just to expand their networks.

➤ **Go to business social events and don't spend all your time talking to people you already know. Make a point of meeting new people who work in other departments.**

Warning: Business social events are business events. There is a difference between a softball game with your friends and one at work. There is a difference between a holiday party with your friends and one at work. The goal of all business social events is to expand networks and to enable people to relate to one another informally. A holiday party is not an opportunity for the company to reward its employees with unlimited free alcohol.

➤ **Party with your friends, but network at business social functions.**

I once managed an exceedingly capable C++ developer who got drunk at the holiday party and made a fool of himself. The next Monday, our business unit manager wanted me to fire him. He was critical to our project, and I was able to help him keep his job. Our relationship, however, was never the same, and his stature at the company fell dramatically.

➤ **Business social functions are business events.**

It is important, too, for students to use social organizations outside of their company for network building. The local chapter of professional accountants or marketers or software entrepreneurs or financial executives is an important source of professional relationships. The best way to build a network is not just to go to a meeting; rather, get involved with the group. Help run a meeting, become an officer, work on the membership committee.

➤ **As the guide points out, there is someone out there who knows someone or something that you need to know. Because you don't and can't know who that person is, your only alternative is to meet as many interesting people as you can.**

❓ SUGGESTED RESPONSES FOR DISCUSSION QUESTIONS

1. The answer depends on the student and your local situation.

2. Use a fraternity or sorority, a student club, a church community, a dorm, a professional group, a job.

3. It's easier to meet Linda because she's in your group. You and she have many acquaintances in common. You also have your department's business in common, so you'll likely have much to say. It's more awkward to meet Eileen. You have no acquaintances in common; you may not know what group she works in or what she does. You may have little to say to one another.

➤ **It may be awkward to meet strangers, but it is important. Try it. Practice while you're in school. Get used to meeting people and talking with them. Learn to be better at it. If you're shy, force yourself to do it.**

4. Business social events are business events, and not treating them as a way of increasing the size of your network is naive.

➤ **Over time, business relationships may evolve into social relationships, but only over time. Assume people you meet in business are just as interested in learning how you can help them as you are in learning how they can help you. This is not a social setting. It's a business setting, and your business function is to meet and greet in such a way so as to make you a more effective employee.**

People do business with people. Are they using one another when they do? Probably. But, that's no surprise to anyone and there should be no deception.

➤ **You probably don't want to treat parties with your friends this way, but a business social function is not a party. It's a business function.**

5. First, regarding the phrase, professionals need to know their profession. Accountants need to know accounting, financial analysts need to know finance, and network administrators need to know TCP/IP–OSI. That said, however, what differentiates two people with about the same level of knowledge? Their relationships!

When you're designing a computer network, knowledge of data communications technology is critical; but when you're an accounts payable manager who's been asked to prepare a high-level management statement of networking alternatives, then knowing who to call for help is more important than your particular knowledge of data communications.

➤ **Knowledge of data communications at the basic level of this chapter will help you better talk with experts in the field. It will help you build your network.**

➤ **Enlarging your networks and using your relationships to be more effective at work is an accepted norm in business. It is therefore ethical.**

6. Get out and meet people. Go to every possible business speaker event. Talk with the speaker afterward. Ask interesting questions about his or her talk. Get that person's business card. Follow up with an email thanking them and asking another pertinent question or two. Join relevant business clubs on campus. Get involved. When businesspeople come to campus, volunteer to greet them and buy them a cup of coffee before or afterward. Do everything you can to expand your network. All these actions increase the likelihood that you'll meet that person who knows about the job that would be ideal for you. And, by the way, your life on campus will be more enjoyable and interesting, too.

Business relationships exist for the purpose of conducting business. You are not abusing a relationship as long as there is no deception as to the purpose of the relationship.

WRAP UP

One way to wrap up is to challenge the students to keep thinking about it:

➤ **Networking is important—very important. In some ways, for the purposes of getting a job, developing a good network is more important than your GPA. Look how much time you put into your GPA. Just put some of that time into building your network.**

➤ **Network building is, by the way, a lifelong activity. It may be that some relationships you build here on campus will pay dividends many years down the road.**

➤ **Think seriously about these ideas. Discuss them with your friends. Determine what you believe about the relative importance of knowledge and networks. When is one more important than the other?**

➤ **Again, it's your life, your career. I'm just trying to coach you into behaviors that will help you become a successful business professional. Give it some thought!**

PART 2 The International Dimension

Global Communication

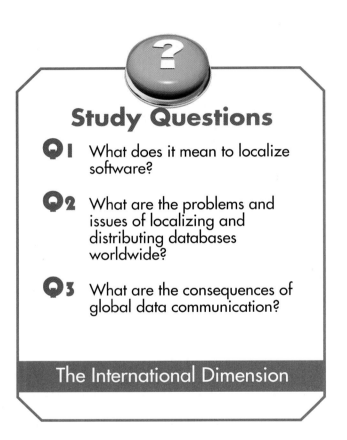

Study Questions

Q1 What does it mean to localize software?

Q2 What are the problems and issues of localizing and distributing databases worldwide?

Q3 What are the consequences of global data communication?

The International Dimension

Q1 What Does It Mean to Localize Software?

The process of making a computer program work in a second language is called **localizing** that software. It turns out to be surprisingly hard to do. If you think about localizing a document or a Web page, all you need to do is hire a translator to convert your document or page from one language to another. The situation is more difficult for a computer program, however.

Suppose, for example, your company has developed its own inventory control database application and that your firm has just acquired a company in Mexico. You want to use that same inventory control program for your Mexican operations. As a new manager, suppose you haven't even considered this matter during the acquisition process. After the acquisition is done, you ask your technical people to give you a time estimate for converting your inventory application into Spanish. Unless that program was designed from the beginning to be localized, you will be shocked at the effort and cost required. Why?

Consider a program you frequently use—say, Microsoft Word—and ask what would need to be done to translate it to a different language. The entire user interface will need to be translated. The menu bar and the commands on the menu bar will need to be translated. It is possible that some of the icons (the small graphics on a menu bar) will need to be changed because some graphic symbols that are harmless in one culture are confusing or offensive in another.

The inventory control application is a database application, so it will have forms, reports, and queries. The labels on each of these will need to be translated. Of course, not all labels translate into words of the same length, and so the forms and reports may need to be redesigned. The questions and prompts for queries, such as "Enter part number for back order," must also be translated.

All of the documentation will need to be translated. That should be just a matter of hiring a translator, except that all of the illustrations in the documentation will need to be redrawn in the second language.

Think, too, about error messages. When someone attempts to order more items than there are in inventory, your application produces an error message. All of those messages will need to be translated. There are other issues as well. Sorting order is one. Spanish uses accents on certain letters, and it turns out that an accented $\acute{o}$ will sort after z when you use the com-

puter's default sort ordering. Your programmers will have to deal with that issue as well.

Figure ID2-1 presents a short list of issues to face when localizing a computer program.

Programming techniques can be used to simplify and reduce the cost of localization. However, those techniques must be used in the beginning. For example, suppose that when a certain condition occurs, the program is to display the message, "Insufficient quantity in stock." If the programmer codes all such mes-

sages into the computer program, then, to localize that program, the programmer will have to find every such message in the code and then ask a translator to change that code. A preferred technique is to give every error message a number and to place the number and text of the error message into a separate file. Then, the code is written to display a particular error number from that file. During localization, translators simply translate the file of error messages into the second language.

The bottom line for you as a future manager is to understand two points: (1) Localizing computer programs is much more difficult, expensive, and time-consuming than translating documents. (2) If a computer program is likely to be localized, then plan for that localization from the beginning. In addition, when considering the acquisition of a company in a foreign country, be sure to budget time and expense for the localization of information systems.

Q2 What Are the Problems and Issues of Localizing and Distributing Databases Worldwide?

Consider the acquisition of the Mexican company just described. You have decided to localize your inventory control application. The next question is, "Do you want to localize your inventory database?"

Figure ID2-1
Issues to Address When Localizing a Computer Program

- Translate the user interface, including menu bars and commands.
- Translate, and possibly redesign, labels in forms, reports, and query prompts.
- Translate all documentation and help text.
- Redraw and translate diagrams and examples in help text.
- Translate all error messages.
- Translate text in all message boxes.
- Adjust sorting order for different character set.
- Fix special problems in Asian character sets and in languages that read and write from right to left.

Assume you have a centralized inventory database in the United States. Do you want the inventory control programs that will run in Mexico to access that same database? With modern data communications, that is entirely possible.

However, your business requirements may dictate that you need to create a second database in Mexico. In that case, there are two issues. First, you will need to localize it. Second, you will need to determine the relationship between the two databases. Do the contents of those two databases refer to a single centralized inventory, or do they refer to two different inventories? If, for example, the two databases both indicate that there are 10 widgets in inventory, is that a single centralized inventory, or are there two separate inventories, one in the United States and one in Mexico, and do they, thus, both happen to have 10 widgets in stock?

Consider database localization first. In most cases, when companies localize databases, they choose to translate the data, but not the metadata. Thus, the contents of the *Remarks* field or the *Description* files are translated. However, the names of tables, the names of fields, the description of the meaning of the fields, and other such metadata are left in English (or whatever the original language was). As stated in the previous section, forms, reports, queries, and database application programs will also need to be localized.

Now consider the relationship between the two databases. If they refer to two separate inventories, then there is no problem. Each database can be processed and administered as an independent entity. If the two databases refer to the *same* inventory, however, then they contain duplicated records. Such databases are said to be **replicated**. In this case, if it is possible to partition the workload so that the inventory application running on a server in Mexico updates different records than the inventory application running on a server in the United States, then the situation can be managed.

If, however, the two inventory applications running on the two servers can update the *same items at the same time*, serious problems occur. Considerable time, expense, and sophisticated programming are necessary to develop and support such databases. Because of the expense, difficulty, and risk, most organizations define their business processes to avoid this situation.

This problem, by the way, is not strictly an international problem. The two separate servers could be running in the same country, and the problem will be the same. The situation arises more frequently, however, in international situations.

Q3 What Are Consequences of Global Data Communication?

We discussed the impact of modern data communications on the development of the global economy in the last part (page 54). In brief, data communications have tremendously expanded the size of the global economy and the global workforce.

In this section, consider the impact of data communications on less-developed countries. One of the most positive aspects of IT is that technology users can skip generations. People can benefit from the most modern technology without having to use the earlier technology. When Microsoft introduces a new version of Word, you can receive the benefit of that new version without having to learn Word 1.0, then Word 2.0, then Word 3.0, and so forth. Similarly, you can buy a cell phone and use it without ever having used a wired phone. You can do instant messaging with your friends without ever having sent an email.

What are the consequences? In many developing countries, cell or satellite phones are the first phones that most people use. There are sections of the world that do not have telephone wires and that will never have them. In some countries, the first weather forecast someone sees will be presented on a Web page that is delivered via a cell phone.

The economic, social, and political consequences of this phenomenon are staggering. A coffee farmer in Kenya, someone who has never sold his or her beans to anyone but a local trader, can suddenly sell them to Starbucks in Seattle. A basket weaver in Cameroon, who has sold her wares only at the local market, can suddenly sell her baskets to collectors in Tokyo. People whose world horizon has been restricted to villages in their neighborhood or streets in their city suddenly find themselves connected to the rest of the world. Local laws and customs become outmoded, even irrelevant.

Furthermore, existing companies, organizations, and governments are seriously challenged. The public telephone utility in many countries has been a profitable monopoly and medium of control. Cell and satellite phones threaten this monopoly and reduce the power of individuals and cartels. In some countries there has been a backlash and restriction of the spread of technology. Such measures only delay the inevitable. How can a country with serious penalties for using a copy machine for political purposes maintain control in the face of email, instant messaging, and the Web?

During your career, these countries will see unprecedented change. This change will create many opportunities for interesting jobs, careers, and new businesses.

Active ? Review

Use this Active Review to verify that you understand the material in the International Dimension. You can read the entire minichapter and then perform the tasks in this review, or you can read the material for just one question and perform the tasks in this review for that question before moving on to the next one.

Q1 What does it mean to localize software?

Explain why information systems, and in particular, software, should be a consideration during the merger and acquisition process. Summarize the work required to localize a computer program. In your own words, explain why it is better to design a program to be localized rather than attempt to adapt an existing single-language program to a second language.

Q2 What are the problems and issues of distributing databases worldwide?

Explain what is required to localize a database. Explain possible relationships of two databases.

Define *replicated databases*. Explain the conditions for which replicated databases are not a problem. Explain the conditions for which replicated databases are a problem. How do most organizations deal with this problem?

Q3 What are the consequences of global data communication?

Explain the statement, "technology users can skip generations." Illustrate this principle with an example from your own life. Describe the economic consequences of this principle on developing countries. Describe the social and political consequences of this principle. Give an example of a job, career, or business opportunity that these changes will present.

Key Terms and Concepts

Localizing software 138
Replicated databases 140

PART 2 review

Consider Your Net Worth

Examine the questions addressed in each chapter and think about how those ideas will pertain to you as a future manager and professional business person. How can you use the knowledge you've gained to increase your net worth both to your employer and yourself?

1. Considering your future goals (use your answer to question 1, "Consider Your Net Worth," page 58), describe how the knowledge you've gained about computer hardware and software helps you. How will it help you specify equipment that you need? How will it help you specify equipment for your employees? How can you use the knowledge about buying decisions? What does the information about viruses tell you to do for yourself and for your employees?

2. As a business professional, when would you choose to use a database? When would you use a spreadsheet? Describe the kind of problem for which you would use a personal DBMS. What kind of problem needs an enterprise-class DBMS? Under what conditions could you get by with just forms, reports, and queries, and under what other conditions would you need to hire someone to develop database application programs?

3. Suppose you manage a department. Under what conditions can the needs of your department be satisfied by a LAN? Besides Internet access, under what conditions would your group need a WAN? When would a network of leased lines be appropriate? Under what conditions would you want your employees to ensure they have the https:// characters in their browser address line? What steps could you take to prevent your employees from accessing a particular Web site? When would a VPN be appropriate? Under what conditions are email and IM protected by encryption?

4. Reflect on Dee's experiences as discussed in Chapters 4 through 6. Even though you are unlikely to start a blog, what can you learn from her? How does knowledge of IT and IS help you better work with the IT department? How does it help you be a better negotiator with personnel?

How can you use knowledge of hardware and software, databases, and data communications to be a better advocate for your needs and the needs of your department? How does such knowledge give you a competitive advantage over other professionals and managers who do not have it?

Career Assignments

1. Dee's consultant played a crucial role in her success. Suppose you decide to become a similar consultant, probably not for creating blogs but, say, for helping people determine their hardware and software needs. You might even do this job as an in-house consultant.

a. Would it be essential to have a strong business background to perform such a service? Why or why not?

b. Would it be essential to have a strong technical background to perform such a service? Why or why not?

c. For this job, which is more important, business knowledge or technical skills? Explain your answer.

d. What courses and other activities could you engage in while you are in college to prepare for this job?

e. Even if you do not perform such a job full time, explain how having the skills to perform such a job would increase your desirability to a departmental manager. How could you use such a skill in a job interview?

 2. Go to the Occupational Outlook Handbook at *stats.bls.gov/oco/home.htm.*

a. Summarize the job outlook for jobs like that in question 1.

b. Describe the educational requirements necessary for this job.

c. What courses and other activities could you engage in while you are in college to prepare you for this job?

d. Answer part c, but suppose your goal is to be or to become a *manager of computer support specialists.*

 3. Sometimes, you will see employee ads that state, "No computer skills required." Instead of searching for such jobs, suppose you attain some degree of proficiency using computers and information systems. Query your favorite Web search engine for the phrase "job opportunities with computer skills." Visit three of the links that seem interesting.

a. You will not find any consistent definition of the term *computer skill.* Summarize several of the definitions (possibly implied rather than stated) that you do find.

b. Considering your answer to part a, how can you improve your job prospects by taking more IS classes in combination with your major (assuming you are not an IS major)?

c. Describe two jobs that involve significant computer skills but that are not strictly in the computer industry. What can you do while you are in college to prepare for one of those jobs?

4. Search the U.S. Department of Labor's Occupational Outlook Handbook (*stats.bls.gov/oco/home.htm*) for the term *database administrator*. Answer the following questions based on the information you find.

   a. What are the job prospects for database administrators in the next five years?

   b. What skills do database administrators need? (*Note:* Sometimes, this handbook groups jobs together. Make sure you find the skills necessary for database administrators in particular.)

   c. What courses could you take or activities could you engage in to prepare you for such a job?

 5. Do a Web search for the term *databases for x*, filling in your major field of study for *x*. If you are majoring in accounting, for example, search for *databases for accounting*. If you are majoring in marketing, fill in *databases for marketing*. Read two or three of the links that you find interesting. Look for articles that are less technical and more managerial.

   a. Summarize your findings.

   b. Describe two or three job opportunities that might exist for someone who has some technical knowledge along with a business degree in a functional area like accounting or marketing. These job opportunities may not be listed as such. Instead, think about what you have read in this chapter and what you learned in part a, and imagine what job opportunities there might be.

   c. Today, business professionals are required to be more actively involved in the development and use of IS. Official job descriptions may not have kept up with this requirement. Explain how you could use this fact and your knowledge of IS to create a competitive advantage over other job applicants.

   d. Your department maintains relationships with professionals who are active in your major field of study. Describe how you could contact one of those professionals to verify the conclusions you reached in parts a through c. What ancillary benefits might accrue if you do this?

 6. Suppose you are interested in working in sales of products and services for computer networking and related industries. Query your favorite Web search engine for job opportunities, such as PSDN sales job opportunities, WAN sales job opportunities, and network sales job opportunities. Also, search the Web sites of communication vendors such as Cisco, Juniper, Redback, Nortel, and others for possible job leads.

   a. Describe the characteristics of jobs that are currently available.

   b. Search the Department of Labor's Occupational Outlook Handbook (*stats.bls.gov/oco/home.htm*) and related resources to determine the outlook for such jobs.

   c. What classes or other activities, such as internships, could you take to prepare for such jobs?

 7. Answer question 6, but suppose you are interested in network customer support job opportunities.

Application Exercises

 1. Suppose that you work in a sales office and your boss asks you to create a "computer file" to keep track of product prices offered to customers. Suppose you decide to use a spreadsheet for this purpose as follows.

a. Create a spreadsheet with the following columns: *CustomerName, CustomerLocation, MeetingDate, ProductName, UnitPrice, Salesperson,* and *Salesperson_Email.*

b. Suppose you have three customers: Ajax, Baker, and Champion. Suppose Ajax is located in New York City, Baker is located in Toronto, and Champion is located in New York City. Assume you have two salespeople: Johnson and Jackson. (Make up email addresses for each.)

Assume you have three products: P1, P2, and P3. Periodically, your salespeople meet with customers, and during these meetings, they agree on product prices. The salespeople pitch one, two, or three products in each of these meetings. Some customers negotiate better prices than others, so the price varies by customer.

Using this information, fill your spreadsheet with at least 20 rows of sample data. Make up the price data. Assume that prices increase and decrease over time. Enter data for some meetings in 2006 and for some meetings in 2007.

c. Copy your spreadsheet to a new worksheet. Suppose that you made a mistake and Champion is based in San Francisco, not New York City. Using this second worksheet, make the necessary changes to correct your mistake.

d. Suppose that you learn that the product P1 was renamed P1-Turbo in 2007. Explain the steps you need to take to correct this mistake.

e. A real sales-tracking application would have hundreds of customers, many salespeople, hundreds of products, and possibly thousands of meetings. For such a spreadsheet, how would you correct the problems in parts c and d? Comment on the appropriateness of using a spreadsheet for such an application.

2. Consider the same problem as in question 1, except use a database to keep track of the price quotations.

a. Create a new database using Microsoft Access and create the following three tables:

CUSTOMER (*CustomerName, Location*)
SALESPERSON (*SalespersonName, Saleperson_Email*)
PRICE_QUOTE (*Date, Product, Price, CustomerName, SalespersonName*)

Assume the following: *CustomerName* is the key of CUSTOMER; *SalespersonName* is the key of SALESPERSON; and the three columns (*Date, Product,* and *CustomerName*) are the key of PRICE_QUOTE. Make appropriate assumptions about the data types for each table column.

b. Use Access to create a 1:N relationship between CUSTOMER and PRICE_QUOTE. Create a 1:N relationship between SALESPERSON and PRICE_QUOTE. Check Enforce Referential Integrity for both relationships. (See Chapter Extension 5, page 363, for an explanation of 1:N relationships.)

c. Fill your tables using the same data that you used in question 1.

d. Make the changes necessary to record the fact that customer Champion is based in San Francisco rather than in New York City. How many items do you need to change?

e. Make the changes necessary to change the name of product P1 to P1-Turbo for all quotes after 2007.

f. Using the Access Help system, learn about update action queries. Create an update action query to make the change in part e.

g. Compare spreadsheets and databases for this application. Which is better? Why? What are the characteristics of an application that would cause you to choose a database over a spreadsheet? A spreadsheet over a database?

3. Suppose you work for a company that installs computer networks. Assume that you have been given the task of creating spreadsheets to generate cost estimates.

a. Create a spreadsheet to estimate hardware costs. Assume that the user of the spreadsheet will enter the number of pieces of equipment and the standard cost for each type of equipment. Assume that the networks can include the following components: NIC cards, WNIC cards, wireless access points, switches of two types—one faster, one slower—at two different prices, and routers. Also assume that the company will use both UTP and optical fiber cable and that prices for cable are stated as per foot.

b. Show how you can use the spreadsheet from part a to estimate the costs of networks having different performances. Use the network layout in Figure 6-6 and assume different kinds of devices at different prices. Make assumptions about distances between computers and devices.

c. Modify your spreadsheet to include labor costs. Assume there is a fixed cost for the installation of each type of equipment and a per foot cost for the installation of cable.

4. Suppose you manage a department of 20 employees and you wish to build an information system to track their computers, the software that resides on those computers, and the licenses for each software product. Assume that employees can have more than one computer and that each computer has multiple software products. Each product has a single license. The license can be either a *site license* (meaning your organization paid for everyone in the company to be able to use that program) or the license is a purchase order number and date for the order that paid for the license.

a. Design a spreadsheet for keeping track of the employees, computers, and licenses. Insert sample data for three employees and at least five computers with typical software.

b. Design a database for keeping track of the employees, computers, and licenses. Assume your database has an EMPLOYEE table, a COMPUTER table, and a SOFTWARE_LICENSE table. Place appropriate columns in these tables and construct the relationship. Insert sample data for three employees, five computers, and multiple software licenses per computer.

c. Compare the spreadsheet and database solutions to this problem. Which is easier to set up? Which is easier to maintain?

d. Use whichever of your solutions you prefer for producing the following two reports:

- A list of employees and their computers, sorted by employee.

- A list of software products, the computers on which they reside, and the employees assigned those computers, sorted by software product name.

PART 2 CASE 2-1

Aviation Safety Network

The mission of the Aviation Safety Network (ASN) is to provide up-to-date, complete, and reliable information on airliner accidents and safety issues to those with a professional interest in aviation. ASN defines an airliner as an aircraft capable of carrying 14 or more passengers. ASN data include information on commercial, military, and corporate airplanes.

ASN gathers data from a variety of sources, including the International Civil Aviation Board, the National Transportation Safety Board, and the Civil Aviation

Figure PC2 1-1
Incidents and Accidents Involving the Airbus 320 from the ASN Aviation Safety Database

ASN Aviation Safety Database results

24 occurrences in the ASN safety database:

date	type	registration	operator	fat.	location	pic	cat
26-JUN-1988	Airbus A.320	F-GFKC	Air France	3	France		A1
14-FEB-1990	Airbus A.320	VT-EPN	Indian Airlines	92	India		A1
20-JAN-1992	Airbus A.320	F-GGED	Air Inter	87	France		A1
27-MAR-1993	Airbus A.320	VT-E..	Indian Airlines	0	India		H2
26-AUG-1993	Airbus A.320	G-KMAM	Excalibur Airways	0	U.K.		I2
14-SEP-1993	Airbus A.320	D-AIPN	Lufthansa	2	Poland		A1
22-OCT-1993	Airbus A.320	F-....	Air Inter	0	France		I2
10-DEC-1993	Airbus A.320	F-GF..	Air France	0	France		H2
19-DEC-1996	Airbus A.320	F-OHMK	Mexicana	0	Mexico		A2
10-MAR-1997	Airbus A.320	A4O-EM	Gulf Air	0	U.A.E.		A1
22-MAR-1998	Airbus A.320	RP-C3222	Philippine Air Lines	0	Philippines		A1
12-MAY-1998	Airbus A.320	SU-GB?	EgyptAir	0	Egypt		A2
21-MAY-1998	Airbus A.320	G-UKLL	Air UK Leisure	0	Spain		I2
12-FEB-1999	Airbus A.320	F-GJVG	Air France	0	France		U2
02-MAR-1999	Airbus A.320	F-G...	Air France	0	France		H2
26-OCT-1999	Airbus A.320	VT-ESL	Indian Airlines	0	Myanmar		A2
11-APR-2000	Airbus A.320	F-OHMD	Mexicana	0	Mexico		O1
05-JUL-2000	Airbus A.320		Royal Jordanian	1	Jordan		H2
23-AUG-2000	Airbus A.320	A4O-EK	Gulf Air	143	Bahrain		A1
07-FEB-2001	Airbus A.320	EC-HKJ	Iberia	0	Spain		A1
17-MAR-2001	Airbus A.320	N357NW	Northwest Airlines	0	USA		A2
20-MAR-2001	Airbus A.320	D-AIP.	Lufthansa	0	Germany		I2
24-JUL-2001	Airbus A.320	4R-ABA	SriLankan Airlines	0	Sri Lanka		O1
28-AUG-2002	Airbus A.320	N635AW	America West	0	USA		A1

Authority. Data are also taken from magazines, such as *Air Safety Week* and *Aviation Week and Space Technology*; from a variety of books; and from prominent individuals in the aviation safety industry.

ASN compiles the source data into a Microsoft Access database. The core table contains over 10,000 rows of data concerning incident and accident descriptions. This table is linked to several other tables that store data about airports, airlines, aircraft types, countries, and so forth. Periodically, the Access data are reformatted and exported to a MySQL database, which is used by programs that support queries on ASN's Web site (*aviation-safety.net*).

On that site, incident and accident data can be accessed by year, by airline, by aircraft, by nation, and in other ways. For example, Figure PC2 1-1 (page 148) shows a list of incidents and accidents that involved the Airbus 320. When the user clicks on a particular accident, such as the one on March 20, 2001, a summary of the incident is presented, as shown in Figure PC2 1-2.

In addition to descriptions of incidents and accidents, ASN also summarizes the data to help its users determine airliner accident trends. For example, Figure PC2 1-3 shows the safest location on the aircraft for a selection of airliner accidents. (A value of *ER* in the *Phase* column means the accident occurred while the aircraft was en route, *LA* means the accident occurred during landing, and *TO* means that

Incident Description   Status: **Final**   [legenda]

Date:	**20 MAR 2001**
Time:	12:00
Type:	Airbus A.320-211
Operator:	Lufthansa
Registration:	D-AIP.
Year built:	1990
Engines:	2 CFMI CFM56-5A1
Crew:	0 fatalities / 6 on board
Passengers:	0 fatalities / 115 on board
Total:	0 fatalities / 121 on board
Airplane damage:	None
Location:	Frankfurt International Airport (FRA) (Germany)
Phase:	Take-off
Nature:	International Scheduled Passenger
Departure airport:	Frankfurt International Airport (FRA)
Destination airport:	Paris

Narrative:
The Airbus 320 hit turbulence just after rotation from runway 18 and the left wing dipped. The captain responded with a slight sidestick input to the right but the aircraft banked further left. Another attempt to correct the attitude of the plane resulted in a left bank reaching ca 22deg. The first officer then said "I have control", and switched his sidestick to priority and recovered the aircraft. The left wingtip was reportedly just 0.5m off the ground. The aircraft climbed to FL120 where the crew tried to troubleshoot the problem. When they found out that the captain's sidestick was reversed in roll, they returned to Frankfurt. Investigation revealed that maintenance had been performed on the Elevator Aileron Computer no. 1 (ELAC). Two pairs of pins inside the connector had accidentally been crossed during the repair.

Figure PC2 1-2
Incident Description Summary from the ASN Aviation Safety Database

Source: Aviation Safety Network, *http://aviation-safety.net*

Figure PC2 1-3
Safest Location on Aircraft from
the ASN Aviation Safety
Database

Source: Aviation Safety Network,
http://aviation-safety.net.

Date	Type	Occupants	Survivors	Phase [1]	Safest location
02 MAY 1970	DC-9	63	40	ER	rear
04 APR 1977	DC-9	85	22	ER	rear
12 AUG 1985	Boeing 747	524	4	ER	rear
11 NOV 1965	Boeing 727	91	48	LA	rear
20 NOV 1967	Convair CV-880	82	12	LA	rear
13 JAN 1969	DC-8	45	30	LA	front
08 DEC 1972	Boeing 737	61	18	LA	rear
29 DEC 1972	Lockheed L-1011	176	77	LA	front & rear
30 JAN 1974	Boeing 707	101	4	LA	center
11 SEP 1974	DC-9	82	12	LA	rear
24 JUN 1975	Boeing 727	124	9	LA	rear
27 APR 1976	Boeing 727	88	51	LA	front
11 FEB 1978	Boeing 737	49	7	LA	rear
28 DEC 1978	DC-8	189	179	LA	rear
02 JUN 1983	DC-9	46	23	LA	center
02 AUG 1985	Lockheed L-1011	163	29	LA	rear
15 SEP 1988	Boeing 737	104	69	LA	rear
08 JAN 1989	Boeing 737	126	79	LA	front
19 JUL 1989	DC-10	296	185	LA	center
01 FEB 1991	Boeing 737	89	67	LA	rear
20 JAN 1992	Airbus A.320	96	9	LA	rear
26 APR 1994	Airbus A.300	271	7	LA	center
01 JUN 1999	DC-9	145	134	LA	front & rear
03 DEC 1990	DC-9	44	36	TA	front
27 NOV 1970	DC-8	229	182	TO	front
13 JAN 1982	Boeing 737	79	5	TO	rear
22 AUG 1985	Boeing 737	137	82	TO	front
15 NOV 1987	DC-9	82	54	TO	rear
31 AUG 1988	Boeing 727	108	94	TO	front & center
22 MAR 1992	Fokker F-28	51	24	TO	front & rear
02 JUL 1994	DC-9	57	20	TO	rear
31 OCT 2000	Boeing 747	179	96	TO	front & rear

accident occurred during takeoff.) According to ASN, "there is no significant difference regarding survival for passengers seated in the front or the rear of the plane."

Hugo Ranter of the Netherlands started the ASN Web site in 1995. Fabian I. Lujan of Argentina has maintained the site since 1998. ASN has more than 10,000 email subscribers in 150 countries, and the site receives over 50,000 visits per week.

Questions

1. All of the data included in this database are available in public documents. Since this is the case, what is the value of the Aviation Safety Network? Why don't users just consult the online version of the underlying

references? In your answer, consider the difference between data and information.

2. What was the cause of the incident shown in Figure PC2 1-2? That incident, in which no one was injured, occurred in an Airbus 320 airplane that was flown by Lufthansa Airlines out of an airport in Germany. It would be illogical to conclude from this one incident that it is dangerous to fly Airbus 320s, Lufthansa, or out of Germany. Suppose, however, that you wanted to determine whether there is a systematic pattern of maintenance problems with the A320, Lufthansa, or airports in Germany. How would you proceed? How would you use the resources of *aviation-safety.net* to make this determination?

3. The ASN database and Web site were created and are maintained by two individuals. The database may be complete and accurate, or it may not be. To what extent should you rely on these data? What can you do to decide whether you should rely on the data at this site?

4. Consider the data in Figure PC2 1-3. Do you agree that there appears to be no significant difference between passengers in the front and the rear of the airplane? Why or why not? There does seem to be a difference between the number of accidents and the phase of the flight. What is that difference, and how can you use it to limit your exposure to aircraft accidents?

5. Suppose you work in the marketing department for an airline. Can you use these data in your marketing efforts? If so, how? What are the dangers of basing a marketing campaign on safety?

6. Suppose you are a maintenance manager for a major airline. How can you use these data? Would it be wise to develop your own, similar database? Why or why not?

CASE 2-2

Computerizing the Ministry of Foreign Affairs

In 1994, the Ministry of Foreign Affairs of a West African country embarked on an ambitious program to computerize its internal services and communications. The project began slowly, with limited funding, and it relied on donated hardware and software. In 1999, the goals of the project were revised to include the development of Web-based applications, and at that point, the project received internal budget allocations. Between 1999 and 2002, a total of $650,000 was allocated.

The system's purpose was to make the organization dynamic and modern via the use of information technology. For example, the United Nations provides data and documents electronically, and the Foreign Affairs Ministry wanted to participate in the use of this new technology.

Another project goal was to facilitate communication between the Ministry of Foreign Affairs home office and its diplomatic missions abroad. In particular, the new system would use an external Web site and email to distribute information and facilitate discussions and decision making between geographically separated participants. A specific objective was to reduce travel costs by half.

Unfortunately, by 2002 the project had delivered few benefits. Data continued to be stored on paper, a local computer network within the Ministry of Foreign Affairs was inoperative, and the diplomatic correspondence bag remained the primary means of exchanging paper-based information. Diplomats continued to travel, and travel expenses were not reduced by the new system. In short, the project was a failure.

In his case study of this application, Kenhago Olivier identified three factors behind the failure of this system:

1. Vendor contracts were awarded not on the basis of competence, but rather on personal relations between Ministry of Foreign Affairs officials and vendor personnel.

2. The major application threatened the perquisites ("perks") of diplomats. Travel is an important source of revenue for headquarters personnel; they compensate for their low salaries by travel compensation and by the opportunity to trade goods.

3. The computing infrastructure was limited; there were a maximum of two personal computers per department at headquarters and only 35 computers in a building housing more than 300 officials.

Source: K. T. Olivier, "Problems in Computerising the Ministry of Foreign Affairs," Success/Failure Case Study No. 23, eGovernment for Development, www.egov4dev.org/mofa.htm (accessed October 2004).

Questions

1. The purpose of this system was for the Ministry of Foreign Affairs "to become a more dynamic, modern organization via the use of information technology." What are the dangers of stating the purpose of a system in this way? How could this statement be improved?

2. Why was the goal of reducing travel costs not achieved? What steps would need to be taken before this goal could ever be achieved? What is the likely outcome in any system in which the goals of the system conflict with the interests of important users? Which is stronger—the momentum of the new system or the resistance of the users?

3. When the features of new information systems conflict with the needs and desires of important user groups, what should be done? Should system development be stopped? If not, should the features be changed? What can be done to reduce the users' resistance? Who is in a position to resolve the conflict—the development team? The business users? Someone else?

4. This case description implies that the project was severely underfunded. Attempting to modernize a department with donated equipment sounds desperate, and trying to change communication patterns using email when 300 officials share 35 personal computers is probably impossible. The desire to use the U.N.'s computer-based systems to reduce travel and to enable email communication are appropriate goals for a governmental organization today. But the limited funding is a reality. If you were placed in charge of a project that was underfunded like this one, what would you do?

5. In most cases, the costs of an information system are not known at the beginning of a project. It is only after specifying requirements and identifying alternative solutions that costs can be approximated. Knowing this, how would you proceed if you were given the responsibility for managing a new

development project? What would you do if you found that the funding available is not nearly enough? What would you do if you found that the funding is 10 to 20 percent too low? What would you do if the funding appeared to be adequate, but you sensed that the cost estimates were optimistically low? In each of these cases, what is the best strategy for your organization? For your career?

IS and Competitive Strategy

This could happen to you

Dorset-Stratford Interiors (DSI) is a partnership located near Manchester, New Hampshire. It leases facilities on the site of a former airbase "surplused" by the U.S. Air Force. Facilities include a large hangar, one capable of handling three aircraft at a time, as well as a machine shop, production facility, and office and inventory space. Eleanor Dorset, one of the partners in DSI,[1] describes the origins of the partnership as follows:

"I came into this business through the backdoor. I was designing interiors for well-to-do clients here in New England, and one of them asked me to design the interior of his airplane. I really enjoyed it and saw that I have an ability to express clients' needs within the space and safety constraints of an airplane. It helps that I've been crazy about aviation all my life.

"John Stratford was running a Boeing 737 aircraft refitting and maintenance company when I met him. In fact, we chose his company for the build-out of the design for my original client. John has the same passion for quality that I have, and he also knows how to manage projects and costs. After we finished that first project, John asked me to provide design services for one of his customers, and DSI was born. I handle the front-end sales and manage the design department; John runs operations and all of the back-office. He also manages customer service and support.

"We specialize in Boeing 737 interiors for individuals, corporations, and governments. Most often, we design and construct what are called *head-of-state* interiors. The projects vary, but usually they include a main cabin with 20 or fewer seats, a deluxe galley, some type of office suite, and a bedroom. Everything is first-rate: the fit and finish of our woodwork, the quality of our fabrics, the overall design

[1]This case is based on a real company, and the problems, situations, and systems described are real. DSI, however, is fictitious. The actual company declined to allow us to publish its name or other identifying data. Company executives decided not to reveal the information about their competitive strategy and the means they use to accomplish that strategy. The actual company, like DSI, provides custom, high-end, high-quality products. It does so, however, to a segment of a different industry.

tailored to the needs of the customer. And, of course, we pay careful attention to the safety systems of the aircraft.

"There are some variances among interiors. Corporations often want more seating and hold back on the more exotic options. For individuals, the sky is literally the limit when it comes to luxury accommodations. Interiors for government aircraft vary; some are Spartan, while others are elaborate.

"We build to the client's needs, and we believe we provide the very highest quality. If you want the lowest possible price, you should go to an off-shore vendor. Its labor will be cheaper, and the company doesn't have our notions of quality. It can do a fine job of crafting a safe interior, but the look and feel will be another quality altogether.

"I don't mean to say we don't care about costs; we do. We want to give our customers the best possible value. So we constantly ask, 'Where can we save?' Everyone pays more or less the same for materials, so DSI is not going to gain an advantage there. The savings have to be in labor. And, in fact, we're constructing interiors for 25 percent less today than when we started. Part of this is due to our specialization on the 737. But most of our labor savings occur because every employee focuses on productivity.

"Three factors account for our high productivity: equipment, processes, and information systems. We use modern manufacturing equipment, computer-guided cutting and milling, specialty welding machines, and so forth. We also carefully design our work processes to make our workers as efficient as we can. For example, we station consumable tool parts like sandpaper as close to workers as possible. Also, for any type of assembly, all the necessary parts and materials are delivered in carts or buckets right to the line. Everything is carefully labeled.

"One of our advantages is that we were able to design new processes as we grew. One of our competitors, which has been in this business since World War II, is hampered by decades-old work processes. It hasn't been able to tear itself away from how something's always been done in order to improve its operations.

"On the other hand, we don't move want to move forward so fast that no one can keep up. If you change too fast, chaos and resistance result. One of our young employees, fresh out of school, wanted to change too many things too fast, and finally, we had to let him go. It's got to be evolution, not revolution.

"The third factor in our productivity is use of information systems. But we need systems that provide real, tangible benefits—and that do so *now*. We're not interested in something just because it's new or is supposed to be great. We're a small builder in a very competitive industry. We can't afford expensive experiments that don't work out."

The employee count at DSI varies from 100 to 200 people, depending on the work in progress. A typical project costs between $5 and $10 million. Project duration from contract signing to rollout is about 6 months. As a privately held partnership, DSI does not release financial data, but we can estimate its revenue. Because the company can work on at most three projects at one time and because each project lasts about 6 months, DSI could complete six projects a year. If each project costs from $5–$10 million, DSI's total revenue runs $30–$60 million a year. Because planning and design do not occupy hangar space, the company actually does more than six projects; in a good year, its revenue would be closer to $60 million.

Ms. Dorset knows the key goal for DSI's competitive advantage is labor productivity, and she understand how IS contributes to that key goal. You may find yourself in that same position at some point in your career. Your key competitive factor may not be labor productivity, but the success of some other competitive factor may be related to the use of IS. To prepare yourself for that day, strive to understand the many ways that IS within the organization (Chapter 7), IS across organizations (Chapter 8), and IS for decision making (Chapter 9) directly contribute to competitive advantage.

7 Competitive Advantage with Information Systems Within Organizations

This could happen to you

In the part-opening pages, Eleanor Dorset stated DSI's competitive strategy: quality differentiation within the 737 high-end refurbishing market. However, many of DSI's customers require competitive bidding. Therefore, the company needs to be cost-conscious. In terms of its value chain, it must ensure that every activity creates demonstrable value that justifies additional costs.

Suppose you have been hired as a summer intern at DSI. You're one of three interns, and when Ms. Dorset hired you, she made it clear that only one of the three of you has a chance at a full-time job. You very much want to be the intern selected for the full-time job.

You're working late one night on a task to support a bid proposal, and your direct supervisor, for whom you've worked very hard, stops by your cubicle.

"Thanks for helping us get out this proposal. If you keep working like this, I'm going to want to offer you a job when you finish school. . . . But there's a problem. Few people know this, but one of the other interns is John Stratford's niece. Don't spread it around, but I wanted you to know that she's got the inside track."

Needless to say, this news is depressing. "Is there no chance, then?" you ask.

"Well, if it's a tie between the two of you in his mind, he'll probably pick her. But John's a good businessman, and if you can show that you're someone DSI just *has* to have on staff, then either he'll pick you, or he and Eleanor will create a job for you. But you've got to show them you're superior."

"How?" you ask.

"Well, I'm not sure. Part of showing that you're superior is for you to figure out something on your own. But here's a thought: Almost everything John does is aimed at making labor more productive. So think along the lines of making our labor more productive. It doesn't necessarily have to be something that he decides to do . . . just some good idea that shows you know what drives our business and you are thinking of innovative ideas to help."

Because this is an MIS class and because Ms. Dorset says the company uses information systems to gain labor productivity, we'll focus on innovative information systems for you to propose. Read this chapter and its extensions with this task in mind because . . . this could happen to you.

Optional Extensions for this chapter are CE9, "Functional Information Systems," and CE10, "Cross-Functional Systems."

Study Questions

Q1 How do organizations gain a competitive advantage using IS inside the organization?

Q2 What are the three fundamental types of IS within organizations?

Q3 How do functional systems relate to the value chain?

Q4 What are the basic types of functional systems?

Q5 What are the problems of functional systems?

Q6 How do cross-functional systems relate to the value chain?

How does the knowledge in this chapter help you at DSI?

Q1 How Do Organizations Gain a Competitive Advantage Using IS inside the Organization?

In Chapter 3, we discussed the ways in which organizations achieve a competitive advantage with IS. To recap, organizations determine a competitive strategy and design value chaines to achieve that strategy. Value chain activities are accomplished using business processes. Organizations develop information systems to support those business processes. In short, information systems exist to help organizations achieve their competitive strategy.

If you were to walk into any organization (say, for example, your first employer), you would find a maze of different information systems. The knowledge in this chapter will help you to make sense out of that maze, to identify different kinds of information systems and what they do, and to understand how IS helps an organization achieve its competitive strategy. The knowledge in this chapter will also help you avoid creating an IS that is unrelated to the organization's competitive strategy.

This chapter considers information systems that facilitate processes *within* the organization. In the next chapter, we will consider systems that facilitate processes *across* organizations.

Q2 What Are the Three Fundamental Types of IS within Organizations?

IS within organizations will be easier to understand if we begin with a short history. Figure 7-1 shows three categories of IS that have evolved over time.

Calculation Systems

The very first information systems, **calculation systems**, seem antiquated today, but they were in use not very long ago. In fact, they could have been used in the business world by your grandfather.

The purpose of those early systems was to relieve workers of tedious, repetitive calculations. The first systems computed payroll and wrote paychecks; they

Figure 7-1
History of IS Within
Organizations

Name	Era	Scope	Perspective	Example	Technology Symbols
Calculation systems	1950–1980 (Your grandfather)	Single purpose	Eliminate tedious human calculations. "Just make it work!"	Payroll General ledger Inventory	Mainframe Punch card
Functional systems	1975–20?? (Your mother)	Business function	Use computer to improve operation and management of individual departments.	Human resources Financial reporting Order entry Manufacturing (MRP and MRP II)	Mainframe Stand-alone PCs Networks and LANs
Integrated systems (also cross-functional or process-based systems)	2000— (You)	Business process	Develop IS to integrate separate departments into organization-wide business processes.	Customer relationship management (CRM) Enterprise resource planning (ERP)	Networked PCs Client-servers The Internet Intranets

applied debits and credits to the general ledger and balanced the company's accounting records. They also kept track of inventory quantities—that is, quantities that were verified by physical item counts about once a quarter. As calculating machines, they were more accurate than humans—as long as the systems actually worked. (Computer failure rates were high.) Those systems were labor-saving devices, but in truth, they produced little information. None of them survive today, and we will not consider them further.

Functional Systems

The **functional systems** of the second era facilitated the work of a single department or function. They grew as a natural expansion of the capabilities of the systems of the first era. For example, payroll expanded to become human resources, general ledger became financial reporting, and inventory was merged into operations or manufacturing. The changes were more than just in name. In each functional area, companies added features and capabilities to information systems to support more functional-area activity.

The problem with functional applications is their isolation. In fact, functional applications are sometimes called **islands of automation** because they work independently of one another. Unfortunately, independent, isolated systems cannot produce the productivity and efficiency necessary for many businesses. Purchasing influences inventory, which influences production, which influences customer satisfaction, which influences future sales. Decisions that are appropriate when considering only a single function like purchasing may create inefficiencies when the entire process is considered.

Integrated, Cross-Functional Systems

The isolation problems of functional systems led to the third era of information systems. In this era, systems were designed not to facilitate the work of a single department or function, but rather to integrate the activities in an entire business process. Because those activities cross departmental boundaries, such systems are sometimes called **cross-departmental** or **cross-functional systems**. Because they support complete business processes, they are sometimes also called **process-based systems**.

Transitioning from single-purpose to functional applications was relatively easy. The newer systems provided increased functionality within a single department or function. The line of authority was clear, and little interdepartmental coordination was necessary. Unfortunately, the transition from functional systems to integrated systems is difficult. Integrated processing requires many departments to coordinate their activities. There is no clear line of authority, peer competition can be fierce, and interdepartmental rivalries can subvert the development of the new system.

Most organizations today are a mixture of functional and integrated systems. To successfully compete internationally, however, organizations must eventually achieve the efficiencies of integrated, cross-departmental, process-based systems. Thus, during your career, you can expect to see an increasing number of integrated systems and fewer functional systems. In fact, you will likely be one of the business leaders asked to implement new integrated systems.

By the way, do not assume that the systems and processes discussed in the remainder of the chapter apply only to commercial, profit-making organizations. Not-for-profit and government organizations have most of these same processes, but with a different orientation. Your state's Department of Labor, for example, has both employees and customers. The Girl Scouts of America has a general ledger

Figure 7-2
Reorganized Porter Value
Chain Model

	Human Resources				
Support Activities	Accounting and infrastructure				
	Procurement and technology				
In-bound Logistics	Operations or Manufacturing	Out-bound Logistics	Marketing and Sales	Service and Support	Margin

Primary Activities

and financial statements, as well as operational systems. Information systems for not-for-profit and for government organizations are oriented toward quality of service and efficiency rather than toward profit, but those systems still exist.

Q3 How Do Functional Systems Relate to the Value Chain?

We can use Porter's value chain model (introduced in Chapter 3) to explain the scope and purposes of different types of information systems within the organization. For our purposes, the value chain model will be more useful if we redraw it as shown in Figure 7-2. The value chain starts with marketing and sales activities. Sales and order activities are followed by in-bound logistics, operations and manufacturing, out-bound logistics, and finally, service and support. Porter termed each of these activities *primary activities* because they relate directly to the organization's customers and products.

The primary activities are facilitated by human resource, accounting and infrastructure, procurement, and technology activities. Porter termed these latter functions *support activities*. As we have redrawn the value chain in Figure 7-2, the primary activities occur in the order shown: They are supported first by the humans that perform work in the primary activities, and the human resources with primary activities are supported, in turn, by accounting and other infrastructure.

Figure 7-3 shows five functional systems and their relationship to the value chain. As you would expect, each functional system is closely allied with

Figure 7-3
Reorganized Porter Value Chain
Model and Its Relationship to
Functional Systems

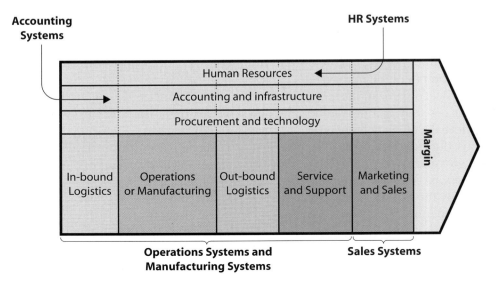

the activities it supports, and there is little cross-over among activities. To help you understand these systems, we will briefly survey them next. For more detailed information, see Chapter Extension 9, "Functional Information Systems."

Q4 What Are the Basic Types of Functional Systems?

Figure 7-4 lists principal functional systems used in five value chain activities. Consider each.

Marketing and Sales Systems

Product management is the primary functional system for marketing. Product managers use such systems to help assess how well their product-marketing efforts are working. In such a system, sales data are summarized by product, product category, and business line. Sales to date are compared to forecasts, sales in past periods, and other expectations. If the data are current enough, adjustments can be made in advertising and promotion programs by moving dollars from, say, overperforming products to underperforming products.

In truth, relatively few functional systems support marketing, but many, like Dee's blog, support sales. Recall how Dee used her blog to share knowledge about sales results and successful sales strategies with the sales force.

Function	Example Information Systems
Marketing & sales	Product management Lead tracking Sales forecasting Customer management
Operations	Order entry Order management Inventory management Customer service
Manufacturing	Inventory Planning Scheduling Manufacturing operations
Human resources	Payroll and compensation Recruiting Assessment Development and training Human resources planning
Accounting and finance	General ledger Financial reporting Accounts receivable Accounts payable Cost accounting Budgeting Cash management Treasury management

Figure 7-4
Typical Functional Systems

Other sales examples, as listed in Figure 7-4, include lead tracking, sales forecasting, customer management, and customer service (shown on the far right in Figure 7-3.) *Lead tracking* records prospects and keeps track of sales contacts with potential customers. *Sales forecasting* is vital not only for planning production or managing inventories, but also for financial reporting by publicly held companies. Wall Street hates surprises and punishes the stock price of companies that miss their sales forecasting.

The major purpose of *customer management* systems is to generate follow-up business from existing customers. Salespeople use such systems to determine what products customers have already purchased, to record all contacts with the customer, and to follow up for additional revenue generation. The *Ethics Guide* on pages 163a–163b shows the misuse of a customer management system to accelerate sales, an ethically questionable activity. It also shows how the misuse of customer management creates problems in manufacturing systems.

Operations Systems

As shown in Figure 7-3, both operations and manufacturing systems support the same primary activities in the value chain. Operations systems are used by non-manufacturers, such as distributors and retailers. Manufacturing systems are used by companies that transform materials into products.

Important operations systems are listed in Figure 7-4. *Order entry* can take place in-house, in which company employees enter orders, or it can be done at Web-based, e-commerce sites such as retailers Amazon.com or REI. *Order management* systems track orders through the fulfillment process, handling back orders and order changes as well as providing order status.

Inventory management systems analyze sales activity and generate product orders as required. Inventory management is a balancing act between the cost of carrying excessive inventory and the cost of lost orders due to product outage. Modern inventory management seeks to minimize the investment in inventory.

Customer service is a fourth operations function. Such systems provide information about the status of orders and are also used to process complaints, to respond to product or service issues, and to receive returned goods.

Manufacturing Systems

Manufacturing information systems support the transformation of materials into products. They process data about inventories for raw materials, work-in-process, and finished goods. They also concern production planning.

Most manufacturers typically choose one of two manufacturing philosophies: With **push production planning**, the organization creates a production plan or schedule and pushes goods through manufacturing and sales. "We're going to produce 500 widgets: Make them and sell them." **Pull production planning** responds to customer demand. As the company sells goods, its finished goods inventories fall, and the reduction in inventory triggers the production of more goods. Whichever philosophy a manufacturer uses, it will choose a *planning system* to match.

Organizations that produce custom, "one-off," expensive products fall outside of the push/pull categories. When aircraft detailer DSI sells a $10 million interior, it plans its activities to build that particular interior. Such manufacturers differ from those that produce, say, tennis shoes, where production is either pushed or pulled through the manufacturer.

Manufacturing scheduling and operations are additional functional systems. A tennis shoe manufacturer that needs to produce 15 types of shoes in various sizes and in various colors has many choices about how to produce those shoes. Some methods require less setup and less idle time for workers or machines and are, therefore, cheaper. *Scheduling systems* help organizations determine the optimal methods. *Manufacturing operations systems* control manufacturing plants and machines. A production line of robots, for example, is controlled by a manufacturing operations system.

Today, both operations and manufacturing activities are beginning to use an important new technology called **radio-frequency identification tags (RFIDs)**. Major retailers, such as Wal-Mart, have specified that their suppliers must place RFIDs on all products they supply. An RFID is a computer chip that transmits data about the container, product, or equipment to which it is attached. RFID data include not just product numbers, but also data about where the product was made, the product's components, special handling requirements, and, for perishable products, when the contents will expire. RFIDs can record and transmit custom, application-specific data as well. Sensors connected to inventory and other functional systems receive RFID signals and automatically record the arrival, departure, or movement of the item. Many innovative applications of RFIDs are being developed today, even as you read this sentence.

Radio-Frequency Indentification Tag (RFIDs)

Human Resources Systems

Functional systems for human resources (HR) include *payroll* and *related compensation systems*, such as sick leave and vacation-time accounting. Other HR functions systems include those used for *recruiting* personnel as well as for *assessing* employee performance.

In organizations with formal development and training programs, such as large corporations, government agencies, and military organizations, functional systems are used to categorize the skills of employees, their training requirements, and the training they have had. Such systems feed *HR planning systems* to ensure that sufficient numbers of workers with appropriate skills will be available to fill needed job requirements. Imagine an organization of 50,000, and you will see the need for such systems.

Accounting Systems

Accounting functional systems support all of the organization's accounting activities. Such systems were some of the earliest calculation systems, and they have continued their importance as functional systems evolved. Examples are *general ledger, financial reporting, accounts receivable*, and *accounts payable systems*. Other important accounting systems include *cost accounting, budgeting, cash management*, and management of the organization's stocks and bonds, borrowings, and capital investments via *treasury management*.

Over the years, one of the key improvements in accounting systems has been a reduction in time required to provide results. Nothing is more

Dialing for Dollars

Suppose you are a salesperson, and your company's sales forecasting system predicts that your quarterly sales will be substantially under quota. You call your best customers to increase sales, but no one is willing to buy more.

Your boss says that it has been a bad quarter for all of the salespeople. It's so bad, in fact, that the VP of Sales has authorized a 20 percent discount on new orders. The only stipulation is that customers must take delivery prior to the end of the quarter so that accounting can book the order. "Start dialing for dollars," she says, "and get what you can. Be creative."

Using your customer management system, you identify your top customers and present the discount offer to them. The first customer balks at increasing her inventory, "I just don't think we can sell that much."

"Well," you respond, "how about if we agree to take back any inventory you don't sell next quarter?" (By doing this, you increase your current sales and commission, and you also help your company make its quarterly sales projections. The additional product is likely to come back next quarter, but you think, "Hey, that's then and this is now.")

"OK," she says, "but I want you to stipulate the return option on the purchase order."

You know that you cannot write that on the purchase order because accounting won't book all of the order if you do. So you tell her that you'll send her an email with that stipulation. She increases her order, and accounting books the full amount.

With another customer, you try a second strategy. Instead of offering the discount, you offer the product at full price, but agree to pay a 20 percent credit in the next quarter. That way you can book the full price now. You pitch this offer as follows: "Our marketing department analyzed past sales using our fancy new computer system, and we know that increasing advertising will cause additional sales. So, if you order more product now, next quarter we'll give you 20 percent of the order back to pay for advertising."

In truth, you doubt the customer will spend the money on advertising. Instead, they'll just take the credit and sit on a bigger inventory. That will kill your sales to them next quarter, but you'll solve that problem then.

Even with these additional orders, you're still under quota. In desperation, you decide to sell product to a fictitious company that is "owned" by your brother-in-law. You set up a new account, and when accounting calls your brother-in-law for a credit check, he cooperates with your scheme. You then sell $40,000 of product to the fictitious company and ship the product to your brother-in-law's garage.

Accounting books the revenue in the quarter, and you have finally made quota. A week into the next quarter, your brother-in-law returns the merchandise.

Meanwhile, unknown to you, your company's manufacturing system is scheduling production. The program that creates the production schedule reads the sales from your activities (and those of the other salespeople) and finds a sharp increase in product demand. Accordingly, it generates a schedule that calls for substantial production increases and schedules workers for the production runs. The production system, in turn, schedules the material requirements with the inventory application, which increases raw materials purchases to meet the increased production schedule.

DISCUSSION QUESTIONS

1. Is it ethical for you to write the email agreeing to take the product back? If that email comes to light later, what do you think your boss will say?

2. Is it ethical for you to offer the "advertising" discount? What effect does that discount have on your company's balance sheet?

3. Is it ethical for you to ship to the fictitious company? Is it legal?

4. Describe the impact of your activities on next quarter's inventories.

aggravating to a manager than to find out—six weeks after the quarter has closed—that his or her department was over budget. Managers need to know the relationship of expenses accrued, encumbered, and budgeted as close to real time as they can. Similarly, management would like to close the books as close to the end of an accounting period as possible. In the history of computing, accounting systems have reduced the time to produce results from months to weeks or even to days. Many systems can now provide near-real time accounting information.

The Sarbanes-Oxley Act

In recent years, legislation known as the **Sarbanes-Oxley Act** has impacted all information systems, but particularly accounting information systems. The Sarbanes-Oxley Act of 2002 is a revision of the Exchange Act of 1934 that governs the reporting requirements of publicly held companies. Sarbanes-Oxley was enacted to prevent corporate frauds like those perpetrated by WorldCom, Enron, and others. It requires management to create internal controls sufficient to produce reliable financial statements and to protect the organization's assets. Management is further required to issue a statement indicating it has done so. The organization's external auditor must also issue an opinion on the quality of the internal controls and the credibility of management's statement. Sarbanes-Oxley exposes both management and the external auditor to financial and potential criminal liability if subsequent events should show that internal controls were defective.

An example of an internal control is **separation of duties and authorities**. In an accounts payable system, for example, three separate individuals are required: one to authorize the expense, one to issue the check, and a third to account for the transaction. No one person should perform two or more of these actions. You will learn about other such controls in your accounting classes.

If management is relying on computer-based accounting information systems for the preparation of financial statements—and all large organizations do—then those computer-based systems must have appropriate controls, and management must assert that those controls are reliable. This places a greater burden on the development and use of IS than was prevalent prior to this act.

Additionally, IS can produce valuable assets that are subject to liability. For example, the database of an order-processing information system that stores customer identities and credit card data contains an organizational asset. If the design of the IS ineffectively prevents unauthorized persons from accessing that data, then a **contingent** (possible) **liability** exists. Without effective controls, someone could steal a customer's name and credit card data and damage the customer. The customer then could sue the organization and likely prevail. The possibility that this might occur makes the liability *contingent*. Even if no one has yet sued, in such a case management is required both to report the liability in its financial statements and to take action to remedy the situation to eliminate the contingent liability.

If you are not yet convinced that you, as a general business major, need the knowledge of this MIS class, the Sarbanes-Oxley Act should convince you. As a senior manager, you will be required to make assertions about the controls on your IS that will expose you to both financial and criminal penalties. When that day arrives, it will be well worth knowing the fundamentals of IS. For a more critical review of the Sarbanes-Oxley Act, see *MIS in Use 7*.

Sarbanes-Oxley: Boon or Bane?

In 2002, in response to the corporate crimes committed by Enron, WorldCom, and others, Congress passed the Sarbanes-Oxley Act. Its goal was to strengthen and upgrade financial reporting and, thus, maintain and improve trust in public companies' financial reports. Such trust is crucial; without it, the investment community and the entire U.S. economy would come to a standstill.

CIO Magazine publishes articles of interest and importance to chief information officers (CIOs, discussed in Chapter 11). If you search for topics on Sarbanes-Oxley at *www.CIO.com*, you'll find a revealing sequence of articles. Initial articles reported confusion and concern among CIOs. Then articles appeared that explained how to comply. Most recently, *CIO Magazine*'s editor, Gary Beach, published an editorial entitled, "Repeal Sarbanes-Oxley." What happened? Surely no one is opposed to accurate financial reporting. According to Mr. Beach, ". . . while foreign companies are free to grab market share, U.S. executives are instead grabbing their Sarbanes-Oxley manuals" to learn how to comply with the act.[1]

According to a poll conducted by *CIO Magazine*, large companies expect to divert more than 15 percent of their IS budgets to Sarbanes-Oxley compliance. That represents a huge investment, and given the importance of a favorable audit report, it is

an expense that organizations view as mandatory, whether or not it is sensible.

Part of the problem is that, even in 2007, no one knows what exactly is necessary to comply with Sarbanes-Oxley. The act requires external auditors to become even more independent than they had been in the past, and thus many will not issue opinions on the specific controls that IS needs. The attitude seems to be, "Show us what you have, and we'll tell you if it's enough." IT managers are understandably frustrated.

Further, the wording of the act is so vague that, to protect themselves, auditors have taken the broadest possible interpretation. Consider, for example, Section 409, which requires disclosure of significant financial events within 48 hours. What characterizes an event as *significant*? If a customer cancels a large order, is that significant? If so, how large must an order be to be considered large? If a supplier is devastated by a hurricane, is that significant? "How," many CIOs ask, "can we determine from our information systems that a significant event has occurred? And within 48 hours? Are we supposed to reprogram our applications to include alerts on all such events? What other events should we look for? And who's paying for all of this?"

One thing is certain, the Sarbanes-Oxley Act will provide full employment for internal auditors in general and for IT auditors in particular. Organizations will have to sponsor a flurry of activity, however uneconomic, to show that they are doing something to comply. No company can afford to ignore the act.

Senators Sarbanes and Oxley are both attorneys, neither of whom has ever worked in a publicly traded company. In the light of the financial disasters at Enron and WorldCom, their law was highly praised by the public. But, is it worth its cost? Will millions, perhaps billions, be wasted in unnecessary compliance? In the long run, will it hamper U.S. corporations that must compete internationally against corporations that are not burdened by this act? Will it ultimately work to reduce investor choices? And given the requirements of the Sarbanes-Oxley Act, why would privately owned companies, like DSI, ever choose to go public?

---

[1]Gary Beach, "Repeal Sarbanes-Oxley," *CIO*, April 1, 2005, *www.CIO.com* (accessed August 2006).

Q5 What Are the Problems of Functional Systems?

Functional systems provide tremendous benefits to the departments that use them, but as stated earlier, their benefits are limited because they operate in isolation. In particular, functional systems have the problems listed in Figure 7-5. First, with isolated systems, data are duplicated because each application has its own database. For example, customer data may be duplicated and possibly inconsistent when accounting and sales/marketing applications are separated. The principal problem of duplicated data is a potential lack of data integrity. Changes to product data made in one system may take days or weeks to reach the other systems. During that period, inconsistent data will cause inconsistent application results. (For more on the data integrity problem, see Chapter Extension 5.)

Additionally, when systems are isolated, business processes are disjointed. There is no easy way for the sales/marketing system, for example, to integrate activity with the accounting system. Just sending the data from one system to the other can be problematic.

Consider the simple example in Figure 7-6. Suppose the order entry and inventory systems define a product number as three characters, a dash, and four numeric digits. Yet, suppose the Manufacturing system in the same company defines a product as four digits followed by characters. Every time parts data are exported from order entry and imported into manufacturing (or the reverse), the data must be converted from one scheme to the other. Multiply this conversion process by several hundred data items, and possibly dozens of other systems, and you can see why processing is disjointed across functional applications.

Figure 7-5
Major Problems of Isolated Functional Systems

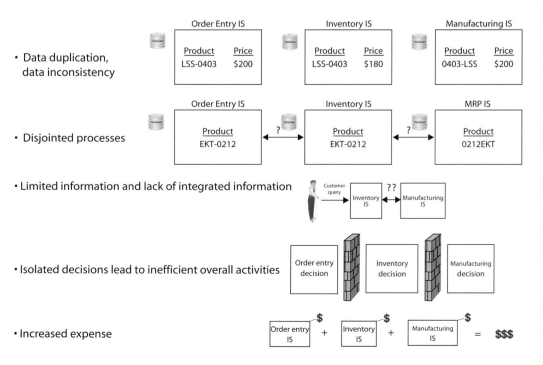

• Order Entry System Product Number:
    Format: ccc–nnnn
    Example: COMP–3344
• Manufacturing System Product Number:
    Format: nnnnccc
    Example: 3344COMP

Figure 7-6
Example of System Integration Problem

A consequence of such disjointed systems is the lack of integrated enterprise information. When a customer inquires about an order, several systems may need to be queried. For example, some order information is in the order entry system, some is in the finished-goods inventory system, and some is in the manufacturing system. Obtaining a consolidated statement about the customer's order will require processing each of these systems, with possibly inconsistent data.

A fourth consequence of isolated systems is inefficiency. When using isolated functional systems, a department can make decisions based only on the isolated data that it has. So, for example, raw materials inventory systems will make inventory replenishment decisions based only on costs and benefits in that single inventory. However, it might be that the overall efficiency of the sales, order entry, and manufacturing activities, considered together across the enterprise, will be improved by carrying a less than optimal number of products in raw materials inventory.

Finally, isolated functional systems can result in increased cost for the organization. Duplicated data, disjointed systems, limited information, and inefficiencies all mean higher costs.

Organizations recognized the problems of isolated systems back in the 1980s, and business consultants began searching for ways to build more integrated systems. We consider those systems next.

Q6 How Do Cross-functional Systems Relate to the Value Chain?

Cross-functional systems were developed to overcome the problems of functional systems. Two types of cross-functional systems are important today: customer relationship management (CRM) and enterprise resource planning (ERP) systems.

As you will see, these types of cross-functional systems provide numerous benefits for organizations. Yet because of the changes required for organization-wide process integration, these systems also at times cause resistance among some employees, as shown in the *Guide* on pages 167a–167b.

CRM Systems and the Value Chain

As you can see in Figure 7-7, **customer relationship management (CRM) systems** integrate all of the primary business activities. They track all interactions with the customer from prospect through follow-up service and support. Vendors of CRM systems claim that using their products makes the organization *customer-centric*. Though that term reeks of sales hyperbole, it does indicate the nature and intent of CRM systems.

TQM

The Flavor-of-the-Month Club

KNOWLEDGE MANAGEMENT

"Oh, come on. I've been here 30 years and I've heard it all. All these management programs. . . . Years ago, we had Zero Defects. Then it was Total Quality Management, and after that, Six Sigma. We've had all the pet theories from every consultant in the Western Hemisphere. No, wait, we had consultants from Asia, too.

ZERO DEFECTS

"Do you know what flavor we're having now? We're redesigning ourselves to be 'customer centric.' We are going to integrate our functional systems into a CRM system to transform the entire company to be 'customer-centric.'

"You know how these programs go? First, we have a pronouncement at a 'kick-off meeting' where the CEO tells us what the new flavor is going to be and why it's so important. Then a swarm of consultants and 'change management' experts tell us how they're going to 'empower' us. Then HR adds some new item to our annual review, such as, 'Measures taken to achieve customer-centric company.'

"So, we all figure out some lame thing to do so that we have something to put in that category of our annual review. Then we forget about it because we know the next new flavor of the month will be along soon. Or worse, if they actually force us

to use the new system, we comply, but viciously. You know, go out of our way to show that the new system can't work, that it really screws things up.

"You think I sound bitter, but I've seen this so many times before. The consultants and rising stars in our company get together and dream up one of these programs. Then they present it to the senior managers. That's when they make their first mistake: They think that if they can sell it to management, then it must be a good idea. They treat senior management like the customer. They should have to sell the idea to those of us who actually sell, support, or make things. Senior management is just the banker; the managers should let us decide if it's a good idea.

"If someone really wanted to empower me, she would listen rather than talk. Those of us who do the work have hundreds of ideas of how to do it better. Now it's customer-centric? As if we haven't been trying to do that for years!

"Anyway, after the CEO issues the pronouncements about the new system, he gets busy with other things and forgets about it for a while. Six months might go by, and then we're either told we're not doing enough to become customer-centric (or whatever the flavor is) or the company announces another new flavor.

"In manufacturing they talk about push versus pull. You know, with push style, you make things and push them onto the sales force and the customers. With pull style, you let the customers' demand pull the product out of manufacturing. You build when you have holes in inventory. Well, they should adapt those ideas to what they call 'change management.' I mean, does anybody need to manage real change? Did somebody have a 'Use the cell phone' program? Did some CEO announce, 'This year, we're all going to use the cell phone'? Did the HR department put a line into our annual evaluation form that asked how many times we'd used a cell phone? No, no, no, and no. Customers pulled the cell phone through. We wanted it, so we bought and used cell phones. Same with color printers, Palm Pilots, and wireless networks.

"That's pull. You get a group of workers to form a network, and you get things going among the people who do the work. Then you build on that to obtain true organizational change. Why don't they figure it out?

"Anyway, I've got to run. We've got the kick-off meeting of our new initiative—something about supply chain management. Now they're going to empower me to buy things from our suppliers. Like I haven't been doing that all these years. Oh, well, I plan to retire soon.

"Oh, wait. Here, take my T-shirt from the knowledge management program two years ago. I never wore it. It says, 'Empowering You Through Knowledge Management.' That one didn't last long."

DISCUSSION QUESTIONS

1. Clearly, this person is bitter about new programs and new ideas. What do you think might have been the cause of his antagonism? What seems to be his principal concern?

2. What does he mean by "vicious" compliance? Give an example of an experience you've had that exemplifies such compliance.

3. Consider his point that the proponents of new programs treat senior managers as the customer. What does he mean? To a consultant, is senior management the customer? What do you think he's trying to say?

4. What does he mean when he says, "If someone wants to empower me, she would listen rather than talk"? How does listening to someone empower that person?

5. His examples of "pull change" all involve the use of new products. To what extent do you think pull works for new management programs?

6. How do you think management could introduce new programs in a way that would cause them to be pulled through the organization? Consider the suggestion he makes, as well as your own ideas.

7. If you managed an employee who had an attitude like this, what could you do to make him more positive about organizational change and new programs and initiatives?

Figure 7-7
CRM and the Value Chain Model

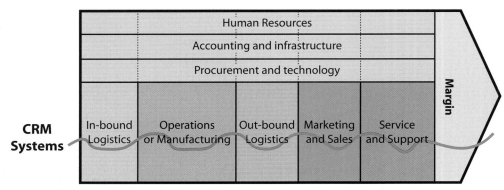

A key element of CRM is that all customer data is stored in a single database. This characteristic eliminates the possibility of inconsistent customer data. It also enables employees in every department to see and know the customer's complete history. For example, when a salesperson calls a customer for follow-up business, he or she will know not only how much the customer has ordered in the past, but also the complaints or issues the customer has had, any existing open orders, the customer's credit status, and other relevant customer data.

ERP Systems and the Value Chain

Enterprise resource planning (ERP) systems provide even more integration than CRM. As Figure 7-8 shows, ERP integrates the primary value chain activities with human resources and accounting. ERP systems are truly enterprise-wide. They track customers, process orders, manage inventory, pay employees, and provide general ledger, payable, receivables, and other necessary accounting functions.

While programs for some functional systems are written in-house by the organization that uses them, almost no CRM or ERP system is. Normally, organizations license CRM or ERP software from vendors such as SAP, Oracle, or Microsoft. In most cases, the conversion to these systems requires the organization to adapt its procedures to the procedures inherent in the software. Such change is disruptive and painful, the more so for ERP because ERP touches every aspect of the organization.

We discuss CRM and ERP and some of these problems in greater detail in Chapter Extension 10, "Cross-functional Systems: CRM, ERP, and EAI," on page 439. There, we also discuss a compromise between functional systems and ERP called *enterprise application integration (EAI)*.

Figure 7-8
ERP Systems and the Value Chain

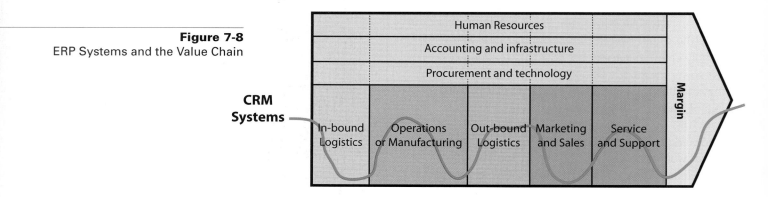

How does the knowledge in this chapter help you at DSI?

You need to close the gap on the niece who has the inside track for the job at DSI. You know that DSI competitive strategy is to differentiate on quality, subject on some projects to a competitive-bidding process.

Theoretically, you could propose a system that increases quality and labor costs, as long as the value generated by the increased quality is sufficiently greater than the marginal cost. But, doing so increases the sales challenges of explaining why the additional costs are a worthy investment for the customer. It is unlikely that DSI wants to increase its sales challenges, no matter how great your idea is, so you decide not to pursue that theoretical possibility.

Instead, you decide to focus directly on what your boss recommended: increase labor productivity and, therefore, reduce labor costs. The text does not say this, but assume DSI does not use ERP. You know ERP could save labor costs, but developing a new ERP system will impact many departments and mean substantial disruption of existing operations. As a summer intern, you're certain you do not have the credibility necessary to obtain serious consideration for a system with such high transition costs.

You begin looking for examples of how DSI currently saves labor. One way is by using recycled vending machines like the one in Figure 7-9. Rather than candy bars and potato chips, this machine vends consumable tools, such as sandpaper, burnishing wheels, and drill bits. These vending machines are located throughout the hangar, within a few steps of the production lines.

When a worker needs a new consumable tool part, he or she walks a few steps to the vending machine, scans the magnetic strip of his or her employee badge with the hand-held scanner, and keys the number of the item needed. The vending machine is connected to an IS that allocates the expense of that item to that employee. Employees are always logged into a particular project, and so the cost of the item is allocated to the project as well. These machines save the labor time of having the welder walk to a centralized tool crib, possibly stand in line, chatting with other workers, before obtaining that same item.

What other systems might increase labor productivity? On your way to your lunch break, you've noticed that DSI maintains a shop where it repairs tools. A broken tool means that whoever was using that tool has lost time. And, if there is no replacement for the broken tool, work may need to be delayed or rescheduled until the tool is fixed or repaired.

You wonder what data is kept about tool repairs. The repair shop has two or three computer monitors, so workers in the tool shop must enter something about the repairs. Perhaps there is a way to process the repair data to determine how much time is lost when a tool is in repair? If so, that might give you an idea of how much time is being lost. If it is a substantial amount of time, maybe the data could be analyzed and a system developed that would recommend the acquisition of backups for frequently breaking tools? You decide to think more about this possibility.

You have also noticed that DSI operates a tool crib from which workers check out portable tools, such as impact hammers, sanders, and grinders. From

Figure 7-9
Vending Machines That
Hold Consumable Tools
Reduce Wasted Labor

time to time, you see a line in front of that tool crib. Workers standing in that line represent lost labor time. You haven't seen any evidence that DSI is using RFID. You begin to wonder if it would be possible to propose a "virtual tool crib." Each item of equipment would have its own RFID chip, and that chip could be used to record and report who has the tool checked out and where it is currently located. You think that idea has potential promise and decide to consider it as well.

Active **?** Review

Use this Active Review to verify that you understand the material in the chapter. You can read the entire chapter and then perform the tasks in this review, or you can read the material for just one question and perform the tasks in this review for that question before moving on to the next one.

Q1 How do organizations gain a competitive advantage using IS inside the organization?

Define *competitive strategy*. Explain the relationship between competitive strategy, value chains, business processes, and information systems.

Q2 What are the three fundamental types of IS within organizations?

Using Figure 7-1, explain the three types of IS. Give an example of each. Describe how each type overcomes problems in the earlier type. Explain which of these systems you are likely to encounter in your career. Describe a problem that is likely to concern you.

Q3 How do functional systems relate to the value chain?

Draw the Porter value chain model as shown in this chapter. Explain the nature of the work performed at each value chain activity. Show how the fundamental types of functional information systems relate to value chain activities.

Q4 What are the basic types of functional systems?

Name five categories of functional systems. Explain the general purpose of each. Explain the differences among manufacturing, operations, scheduling, inventory, and planning systems. Explain the role of RFID tags.

Q5 What are the problems of functional systems?

Name five problems of functional systems and describe each. Give an example of a data integration problem. Describe the consequences of a lack of data integration.

Q6 How do cross-functional systems relate to the value chain?

Name the two cross-functional systems discussed in this chapter and describe the purpose of each. Explain how the scope of these two systems differs. Show how each type relates to the value chain model.

How does the knowledge in this chapter help you at DSI?

State DSI's competitive strategy. Explain how that strategy influences the development of IS. Explain how a system that adds value and cost could be a wise investment. Describe how such a system increases DSI's sales challenges. Explain why it is probably unwise for the intern to propose such a system. Explain why the intern decided not to propose an ERP system.

State the primary criterion the intern decided to use in thinking about a new IS. Explain why the vending machine system exemplifies that criterion. Explain why tool repair represents a potential loss of labor time and describe how tool repair data could be processed to determine if this is a substantial loss. Summarize the two opportunities the intern decided to pursue. Explain the term *virtual tool crib*.

Key Terms and Concepts

Using Your Knowledge

1. Choose one of the following basic business processes: inventory management, operations, manufacturing, HR management, or accounting/financial management. Use the Internet to identify three vendors that license a product to support that process. Compare offerings from the three vendors as follows.
   a. Determine differences in terminology, especially differences in the ways that the vendors use the same terms.
   b. Compare features and functions of each of the product offerings.
   c. For each vendor, specify the characteristics of a company for which that vendor's offering would be ideal.

2. Suppose you are the intern at DSI. Do you agree with the conclusions reached? Do you agree with the statement of competitive advantage? Do you agree with the decision not to explore a system that adds both value and cost? Do you agree not to propose an ERP system? Do you agree with the decision to explore the tool repair data and the possible virtual tool crib? For each of these questions, say why or why not.

3. Examine the list of problems of functional systems in Figure 7-5. Assuming that DSI uses only functional systems, give an example of each one of these problems. You do not have all of the data necessary to know whether or not DSI has those problems, but describe problems that are plausible. State your assumptions when necessary.

4. Consider the possibility of processing the tool repair data to determine possible wasted labor costs. Does the fact that a tool is in the repair shop necessarily indicate that labor was lost? How could you find out if that was the case? Acquiring backup tools could be expensive. How would you go about justifying the additional expense? What economic argument would you make to justify the purchase of the backups? How do the cost of the tool and the frequency of the failure impact the decision to buy a backup? Does the length of time to repair a tool impact this decision? How could a system of priorities for tool repair also save labor hours?

5. Investigate the possibility of a virtual tool crib. Assume each tool has an RFID. (Google RFID to learn more if you need to.) Assume that each production facility has racks on which tools can be placed when not in use. Assume that tools reside in only one of those racks; there is no centralized tool crib or other repository. Describe the nature of an IS for tracking tools. Could that system prevent tool theft? If so, how? How would an employee obtain a tool when needed? How would the IS help employees learn the location of tools? On balance, does this seem like a workable idea? Or, is it just some high-tech option that would create confusion?

6. Explain how the Sarbanes-Oxley Act impacts DSI.

Case Study 7 _____

Manufacturing Planning at the Brose Group

Reread *MIS in Use 2*, about the Brose Group (page 31) before you proceed with this case.

Modern manufacturing seeks to improve productivity by reducing waste, which means eliminating:

- Overproduction that leads to excess inventories
- Unavailable needed parts, which idle workers and facilities
- Wasted motion and processing due to poorly planned materials handling and operations activities

Manufacturing that eliminates these wastes is called *lean manufacturing*.

To accomplish lean manufacturing, SAP has invented a business process it calls just-in-sequence (JIS) manufacturing. JIS is an extension to just-in-time (JIT), the pull manufacturing philosophy described in this chapter. JIS extends JIT so that parts not only arrive just in time, but also arrive in just the correct sequence.

For example, the Brose Group factory in Brazil manufactures doors for General Motors. When General Motors starts the construction of a new auto, it sends a signal of the need for doors to the Brose Group. That signal starts the construction of the four doors on four separate production lines in Brazil. Brose schedules the work on each of these lines so as to produce the four doors and their related equipment and deliver them at the correct time and in the correct sequence at General Motors. Thus, if General Motors needs the rear-door frames, then the front-door frames, then the front doors, and finally the rear doors, Brose will schedule manufacturing and delivery accordingly.

To achieve JIS, Brose used SAP R/3 combined with a supplementary SAP module called SAP for Automotive with JIS. Like all ERP software, these applications include inherent (that is, built-in) processes that the organization does not need to design separately. In this case, those business processes include manufacturing planning methods and procedures for JIS performance.

Sources: brose.de/en/pub/company (accessed November 2004); sap.com/industries/automotive/pdf/CS_Brose_Group.pdf, 2003 (accessed March 2005).

Questions

1. Reflect on the nature of JIS planning. In general terms, what kinds of data must Brose have in order to provide JIS to its customers? What does Brose need to know? It certainly needs a bill of materials for the items it produces. What other categories of information will Brose need?

2. According to the description on page 31, the SAP system included applications for sales and distribution, materials management, production planning, quality management, and financial accounting and control. Describe, in general terms, features and functions of these applications that are necessary to provide JIS.

3. The Brose factory in Brazil produces more than doors for General Motors. The factory must coordinate the door orders with orders for other products and orders from other manufacturers. What kinds of IS are necessary to provide such coordinated manufacturing planning?

4. Brazilians speak Portuguese, workers in the United States speak English and Spanish, and personnel at the Brose headquarters speak German. Summarize

challenges to Brose and SAP Consulting when implementing a system for users who speak four different languages and live in four (at least) different cultures.

5. Visit *sap.com/industries/automotive* and investigate SAP for Automotive with JIS. What features and functions does this product have that standard SAP R/3 does not have? What advantages does SAP obtain by creating and licensing this product? What advantages do SAP's customers obtain from this product? In your response, consider both R/3 customers who are and who are not automotive manufacturers.

6. Brose seeks to provide JIS service to its customers. Does this goal necessitate that Brose suppliers also provide JIS service to Brose? What can Brose do if its suppliers do not provide such service? Is there any reason why Brose would not want them to provide such service? Do you think that before one company in a supply chain can offer JIS, all companies in the supply chain must offer the service?

Dorset-Stratford Interiors, Part 3 and Chapter 7

GOALS

Use Dorset-Stratford Interiors (DSI) to:

* Help students relate IT and IS to real business problems.

* Demonstrate how information systems contribute to competitive strategy.

* Understand how students can use knowledge of MIS to gain a personal competitive advantage.

BACKGROUND

1. The company behind DSI is incredibly successful. It is small and very well run, and it has a superior reputation for quality. When I visited, its production facilities were spotless, employees were working hard, and no one was standing around looking for something to do. The place exuded good management.

2. The real John Stratford is a very no-nonsense person who is used to command. During our interviews, he sat behind his very large desk and kept me at quite a distance. It was clear he liked being in charge. He was friendly, very professional, but somewhat condescending. After he read the case, he was incredulous that I would expect him to allow me to publish it. Because he'd given me most of the material, I, in turn, was surprised at his reaction. I thought he would be pleased that I had captured the company's competitive strategy, etc. I didn't think what I'd written (essentially what is here in the book, but disguised as DSI) was all that revealing. I suspect he was concerned in part because the company is private and not used to public disclosure. A public company, like Dell, for example, is pleased to publish its competitive strategy widely and broadly. The company behind DSI is unused to the spotlight.

3. The business dynamics of DSI and the actual company are very similar. They both manufacture high-quality, custom, complicated products. I chose them for this text because their business is complicated enough to have business-process problems, complicated enough to discuss IS within the organization and IS across organizations, but not so complicated that students cannot comprehend them.

4. The intern in the case is a device to cause the students to engage the situation vicariously. (See the Instructor Preface.) I want the students to place themselves in that company and think about the issues raised. I want them to think, "This could happen to me." The niece is fictitious, but I added her to attempt to raise the students' emotional involvement a bit.

5. One of the more interesting scenes at DSI was employees obtaining small parts from recycled vending machines. You can find examples at: *www.cribmaster.com/toolbox.htm.* As of October 2006, that Web page has a link to a video that illustrates perfectly an innovative application of information systems and business activities. It is worth playing in class.

6. One of the ideas the DSI intern considers is a virtual tool crib using RFID. The Web site above actually offers such a product . . . or one close to it. It also is worth checking out.

7. High-end airplane interiors are spectacular to view. They sure make seat 11B (or whatever) on a commercial flight look dreary—at least to my eye. Check out: *www.goredesign.com/portfolio.html* and *www.completioncenter.com* for examples. (DSI is **not** based on either of these companies.) Also, Google head-of-state aircraft interior for more examples.

8. DSI uses only functional systems. The company has no CRM and no ERP. When I asked "John Stratford" if his company uses ERP or SAP, he responded, "What are they?" I was astounded, but, hey, he's incredibly successful at what he does. But, could he be more so? What he's doing works, and he's happy with it though.

HOW TO GET THE STUDENTS INVOLVED

1. I start with the sizzle. Go out to one of the Web sites in item 7 and show the students what the interior of a private airplane looks like.

   a. It beats flying commercial, doesn't it?

   b. Any of you could ride in—or own—one of these. Just start thinking about innovative applications of IS and IT in an important industry . . . that's really how Michael Dell got started.

2. One way to think about this business is to identify value chains:

   a. How has the author redrawn the Porter value chain model?

   b. What do we know or what can we surmise about sales and marketing at DSI?

c. What do we know or what can we surmise about in-bound logistics at DSI?

d. What do we know or what can we surmise about manufacturing at DSI? (Think especially about problems due to high-end, custom manufacturing.)

e. What do we know or what can we surmise about out-bound logistics at DSI?

f. What do we know or what can we surmise about service and support at DSI?

g. What do we know or what can we surmise about support activities?

3. Next, think about information systems to support each of the primary activities in the value chain:

a. For each value chain activity at DSI, give an example of a functional system that would support that value chain.

b. Score that functional system against DSI's competitive strategy

4. Now, consider cross-functional systems:

a. How could DSI use a CRM application?

b. How would that application at DSI differ from CRM at, for example, Dell or Amazon.com?

c. How could DSI use an ERP system?

d. How would that application at DSI differ from ERP at, for example, Toyota?

5. Ask the students to consider the intern's two ideas: analyzing the tool repair data and a virtual tool crib.

a. Summarize the project to analyze tool repair data.

b. How would it contribute to DSI's competitive strategy?

c. How well do you like that idea?

d. Summarize the virtual tool crib idea.

e. How would it contribute to DSI's competitive strategy?

f. How well do you like that idea?

g. What other system ideas might make sense?

BOTTOM LINE

* You can use information systems to gain a competitive advantage both personally and as an organization. Remember to think of innovative applications of IS and IT; they will be key during your career.

Using the Ethics Guide: Dialing for Dollars *(page 163a)*

GOALS

* Understand how business pressures motivate people to act unethically and sometimes illegally.

* Discuss ethical principles among three different aggressive sales techniques.

* Illustrate how deception in the use of an interdepartmental information system may cause unintended consequences.

BACKGROUND AND PRESENTATION STRATEGIES

The stock market is *brutal to companies that miss their quarterly sales projections*. The pressure on a company to make its numbers can be over the top—especially on small-cap companies that are new, have a limited track record, and have limited cash reserves. Stock prices on such companies can fall by two-thirds of their value in a day.

The software industry has used all three of the techniques in this guide, especially during the 1990s and early 2000s. These techniques, when applied to distributor-customers, are often referred to as *stuffing the channel*. It's a risky strategy; the company is just putting this quarter's problem into the next quarter, where, unless there is a substantial increase in sales demand, the problem will be worse. Managers do it or look the other way when it's being done, because putting off the stock price slaughter for one quarter is at least putting it off for one quarter.

The three techniques used here are:

1. The side letter
2. The delayed discount
3. The fictitious account

I believe that *all three of the stuffing techniques are unethical*. Furthermore, the first and third violate SEC rules and regulations, and the *last one is criminally fraudulent*.

In class, I've used the following sequence of questions to introduce this guide:

➤ **Why is the company doing this?**

➤ **What are the techniques used here?**

➤ **Which of these techniques is criminally fraudulent?**

➤ **Which are violations of SEC rules and regulations?**

➤ **Which are unethical?**

The *surprise in this guide* is the impact these actions have on manufacturing scheduling. Given cross-departmental systems, the fictitious increased sales activity *generates increased production activity*, thus compounding the company's problems in the next quarter. The company will have a huge finished goods inventory—from returns and also from the increased production activity. The stock market will note the increased inventory, and even more pressure will come to the beleaguered company (though they brought it on themselves).

Such ethical issues are, by the way, not new: *"Oh, the tangled web we weave, when first we practice to deceive!"* (Sir Walter Scott, *Marmion*). Here, we've automated the tangled web—*increased the productivity of entanglement.*

This company is in serious trouble. At this point, *all choices are bad*. It's a "pick your least regret" situation. I believe that this company, unlike DSI, is a company to leave, and soon. These practices are unethical, and the company will ultimately fail. The bloodbath, when it happens, will be huge.

? SUGGESTED RESPONSES FOR DISCUSSION QUESTIONS

1. To me, *the email involves deception*. The reason for writing it is to avoid a control placed by the accounting department. In almost every case, actions taken for the purpose of deception are unethical. The second part of this question is a good one to ask the class:

   ➤ **If the email comes to light later, what will your boss say?**

   Your boss will likely deny direct involvement. Your boss won't deny that such letters are written, but he or she will never admit (nor will there be evidence to prove) that it was encouraged. You'll be left holding the bag, so to speak.

   Additional questions to add reality to this vignette:

   ➤ **What would you do if you found yourself employed by a company that encouraged such practices?**

   Suppose you like where you live, your kids are happy in school, and your spouse has a great job.

   ➤ **Would you change jobs just because of this problem?**

2. I think the delayed discount via the advertising letter is deceptive, and hence unethical. But sometimes I play devil's advocate as follows:

➤ **Is this clearly less unethical than the email? The customer might use the discount for advertising. If they don't, it's not my fault.**

Yes, that might be, but the entire action is based on deception. And there's an additional lie:

➤ **How likely is it that the salesperson's "fancy CRM" produced information about the utility of advertising?**

➤ **Can any course of action that involves a lie ever be ethical? Why or why not?**

To answer the rest of the question in the text, the impact on the balance sheet is to overstate revenue in this quarter.

3. Shipping to the fictitious company is both *illegal and unethical*. This is *"Go to jail"* activity. DO NOT engage in such activity! Enough said.

4. The email and the fictitious company actions will cause excessive inventory next quarter. All this is "behind the scenes," so no information system will have been programmed to expect the large returns that are going to occur. And, as pointed out in the next question, the sales this quarter may cause the MPS to increase production.

Another question to ask:

➤ **What would you do if you worked as an inventory manager in this company? How would you plan your inventory?**

This organization *is in a very interesting bind*. Inventories are going to go up unless someone tells production to ignore the depletion of inventory. But this means that someone has to explain to why. If they explain why, however, then what was a "dirty little secret" *in sales* becomes a "dirty little secret" *across the company*. Is this the culture that any company wants to create? And yet, if they miss their numbers badly, the organization will be in trouble.

➤ **Which is better: Work in a company with a culture of keeping "dirty little secrets" or work in a troubled company?**

5. The sales manager will probably begin to reduce sales activity by some factor in his planning. He'll have to guess because no one is likely to tell him which sales are phony. Long-term production planning becomes impossible.

To me, this is a fascinating consequence of these unethical practices. If top management is not aware of the channel stuffing that sales is doing (unlikely, but possible), the production manager might be called on the carpet—at least for increasing production because of the perceived phony sales.

In my experience, *production people and sales people have very different personalities with very different values*. Production people crave organization, accuracy, and quality. Sales people crave human interaction, flexibility, optimism, and "we can do it" attitudes. The two types are like oil and water. I see a possibly explosive meeting between these two groups.

If the class is willing, it might be worthwhile to *conduct a mock hallway interchange*—have one student (majoring in, for example, marketing) represent the sales person and another (majoring in, for example, production management) represent the production manager. You can be the CEO!

Cue the students: *The production manager is irate and righteous;* the salesperson is *guilty*, but thrilled to have *made the numbers*. The salesperson feels like he or she has *pulled the company* out of a disaster.

6. It will take a miracle to stop this cycle. The company will have to have an incredibly strong next quarter. Without that, they'll be dialing for dollars again. And next quarter, the problem will be amplified; they'll be dialing for even more dollars. This cannot go on. Ultimately, they will have a bad quarter—with consequences much worse than they would have had if they'd have taken the hit in the first bad quarter.

WRAP UP

➤ **The easiest response to this scenario is to say "I'll never work for a company like that." But, what if you like the company and situations like this only come around every 18 months or so—and then it's only the occasional side letter?**

➤ **Would you stay here?**

➤ **Last point: With process-based, interdepartmental systems, the actions of one department influence those of another. In this case, deception breeds deception (and disaster!).**

Using the Guide: The Flavor-of-the-Month Club *(page 167a)*

GOALS

* Understand sources of resistance to change-management activities.

* Encourage students to think about the reality of change management and how to deal with forces that oppose it.

BACKGROUND AND PRESENTATION STRATEGIES

The person on whom this vignette is based believed that *management never listened* to him. He thought he was *smarter than management* (and he probably was), and he thought most attempts at change management were silly—almost as if management went to a training program, learned certain words to recite, and then recited those words, without any real care for the employees.

People who deal closely with the customer often identify more with the customers' needs and problems than they do with their own management. Because they spend more time with the customer than they do with their managers, they begin to identify more with the customer than with the company. They blame management for the customers' problems. This is especially true if they have no ready fix for the customers' problems.

Outside consultants can be highly demotivating to employees. Employees quite naturally feel resentful when some highly paid person from outside comes along and "tells management what I've been telling them all along." They feel, "Management won't listen to me, but they will listen to them."

A single "kick-off" meeting is insufficient to launch a new program. The program must have *regular, recurring follow-up* at all levels of management (especially first-line management).

Companies sometimes encounter *vicious compliance:* "You control my paycheck, but you don't control my heart and mind. I'll do what you say, but angrily, and I won't do a very good job at it." This is an incredibly immature response, but sometimes employees feel that is their only possible response. Communication is nil.

Scenario for class discussion: To illustrate how difficult change management can be, consider the following scenario: Suppose an organization changes its competitive strategy from a *differentiating strategy* to a *cost-leader strategy.*

➤ **How will this change alter the way the organization treats its existing customers?**

➤ **How will the customers respond to those changes?**

➤ **How will the employees respond to the customers' responses?**

➤ **What kind of change-management program needs to be created when shifting to a cost-leader strategy?**

➤ **What changes, besides customer service, will be affected? For example, how might that strategy change employee travel accommodations or computer equipment?**

➤ **How will the employees respond to those changes?**

Ask the students to specify five or six features of a change-management program to implement a change to a cost-leader strategy.

➤ **Even with such a program, how popular will such a change be?**

➤ **Is it conceivable that there could be a pull style of change management? If so, how?**

➤ **Is it even possible for an organization to make the shift from a differentiation strategy to a cost-leadership strategy?**

➤ **How popular will management be during such a change? Does unpopularity justify not making the change?**

 SUGGESTED RESPONSES FOR DISCUSSION QUESTIONS

1. Begin by asking the students:

   ➤ **What causes someone to have such an attitude?**

   ➤ **What has management done in the past to cause him to feel this way?**

   ➤ **What would you do if you had an employee like this?**

   Some of the causes I perceive: Management doesn't listen to his good ideas, but they will listen to an outside consultant. Management is insincere in its efforts to help employees deal with changes.

2. Vicious compliance means employees do something because they have to. They don't believe in it, but they'll do it because they want their paychecks. It is horrible to feel like this and horrible to manage people who act like this.

> ➤ **Have you every worked in an organization in which vicious compliance was practiced?**

> ➤ **What causes vicious compliance?**

> ➤ **What would you do if you managed a department with employees who were complying viciously?**

> ➤ **Can information systems play a role in causing vicious compliance?**

3. He wants to focus on the needs of the company's customers, not the needs of the company's managers. Sometimes, senior management is treated as the person to convince, yet revenue depends on the customers' response.

   For example, you can convince management that a new IS will be terrific, but if its features cause employees to hate it, then it was not terrific. By the way, employees have a different relationship to senior managers than consultants do. If management buys the consultants' story, the consultants have convinced their customer, but the employees will be left with the duty of convincing the company's customers.

   > ➤ **What does he mean by the statement, "Senior management is just the banker"?**

   > ➤ **What happens when employees are more focused on pleasing their management than on pleasing the customer?**

   > ➤ **What is the proper balance between pleasing management and pleasing the customer?**

4. The employee is saying that he has great ideas that he believes no one listens to. He doesn't need someone to give him more power, he needs someone to let him use the power he already has.

   > ➤ **How does listening to someone empower them?**

   > ➤ **What is the difference between *telling* someone what they should do and *listening* to them say what they want to do?**

   > ➤ **How does that difference empower someone?**

5. The contrarian has a point: When people truly see the benefit of something, there really is no need to manage change. But, is all change like that?

> ➤ **Is there a way, for example, to pull the changes to implement a new ERP system through the organization? How?**

> ➤ **If not, how could management push the changes for the new ERP system?**

   Pull can work if employees have been the source of a change or have had a vital role in implementing that change. Maybe quality circles succeed because employees will pull the change to them.

6. Management could listen to the employees, incorporate employees' ideas for implementation, communicate early and often, and take active steps to show value for employees. Management also must deal with self-efficacy issues (see the Guide on page 441a, "Thinking About Change").

7. He needs to be listened to, and more than once. He will be quick to sense any insincerity, and if he's promised anything, he'll be furious (as well as smug because he *knew* it was only a ruse) that management has let him down once again. Involve him in a leadership role for new programs and initiatives. This employee will be high-maintenance for a long time. The extra effort might be worth the manager's time, if he has lots to add to the group.

WRAP UP

> ➤ **What did you learn about change management from this exercise?**

> ➤ **How does change management pertain to IS in particular?**

> ➤ **Side note: Interesting career opportunities are available in helping organizations adapt to changes brought by information systems, but such jobs can be hard to find. Not all go by the title of change-management consultant. Sometimes the titles are user support, user training, systems analyst, and related titles. If you're interested in this topic, you should take our systems development class.**

8 Competitive Advantage with Information Systems Across Organizations

This could happen to you

You're working as the intern at DSI, and you're competing for a full-time job. One day, walking back to your desk to eat your sack lunch, you walk past a window overlooking the parking lot and see Mr. Stratford, his sister, and the niece-intern against whom you are competing. She's "dressed to the nines," and they are chatting and laughing together as they get into Mr. Stratford's big, black Mercedes.

"Aaah," you scream to yourself, "they're probably going to the country club for lunch."

You've lost your appetite for the tuna sandwich in your brown bag, and you decide to focus even harder on an innovative IS to increase labor productivity.

DSI designs and builds Boeing 737 interiors. It specializes in high-quality, head-of-state-caliber fit and finish. The company does not make aluminum, nor does it cut and bend aluminum into needed shapes. Further, it doesn't manufacture fabrics, carpets, furniture, air filtration systems, or other components. Instead, DSI relies on other companies for those products.

Thus, DSI relies on its in-bound logistics activity to obtain needed components and materials. It follows then that some DSI business processes and some portions of the information systems that support those processes cross into other organizations.

Is there some way to use cross-organizational information systems to gain labor productivity? You developed two interesting possibilities for new systems within the firm in Chapter 7. Those ideas were okay, maybe even good enough to propose, but is there some better system involving suppliers or customers?

Consider that possibility as you read this chapter.

Optional Extensions for this chapter are CE11, "E-Commerce," CE12, "Supply Chain Management," and CE13, "Information Technology for Data Management."

Study Questions

Q1 How do interorganizational information systems provide competitive advantages?

Q2 What is the potential conflict concerning information systems between customers and vendors?

Q3 What are the major categories of interorganizational information systems?

Q4 What technology is required for interorganizational IS?

Q5 How do interorganizational information systems benefit small businesses?

Q6 How will the increasing use of interorganizational information systems change organizational structures?

How does the knowledge in this chapter help you at DSI?

Q1 How Do Interorganizational Information Systems Provide Competitive Advantages?

Many types of information systems cross organizations. The most common type involves selling and purchasing, and we will consider that type in this section. In addition to selling and purchasing, however, other interorganizational systems, such as check clearing or credit card processing, integrate multiple-company operations. We will not attempt to discuss every type of interorganizational IS here. Instead, we will use the example of selling and purchasing to discuss and illustrate basic ideas and concepts.

Figure 8-1 shows value chain activities that involve business processes for selling and purchasing. The black arrows show flows of data, information, and products between organizations. The blue arrows show similar flows within the organization. In this chapter, we are concerned only with business processes across organizations, those shown with black arrows.

This diagram represents both manufacturers and nonmanufacturers, though it should be interpreted differently for each type. For manufacturers, in-bound logistics is primarily concerned with the acquisition, inventory, and con-

Figure 8-1
Value Chain Activities Across Organizations

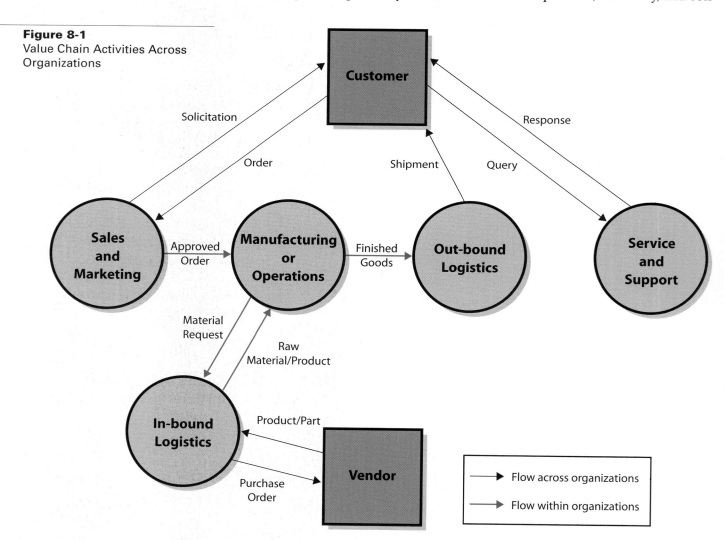

trol of *raw materials and parts.* For nonmanufacturers, such as distributors and retailers, in-bound logistics is primarily concerned with the acquisition, inventory, and control of *finished products* for sale. Of course, for nonmanufacturers, there is no manufacturing activity; there are only operations activities.

As shown in Figure 8-1, three principal flows concern activities with the customer: *Solicitation/Order, Shipment,* and service *Query/Response.* Information systems that support these flows must facilitate the organization's competitive strategy. If, for example, that strategy is to be the lowest-cost vendor across an industry, then information systems that support solicitation and ordering, shipping, and service must all be designed to minimize cost. The organization must ask questions like: "How can we structure our solicitation and ordering system so as to minimize the cost of processing an order?" For example, it might decide to develop a Web site with customer self-help features.

Consider Dell Computer. Dell structures its Web site so that almost anyone can configure and order a computer online, with no human assistance from Dell. The site guides home users, novice business users, and expert users into different parts of the site that provide different experiences. Dell offers home users packages with easy-to-understand options. Experts, who are more likely to be buying, say, high-performance server computers, can choose base computers and select from a complex array of options and choices. Dell's site gives extensive support with definitions and explanations, all online. In this way, Dell nearly automates ordering and, thus, dramatically reduces the cost of processing an order. This system is consistent with Dell's competitive strategy, which is to provide the lowest-cost computers across the computer industry. Go to *www.dell.com* and investigate the ordering experience it provides. As you use Dell's site, look for ways it has structured the site to reduce the cost of processing an order.

A vendor whose competitive strategy is to differentiate on quality within a market segment would develop a different type of solicitation and ordering system. Laguna Tools sells very expensive, high-end woodworking tools to serious hobbyists and professional woodworkers. Visit its site at *www.lagunatools.com,* and you'll see that it is designed to engender excitement about its products and to obtain leads for salespeople. Laguna offers product CDs and training materials in exchange for prospects' contact information. All of this data is input into a CRM system that enables salespeople to view a complete customer history. Its cost of sales is considerably higher than Dell's, but that difference reflects the company's competitive strategy.

Q2 What Is the Potential Conflict Concerning Information Systems Between Customers and Vendors?

According to Figure 8-1, the in-bound logistics process issues purchase orders to vendors, and receives products and parts in response. This diagram is drawn the way such diagrams are normally drawn, and it reflects typical thinking about the value chain and business processes. However, this diagram contains an inconsistency.

Suppose we work for DSI. We have vendors, such as Alcan Aluminum, that sell products to us. We perceive Alcan as a vendor, but Alcan perceives us as a customer. Thus, whatever processes and flows exist between a company and its customers must also exist between a company and its vendors. Figure 8-1 shows *Solicitation/Order, Shipping,* and *Query/Response* processes between the company and its customers. For consistency, we should redraw that figure as shown

Figure 8-2
Alternate Model of Value Chain
Activities Across Organizations

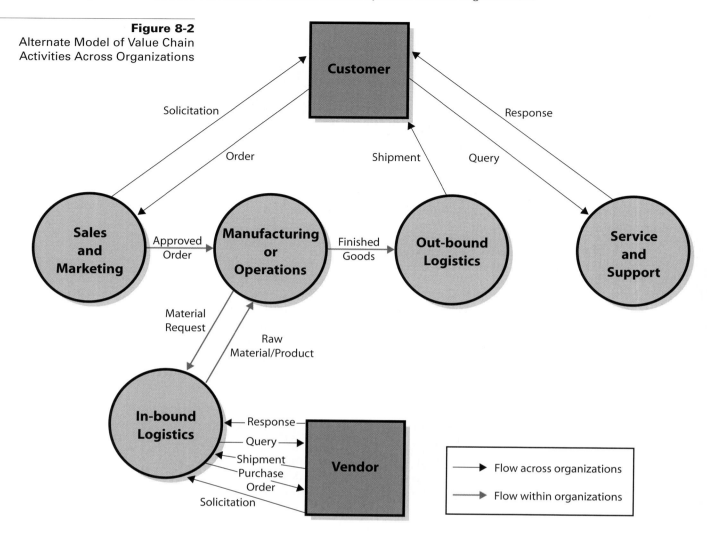

in Figure 8-2 to show those same processes between the company and its vendors. Normally, Figure 8-1 is preferred because it is drawn from the point of view of the party that is buying from the vendor. However, the additional flows shown in Figure 8-2 are assumed.

This clarification brings a potential conflict to light. As Figure 8-3 shows, employees at DSI view Alcan as a vendor. Alcan, on the other hand, views DSI as a customer. A potential conflict arises if DSI seeks to minimize the cost of ordering, and Alcan seeks to minimize the cost of selling. For example, DSI might want to send an engineering diagram to Alcan and ask Alcan employees to extract from it the necessary aluminum parts and pieces. Alcan, on the other hand, may want to receive orders in the form of parts and pieces, already diagrammed for cutting and bending. Alcan may resist (or place a surcharge for) extracting that information from DSI's diagram.

That conflict is only a *potential* conflict, however, because information systems can often be designed to minimize processing costs for both the customer and supplier. For example, DSI uses AutoCad to create its engineering drawings. AutoCad has the ability to transform engineering drawings into instructions for numerically controlled cutting equipment. Thus, if DSI submits its orders in the form of AutoCad files, Alcan can use those files to drive its cutting equipment. DSI reduces the cost of buying, and Alcan reduces the cost of selling. (Actually, in this case, Alcan reduces the cost of both selling and manufacturing.)

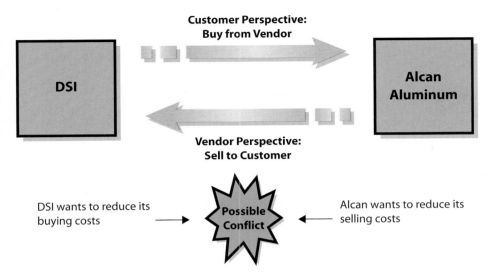

Figure 8-3
Two Perspectives on Customer/Vendor Processes

In situations when no off-the-shelf software provides a solution to benefit both parties, the customer and vendor sometimes develop custom software to achieve mutual benefit. A new technology called XML Web Services is designed to facilitate the development and sharing of such applications, as you can learn in Chapter Extension 13, "Information Technology for Data Exchange: EDI and XML," on page 473.

Q3 What Are the Major Categories of Interorganizational Information Systems?

The four major categories of interorganizational IS are:

1. E-commerce
2. Customer relationship management (CRM)
3. Supply chain management (SCM)
4. Interorganizational transaction processing

E-commerce

E-commerce concerns the buying and selling of goods and services over the Web. With e-commerce, vendors sell from Web storefronts, which are Web servers that process the http protocol, and operate order-entry application software connected to product and customer databases. A key characteristic of e-commerce sites is that the client (the customer, in this case) only needs to run an Internet browser such as Internet Explorer or Firefox. No special software needs to be installed on an e-commerce customer's computer. Thus, e-commerce clients are *thin*.

B2C e-commerce supports sales from business to consumers—*www. Amazon.com* is a typical example. **B2B e-commerce** concerns sales from one business to another. Visit *www.experian.com* for information about B2B vendor relationships. Finally, **B2G e-commerce** concerns sales from businesses to government. The site *www.govcommerce.net* provides a clearinghouse for business and government commerce. For more about e-commerce systems, see Chapter Extension 11, "E-commerce," on page 451. For an example of how companies are conducting e-commerce, see *MIS in Use 8* (page 182).

8

Dun and Bradstreet Sells Reports Using E-Commerce

Dun and Bradstreet (D&B) collects and publishes corporate and financial data and data analysis about public and private companies. Customers use D&B's products to assess the creditworthiness of potential customers, to find and evaluate customer leads, to select potential suppliers, and to facilitate supplier negotiations. In business for over 160 years, D&B stores data about 80 million businesses in over 200 countries worldwide. To provide the latest, most up-to-date information, D&B updates its databases more than one million times a day.

Throughout the years, D&B has used the latest technology to deliver its reports. In the beginning, reports were on paper and delivered via mail. Later, reports were faxed to customers, and still later they were delivered via private communications networks. With the advent of the Internet, however, D&B has an even more effective delivery medium: Web-based e-commerce.

Figure 1 shows a search page from the D&B Web site (*www.dnb.com*). The user has selected a credit report and is using the form shown to find a credit report available for Georgia-Pacific, a building-products company located in the state of Georgia in the United States. Available reports are shown in the response in Figure 2. These reports can be purchased online via the D&B commerce server.

Consider the advantages to D&B of delivering these reports via the Web. First, the site is up and running 24/7, including holidays. Second, to purchase a report the user enters all customer data, saving D&B data entry and related administrative costs. Furthermore, by using Web-based e-commerce, D&B

can change or extend its product offerings simply by making a few changes to its commerce server database. There is no need to create, print, inventory, or mail a new catalog. Finally, the commerce server records customer purchase data that can be mined for information to guide future product offerings. Thus, by using e-commerce technology, D&B sells 24/7, saves costs, distributes more current data, and gains marketing information.

Figure 1
D&B Web Storefront
Source: Used with permission of D&B Corporation.

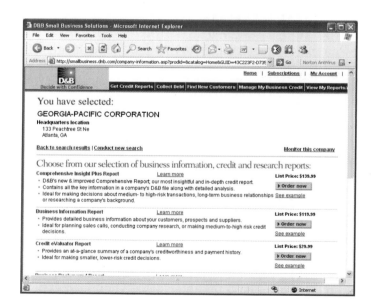

Figure 2
Example of D&B Product Offerings
Source: Used with permission of D&B Corporation.

Customer Relationship Management (CRM)

As you learned in Chapter 7, **customer relationship management (CRM)** systems integrate all of the primary business activities. They track all interactions with the customer from prospect through follow-up service and support. (CRM applications are also discussed in Chapter Extension 10.) Here, we extend that discussion to consider CRM from the standpoint of the customer.

As shown in Figure 8-3, the vendor's CRM is the other side of the customer's purchasing system. To facilitate purchasing, customers sometimes choose to install a portion of their vendor's CRM system on their own computers. Hospitals and pharmacies, for example, sometimes install thick-client software on their purchasing computers. Such software provides functionality to manage the hospital's inventory, to automatically schedule reorders, to detect unusual patterns of usage, and so forth. It adds sufficient value to overcome the risks of installing unknown software from another company. The *Guide* on pages 183a–183b discusses some of the risks associated with using another company's software programs.

To the vendor, placing a portion of its CRM on the customers' computers engenders a competitive advantage by creating high *switching costs*. A hospital, for example, that has trained its professional staff on the use of a particular vendor's CRM will be reluctant to change to a different vendor. Such a change would necessitate retraining doctors, nurses, pharmacists, and other medical professionals. The opportunity cost of these professionals' time is huge.

Supply Chain Management (SCM)

Supply chain management (SCM) systems integrate the primary in-bound logistics business activity. SCM applications have features and functions to source, order, and settle. Figure 8-4 shows the specific functions.

- **Sourcing Function**
  Find Vendors:
  - Who have the products we need
  - Who will give us a favorable price
  - Who are reliable regarding schedule and quality
  - Who will stand behind their product

- **Ordering Function**
  Send and Receive:
  - Requests for information (RFI)
  - Quotes
  - Proposals
  - Orders

- **Settlement Function**
  Process:
  - Receipt of goods
  - Reconciling goods received with purchase orders
  - Schedule payment

Figure 8-4
Specific Functions of SCM Systems

A Trojan Horse?

Suppose you work for a distributor that manages its inventory very closely. One of your major manufacturers says that it can dramatically shorten the lead time on most of its products if your purchasing personnel order directly from the manufacturer's CRM. To make that possible, the manufacturer needs to install some of its programs on the computers in your purchasing department. Your staff will use those programs to order from the manufacturer's system.

Reduced lead time has high value to you because it translates directly into a smaller inventory, something your company is fanatical about. You contact other companies that have allowed the manufacturer to install such programs, and no one reports any difficulty. There were a few installation glitches, and once in a while the manufacturer's CRM is unavailable, but no one has reported serious problems. Given all that, you agree to try it for a three-month period.

You negotiate the details of your agreement with the manufacturer, and the legal departments of both companies sign an agreement. All is proceeding smoothly until the chief information officer (CIO) of your company gets wind of this project. He refuses to allow the programs to be installed on the computers in purchasing. He also directs building security personnel not to allow anyone from the manufacturer into your company's building.

When you learn of the CIO's actions, you immediately schedule an appointment with him. At the meeting, you can tell he's barely controlling his fury. "First," he says, "have you thought about the consequences of putting someone else's programs on our network? Behind our firewall? We go to huge trouble and enormous expense to build these firewalls, and then you put somebody else's software inside them? Do you know what a Trojan horse is?"

"But," you stammer, "other companies have done this without a problem."

"Maybe so, and maybe they've had security problems that they don't know about. I can't believe you got this far on this project and no one thought to even contact me. It's unbelievable!"

"Well," you counter, "I see your point and I'm sorry we didn't contact you sooner. But what can we do now? Using their system could mean huge cost savings to us."

DISCUSSION QUESTIONS

1. Why is the CIO so concerned? The company regularly installs software from Microsoft, Oracle, IBM, Sun, and other vendors. Why is he so worried about this one?

2. In your own words, explain the problems of installing another company's software inside your own network. How does the term *Trojan horse* apply here?

3. Was it irresponsible not to involve the CIO in this project? Even if you didn't know to contact the CIO, should the legal department have done so? What does this situation tell you about the position of the IS department at this company?

4. What can be done? Is this issue serious enough to cause the cancellation of this project? What steps can the CIO take to reduce the risk? What steps can you take? How about the legal department? Or accounting? If your firm has a risk-management department, how should it be involved?

5. At some point, so much extra work is involved to protect the security of your computer system that you begin to wonder if the direct order-entry system is worth it. Is the CIO wrong? If you can't manage your inventory effectively, you won't be in business anyway. Is the CIO being too restrictive? Why or why not?

Chapter Extension 12, "Supply Chain Management," on page 463, further discusses SCM systems.

Interorganizational Transaction Processing

Interorganizational transaction processing involves systems that process routine transactions among two or more organizations. It is the oldest form of cross-organization information systems. The first such systems automated check clearing for banks and other financial institutions. When you write a check to pay a local supplier, the supplier deposits your check with its bank. That bank, in turn, deposits the check with another bank, possibly a Federal Reserve bank, and so forth, all the way back to your bank, the bank on which you wrote the check.

Prior to automation, the check clearing required hundreds of thousands of hours of repetitive, boring, clerical labor. Accordingly, the banking industry had a substantial incentive to automate that process, and it developed transaction processing systems networked by private WANs just for that purpose. Many such WANs (or their descendants) are still in use. With the advent of the Internet, however, some financial processing is also done using VPNs and other private networks based on Internet infrastructure.

The technology and example of check-clearing transaction processing spawned numerous other forms of interorganizational transaction processing. Some examples are automatic payroll deposits using electronic payroll, automatic payroll-deduction processing, credit-card processing, and more recently, debit-card processing.

You can read more about the technology that underlies such applications in Chapter Extension 13, "Information Technology for Data Exchange: EDI and XML," on page 473.

Q4 What Technology Is Required for Interorganizational IS?

Because ordering/selling systems are two sides of the same coin, we can view an interorganizational system from either the buyers' or the sellers' perspective. In most cases, it is the seller who wants to induce the buyer to use its system. E-commerce and CRM are two examples. With supply chain management, however, it is normally the buyer who wants the seller to utilize its system. In either case, one party has a system that it wants the other party to use. Here, we will say that the organization with the system it wants to be used is the *server*, and the organization that utilizes the system is the *client*. Thus, when you buy from Amazon.com, Amazon.com is the server, and you are the client.

Figure 8-5 shows a continuum of alternative technologies, ranked in order of difficulty and cost to the client. The simplest technology is email. The buyer and seller conduct their transaction by exchanging emails. Almost every employee in the world has an email address and knows how to use it. The development cost of such a system is nil.

While email is the easiest to use, it has limited capacity. Emails with megabyte attachments are slow to deliver, and many ISPs refuse to transmit large attachments. Email is also almost never encrypted. Sending credit card numbers, PO numbers, or other sensitive data over open email is unwise and

Easier, Lower Cost   **More Difficult, Higher Cost**

| Email | FTP | Thin-client Applications (E-commerce) | Thick-client Applications (Classic CRM) | XML Web Services (Modern SCM) | Joint Custom Applications (Check Clearing) |

Figure 8-5
Continuum of Client's Investment in Interorganizational Technology Alternatives

needlessly risky. If nothing else, choose to use the telephone to transmit sensitive numbers.

The next easiest alternative, **ftp**, has greater capacity than email. Using ftp, buyers and sellers can exchange large files. DSI's buyers, for example, can use ftp to send large AutoCad files to suppliers for processing. Using ftp is almost as easy as using email. To access an ftp site from a browser, all you need to do is to key *ftp://* followed by an IP address. The browser will open to that directory as if it were a directory on your system. You can copy and paste as if that directory were local. Organizations can secure ftp sites with a user name and password.

The third easiest alternative is **thin-client e-commerce**. *Thin-client* means that the client needs only a browser to participate. No software must be preinstalled on the client computer. When you order from Amazon.com, REI.com, or any other Web retailer, you use thin-client e-commerce.

Thick-client e-commerce requires that software in addition to a browser be installed on the client's computer. Usually, the installation is not difficult, but such software poses significant security risks. Any time foreign software is installed behind the organization's firewall, there is the danger that the software contains a **Trojan horse**, a virus that masquerades as useful programs or files (remember the *Guide* on pages 183a–183b). Also, installing thick-client software on, say, 500 user computers is an administrative hassle, especially when organizations do not give users administrative permission for their computers. In such a case, someone from the IT department, who does have administrator permission, must install the software. Later, when a new version is created, the software must be reinstalled on those same 500 computers. The last two alternatives are the most difficult and expensive because they require the client organization to develop software. A new technology and standards called *XML Web services* greatly simplifies the process of writing such software, but it still is expensive and it still requires a systems development project.

The final, and most expensive technology, is *joint custom applications*. Here, personnel from two or more organizations meet, establish the requirements for the system, jointly design the system, and then implement it. The banking and financial services industry used this alternative to create the check clearing and financial transactions systems. The value and importance of such systems justified their high cost. On the other hand, it would be difficult for DSI to justify the cost of developing a custom application to share drawings with its suppliers. Instead, it sends AutoCad files using ftp.

The technology used by XML Web services and custom applications is discussed in Chapter Extension 13, "Information Technology for Data Exchange: EDI and XML," on page 473.

Q5 How Do Interorganizational Information Systems Benefit Small Businesses?

The availability of interorganizational information systems allows organizations to focus their activities on their core competencies. By facilitating interorganizational processes, information systems enable the outsourcing of all but the most critical and important activities. This phenomenon benefits all businesses, but it helps small businesses in particular. Using interorganizational IS, small businesses can avoid the time and expense of building infrastructure for non–core-competency activities. This reduces the capital requirements for a new business and shortens the time to market.

To better understand these statements, consider a simple scenario: Suppose you realize that people often pay more for new items on eBay than they would pay if they shopped for bargains on the Internet. Either they don't like to e-shop, or perhaps they become entangled in the excitement of an auction, lose a bid, and decide to pay the *BuyItNow* price for a similar item in another auction. For whatever reason, you notice an inefficiency in the flow of price information among Internet users.

Let's suppose you see that inefficiency as a business opportunity. What sort of a business can you run to take advantage of that inefficiency? Assume you are willing to invest no more than $700 in a computer, $49 per month for a DSL line, and a few hours of your time each day. How many of the value chain activities can you outsource using interorganizational information systems?

Begin with market research. Using your Internet connection to the Web, you can investigate auctions, product categories, and related market segments. Doing this work saves hiring market research firms to produce this information for you. You do not need to conduct extensive and expensive market surveys; the information you need is on the Internet. Suppose you notice that there are opportunities on the sale of high-end motorcycle parts. The baby boomers are

Figure 8-6
Baby Boomer Bike Market

reliving their childhoods, but now have considerable disposable income to spend. They can't stand losing an auction and will pay to get what they want, right now. You decide to focus on this opportunity.

Using the Internet, you find sources for motorcycle parts. Sourcing is a typical supply chain activity; and again, by using the Internet, you have avoided hiring someone else to do this work for you. You search for sites that offer the products you want, have free shipping, and (if possible) for which you do not need to pay taxes.

When you find an item offered at a bargain price, you set up an auction for that item on eBay. You have not yet purchased the item; you just know where you can buy it. You set a price and the terms of the auction so that, at whatever price the item sells, you will make some profit (after deducting the cost of the auction). Avoiding the expense of hiring a photo team to take photos, you download pictures of the item from your vendor, and copy those photos into your auction. Your only financial exposure if the item does not sell is the cost of the auction.

Suppose the item sells. You then buy it from the vendor you've located, paying for it using PayPal or a credit card, and you request the vendor to ship the item directly to your customer, a process called **drop shipping**. If you pay with a credit card, it's possible you will receive payment from your customer before you pay for the item you sold. Because the item is new, and because you sell only high-quality items, all service and support are handled by the manufacturer.

Review this scenario in terms of the value chain model in Figure 8-7. You did market research, but you outsourced all of the data-gathering activities to eBay, PriceGrabber, etc. You set up the auction on eBay and, thus, outsourced the sales infrastructure to eBay. You did the product-sourcing yourself, but again, you had considerable help from the Internet. Because you drop-shipped the item to your customer, you outsourced all inventory, operations, and shipping activities to that vendor. If the customer pays you before you pay your credit card, you can even earn interest on the customer's money. You outsourced service and support to the manufacturer.

Figure 8-7
Interorganizational Information Systems Enable Outsourcing of Value Chain Activities

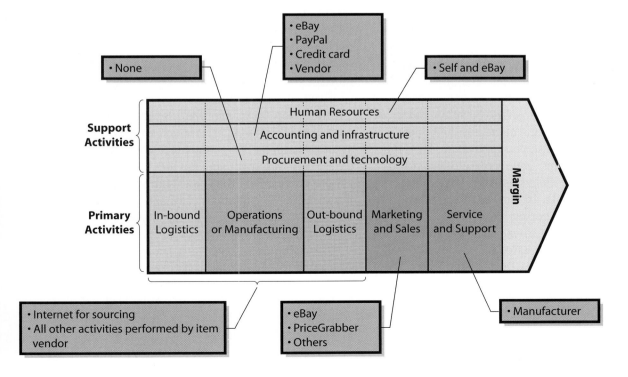

The Ethics of Supply Chain Information Sharing

Suppose that you work for a distributor that has developed information systems to read inventory data both up and down the supply chain. You can query the finished goods inventories of your manufacturers and the store inventories of your retailers. These systems were developed to increase supply chain efficiency and profitability. Consider the following situations:

Situation A: You notice that the store inventories of all retailers are running low on items in a particular product family. You know the retailers will soon send rush orders for some of those items, and in anticipation, you accumulate an oversupply of those items. You query the manufacturers' inventory data, and you find that the manufacturers' finished goods inventories are low. Because you believe you have the only supply of those items, you increase their price by 15 percent. When the retailers ask why, you claim extra transportation costs. In fact, all of the increase is going straight to your bottom line.

Situation B: Unknown to you, one of your competitors has also accumulated a large inventory of those same items. Your competitor does not increase prices on those items, and consequently you sell none at your increased price. You decide you need to keep better track of your competitors' inventories in the future.

You have no direct way to read your competitors' inventories, but you can infer their inventories by watching the decrease of inventory levels on the manufacturer side and comparing that decrease to the sales on the retail side. You know what's been produced, and you know what's been sold. You also know how much resides in your inventory. The difference must be held in your competitor's inventories. Using that process, you now can estimate your competitors' inventories.

Situation C: Assume that the agreement that you have with the retailers is that you are able to query all of their current inventory levels, but only for the orders they have with you. You are not supposed to be able to query orders they have with your competitors. However, the IS contains a flaw, and by mistake, you are able to query everyone's orders, your own as well as those of your competitors.

Situation D: Assume the same agreement with your retailers as in situation C. One of your developers, however, notices a hole in the retailer's security system and writes a program to exploit that hole. You now have access to all of the retailers' sales, inventory, and order data.

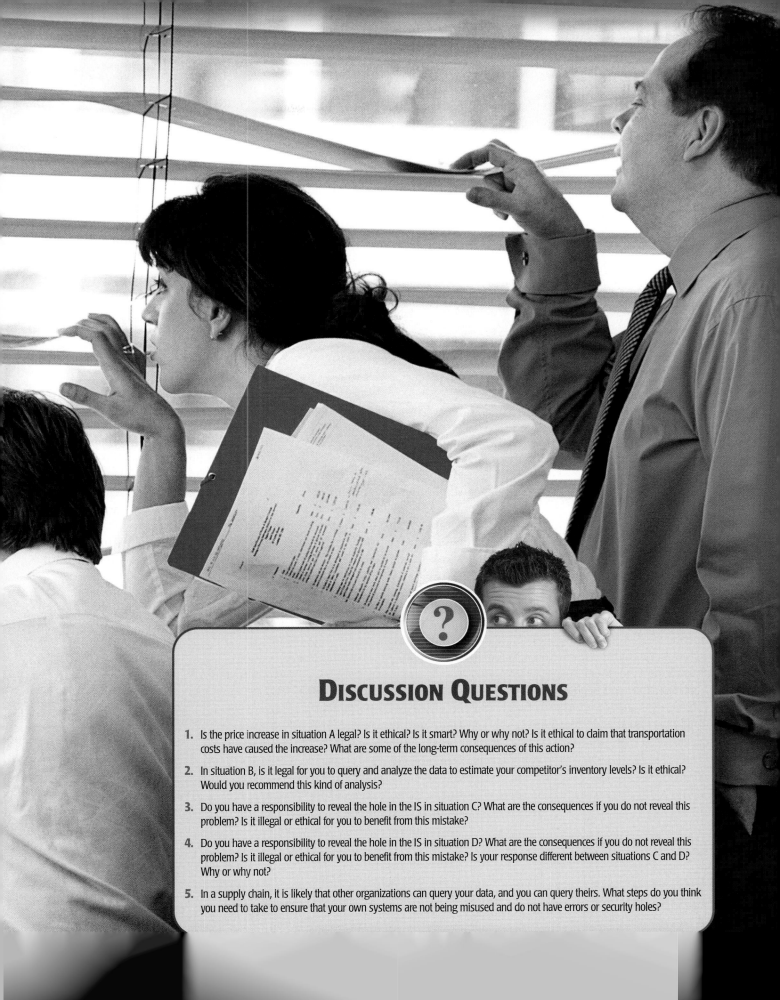

DISCUSSION QUESTIONS

1. Is the price increase in situation A legal? Is it ethical? Is it smart? Why or why not? Is it ethical to claim that transportation costs have caused the increase? What are some of the long-term consequences of this action?

2. In situation B, is it legal for you to query and analyze the data to estimate your competitor's inventory levels? Is it ethical? Would you recommend this kind of analysis?

3. Do you have a responsibility to reveal the hole in the IS in situation C? What are the consequences if you do not reveal this problem? Is it illegal or ethical for you to benefit from this mistake?

4. Do you have a responsibility to reveal the hole in the IS in situation D? What are the consequences if you do not reveal this problem? Is it illegal or ethical for you to benefit from this mistake? Is your response different between situations C and D? Why or why not?

5. In a supply chain, it is likely that other organizations can query your data, and you can query theirs. What steps do you think you need to take to ensure that your own systems are not being misused and do not have errors or security holes?

Consider support activities: Because you avoided building infrastructure, you only have one part-time employee, yourself; you have no payroll or other compensation needs. You might want insurance, but if you sell enough using eBay, you can buy life and medical insurance from eBay at attractive terms, so you can outsource those functions as well.

Consider accounting: eBay, PayPal, your credit card company, and the vendor will do most of the work. All you need to do is maintain records to track your income for tax reporting. You can even pay your taxes online if you choose. All of this is possible only because of the prevalence of interorganizational information systems.

This scenario is an extreme case, but it illustrates how small businesses can avoid building infrastructure, reduce capital requirements, and get to market sooner by taking advantage of interorganizational IS. See Chapter Extension 20, "Outsourcing," page 559, for more information.

Q6 How Will the Increasing Use of Interorganizational Information Systems Change Organizational Structures?

Interorganizational information systems enable outsourcing to the point of creating **virtual organizations**, the term *virtual* meaning something appears to exist that does not, in fact, exist. In the eBay scenario just described, from whom did the customer buy the motorcycle part? She bought it via eBay, and from you, except that, unknown to her, you were just a broker in the transaction. The part was inventoried and shipped from some other party. The value chain activities in Figure 8-7, which Porter envisioned in 1980 to occur within a single organization, are now shared among several entities. The customer bought the motorcycle part from a virtual organization.

You might think this is a special case, an academic puzzle, but it is not. Consider DSI. Its expertise is designing and building aircraft interiors. The company knows, for example, that a galley constructed in one location on a 737 costs X, but that if the galley is moved aft two feet, it costs one-half X. In the first location, the galley interferes with critical structural members of the 737, and in the second it does not. DSI's expertise enables it to provide a less-expensive and better solution for its clients.

DSI wishes to sell that valuable expertise. It does not wish to spend its time and money building infrastructure that does not involve the company's core competency. So, wherever possible, DSI will use interorganizational information systems to off-load noncritical work. Even if that off-loading increases costs, DSI will be ahead if the *opportunity cost* of the time for DSI employees to perform the off-loaded activity is greater than the cost of outsourcing.

The development of interorganizational information systems and the rise of outsourcing will cause major changes in organizational structures during your career. Pay attention to this trend. In any organization, strive to work in a business activity that is directly in line with the organization's specialty. If not, your job is at risk of being outsourced. If you want to work in a hospital, be a doctor or a nurse. If you want to work at a design firm, be a designer. One last point: Some interesting ethical situations can arise as a result of the increasing use of interorganizational information systems. See the *Ethics Guide* on pages 187a–187b for a discussion of the ethics of interorganizational information sharing.

How does the knowledge in this chapter help you at DSI?

We left you at the start of this chapter agonizing over your tuna sandwich and pondering information systems to increase labor productivity. At the end of Chapter 7, you had developed ideas for two functional systems, one to process tool repair data and a second to use RFID to create a virtual toolcrib. Those ideas seem okay, but they don't sizzle. Is there some more interesting possibility for an interorganizational IS? You decide to examine possibilities for each activity in the value chain.

You don't see any exciting opportunities for interorganizational systems in marketing and sales. You believe the DSI Web site could be more exciting, but proposing a Web site upgrade is hardly innovative.

In-bound logistics, however, has possibilities. Currently, DSI purchasing agents send ftp AutoCad files to manufacturers and metal fabricators. Those companies use AutoCad to extract instructions for automated cutting and bending machines from the files they receive.

In addition to cutting and bending, DSI requires its contractors to mark the locations for welding and other attachment of adjacent bulkheads, lockers, lighting, and so forth. The extracted AutoCad instructions direct automated machines to place these marks, and they are exceedingly accurate. This marking saves DSI considerable labor, and the marginal cost to the manufacturer or fabricator is near zero.

One DSI innovation was to establish a color for each project. One project might have red, another blue, another green. DSI requires its vendor to mark the aluminum or other product in the color that is associated with the project on which the part will be used. That way, when a component arrives at the DSI hangar, employees know, just from the color of the marking, which project will use it. They can then store the component in the correct section of the raw materials inventory. (Reflect for a moment on this: The bulkhead or other part is itself carrying information, which makes it part of the interorganizational IS. Some of the hardware for this IS is not computers, but markings on cut aluminum, instead!)

In spite of the coloring system, however, you have noticed considerable moving of components in inventory. DSI does not practice just-in-time (JIT) inventory, and components arrive in the order in which the manufacturers and fabricators happen to produce and deliver them. A large bulkhead that will be used late in the project might arrive early and need to be moved again and again in inventory as other components arrive. That looks like an opportunity for an interorganizational IS. You could propose that DSI practice JIT, but that would involve a commitment to serious procedural changes. You know from Chapter 7 that such changes can be difficult, so you decide not to pursue JIT.

Another possibility occurs to you. Why not use RFID tags to record the construction phase in which a component will be used? DSI could build an IS that would read the RFID tag as the component arrives, and allocate that component to a location in the raw materials inventory that would minimize the subsequent moving of components. Such a system would not only save the labor of the movement, it also reduces the likelihood that components will be damaged while in inventory.

You like this possibility but want to consider the other value chain activities as well. There might be opportunities in manufacturing, but John Stratford seems to manage that function very well. You decide not to look further there. You know that out-bound logistics is more than just the runway, but you still don't see any exciting interorganizational systems for out-bound logistics, given the nature of DSI's product. You come to the same conclusion regarding service and support.

So you conclude that your best bet is to pursue the use of RFID on components to reduce their movement in inventory and save potential damage.

As you take the remains of your tuna sandwich to the trash, you glance out the window and notice the big Mercedes is still not back. You like the ideas you have so far, but you wonder if they are enough. Is there something more interesting than what you've got so far? Think about it . . . because this could happen to you!

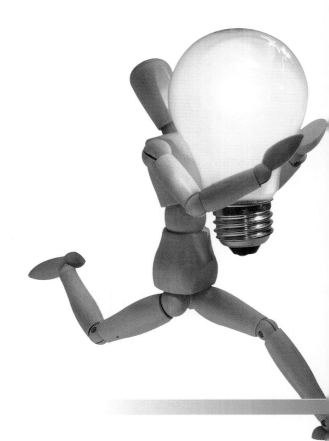

Active ? Review

Use this Active Review to verify that you understand the material in the chapter. You can read the entire chapter and then perform the tasks in this review, or you can read the material for just one question and perform the tasks in this review for that question before moving on to the next one.

Q1 How do interorganizational information systems provide competitive advantages?

Using the example of buying and selling, diagram the flows of data, information, and products between organizations. Explain how your diagram should be interpreted for manufacturers and for nonmanufacturers, such as distributors. Describe ways that organizations can gain a competitive advantage using customer processes. Explain how the differences described for customer information systems at Dell and at Laguna Tools reflect their competitive strategies.

Q2 What is the potential conflict concerning information systems between customers and vendors?

Explain the differences between Figure 8-1 and Figure 8-2. Explain why Figure 8-2 is more accurate. Describe two different perspectives on interorganizational systems that involve buying and selling. Explain why the conflict is only a *potential* conflict.

Q3 What are the major categories of interorganizational information systems?

Name four categories of interorganizational information systems and describe the characteristics of each.

Q4 What technology is required for interorganizational IS?

Describe which party is the client in an interorganizational information system. List technology alternatives for interorganizational IS in increasing order of difficulty and cost to the client. Briefly explain each alternative.

Q5 How do interorganizational information systems benefit small businesses?

Summarize the ways that interorganizational information systems benefit small businesses. Using the example of the eBay auction, explain how the availability of interorganizational information systems reduces the need for infrastructure. Explain to yourself what is keeping you from starting that business, or one like it, tonight.

Q6 How will the increasing use of interorganizational information systems change organizational structures?

Define the term *virtual organization*. Explain why the customer purchased the motorcycle part from a virtual organization. Describe why DSI will seek to off-load as many non–core-competency activities as possible. Explain why it might even be worthwhile to outsource activities when DSI can perform that activity more cheaply itself. Explain how the statement, "If you work in a hospital, you want to be a doctor or a nurse" pertains to your career choices.

How does the knowledge in this chapter help you at DSI?

Explain the opportunities for interorganizational systems for DSI. Summarize how DSI uses interorganizational information systems to facilitate in-bound logistics. Describe how the aluminum parts became part of the hardware of an IS. Justify the decision not to explore JIT. Explain one potential use for RFID at DSI.

Key Terms and Concepts

B2B e-commerce 181
B2C e-commerce 181
B2G e-commerce 181
Customer relationship management
(CRM) 183
Drop shipping 187

E-commerce 181
ftp 185
Interorganizational transaction
processing 184
Supply chain management (SCM)
183

Thick-client e-commerce 185
Thin-client e-commerce 185
Trojan horse 185
Virtual organization 188

Using Your Knowledge

1. Distance learning is an application of interorganizational information systems. Although it may seem odd to label students as organizations, they are customers, in the same sense that consumers are customers in B2C e-commerce systems.

   a. Draw a process diagram of a regular, non–distance-learning class using a format like that in Figure 8-1. Label the activities and the flows among the activities.

   b. Draw a second process diagram of a distance-learning class. In what ways are the two diagrams similar? In what ways are they different?

   c. What is the competitive strategy of your university? How do distance-learning classes contribute to that competitive strategy?

   d. Assuming that no face-to-face meeting is required to successfully teach a successful distance-learning class, neither students nor professors need live near campus. In fact, they do not need to even reside on the same continent. What opportunities does that fact present to your university? What new educational products might your university develop?

   e. Considering your answer to question d, what opportunities does distance learning provide your professor? Is there any reason a professor should not teach for more than one university? Do you think there is a realistic opportunity for a group of professors from different universities to band together to form a virtual college? What competitive advantage might they accrue by doing so?

2. Suppose you are the chancellor of a small, private university about to go bankrupt. Your principal assets are your name and your authority to grant degrees. Suppose you outsource the teaching of classes to distance-learning programs at any other respectable university. Students can enroll at your university in some educational program—say, general business—by paying your institution a fee. Students then take a set of distance-learning classes from other universities. When students have completed necessary classes, they pay your institution a second fee, you verify the student has passed the classes, and you grant the student a degree.

   a. Compare this situation to the situation of the person who is selling goods at eBay. In what ways have you, as chancellor, simply taken advantage of interorganizational information systems to maximize outsourcing?

   b. Compare the quality of education delivered via this method to a distance-learning program in which all classes are taught by a single university. In what ways might the quality be higher? In what ways might it be less?

c. Do you think this is a realistic scenario? Why or why not? If you think unrealistic, what changes could you make to cause it to be realistic?

d. Question 6 of this chapter (see page 188) addresses changes that inter-organizational information systems will cause to organizational structure. In what ways do you think such systems will cause changes in the structure of universities?

3. Consider the opportunity of selling goods on eBay as described in Question 5 (see page 186).

   a. Investigate auctions on eBay and, for any category of product in which you have knowledge or interest, compare selling prices to prices of new goods from e-commerce sites. Attempt to find one or more products in which the item sold on eBay costs more than if it had been purchased from a vendor. State the price differential(s). If you find no such products, list the products' eBay prices, and vendor prices for five of the products you investigated.

   b. Go to *www.eBay.com* and learn how eBay charges for its auctions. You have many options to choose from; select the option(s) that you believe will be best for selling goods using this strategy. Explain why you think that option is the best.

   c. Using price comparison sites (such as PriceGrabber, Cnet.com, or Frugle), identify three sources for products that you identified in question a. If you did not find any qualifying products in that question, identify sources for some product in which you have an interest. Seek sources that provide free shipping and to which you do not need to pay taxes.

   d. Either by yourself or with a group of classmates, find some product from your answer in c that seems to you to be a good bargain. Set up an auction for that item on eBay with terms that will enable you to make some profit, even if the product sells at the lowest price.

   e. Run the auction. If you make some profit, celebrate. If not, state why and what you would do differently were you to do this again.

4. Investigate the use of RFIDs for reducing the amount of labor required to move components that are waiting for final assembly. Ideally, you want your system to recommend a location so that a component could be received, placed once, and not moved again until it is needed.

   a. Describe, in general terms, how you think this system would work. Assume that DSI already breaks its projects into phases, and each component is labeled in AutoCad with the name of the phase in which it will be used.

   Using resources on the Web:

   b. Determine the cost of RFIDs.

   c. Identify software packages that will write and read RFID devices. What hardware is required?

   d. What is the approximate cost to the vendor of storing project phase data in an RFID on a component? Assume that AutoCad can interface with the software that writes the RFID.

   e. What is the approximate cost to DSI of reading RFID data?

   f. Assume that you can physically organize inventory space to correspond to the phases of a project. Describe in general terms how the RFID data could be used to determine the location of a component when it is received.

g. Write a report to give to Ms. Dorset and Mr. Stratford. In your report, describe the idea and its costs and benefits. Explain what you have been able to learn and what else you need to know. Describe how you would go about obtaining answers to the remaining questions.

Case Study 8

Fine Woodworking Versus *Wooden Boat*

Fine Woodworking is a high-quality, bimonthly publication that addresses topics of interest to serious woodworking enthusiasts. Issues include woodworking techniques, project descriptions, tool reviews, classified ads, and considerable advertising. *Fine Woodworking* has been published for about 30 years.

Wooden Boat is also a high-quality, bimonthly publication, but it concerns the design and construction of wooden boats. Issues include boat-building techniques; project descriptions; reviews of tools, books, and boats; classified ads; and considerable advertising. It, too, has been published for about 30 years.

These two publications, which are very similar, are owned and published by different companies. In recent years, both publications have sought to use the Internet to leverage the value of their past issues, but they have done so in two different ways.

Wooden Boat provides an online index to past issues at *www.woodenboat. com*. Subscribers who have kept past issues frequently access this site to locate an article about some topic. While readers are at the site, *Wooden Boat* offers to sell them a number of products, as you can see when you visit the site. One of the products for sale is past issues of the magazine. Thus, using the online index, if you locate an article you want, and if you do not have that issue, you can buy it from the Web site.

Fine Woodworking has taken a different approach. It offers an online subscription to the magazine and its archives for an annual fee. Go to *www. finewoodworking.com* to see the current offer. Anyone who has paid that fee can access the site, search for topics of interest, and download articles about that topic in pdf format. If you want to know how, for example, to sharpen a hand plane, you can search for that topic and download quite a number of articles from their archive.

Questions

1. These two very similar publications have taken two different approaches for using the Internet to gain revenue from their archives. Describe what you believe are the advantages and disadvantages of each approach.

2. Visit *www.woodenboat.com* and *www.finewoodworking.com.* What do you think is the competitive strategy of these two publications? Justify your response.

3. Given your answer to question 2, does competitive strategy explain why they have chosen different ways of using the Internet to gain revenue from their archives?

4. Has *Wooden Boat* chosen its method because it has a store? Is it using its index as bait to attract prospects to the store? Is this technique necessarily any better than a subscription? Why or why not?

5. Under what conditions do you think the *Wooden Boat* strategy is superior?

6. Is *Fine Woodworking* in danger of losing subscriptions to its paper magazine to the online magazine? Does it matter? Might *Fine Woodworking* be attempting to move its readership to an online publication?

7. Under what conditions do you think the *Fine Woodworking* strategy is superior?

Teaching Suggestions

Dorset-Stratford Interiors, Chapter 8

GOALS

Use Dorset-Stratford Interiors (DSI) to:

✳ Encourage students to think about the application of information systems across organizations.

✳ Vicariously motivate students to use MIS knowledge to increase their personal competitive advantage.

BACKGROUND

1. Interorganizational systems typically involve sales and marketing, and in-bound and out-bound logistics functions. The nature of DSI business precludes using e-commerce for sales and marketing; DSI can hardly sell head-of-state interiors in the same ways that Amazon.com sells books. It's hard to imagine DSI on the PriceGrabber.com site.

2. Mr. Stratford pointed down the runway and said, "There's our out-bound logistics function." Clearly, he was exaggerating, but out-bound logistics is probably not where the best innovative applications of MIS lie for DSI.

3. In-bound logistics is complicated, however. The real company behind DSI does, indeed, use colors as explained in the text. It also has an inventory of large and heavy items in its raw-materials inventory, and it wants to minimize unnecessary movement of those items. At DSI, that inventory is constrained to the available space in the hangar, and at times DSI needs to pack it tightly. That can mean considerable wasted labor when workers need to move items out of that inventory.

4. Just-in-time inventory policy would be a good idea. The intern decides not to pursue that idea because of the need to make many procedural changes, but that might not be the intern's best decision. This point is a good candidate for class discussion.

5. Regarding Stratford's luncheon with his niece, the "best revenge is a life well lived." The intern should forget about it and focus on having a productive experience at DSI. It might have been nice to eat at the country club, but, oh well—focusing on finding an innovative application of technology is at least not fattening.

HOW TO GET THE STUDENTS INVOLVED

1. I think the best way for the class to use this case is to think about each of the activities in the value chain. You might split up the class into groups and have each group consider innovative interorganizational IS for each value chain activity. If there aren't any such applications, the group should say why and then find a value chain activity for which there are such applications. Service and support activities might contain some interesting possibilities. What does DSI do when something doesn't work? They need to know what's on the plane, how it's configured, etc. And their customers are likely to be quite demanding.

   a. What are interorganizational applications for sales and marketing?

   b. What are interorganizational applications for in-bound logistics?

   c. What are interorganizational applications for manufacturing?

   d. What are interorganizational applications for out-bound logistics?

   e. What are interorganizational applications for service and support?

2. I think it's worthwhile to revisit the intern's conclusion of not exploring JIT:

   a. What is JIT?

   b. Why did the intern not explore JIT?

   c. If you were the intern, and you decided to explore JIT, what would you need to do? List major tasks to accomplish.

   d. Does JIT seem like a better idea than using RFID to place items in inventory?

3. Let's explore the RFID idea. An interesting use of RFID can be found here: *www.cribmaster.com/ rfidentry.htm*. It's not quite what the intern has in mind, but it might suggest ideas.

   a. What is an RFID?

   b. What kind of data can be stored by an RFID?

   c. What data would be needed to determine how to locate an item in inventory?

d. What logic could be used to determine where to place something in relation to other items?

e. What data, other than data on the RFID, would be needed? Where would that data come from?

BOTTOM LINE

Same as Chapter 7:

* **Seek innovative applications of IS and IT in order to gain a competitive advantage . . . for you and for your organization.**

Using the Guide: A Trojan Horse? (page 183a)

GOALS

* Sensitize students to the problems of installing other companies' software.

* Illustrate problems that can occur when not involving the CIO or other IS professionals in business initiatives that involve computing infrastructure.

BACKGROUND AND PRESENTATION STRATEGIES

Warning: This guide uses the term *firewall*, but we won't discuss firewalls until Chapter 12. For now, I explain that a *firewall* is a computing device that filters Internet and other network traffic for security.

Unfortunately, the problem presented in this scenario is common. Recently I visited my doctor's office for routine blood tests. While sitting in the office laboratory, I noticed that the lab technician's computer was running an application program from an independent medical lab. (The screen showed a logo that I recognized from the lab's billing statements.)

I asked the technician if that program belonged to the doctors' group or if it was from the lab. She said, "Oh, it's not ours, it's one the lab wrote." I asked if they sent her an installation disk with the program or if she installed it over the Internet. "Oh, no, they come over here from time to time and install their programs on our computers."

This doctors' group, consisting of 30+ physicians and staff, is located in a major medical center in Seattle, and the doctors have privileges at a major university teaching hospital. I would think they are in at least the top quartile of their business (I hope so, anyway), and they send me all sorts of notices about how they protect my data according to HIPAA standards, and so on. While I sat there, a number of questions popped into my mind. But, first, ask the students:

➤ **What questions pop into your mind when you hear this scenario?**

Here are some of the questions I was asking:

➤ **How do they know that program is free of viruses, malicious Trojan horses, and other malware?**

➤ **How do they know that the people from the lab who install those programs aren't installing some other, malicious program as well?**

➤ **Their computers are connected to a network and via that network to the Internet. How do they know that a program installed by the lab software person is not sending patient data out the door?**

➤ **What stipulations exist in their contract with the lab to protect the doctors in case of a malicious Trojan horse or other malware?**

➤ **Does their insurance policy protect them for this type of liability?**

➤ **What do they know about the personnel who are installing these programs on their computers? Are they employees of the lab? Are they employees of another company? Are they recent graduates of the state's white-collar crime incarceration program?**

➤ **Here's a pertinent announcement:**

➤ **Do NOT let ANYONE outside your IS organization install programs on your computers!**

➤ **Compare this guide to the situation at Emerson in which Dee's consultant was allowed to work inside the network. What problems might have occurred?**

➤ **One more time, do you think it was a wise decision for the VP of Sales at Emerson to force the CIO into allowing the consultant access inside the Emerson network?**

ⓘ SUGGESTED RESPONSES FOR DISCUSSION QUESTIONS

1. The CIO is right to be very concerned.

   ➤ **What's the difference between software from Microsoft or Oracle and software from ABC Manufacturing?**

   (The answer is not what one student quipped in my class, "Software from ABC Manufacturing actually works.") The difference is that Microsoft and Oracle are very experienced vendors with substantial talent and expertise for ensuring that their software does not contain malware. ABC Manufacturing may or may not have such talent and expertise.

2. Once inside the organization's network, the Trojan horse program can wreak havoc on the organization's computing infrastructure. It can steal data; it can disrupt operations; it can maliciously destroy data. As the CIO says, they go to incredible effort and expense

to protect the perimeter of the organization's network, and this installation will bypass all those protections.

3. Yes, it was incredibly irresponsible not to involve the CIO!

> **Do not install any programs on your computer that have not been approved by your IT department. Do not let anyone you manage install them, either.**

I hope this was just an oversight on the part of a junior person in the legal department. Every organization should have a policy of notifying the CIO of any initiative that involves installing computer software on the organization's computers.

If this was not an oversight, then the CIO has little stature in the organization. Some corrective action needs to be taken.

4. It will be interesting to see how the students respond. I think it is potentially serious enough to cause cancellation of the project. The CIO needs a chance to have his or her staff check into the program and find out who wrote it, what it does, how it's been tested, the experience of the manufacturer, and the experiences of other businesses that use the program. Perhaps, too, computers that use this program can be set up in a special security zone within the organization's network. Lots can be done, but the CIO needs time and a chance to participate.

To avoid such problems, you could be certain to involve the CIO from the start. Legal could ensure that the contract protects the organization from problems in the manufacturer's software. Accounting could be instructed not to approve the budget for projects that involve computer software without concurrence from the IT department. If there is a

separate risk management department, it too should be notified of this issue; there may be a need to obtain a special liability insurance policy or take other risk-reduction action.

5. Questions to ask the class:

> **Is the CIO being too restrictive?**

> **Should the company just install the software and hope for the best?**

> **If you were a proponent of the direct order-entry system, what would you do?**

I don't think the CIO is too restrictive at all. The company should not install the software and just hope for the best. That's no way to run a business!!! There are many alternatives between closing one's eyes to the risk and canceling the project.

WRAP UP

> **In this world of viruses, worms, Trojan horses, spyware, adware, data thefts, identity thefts, and other problems, the CIO and the IT department have every right—even duty—to restrict the installation of programs on computers within the organization's network.**

> **Work with the IT department when you have an initiative that will require new software. Give them fair notice.**

> **Consider these problems whenever you are faced with the need to allow someone access inside your organizational network (as Dee should have done).**

> **We will be discussing these issues further when we discuss IT management in Chapter 11 and information security in Chapter 12.**

Chapter 8

Using the Ethics Guide: The Ethics of Supply Chain Information Sharing (page 187a)

GOAL

* Investigate the differences between aggressive, unwise, unethical, and illegal activity using information systems in the supply chain.

BACKGROUND AND PRESENTATION STRATEGIES

The situations are sorted in increasing order of questionability. The first one is certainly legal and ethical; it may or may not be wise. The last one is certainly unethical, and it may be illegal, or at least a violation of a contract.

These scenarios are similar to those in the "Ethics Guide" in Chapter 1. They involve the use or misuse of information. The difference is that the information systems here are far more sophisticated than the email systems described in Chapter 1.

One of the challenges in attempting to view systems from a supply-chain-wide perspective is that there is no Supply Chain Company. The supply chain has no owners, no stockholders, and no employees, and no organization is concerned about the economic welfare of the supply chain to the exclusion of its own economic welfare.

Because of this characteristic, every organization views the supply chain through the prism of its own goals and objectives. Any information system developed to support supply-chain-wide integration is subject to use or misuse to further the goals of the individual companies. An information system might provide information to enable supply-chain-wide optimization, but an organization could use that same system to further its own interests, as in the examples described here.

A supply chain is a complex network. Adding information systems to this network further increases the complexity of the interactions. It would be exceedingly difficult, probably impossible, to predict the consequences of the addition of a new information system. Therefore, companies in the supply chain are wise to proceed slowly when sharing information about their inventories, orders, demand patterns, and related

matters. The consequences could be surprising, and possibly undesirable.

As a result, supply-chain-wide information systems are likely to be implemented much more slowly than the technology could possibly support.

➤ **Using terms from Chapter 10, all these concerns fall into the category of organizational feasibility. Supply chain information systems can be cost, schedule, and technically feasible, but fail organizationally because of the lack of control over the side consequences of sharing information.**

 SUGGESTED RESPONSES FOR DISCUSSION QUESTIONS

1. I think situation A is both legal and ethical. At least the action of using the information to know to accumulate inventory is legal and ethical. Increasing prices also is legal and ethical.

   ➤ **Is lying to provide a justification of the price increase ethical?**

   It does not seem ethical to me. I think the need to lie is an indication that something has been done that is not right—or that needs to be sheltered from the hard light of truth.

   Probably the best question here, though, is:

   ➤ **Setting aside the lie and assuming that all this behavior is otherwise ethical, is increasing the prices in this situation wise?**

   So much depends on the perceptions of the retailers. They might view it as smart—as your ability to read trends and to increase prices on scarce goods. They might respect your operations more because of it. However, they might perceive it as greedy and ruthless. It could reduce trust and encourage the retailers to find a different distributor, one that wouldn't "put the screws to them" when it could.

2. I see no legal or ethical problem in any of this analysis. It's an analysis that's available to everyone in the supply chain. You're just using the information that you have at your disposal to better run your business.

3. Much depends on whatever contracts exist among the organizations in the supply chain. If you have signed a contract that stipulates that you will query only your own orders, then using this flaw violates that contract. Even if you have just agreed verbally to this limitation, that verbal agreement could be

binding. Even if it is not binding, if you did agree verbally to read data only about your orders, then using the flaw is unethical.

> **Setting aside contractual or ethical obligations, do you see a problem in not revealing the flaw?**

As long as the flaw exists, there is the possibility that other distributors are using it to query the retailers' orders with you. It's a double-edged sword that can cut both ways. All in all, it would seem a wise course of action to reveal the flaw, possibly for contractual reasons, certainly for ethical reasons. As long as the flaw exists, you cannot control its consequences.

> **By the way, if one such flaw exists, there's always the possibility of two such flaws. You don't know about the ethics of your competitors. What are the consequences?**

> **How do you spell paranoia? This flaw could be the downfall of the information-sharing initiative in this supply chain.**

See also question 5.

4. You may or may not have a contractual obligation to reveal the hole in situation D, but, in my opinion, you certainly have an ethical responsibility to reveal the hole. Also:

> **Where there is one hole, there may be two. How do you know that other organizations are not exploiting it to obtain data about your operations?**

You have culpability here that you did not have in situation C. In this situation, your developer actively sought a way to obtain unauthorized access.

> **Do you think other organizations in the supply chain would see a difference in your behavior between situations C and D?**

You bet they would. The one in C just happened. The other you caused!

5. This is a very tough question. Whenever you open any of your information systems to the outside, you run a risk of inadvertently releasing confidential information. There is no way around it. Some thoughts about possible safeguards are:

- Use a careful and methodical development process (see Chapter 10).

- Thoroughly test the systems you implement.

- Observe usage patterns in your data. Attempt to identify spurious queries.

- Protect your network from unauthorized access.

- Hire a white-hat hacker (see Chapter 12).

- Buy insurance.

- Other???

WRAP UP

> **We've considered two types of integration in this and in the prior chapter. In Chapter 7, we examined interdepartmental, cross-functional systems that integrated departmental activity and eliminated the silos of isolation caused by functional systems.**

> **In this chapter, we considered systems that provide a similar integrative function, but across businesses in a supply chain, and not just departments in an organization.**

> **From the standpoint of databases to build, applications to write, and procedures to develop, the integration of departments into process-based systems and the integration of separate organizational information systems into supply chain systems are very similar.**

> **Yet, there are substantial differences—differences that we can state in different ways. In terms of systems development, we can say that supply chain systems have organizational feasibility issues that interdepartmental, intracompany systems don't have.**

> **What are some examples of organizational feasibility issues that supply chain systems have but that interdepartmental, intracompany systems do not have? (Many important differences among companies may become problematical: company objectives, goals, competitive strategy, priorities, and culture are just a few.)**

> **How do those differences impact supply chain information systems development?**

(Different companies will value the supply chain IS differently; some may see it as essential, and some may see it as barely worthwhile. They will have different priorities, varying degrees of willingness to invest, different requirements, various levels of patience with delays, and others.)

9 Competitive Advantage with Information Systems for Decision Making

This could happen to you

You're getting depressed. Three weeks have gone by since you saw the niece-intern-competitor go out to lunch with Mr. Stratford, and there haven't been any lunch invitations for you. You've got to find a way to distinguish yourself, and while you've thought of three interesting possible systems for increasing labor productivity, you're not sure any of them is outstanding. What to do?

You might take another tack. Chapters 7 and 8 discussed the ways information systems support business processes; Chapter 7 addressed processes within the organization, and Chapter 8 addressed processes across organizations. What about considering ways in which information systems improve decision making?

Of course, business processes and decision making are closely allied. Every business process involves decision making, and every business decision occurs in the context of a business process. The distinction is one of perspective. From the process perspective, we consider how information systems facilitate competitive strategy by adding value to or reducing the costs of processes. From the decision-making perspective, we consider how information systems add value or reduce costs by improving the quality of human decisions.

Consider your situation at DSI. You want to propose a system that increases labor productivity. You've thought about systems that facilitate processes. Is there an information system that improves decision making?

For example, last week DSI learned that one of its suppliers was leveled by a hurricane. The supplier expects to be back in business soon, but there is no way it can produce components for DSI's current projects on time. DSI had to select a different vendor, and fast. Is there a way to build an IS to select a supplier based on past supplier performance?

That's a possibility you need to consider. But, what would you recommend? A reporting system? A data-mining system? A knowledge management system? An expert system? In responding to this task, how would you describe the alternative you recommend? The knowledge you gain from this chapter will help.

Optional Extensions for this chapter are CE14, "Database Marketing," CE15, "Reporting Systems and OLAP," and CE16, "Data Mining and Counter-Terrorism."

Study Questions

Q1 How big is an exabyte, and why does it matter?

Q2 How do BI systems provide competitive advantages?

Q3 What problems do operational data pose for BI systems?

Q4 What are the purpose and components of a data warehouse?

Q5 What is a data mart, and how does it differ from a data warehouse?

Q6 What are the characteristics of data-mining systems?

How does the knowledge in this chapter help you at DSI?

Q1 How Big Is an Exabtye, and Why Does It Matter?

According to a study done at the University of California at Berkeley,[1] a total of 403 petabytes of new data was created in 2002. Undoubtedly, even greater amounts are being generated today, but just consider that number. As shown in Figure 9-1, 403 **petabytes** is roughly the amount of all printed material ever written. The print collection of the Library of Congress is .01 petabytes, so 400 petabytes equals 40,000 copies of the print collection of the Library of Congress. That is indeed a lot of data, and it's the amount generated in just one year. By 2007, nearly 2,500 petabytes, or 2.5 **exabytes**, of data will have been generated.

The generation of all these data has much to do with Moore's Law. The capacity of storage devices increases as their costs decrease. Today, storage capacity is nearly unlimited. Figure 9-2 shows that at the end of 2003, total hard-disk storage capacity exceeded 41 exabytes, which is eight times the number of words ever spoken by all human beings throughout history. Not all of that storage is used for business. Much of it is used to store music, digital pictures, video, and phone conversations. However, much of that capacity is also used to store the data from business information systems. For example, in 2004 Verizon's SQL

Figure 9-1
How Big Is an Exabyte?

Source: sims.berkeley.edu/research/projects/how-much-info/datapowers.html (assessed May 2005). Used with the permission of Peter Lyman and Hal R. Varian, University of California at Berkeley.

Kilobyte (KB)	*1,000 bytes OR 10^3 bytes* 2 Kilobytes: A typewritten page 100 Kilobytes: A low-resolution photograph
Megabyte (MB)	*1,000,000 bytes OR 10^6 bytes* 1 Megabyte: A small novel OR a 3.5-inch floppy disk 2 Megabytes: A high-resolution photograph 5 Megabytes: The complete works of Shakespeare 10 Megabytes: A minute of high-fidelity sound 100 Megabytes: One meter of shelved books 500 Megabytes: A CD-ROM
Gigabyte (GB)	*1,000,000,000 bytes OR 10^9 bytes* 1 Gigabyte: A pickup truck filled with books 20 Gigabytes: A good collection of the works of Beethoven 100 Gigabytes: A library floor of academic journals
Terabyte (TB)	*1,000,000,000,000 bytes OR 10^{12} bytes* 1 Terabyte: 50,000 trees made into paper and printed 2 Terabytes: An academic research library 10 Terabytes: The print collections of the U.S. Library of Congress 400 Terabytes: National Climactic Data Center (NOAA) database
Petabyte (PB)	*1,000,000,000,000,000 bytes OR 10^{15} bytes* 1 Petabyte: Three years of EOS data (2001) 2 Petabytes: All U.S. academic research libraries 20 Petabytes: Production of hard-disk drives in 1995 200 Petabytes: All printed material
Exabyte (EB)	*1,000,000,000,000,000,000 bytes OR 10^{18} bytes* 2 Exabytes: Total volume of information generated in 1999 5 Exabytes: All words ever spoken by human beings

[1]"How Much Information, 2003," *sims.berkeley.edu/research/projects/how-much-info-2003* (accessed May 2005).

Year	Disks Sold (Thousands)	Storage Capacity (Petabytes)
1992	42,000	
1995	89,054	104.8
1996	105,686	183.9
1997	129,281	343.63
1998	143,649	724.36
1999	165,857	1394.60
2000	200,000 (IDEMA)	4,630.5
2001	196,000 (Gartner)	7,279.14
2002	213,000 (Gartner projection)	10,849.56
2003	235,000	15,892.24
TOTAL	**1,519,527 (1.5 billion drives)**	**41,402.73 (41 exabytes)**

Figure 9-2
Hard-Disk Storage Capacity

Source: sims.berkeley.edu/research/projects/how-much-info/datapowers.html (assessed May 2005). Used with the permission of Peter Lyman and Hal R. Varian, University of California at Berkeley.

Server database contained more than 15 terabytes of data. If that data were published in books, a bookshelf 450 miles long would be required to hold them.

Why does this exponential growth in data matter to us? First, understand that the phenomenal data growth occurs inside organizations just as much as outside of them. Every time DSI builds another airplane interior, its information systems generate megabytes of data about designs, bills of materials, supplier performance, production costs, employee productivity, customer payment patterns, market and product trends, and so forth.

Now buried in all of this data is information that, if found and made available to the right people at the right time, can improve the decisions DSI makes. For example, when negotiating with a prior customer, how flexible does Ms. Dorset want to be when negotiating price? The decision to reduce price must be based, in part, on past experience with that customer. How stable were that customer's requirements? How many change-orders did that customer require? How quickly did the customer pay? How much service and support has the customer needed?

For another example, consider the 15+ terabytes in Verizon's customer database. Buried in all of that data is a pattern that can help the company decide which customers are at risk of switching to another company. The same data can forecast the revenue impact of alternative cell phone prices and programs. Either analysis will improve Verizon's decisions, and by doing so, will increase Verizon's competitive strength.

Q2 How Do BI Systems Provide Competitive Advantages?

A **business intelligence (BI) system** is an information system that provides information for improving decision making. BI systems vary in their characteristics and capabilities and in the way they foster competitive advantage.

Figure 9-3 (page 200) summarizes the characteristics and competitive advantages of four categories of business intelligence systems. **Reporting systems** integrate data from multiple sources, and they process that data by sorting,

Business Intelligence System	Characteristics	Competitive Advantage	To Learn More, Read
Reporting Systems	Integrate and process data by sorting, grouping, summing, and formatting. Produce, administer, and deliver reports.	Improve decisions by providing relevant, accurate, and timely information to the right person.	Chapter Extension 15, "Reporting Systems and OLAP"
Data-Mining Systems	Use sophisticated statistical techniques to find patterns and relationships.	Improve decisions by discovering patterns and relationships in data to predict future outcomes.	Chapter Extension 14, "Database Marketing," and Chapter Extension 16, "Data mining and Counterterrorism"
Knowledge Management Systems	Share knowledge of products, product uses, best practices, etc., among employees, managers, customers, and others.	Improve decisions by publishing employee and others' knowledge. Create value from existing intellectual capital. Foster innovation, improve customer service, increase organizational responsiveness, and reduce costs.	Chapter Extension 3, "Knowledge Management and Expert Systems"
Expert Systems	Encode human knowledge in the form of If/Then rules and process those rules to make a diagnosis or recommendation.	Improve decision making by nonexperts by encoding, saving, and processing expert knowledge.	Chapter Extension 3, "Knowledge Management and Expert Systems"

Figure 9-3
Characteristics and Competitive
Advantage of BI Systems

grouping, summing, averaging, and comparing. Such systems format the results into reports and deliver those reports to users. Reporting systems improve decision making by providing the right information to the right user at the right time. You can learn more about reporting systems in Chapter Extension 15, "Reporting Systems and OLAP," on page 493.

Data-mining systems process data using sophisticated statistical techniques like regression analysis and decision tree analysis. Data-mining systems find patterns and relationships that cannot be found by simpler reporting operations like sorting, grouping, and averaging. Data-mining systems improve decision making by using the discovered patterns and relationships to *anticipate* events or to *predict* future outcomes. An example of a data-mining system is one that predicts the likelihood that a prospect will donate to a cause or political campaign based on the prospect's characteristics, such as age, sex, and home Zip code. **Market-basket analysis** is another data-mining system, which computes correlations of items on past orders to determine items that are frequently purchased together.

We will discuss data mining in more detail at the end of this chapter. In addition, you can learn practical applications of data-mining systems in two chapter extensions: Chapter Extension 14, "Database Marketing" (page 483), and Chapter Extension 16, "Information Systems and Counterterrorism" (page 507).

Knowledge-management (KM) systems create value from intellectual capital by collecting and sharing human knowledge of products, product uses, best practices, and other critical knowledge with employees, managers, customers, suppliers, and others who need it. Knowledge management is a process supported by the five components of an information system. As you can learn in Chapter Extension 3, "Knowledge Management and Expert Systems," starting on page 335, by sharing knowledge, KM systems foster innovation, improve customer service, increase organizational responsiveness by getting products and services to market faster, and reduce costs.

Expert systems are the fourth category of BI system in Figure 9-3. Expert systems encapsulate the knowledge of human experts in the form of *If/Then* rules. In a medical diagnosis system, for example, an expert system might have a rule such as:

If Patient_Temperature > 103, *Then* Initiate High_Fever_Procedure

Operational expert systems can have hundreds or even thousands of such rules. While few expert systems have demonstrated a capability equivalent to a human expert, some are good enough to considerably improve the diagnosis and decision making of non-experts. You can learn more about expert systems in Chapter Extension 3, "Knowledge Management and Expert Systems" (page 340).

As with all information systems, it is important to distinguish between business intelligence tools and business intelligence systems. Business Objects licenses the reporting tool Crystal Reports. SPSS licenses the data-mining suite Clementine, and Microsoft offers SharePoint Server as, in part, a knowledge-management system. All of these products are, however, just software. They represent just one of the five components.

To gain the promise of improved decision making, organizations must incorporate data-mining products into complete information systems. A reporting tool can generate a report that shows a customer has cancelled an important order. It takes a reporting *system*, however, to alert the customer's salesperson to this unwanted news in time for the salesperson to attempt to reverse the decision. Similarly, a data-mining tool can create an equation that computes the probability that a customer will default on a loan. A data-mining *system*, however, uses that equation to enable banking personnel to approve or reject a loan on the spot.

Q3 What Problems Do Operational Data Pose for BI Systems?

Data from transaction processing and other operational systems can be processed to create basic reports without problem. If we want to know, for example, current sales and how those sales relate to sales projections, we simply process data in the order-entry database.

However, raw operational data is seldom suitable for more sophisticated reporting or data mining. Figure 9-4 lists the major problem categories. First, although data that are critical for successful operations must be complete and accurate, data that are only marginally necessary do not need to be. For example, some systems gather demographic data in the ordering process. But because such data are not needed to fill, ship, and bill orders, their quality suffers.

Problematic data are termed **dirty data**. Examples are values of *B* for customer gender and of *213* for customer age. Other examples are a value of *999-999-9999* for a U.S. phone number, a part color of *gren*, and an email address of *WhyMe@GuessWhoIAM.org*. All of these values can be problematic for data-mining purposes.

• Dirty data	• Wrong granularity
• Missing values	– Too fine
• Inconsistent data	– Not fine enough
• Data not integrated	• Too much data
	– Too many attributes
	– Too many data points

Figure 9-4
Problems of Using Operational
Data for BI Systems

Missing values are a second problem. A nonprofit organization can process a donation without knowing the donor's gender or age, but a data-mining application will suffer if there are many such values.

Inconsistent data, the third problem in Figure 9-4, are particularly common for data that have been gathered over time. When an area code changes, for example, the phone number for a given customer before the change will not match the customer's number after the change. Likewise, part codes can change, as can sales territories. Before such data can be used, they must be recoded for consistency over the period of the study.

Some data inconsistencies occur from the nature of the business activity. Consider a Web-based order-entry system used by customers worldwide. When the Web server records the time of order, which time zone does it use? The server's system clock time is irrelevant to an analysis of customer behavior. Coordinated Universal Time (formerly called Greenwich Mean Time) is also meaningless. Somehow, Web server time must be adjusted to the time zone of the customer.

Another problem is nonintegrated data. Suppose, for example, that an organization wants to perform an analysis of customer purchase and payment behavior. Unfortunately, the organization records payment data in an Oracle financial management database that is separate from the Microsoft CRM database that has the order data. Before the organization can perform the analysis, the data must be integrated.

Data can also be too fine or too coarse. Data **granularity** refers to the degree of summarization or detail. Coarse data is highly summarized; fine data express precise details. For example, suppose we want to analyze the placement of graphics and controls on an order-entry Web page. It is possible to capture the customers' clicking behavior in what is termed **clickstream data**. Those data are very fine, however, including everything the customer does at the Web site. In the middle of the order stream are data for clicks on the news, email, instant chat, and a weather check. Although all of that data is needed for a study of consumer computer behavior, such data will be overwhelming if all we want to know is how customers respond to ad locations. Because the data are too fine, the data analysts must throw away millions and millions of clicks.

Data can also be too coarse. For example, a file of order totals cannot be used for a market-basket analysis. For market-basket analysis, we need to know which items were purchased with which others. This doesn't mean the order-total data are useless. They can be adequate for other purposes; they just won't do for a market-basket analysis.

Generally, it is better to have too fine a granularity than too coarse. If the granularity is too fine, the data can be made coarser by summing and combining. Only analysts' labor and computer processing are required. If the granularity is too coarse, however, there is no way to separate the data into constituent parts.

The final problem listed in Figure 9-4 concerns too much data. As shown in the figure, we can have either too many attributes or too many data points. Think of the tables in Chapter 5. We can have too many columns or too many rows.

Consider the first problem: too many attributes. Suppose we want to know the factors that influence how customers respond to a promotion. If we combine internal customer data with customer data that we can purchase, we could have more than a hundred different attributes to consider. How do we select among them? Because of a phenomenon called the **curse of dimensionality**, the more attributes there are, the easier it is to build a model that fits the sample data but that is worthless as a predictor. There are other good reasons for reducing the number of attributes, and one of the major activities in data mining concerns efficient and effective ways of selecting attributes.

The second way to have too much data is to have too many data points—too many rows of data. Suppose we want to analyze clickstream data on CNN.com. How many clicks does that site receive per month? Millions upon millions! In order to meaningfully analyze such data, we need to reduce the amount of data. There is a good solution to this problem: statistical sampling. Organizations should not be reluctant to sample data in such situations, as explained in the *Guide* on pages 203a–203b.

Q4 What Are the Purposes and Components of a Data Warehouse?

The purpose of a **data warehouse** is to extract and clean data from operational systems and other sources, and to store and catalog that data for processing by BI tools. Figure 9-5 shows the basic components of a data warehouse. Programs read operational data and extract, clean, and prepare that data for BI processing. The prepared data are stored in a data-warehouse database using a data-warehouse DBMS, which can be different from the organization's operational DBMS. For example, an organization might use Oracle for its operational processing, but use SQL Server for its data warehouse. Other organizations use SQL Server for operational processing, but use DBMSs from statistical package vendors, such as SAS or SPSS, in the data warehouse.

Data warehouses include data that are purchased from outside sources. A typical example is customer credit data. Figure 9-6 (page 204) lists some of the consumer data than can be purchased from commercial vendors today. An amazing (and from a privacy standpoint, frightening) amount of data is available.

Metadata concerning the data—its source, its format, its assumptions and constraints, and other facts about the data—is kept in a data-warehouse metadata database. The data-warehouse DBMS extracts and provides data to business intelligence tools, such as data-mining programs.

By the way, do not interpret the term *warehouse* literally. It is a warehouse only in the sense that it is a facility for storing data for use by others. It is *not* a

Video

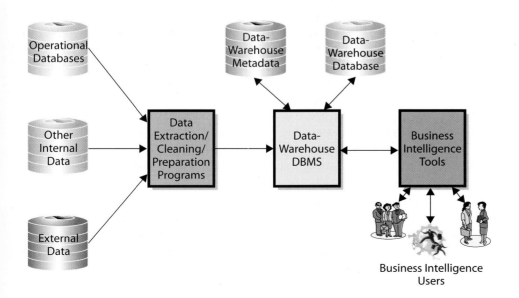

Figure 9-5
Components of a Data Warehouse

Counting and Counting and Counting

Not long ago, in a very large software company, a meeting occurred between a group of highly competent product managers and a group of equally competent data miners. The product managers wanted the data miners to analyze customer clicks on a Web page to determine customer preferences for particular product lines. The products were competing with one another for resources, and the results of the analysis were important in allocating those resources.

The meeting progressed well until one of the data miners started to explain the sampling scheme that they would use.

"Sampling?" asked the product managers in a chorus. "Sampling? No way. We want all the data. This is important, and we don't want a guess."

"But there are millions, literally, millions of ad clicks to analyze. If we don't sample, it will take hours, maybe even days, to perform the calculations. You won't see the results from each day's analysis until several days later if we don't sample." The data miners were squirming.

"We don't care," said the product managers. "We must have an accurate study. Don't sample!"

This leads us to a statistical concept you need to know: *There's nothing wrong with sampling.* Properly done, the results from a sample are just as accurate as results from the complete data set. Studies done from samples are also cheaper and faster. Sampling is a great way to save time and money.

Suppose you have a bag of blue and red balls randomly mixed. Let's say the bag is big enough to contain 100,000 balls. How many of those balls do you need to examine to calculate, accurately, the proportion of each color?

You go to the park on a sunny day, sit down with your bag, and start pulling balls out of the bag. After 100 balls, you conclude the ratio of blue to red is 3 to 4. After 500 balls, you conclude the ratio of blue to red balls is 3 to 4. After 5,000 balls, you conclude the ratio of blue to red balls is 3 to 4. After 10,000 balls, you conclude the ratio of blue to red balls is 3 to 4. Do you really need to sit there until next week, counting balls day and night, to examine every ball in the bag? And, if you're the manager who needs to know that ratio, do you really want to pay someone to count all those balls? You knew the answer after you had counted 100 balls.

That's why the data miners were so depressed after their meeting with the product managers. They knew they had to count Web clicks long, long after there was any more information to be gained from continuing to count. To add to the pain of their situation, they had to do it only because of the product managers' ignorance.

In truth, skill is required to develop a good sample. The product managers should have listened to the data miners' sampling plan and ensured that the sample would be appropriate, given the goals of the

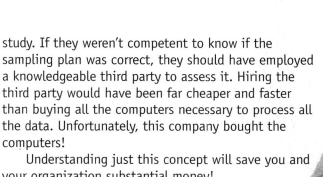

study. If they weren't competent to know if the sampling plan was correct, they should have employed a knowledgeable third party to assess it. Hiring the third party would have been far cheaper and faster than buying all the computers necessary to process all the data. Unfortunately, this company bought the computers!

Understanding just this concept will save you and your organization substantial money!

DISCUSSION QUESTIONS

1. In your own words, explain why a sample can give the same accuracy of results as the entire data set. Under what circumstances would it not give the same results?

2. Suppose you want to predict the demand for toothbrushes from past sales data. Suppose there are 5 colors and 10 styles. If you want to predict the sales for all types of toothbrushes, how should you sample? If you want to predict the sales for each color and style, would you sample differently? Why or why not?

3. The data miners tried to sell the idea of sampling based on the reduction of work. Suppose instead they had tried to sell the idea based on the idea of equal accuracy. Would the result have been different?

Figure 9-6
Consumer Data Available for
Purchase from Data Venders

• Name, address, phone	• Catalog orders
• Age	• Marital status, life stage
• Gender	• Height, weight, hair and
• Ethnicity	eye color
• Religion	• Spouse name, birth date
• Income	• Children's names and
• Education	birth dates
• Voter registration	
• Home ownership	
• Vehicles	
• Magazine subscriptions	
• Hobbies	

large building with shelves and forklifts buzzing through aisles loaded with pallets. Physically, a data warehouse consists of a few fast computers with very large storage devices. The data warehouse is usually staffed by a small department consisting of both technical personnel and business analysts. The technical personnel work to develop the best ways of storing and cataloging the data warehouse's contents. The business analysts work to ensure the contents are relevant and sufficient for the business needs of BI system users.

Q5 What Is a Data Mart, and How Does It Differ from a Data Warehouse?

A **data mart** is a data collection that is created to address the needs of a particular business function, problem, or opportunity. An e-commerce company, for example, might create a data mart storing clickstream data that is presampled and summarized in such a way to enable the analysis of Web page design features.

That same company might have a second data mart for market-basket analysis. This second data mart would contain records of past sales data organized to facilitate the computation of item-purchase correlations. A third data mart could contain inventory data and be organized to support a BI system used to plan the layout of inventory.

So how is a data warehouse different from a data mart? In a way, you can think of a *data warehouse* as a distributor in a supply chain. The data warehouse takes data from the data manufacturers (operational systems and purchased data), cleans and processes the data, and locates the data on its shelves, so to speak—that is, on the disks of the data warehouse computers. The people who work with a data warehouse are experts at data management, data cleaning, data transformation, and the like. However, they are not usually experts in a given business function.

As stated, a *data mart* is a data collection, smaller than the data warehouse, that addresses a particular component or functional area of the business. If the data warehouse is the distributor in a supply chain, then a data mart is like a retail store in a supply chain. Users in the data mart obtain data that pertain to a particular business function from the data warehouse. Such users do not have the data management expertise that data warehouse employees have, but they are knowledgeable analysts for a given business function. Figure 9-7 illustrates these relationships.

As you can imagine, it is expensive to create, staff, and operate data warehouses and data marts. Only large organizations with deep pockets can afford to

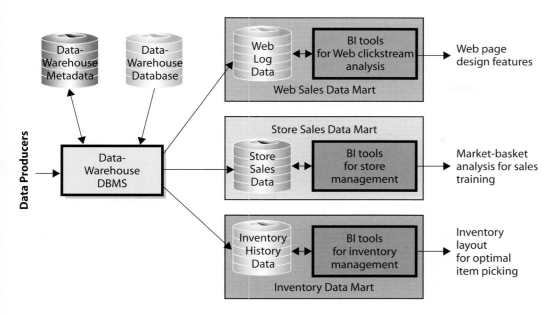

Figure 9-7
Data Mart Examples

operate a system like that shown in Figure 9-7. Smaller organizations operate subsets of this system; they may have just a simple data mart for analyzing promotion data, for example.

Q6 What Are the Characteristics of Data-mining Systems?

We now return to the concept of data mining. **Data mining** is the application of statistical techniques to find patterns and relationships among data and to classify and predict. As shown in Figure 9-8 data mining represents a convergence of disciplines. Data-mining techniques emerged from statistics and mathematics and from artificial intelligence and machine-learning fields in computer science. As a result, data-mining terminology is an odd blend of terms from these different disciplines. Sometimes people use the term *knowledge discovery in databases* (*KDD*) as a synonym for *data mining*.

Data-mining techniques take advantage of developments in data management for processing the enormous databases that have emerged in the last

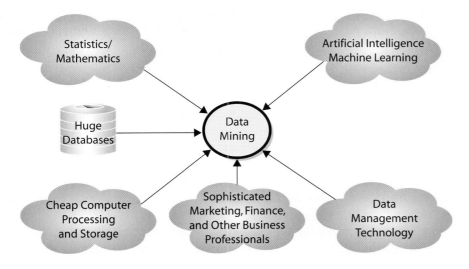

Figure 9-8
Convergence Disciplines for Data Mining

10 years. Of course, these data would not have been generated were it not for fast and cheap computers, and without such computers, the new techniques would be impossible to compute.

Most data-mining techniques are sophisticated, and many are difficult to use as well. Such techniques are valuable to organizations, however, and some business professionals, especially those in finance and marketing, have become expert in their use. Today, in fact, there are many interesting and rewarding careers for business professionals who are knowledgeable about data-mining techniques.

Data-mining techniques fall into two broad categories: unsupervised and supervised. We explain both types below.

Unsupervised Data Mining

With **unsupervised data mining**, analysts do not create a model or hypothesis before running the analysis. Instead, they apply the data-mining technique to the data and observe the results. With this method, analysts create hypotheses after the analysis to explain the patterns found.

One common unsupervised technique is **cluster analysis**. With it, statistical techniques identify groups of entities that have similar characteristics. A common use for cluster analysis is to find groups of similar customers from customer order and demographic data.

For example, suppose a cluster analysis finds two very different customer groups: One group has an average age of 33, owns at least one laptop and at least one PDA, drives an expensive SUV, and tends to buy expensive children's play equipment. The second group has an average age of 64, owns vacation property, plays golf, and buys expensive wines. Suppose the analysis also finds that both groups buy designer children's clothing.

These findings are obtained solely by data analysis. There is no prior model about the patterns and relationship that exist. It is up to the analyst to form hypotheses, after the fact, to explain why two such different groups are both buying designer children's clothes.

Supervised Data Mining

With **supervised data mining**, data miners develop a model prior to the analysis and apply statistical techniques to data to estimate parameters of the model. For example, suppose marketing experts in a communications company believe that cell phone usage on weekends is determined by the age of the customer and the number of months the customer has had the cell phone account. A data-mining analyst would then run an analysis that estimates the impact of customer and account age. One such analysis, which measures the impact of a set of variables on another variable, is called a **regression analysis**. A sample result for the cell phone example is:

```
CellPhoneWeekendMinutes =
12 + (17.5 * CustomerAge) + (23.7 * NumberMonthsOfAccount)
```

Using this equation, analysts can predict the number of minutes of weekend cell phone use by summing 12, plus 17.5 times the customer's age, plus 23.7 times the number of months of the account.

As you will learn in your statistics classes, considerable skill is required to interpret the quality of such a model. The regression tool will create an equation, such as the one shown. Whether that equation is a good predictor of future cell phone usage depends on statistical factors like t values, confidence intervals, and related statistical techniques.

Neural networks are another popular supervised data-mining technique used to predict values and make classifications, such as "good prospect" or "poor prospect" customers. The term *neural networks* is deceiving because it connotes a biological process similar to that in animal brains. In fact, although the original *idea* of neural nets may have come from the anatomy and physiology of neurons, a neural net is nothing more than a complicated set of possibly nonlinear equations. Explaining the techniques used for neural networks is beyond the scope of this text. If you want to learn more, search *kdnuggets.com* for the term *neural network.*

Chapter Extension 14, ""Database Marketing," and Chapter Extension 16, "Information Systems and Counterterrorism," demonstrate the use of some data-mining techniques. These chapter extensions should give you, a future manager, a sense of the possibilities of data-mining techniques. You will need additional coursework in statistics, data management, marketing, and finance, however, before you will be able to perform such analyses yourself. As useful as data mining and business intelligence can be for organizations, they are not without problems, as discussed in the *Ethics Guide* on pages 207a–207b.

Data Mining in the Real World

"I'm not really a contrarian about data mining. I believe in it. After all, it's my career. But data mining in the real world is a lot different from the way it's described in textbooks.

"There are many reasons it's different. One is that the data are always dirty, with missing values, values way out of the range of possibility, and time values that make no sense. Here's an example: Somebody sets the server system clock incorrectly and runs the server for a while with the wrong time. When they notice the mistake, they set the clock to the correct time. But all of the transactions that were running during that interval have an ending time before the starting time. When we run the data analysis, and compute elapsed time, the results are negative for those transactions.

"Missing values are a similar problem. Consider the records of just 10 purchases. Suppose that two of the records are missing the customer number and one is missing the year part of the transaction date. So you throw out three records, which is 30 percent of the data. You then notice that two more records have dirty data, and so you throw them out, too. Now you've lost half your data.

"Another problem is that you know the least when you start the study. So you work for a few months and learn that if you had another variable, say the customer's Zip code, or age, or something else, you could do a much better analysis. But those other data just aren't available. Or, maybe they are available, but to get the data you have to reprocess millions of transactions, and you don't have the time or budget to do that.

"Overfitting is another problem, a huge one. I can build a model to fit any set of data you have. Give me 100 data points and in a few minutes, I can give you 100 different equations that will predict those 100 data points. With neural networks, you can create a model of any level of complexity you want, except that none of those equations will predict new cases with any accuracy at all. When using neural nets, you have to be very careful not to overfit the data.

"Then, too, data mining is about probabilities, not certainty. Bad luck happens. Say I build a model that predicts the probability that a customer will make a purchase. Using the model on new-customer data, I find three customers who have a .7 probability of buying something. That's a good number, well over a 50-50 chance, but it's still possible that none of them will buy. In fact, the probability that none of them will buy is $.3 \times .3 \times .3$, or .027, which is 2.7 percent.

"Now suppose I give the names of the three customers to a salesperson who calls on them, and sure enough, we have a stream of bad luck and none of them buys. This bad result doesn't mean the model is wrong. But what does the salesperson think? He thinks that the model is worthless and that he can do better on his own. He tells his manager who tells her associate, who tells the northeast region, and sure enough, the model has a bad reputation all across the company.

"Another problem is seasonality. Say all your training data are from the summer. Will your model be valid for the winter? Maybe, but maybe not. You might even know that it won't be valid for predicting winter sales, but if you don't have winter data, what do you do?

"When you start a data-mining project, you never know how it will turn out. I worked on one project for six months, and when we finished, I didn't think our model was any good. We had too many problems with data: wrong, dirty, and missing. There was no way we could know ahead of time that it would happen, but it did.

"When the time came to present the results to senior management, what could we do? How could we say we took six months of our time and substantial computer resources to create a bad model? We had a model, but I just didn't think it would make accurate predictions. I was a junior member of the team, and it wasn't for me to decide. I kept my mouth shut, but I never felt good about it."

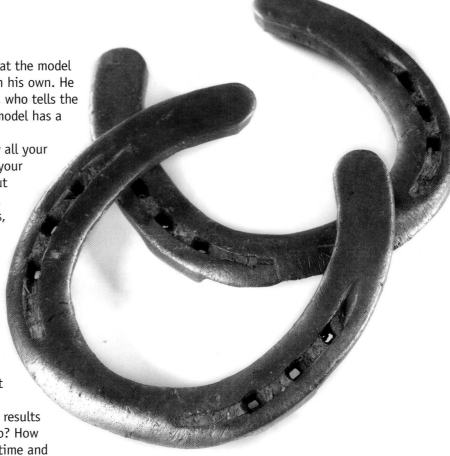

DISCUSSION QUESTIONS

1. Did this employee have an ethical responsibility to speak up regarding his belief about the quality of the data-mining model? Why or why not?

2. If you were this employee, what would you have done?

3. The case doesn't indicate how the data-mining model was to be used. Suppose it was to be used at a hospital emergency room to predict the criticality of emergency cases. In this case, would you change your answers to questions 1 and 2? Why or why not?

4. Suppose the data-mining model was to be used to predict the likelihood that sales prospects respond to a promotional postal mailing. Say the cost of the mailing is $10,000 and will be paid by a marketing department having an annual budget of $25 million. Do your answers to questions 1 and 2 change for this situation? Why or why not?

5. If your answers are different for questions 3 and 4, explain why. If they are not different, explain why not.

6. Suppose you were this employee and you spoke to your direct boss about your misgivings. Your boss said, "Forget about it, junior." How would you respond?

7. Suppose your boss told you to forget about it, but in a meeting with your boss and your boss's boss, the senior manager asks you what you think of the predictive ability of this model. How do you respond?

How does the knowledge in this chapter help you at DSI?

You're still seeking an IS that will provide higher labor productivity for DSI. Your most recent idea has been to focus on a system that would analyze past supplier performance to help DSI select suppliers. Using the knowledge in this chapter, you can describe four categories of possible information systems and describe, at least at a high level, the advantages and disadvantages of each.

A reporting system would process the data about past suppliers, the products they've supplied, and the timeliness of component delivery. If quality data is kept in the manufacturing systems, the reporting system can process that data to rank supplier quality.

A data-mining system would search for patterns and relationships for predicting future events. You could use such a system to predict the likelihood of a delivery delay or of a quality problem. Knowledge-management systems enable humans to share their knowledge, and you might be able to construct one that would enable buyers and manufacturing managers to rank suppliers or to share their experiences working with suppliers.

Finally, you could conceivably build an expert system containing rules for selecting a supplier, given a component or part need. Anticipating questions Mr. Stratford might ask, you probably should also describe the advantages and disadvantages of each. (See Exercise 6.)

In addition to these systems, you might also consider a data warehouse or data mart. DSI is probably too small for a data warehouse, but it might make sense for it to gather in-bound logistics and manufacturing data into some type of data mart. Doing so would facilitate not just the selection of suppliers, but also the process of creating a bid. (See Exercise 7.)

Once you have all of this analysis, what should you do with it? Which of the systems you've investigated should you recommend for use at DSI? For answers to these questions, and to continue the story, you'll have to read Chapter 10. Meanwhile, answer the questions in the exercises that follow—answer them well because. . . this could happen to you.

Active ? Review

Use this Active Review to verify that you understand the material in the chapter. You can read the entire chapter and then perform the tasks in this review, or you can read the material for just one question and perform the tasks in this review for that question before moving on to the next one.

Q1 How big is an exabyte, and why does it matter?

State the total disk storage capacity as of 2003. Compare this storage capacity to the number of words ever spoken by human beings. Compare this capacity to the contents of all the U.S. academic libraries. Explain how this phenomenon impacts organizations today; use DSI as an example.

Q2 How do BI systems provide competitive advantages?

Define *business intelligence systems*. Name four categories of BI systems, and describe the basic characteristics of each. Explain how systems in each category contribute to competitive advantage.

Q3 What problems do operational data pose for BI systems?

List problems that occur when using operational data for BI systems. Briefly summarize each problem. Define *granularity*. Explain the problem posed by the curse of dimensionality.

Q4 What are the purpose and components of a data warehouse?

State the purpose of a data warehouse. Explain the role of each component in Figure 9-5. Of the many different types of data that can be purchased, name five that you think are the most concerning from a privacy standpoint. State reasons why some businesses might want to purchase this data. Explain why the term *warehouse* is misleading.

Q5 What is a data mart, and how does it differ from a data warehouse?

Define *data mart*, and give an example of one not described in this chapter. Explain how data warehouses and data marts are like components of a supply chain. Under what conditions does an organization staff a data warehouse with several data marts?

Q6 What are the characteristics of data-mining systems?

State the purpose of data-mining systems. Explain how data mining emerged from the convergence of different disciplines. Describe the impact this history had on data-mining terminology. Explain the characteristics and uses of unsupervised data mining. Explain the characteristics and uses of supervised data mining. Explain why the term *neural network* is a misnomer.

How does the knowledge in this chapter help you at DSI?

Describe how you would use the knowledge in this chapter to respond to your challenge at DSI.

Key Terms and Concepts

Using Your Knowledge

1. The data in Figure 9-2 is as of 2003. Using the trend of the years from 2000 to 2003, estimate the storage capacity sold during 2007. Search the Web for an estimate of the same number. Compare your estimate to the size of all printed material (shown in Figure 9-1). Do you agree with the statement, "Today, disk storage is essentially free"? Describe two business opportunities that this trend creates. How does YouTube benefit from this trend?

2. How does the data storage trend described in question 1 impact your university? What types of data are growing the fastest? Of the fast-growing data, how much is generated by students? How much is generated by classroom activities? How much is generated by administration? How much is generated by research?

3. Suppose you work for the university and have access to student, class, professor, department, and grade data. Suppose you want to determine whether grade inflation exists, and, if so, where it seems to be the greatest. Describe a reporting system that would produce evidence of grade inflation. How would you structure the reports to determine where it is the greatest?

4. Suppose you work for the university and have access to student, class, professor, department, and grade data. Assume the student data includes students' home address, high school, and prior college performance (if any). Describe an unsupervised data-mining technique that could be used to predict college applicants who are likely to succeed academically. Is it responsible or irresponsible to use an unsupervised technique for such a problem?

5. Same as exercise 4, but describe a supervised data-mining technique that could be used to predict the success of applicants. Is using a supervised technique more justifiable than using an unsupervised technique? Explain your answer.

6. Explain how a set of If/Then rules could be used to select a supplier. Give an example of five rules that would be pertinent to this problem. Given the nature of DSI's product, and the size and culture of the organization, do you think it is likely that DSI would embrace an expert system? Consider Ms. Dorset's commentary at the start of Part III (page 154) as you formulate your answer.

7. Do you think a data warehouse is appropriate for DSI? Why or why not? Figure 9-7 implies that data marts require the existence of a data warehouse, but this is not always true. DSI could construct a data mart containing inbound logistic and manufacturing data without a data warehouse. In this case, the data mart would need to clean and prep its own operational data. Given DSI's product and the nature of its business, what value might such a data mart provide? List seven decisions that such a data mart might support. Describe the BI system that would support each decision. Explain how such BI systems contribute to DSI's competitive strategy.

8. Summarize the four systems proposed for use at DSI. Compare and contrast the features and functions of each. Rate these systems on their ability to

increase labor productivity. Which system would you choose to propose for DSI to use? Write a short (no more than one page) description of the alternatives, your analysis, and the rationale for your recommendation. Do you think your analysis demonstrates innovative thinking on ways to facilitate DSI's competitive strategy?

Case Study 9

Building Data for Decision Making at Home Depot

Home Depot is a major retail chain specializing in the sale of construction and home repair and maintenance products. The company has over 2,000 retail stores in North America from which it generated $81.5 billion in sales in 2005. Home Depot carries more than 40,000 products in its stores and employs 355,000 people worldwide.

Suppose you are a buyer for the clothes washer and dryer product line at Home Depot. You work with seven different brands and numerous models within each brand. One of your goals is to turn your inventory as many times a year as you can, and to do so, you want to identify poorly selling models (and even brands) as quickly as you can. This identification is not as easy as you might think because competition is intense among washer and dryer manufacturers, and a new model can quickly capture a substantial portion of another model's market share. Thus, a big seller this year can be "a dog" (a poor seller) next year.

Another problem is that while some sales trends are national, others pertain to specific regions. A strong seller in the Southeast may not sell as well in the Northwest. Thus, a brand can be a big seller in one region and a dog in another.

In answering the following questions, assume you have total sales data for each brand and model, for each store, for each month. Assume also that you know the store's city and state.

Questions

1. Explain how reporting systems could be helpful to you.

2. Show the structure of one or two reports that you could use to identify poorly selling models. How would you structure the reports to identify different sales trends in different regions?

3. For one of your reports in question 2, write a description of your requirements suitable for giving to an IT professional. Be as complete and thorough as you can in describing your needs.

4. Explain how data-mining systems could be helpful to you.

5. How could cluster analysis help you identify poorly selling brands? How could cluster analysis help you determine differences in sales for different geographic regions? Is the unsupervised nature of cluster analysis an advantage or disadvantage for you?

6. How could regression analysis help you determine poorly selling brands?

7. Do you believe there is an application for a KM system for identifying poorly selling brands? Why or why not?

8. Do you believe there is an application for an expert system for identifying poorly selling brands? Why or why not?

Dorset-Stratford Interiors, Chapter 9

GOALS

Use Dorset-Stratford Interiors (DSI) to:

* Illustrate the difference between information systems that support business processes and information systems that support decision making.

* Deepen understanding of four types of business intelligence systems by applying each to the DSI situation.

* Vicariously motivate students to use MIS knowledge to increase their personal competitive advantage (through the challenges of the internship).

BACKGROUND

1. Chapters 7 and 8 focused on how information systems support business processes. This chapter considers information systems that support *decision making*. As the text indicates, however, the difference is only one of perspective. Every business process includes decisions, and every decision is part of a business process. It's really just a question of the primary focus of the system: Are we using the IS to support the sales process, or are we using the IS to decide customer creditworthiness? Both are part of CRM, but with different orientations.

2. Figure 9-3 compares the four basic types of business intelligence systems. Knowledge management and expert systems are not described in this chapter, but are discussed in Chapter Extension 3. While that extension is not required to address DSI in this chapter, it would help.

3. The text suggests investigating a business intelligence system to evaluate and choose suppliers. A good question to ask is, how does such a system contribute to DSI's competitive strategy of making its labor more productive? It might make the buyers more productive, and having the right materials on hand will reduce labor inefficiency. Also, having materials delivered on schedule will reduce idle time and the need to reschedule work. Further, why does DSI want to make its labor more productive? To reduce costs. Making the right decision on a supplier will certainly reduce costs.

4. DSI is way too small to think about a data warehouse. The text suggests DSI might gather data to create a small data mart. That's probably not too much of a stretch of the term, and calling the collected data a *data mart* will bring positive attention to that data and its uses.

HOW TO GET THE STUDENTS INVOLVED

1. The purpose of DSI in Part 3 is to cause the students to think about potential applications of IS, using the foil of a student intern. To make sure they're on board, it might be good to start with a review so far:

   a. **What was the subject of Chapter 7? Chapter 8?**

   b. **What is the subject of Chapter 9, and how does it differ from Chapters 7 and 8?**

   c. **In your own words, explain the difference between an IS that supports a business process and one that supports decision making.**

   d. **If I were to say to you, "No the purpose of all IS is to support decision making," how would you respond? If I were to say, "The purpose of all IS is to support business processes," how would you respond?**

   e. **How is this distinction useful?**

   (I think because, when we're looking for innovative applications of IS, considering these two perspectives helps us think of more alternatives. I suspect there are other reasons, too, but that's why it matters to me.)

2. Now consider the DSI intern's work, so far:

   a. **What two ideas did the intern develop for IS within the DSI organization?**

   b. **What idea did the intern have for IS across organizations?**

   c. **How well do you like those ideas?**

3. In this chapter, the intern is seeking information systems that improve decision making.

   a. **Describe the business intelligence system the intern is considering.**

   b. **How does that information system idea support business processes? How does it support better decision making?**

   c. **One of the systems from Chapter 7 is actually a type of business intelligence system. Which one?**

4. Now let's consider innovative applications of business intelligence systems at DSI:

   a. **What IS idea did the intern develop?**

   b. **How would that IS support decision making?**

   c. **How would that IS support DSI's competitive strategy?**

5. Now attempt to do better than the intern:

   a. What are the four types of BI system described in the book?

   b. What are the purpose and characteristics of each type?

   c. Give an example of a reporting system (other than the one from Chapter 7) that supports DSI's competitive strategy.

   d. Give an example of a data-mining system that supports DSI's competitive strategy.

   e. Give an example of a knowledge-management system that supports DSI's competitive strategy.

   f. Give an example of an expert system that supports DSI's competitive strategy.

   g. Which is best, and why?

BOTTOM LINE

Same as Chapters 7 and 8:

* Seek innovative applications of IS and IT in order to gain a competitive advantage . . . for you and for your organization.

Using the Guide: Counting and Counting and Counting (page 203a)

GOALS

✳ Teach the students that:
- Proper sampling leads to valid results and can save time and money.
- Not all sampling plans are valid. The sampling plan should be evaluated.

✳ Illustrate a practical application of empathetic thinking.

BACKGROUND AND PRESENTATION STRATEGIES

As the start of the chapter indicates, information systems are generating enormous amounts of data. Attempts to process all the data are wasteful, time consuming, and foolish. There is nothing wrong with a proper sample!

The marketing analysts in this guide were MBA-level analysts working for a famous and very successful software company. They were highly paid and very successful in their careers. In this case, they also caused their employer to waste a large amount of money.

One caveat: Sampling is every bit as accurate as nonsampling, *as long as the sampling plan is valid.* So, rather than refusing to allow sampling, the product managers should have evaluated the sampling plan—or hired someone to do it if they were not qualified. What a waste!

Question 2 can't be answered based on the information in this guide. Its purpose is to show *the need for a sampling plan* and possibly the need to bring in outside expertise to evaluate that plan.

I wasn't in the meeting between the data miners and the product managers, but from the reports I heard, I think the data miners erred in stating their objection as avoiding useless work. The product managers didn't care about the data miners' workload; they cared about their products. If the data miners thought empathetically, they would have explained how sampling would enable them to do more studies, faster, with quicker turnaround, and thus provide better guidance to the product managers. In fairness to the data miners, however, they were blindsided by this issue. They didn't expect to have any resistance to sampling, and responded extemporaneously with their concerns. See question 3.

 ### SUGGESTED RESPONSES FOR DISCUSSION QUESTIONS

1. Once you have sampled enough items, additional sampling does not add more value. You're just wasting your time and money.

   ➤ **How do you know if you've sampled enough?**

   Intuitively, you know you've sampled enough when continued sampling provides little new information. Principles and formulas exist that specify how many items you need to sample. They are the subject of a statistics class, not this class. For now, just understand that sampling can provide accurate results.

   By the way, the number required for a good sample is surprisingly small. Many good samples for political attitudes for the U.S. population use fewer than 4,000 people.

2. The question indicates the need for a sampling plan, and, as should have happened in this guide, for someone with statistical expertise to evaluate the appropriateness of the sampling plan. The answer to this question cannot be determined from the information in this guide. The point:

   ➤ **Sampling can be tricky: If you don't know what you're doing, hire someone who does.**

   The following sequence of questions will indicate the general nature of a solution to the problem. Suppose 1 out of every 1,000 toothbrush sales is for the style Macho and the color Pink.

   ➤ **If we sample 1,000 items, how likely are we to find a sale for Macho, Pink toothbrushes?**

   (Very unlikely.)

   Suppose that we sample 100,000 items. Suppose the most popular color and style is {Pink, Grandmother}, and it accounts for 70 percent of our sales. On average then, 70,000 of those in the sample will be sales for {Pink, Grandmother} toothbrushes. With a straight sample of 100,000, we oversampled {Pink, Grandmother} and likely undersampled {Pink, Macho}.

   The conclusion: Sampling is fine, but if there is any complexity at all, and if you don't know what you're doing, call in an expert.

3. I think the result would have been different. This answer takes us back to empathetic thinking, which

was first discussed in Chapter 2 (page 31a). The data miners responded with what was important to *them*, which was all the unnecessary work that they had to do. But the product managers didn't care about how much work the data miners had; they cared about the future of their products.

If the data miners had thought about the problem from the perspective of the product managers, they would have focused on the benefit of *equal accuracy with results available faster*. They needed to focus on benefits *to the product managers* instead of cost to *them*.

➤ **After the meeting was over, was there anything the data miners might have done to reverse the nonsampling decision?**

Product managers are incredibly busy people with packed schedules. It might be impossible to reschedule a meeting with the product managers to revisit this issue. But the issue might be too loaded to revisit via email. This could well be a decision that needs to be reversed but never will be because the necessary people cannot be regrouped to revisit it. Because of the way the matter was left, the product managers think the data miners are just trying to avoid work; they won't agree to remeet for that reason.

➤ **How would you write an email to justify a subsequent meeting?**

➤ **How likely is this email to succeed?**

(I think unlikely. In this situation, the data miners had one shot, and they missed. I doubt they'll get another.)

➤ **When you're not getting the decision you want, remember to reframe the question using empathetic thinking. Doing so, you might avoid situations like this!**

WRAP UP

The conclusions of this guide are simple:

➤ **Use sampling and, if you need to, hire an expert to evaluate the sampling plan.**

➤ **Possibly the most important learning in this guide, though, is the ineffective communication strategy used by the data miners (see question 3). They should have sold sampling by focusing on the benefit of equally accurate results, delivered faster.**

Using the Ethics Guide: Data Mining in the Real World (page 207a)

GOAL

* Teach real-world issues and limitations for data mining.

* Investigate the ethics of working on projects of doubtful or harmful utility to the sponsoring organization.

BACKGROUND AND PRESENTATION STRATEGIES

The contrarian whom I interviewed for this guide had 15 years' experience as a data miner, most of that in the automotive industry. He'd come back to the university because he was having a career crisis. He wasn't sure that data mining was worth it. He'd begun to question the validity of many data-mining techniques. His concerns and misgivings are summarized in this guide.

Judging by his experience, especially his last comment about luck, we can conclude that data mining shares risk characteristics with other forms of mining. Sometimes you find the gold or the oil, and sometimes you do not.

A *difficult ethical dilemma* is buried in this guide—one that I softened in writing the text. At the end of six months, this person had determined that the model that he had developed was, in fact, useless. They had overfit the data, and *he believed the predictive power of the model was nil.* He did not believe that the model should be implemented. But he was a junior member of the team, and his boss did not want to admit the model they had developed would be a bad predictor. His response was to leave that company within a few months. He still feels guilty about it—guilty that he didn't get a better result and guilty that he wasn't more honest and forthcoming.

 SUGGESTED RESPONSES FOR DISCUSSION QUESTIONS

1. This employee was in a bind.

   ➤ **As a junior person, did he have the authority to "blow the whistle" about this project?**

➤ **Did this employee have an ethical obligation to take more action than he did?**

So much depends on this person's position in the company and in the project. If he was a very junior person, he probably can just put this down as "gaining experience." If he was part of the management of the project, he has a harder dilemma. I don't think there is a clear answer.

2. Ask the students for their responses. Recall that ethical behavior is behavior that is consistent with the norms of some group. What norms applicable here?

   ➤ **If you, as a junior employee, were in his circumstances and had developed a model that you didn't believe was useful, what would you do?**

   Some possible responses:
   First would be to discuss your misgivings with your boss. Maybe you are wrong about the quality of the model. Maybe there are other factors in the background that make your fears ungrounded. Maybe your boss agrees and wants to strategize with you about what to do.

   ➤ **If your boss disagrees, would you go higher in the organization?**

   Maybe. But only after very careful questioning of my situation and motives. I'd ask myself whether the problems and risks of going higher are worth the gain.

   Risks:

   * This will end my relationship with my boss.

   * My boss will become my enemy within the company.

   * I may expose both of us to the risk of being fired.

   * My boss's boss may think I'm a whiner and a problem maker.

   * My boss's boss may not want to know.

   Gain:

   * Saving the organization time and money.

   * If the data-mining project involves people, saving the harm that will be done by miscategorizing people.

   * Preserving the reputation of data mining within the organization.

   Other courses of action are to quit the company, to transfer to another group, or to not do anything at all.

All in all, this is a very difficult situation with no clear and obvious solution.

3. Using the definition of ethical as conforming to a group norm, most people would say that the employee has a responsibility to speak up if the system is going to be used for life-threatening situations. In that case, his management would most likely be much more concerned as well. If not, the ethics of this organization are questionable.

4. Yes, in this case, the potential loss is minimal—probably less than the cost of the data mining system's development.

➤ **Why would a company choose such an elaborate data-mining application for predicting the response on a $10,000 mailing?**

Perhaps the company is testing the quality of the data model.

5. Again, this goes back to the definition of ethical. I would think most people would agree that the situation in question 3 is far more serious than that in question 4.

6. See the answer to question 2. I would think that much depends on the employees role in the project. If you are very junior and your boss says, "Forget about it," I think you are justified in doing so. If you are more senior in the project, you may have an ethical responsibility to go higher in the organization. Again, though, it depends on the nature of the application.

7. Unless the employee was specifically directed not to express his opinion, I think it is appropriate to respectfully state his concerns.

➤ **Suppose your boss asks you to attend the meeting with your boss's boss, and instructs you not to express your opinion on the data-mining system. What do you do?**

This is very tough. A logical question to ask is, "Why are you being invited to the meeting if you are not to express your opinion?" However, asking that question may be construed as impertinent.

Probably the best you can do is to go to the meeting, stay quiet, and work diligently to find a new boss.

WRAP UP

➤ **This case has two major themes: realistic problems in data mining and an ethical dilemma—when you know something that will be possibly self-defeating to reveal. Both are important.**

➤ **You may not be a data miner in your career, but you will most likely encounter, sometime during your career, a situation when you may have to take self-defeating actions in order to act ethically. You need to keep thinking about such situations and what YOU will do.**

PART 3 The International Dimension

Global IS and the Value Chain

Study Questions

Q1 How do global information systems benefit the value chain?

Q2 Why do global information systems impact functional and cross-functional systems differently?

Q3 How do global information systems affect supply chain profitability?

Q4 What is the economic impact of global manufacturing?

Q5 Should information systems be instruments for exporting cultural values?

The International Dimension

Q1 How Do Global Information Systems Benefit the Value Chain?

Because of information systems, any or all of the value chain activities in Figure 7-2 (page 160) can be performed anywhere in the world. An international company can conduct sales and marketing efforts locally, for every market in which it sells. Emerson Pharmaceutical, for example, sells in the United States with a U.S. sales force, in France with a French sales force, and in Argentina with an Argentinean sales force. Depending on local laws and customs, those sales offices may be owned by Emerson, or they may be locally owned entities with which Emerson contracts for sales and marketing services. Emerson can coordinate all of the sales efforts of these entities using the same CRM system. When Emerson managers need to roll up sales totals for a sales projection, they can do so using an integrated, worldwide system.

Manufacturing of a final product is frequently distributed throughout the world. Components of the Boeing 787 are manufactured in Italy, China, England, and numerous other countries and delivered to Everett, Washington, for final assembly. Each manufacturing facility has its own in-bound logistics, manufacturing, and out-bound logistics activity, but those activities are linked together via information systems.

For example, Rolls Royce manufactures an engine and delivers that engine to Boeing via its out-bound logistics activity. Boeing receives the engine using its in-bound logistics activity. All of this activity is coordinated via shared, interorganizational information systems.

Rolls Royce's CRM is connected, using techniques described in Chapter Extension 10, cross-functional systems: CRM, ERP, and EAI (page 439), with Boeing's SRM.

Because of the abundance of low-cost, well-educated, English-speaking professionals in India, many organizations have chosen to outsource their service and support functions to India. Some accounting functions are outsourced to India as well.

Because of world time differences, global virtual companies operate 24/7. Boeing engineers in Los Angeles can develop a design for an engine support strut and send that design to Rolls Royce in England at the end of their day. The design will be waiting for Rolls Royce engineers at the start of their day. They review the design, make needed adjustments, and send it back to Boeing in Los Angeles, where the reviewed, adjusted design arrives at the start of the workday in Los Angeles. The ability to work around the clock by moving work into other time zones has greatly increased productivity.

Q2 Why Do Global Information Systems Impact Functional and Cross-functional Systems Differently?

As you learned in Chapter 7, functional information systems support business processes within a given value chain activity or business function. Because the systems operate independently, the organization suffers from a lack of data integration. Sales and marketing data, for example, are not integrated with operations or manufacturing data.

This lack of integration has *advantages*, however, for international organizations and international systems. Because the order-processing functional system in the United States is separate from and independent of the manufacturing systems in Taiwan, it is unnecessary to accommodate language, business and cultural differences in a single system. U.S. order-processing systems can operate in English and reflect the practices and culture of the United States. Taiwanese manufacturing information systems can operate in Chinese and reflect the business practices and culture of Taiwan. As long as there is an adequate data interface between the two systems, they can operate independently, sharing data when necessary.

Cross-functional, integrated systems such as ERP solve the problems of data isolation by integrating data into databases that provide a comprehensive and organization-wide view. However, because they are integrated, cross-functional systems do not readily accommodate differences in language, business practices, and cultural norms.

For example, consider the ERP system, SAP. SAP software is developed and licensed by SAP, a German software company. Because SAP addresses a global market, SAP software was localized long ago into English and numerous other foreign languages. Suppose that a multinational company with operations in Spain, Italy, Taiwan, Singapore, and Los Angeles uses SAP. Should this company allow the use of different language versions of SAP? As long as the functionality of the versions is the same, no harm occurs by doing so.

But what if employees enter data in different languages? If this is allowed, much of the value of an integrated database is lost. If you speak English, what good are customer contact data recorded in Spanish, Italian, Chinese, and English? Data isolation entered the ERP system via the back door.

Inherent processes are even more problematic. As you learned in Chapter 7, each software product assumes that the software will be used by people filling particular job functions and performing their actions in a certain way. ERP vendors justify this standardization by saying that their procedures are based on industrywide best practices and that the organization will benefit by following these standard processes. That statement may be true, but some inherent processes may conflict with cultural norms. If they do, it will be very difficult for management to convince the employees to follow those inherent processes. Or at least, it will be difficult in some cultures to do so.

Inherent processes are standardizing business processes worldwide. Over time, conflicting cultural differences will be eliminated, and the world of commerce will become uniform, worldwide. One can debate whether this standardization is beneficial or harmful. See question Q5 (page 215).

Q3 How Do Global Information Systems Affect Supply Chain Profitability?

In short, global information systems increase supply chain profitability. As stated in Chapter Extension 10, supply chain performance is driven by four factors: facilities, inventories, transportation, and information. Every one of these drivers is positively affected by global information systems. Because of global IS, facilities can be located anywhere in the world. If Amazon.com finds it economically advantageous to warehouse books in Iceland, it can do so. If Rolls Royce can more cheaply manufacture its engine turbine blades in Poland, it can do so.

Furthermore, information systems reduce inventories and hence save costs. They can be used to reduce or eliminate the *bullwhip effect*, a phenomenon in which the variability in the size and timing of orders increases at each stage of the supply chain. (For more on this topic, see Chapter Extension 12, "Supply Chain Management," on page 463.) They also support JIT inventory techniques worldwide. Using information systems, the order of a Dell computer from a user in Bolivia triggers a manufacturing system at Dell, which, in turn, triggers the order of a component from a warehouse in Taiwan—all automatically.

To underscore this point, consider the inventories that exist at this moment in time, worldwide. Every component in one of those inventories represents a waste of the world's resources. Any product or component sitting on a shelf is not being used and is adding no value to the global economy. In the perfect world, a customer would think, "I want a new computer" and that thought would trigger systems all over the world to produce and assemble necessary components, instantly. Given that we live in a world bound by time and space, instantaneous production is forever unreachable. But the goal of worldwide information systems for supply chain inventory management is to come as close to instantaneous as possible.

Consider transportation, the third driver. When you order a book from Amazon.com, you are presented with at least four shipping options. You can choose the

speed and attendant price that is appropriate for your needs. Similar systems for businesses allow them to choose the delivery option that optimizes the value they generate. Further, automated systems enable suppliers and customers to track the shipment's location, 24/7, worldwide.

Finally, global information systems produce comprehensive, accurate, and timely information. As you learned in Chapter 9, information systems produce data at prodigious rates, worldwide. That data facilitates operations as just discussed, but it also produces information for planning, organizing, deciding, and other analyses.

Next time you walk into Wal-Mart, think about the impact global information systems had in producing, ordering, and delivering the thousands of items you see.

Q4 What Is the Economic Impact of Global Manufacturing?

Henry Ford pioneered modern manufacturing methods, and in the process, he reduced the price of automobiles to the point they were no longer the playthings of the very rich but were affordable to the general population. In 1914, Ford took the unprecedented step of unilaterally increasing his workers' pay from $2.50 per day for 10 hours' work to $5 per day for 8 hours' work. As a consequence, many of his workers could soon afford to purchase an automobile. By paying his workers more, Ford increased demand.

The increase in demand was not due only to purchases by his workers, of course. Because of what economists call the *accelerator effect*, a dollar spent will contribute two or three dollars of activity to the economy. Ford's workers spent their increased pay not just on autos, but also on goods and services in their local community, which benefited via the accelerator effect. That benefit enabled non-Ford workers also to afford an auto. Further, because of the positive publicity he achieved with the pay increase, the community was strongly disposed to purchase a Ford automobile.

Consider those events in light of global manufacturing. For example, if Boeing manufactures airplanes entirely in the United States, the U.S. economy will be the sole beneficiary of that economic activity. If an Italian airline chooses to buy a Boeing plane, the transaction will be a cost to the Italian economy. There will be no accelerator effect, and the transaction will have no consequence on Italians' propensity to fly.

However, if Boeing purchases major components for its airplanes from Italian companies, then that purchase will generate an accelerator effect for the Italian economy. By buying in Italy, Boeing contributes to Italy's economy, and ultimately increases Italians' propensity to fly. That foreign-component purchase will, of course, reduce economic activity in the United States, but if it induces Italians to purchase sufficiently more Boeing airplanes, then it is possible that the loss will be compensated by the increase in airplane sales volume. That purchase will also benefit Boeing's image among Italians and increase the likelihood of sales to the Italian government.

The same phenomenon pertains to Dell computers, Cisco routers, and Microsoft programmers. It also explains why Toyota manufactures cars in the United States.

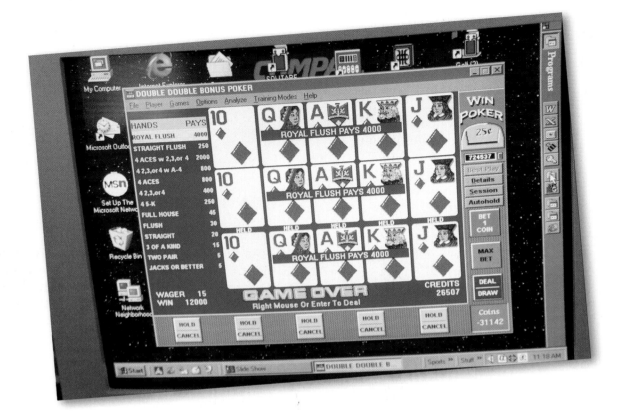

Q5 Should Information Systems Be Instruments for Exporting Cultural Values?

This question of whether information systems *should be* instruments for exporting cultural values is complex and difficult. As discussed under Q2, it is undeniable that information systems *do* export cultural values. When an organization installs an ERP system, it installs inherent processes. According to ERP vendors, everyone ultimately benefits because these processes encode each industry's "best practices." But what is deemed a best practice depends heavily on culture. Speed and efficiency may be highly valued in one culture, whereas warm and engaging interpersonal relationships may be highly valued in another. The inherent process, however, will simply encode the cultural values of the designers of the system.

One might say that exporting such cultural values is innocent, and ultimately, if someone doesn't like the procedures in place at his or her employer, he or she can choose to work elsewhere. But what about values such as freedom of speech? In the spring of 2006, the Chinese government asked MSN to shut down IP support for blog sites that it deemed offensive. The sites, located in China, were criticizing the Chinese government. Had the sites been located in the United States, the First Amendment of the Constitution would have protected their activities.

The question for MSN was whether it should comply with the Chinese government's request. The values of most—if not all—of the people who constructed the MSN system would support freedom of speech. But the site was operating in China, and as a sovereign government, China has the right to enact laws as it sees fit. MSN chose to shut down the sites, and many in the United States criticized that decision. Google experienced similar criticism when, under pressure from China and other countries, it agreed not to allow searching on terms such as *democracy*.

But consider a site that offers online gambling. Gambling is legal in many countries and is considered culturally positive in some. Most European nations allow online gambling. The U.S. federal government, however, outlawed online sports betting, and no state has licensed any form of online games of chance. If a Chinese company were to offer either form of online gambling from a site in the United States, the U.S. government or a state would certainly shut it down.

Is this a double standard? Does the United States want the right to shut down information systems that violate its laws, but disallow other nations from doing the same? Some would say the comparison fails because gambling is a vice and freedom of speech is a basic human right. But, not every nation or culture agrees.

Information systems project human values. The question is, "Whose values?"

Active ? Review

Use this Active Review to verify that you understand the material in the chapter. You can read the entire chapter and then perform the tasks in this review, or you can read the material for just one question and perform the tasks in this review for that question before moving on to the next one.

Q1 How do global information systems benefit the value chain?

Using Figure 7-2 (page 160) as a guide, explain how each primary value chain activity can be performed anywhere in the world. Explain how global, virtual companies operate 24/7. Using the answers to this question, explain three ways that DSI can benefit from a global information system.

Q2 Why do global information systems impact functional and cross-functional systems differently?

In your own words, explain the difference between functional systems and cross-functional systems. Explain the problem of functional systems that cross-functional systems overcome. Explain how this problem can actually be an advantage for global information systems. Describe how different language, business practices, and cultural norms pose a problem for cross-functional systems. Describe how inherent processes standardize business processes worldwide. State whether you think standardization is beneficial or harmful.

Q3 How do global information systems affect supply chain profitability?

State the short answer to this question. Name the four drivers of supply chain profitability. Discuss how global information systems affect each driver. Explain how inventories represent waste. Summarize the ways that you think global information systems have in filling the shelves at Wal-Mart.

Q4 What is the economic impact of global manufacturing?

Summarize the impact that Henry Ford's act of increasing his workers' pay had on Ford auto sales. Describe how the accelerator effect contributed to the increase in demand. Explain how this same phenomenon pertains to Boeing acquiring major subsystems from manufacturers in Italy or to Toyota building autos in the United States.

Q5 Should information systems be instruments for exporting cultural values?

Describe how information systems export cultural values. Explain how the term *best practice* encodes a cultural bias. State whether or not you think MSN should have shut down the IP addresses for the blogs in China. Explain the costs and benefits to MSN of its decision. Describe the difference between MSN shutting down the Chinese blog and the United States shutting down an online sports-betting site. If you see no difference, explain why.

PART 3 review

Consider Your Net Worth

Examine the questions addressed in Chapters 7 through 9 and consider how those ideas will pertain to you as a future manager and professional businessperson. How can you use the knowledge you've gained to increase your net worth both to your employer and yourself?

1. Considering your future goals (refer back to your answer to question 1 in "Consider Your Net Worth," page 58), how does the knowledge you've gained from Chapters 7 through 9 help you? What are the advantages of CRM and ERP over functional systems? How do information systems that span organizations differ from those that exist within an organization? What special problems exist for interorganizational systems? What kinds of information systems facilitate decision making, and what are the characteristics of each? How might you use reporting and data-mining systems in your career? How does knowledge of these topics give you a competitive advantage over others who do not have this knowledge?

2. Suppose that six months into your first job, your company announces that it is about to transition from functional systems to an ERP system. Say you are managing a small group in your business subject area (it could be sales, marketing, operations, finance, or accounting). Based on the information in Chapter 7 and Chapter Extension 10 (on CRM, ERP, and EAI), what do you think is likely to occur? What challenges will you soon face? How will you be able to tell how well management has prepared the organization for this change? What actions can you take to facilitate the changeover and to help your employees?

3. The primary orientation of Chapters 7 and 8 was manufacturing and operations enterprises. However, service organizations and government organizations also have business processes, and they also use information systems. Describe an example of three primary business processes for either a service or government organization. Compare and contrast the information systems in your example to those at DSI. Explain how this knowledge will help professionals who work in service or governmental organizations.

4. Page 188 of Chapter 8 contains the statement, "If you want to work in a hospital, be a doctor or a nurse. If you want to work at a design firm, be a designer." What is the logical basis for these statements? Clearly, these statements do not mean that one should not be a general manager or an accountant, nor do they mean that people should not own small businesses. What, then, do they mean? What warnings and guidance do they provide? In what ways have information systems changed the workplace? How do you think they will continue to change the workplace? In light of these trends, under what conditions would one choose to be a general manager or an accountant? Describe, as specifically as you can, how you can use the guidance in these statements for your own career planning.

5. Describe the job you most want to obtain after you graduate. Name the position, the industry, and describe the primary responsibilities you want to have. Explain how the explosion of data created by information systems impacts that job. How will this impact continue into the future? In what ways will this explosion present problems for you? In what ways will it present opportunities? Describe one way that you could use a reporting system to gain an advantage from this trend. Describe one way you can use a data-mining application to gain an advantage from this trend.

6. The data explosion described in Chapter 9 occurs, in part, because the cost of data storage is essentially zero. That fact, combined with ubiquitous and nearly free data communications, is creating many new business opportunities. Describe such a business opportunity in a field in which you are interested. If possible, describe a business that you could start that would take advantage of this opportunity. If the opportunity is too large to reasonably accomplish on your own, describe an existing business that might want to take advantage of it.

Career Assignments

 1. Use your favorite search engine to search the Web for the term *MRP job opportunities*. Investigate several of the sites that you find to answer the following questions.

   a. Describe the two jobs in the search results that you find to be the most interesting.

   b. Describe the educational requirements for each of these jobs.

   c. Describe internships and other experiences that you could gain to better prepare you for each of these jobs.

   d. Using both Web resources and your own experience, describe the employment outlook for these jobs.

 2. Same as question 1, but search for the term *ERP job opportunities*.

 3. Same as question 1, but search for the term *change management consultant*.

 4. Search the Web for innovative applications of RFID technology to your major field of interest. For example, search for the term *using RFID in accounting systems*. If you find nothing of interest, search instead for the

more general term *innovations in RFID*. Describe the innovations you find. How will innovations like these create job opportunities? How could you take advantage of these opportunities, either working for a user of RFID or working for a vendor of RFID products and consulting services?

 5. Same as question 1, but search for the term *XML job opportunities*.

6. Consider question 6 in "Consider Your Net Worth." Nearly free data storage and data communications not only are creating new business opportunities; they are also creating new career opportunities. Describe two such job opportunities that will arise. Explain how you might find such a job opportunity. What education and experience would you need in order to qualify for such an opportunity?

 7. Same as question 1, but search for the term *database marketing job opportunities*.

Application Exercises

1. Suppose your manager asks you to create a spreadsheet to compute a production schedule. Your schedule should stipulate a production quantity for seven products that is based on sales projections made by three regional managers at your company's three sales regions.

a. Create a separate worksheet for each sales region. Assume that each sheet contains monthly sales projections for each of the past four quarters. Assume that it also contains actual monthly sales for each of those past 4 quarters. Finally, assume that each sheet contains a projection for each month in the coming quarter.

b. Fill in sample data for each of the worksheets in part a.

c. On each of the worksheets, use the data from the prior four quarters to compute the discrepancy between the actual sales and the sale projections. This discrepancy can be computed in several ways: You could calculate an overall average, or you could calculate an average per quarter or per month. You could also weigh recent discrepancies more heavily than earlier ones. Choose a method that you think is most appropriate. Explain why you chose the method you did.

d. Modify your worksheets to use the discrepancy factors to compute an adjusted forecast for the coming quarter. Thus, each of your spreadsheets will show the raw forecast and the adjusted forecast for each month in the coming quarter.

e. Create a fourth worksheet that totals sales projections for all of the regions. Show both the unadjusted forecast and the adjusted forecast for each region and for the company overall. Show month and quarter totals.

f. Create a bar graph showing total monthly production. Display the unadjusted and adjusted forecasts using different colored bars.

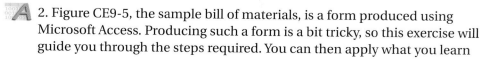 2. Figure CE9-5, the sample bill of materials, is a form produced using Microsoft Access. Producing such a form is a bit tricky, so this exercise will guide you through the steps required. You can then apply what you learn

to produce a similar report. You can also use Access to experiment on extensions of this form.

a. Create a table named PART with columns *PartNumber, Level, Description, QuantityRequired,* and *PartOf. Description* and *Level* should be text, PartNumber should be AutoNumber, and *QuantityRequired* and *PartOf* should be numeric, long integer. Add the PART data shown in Figure CE9-5 to your table.

b. Create a query that has all columns of PART. Restrict the view to rows having a value of 1 for *Level*. Name your query **Level1**.

c. Create two more queries that are restricted to rows having values of 2 or 3 for *Level*. Name your queries **Level2** and **Level3**, respectively.

d. Create a form that contains *PartNumber, Level,* and *Description* from **Level1**. You can use a wizard for this if you want. Name the form **Bill of Materials**.

e. Using the subform tool in the Toolbox, create a subform in your form in part d. Set the data on this form to be all of the columns of **Level2**. After you have created the subform, ensure that the Link Child Fields property is set to *PartOf* and that the Link Master Fields property is set to *PartNumber.* Close the Bill of Materials form.

f. Open the subform created in part e and create a subform on it. Set the data on this subform to be all of the columns of **Level3**. After you have created the subform, ensure that the Link Child Fields property is set to *PartOf* and that the Link Master Fields property is set to *PartNumber.* Close the Bill of Materials form.

g. Open the Bill of Materials Form. It should appear as in Figure CE9-5. Open and close the form and add new data. Using this form, add sample BOM data for a product of your own choosing.

h. Following the process similar to that just described, create a Bill of Materials Report that lists the data for all of your products.

i. (**Optional, challenging extension**) Each part in the BOM in Figure CE9-5 can be used in at most one assembly (there is space to show just one *PartOf* value). You can change your design to allow a part to be used in more than one assembly as follows. First, remove *PartOf* from PART. Next, create a second table that has two columns: *AssemblyPartNumber* and *ComponentPartNumber.* The first contains a part number of an assembly and the second a part number of a component. Every component of a part will have a row in this table. Extend the views described earlier to use this second table and to produce a display similar to Figure CE9-5.

3. Assume you have been asked to create a spreadsheet to help make a buy-versus-lease decision for the servers on your organization's Web farm. Assume you are considering the servers for a five-year period, but that you do not know exactly how many servers you will need. Initially, you know you will need 5 servers, but you might need as many as 50, depending on the success of your organization's e-commerce activity.

a. For the buy-alternative calculations, set up your spreadsheet so that you can enter the base price of the server hardware, the price of all software, and a maintenance expense that is some percentage of the hardware price. Assume that the percent you enter covers both hardware and software maintenance. Also assume that each server has a three-year life, after which it has no value. Assume straight-line depreciation for computers used less than three years, and that at the end of the five years, you can sell the computers you have used for less than three years for their depreciated value. Also assume that your organization pays 2 percent interest on capital expenses. Assume the servers cost $5,000 each, and the needed software costs $750. Assume maintenance expense varies from 2 to 7 percent.

b. For the lease-alternative calculations, assume that the leasing vendor will lease the same computer hardware as you can purchase. The lease includes all the software you need as well as all maintenance. Set up your spreadsheet so that you can enter various lease costs, which vary according to the number of years of the lease (one, two, or three). Assume the cost of a three-year lease is $285 per machine per month, of a two-year lease is $335 per machine per month, and of a one-year lease is $415 per machine per month. Also, the lessor offers a 5 percent discount if you lease from 20 to 30 computers and a 10 percent discount if you lease from 31 to 50 computers.

c. Using your spreadsheet, compare the costs of buy versus lease under the following situations. (Assume you either buy or lease. You cannot lease some and buy some.) Make assumptions as necessary and state those assumptions.

  i. Your organization requires 20 servers for five years.

  ii. Your organization requires 20 servers for the first two years and 40 servers for the next three years.

  iii. Your organization requires 20 servers for the first two years, 40 servers for the next two years, and 50 servers for the last year.

  iv. Your organization requires 10 servers the first year, 20 servers the second year, 30 servers the third year, 40 servers the fourth year, and 50 servers the last year.

  v. For the previous case, does the cheaper alternative change if the cost of the servers is $4,000? If it is $8,000?

4. Assume you have been given the task of compiling evaluations that your company's purchasing agents make of their vendors. Each month, every purchasing agent evaluates all of the vendors that it has worked with in the past month on three factors: price, quality, and responsiveness. Assume the ratings are from 1 to 5, with 5 being the best. Because your company has hundreds of vendors and dozens of purchasing agents, you decide to use Access to compile the results.

a. Create a database with three tables: VENDOR (*VendorNumber, Name, Contact*), PURCHASER (*EmpNumber, Name, Email*), and RATING (*EmpNumber, VendorNumber, Month, Year, PriceRating, QualityRating, ResponsivenessRating*). Assume *VendorNumber* and *EmpNumber* are the keys of VENDOR and PURCHASER, respectively. Decide what you think is the appropriate key for RATING.

b. Create appropriate relationships using Tools/Relationships.

c. Using the table view of each table, enter sample data for vendors, employees, and ratings.

d. Create a query that shows the names of all vendors and their average scores.

e. Create a query that shows the names of all employees and their averages scores. *Hint:* In this and in question f, you will need to use the Group By function in your query.

f. Create a parameterized query that you can use to obtain the minimum, maximum, and average ratings on each criterion for a particular vendor. Assume you will enter *VendorName* as the parameter.

 5. OLAP cubes are very similar to Microsoft Excel *pivot tables.* If you are unfamiliar with pivot tables, open Excel and search the help system for pivot tables. Select one of the demos to see how pivot tables work. Or you can just follow the instructions that follow. For this exercise, assume that in your organization the purchasing agents rate vendors. You can use a pivot table to display the data in flexible and informative ways.

a. Open Excel and add the following column headings to your spreadsheet: *VendorName, EmployeeName, Date, Year,* and *Rating.* Enter sample data under these headings. Add ratings for at least three vendors and at least three rows for each vendor. Add sufficient data so that each vendor will have at least five ratings, and each employee will have entered at least five ratings. Also, add data for at least two different months and two different years.

b. Under the Data tab in Excel, select Pivot Table and Pivot Chart. (From here on, the exact menu names may vary depending on the version of Excel you have. Look for names that are close to those used here.) A wizard will open. Select Excel and Pivot table in the first screen. Click Next.

c. When asked to provide a data range, drag your mouse over the data you entered so as to select all of the data. Be sure to include the column headings. Excel will fill in the range values in the open dialog box. Click Next, Select New worksheet, and then Finish.

d. Excel will create a field list on the right-hand side of your spreadsheet. Drag and drop the field named *VendorName,* on the words "Drop Row Fields Here." Drag and drop *EmployeeName,* on the words "Drop Column Fields Here." Now drag and drop the field named *Rating* on the words "Drop Data Items Here." Voilà! You have a pivot table.

e. To see how the table works, drag and drop more fields on the various sections of your pivot table. For example, drop *Year* on top of *Employee.* Then move *Year* below *Employee.* Now move *Year* below *Vendor.* All of this action is just like an OLAP cube—and, in fact, OLAP cubes are readily displayed in Excel pivot tables. The major difference is that OLAP cubes are usually based on thousands or more rows of data.

f. (**Extra credit**) If you answered question 4 earlier, you can import the data you created there into a pivot table. To do that, select External data in the first panel of the wizard. Then, use the Excel Help system to figure out how to import your data. Your job will be easier if you first create a query in Access that contains the data from all three tables.

 6. It is surprisingly easy to create a market-basket report using table data in Access. To do so, however, you will need to enter SQL expressions into the Access query builder. Here, you can just copy SQL statements to type them in. If you take a database class, you will learn how to code SQL statements like those you will use here.

   a. Create an Access database with a table named ORDERS having columns *OrderNumber, ItemName*, and *Quantity*, with data types Number (*LongInteger*), Text (50), and Number (*LongInteger*), respectively. The key of this table is (*OrderNumber, ItemName*), but you will not need to define it for this exercise. (If you want to know how to define it, after you have entered the data type definitions of those two columns, drag your mouse to highlight both of them in the design window and then click the key icon.)

   b. Now enter sample data. Make sure that there are several items on each order and that some orders have items in common. For example, you might enter [100, 'Cup', 4], [100, 'Saucer', 4], [200, 'Fork', 2], [200, 'Spoon', 2], [200, 'Knife', 2], and [200, 'Cup', 3]. Enter data for at least five orders.

   c. Now, to perform the market basket analysis, you will need to enter several SQL statements into Access. To do so, click the queries tab and select Create query in Design view. Click Close when the Show Table dialog box appears. Now right-click in the gray section above the grid in the Select Query window. Select SQL View. Now enter the following expression exactly as it appears here:

```
SELECT T1.ItemName as FirstItem, T2.ItemName as
SecondItem
FROM ORDERS T1, ORDERS T2
WHERE T1.OrderNumber = T2.OrderNumber
AND T1.ItemName <> T2.ItemName;
```

   Click the red exclamation point in the toolbar to run the query. Correct any typing mistakes and, once it works, save the query using the name **TwoItemBasket**.

   d. Now enter a second SQL statement. Again, click the queries tab and select Create query in Design view. Click Close when the Show Table dialog box appears. Now right-click in the gray section above the grid in the Select Query window. Select SQL View. Now enter the following expression exactly as it appears here:

```
SELECT TwoItemBasket.FirstItem,
TwoItemBasket.SecondItem, Count(*) AS SupportCount
FROM TwoItemBasket
GROUP BY TwoItemBasket.FirstItem,
TwoItemBasket.SecondItem;
```

   Correct any typing mistakes and, once it works, save the query using the name **SupportCount**.

e. Examine the results of the second query and verify that the two query statements have correctly calculated the number of times that two items have appeared together. Explain further calculations you need to make to compute support.

f. Explain the calculations you need to make to compute lift. Although you can make those calculations using SQL, you need more SQL knowledge to do it, and we will skip that here.

g. Explain, in your own words, what the query in part c seems to be doing. What does the query in part d seem to be doing? Again, you will need to take a database class to learn how to code such expressions, but this exercise should give you a sense of the kinds of calculations that are possible with SQL.

PART 3 CASE 3-1

Laguna Tools

Laguna Tools is a privately held reseller of high-end woodworking equipment. Based in Irvine, California, Laguna imports table saws, lathes, and other machines from top-quality European manufacturers. It resells those machines in the United States and Canada. Laguna is especially known for the comprehensive line of band saws that are constructed to its own specifications by factories in Italy and Poland.

Laguna's competitive strategy is to provide the highest-quality tools for woodworking professionals, including cabinet makers, artists, and wood fabricators. It also sells to high-end, "carriage trade" amateur woodworkers. With prices ranging from $2,000 to $20,000 per machine, Laguna's machines are among the most expensive woodworking equipment sold.

Most woodworking shops have a need for multiple machines. A common shop has table saw, band saw, jointer, planer, shaper, lathe, and mortise machines. Accordingly, once a customer orders one machine from Laguna, he or she is quite likely to buy a second.

Laguna advertises in popular woodworking magazines, and it uses its Web site at *www.lagunatools.com* to gather leads. The company follows up on all leads with phone conversations and promotional literature. (So, out of courtesy to the company, do not fill out the customer information form on its Web site unless you are in the market for very high-quality machinery.)

Questions

1. What information should Laguna keep in its database of prospective customers?

2. What information should Laguna keep about customers who order?

3. When a salesperson is talking with a potential or actual customer, what data should he or she have available during the conversation?

4. Describe how Laguna could use an RFM analysis. What should it do with a [1, 1, 1] customer? What should it do with a [2, 2, 5] customer? What should it do with a [5, 1, 1] customer? (RFM is discussed in Chapter Extension 14, "Database Marketing," on page 483.)

5. Explain how Laguna could use a market-basket analysis. What information must Laguna have to effectively use a market-basket analysis? (Market-basket analysis is discussed in Chapter Extension 14, "Database Marketing," on page 483.)

6. Explain how Laguna could use an OLAP analysis. Identify possible measures, dimensions, and cubes. What information would the company obtain from the OLAP analysis? (OLAP analysis is discussed in Chapter Extension 15, "Reporting Systems and OLAP," on page 493.)

7. Examine your answers to the previous questions, and specify whether you think RFM, market-basket, or OLAP analysis would be the most useful to Laguna.

CASE 3-2

Dun and Bradstreet Data via Web Services

As stated in the Dun and Bradstreet (D&B) case on page 182, D&B collects data on more than 80 million businesses and sells it to customers who use the data for analyzing customer credit, selecting customer prospects, and identifying potential suppliers.

Some customers are willing to buy company reports using the commerce server illustrated in the previous D&B case. For others, this process is too slow and cumbersome. For example, consider the customers that use D&B data to assess creditworthiness. Because of competitive pressure, some companies must make credit assessments immediately, in real time, while interacting with their customers. For such applications, buying a prewritten report over the D&B commerce server will not suffice.

Instead, these customers want to use automated processes to access the D&B databases. They want to write credit-analysis programs that obtain needed data from D&B in real time. Consider, for example, the needs of a computer distributor or retailer. The distributor's customers can place large orders using the distributor's Web storefront. The equipment price for a medium-sized network could total $40,000 or $50,000, and before accepting the order, the distributor needs to assess the creditworthiness of the customer. In situations like this, the distributor wants its commerce server programs to access D&B data and to use it to evaluate credit programmatically.

To meet this need, D&B developed a version of Web services that its customers' programs can access. Although the D&B version uses XML documents for data exchange, it does not use all of the XML Web service standards. (XML Web services are discussed in Chapter Extension 13, "Information Technology for Data Exchange: EDI amd XML," on page 473.) In particular, it does not provide a standard service description nor use standard services protocols. Instead, the D&B service provides a proprietary interface for customers. The D&B Web service could not use the current, modern standards because those standards were not finalized when D&B developed its Web services system.

Still, D&B's Web services do use XML. Consequently, its users can realize the advantages of schema validation, and both D&B and its customers can use XML standards to reformat documents automatically.

In order to use the D&B Web services, customers must enter into an agreement with D&B that specifies which data will be accessed and what and how they will pay for that data access. Then, the customers must learn the D&B interface and develop programs accordingly. D&B provides some technical assistance to customer program developers.

By using Web services to obtain data, customers obtain the latest, up-to-the-minute data. This advantage is important because D&B makes over a million updates to its database every day. Furthermore, D&B Web services provide a single, consistent interface for customers to use. Customers save costs because they need to develop D&B access programs only once; all applications can use those programs to obtain D&B data. Finally, D&B customers can use the Web services interface to request alerts when particular data are updated. Alerts enable customers to update their own databases with the most current data.

Sources: Sean Rhody, "Dun and Bradstreet," **Web Services Journal**, Vol. 1, Issue 1, *sys-con.com/webservices* (accessed December 2004); Dun and Bradstreet, "Data Integration Toolkit," PowerPoint Presentation, *globalaccess.dnb.com* (accessed December 2004).

Questions

1. Summarize the difference between obtaining D&B data by purchasing reports from the D&B Web server and by obtaining D&B data via Web services. (Web services are discussed in Chapter Extension 11, "E-Commerce," on page 451. Web services are discussed in Chapter Extension 13, "Information Technology for Data Exchange: EDI and XML," on page 473.)

2. Explain how schema validation improves the quality of the data exchange. How can D&B and its Web services customers use schema validation to their advantage?

3. As stated, D&B did not describe their Web services in the standard way. What are the consequences to D&B? What are the consequences to D&B's customers? D&B could upgrade its Web services to use these standards. If you worked at D&B, how would you decide whether to make that upgrade? Consider the consequences of the upgrade on both new and existing D&B Web services customers.

4. Besides credit reporting, D&B customers use D&B data to find and assess customer prospects and to determine potential sources of suppliers. Explain how Web services could be used for these applications as well as for credit analysis.

5. D&B is an international organization that provides data to customers worldwide. What advantages does the use of Web services provide for non-U.S. customers?

6. How does the D&B Web services interface give D&B a competitive advantage over other data providers?

PART 4

Information Systems Management

This could happen to you

Emerson Pharmaceuticals and DSI are very different companies. Emerson is a multinational organization with a billion dollars in sales and with facilities, offices, and personnel throughout the world. Emerson U.S. (its U.S. division) has 450 salespeople, plus thousands of other employees in labs, production facilities, and headquarters. DSI is a company with a single facility and an estimated $50 million in sales (as a private company, it does not release financial data). The total number of DSI employees is less than half the number of sales people at Emerson.

Both Emerson and DSI use information systems, but they manage them very differently. Emerson U.S. has more than 200 employees in its IT department, and it outsources several important functions to other vendors as well. DSI has one employee in its "IT department" (and the day I interviewed him, I found him sitting on the floor repairing a computer).

In Part 4, we will consider how both of the companies develop information systems, how they manage their IT and IS resources, and how they protect their systems with security. Not surprisingly, the two companies take very different approaches to all three of these topics.

10 Information Systems Development

This could happen to you

Dee Clark wanted to develop a blog to communicate to her sales force. She had a focused goal and a short time frame. Her employer, Emerson, has extensive IT resources, including a large corporate network, and Dee needed to integrate her blog into that network. She proceeded by fits and starts and, with the help of her consultant, was successful. However, in the process she exposed her organization to an enormous security risk, as you will learn in Chapter 12.

Dee was successful only because her system was simple. She was the only person contributing to the blog. While the 450 salespeople did use the blog, they needed no training to do so. The salespeople were passive readers who needed no more skill than the ability to read news on a browser. Had Dee been developing a more complicated system with more users and greater functionality, she could not have succeeded proceeding as she did. She needed to know and understand a process for developing information systems.

Now, consider your situation at DSI. Suppose you pitch the RFID information system you have in mind: Vendors place RFID chips on components they produce, and a computer program at DSI processes the RFID data to determine where to place the component into raw materials inventory. This system is not nearly as simple as building a blog.

What would you do if Mr. Stratford says to you, "Great idea. Tell me how to proceed. What do we do next?"

How do you answer him? How *should* DSI proceed? Do you tell him to start buying RFID chips? Not likely. But, what do you say? The information in this chapter should help, if you find yourself in a situation in which this happens to you.

Optional Extensions for this chapter are CE17, "Small-Scale Systems Development," CE18, "Large-Scale Systems Development," and CE19, "Alternative Development Techniques."

?

Study Questions

Q1 What is systems development?

Q2 Why is systems development difficult and risky?

Q3 What are the five phases of the systems development life cycle?

Q4 How is system definition accomplished?

Q5 What is the users' role in the requirements phase?

Q6 How are the five components designed?

Q7 How is an information system implemented?

Q8 What are the tasks for systems maintenance?

Q9 What are problems with the SDLC?

How does the knowledge in this chapter help you at DSI?

Q1 What Is Systems Development?

Systems development, or **systems analysis and design** as it is sometimes called, is the process of creating and maintaining information systems. Notice that this process concerns *information systems*, not just computer programs. Developing an *information system* involves all five components: hardware, software, data, procedures, and people. Developing a *computer program* involves software programs, possibly with some focus on data and databases. Figure 10-1 shows that systems development has a broader scope than computer program development.

Because systems development addresses all five components, it requires more than just programming or technical expertise. Establishing the system's goals, setting up the project, and determining requirements require business knowledge and management skill. Tasks like building computer networks and writing computer programs require technical skills, but developing the other components requires nontechnical, human relations skills. Creating data models requires the ability to interview users and understand their view of the business activities. Designing procedures, especially those involving group action, requires business knowledge and an understanding of group dynamics. Developing job descriptions, staffing, and training all require human resource and related expertise.

Thus, do not suppose that systems development is exclusively a technical task undertaken by programmers and hardware specialists. Rather, it requires coordinated teamwork of both specialists and nonspecialists with business knowledge.

So far in the consideration of Dee's blog and in the situation at DSI, we have discussed only the development of small-scale IS. *MIS in Use 10* discusses the nature of large-scale corporate information systems and why such systems need formal methods of development.

In Chapter 4, you learned there are three sources for software: off-the-shelf, off-the-shelf with adaptation, and tailor-made. Although all three sources pertain to software, only two of them pertain to information systems. Unlike software, *information systems are never off-the-shelf.* Because information systems involve your company's people and procedures, you must construct or adapt procedures to fit your business and people, regardless of how you obtain the computer programs.

As a future business manager, you will have a key role in information systems development. In order to accomplish the goals of your department, you need to ensure that effective procedures exist for using the information system. You need to ensure that personnel are properly trained and are able to use the IS effectively. If your department does not have appropriate procedures and trained personnel, you must take corrective action. Although you might pass off hardware, program, or data problems to the IT department, you cannot pass off procedural or personnel problems to that department. Such problems are your problems. The single most important criterion for information systems success is for users to take ownership of their systems.

Figure 10-1
Systems Development Versus
Program Development

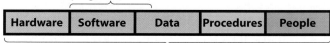

Thinking Big About Systems Development

Many students do not appreciate the need for systems development processes. You may have worked only with an accounting spreadsheet or a single-user contact manager database. These are small systems with easily understood requirements. If you have not worked with large-scale corporate information systems, you have not seen their scope, and so you may not know why systems development processes are so important.

Consider the IRS case discussed in Chapter 1. The IRS has over 100,000 employees at more than a thousand sites. The development team for the IRS system includes more than 500 professionals. How do you manage them? How do you ensure that they are working to the same set of goals and requirements and using the same design? (See the case starting on page 311 for more on this situation.)

Or consider the problems of international organizations. Suppose the Coca-Cola Corporation wants to standardize on a single information system for beverage production. Coca-Cola plants exist in almost every country in the world; a new system will involve tens of thousands of people and more than 50 different languages. How do you develop such a system? Clearly, you must follow a comprehensive process, and you must do so consistently, despite the different languages and cultures.

Or think about a company like 3M. This company has over 50 business units that sell thousands of products in more than 90 nations. 3M is concerned about the proper and safe use of its products worldwide. Suppose the 3M legal department asks you to develop an information system that stores product information, product safety requirements, and the relationship of product requirements to international, national, and local labor laws. Suppose you are given three years and a $10 million budget for the new system. How do you proceed?

As you learned in Part 3, enterprise-wide information systems seldom just automate existing procedures. Instead, most information systems are *process-design oriented*. The idea is first to modernize and streamline the underlying business processes and then to develop an information system to support and enforce those new business processes. However, the new system will change the way people work; it will change habits, authorities, reporting structures, and the like. These are very difficult changes for people to make. Designing such a system for a global organization is a monumental task.

Large-scale systems have wide-reaching effects. Therefore, development of such projects must be carefully planned and executed, using an effective and comprehensive development process. Without such a process, chaos and disaster are the likely result.

Q2 Why Is Systems Development Difficult and Risky?

Systems development is difficult and risky. Many projects are never finished. Of those that are finished, some are 200 or 300 percent over budget. Still other projects finish within budget and schedule, but never satisfactorily accomplish their goals.

You may be amazed to learn that systems development failures can be so dramatic. You might suppose that with all the computers and all the systems developed over the years, by now there must be some methodology for successful systems development. In fact, there *are* systems development methodologies that can result in success, and we will discuss four of them in this chapter and in

Chapter Extension 19, "Alternative Development Techniques." But, even when competent people follow one of these methodologies, the risk of failure is still high.

In the following sections, we will discuss the following major challenges to systems development:

- The difficulty of determining requirements
- Changes in requirements
- Scheduling and budgeting difficulties
- Changing technology
- Diseconomies of scale

The Difficulty of Requirements Determination

First, requirements are difficult to determine. Consider the proposed new system at DSI. What does it mean to use RFID data to determine where to place a component in inventory? What specific data will be used? How will the data be used? Should the system consider only open locations in the hangar? Should the system examine the existing contents of raw materials inventory and suggest inventory rearrangements? Should every item in raw materials inventory be involved in this new system? If not, which components will be?

Consider the impact on suppliers and component manufacturers. How are the suppliers to obtain the data that they are to place on the RFID devices? Does DSI provide that data on the AutoCad files it sends to the suppliers and manufacturers? Does DSI even send AutoCad files to suppliers?

The questions go on and on. One of the major purposes of the systems development process is to ensure that such questions are both asked and answered.

Changes in Requirements

Even more difficult, systems development aims at a moving target. Requirements change as the system is developed, and the bigger the system and the longer the project, the more the requirements change.

When requirements do change, what should the development team do? Stop work and rebuild the system in accordance with the new requirements? If they do that, the system will develop in fits and starts and may never be completed. Or should the team finish the system, knowing that it will be unsatisfactory the day it is implemented and will, therefore, need immediate maintenance?

Scheduling and Budgeting Difficulties

Other challenges involve scheduling and budgeting. How long will it take to build a system? That question is not easy to answer. Suppose you are adopting the raw-materials database at DSI. How long will it take to create the data model? Even if you know how long it takes to make those changes, DSI employees may disagree with you and each other. How many times will you need to rebuild the data model until everyone agrees?

Consider the applications. How long will it take to build the forms, reports, queries, and application programs? How long will it take to test all of them? What about procedures and people? What procedures need to be developed, and how much time should be allowed to create and document them, develop training programs, and train the personnel?

Further, how much will all of this cost? Labor costs are a direct function of labor hours; if you cannot estimate labor hours, you cannot estimate labor costs. Moreover, if you cannot estimate how much a system costs, then how do you perform a financial analysis to determine if the system generates an appropriate rate of return? (See Chapter Extension 21, "Financing and Accounting for IT Projects," for more on this topic.)

Changing Technology

Yet another challenge is that while the project is underway, technology continues to change. For example, while you are developing DSI's new system, Microsoft, Sun, and IBM are working on new versions of XML Web Services. You learn that these new versions could drastically shorten your development time, halve the costs, and result in a better system. That is, it will do those things if it actually works the way vendors say it will.

Even if you believe the new technology is a viable answer, do you want to stop your development to switch to the new technology? Would it be better to finish developing according to the existing plan?

Diseconomies of Scale

Unfortunately, as development teams become larger, the average contribution per worker decreases. This is true because as staff size increases, more meetings and other coordinating activities are required to keep everyone in sync. There are economies of scale up to a point, but beyond a workgroup of, say, 20 employees, diseconomies of scale begin to take over.

A famous adage known as **Brooks's Law** points out a related problem: *Adding more people to a late project makes the project later.*[1] Brooks's Law is true not only because a larger staff requires increased coordination, but also because new people need training. The only people who can train the new employees are the existing team members, who are, thus, taken off productive tasks. The costs of training new people can overwhelm the benefit of their contribution.

In short, managers of software development projects face a dilemma: They can increase work per employee by keeping the team small, but in doing so, they extend the project's timeline. Or they can reduce the project's timeline by adding staff, but because of diseconomies of scale, they will have to add 150 or 200 hours of labor to gain 100 hours of work. And, due to Brooks's Law, once the project is late, both choices are bad.

Furthermore, schedules can be compressed only so far. According to one other popular adage, "Nine women cannot make a baby in one month."

Is It Really So Bleak?

Is systems development really as bleak as the list of challenges makes it sound? Yes and no. All of the challenges just described do exist, and they are all significant hurdles that every development project must overcome. As noted previously, once the project is late and over budget, no good choice exists. "I have to pick my regrets," said one beleaguered manager of a late project.

---

[1]Fred Brooks was a successful senior manager at IBM in the 1960s. After retiring from IBM, he wrote a classic book on IT project management called *The Mythical Man-Month.* Published by Addison-Wesley in 1975, the book is pertinent today and should be read by every IT or IS project manager. It's an enjoyable book, too.

The IT industry has over 50 years of experience developing information systems, and over those years, methodologies have emerged that successfully deal with these problems. In the next study question, we will consider the systems development life cycle (SDLC), the classic process for systems development. In addition, Chapter Extension 19, "Alternative Development Techniques," addresses three other development methods:

- Rapid application development (RAD)
- Object-oriented systems development (OOD)
- Extreme programming (XP)

You may be wondering why there are *four* different methodologies. Why not just one? Because information systems differ, no single process works for all situations. Some systems automate business processes and decision making, whereas others augment them. An automated system must be a complete solution; an augmentation system can have gaps that users fill.

Also, the scale of information systems varies widely. Personal systems support one person with a limited set of requirements. Workgroup systems support a group of people, normally with a single application. Enterprise systems support many workgroups with many different applications. Interenterprise systems support many different organizations with different organizational cultures; some support users in different countries with different cultural heritages.

Given the variety of possible systems, it is not surprising that there are different development processes. Different processes are appropriate for different types of systems. We begin with the classical systems development process.

Q3 What Are the Five Phases of the SDLC?

The **systems development life cycle (SDLC)** is the classical process used to develop information systems. The IT industry developed the SDLC in the "school of hard knocks." Many early projects met with disaster, and companies and systems developers sifted through the ashes of those disasters to determine what went wrong. By the 1970s, most seasoned project managers agreed on the basic tasks that need to be performed to successfully build and maintain information systems. These basic tasks are combined into phases of systems development.

Different authors and organizations package the tasks into different numbers of phases. Some organizations use an eight-phase process, others use a seven-phase process, and still others use a five-phase process. In this text, we will use the following five-phase process:

1. System definition
2. Requirements analysis
3. Component design
4. Implementation
5. System maintenance

Figure 10-2 shows how these phases are related. Development begins when a business-planning process identifies a need for a new system. We address IS

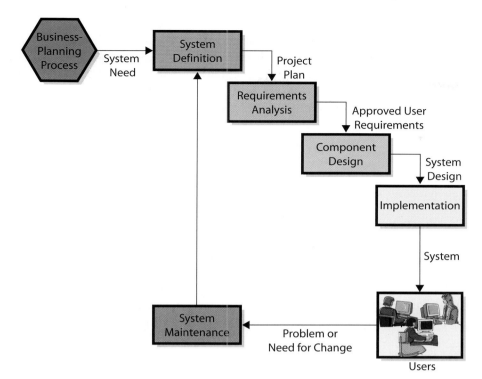

Figure 10-2
Phases in the SDLC

planning processes in Chapter 11. For now, suppose that management has determined, in some way, that the organization can best accomplish its goals and objectives by constructing a new information system.

Developers in the first SDLC phase, system definition, use management's statement of the system needs in order to begin to define the new system. The resulting project plan is the input to the second phase, requirements analysis. Here, developers identify the particular features and functions of the new system. The output of that phase is a set of approved user requirements, which become the primary input used to design system components. In phase 4, developers implement, test, and install the new system.

Over time, users will find errors, mistakes, and problems. They will also develop new requirements. The description of fixes and new requirements is input to a system maintenance phase. The maintenance phase starts the process all over again, which is why the process is considered a cycle.

In the following sections, we will consider each phase of the SDLC in more detail.

Q4 How Is System Definition Accomplished?

In response to the need for the new system, the organization will assign a few employees, possibly on a part-time basis, to define the new system, to assess its feasibility, and to plan the project. Typically, someone from the IS department leads the initial team, but the members of that initial team are both users and IS professionals.

Figure 10-3
SDLC: System Definition Phase

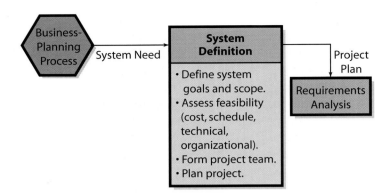

Define System Goals and Scope

As Figure 10-3 shows, the first step is to define the goals and scope of the new information system. As you learned in Part 3, information systems exist to facilitate an organization's competitive strategy by supporting business processes or by improving decision making. At this step, the development team defines the goal and purpose of the new system in terms of these purposes.

Consider the materials inventory RFID system at DSI. What is the purpose of that system? To reduce costs in two ways: First, it will lower labor costs by eliminating (or reducing) the number of times raw materials inventory needs to be reorganized to fit in parts and components. Second, it will reduce material costs by eliminating damage to materials and components incurred when items are moved in raw materials inventory.

Another task is to define the project's scope. For the DSI system, are all parts and components to be managed? Or are only major assemblies and components to be managed? How is *major* defined? By size? By cost? Is this system to be effective for all future projects or only certain future projects? Furthermore, which parts of the system are to be implemented at DSI, and which parts will be implemented at the suppliers and manufacturers?

In other systems, the scope might be delineated by specifying the users that will be involved, or the business processes that will be involved, or the plants, offices, and factories that will be involved. At Emerson, for example, Dee might have defined the scope of her blog so as to include only U.S. salespeople, or only U.S. salespeople that sell certain products.

A clear definition of project scope greatly simplifies requirements determination and other subsequent development work.

Assess Feasibility

Once we have defined the project's goals and scope, the next step is to assess feasibility. This step answers the question, "Does this project make sense?" The aim here is to eliminate obviously nonsensible projects before forming a project development team and investing significant labor.

Feasibility has four dimensions: **cost**, **schedule**, **technical**, and **organizational**. Because IS development projects are difficult to budget and schedule, cost and schedule feasibility can be only an approximate, back-of-the-envelope analysis. The purpose is to eliminate any obviously infeasible ideas as soon as possible.

For example, for the DSI system, you might investigate how much the hardware for RFID scanning costs. If the answer is a minimum of $30,000, then you can decide if DSI can reasonably expect to receive benefits to justify this expense. If you do not expect sufficient benefits, DSI can cancel the project or agree to accomplish your goals using some other system. For a discussion of ethical issues relating to estimation, see the *Ethics Guide* on pages 241a–241b.

Like cost feasibility, *schedule feasibility*, is difficult to determine because it is difficult to estimate the time it will take to build the system. However, if, for example, you determine that it will take no less than six months to develop the system and put it into operation, DSI can then decide if it can accept that minimum schedule. At this stage of the project, the company should not rely on either cost or schedule estimates; the purpose of these estimates is simply to rule out any obviously unacceptable projects.

Technical feasibility refers to whether existing information technology is likely to be able to meet the needs of the new system. At DSI, you might ask whether it is possible to use RFID to organize inventory. Is there sufficient regularity in the way inventory is accessed to determine where goods should be placed? You know it is technically feasible to read RFID data. The question is, can you do something useful with that data?

The team that proposed the database subsystem for the IRS (see Chapter 1, page 9) should have investigated technical feasibility in greater depth. From the public documents, it appears that senior IRS managers were not aware they were pushing the limits of technology when they agreed to the CADE system. See *Part Case Study 4-1* page 311, for more.

Finally, *organizational feasibility* concerns whether the new system fits within the organization's customs, culture, charter, or legal requirements. For example, if DSI has contracts that prohibit suppliers from providing the RFID data, the proposed system is organizationally infeasible. Or if the combined data violate antitrust law, the new system would be organizationally infeasible.

Form a Project Team

If the defined project is determined to be feasible, the next step is to form the project team. Normally the team consists of both IT personnel and user representatives. The project manager and IT personnel can be in-house personnel or outside contractors. We will describe various means of obtaining IT personnel using outside sources and the benefits and risks of outsourcing when we discuss IS management in Chapter 11.

Typical personnel on a development team are a manager (or managers for larger projects), system analysts, programmers, software testers, and users. **Systems analysts** are IT professionals who understand both business and technology. They are active throughout the systems development process and play a key role in moving the project through the systems development process. Systems analysts integrate the work of the programmers, testers, and users. Depending on the nature of the project, the team may also include hardware and communications specialists, database designers and administrators, and other IT specialists.

The team composition changes over time. During requirements definition, the team will be heavy with systems analysts. During design and implementation, it will be heavy with programmers, testers, and database designers. During integrated testing and conversion, the team will be augmented with testers and business users.

User involvement is critical throughout the system development process. Depending on the size and nature of the project, users are assigned to the project either full or part time. Sometimes users are assigned to review and oversight committees that meet periodically, especially at the completion of project

Estimation Ethics

A *buy-in* occurs when a company agrees to produce a system or product for less than it knows the project will require. An example for DSI would be if a consultant agreed to build the system for $50,000 when good estimating techniques indicate it will take $75,000.

If the contract for the system or product is written for "time and materials," the customer will ultimately pay the $75,000 for the finished system. Or the customer will cancel the project once the true cost is known. If the contract for the system or product is written for a fixed cost, then the developer will absorb the extra costs. The latter strategy is used if the contract opens up other business opportunities that are worth the $25,000 loss.

Buy-ins always involve deceit. Most would agree that buying in on a time-and-materials project, planning to stick the customer with the full cost later, is unethical and wrong. Opinions vary on buying in on a fixed-priced contract. Some would say buying in is always deceitful and should be avoided. Others say that it is just one of many different business strategies.

What about in-house projects? Do the ethics change if an in-house development team is building a system for use in house? If team members know there is only $50,000 in the budget, should they start the project if they believe its true cost is $75,000? If they do start, at some point senior management will either have to admit a mistake and cancel the project or find the additional $25,000. Project sponsors can make all sorts of excuses for such a buy-in. For example, "I know the company needs this system. If management doesn't realize it and fund it appropriately, then we'll just force their hand."

These issues become even stickier if team members disagree about how much the project will cost. Suppose one faction of the team believes the project will cost $35,000, another faction estimates $50,000, and a third thinks $65,000. Can the project sponsors justify taking the average? Or, should they describe the range of estimates?

Other buy-ins are more subtle. Suppose you are a project manager of an exciting new project that is possibly a career-maker for you. You are incredibly busy, working six days a week and long hours each day. Your team has developed an estimate for $50,000 for the project. A little voice in the back of your mind says that maybe not all costs for every aspect of the project are included in that estimate. You mean to follow up on that thought, but more pressing matters in your schedule take precedence. Soon you find yourself in front of management, presenting the $50,000 estimate. You probably should have found the time to investigate the estimate, but you didn't. Is your behavior unethical?

Or suppose you approach a more senior manager with your dilemma. "I think there may be other costs, but I know that $50,000 is all we've got. What should I do?" Suppose the senior manager says something like, "Well, let's go forward. You don't know of anything else, and we can always find more budget elsewhere if we have to." How do you respond?

You can buy in on schedule as well as cost. If the marketing department says, "We have to have the new product for the trade show," do you agree, even if you know it's highly unlikely? What if marketing says, "If we don't have it by then, we should just cancel the project." Suppose it's not impossible to make that schedule, it's just highly unlikely. How do you respond?

DISCUSSION QUESTIONS

1. Do you agree that buying in on a cost-and-materials project is always unethical? Explain your reasoning. Are there circumstances in which it could be illegal?

2. Suppose you learn through the grapevine that your opponents in a competitive bid are buying in on a time-and-materials contract. Does this change your answer to question 1?

3. Suppose you are a project manager who is preparing a request for proposal on a cost-and-materials systems development project. What can you do to prevent buy-ins?

4. Under what circumstances do you think buying in on a fixed-price contract is ethical? What are the dangers of this strategy?

5. Explain why in-house development projects are always time-and-materials projects.

6. Given your answer to question 5, is buying in on an in-house project always unethical? Under what circumstances do you think it is ethical? Under what circumstances do you think it is justifiable, even if it is unethical?

7. Suppose you ask a senior manager for advice as described in the guide. Does the manager's response absolve you of guilt? Suppose you ask the manager and then do not follow her guidance. What problems result?

8. Explain how you can buy in on schedule as well as costs.

9. For an in-house project, how do you respond to the marketing manager who says that the project should be cancelled if it will not be ready for the trade show? In your answer, suppose that you disagree with this opinion—suppose you know the system has value regardless of whether it is done by the trade show.

STANDARD VEHICLE PRICE
Options Installed by Manufacturer

MANUFACTURER'S SUGGESTED RETAIL PRICE

CONVENIENCE PACKAGE
• REMOTE KEYLESS ENTRY W/ALARM $14,410.00
• POWER WINDOWS
• POWER REMOTE EXTERIOR MIRRORS
• CRUISE CONTROL
TRAVEL PACKAGE   825.00
• MAP LIGHTS
• AUTO-DIMMING INSIDE MIRROR
EXTERIOR TEMPERATURE GAUGE
DIGITAL COMPASS
FLOOR MATS - FRONT AND REAR   200.00
POWER SUNROOF
ANTI-LOCK BRAKES W/TRAC CTRL
50-STATE EMISSIONS
TOTAL OPTIONS

                                             80.00
                                            725.00
                                            400.00
                                            N/C
                                          2,230.00

phases and other milestones. Users are involved in many different ways. *The important point is for users to have active involvement and to take ownership of the project throughout the entire development process.* DSI has only one person in its IT department, so the development team will consist, at least initially, of that person and users. As the project progresses, DSI will need to outsource for professional systems developers and programmers (or hire additional IT personnel).

The first major task for the assembled project team is to plan the project. Members of the project team specify tasks to be accomplished, assign personnel, determine task dependencies, and set schedules. You will learn more about project planning in your operations management classes, if you have not done so already.

Q5 What Is the Users' Role in the Requirements Phase?

The primary purpose of the requirements analysis phase is to determine and document the specific features and functions of the new system. For most development projects, this phase requires interviewing dozens of users and documenting potentially hundreds of requirements. Requirements definition is, thus, expensive. It is also difficult, as you will see.

Determine Requirements

Determining the system's requirements is the most important phase in the systems development process. If the requirements are wrong, the system will be wrong. If the requirements are determined completely and correctly, then design and implementation will be easier and more likely to result in success.

Examples of requirements are the contents of a report or the fields in a data entry form. Requirements include not only what is to be produced, but also how frequently and how fast it is to be produced. Some requirements specify the volume of data to be stored and processed.

If you take a course in systems analysis and design, you will spend weeks on techniques for determining requirements. Here, we will just summarize that process. Typically, systems analysts interview users and record the results in some consistent manner. Good interviewing skills are crucial; users are notorious for being unable to describe what they want and need. Users also tend to focus on the tasks they are performing at the time of the interview. Tasks performed at the end of the quarter or end of the year are forgotten if the interview takes place mid-quarter. Seasoned and experienced systems analysts know how to conduct interviews to bring such requirements to light.

As listed in Figure 10-4, sources of requirements include existing systems as well as the forms, reports, queries, and application features and functions desired in the new system. Security is another important category of requirements.

If the new system involves a new database or substantial changes to an existing database, then the development team will create a data model. As you learned in Chapter 5, that model must reflect the users' perspective on their business and business activities. Thus, the data model is constructed on the basis of user interviews and must be validated by those users.

Sometimes, the requirements determination is so focused on the software and data components that other components are forgotten. Experienced project

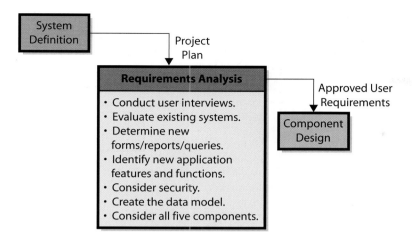

Figure 10-4
SDLC: Requirements Analysis
Phase

managers ensure consideration of requirements for all five IS components, not just for software and data. Regarding hardware, the team might ask: Are there special needs or restrictions on hardware? Is there an organizational standard governing what kinds of hardware may or may not be used? Must the new system use existing hardware? What requirements are there for communications and network hardware?

Similarly, the team should consider requirements for procedures and personnel: Do accounting controls require procedures that separate duties and authorities? Are there restrictions that some actions can be taken only by certain departments or specific personnel? Are there policy requirements or union rules that restrict activities to certain categories of employees? Will the system need to interface with information systems from other companies and organizations? In short, requirements need to be considered for all of the components of the new information system.

These questions are examples of the kinds of questions that must be asked and answered during requirements analysis.

Approve Requirements

Once the requirements have been specified, the users must review and approve them before the project continues. The easiest and cheapest time to alter the information system is in the requirements phase. Changing a requirement at this stage is simply a matter of changing a description. Changing a requirement in the implementation phase may require weeks of reworking applications components and the database.

Q6 How Are the Five Components Designed?

Each of the five components is designed in this stage. Typically, the team designs each component by developing alternatives, evaluating each of those alternatives against the requirements, and then selecting among those alternatives. Accurate requirements are critical here; if they are incomplete or wrong, then they will be poor guides for evaluation. Figure 10-5 (page 244) shows that design tasks pertain to each of the five IS components.

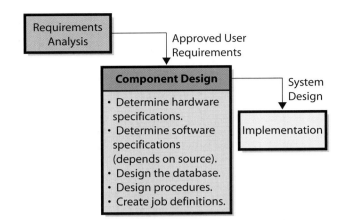

Figure 10-5
SDLC: Component Design Phase

Hardware Design

For hardware, the team determines specifications for the hardware that they want to acquire. (The team is not designing hardware in the sense of building a CPU or a disk drive.)

For the DSI system, the team would need to determine what hardware is required to read and write to the RFID devices. They also need to specify the computer and network connections that will process the RFID data and compute inventory locations for incoming components.

Software Design

Software design depends on the source of the programs. For off-the-shelf software, the team must determine candidate products and evaluate them against the requirements. For off-the-shelf-with alteration software with alteration software, the team identifies products to be acquired off-the-shelf and then determines the alterations required. For custom-developed programs, the team produces design documentation for writing program code.

Database Design

If developers are constructing a database, then during this phase they convert the data model to a database design using techniques like those described in Chapter 5. If developers are using off-the-shelf programs, then little database design needs be done; the programs will handle their own database processing.

Procedure Design

For a business information system, the system developers and the organization must also design procedures for both users and operations personnel. Procedures need to be developed for normal, backup, and failure recovery operations, as summarized in Figure 10-6. Usually, teams of systems analysts and key users design the procedures.

Design of Job Descriptions

With regard to people, design involves developing job descriptions for both users and operations personnel. Sometimes new information systems require new jobs. If so, the duties and responsibilities for the new jobs need to be defined in

	Users	Operations Personnel
Normal processing	• Procedures for using the system to accomplish business tasks	• Procedures for starting, stopping, and operating the system
Backup	• User procedures for backing up data and other resources	• Operations procedures for backing up data and other resources
Failure recovery	• Procedures to continue operations when the system fails • Procedures to convert back to the system after recovery	• Procedures to identify the source of failure and get it fixed • Procedures to recover and restart the system

Figure 10-6
Procedures to Be Designed

accordance with the organization's human resources policies. More often, organizations add new duties and responsibilities to existing jobs. In this case, developers define these new tasks and responsibilities in this phase. Sometimes, the personnel design task is as simple as statements like, "Jason will be in charge of making backups." As with procedures, teams of systems analysts and users determine job descriptions and functions.

Q7 How Is an Information System Implemented?

Once the design is complete, the next phase in the SDLC is implementation. Tasks in this phase are to build, test, and convert the users to the new system (see Figure 10-7). Developers construct each of the components independently. They obtain, install, and test hardware. They license and install off-the-shelf programs; they write adaptations and custom programs as necessary. They construct a

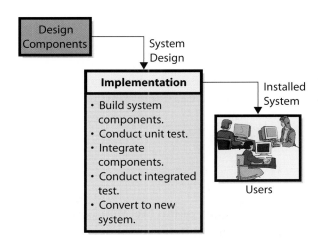

Figure 10-7
SDLC: Implementation Phase

database and fill it with data. They document, review, and test procedures, and they create training programs. Finally, the organization hires and trains needed personnel.

System Testing

Once developers have constructed and tested all of the components, they integrate the individual components and test the system. So far, we have glossed over testing as if there is nothing to it. In fact, software and system testing are difficult, time-consuming, and complex tasks. Developers need to design and develop test plans and record the results of tests. They need to devise a system to assign fixes to people and to verify that fixes are correct and complete.

A **test plan** consists of sequences of actions that users will take when using the new system. Test plans include not only the normal actions that users will take, but also incorrect actions. A comprehensive test plan should cause every line of program code to be executed. The test plan should cause every error message to be displayed. Testing, retesting, and re-retesting consume huge amounts of labor. Often, developers can reduce the labor cost of testing by writing programs that invoke system features automatically.

Today, many IT professionals work as testing specialists. Testing, or **product quality assurance (PQA)** as it is often called, is an important career. PQA personnel usually construct the test plan with the advice and assistance of users. PQA test engineers perform testing, and they also supervise user test activity. Many PQA professionals are programmers who write automated test programs.

In addition to IT professionals, users should be involved in system testing. Users participate in the development of test plans and test cases. They also can be part of the test team, usually working under the direction of PQA personnel. Users have the final say on whether the system is ready for use. If you are invited to participate as a user tester, take that responsibly seriously. It will become much more difficult to fix problems after you have begun to use the system in production.

Beta testing is the process of allowing future system users to try out the new system on their own. Software vendors like Microsoft often release beta versions of their products for users to try and to test. Such users report problems back to the vendor. Beta testing is the last stage of testing. Normally products in the beta test phase are complete and fully functioning; they typically have few serious errors. Organizations that are developing large new information systems sometimes use a beta-testing process just as software vendors do.

System Conversion

Once the system has passed integrated testing, the organization installs the new system. The term **system conversion** is often used for this activity because it implies the process of *converting* business activity from the old system to the new.

Organizations can implement a system conversion in one of four ways:

- Pilot
- Phased
- Parallel
- Plunge

IS professionals recommend any of the first three, depending on the circumstances. In most cases, companies should avoid "taking the plunge!"

With **pilot installation**, the organization implements the entire system on a limited portion of the business. An example would be for DSI to use the system for one of two component manufacturers. The advantage of pilot implementation is that if the system fails, the failure is contained within a limited boundary. This reduces exposure of the business and also protects the new system from developing a negative reputation throughout the organization(s).

As the name implies, with **phased installation** the new system is installed in phases across the organization(s). Once a given piece works, then the organization installs and tests another piece of the system, until the entire system has been installed. Some systems are so tightly integrated that they cannot be installed in phased pieces. Such systems must be installed using one of the other techniques. DSI's RFID system falls into this category.

With **parallel installation**, the new system runs in parallel with the old one until the new system is tested and fully operational. Parallel installation is expensive because the organization incurs the costs of running both systems. Users must work double time, if you will, to run both systems. Then, considerable work is needed to determine if the results of the new system are consistent with those of the old system.

However, some organizations consider the costs of parallel installation to be a form of insurance. It is the slowest and most expensive style of installation, but it does provide an easy fallback position if the new system fails.

The final style of conversion is **plunge installation** (sometimes called *direct installation*). With it, the organization shuts off the old system and starts the new system. If the new system fails, the organization is in trouble: Nothing can be done until either the new system is fixed or the old system is reinstalled. Because of the risk, organizations should avoid this conversion style if possible. The one exception is if the new system is providing a new capability that is not vital to the operation of the organization.

Figure 10-8 summarizes the tasks for each of the five components during the design and implementation phases. Use this figure to test your knowledge of the tasks in each phase.

Figure 10-8
Design and Implementation for the Five Components

	Hardware	Software	Data	Procedures	People
Design	Determine hardware specifications.	Select off-the-shelf programs. Design alterations and custom programs as necessary.	Design database and related structures.	Design user and operations procedures.	Develop user and operations job descriptions.
Implementation	Obtain, install, and test hardware.	License and install off-the-shelf programs. Write alterations and custom programs. Test programs.	Create database. Fill with data. Test data.	Document procedures. Create training programs. Review and test procedures.	Hire and train personnel.
Integrated Test and Conversion					

Unit test each component

Q8 What Are the Tasks for System Maintenance?

The last phase of the SDLC is maintenance. Maintenance is a misnomer; the work done during this phase is either to *fix* the system so that it works correctly or to *adapt* it to changes in requirements.

Figure 10-9 shows tasks during the maintenance phase. First, there needs to be a means for tracking both failures[2] and requests for enhancements to meet new requirements. For small systems, organizations can track failures and enhancements using word-processing documents. As systems become larger, however, and as the number of failure and enhancement requests increases, many organizations find it necessary to develop a failure tracking database. Such a database contains a description of each failure or enhancement. It also records who reported the problem, who will make the fix or enhancement, what the status of that work is, and whether the fix or enhancement has been tested and verified by the originator.

Typically, IS personnel prioritize system problems according to their severity. They fix high-priority items as soon as possible, and they fix low-priority items as time and resources become available.

With regard to the software component, software developers group fixes for high-priority failures into a **patch** that can be applied to all copies of a given product. As described in Chapter 4, software vendors supply patches to fix security and other critical problems. They usually bundle fixes of low-priority problems into larger groups called **service packs**. Users apply service packs in much the same way that they apply patches, except that service packs typically involve fixes to hundreds or thousands of problems.

By the way, you may be surprised to learn this, but all commercial software products are shipped with known failures. Usually vendors test their products and remove the most serious problems, but they seldom, if ever, remove all of the defects they know about. Shipping with defects is an industry practice;

Figure 10-9
SDLC: System Maintenance Phase

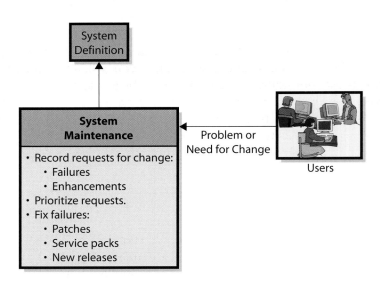

---

[2]A *failure* is a difference between what the system does and what it is supposed to do. Sometimes, you will hear the term *bug* used instead of *failure*. As a future user, call failures *failures*, for that's what they are. Don't have a *bugs list*, have a *failures list*. Don't have an *unresolved bug*, have an *unresolved failure*. A few months of managing an organization that is coping with a serious failure will show you the importance of this difference in terms.

Microsoft, Adobe, Oracle, RedHat, and many others all ship products with known problems.

Because an enhancement is an adaptation to new requirements, developers usually prioritize enhancement requests separate from failures. The decision to make an enhancement includes a business decision that the enhancement will generate an acceptable rate of return. Although minor enhancements are made using service packs, major enhancement requests usually result in a complete new release of a product.

As you read this, keep in mind that although we usually think of failures and enhancements as applying to software, they can apply to the other components as well. There can be hardware or database failures or enhancements. There can also be failures and enhancements in procedures and people, though the latter is usually expressed in more humane terms than failure or enhancement. The underlying idea is the same, however.

As stated earlier, note that the maintenance phase starts another cycle of the SDLC process. The decision to enhance a system is a decision to restart the systems development process. Even a simple failure fix goes through all of the phases of the SDLC; if it is a small fix, a single person may work through those phases in an abbreviated form. But each of those phases is repeated, nonetheless.

Q9 What Are Problems with the SDLC?

Although the industry has experienced notable successes with the SDLC process, there have also been many problems with it, as discussed next.

The SDLC Waterfall

One of the reasons for SDLC problems is due to the **waterfall** nature of the SDLC. Like a series of waterfalls, the process is supposed to operate in a sequence of nonrepetitive phases. For example, the team completes the requirements phase and goes over the waterfall into the design phase, and on through the process (look back to Figure 10-2, page 239).

Unfortunately, systems development seldom works so smoothly. Often, there is a need to crawl back up the waterfall, if you will, and repeat work in a prior phase. Most commonly, when design work begins and the team evaluates alternatives, they learn that some requirements statements are incomplete or missing. At that point, the team needs to do more requirements work, yet that phase is supposedly finished. On some projects, the team goes back and forth between requirements and design so many times that the project seems to be out of control.

Requirements Documentation Difficulty

Another problem, especially on complicated systems, is the difficulty of documenting requirements in a usable way. I once managed the database portion of a software project at Boeing in which we invested more than 70 labor-years into a requirements statement. The requirements document was 20-some volumes that stood 7 feet tall when stacked on top of one another.

When we entered the design phase, no one really knew all the requirements that concerned a particular feature. We would begin to design a feature

The Real Estimation Process

"I'm a software developer. I write programs in an object-oriented language called C++. I'm a skilled object-oriented designer, too. I should be—I've been at it 12 years and worked on major projects for several software companies. For the last 4 years, I've been a team leader. I lived through the heyday of the dot-com era and now work in the IT department of a giant pharmaceutical company.

"All of this estimating theory is just that—theory. It's not really the way things work. Sure, I've been on projects in which we tried different estimation techniques. But here's what really happens: You develop an estimate using whatever technique you want. Your estimate goes in with the estimates of all the other team leaders. The project manager sums all those estimates together and produces an overall estimate for the project.

"By the way, in my projects, time has been a much bigger factor than money. At one software company I worked for, you could be 300 percent over your dollar budget and get no more than a slap on the wrist. Be two weeks late, however, and you were finished.

"Anyway, the project managers take the project schedule to senior management for approval, and what happens? Senior management thinks they are negotiating. 'Oh, no,' they say, 'that's way too long. You can surely take a month off that schedule. We'll approve the project, but we want it done by February 1 instead of March 1.

"Now, what's their justification? They think that tight schedules make for efficient work. You know that everyone will work extra hard to meet the tighter timeframe. They know Parkinson's Law—'the time required to perform a task expands to the time available to do it.' So, fearing the possibility of wasting time because of too-lenient schedules, they lop a month off our estimate.

"Estimates are what they are; you can't knock off a month or two without some problem, somewhere. What does happen is that projects get behind, and then management expects us to work longer and longer hours. Like they said in the early years at Microsoft, 'We have flexible working hours. You can work any 65 hours per week you want.'

"Not that our estimation techniques are all that great, either. Most software developers are optimists. They schedule things as if everything will go as planned, and things seldom do. Also, schedulers usually don't allow for vacations, sick days, trips to the dentist, training on new technology, peer reviews, and all the other things we do in addition to writing software.

"So we start with optimistic schedules on our end, then management negotiates a month or two off, and voilà, we have a late project. After a while, management has been burned by late projects so much that they mentally add the month or even more back onto the official schedule. Then both sides work in a fantasy world, where no one believes the schedule, but everyone pretends they do.

"I like my job. I like software development. Management here is no better or worse than in other places. As long as I have interesting work to do, I'll stay here. But I'm not working myself silly to meet these fantasy deadlines."

DISCUSSION QUESTIONS

1. What do you think of this developer's attitude? Do you think he's unduly pessimistic or do you think there's merit to what he says?

2. What do you think of his idea that management thinks they're negotiating? Should management negotiate schedules? Why or why not?

3. Suppose a project actually requires 12 months to complete. Which do you think is likely to cost more: (a) having an official schedule of 11 months with at least a 1-month overrun or (b) having an official schedule of 13 months and following Parkinson's Law, having the project take 13 months?

4. Suppose you are a business manager and an information system is being developed for your use. You review the scheduling documents and see that little time has been allowed for vacations, sick leave, miscellaneous other work, and so forth. What do you do?

5. Describe the intangible costs of having an organizational belief that schedules are always unreasonable.

6. If this developer worked for you, how would you deal with his attitude about scheduling?

7. Do you think there is something different when scheduling information systems development projects than when scheduling other types of projects? What characteristics might make such projects unique? In what ways are they the same as other projects?

8. What do you think managers should do in light of your answer to question 7?

249b

only to find that we had not considered a requirement buried somewhere in the documentation. In short, the requirements were so unwieldy as to be nearly useless. Additionally, during the requirements analysis interval, the airplane business moved on. By the time we entered the design phase, many requirements were incomplete and some were obsolete. Projects that spend so much time documenting requirements are sometimes said to be in **analysis paralysis**.

Scheduling and Budgeting Difficulties

For a new, large-scale system, schedule and budgeting estimates are so approximate as to become nearly laughable. Management attempts to put a serious face on the need for a schedule and a budget, but when you are developing a large multiyear, multimillion-dollar project, estimates of labor hours and completion dates are approximate and fuzzy. The employees on the project, who are the source for the estimates, know little about how long something will take and about how much they had actually guessed. They know that the total budget and timeline is a summation of everyone's similar guesses. Many large projects live in a fantasy world of budgets and timelines. The *Guide* on pages 249a–249b states the difficulties with project estimation.

In truth, the software community has done much work to improve software development forecasting. But for large projects with large SDLC phases, just too much is unknown for any technique to work well. So, development methodologies other than the SDLC have emerged for developing systems through a series of small, manageable chunks. Rapid application development, object-oriented development, and extreme programming are three such methodologies, as described in Chapter Extension 19, "Alternative Development Techniques."

How does the knowledge in this chapter help you at DSI?

Knowledge of the SDLC will be invaluable to you at DSI. When Mr. Stratford says, "Great idea, what do we do next?" you know exactly what to say. You can give him a quick summary of the phases of the SDLC and then describe tasks in the definition phase more specifically. You could also say that, as a summer intern, you'll have time to do work on the definition phase, but that if DSI wants to go forward beyond that, they'll need to involve other personnel and probably professional systems developers. However, during the summer, you should be able to gather the data to help DSI decide whether or not this project is cost (and otherwise) feasible.

If you get this far, I'd say the full-time job has to be yours. It would be very hard for any intern, niece or otherwise, to compare to this performance!

Active ? Review

Use this Active Review to verify that you understand the material in the chapter. You can read the entire chapter and then perform the tasks in this review, or you can read the material for just one question and perform the tasks in this review for that question before moving on to the next one.

Q1 What is systems development?

Define *systems development*. Explain how systems development differs from program development. Describe the types of expertise needed for systems development projects. Explain why the systems development process is important for large organizations.

Q2 Why is systems development difficult and risky?

Describe the risk in systems development. Summarize the difficulties posed by: requirements definition, requirements changes, scheduling and budgeting, changing technology, and diseconomies of scale.

Q3 What are the five phases of the systems development life cycle?

Name the five phases in the systems development life cycle, and briefly describe each.

Q4 How is system definition accomplished?

Using Figure 10-3 as a guide, explain how you would describe to Mr. Stratford the systems definition task for DSI's RFID system. Name and describe four elements of feasibility. (*Hint:* The four types of feasibility can be arranged as Cost, Operational, Schedule, Technical; arranged this way, the first letter of each makes the acronym *COST*.)

Q5 What is the users' role in the requirements phase?

Summarize the tasks in the requirements phase. Describe the role for users in this phase. Discuss what you believe will happen if users are not involved or if users do not take this work seriously. Describe the role users play in requirements approval.

Q6 How are the five components designed?

Summarize design activities for each of the five components of an information system. Explain six categories of procedure that need to be designed.

Q7 How is an information system implemented?

Name the two major tasks in systems implementation. Summarize the system testing process. Describe the difference between system and software testing. Explain testing tasks for each of the five components. Name four ways of system conversion. Describe each way, and give an example of when each would be effective.

Q8 What are the tasks for systems maintenance?

Explain why the term *maintenance* is a misnomer. Summarize tasks in the maintenance phase.

Q9 What are problems with the SDLC?

Explain why the SDLC is considered a waterfall process, and describe why this characteristic can be a problem. Describe problems that occur when attempting to develop requirements using the SDLC. Summarize scheduling and budgeting difficulties that the SDLC presents.

Key Terms

Analysis paralysis 250
Beta testing 246
Brooks's law 237
Component design phase 244f
Cost feasibility 240
Implementation phase 245f
Maintenance phase 248f
Organizational feasibility 240
Parallel installation 247

Patch 248
Phased installation 247
Pilot installation 247
Plunge installation 247
Product quality assurance (PQA) 246
Requirements analysis phase 243f
Schedule feasibility 240
Service pack 248
System conversion 246

System definition phase 240f
Systems analysis and design 234
Systems analysts 241
Systems development 234
Systems development life cycle (SDLC) 238
Technical feasibility 240
Test plan 246
Waterfall 249

Using Your Knowledge

1. Assume Mr. Stratford said to you, "Great idea, what do we do next?" with regard to the project to use RFID on arriving components to assess where to place those components in raw materials inventory.
   a. Develop a plan for this project using the SDLC.
   b. Specify in detail the tasks to accomplish during the systems definition phase.

2. Consider the DSI project in Chapter 7 (pages 169–170) in which you were going to analyze tool repair data to determine if tool outages are causing substantial labor losses. Assume that these tools are kept in a centralized tool crib. The tool crib assigns a unique identifier to each tool and maintains records that indicate whether a tool is (a) checked out to an employee, (b) in repair, or (c) available and unused. Further assume that the records for each tool include a tool type, such as 10-inch grinder or 4-inch belt sander. Finally, assume you are to build a system that will produce a quarterly report that shows for each tool and each tool type, the number of days in use, the number of days in repair, and the number of days available and unused. Further, for each type, your report should show the number of days that all tools of a given type were in repair.
   a. Describe the tasks that need to be accomplished for each phase of the SDLC to build such a system.
   b. Specify in detail the tasks to accomplish during the systems definition phase.

3. Suppose Mr. Stratford has asked you to recommend a system for ranking and selecting suppliers (see page 196).
   a. Consider a reporting system. Specify in detail the tasks to accomplish during the systems definition phase.
   b. Consider a data-mining system. Specify in detail the tasks to accomplish during the systems definition phase.
   c. Consider a knowledge-management system. Specify in detail the tasks to accomplish during the systems definition phase.
   d. Consider an expert system. Specify in detail the tasks to accomplish during the systems definition phase.
   e. Assume you have accomplished all of the tasks you identify in tasks a through d. Explain how you would use the results to recommend a particular system type.

4. Read the description for developing a database to track volunteers for the public TV station in Chapter Extension 5, "Database Design."
   a. Develop a brief plan for this project using the SDLC. List major tasks to perform at each stage.
   b. Specify in detail the tasks to accomplish during the systems definition phase.

Case Study 10

Slow Learners, or What?

In 1974, when I was teaching at Colorado State University, we conducted a study of the causes of information systems failures. We interviewed personnel on several dozen projects and collected survey data on another 50 projects. Our analysis of the data revealed that the single most important factor in IS failure was a lack of user involvement. The second major factor was unclear, incomplete, and inconsistent requirements.

At the time, I was a devoted computer programmer and IT techie, and frankly, I was surprised. I thought that the significant problems would have been technical issues.

I recall one interview in particular. A large sugar producer had attempted to implement a new system for paying sugar-beet farmers. The new system was to be implemented at some 20 different sugar-beet collection sites, which were located in small farming communities, adjacent to rail yards. One of the benefits of the new system was significant cost savings, and a major share of those savings occurred because the new system eliminated the need for local comptrollers. The new system was expected to eliminate the jobs of 20 or so senior people.

The comptrollers, however, had been paying local farmers for decades; they were popular leaders not just within the company, but in their communities as well. They were well liked, highly respected, important people. A system that caused the elimination of their jobs was, using a term from this chapter, *organizationally infeasible*, to say the least.

Nonetheless, the system was constructed, but an IS professional who was involved told me, "Somehow, that new system just never seemed to work. The data were not entered on a timely basis, or they were in error, or incomplete; sometimes the data were not entered at all. Our operations were falling apart during the key harvesting season, and we finally backed off and returned to the old system." Active involvement of system users would have identified this organizational infeasibility long before the system was implemented.

That's ancient history, you say. Maybe, but in 1994 the Standish Group published a now famous study on IS failures. Entitled "The CHAOS Report," the study indicated the leading causes of IS failure are, in descending order, (1) lack of user input, (2) incomplete requirements and specifications, and (3) changing requirements and specifications (*standishgroup.com*). That study was completed some 20 years after our study.

In 2004, Professor Joseph Kasser and his students at the University of Maryland analyzed 19 system failures to determine their cause. They then correlated their analysis of the cause with the opinions of the professionals involved in the failures. The correlated results indicate the first-priority cause of system failure was "Poor requirements"; the second-priority cause was "Failure to communicate with the customer" (*softwaretechnews.com/technews2-2/trouble.html*).

In 2003, the IRS Oversight Board concluded the first cause of the IRS BSM failure (see Case Study 1) was "inadequate business unit ownership and sponsorship of projects. This resulted in unrealistic business cases and continuous project scope 'creep.' "

For over 30 years, studies have consistently shown that leading causes of system failures are a lack of user involvement and incomplete and changing requirements. Yet failures from these very failures continue to mount.

Sources: www.standishgroup.com; www.softwaretechnews.com/technews2-2/trouble.html.

Questions

1. Using the knowledge you have gained from this chapter, summarize the roles that you think users should take during an information systems development project. What responsibilities do users have? How closely should they work with the IS team? Who is responsible for stating requirements and constraints? Who is responsible for managing requirements?

2. If you ask users why they did not participate in requirements specification, some of the common responses are the following:
   a. "I wasn't asked."
   b. "I didn't have time."
   c. "They were talking about a system that would be here in 18 months, and I'm just worried about getting the order out the door today."
   d. "I didn't know what they wanted."
   e. "I didn't know what they were talking about."
   f. "I didn't work here when they started the project."
   g. "The whole situation has changed since they were here; that was 18 months ago!"

   Comment on each of these statements. What strategies do they suggest to you as a future user and as a future manager of users?

3. If you ask IS professionals why they did not obtain a complete and accurate list of requirements, common responses are:
   a. "It was nearly impossible to get on the users' calendars. They were always too busy."
   b. "The users wouldn't regularly attend our meetings. As a result, one meeting would be dominated by the needs of one group, and another meeting would be dominated by the needs of another group."
   c. "Users didn't take the requirement process seriously. They wouldn't thoroughly review the requirements statements before review meetings."
   d. "Users kept changing. We'd meet with one person one time and another person a second time, and they'd want different things."
   e. "We didn't have enough time."
   f. "The requirements kept changing."

   Comment on each of these statements. What strategies do they suggest to you as a future user and a future manager of users?

4. If it is widely understood that one of the principal causes of IS failures is a lack of user involvement, and if that factor continues to be a problem after 30+ years of experience, does this mean that the problem cannot be solved? For example, everyone knows that you can maximize your gains by buying stocks at their annual low price and selling them at their annual high price, but doing so is very difficult. Is it equally true that although everyone knows that users should be involved in requirements specification, and that requirements should be complete, it just cannot be done? Why or why not?

Teaching Suggestions

Emerson Pharmaceuticals and Dorset-Stratford Interiors, Part 4 and Chapter 10

GOALS

Use Dee's blog and Dorset-Stratford Interiors (DSI) to:

* Compare and contrast Emerson and DSI to demonstrate different scales of IT management.

* Motivate learning the SDLC (use DSI).

* Demonstrate a practical application of the early phases of the SDLC (use DSI).

BACKGROUND

1. The text explains the SDLC in Chapter 10 and provides a description of additional development methodologies in Chapter Extension 19. Depending on how far you want to go with the DSI case, you could explore the use of alternative development, such as RAD or XP.

2. There is one SDLC, but it varies considerably according to the scale of the project. The SDLC can be used for Dee's blog, or it could be used for the development of a large, complicated system. We can use the Emerson and DSI cases to explore these differences. Dee worked with her consultant and a few IS personnel to develop her blog. The few people, simple requirements, and readily available software to license made the development process simple. DSI has even more complicated systems, and the SDLC will be correspondingly more complicated. Finally, when Emerson builds a new IS, for example a CRM, the project will be enormous. Although the phases of the SDLC will be the same for an organization-wide system at Emerson, their implementation will be far more complex and requires years, not weeks, of development. See Chapter Extensions 17 and 18 for more on using the SDLC for different-sized projects.

3. The "takeaway" for the student is that the SDLC is a good way to think about systems development, but it will vary in nature and character from project to project. The SDLC that students encounter on the job may fall anywhere on the continuum of complexity. Again, see Chapter Extensions 17 and 18.

4. I try to use the intern's project at DSI as a way of having the students experience why the users' role is so important in the definition and requirements phases.

HOW TO GET THE STUDENTS INVOLVED

1. I start with the intern:
   a. **Ever hear the adage, "Be careful what you ask for?" What does it mean?**
   b. **How does that adage pertain to the intern at DSI?**
   c. **Suppose you pitch Mr. Stratford on one of your ideas, and he says, "Great. What do we do next?" How do you respond?**
   d. **Suppose he says, "Give me a memo on what you think we should do?" What would you say in that memo?**
   (Use the phases of the SDLC to structure your response.)

2. Consider one of the projects you've defined for DSI:
   a. **The text uses the RFID project for staging components in raw materials inventory.**
   b. **What were the other three ideas?**
   (They were:
   • a reporting system to determine how much labor is lost to tool downtime,
   • a virtual tool crib, and
   • a BI system to select vendors.)
   c. **Which of these is the best? Which should we explore? Why?**
   d. **How does the system we've chosen contribute to DSI's competitive strategy?**

3. Now consider how to apply the SDLC to this system:
   a. **Describe, in general terms, the kind of work that needs to be done for this project for each phase of the SDLC.**
   b. **You're an intern. How much of the SDLC can you do?**
   c. **What is a reasonable goal for you at DSI?**
   d. **What would be a reasonable goal for you at DSI if you managed, for example, the business function most directly involved in the new system?**

4. Now consider the definition phase, goals and scope:
   a. **What are the four steps identified in the text for this phase?**
   b. **What work needs to be done to define the system goals and scope?**
   c. **What questions do you need to ask to accomplish that work?**
   d. **How will you get answers to those questions?**

5. Now consider the feasibility part of the definition phase:

   a. **What are the four elements of feasibility defined in the text?**

   b. **What work needs to be done for each?**

   c. **What questions do you need to ask to accomplish that work?**

   d. **How will you get answers to those questions?**

6. Now consider the rest of the definition phase. (Chapter Extension 18, addresses project planning. See, in particular, Figure CE18-3.)

   a. **What else do you need to do to complete the definition phase?**

   b. **What work needs to be done?**

   c. **What questions do you need to ask to accomplish that work?**

   d. **How will you get answers to those questions?**

7. Now consider transfer of this knowledge to other domains:

   a. **What have you learned from this process?**

   b. **How can you use the SDLC in the future?**

   c. **Could you use the SDLC for other than IS projects?**

   d. **Give me some examples.**

BOTTOM LINE

* The SDLC is an excellent way to organize your thinking about new systems development projects. As a user, you will be primarily involved in the definition and requirements phases. Get involved! Also, use the SDLC for any type of project development.

Using the Ethics Guide: Estimation Ethics (page 241a)

GOALS

✳ Introduce the concept of *buy-in* as it pertains to information systems.

✳ Assess the ethics of buy-ins in different settings.

BACKGROUND AND PRESENTATION STRATEGIES

I was first introduced to *buy-in* when I worked in procurement in the defense industry in the late 1960s. At that time, it was common for large government contractors to buy-in on initial system production and to make up the difference by selling expensive spare parts over the 20-year or more life of that system. Senator Proxmire attained national prominence when he discovered the U.S. Navy was paying $250 for submarine toilet seats. Another cost-recovery technique was to claim that all but the most obvious corrections to plans were "out of scope" changes that required supplemental payment.

I was a very junior person, and I do not know what the thinking was at senior levels. But, I suspect it involved a degree of "wink-wink" collusion between high-level defense and aerospace executives. Congress had only so much money in the budget for a given system. The contractor would bid within that limit and make up the differences via supplemental appropriations in later years. I suspect that none of this was a surprise to Congress. It was a way of obtaining a system in the face of competing demands for the government budget. Some called it a "game that we must play." It was not illegal, and it involved some risk on the contractor's part; there was always the chance that a project would be cancelled before the buy-in costs could be recovered.

Buy-ins are prevalent in everyday life, too. We all know the ads for cars that loudly announce a price of $15,000, but the small print indicates that there will be supplemental charges for "additional items."

All types of custom building also can involve buy-ins. Building a custom home, a custom boat, a custom airplane initerior—all are susceptible to buy-ins.

The best defense against buy-ins is experience in the industry. Or, as Donald Trump put it during his Senate testimony on the United Nations remodeling project, if

you don't have experience working with New York construction contractors, "You'll go to school while they eat your lunch."

So, one of the major goals of this guide is to see how buy-ins apply to information systems projects. Future managers need to know this so that they can guard against, or at least consider the possibility of a buy-in.

Future managers also need to consider their own values and principles. At what point is a buy-in within accepted boundaries of conduct, and when does it exceed those boundaries? When will you be willing to put your job on the line when resisting a buy-in on ethical principles?

Finally, note that the guide points out that buy-ins can occur for both cost and schedule. They also can occur for technical feasibility when a team asserts that some new technology is further developed than it is. (I suspect that happened with the IRS CADE project discussed at the end of Chapter 1.) Ultimately, however, technical buy-ins become both cost and schedule buy-ins.

 SUGGESTED RESPONSES FOR DISCUSSION QUESTIONS

1. Again, using the definition of *ethical* as "consistent with agreed principles of correct moral conduct," I don't think it's possible to say that every buy-in is unethical. All buy-ins involve deceit, but that deceit may be an accepted practice in the industry (see previous comments). It's a very slippery slope, however. What level of deceit is allowable? Senator Proxmire's discovery of a $250 submarine toilet seat seems to indicate that someone went over the line.

   Yes, a buy-in could be illegal, especially for public projects. The contractor might have agreed to comply with a law that pertains to honesty in bidding. Also, some states may have enacted laws that require a certain level of truth in advertising. Such laws lie behind the auto ads in which someone quickly reads the serial number of autos that are being advertised.

2. First, your company may have a policy about buy-ins that requires you to submit a complete and honest bid. If so, you should follow that policy. If not, you need to wonder how reliable the grapevine is and assess how widespread and accepted buy-ins are in your industry. You also need to check with your management. Consider the impact of a buy-in on your reputation for future jobs (see question 3). As a

general rule, I'd say avoid the buy-in, bid honestly, and keep looking for other jobs on which to bid.

3. Create as comprehensive a list of features and functions as you can. Ensure that the proposal requires an estimate for every feature and function. Check bids to ensure that every item was included. Employ experts to determine the reasonableness of the bid items. For this activity, there is no substitute for experience. Check the reputation of the vendor. Are they known for buy-ins or for honest bids? What percent overrun is typical for the vendor's projects?

4. The obvious danger is that you never have a chance to get your money back. The customer never approves any "out of scope" changes and cancels the project before you have a chance to recoup losses on spare or replacement parts.

   Some vendors buy-in in order to gain experience and/or reputation on a particular technology. Someone might buy-in, for example, on building a database for a Web site so as to learn how to build such databases. If the vendor considers the difference between the buy-in bid and the actual cost as an investment and has no intent of recovering that loss, then the behavior is ethical, at least to my mind. Otherwise, is the buy-in consistent with agreed-on principles in that industry?

5. There is no fixed bid.

6. What hard questions! Is it ever appropriate to deceive your own management? If so, when? I think, over the long haul, nothing is more serviceable than the truth. I don't think I'd ever recommend deceiving one's own management. There may be exceptions to that, but I'd say they'd be very rare. I'd say it's unethical, unwise, and seldom justifiable. In some organizations, that attitude might be called naïve. (If so, I'd rather work somewhere else.)

7. If I were the junior person, I'd go with the manager's recommendation. The statement, "We can always find the money someplace else," suggests to me that the manager has flexibility in the budget that I don't know about. I think the statement "absolve you of guilt" puts it a little strongly, but, yes, I think I could go forward on solid ethical ground. Not following the advice is a form of betrayal. If you aren't going to follow that advice, at least tell your manager ahead of time and explain why you cannot. Or, determine the other costs and show them to your manager.

8. You can buy-in on schedule by agreeing to produce something on a schedule that you believe you cannot meet. When schedule delays occur, the customer is so committed to the project that they cannot cancel it.

9. Again, nothing is more serviceable than the truth. I'd call the marketing manager's bluff: "OK, let's cancel the project." If the project is important enough, that person will back down. Then, I'd say, "We'll do the best we can, but we operate under the risk that it won't be done by then. Plan accordingly." I'd then try to negotiate having some limited version of the project ready by the trade show.

   This happened to me once when a senior sales manager said a version of a software product had to be ready by that year's fall Comdex show. I did exactly as described previously. It turned out he was speaking rashly and backed down. We delivered a solid working version for use in the computers in the trade-show booth. The full version was shipped to customers two months later.

WRAP UP

➤ **Be aware that buy-ins occur and that some vendors make a practice of them. Scrutinize unbelievably low bids. They probably are unbelievable.**

➤ **There is no substitute for experience. Hire expertise to evaluate bids.**

➤ **Consider your own position on buy-ins. When can you justify one? Ever? If so, when?**

Using the Guide: The Real Estimation Process (page 249a)

GOALS

✱ Sensitize students to the challenges of software scheduling.

✱ Alert students to possible consequences when negotiating a schedule.

BACKGROUND AND PRESENTATION STRATEGIES

There are many formal methods for scheduling, and I've worked at companies that have attempted to implement some of those methods. But invariably, requirements change, personnel depart, management loses patience with the discipline required to manage to schedules, or some other factor invalidates the good intentions of the project's managers. Companies that have an effective process for scheduling software projects are extremely rare.

If anyone had figured software scheduling out, you'd think it would be Microsoft. But look how late both Vista is and SQL Server 2005 was. Clearly, they don't know how to do it, either.

The Software Institute at Carnegie Mellon developed the software maturity model that rates organizations on their use of effective development processes. Perhaps some of that model's level-4 or level-5 companies know how to schedule software development and how to manage to that schedule.

For complex software, with real users and with real requirements-management problems, I'm skeptical that anyone has figured it out. I think schedule risk is one of the major reasons that organizations choose to license software. The schedule (and attendant cost) risks of in-house software development are just too great.

Perhaps there's something about the nature of software that means you can't know how long it will take until you've done it. If so, the only organizations that can afford that kind of risk are vendors who can amortize the cost (whatever it turns out to be) over hundreds or thousands of users.

The protagonist of this guide has been burned many times. He's been asked to work weekends, holidays, and nights and to put in 80- and 90-hour work weeks during

"crunch time," and he's not doing it anymore. He'll give what he thinks is a fair contribution—and he'll probably do quite a bit more than that—but he no longer believes in heroics. "The more rabbits you pull out of the hat, the more rabbits they expect you to pull out of a hat, until all you're doing is pulling rabbits out of the hat. Nope, not anymore!"

Two important takeaways for the students:

➤ **Software developers are optimists. Ensure that they have not planned schedules assuming that people work full time. People can't work all the time—they get sick, go to the dentist, serve jury duty, write employee evaluations, sit on design reviews, apply for patents, and so on. Plans should apply a factor like 0.6 to compute the number of effective labor hours for each employee.**

➤ **Be aware of the consequences of negotiating a schedule. If the developers have used a sensible process for creating the schedule, it is seldom worth reducing it. They're optimists, anyway, and chances are the project will take longer than they think. If you trust that developer management is making effective use of the developers' time, leave the schedules alone.**

One important point not brought out by this guide: *Large projects are much harder to schedule than small ones.* Also, if the project lasts longer than a year, watch out! Longer projects mean more chance for technology change, requirements change, and employee turnover. All these factors increase the likelihood of schedule delays.

 SUGGESTED RESPONSES FOR DISCUSSION QUESTIONS

1. I think the developer has been burned many times. We can learn a lot by understanding his points.

2. There's a risk when management attempts to negotiate schedules. As stated in the takeaway, noted previously, if management trusts that development management has used a sensible process to obtain the schedules, and if they trust development management to effectively utilize developers' time, leave the schedule alone.

   Alternatively, if the product must be produced more quickly, remove requirements. But do so realistically, and not as part of a negotiating ploy.

   As a manager, consider, too, the implications of negotiating a schedule. You're essentially telling the developers that you do not trust them, that you think they're attempting to deceive you with a relaxed schedule.

Rather than a harsh negotiation with the implications just stated, you might ask the developers to show you their schedule, to discuss their scheduling methodology with you, and then, as a team, work together to determine if there are any tasks for which the schedule could be compressed, or ways of rearranging tasks for greater schedule efficiency.

3. Without any further information about the costs of the one-month difference, I'd prefer the 13-month shipment. Software that is produced when in "late mode" is typically lower in quality than software that is produced on a planned schedule. I'd bet (absent more information) that such quality matters will translate into costs high enough to swamp the costs of the two extra months of development.

4. Return the plan to development management and tell them to plan more realistically. This planning mistake would raise serious flags in my mind about the competency of the development team. I'd do something to get that team more training, bring in consulting expertise, or start looking for new development managers.

5. If schedules are always unreasonable, then nobody believes anything. Schedules lose relevance, importance, and meaning. "Everybody knows this is a phony schedule. Don't knock yourself out."

6. I'd listen. I'd ask them to help me develop a plan and a process that would not have the result they fear. I'd work with them to develop that plan and to implement it.

7. This is a good question for the students to discuss. Some factors that may make software scheduling harder are:

   - Changing technology.
   - Changing requirements.

- Software is mental—it's logical poetry. It's as varied as the human mind.
- Large differences exist in the amount of quality code that different developers generate. These differences complicate planning.
- Different tasks require different amounts of time. Writing an application where the tools and techniques are known is far simpler than inventing or applying a new technology. This complicates the planning process. Consider the IRS's CADE example.

In other ways, software is similar to managing any other complex project. It requires clearly defined tasks and schedules, unambiguous assignments of personnel to tasks, careful follow-up on assignments, management of critical paths and schedules, effective communication, and other skills students will learn in their project management classes.

8. Learn project management skills. Be aware of the difficulty of scheduling software projects. Understand the need to manage requirements creep. Be willing to remove features and functions if the schedule must be kept. Always plan on delays in software projects. Don't assume that because a project is late that software management is incompetent. It may be, but it may also be that unavoidable factors intervened.

WRAP UP

➤ **What did you learn from this guide?**

➤ **As a future manager, how will you plan your activities around software schedules?**

➤ **How useful are the insights of this contrarian?**

➤ **What characteristics make some contrarians' comments more useful than others?**

11 Information Systems Management

This could happen to you

Dee Clark created a blog for communicating to her sales force, and she wanted to restrict access to that blog to authorized Emerson personnel. The easiest way to protect her blog from outside eyes was to put it inside the corporate network where the salespeople could access it using Emerson's VPN.

Of course, to place the blog software on an Emerson server, Dee needed the permission and help of the IT department. Dee didn't understand the IT department's mission and was surprised when she met substantial resistance. Her response was to use her manager's manager to bludgeon the IT department into submission. In the process, her management chain exposed Emerson to an enormous security risk. Once Dee's consultant, Don Gray, was inside the system, given his knowledge and experience, he could have played havoc with their internal information systems. Dee should have known about that risk. Even if she didn't know, her boss's boss ought to have known about it.

Dee's problems were compounded because she did not understand the IT department's responsibilities, nor did she know their problems and concerns. Consequently, she didn't know how to talk with them. Dee's strength was not empathy, and with no knowledge of their responsibilities of the IT department, she was unable to practice empathetic thinking (see page 31a) when she made her request. Had she approached the IT department with a knowledge of its concerns, she would have had a more supportive response and could have avoided exposing Emerson to such risk. This chapter will explain the organization and operation of typical IT departments. If you find yourself in the position Dee was, you will have the knowledge to interact with IT personnel in a more professional and effective way.

Optional Extensions for this chapter are CE20, "Outsourcing," and CE21, "Financing and Accounting for IT Projects."

Study Questions

Q1 Why do you need to know about the IT department?

Q2 What are the responsibilities of the IT department?

Q3 How is the IT department organized?

Q4 What IS-related job positions exist?

Q5 How do organizations decide how much to spend on IT?

Q6 What are your rights and responsibilities?

How does the knowledge in this chapter help you at Emerson or DSI?

Q1 Why Do You Need to Know About the IT Department?

You need to know about the IT department for two principal reasons. First, like Dee, you need to understand the responsibilities and duties of the IT department so you can be an effective consumer of the IT department's resources. If you understand what the IT department does and how it is organized, you'll know how better to obtain the equipment, services, or systems you (and organizations you manage) need.

Second, you need to know about the functions of the IT department to be a better informed and effective manager or executive. For example, more than one merger or acquisition has been negotiated, signed, and planned, without anyone thinking of the IT departments. As you can now understand, marrying the infrastructure and systems of two organizations requires extensive planning. As *MIS in Use 11* indicates, just merging the email lists of two large organizations is a sizable task. If you understand the functions of the IT department, you will know to raise the issues of IT very early in any plan to acquire or merge with another organization.

Or suppose you sponsor a new business initiative, or work on a team that is sponsoring a new initiative. You need to know to think about the needs of the IT department in supporting that new initiative. Dee's blog is an example of a very small initiative. Suppose, instead, you're working on a team to set up selling in teams with, say, the supplier of a companion product. Perhaps your company sells DSL (digital subscriber line) modems, and you're thinking of partnering sales efforts with a phone company that leases DSL lines to business customers. Many questions arise, one of which is, "Which company will provide customer support?" With knowledge of the IT department's functions, you'll know to ask how this new initiative will impact your existing customer support systems.

Q2 What Are the Responsibilities of the IT Department?

The IT department has four primary responsibilities:

1. Plan for information systems and IT infrastructure.
2. Develop and adapt information systems and IT infrastructure.
3. Maintain information systems and operate and maintain IT infrastructure.
4. Protect infrastructure and data.

We'll consider each.

Plan for Information Systems and IT Infrastructure

Information systems exist to further the organization's competitive strategy. They exist to facilitate business processes and to help improve decision making. As stated in Chapter Extension 18, "Large-Scale Systems Development" (page 529), there are no IS projects; instead, all IS projects are a part of some other business system or facilitate some business goal.

The IT department has the responsibility of aligning all of its activities with the primary goals and objectives of the organization. As new technology emerges, the IT department is responsible to assess that technology and to

11

Cingular Wireless CIO Plans for Successes

SBC Communications and BellSouth merged in 2000 to form Cingular Wireless. In 2004, Cingular purchased AT&T Wireless, creating the largest U.S. wireless carrier, with more than 49 million customers and revenues in excess of $15.4 billion. A key player in the success of the activities was F. Thaddeus Arroyo, Cingular's CIO.

The CIO's first major challenge was blending the 1,400 different information systems and 60 separate call centers that existed when Cingular was born. For example, there were 11 different and separated billing systems. Since then, Cingular has consolidated those 11 systems into 1 and has replaced the 60 call centers with 20 new ones.

Cross-functional teams composed of both users and IT personnel played key roles in the consolidation. According to Arroyo, the IT professionals did not choose the computer systems for the users, but instead consulted with the cross-functional teams to make decisions. Of course, business didn't stop dur-

ing this integration; in fact, the wireless industry was expanding tremendously. Arroyo says, "During the growth period, we were rushing to keep the shelves stocked . . . It exasperated the complex infrastructure we had to support" (*www.cingular.com*, 2005).

To add complexity, in 2003 while the integration projects were underway, the Federal Communications Commission (FCC) created new regulations requiring the top 100 wireless companies to allow customers to keep their phone numbers when they changed carriers. The new regulation required Cingular to make major modifications to its billing and customer service applications—and to do so on short notice.

Even before the dust settled on that project, Cingular bought AT&T Wireless. Arroyo, as CIO, participated in months of merger preplanning involving more than 100 different and complex projects. For example, according to Arroyo, "the day after the deal was closed, over 70,000 employees were merged into one email directory. Also, we had to merge our corporate intranets within 24 hours of closing" (Phillips, 2005). The company needed to accomplish dozens of other, similar projects as well.

In light of his accomplishments, Arroyo has earned numerous industry awards. In 2004, the magazine *Business 2.0* selected him as a member of its "Dream Team." His keys to success in managing all these programs are to build strong teams, to work hard, and "to plan, plan, plan."

Sources: *www.cingular.com/download/business_solutions_cio.pdf* (accessed March 2005); Bruce E. Phillips, "Thaddeus Arroyo, Chief Information Officer, Cingular Wireless," January 13, 2005, *www.hispanicengineer.com* (accessed July 2005).

---

determine if it can be used to advance the organization's goals. Furthermore, as the business changes, the IT department is responsible for adapting infrastructure and systems to the new business goals.

Several years ago, Microsoft began to use the phrase **agile enterprise** in its advertising. The term caught on, and today many executives use it to refer to an organization that can quickly adapt to changes in the market, industry, product, law, or other significant external factors. Microsoft used this term because IT infrastructure and systems are known to be particularly difficult to adapt to change, and it claimed its products would change this characteristic. Possibly so, but the one certain effect of its campaign was to tune IT managers and business executives into the need to be agile.

Develop and Adapt Information Systems and IT Infrastructure

Given a plan, the next task for the IT department is to create, develop, and adapt both information systems and IT infrastructure. We discussed systems development in Chapter 10 and in Chapter Extensions 17 and 18 (on small-scale and large-scale systems development). Consequently, we need not say any more about systems development here.

In addition to systems development, the IT department is responsible for creating and adapting infrastructure, such as computer networks, servers, data centers, data warehouses, data marts, and other IT resources. The IT department is also charged with creating systems infrastructures, such as email systems, VPNs, instant messaging, blogs, net meetings, and any other IT-based infrastructure the company needs.

In most organizations, user departments pay for computers and related equipment out of their own budgets. However, because the IT department is responsible for maintaining that equipment and for connecting it to the organizational networks, the IT department will specify standard computer systems and configurations that it will support. The IT department is responsible for defining those specifications.

Maintain Information Systems and Operate and Maintain Infrastructure

We discussed information systems maintenance in Chapter 10 and will not repeat that discussion here. Regarding the operation and maintenance of infrastructure, realize that IT infrastructure is not like the building's plumbing or wiring. You cannot install a network or a server and then forget it. IT infrastructure must be operated and maintained. Networks and servers need to be powered on, and they need to be monitored. From time to time, they need to be adjusted or **tuned** to changes in the workload. Components fail, and when they do, the IT department is called upon to repair the problem.

To understand the importance of this function, consider what happens when a network fails. Users cannot connect to their local servers; they cannot run the information systems they need to perform their jobs. Users cannot connect with the Internet or send or receive email. Users may not even be able to reach their contact lists to find phone numbers to make telephone calls to explain why they are not responding. Truly, the business stops. And if, like Emerson, information systems have been distributed to customers or suppliers, personnel in other businesses are impacted as well.

Because of the high cost and serious disruption of system outages, information systems personnel are particularly sensitive to possible threats to that infrastructure. The Emerson IT personnel had every right to object to Dee's allowing a consultant to access their network. And, had a problem occurred, had the consultant done something to disrupt the network, the IT department would be accountable. Most of the company would judge the problem to have been an IT failure, even though Dee and her bosses were the true source of the problem. No one—including the CEO or even the sales vice president—who applied the pressure would care. This point leads to the last IT department responsibility.

Protect Infrastructure and Data from Threats

The IT department is responsible to protect infrastructure and data from threats. We will discuss threats and safeguards against them in Chapter 12. For now, just understand that threats to infrastructure and data arise from three sources: human error and mistakes, malicious human activity, and natural events and disasters.

The IT department helps the organization manage risk. The department needs to identify potential threats, estimate both financial and other risks, and specify appropriate safeguards. Nothing is free, including safeguards, and, indeed, some safeguards are very expensive. The IT department works with the

CFO and others in the organization to determine what safeguards to implement, or stated differently, what level of risk to assume. See Chapter 12 for more information.

Q3 How Is the IT Department Organized?

Figure 11-1 shows typical top-level reporting relationships. As you will learn in your management classes, organizational structure varies depending on the organization's size, culture, competitive environment, industry, and other factors. Larger organizations with independent divisions will have a group of senior executives like those shown here for each division. Smaller companies may combine some of these departments. Consider the structure in Figure 11-1 as a typical example.

The title of the principal manager of the IT department varies from organization to organization. A common title is **chief information officer (CIO)**. Other common titles are *vice president of information services, director of information services*, and, less commonly, *director of computer services*.

In Figure 11-1, the CIO, like other senior executives, reports to the chief executive officer (CEO), though sometimes these executives report to the chief operating officer (COO), who in turn reports to the CEO. In some companies, the CIO reports to the chief financial officer (CFO). That reporting arrangement may make sense if the primary information systems support accounting and finance activities. In organizations such as manufacturers that operate significant nonaccounting information systems, the arrangement shown in Figure 11-1 is more common and effective.

The structure of the IT department also varies among organizations. Figure 11-1 shows a typical IT department with four groups and a data administration staff function.

Most IT departments include a *technology* office that investigates new information systems technologies and determines how the organization can benefit from them. For example, today many organizations are investigating

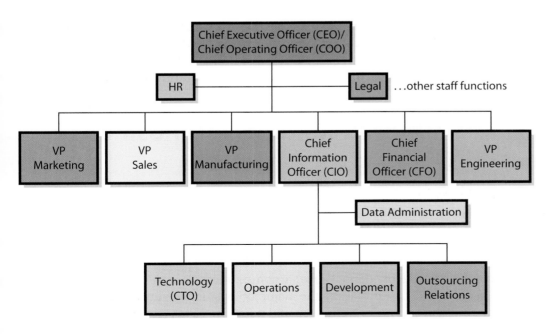

Figure 11-1
Typical Senior-Level
Reporting Relationships

Web services technology and planning on how they can best use that technology to accomplish their goals and objectives. An individual called the **chief technology officer (CTO)** often heads the technology group. The CTO sorts through new ideas and products to identify those that are most relevant to the organization. The CTO's job requires deep knowledge of information technology and the ability to envision how new IT will affect the organization over time.

The next group in Figure 11-1, *operations*, manages the computing infrastructure, including individual computers, computer centers, networks, and communications media. This group includes system and network administrators. As you will learn, an important function for this group is to monitor user experience and respond to user problems.

The third group in the IT department in Figure 10-1 is *development*. This group manages the process of creating new information systems as well as maintaining existing information systems. (Recall from Chapter 10 that in the context of information systems, maintenance means either removing problems or adapting existing information systems to support new features and functions.)

The size and structure of the development group depends on whether programs are developed in-house. If not, this department will be staffed primarily by systems analysts who work with users, operations, and vendors to acquire and install licensed software and to set up the system components around that software. If the organization develops programs in-house, then this department will include programmers, test engineers, technical writers, and other development personnel.

The last IT department group in Figure 11-1 is *outsourcing relations*. This group exists in organizations that have negotiated outsourcing agreements with other companies to provide equipment, applications, or other services. You will learn more about outsourcing later in this chapter.

Figure 11-1 also includes a *data administration* staff function. The purpose of this group is to protect data and information assets by establishing data standards and data management practices and policies.

There are many variations on the structure of the IT department shown in Figure 11-1. In larger organizations, the operations group may itself consist of several different departments. Sometimes, there is a separate group for data warehousing and data marts.

As you examine Figure 11-1, keep the distinction between IS and IT in mind. Information systems (IS) exist to help the organization achieve its goals and objectives. Information systems have the five components we have discussed throughout this text. Information technology (IT) is just technology. It concerns the products, techniques, procedures, and designs of computer-based technology. IT must be placed into the structure of an IS before an organization can use it.

Q4 What IS-Related Job Positions Exist?

The IS industry has a wide range of interesting and well-paying jobs. Many students enter the MIS class thinking that the IS industry consists only of programmers and computer technicians. If you reflect on the five components of an information system, you can understand why this cannot be true. The data, procedure, and people components of an information system require professionals with highly developed interpersonal communications skills.

Figure 11-2 summarizes the major job positions in the IS industry. With the exception of computer technician and possibly of PQA test engineer, all of these

Title	Responsibilities	Knowledge, Skill, and Characteristics Requirements	2006 U.S. Salary Range (USD)
System analyst	Work with users to determine system requirements, design and develop job descriptions and procedures, help determine system test plans.	Strong interpersonal and communications skills. Knowledge of both business and technology. Adaptable.	$65,000–$150,000
Programmer	Design and write computer programs.	Logical thinking and design skills, knowledge of one or more programming languages.	$50,000–$150,000
PQA test engineer	Develop test plans, design and write automated test scripts, perform testing.	Logical thinking, basic programming, superb organizational skills, eye for detail.	$40,000–$95,000
Technical writer	Write program documentation, help-text, procedures, job descriptions, training materials.	Quick learner, clear writing skills, high verbal communications skills.	$40,000–$95,000
User support representative	Help users solve problems, provide training.	Communications and people skills. Product knowledge. Patience.	$40,000–$65,000
Computer technician	Install software, repair computer equipment and networks.	Associate degree, diagnostic skills.	$30,000–$65,000
Network administrator	Monitor, maintain, fix, and tune computer networks.	Diagnostic skills, in-depth knowledge of communications technologies and products.	$65,000–$150,000+
Consultant	Wide range of activities: programming, testing, database design, communications and networks, project management, security and risk management, strategic planning.	Quick learner, entrepreneurial attitude, communications and people skills. Respond well to pressure. Particular knowledge depends on work.	From $35 per hour for a contract tester to more than $500 per hour for strategic consulting to executive group.
Salesperson	Sell software, network, communications, and consulting services.	Quick learner, knowledge of product, superb professional sales skills.	$65,000–$200,000+
Small-scale project manager	Initiate, plan, manage, monitor, and close down projects.	Management and people skills, technology knowledge. Highly organized.	$75,000–$150,000
Large-scale project manager	Initiate, plan, monitor, and close down complex projects.	Executive and management skills. Deep project management knowledge.	$150,000–$250,000+
Database administrator	Manage and protect database (see Chapter 12).	Diplomatic skills, database technology knowledge.	$75,000–$200,000
Chief technology officer (CTO)	Advise CIO, executive group, and project managers on emerging technologies.	Quick learner, good communication skills, deep knowledge of IT.	$125,000–$250,000+
Chief information officer (CIO)	Manage IT department, communicate with executive staff on IT- and IS-related matters. Member of the executive group.	Superb management skills, deep knowledge of business, and good business judgment. Good communicator. Balanced and unflappable.	$150,000–$300,000, plus executive benefits and privileges

Figure 11-2
Job Positions in the Information Systems Industry

Jumping Aboard the Bulldozer

A recent popular theme in the media is how overseas outsourcing is destroying the U.S. labor market. The "jobless recovery" is how it's headlined. However, a closer look reveals that overseas outsourcing is not the culprit. First, Brainard and Litan cite research that indicates that organizations will move about 250,000 jobs per year overseas between now and 2015.[1] Although that may sound like a lot, in the context of the 137 million U.S. workers, and in the context of the 15 million Americans who lose their jobs due to other factors, 250,000 jobs overseas is not much.

The culprit—if culprit is the right word—is not overseas outsourcing; it is productivity. Because of information technology, Moore's Law, and all the information systems that you have learned about in this book, worker productivity continues to increase, and it is possible to have an economic recovery without a binge of new hiring.

The Austrian economist Joseph Schumpeter called such processes "creative destruction" and said that they are the cleansers of the free market.[2] Economic processes operate to remove unneeded jobs, companies, and even industries, and thereby keep the economy growing and prospering. In fact, the lack of such processes hindered the growth of Japan and some European nations in the 1990s.

(By the way, there's a historical irony here because creative destruction gave rise to one of the first information systems. This system consisted of a group of human "calculators" who were employed by the French in the 1790s to compute scientific tables for the then-new metric system. According to Ken Alder, the human calculators were wigmakers, made unemployed by the French Revolution.[3] The guillotine not only reduced the size of the market for wigs, but also made aristocratic hairstyles less popular. And so wigmakers became human calculators.)

This idea of creative destruction is all well and good for an economic theory, but what do you, as a student in the first decade of the twenty-first century, do? How do you respond to the dynamics of shifting work and job movements? You can take a lesson from the railroads in the 1930s. They were blindsided by air transportation. In a now-classic marketing blunder, the railroads perceived themselves as purveyors of railroad transportation instead of purveyors of transportation more generally. The railroads were well positioned to take advantage of air transportation, but they did nothing and were overtaken by the new airline companies.

How does this apply to you? As you have learned, MIS is the development and use of information systems that enable organizations to achieve their goals and objectives. When you work with information systems, you are not a professional of a particular system or technology; rather, you are a developer or

---

[1] Lial Brainard and Robert Litan, "Services Offshoring Bane or Bone and What to Do?" *CESifo Forum*, Summer 2004, Vol. 5, Issue 2, p. 307.

[2] Joseph Schumpeter, *Capitalism, Socialism, and Democracy* (New York: Harper, 1975), pp. 82–85.

[3] Ken Alder, *The Measure of All Things* (New York: The Free Press, 2002), p. 142.

user of a system that helps your organization achieve its goals and objectives.

Suppose, for example, you work with an EDI-based purchasing information system. If you view yourself as an expert in EDI, then you are doomed, because EDI will be supplanted by XML, as you learned in Chapter Extension 13, "Information Technology for Data Exchange: EDI and XML" (page 473). Are you better off to define yourself as an expert in XML? No, because XML will someday be replaced with something else. Writing XML schemas is work that can easily be moved offshore. Instead, define yourself more generally as someone who specializes in the use of EDI or XML or Gizmo 3.0 to help your business achieve its goals and objectives.

From this perspective, the technology you learned in this class can help you start your career. If IS-based productivity is the bulldozer that is mowing down traditional jobs, then use what you have learned here to jump aboard that bulldozer. Not as a technologist, but as a business professional who can determine how best to use that bulldozer to enhance your career.

In the case of purchasing, learn something about XML and apply that knowledge to gain employment in a company that uses XML to accomplish its goals and objectives. But realize that XML only helps you get that job; it just gets you started. Your long-term success depends not on your knowledge of XML, but rather on your ability to think, to solve problems, and to use technology and information systems to help your organization achieve its goals and objectives.

DISCUSSION QUESTIONS

1. Describe five ways that the overseas outsourcing problem is overstated.

2. Summarize the argument that the "culprit" is not overseas outsourcing, but rather productivity.

3. Why is it incorrect to consider productivity as a culprit?

4. Explain the phenomenon of creative destruction.

5. Why are your career prospects doomed if you define yourself as an expert in EDI? In XML? How should you define yourself?

6. Apply the line of reasoning you used in your answer to question 5 to some other technology or system. Use IPv6, CRM, SCM, decision trees, or some other technology.

7. Explain how you can use one of the technologies in question 6 to help you start your career. To be successful, what perspective must you then maintain?

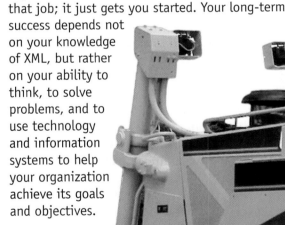

KP200557

positions require a four-year degree. Furthermore, with the exception of programmer and PQA test engineer, all of these positions require business knowledge. In most cases, successful professionals have a degree in business. Note, too, that most positions require good verbal and written communications skills. Business, including information systems, is a social activity.

Many of the positions in Figure 11-2 have a wide salary range. Lower salaries are for professionals with limited experience, or for those who work in smaller companies or work on small projects. The larger salaries are for those with deep knowledge and experience who work for large companies on large projects. Do not expect to begin your career at the high end of these ranges. As noted, all salaries are for positions in the United States and are shown in U.S. dollars.

In the nearly 40 years of my career, I have worked as a systems analyst, programmer, small- and large-scale project manager, consultant, and chief technology officer (CTO). It's been great fun, and the industry becomes more and more interesting each year. Give these careers some thought. Keep in mind that the changing nature of technology—and of business generally—will demand that you remain agile, as the *Guide* on pages 263a–263b discusses.

By the way, for all but the most technical positions, knowledge of a business specialty can add to your marketability. If you have the time, a dual major can be an excellent choice. Popular and successful dual majors are: accounting and information systems, marketing and information systems, and management and information systems.

Q5 How Do Organizations Decide How Much to Spend on IT?

Information systems and information technology are expensive. Consequently, organizations need to address the investment in IS and IT in the same way that they address investments in plant, inventories, or any other substantial project. Typically, decisions to invest in any business project involve an analysis of the costs and benefits. Chapter Extension 21, "Financing and Accounting for IT Projects," describes some of the common techniques.

All such techniques require estimates of the costs and benefits of the project. However, to compare costs to benefits, both the costs and benefits need to be expressed in dollars, or other currency. Estimating dollar costs of IS or IT projects is not more difficult than estimating them for other projects. The difficulty arises when attempting to place a dollar value on benefits.

For example, what is the dollar value of an email system? Employees require access to email in order to do any work. Asking the dollar value of the email system is like asking the dollar value of the restroom. How can you compute it?

Other value computations are difficult, but possible. For example, if a customer support information system reduces the likelihood of losing a customer, then the value of that system can be computed by multiplying the probability of loss times the lifetime value of that customer. Or, if an information system enables customer support representatives to service customers 10 percent faster, then the dollar value of that system is 10 percent of the anticipated customer support costs.

Most IS and IT investment analyses divide benefits into tangible and intangible. **Tangible benefits** are those for which a dollar value can be computed. Reducing customer support costs by 10 percent is a tangible benefit. **Intangible benefits** are those for which it is impossible to compute a dollar value. The benefits of the email system are intangible.

One common method for justifying IS and IT projects is to compute the costs and tangible benefits of the system and to perform a financial analysis. If the project can be justified on tangible benefits alone, then the favorable decision is made. If it cannot be justified on the basis of tangible benefits, then the intangible benefits are considered, and a subjective decision is made as to whether or not the intangibles are sufficiently valuable to overcome the missing tangible benefits that would be required.

You can learn more about these techniques in Chapter Extension 21, "Financing and Accounting for IT Projects."

Q6 What Are Your Rights and Responsibilities?

We conclude this chapter with a summary of your rights and responsibilities with regard to the IT department. The items in Figure 11-3 list what you are entitled to receive and indicate what you are expected to contribute.

Your Rights

You have a right to have the computing resources you need to perform your work as proficiently as you want. You have a right to the computer hardware and programs that you need. If you process huge files for data-mining applications, you have a right to the huge disks and the fast processor that you need. However, if you merely receive email and consult the corporate Web portal, then your right is for more modest requirements (leaving the more powerful resources for those in the organization who need them).

You have a right to reliable network and Internet services. Reliable means that you can process without problems almost all of the time. It means that you never go to work wondering, "Will the network be available today?" Network problems should be a rare occurrence.

You also have a right to a secure computing environment. The organization should protect your computer and its files, and you should not normally even need to think about security. From time to time, the organization may ask you to take

Figure 11-3
User Information Systems Rights and Responsibilities

You have a right to:
- Computer hardware and programs that allow you to perform your job proficiently
- Reliable network and Internet connections
- A secure computing environment
- Protection from viruses, worms, and other threats
- Contribute to requirements for new system features and functions
- Reliable systems development and maintenance
- Prompt attention to problems, concerns, and complaints
- Properly prioritized problem fixes and resolutions
- Effective training

You have a responsibility to:
- Learn basic computer skills
- Learn standard techniques and procedures for the applications you use
- Follow security and backup procedures
- Protect your password(s)
- Use computer resources according to your employer's computer-use policy
- Make no unauthorized hardware modifications
- Install only authorized programs
- Apply software patches and fixes when directed to do so
- When asked, devote the time required to respond carefully and completely to requests for requirements for new system features and functions
- Avoid reporting trivial problems

Using the Corporate Computer

uppose you work at a company that has the following computer-use policy:

Computers, email, and the Internet are to be used primarily for official company business. Small amounts of personal email can be exchanged with friends and family, and occasional usage of the Internet is permitted, but such usage should be limited and never interfere with your work.

Suppose you are a manager, and you learn that one of your employees has been engaged in the following activities:

1. Playing computer games during work hours
2. Playing computer games on the company computer before and after work hours
3. Responding to emails from an ill parent
4. Watching DVDs during lunch and other breaks
5. Sending emails to plan a party that involves mostly people from work
6. Sending emails to plan a party that involves no one from work
7. Searching the Web for a new car
8. Reading the news on CNN.com
9. Checking the stock market over the Internet
10. Bidding on items for personal use on eBay
11. Selling personal items on eBay
12. Paying personal bills online
13. Paying personal bills online when traveling on company business
14. Buying an airplane ticket for an ill parent over the Internet
15. Changing the content of a personal Web site
16. Changing the content of a personal business Web site
17. Buying an airplane ticket for a personal vacation over the Internet

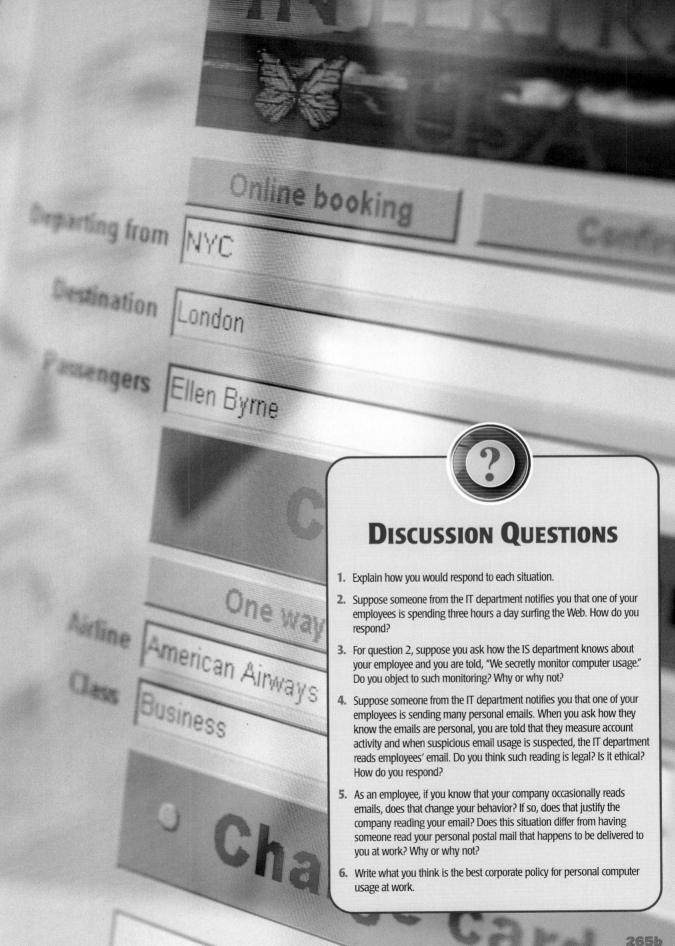

Online booking

Departing from NYC

Destination London

Passengers Ellen Byrne

One way

Airline American Airways

Class Business

Confirm

DISCUSSION QUESTIONS

1. Explain how you would respond to each situation.

2. Suppose someone from the IT department notifies you that one of your employees is spending three hours a day surfing the Web. How do you respond?

3. For question 2, suppose you ask how the IS department knows about your employee and you are told, "We secretly monitor computer usage." Do you object to such monitoring? Why or why not?

4. Suppose someone from the IT department notifies you that one of your employees is sending many personal emails. When you ask how they know the emails are personal, you are told that they measure account activity and when suspicious email usage is suspected, the IT department reads employees' email. Do you think such reading is legal? Is it ethical? How do you respond?

5. As an employee, if you know that your company occasionally reads emails, does that change your behavior? If so, does that justify the company reading your email? Does this situation differ from having someone read your personal postal mail that happens to be delivered to you at work? Why or why not?

6. Write what you think is the best corporate policy for personal computer usage at work.

particular actions to protect your computer and files, and you should take those actions. But such requests should be rare and related to specific outside threats.

You have a right to participate in requirements meetings for new applications that you will use and for major changes to applications that you currently use. You may choose to delegate this right to others, or your department may delegate that right for you, but if so, you have a right to contribute your thoughts through that delegate.

You have a right to reliable systems development and maintenance. Although schedule slippages of a month or two are common in many development projects, you should not have to endure schedule slippages of six months or more. Such slippages are evidence of incompetent systems development.

Additionally, you have a right to receive prompt attention to your problems, concerns, and complaints about information services. You have a right to have a means to report problems, and you have a right to know that your problem has been received and at least registered with the IT department. You have a right to have your problem resolved, consistent with established priorities. This means that an annoying problem that allows you to conduct your work will be prioritized below another's problem that interferes with his or her ability to do the job.

Finally, you have a right to effective training. It should be training that you can understand and that enables you to use systems to perform your particular job. The organization should provide training in a format and on a schedule that is convenient to you.

Your Responsibilities

You also have responsibilities toward the IT department and your organization. Specifically, you have a responsibility to learn basic computer skills and to learn the basic techniques and procedures for the applications you use. You should not expect hand-holding for basic operations. Nor should you expect to receive repetitive training and support for the same issue.

You have a responsibility to follow security and backup procedures. This is especially important because actions that you fail to take may cause problems for your fellow employees and your organization as well as for you. In particular, you are responsible for protecting your password(s). In the next chapter, you will learn that this is important not only to protect your computer, but, because of intersystem authentication, it is important to protect your organization's networks and databases as well.

You have a responsibility for using your computer resources in a manner that is consistent with your employer's policy. Many employers allow limited email for critical family matters while at work, but discourage frequent and long casual email. You have a responsibility to know your employer's policy and to follow it. See the *Ethics Guide* on pages 265a–265b for additional discussions on computer-use policy.

You also have a responsibility to make no unauthorized hardware modifications to your computer and to install only authorized programs. One reason for this policy is that your IT department constructs automated maintenance programs for upgrading your computer. Unauthorized hardware and programs may interfere with these programs. Additionally, the installation of unauthorized hardware or programs can cause you problems that the IT department will have to fix.

You have a responsibility to install computer patches and fixes when asked to do so. This is particularly important for patches that concern security and backup and recovery. When asked for input to requirements for new and adapted systems, you have a responsibility to take the time necessary to provide thoughtful and complete responses. If you do not have that time, you should delegate your input to someone else.

Finally, you have a responsibility to treat information systems professionals professionally. Everyone works for the same company, everyone wants to succeed, and professionalism and courtesy will go a long way on all sides. One form of professional behavior is to learn basic skills so that you avoid reporting trivial problems.

How does the knowledge in this chapter help you at Emerson or DSI?

We have already discussed how you, in Dee's position, could use the knowledge in this chapter. By understanding the need for the IT department to protect the network infrastructure, you would be sensitive to the problem of allowing non-employees to work within the network. You might suggest alternatives, such as having your consultant develop the software on his computer and then having the IT department install it on its network. You might also hire a consultant who is bonded or who can provide some other form of assurance or insurance to the IT department.

The situation at DSI is puzzling; the IT department consists of one employee. Recall the four primary responsibilities for an IT department, and consider that DSI is a $50-million-plus company. The IT job would seem too large for one individual to perform. Either (a) the sole IT person works 200 hours a week, or (b) users are performing some of the IT department's work, or (c) some tasks are not being done.

Clearly, the first is impossible, so either the users are performing the IT department's function or work is not being done. As you learned in Q1, the IT department has four major functions: plan (align), create and develop, operate and maintain, and protect. DSI runs successfully, so the operate-and-maintain function must be adequate, at least as far as the infrastructure is concerned. DSI uses only licensed software, so there is no need for in-house software development and testing.

However, systems that use only licensed software still require project management. One individual cannot perform that task, so users must be doing much of it. Similarly, the sole person cannot be doing much planning. He seemed to be a technically oriented person, one who repairs hardware and installs network gear, so he probably does not have the interest or background to think about strategic uses of IT. Possibly, the DSI partners perform that function themselves.

Most likely, the protect function either is not being performed or is not performed adequately. No one at DSI will know that they have inadequate protection until a crime, natural disaster, or other problem occurs. At that point, actions that should have been done will be visible. Considerable loss is likely. We will consider this topic further in the next chapter.

If you were the intern at DSI, you might realize that no one seems to be thinking strategically about the use of IS. The various proposals that you developed in Part 3 of this text might be very well received. At least it would be worth advocating them. You might even mention the IT functions and wonder whether it is possible for one person to perform all of them. You should use care, however, because such statements could be perceived as meddling or unwarranted criticism.

It is a delicate matter for you as an intern to raise the protection issue. You are a very junior, part-time person, who is under review for possible full-time employment. Your comments about inadequate security may not be appreciated. If my weight is endangering my health, I want my doctor, and not my summer intern, to tell me that. You might raise the possibility of improving security and then drop it if there is no positive response.

If you believe that DSI is not properly protecting its data, you should be careful about the data, especially personal data, you store on your work computer. Understand that it could find its way to a criminal by tomorrow.

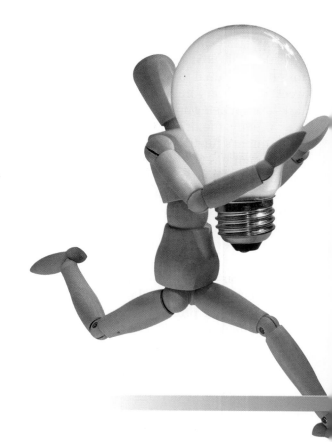

Active ? Review

Use this Active Review to verify that you understand the material in the chapter. You can read the entire chapter and then perform the tasks in this review, or you can read the material for just one question and perform the tasks in this review for that question before moving on to the next one.

Q1 Why do you need to know about the IT department?

Describe two reasons why you need to know about the IT department. Summarize why Dee needed to know. Give an example of a business initiative that involves IT support. Explain why knowing the functions of IT will help you develop that initiative.

Q2 What are the responsibilities of the IT department?

Name four responsibilities of the IT department. Briefly describe each.

Q3 How is the IT department organized?

Draw an organization chart for a typical IT department. Explain the functions of the CIO and the CTO. State reporting relationships of the IT department and the CIO.

Q4 What IS-related job positions exist?

Name positions in the IT department that do not require a four-year degree. Name positions that do not require substantial knowledge of business. State your conclusions from these observations. Select two positions in Figure 11-2 that have interest to you. Describe

what you think you could do to prepare yourself for these positions. Explain why a joint major of IS and another functional discipline may make sense.

Q5 How do organizations decide how much to spend on IT?

Explain the general principles that organizations uses for justifying investments in information technology. Explain the difference between tangible and intangible benefits. Describe the problem of intangible benefits and one way of assessing projects that cannot be justified on their tangible benefits.

Q6 What are your rights and responsibilities?

Using Figure 11-3 as a guide, summarize the rights you have with regard to information systems and technology. Summarize the responsibilities that you have toward the IT department as well.

How does the knowledge in this chapter help you at Emerson or DSI? Discuss why Emerson's IT department did not want nonemployees to work within the network. Describe alternatives you could suggest that would enable Dee to get her blog without ruffling feathers within the IT department. Explain why one person may not be enough to provide IT department functions at DSI. Discuss which IT department functions may not be adequately performed by the one-person "department."

Key Terms and Concepts

Agile enterprise 259
Chief information officer (CIO) 261
Chief technology officer (CTO) 262
Intangible benefit 264
Tangible benefit 264
Tuned 260

Using Your Knowledge

1. Explain Dee's mistake. Explain the mistake of her management. Describe what Dee should have done.

2. Explain how you can use the definition of the four major responsibilities of the IT department to bolster the proposal to develop one of the innovative

information systems you considered in Part 3. Suppose DSI chooses to develop one of those systems; explain how the new system will impact DSI's current IT personnel.

3. Read the Baker, Barker, and Bickel case in Chapter Extension 17, "Small-Scale Systems Development" (starting on page 519). If BBB decides to develop a joint property sales system, who will run it? Using the four functions of the IT department, describe potential problems that might arise for this system. In your opinion, what should BBB do about IT support if they decide to proceed?

4. Consider the information system that your university uses to schedule classes. List 10 benefits. For each, indicate whether it is a tangible or an intangible benefit. For the tangible benefits, briefly explain how you could compute their value. For the intangible ones, indicate why they are intangible.

5. Suppose you work for an organization that you believe does not adequately protect its data and IT assets. Assume you manage the telesales department and you have raised your concerns several times with your management, all to no avail. Describe how you would protect yourself and your department.

6. Suppose you represent an investor group that is acquiring hospitals across the nation and integrating them into a unified system. List five potential problems and risks concerning information systems. How do you think IS-related risks compare to other risks in such an acquisition program?

Case Study 11

Marriott International, Inc.

Marriott International, Inc., operates and franchises hotels and lodging facilities throughout the world. Its 2005 revenue was just over $11.5 billion. Marriott groups its business into segments according to lodging facility. Major business segments are full-service lodging, select-service lodging, extended-stay lodging, and timeshare properties. Marriott states that its three top corporate priorities are profitability, preference, and growth.

In the mid-1980s, the airlines developed the concept of *revenue management*, which adjusts prices in accordance with demand. The idea gained prominence in the airline industry, because an unoccupied seat represents revenue that is forever lost. Unlike a part in inventory, an unoccupied seat on today's flight cannot be sold tomorrow. Similarly, in the lodging industry, today's unoccupied hotel room cannot be sold tomorrow. So, for hotels, revenue management translates to raising prices on Monday when a convention is in town and lowering them on Saturday in the dead of winter when few travelers are in sight.

Marriott had developed two different revenue-management systems, one for its premium hotels and a second one for its lower-priced properties. It developed both of these systems using pre-Internet technology; systems upgrades required installing updates locally. The local updates were expensive and problematic. Also, the two systems required two separate interfaces for entering prices into the centralized reservation system.

In the late-1990s, Marriott embarked on a project to create a single revenue-management system that could be used by all of its properties. The new system, called OneSystem, was custom developed in-house, using a process similar to those you learned about in Chapter 10. The IT professionals understood the importance of user involvement, and they formed a joint IT–business user team that developed the business case for the new system and jointly managed its development. The team was careful to provide constant communication to the system's future users, and it used prototypes to identify problem areas early. Training is a continuing activity for all Marriott employees, and the company integrated training facilities into the new system.

OneSystem recommends prices for each room, given the day, date, current reservation levels, and history. Each hotel property has a revenue manager who can override these recommendations. Either way, the prices are communicated directly to the centralized reservation system. OneSystem uses Internet technology so that when the company makes upgrades to the system, it makes them only at the Web servers, not at the individual hotels. This strategy saves considerable maintenance cost, activity, and frustration.

OneSystem computes the theoretical maximum revenue for each property and compares actual results to that maximum. Using OneSystem, the company has increased the ratio of actual to theoretical revenue from 83 percent to 91 percent. That increase of 8 percentage points has translated into a substantial increase in revenues.

Source: Reprinted through the courtesy of CIO. Copyright 2005 CXO Media, Inc.

Questions

1. How does OneSystem contribute to Marriott's objectives?

2. What are the advantages of having one revenue-management system instead of two? Consider both users and the IT department in your answer.

3. At the same time it was developing OneSystem in-house, Marriott chose to outsource its human relations information system. (See Chapter Extension 20, "Outsourcing," on page 559.) Why would it choose to develop one system in-house but outsource the other? Consider the following factors in your answer.

   - Marriott's objectives
   - The nature of the systems
   - The uniqueness of each system to Marriott
   - Marriott's in-house expertise

4. How did outsourcing HR contribute to the success of OneSystem?

Emerson Pharmaceuticals and Dorset-Stratford Interiors, Chapter 11

GOALS

Use Dee's blog and Dorset-Stratford Interiors (DSI) to:

* Compare and contrast Emerson and DSI's IT departments.

* Explore the responsibilities of the IT department by pondering how DSI can be supported by a one-person department.

* Determine a better way to start Dee's blog project (use the knowledge of IT management).

BACKGROUND

1. *Warning:* The Emerson and DSI cases overlap Chapters 11 and 12. We consider both cases in Chapter 11 because comparing them brings out different aspects of IT management. That consideration, however, reveals security problems in both companies that are better addressed in Chapter 12. The danger is that the cases in this chapter will tend to pull you into discussing security now. For example, because Dee didn't know how to work with IT, she exposed the company to a serious security risk. It is probably cleanest just to identify that risk at the outset but explain that you will pick it up in the next chapter. Similarly, DSI is not staffing the "protect" function, which is creating security risks. Again, I recommend identifying that danger and picking it up again in Chapter 12.

2. Truly, the IT department at the company behind DSI consists of one person. Even more dramatic, the real company is larger than DSI ($120+ million in sales), with 300 employees. As stated in the text, the day I met the IT manager, he was sitting on the floor, repairing a computer. How does DSI succeed? I'm certain there are serious protection flaws at that company, though the CEO ran me off before I could explore them.

3. The lack of protection at DSI (I assume there is a lack, otherwise, how could one person be doing the IT department's job) is serious. The end of the chapter explores why it is delicate for the intern to bring it up. Probably it is fruitless for an intern to do. Most likely, DSI will not do anything about security planning until a disaster occurs. Again, one approach is

to identify this problem now and address it in the next chapter.

4. The chapter suggests that had Dee known something about IT management, she would have known better how to work with the IT department. This is true for two reasons: First, she would have known better how to approach them in the first place. Second, she would have known how serious it was for her to force IT to allow her consultant inside the network. I recommend saving the second reason for the next chapter.

HOW TO GET THE STUDENTS INVOLVED

1. Compare and contrast IT at DSI and IT at Emerson:

   a. How do the IT departments at DSI and Emerson differ?

   b. Can you explain this difference by the different sizes of the two organizations?

   c. Can you explain this difference by the different industries of the two organizations?

   d. Consider the four functions of IT. In what ways are these functions more difficult and challenging for Emerson than for DSI? Do these differences explain the different sizes of the two IT departments?

   e. How do you explain the differences in size?

2. Explore the DSI IT department's capabilities:

   a. How many employees are in the IT department at DSI?

   b. What do you think about that?

   c. What are the four functions of the IT department?

   d. How does one person do all of that for a company the size of DSI?

   e. What do you think is not getting done?

3. What should the intern do?

   a. Suppose you're the intern. Knowing what you know from Chapter 11, what would you do when you learn DSI has a one-person IT department?

   b. Chances are, little IT planning is done at DSI—at least little is done by the IT department. How does that create an opportunity for a non-IS business professional who knows something about IS?

   c. Given what you learned from Chapter 10, how do you suppose DSI develops new information systems?

d. Clearly, DSI has information systems. How must they be constructed? Who must run the projects?

e. How would having a solid knowledge of IT be particularly advantageous to you as an employee at DSI?

4. Consider a solution for DSI:

a. Does DSI have a problem? If so, what?

b. Suppose you, as an employee, not as a summer intern, were concerned about a one-person IT department. What should you do first?

(Contact the current IT manager and see if he thinks he has a problem.)

c. Suppose you manage the purchasing department at DSI. Would you be concerned about a one-man IT department? How?

d. If you manage purchasing, what would you do to compensate for the one-man IT department?

e. Do you think Mr. Dorset or Mr. Stratford think DSI has a problem?

f. From what we know of the two people, who would be more open to discussing the IT situation?

g. Suppose you, as the manager of purchasing, and with the support of the current IT manager, decide to approach Mr. Stratford about the need for a larger IT department. What would you say? Is the real issue the number of people, or is it something else?

h. What would you do if he ignored all that you said?

5. Consider Dee's project at Emerson:

a. How would knowledge of the functions of the IT department have helped Dee?

b. Part of Dee's problem was the way she started. She contacted someone in IT who happened to be known by one of Dee's friends. Whom should she have contacted in that department?

c. Had she contacted a more senior and professional person, how do you think Dee's results might have differed?

d. The IT department likely would have said that Dee's schedule was unrealistic. In what ways would it have been better for Dee to use the influence of her boss's boss to obtain a high priority for her project rather than to use that boss to bludgeon the IT department into allowing network access for her consultant

BOTTOM LINE

* Some IT functions can be ignored for a while, but lack of planning and security will be a problem in the long run.

* Knowing how the IT department is organized will help you know whom to contact for what services.

Using the Guide: Jumping Aboard the Bulldozer (page 263a)

GOAL

✱ Motivate students to use knowledge of IS and IT to create and *sustain* competitive professional advantages.

BACKGROUND AND PRESENTATION STRATEGIES

This guide is among the most important guides in the textbook. It may be *the* most important guide.

I like to emphasize the following two points in this guide:

➤ **Knowledge of information systems and information technology can provide a competitive professional advantage—to all businesspeople, not just IS majors. This advantage accrues to those who know how to apply IS in innovative ways in the organizations in which they work.**

But:

➤ **That competitive advantage is sustainable only if the students learn how to efficiently learn *new technology* and learn *new ways to apply that new technology* to emerging opportunities. What you know now will open the door, but what you learn in the future will keep that door, in fact the whole building, open to you.**

The seventeenth-century philosopher Baruch Spinoza wrote that happiness does not occur by living on a high level of existence (wealth, health, family, etc.), but rather it occurs by *moving from one level of existence to one that is perceived to be higher*. Similarly, sorrow is not life on a low level of existence, but movement from one level to another that is perceived to be lower. According to this theory, people with $50 million in net worth can be miserable if they believe their life is degrading; likewise, people with $100,000 in net worth can be exceedingly happy if they believe their life is improving.

Thus, Spinoza defined happiness as *movement*—in math terms, as the derivative—in an upward direction. He defined sorrow as movement, the derivative, in a downward direction.

Now, what does this have to do with information systems? A particular level of IS knowledge gives a business professional a certain level of competency. That level is *sustainable, however, only to the extent that the businessperson continues to learn, to think, to imagine* new applications and new opportunities. It is the derivative in one's knowledge that matters most. Without continuously learning, and continuously increasing one's ability to apply IS to new opportunities, the competitive advantage will erode. The true competitive advantage is thus not any particular level of knowledge, but an ability to increase one's level of knowledge. It is the movement, the derivative, in a positive direction.

In 1971, I was an expert, a true guru, on IBM Job Control Language (JCL):

```
//DD1 DD DSN=MYFILE,DISP=(NEW,KEEP),
  UNIT=2314,SPACE=(CYL,(2,3,10))
```

What good is that knowledge today? Or knowledge of the shortcut keys for the Wang word processor I once used? Or the knowledge I once had of Total, a popular DBMS product in 1975? It's *worthless* for solving any business problem today.

The great news, the *fantastic news*, is that the continual change in technology constantly *opens new opportunities*. The playing field is continually being releveled. The huge competitive advantage that Lotus once had in the spreadsheet market was wiped out by the emergence of GUI systems like the Macintosh. The huge competitive advantage that Microsoft Access had for Windows applications was wiped out by the emergence of the Web, which opened the door for languages like PHP and DBMS products like MySQL. Without technology change, IBM would still dominate the computer business; Bill Gates would be an aging systems engineer in an IBM office; Michael Dell would be watering golf courses; and thousands of incredibly bored clerks would punch computer cards.

Technological change is every ambitious person's friend. It is the *great equalizer*, the *marvelous opportunity creator*, the ultimate door opener. But this is true only for those who, to use the analogy of this guide, learn to jump aboard that bulldozer and use it creatively throughout their careers!

❓ SUGGESTED RESPONSES FOR DISCUSSION QUESTIONS

1. It's overstated because the 250,000 jobs lost per year is a small percentage of the 137 million U.S. workers.

2. Outsourcing does not impact a high percentage of U.S. jobs. Rather, it is increased productivity that

enables fewer people to accomplish more. The same level of output can be achieved with fewer people. The Web and email enable people to communicate not just faster and more conveniently, but it also reduces the amount of physical paper that needs to be produced, printed, and transported. More ideas are exchanged with fewer resources.

3. Productivity is not a "culprit"; rather, it enhances the material quality of everyone's life. It enables society to do more with less. Productivity makes existing means of operation obsolete; organizations must adapt to more efficient processes, or Schumpeter's creative destruction will clean them up and out.

4. Creative destruction occurs when economic factors remove organizations that have become inefficient. For example, Dell's direct-marketing model drove IBM to sell its personal computer business to Lenovo Group, Limited, a Chinese company. That acquisition will eliminate inefficient competitors in China, or if the acquisition was unwise, creative destruction will reduce or remove the Lenovo Group. However, creative destruction will occur only if the Chinese government allows capitalistic market forces to operate in China. If not, China will compete at a disadvantage on the world's markets, ultimately to its own disadvantage.

5. You should not define yourself in terms of a particular technology because those technologies will be replaced by others. Define yourself as someone who can use the latest interorganizational communications technology (whether that's EDI, XML, or Gizmo 3.0) to help your business achieve its goals and objectives. Find innovative ways to use that technology for supply chain management, for e-commerce, or for some other interorganizational communication problem. If your organization is a cost leader, find innovative ways to save costs with that technology. If your organization has a differentiation strategy, find innovative ways to differentiate your product or service with those technologies.

6. The principle is the same for each of these systems and technologies. Knowledge of the system or technology will open the door, but that door will stay open only as long as the business professional continues to learn new systems and technology and new applications of those systems and technology. Or, as one pundit put it, "In this business, you are never finished until you're finished."

7. I use the example of IPv6 from this list because most students think they'd have to be a real techie to use it to get an interesting job. Not so!

➤ **How could you use knowledge of IPv6 to obtain a job? Write a great paper on why IPv6 is going to be the greatest thing since sliced bread. Or, write a great paper on why IPv6 is not going to be the greatest thing since sliced bread.**

(Take the data communications class to learn more. Negotiate credit for the paper with the data communications professor, thus killing two birds with one stone.)

➤ **Google the Web and identify interesting vendors and companies that have a vested interest in IPv6. While writing the paper, email as many people in those companies as possible, claiming status as a student who's writing a paper and who has a few questions. Build your contact list. Write the paper. While writing it, think of opportunities in marketing, sales, customer support, training, installation, or other personal interest. Slant the paper toward those opportunities. Send the finished paper to every contact you've made while writing it. Follow up with email querying the people about what they thought of it. Be sure to talk about the paper in every job interview.**

(By the way, this is a good place to remind the students of the advantages of never plagiarizing *anything* from any source. The people to whom they send this report will be widely read in the literature. Any attempt at plagiarism will be quickly detected. This is a good habit to have in all cases, but especially here.)

I would be exceedingly surprised if students who seriously embarked upon this course of action did not have more job opportunities than they would ever imagine.

WRAP UP

➤ **If you have enjoyed any aspect of this class, you owe it to yourself to take more IS classes. The future belongs to people who can apply information systems to business in innovative ways!**

➤ **Even if you don't want to become an IS major, think about combining IS knowledge with your major. Take a few of our classes, and while you're taking them, keep thinking about innovative ways to apply what you're learning to your major area of study. Ask the professor for help with that agenda. See if you can do projects for credit that apply what you're learning in those classes to your major field of interest.**

➤ **And, most important, learn how to learn ways of applying IS to your business interests! And keep on learning!**

Using the Ethics Guide: Using the Corporate Computer *(page 265a)*

GOALS

* Evaluate the ethics of employee activities in terms of a particular computer-use policy.

* Forewarn students that employers have the right to monitor computer usage, and many do.

* Develop techniques for managing employees' computer use.

BACKGROUND AND PRESENTATION STRATEGIES

This discussion considers a specific computer-use policy. It also focuses on the student's role as a manager rather than as a computer user.

Many students use their computers in the classroom for email, Web surfing, and instant messaging. If that is the case in your classroom, you might consider the *following hoax*:

➤ **Did you know that the university monitors your use of its network? In fact, I receive a report after each class period on the emails you've sent, the Web sites you've visited, and the number of minutes you've spent in IM chat.**

➤ **Frankly, I'm a little shocked. The content of some of your emails is, well, embarrassing. . . . What is this world coming to, anyway?**

Pause. Let those statements settle in . . .

➤ **OK, those statements *are not true*, but they *could be at your job*. What do you think about that?**

* **If you choose to spend your time in class surfing the Web or chatting with friends, that's your choice. You're wasting your time and money, but that's your choice.**

* **However, if I were paying you to be here, if you were my employees, I'd want to know that you are actually engaged in accomplishing your job and not gossiping about your fellow employees with your sister-in-law across the state.**

➤ **How intrusive do you think an employer should be in making assessments about computer use?**

➤ **Suppose you manage a department and you suspect your employees are wasting time on their computers at work. What would you do?**

➤ **What do you think causes employees to waste time on their computers at work? Would they be wasting time staring out the window, if they did not have a computer?**

By the way, I disagree with that last justification. The Web, IM, email, and computer games are attractive, even addictive, in ways that staring out the window is not.

➤ **In theory at least, if employees have been given appropriate assignments, and if there is regular follow-up on employee progress on those assignments, then employees ought not to have time to waste on their computers. They should be so busy doing their work that there isn't time to surf or chat.**

➤ **This may be naïve, but excessive personal computer use is a symptom of poorly directed or poorly motivated employees. Put everyone in the right job, get them excited about what they're doing, follow up on their progress on a regular basis, and excessive personal computer use will not be a problem.**

➤ **Some senior managers will agree with that statement, too. So, if your department is known to have many employees excessively using their computers for personal work, that fact will reflect negatively on your management ability.**

On August 11, 2005, the blogger Michelle Malkin received a series of abusive, racist, and sexist emails in response to one of her blog entries. One of those exceedingly offensive emails was generated by a legal secretary from his desk at a law office in Los Angeles. The email system automatically generated a trailer that included the name of the law firm. Ms. Malkin posted the abusive email in its entirety, including the trailer with the firm's name, on her Web site. The law firm was inundated with criticism for its employee's behavior. The employee was promptly fired, but the public relations scandal continued to plague the firm for weeks.

➤ **If you managed that law firm, how would you have responded to this situation?**

 ### SUGGESTED RESPONSES FOR DISCUSSION QUESTIONS

1. This is a long list of situations. One approach is to ask the students to group the situations into categories according to the severity of the violation. Three pos-

sible categories are: *OK, Questionable,* and *Definitely Wrong*. I'd put the following in the *Definitely Wrong* category: situations a, f, g, k, l, and p. In the *OK* category, I'd put situations c, e, and m. I'd place all of the others in the *Questionable* category.

It will be interesting to see how your students respond to this!

2. If I was told that an employee was spending three hours a day on the Web, I'd evaluate that employee's recent performance. I'd find out what jobs the employee was supposed to have been doing and find out how well those jobs were done. Clearly, something's wrong. I'd talk with the employee. Perhaps this person is ready for new responsibilities; perhaps the employee has lost interest in work. I'd try to get to the root of the problem and make a change.

3. I personally find secret monitoring of employees computer use a bit creepy, but the employer *is* paying for the employees' time and for the equipment. I grant an employer's right to perform such monitoring. I think that the monitoring ought to be done in such a way, however, so as to minimize the intrusion on the employees' privacy. If someone is using the Web for personal business, neither I nor the company needs to know what sites were visited. Similarly, the company may monitor email, but the intrusion should be limited to the minimum possible needed to accomplish the company's goals.

4. It is certainly legal for companies to read employees' emails, and because the employer is paying for the employees' time and the computer and network equipment, I think it's ethical. When employees use their employer's equipment for personal use, I believe they give up any right to privacy. But, see the limitations stated for question 3.

5. I personally dislike a style of management that relies on the hammer of discovery to limit employees' misuse of computers. I'd prefer to manage by giving people work they want to do, by creating tight but not impossible schedules, by following up with them on

progress, and by focusing on what they *should be* doing rather than on what they *ought not* to be doing.

But, my management experience is limited to managing highly skilled, motivated, ambitious employees in the software business. When employees must spend hours performing dreary, repetitive work, the motivational situation is entirely different. I can see how the hammer might need to be used in those circumstances.

I think the postal mail situation is different. For one, postal mail uses few company resources. Also, an employee reading a single letter is different from an employee sending out hundreds of emails.

6. I like the policy at the start of the guide. One could say it should be more specific, but the problem with that is that employees will be able to say about some behavior, "Well, that's not on the list." I think the key phrase is *never interfere with your work*. One could strengthen that statement by specifically excluding the use of the computer for personal business. Some of the wording depends on other HR policies as well.

WRAP UP

➤ **As a future employee, be forewarned that employers have the right, both legally and ethically, to monitor your computer use. Many do.**

➤ **As a future manager, consider how you will deal with employees who are misusing their computer resources. Know the organization's official policy.**

➤ **Understand, too, that excessive personal computer use by your employees reflects negatively on your management ability.**

➤ **If possible, manage positively. Give the employees sufficient work that they will not have time to misuse computer resources. Follow up with schedules and deadlines. Make sure that missed schedules are not caused by computer misuse.**

12 Information Security Management

"One person?" That's what I asked myself when I met the one and only IT person at DSI. "How can one person perform the whole IT job for a $50-million-plus in sales company?" Dee's division of Emerson sells about $800 million per year and is supported by an IT department with 200 people. Divide sales by the number of IT personnel, and Emerson supports $4 million of revenue per IT person. DSI supports $50 million or so with one person. Is Emerson inefficient, or is something out of whack at DSI?

I commented to DSI's IT person, Chris, that he must be pretty busy.

"Not really," he said. "Oh, sometimes, if one of our servers fails. But, most of the time, I work fairly regular hours."

I learned that DSI develops no software in-house; it uses only licensed software. I also found that John Stratford employs directors and project managers that are IT self-sufficient. Apparently, the only support users want from DSI's IT department is reliable infrastructure. The company has a wired/wireless LAN with two servers. One supports sales and marketing and includes the DSI Web site; the other supports design, inventory, and manufacturing. Seemingly, as long as the servers work, the users are happy.

As stated at the end of Chapter 11, I would bet that something is falling through the cracks at DSI. How secure is the company's system? How well is its data protected? How well is the data backed-up? Is DSI prepared for a natural disaster like a flood or hurricane? What plan does it have to respond to a security incident?

As a summer intern, you probably cannot raise these issues yourself. But suppose that Mr. Stratford asked you about them. Or, suppose you work in accounting, and your boss asked you to help prepare for the annual audit. You know that security is part of that audit. What should DSI be doing about security? What are the risks, and what can the company do about them?

Optional Extensions for this chapter are CE22, "Managing Computer Security Risk," CE23, "SSL/TLS and https," and CE24, "Computer Crime and Forensics."

Study Questions

Q1 What are the sources and types of security threats?

Q2 What are the elements of a security program?

Q3 How can technical safeguards protect against security threats?

Q4 How can data safeguards protect against security threats?

Q5 How can human safeguards protect against security threats?

Q6 What is necessary for disaster preparedness?

Q7 How should organizations respond to security incidents?

How does the knowledge in this chapter help you at DSI?

Q1 What Are the Sources and Types of Security Threats?

We begin by describing security threats. We will first summarize the sources of threats and then describe specific problems that arise from each source.

Three sources of **security threats** are human error and mistakes, malicious human activity, and natural events and disasters.

Human errors and mistakes include accidental problems caused by both employees and nonemployees. An example is an employee who misunderstands operating procedures and accidentally deletes customer records. Another example is an employee who, in the course of backing up a database, inadvertently installs an old database on top of the current one. This category also includes poorly written application programs and poorly designed procedures. Finally, human errors and mistakes include physical accidents like driving a forklift through the wall of a computer room.

The second source of security problems is *malicious human activity*. This category includes employees and former employees who intentionally destroy data or other system components. It also includes both hackers who break into a system as well as virus and worm writers who infect computer systems. Malicious human activity also includes outside criminals who break into a system to steal for financial gain; it also includes terrorism.

Natural events and disasters are the third source of security problems. This category includes fires, floods, hurricanes, earthquakes, tsunamis, avalanches, and other acts of nature. Problems in this category include not only the initial loss of capability and service, but also losses stemming from actions to recover from the initial problem.

Figure 12-1 summarizes threats by type of problem and source. Five types of security problems are listed: unauthorized data disclosure, incorrect data modification, faulty service, denial of service, and loss of infrastructure. We will consider each type.

Figure 12-1
Security Threats

		Source		
		Human Error	**Malicious Activity**	**Natural Disasters**
Problem	**Unauthorized data disclosure**	Procedural mistakes	Pretexting Phishing Spoofing Sniffing Computer crime	Disclosure during recovery
	Incorrect data modification	Procedural mistakes Incorrect procedures Ineffective accounting controls System errors	Hacking Computer crime	Incorrect data recovery
	Faulty service	Procedural mistakes Development and installation errors	Computer crime Usurpation	Service improperly restored
	Denial of service	Accidents	DOS attacks	Service interruption
	Loss of infrastructure	Accidents	Theft Terrorist activity	Property loss

Unauthorized Data Disclosure

Unauthorized data disclosure can occur by human error when someone inadvertently releases data in violation of policy. An example at a university would be a new department administrator who posts student names, numbers, and grades in a public place, when the releasing of names and grades violates state law. Another example is employees who unknowingly or carelessly release proprietary data to competitors or to the media.

The popularity and efficacy of search engines has created another source of inadvertent disclosure. Employees who place restricted data on Web sites that can be reached by search engines may mistakenly publish proprietary or restricted data over the Web.

Of course, proprietary and personal data can also be released maliciously. **Pretexting** occurs when someone deceives by pretending to be someone else. A common scam involves a telephone caller who pretends to be from a credit card company and claims to be checking the validity of credit card numbers: "I'm checking your MasterCard number; it begins 5491. Can you verify the rest of the number?" All MasterCard numbers start with 5491; the caller is attempting to steal a valid number.

Phishing is a similar technique for obtaining unauthorized data that uses pretexting via email. The *phisher* pretends to be a legitimate company and sends an email requesting confidential data, such as account numbers, Social Security numbers, account passwords, and so forth. Phishing compromises legitimate brands and trademarks. *MIS in Use 12* (page 276) looks in more detail at some examples of phishing.

Spoofing is another term for someone pretending to be someone else. If you pretend to be your professor, you are spoofing your professor. **IP spoofing** occurs when an intruder uses another site's IP address as if it were that other site. **Email spoofing** is a synonym for phishing.

Sniffing is a technique for intercepting computer communications. With wired networks, sniffing requires a physical connection to the network. With wireless networks, no such connection is required: **Drive-by sniffers** simply take computers with wireless connections through an area and search for unprotected wireless networks. They can monitor and intercept wireless traffic at will. Even protected wireless networks are vulnerable, as you will learn. Spyware and adware are two other sniffing techniques discussed later in this chapter.

Other forms of computer crime include breaking into networks to steal data such as customer lists, product inventory data, employee data, and other proprietary and confidential data.

Finally, people may inadvertently disclose data during recovery from a natural disaster. Usually, during a recovery, everyone is so focused on restoring system capability that they ignore normal security safeguards. A request like "I need a copy of the customer database backup" will receive far less scrutiny during disaster recovery than at other times.

Incorrect Data Modification

The second problem category in Figure 12-1 is *incorrect data modification.* Examples include incorrectly increasing a customer's discount or incorrectly modifying an employee's salary, earned days of vacation, or annual bonus. Other examples include placing incorrect information, such as incorrect price changes, on the company's Web site or company portal.

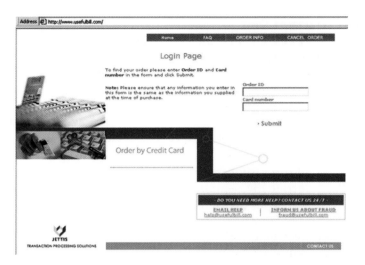

Figure 2
Fake Phishing Screen

Phishing for Credit Card Accounts

Before you read further, realize that the graphics in this case are fake. They were not produced by a legitimate business, but were generated by a phisher. A *phisher* is an operation that spoofs legitimate companies in an attempt to illegally capture credit card numbers, email accounts, driver's license numbers, and other data. Some phishers even install malicious program code on users' computers.

Phishing is usually initiated via an email. Go to *www.fraudwatchinternational.com/internet/phishing.shtml*, and page down two screens. You will see an example that appears to be an email message from PayPal. It fact, that message is a fake. To see even more examples, follow the five-step tour displayed on that site.

The most common phishing attack is initiated with a bogus email. For example, you might receive the email shown in Figure 1.

This bogus email is designed to cause you to click on the "See more details here" link. When you do so, you will be connected to a site that will ask you for personal data, such as credit card numbers, card

expiration dates, driver's license number, Social Security number, or other data. In this particular case, you will be taken to a screen that asks for your credit card number (see Figure 2).

This Web page is produced by a nonexistent company and is entirely fake, including the link "Inform us about fraud." The only purpose of this site is to illegally capture your card number. It might also install spyware, adware, or other malware (see page 281) on your computer.

If you were to get this far, you should immediately close your browser and restart your computer. You should also run anti-malware scans on your computer to determine if the phisher has installed program code on your computer. If so, use the anti-malware software to remove that code.

How can you defend yourself from such attacks? First, you know that you did not purchase two first class tickets to Cozumel. (Had you by odd circumstance just purchased airline tickets to Cozumel, you should contact the legitimate vendor's site *directly* to determine if there had been some mix up.) Because you have not purchased such tickets, suspect a phisher.

Second, notice the implausibility of the email. It is exceedingly unlikely that you can buy two first-class tickets to any foreign country for $349. Additionally, note the misspelled word and the poor grammar ("cortact with us"). All of these facts should alert you to the bogus nature of this email.

Third, do not be misled by legitimate-looking graphics. Phishers are criminals; they do not bother to respect international agreements on legitimate use of trademarks. The phisher might use names of legiti-

---

Your Order ID: "17152492"
Order Date: "09/07/07"
Product Purchased: "Two First Class Tickets to Cozumel"
Your card type: "CREDIT"
Total Price: "$349.00"

Hello, when you purchased your tickets you provided an incorrect mailing address.
See more details here
Please follow the link and modify your mailing address or cancel your order. If you have questions, feel free to cortact with us account@usefulbill.com

Figure 1
Fake Phishing Email

mate companies like Visa, MasterCard, Discover, and AmericanExpress on the Web page, and the presence of those names might lull you into thinking this is legitimate. The phisher is illegally using those names. In other instances, the phisher will copy the entire look and feel of a legitimate company's Web site.

Phishing is a serious problem. To protect yourself, be wary of unsolicited email, even if the email appears to be from a legitimate business. If you have questions about an email, contact the company directly (*not* using the addresses provided by the phisher!) and ask about the email. And above all, never give confidential data such as account numbers, Social Security numbers, driver's license numbers, or credit card numbers in response to any *unsolicited* email.

The discussion of phishing is continued in Case Study 12, page 295.

Incorrect data modification can occur through human error when employees follow procedures incorrectly or when procedures have been incorrectly designed. For proper internal control on systems that process financial data or that control inventories of assets like products and equipment, companies should ensure separation of duties and authorities and have multiple checks and balances in place.

A final type of incorrect data modification caused by human error includes *system errors*. An example is the lost-update problem discussed in Chapter 5 (pages 104–105).

Hacking occurs when a person gains unauthorized access to a computer system. Although some people hack for the sheer joy of doing it, other hackers invade systems for the malicious purpose of stealing or modifying data. Computer criminals invade computer networks to obtain critical data or to manipulate the system for financial gain. Examples are reducing account balances or causing the shipment of goods to unauthorized locations and customers.

Finally, faulty recovery actions after a disaster can result in incorrect data changes. The faulty actions can be unintentional or malicious.

Faulty Service

The third problem category, *faulty service*, includes problems that result because of incorrect system operation. Faulty service could include incorrect data modification, as just described. It also could include systems that work incorrectly by sending the wrong goods to the customer or the ordered goods to the wrong customer, incorrectly billing customers, or sending the wrong information to employees. Humans can inadvertently cause faulty service by making procedural mistakes. System developers can write programs incorrectly or make errors during the installation of hardware, software programs, and data.

Usurpation occurs when unauthorized programs invade a computer system and replace legitimate programs. Such unauthorized programs typically shut down the legitimate system and substitute their own processing. Faulty service can also result from mistakes made during the recovery from natural disasters.

Denial of Service

Human error in following procedures or a lack of procedures can result in **denial of service (DOS)**. For example, humans can inadvertently shut down a Web server or corporate gateway router by starting a computationally intensive application. An OLAP application that uses the operational DBMS can consume so many DBMS resources that order-entry transactions cannot get through.

Denial-of-service attacks can be launched maliciously. A malicious hacker can flood a Web server, for example, with millions of bogus service requests that so occupy the server that it cannot service legitimate requests. As you learned in Chapter 4 (page 84), computer worms can infiltrate a network with so much artificial traffic that legitimate traffic cannot get through. Finally, natural disasters may cause systems to fail, resulting in denial of service.

Loss of Infrastructure

Human accidents can cause *loss of infrastructure*. Examples are a bulldozer cutting a conduit of fiber-optic cables and the floor buffer crashing into a rack of Web servers.

Theft and terrorist events also cause loss of infrastructure. A disgruntled, terminated employee can walk off with corporate data servers, routers, or other crucial equipment. Terrorist events can also cause the loss of physical plants and equipment.

Natural disasters present the largest risk for infrastructure loss. A fire, flood, earthquake, or similar event can destroy data centers and all they contain. The devastation of the Indian Ocean tsunami in December 2004 and of hurricanes Katrina and Rita in the fall of 2005 are potent examples of the risks to infrastructure from natural causes.

You may be wondering why Figure 12-1 does not include viruses, worms, and Trojan horses. The answer is that viruses, worms, and Trojan horses are *techniques* for causing some of the problems in the figure. They can cause a denial-of-service attack, or they can be used to cause malicious, unauthorized data access, or data loss.

Q2 What Are the Elements of a Security Program?

All of the problems listed in Figure 12-1 are real and as serious as they sound. Accordingly, organizations must address security in a systematic way. A security program[1] has three components: senior management involvement, safeguards of various kinds, and incident response.

The first component, senior management, has two critical security functions: First, senior management must establish the security policy. This policy sets the stage for the organization's response to security threats. However, because no security program is perfect, there is always risk. Management's second function, therefore, is to manage risk by balancing the costs and benefits of the security program. See Chapter Extension 22, "Managing Computer Security Risk" (page 579), for more information on management's role.

Safeguards are protections against security threats. A good way to view safeguards is in terms of the five components of an information system, as shown in Figure 12-2. Some of the safeguards involve computer hardware and software. Some involve data; others involve procedures and people. In addition to these safeguards, organizations must also consider disaster recovery safeguards. An effective security program consists of a balance of safeguards of all these types.

---

[1]Note the word *program* is used here in the sense of a management program that includes objectives, policies, procedures, directives, and so forth. Do not confuse this term with a *computer program*.

Hardware	Software	Data	Procedures	People

Technical Safeguards	Data Safeguards	Human Safeguards
Identification and authorization Encryption Firewalls Malware protection Application design	Data rights and responsibilities Passwords Encryption Backup and recovery Physical security	Hiring Training Education Procedure design Administration Assessment Compliance Accountability

Effective security requires balanced attention to all five components!

Figure 12-2
Security Safeguards as They Relate to the Five Components

The final component of a security program consists of the organization's planned response to security incidents. Clearly, the time to think about what to do is not when the computers are crashing all around the organization. We will discuss incident response in the last section of this chapter.

Q3 How Can Technical Safeguards Protect Against Security Threats?

Technical safeguards involve the hardware and software components of an information system. Figure 12-3 lists primary technical safeguards. We have discussed all of these in prior chapters. Here we will just supplement those prior discussions.

Identification and Authentication

Every information system today should require users to sign on with a user name and password. The user name *identifies* the user (the process of **identification**), and the password *authenticates* that user (the process of **authentication**). Review the material on strong passwords and password etiquette in Chapter 1 (pages 13–14) if you have forgotten that discussion.

Passwords have important weaknesses. For one, users tend to be careless in their use. Despite repeated warnings to the contrary, yellow sticky notes holding written passwords adorn many computers. In addition, users tend to be free in

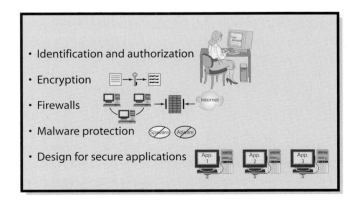

Figure 12-3
Technical Safeguards

sharing their passwords with others. Finally, many users choose ineffective, simple passwords. With such passwords, intrusion systems can very effectively guess passwords.

These deficiencies can be reduced or eliminated using smart cards and biometric authentication.

Smart Cards

A **smart card** is a plastic card similar to a credit card. Unlike credit, debit, and ATM cards, which have a magnetic strip, smart cards have a microchip. The microchip, which holds far more data than a magnetic strip, is loaded with identifying data. Users of smart cards are required to enter a **personal identification number (PIN)** to be authenticated.

Biometric Authentication

Biometric authentication uses personal physical characteristics such as fingerprints, facial features, and retinal scans to authenticate users. Biometric authentication provides strong authentication, but the required equipment is expensive. Often, too, users resist biometric identification because they feel it is invasive.

Biometric authentication is in the early stages of adoption. Because of its strength, it likely will see increased usage in the future. It is also likely that legislators will pass laws governing the use, storage, and protection requirements for biometric data. For more on biometrics, see *searchsecurity.techtarget.com*.

Note that authentication methods fall into three categories: what you know (password or PIN), what you have (smart card), and what you are (biometric).

Single Sign-on for Multiple Systems

Information systems often require multiple sources of authentication. For example, when you sign on to your personal computer, you need to be authenticated. When you access the LAN in your department, you need to be authenticated again. When you traverse your organization's WAN, you will need to be authenticated to even more networks. Also, if your request requires database data, the DBMS server that manages that database will authenticate you yet again.

It would be annoying to enter a name and password for every one of these resources. You might have to use and remember five or six different passwords just to access the data you need to perform your job. It would be equally undesirable to send your password across all of these networks. The further your password travels, the greater the risk it can be compromised.

Instead, today's operating systems have the capability to authenticate you to networks and other servers. You sign on to your local computer and provide authentication data; from that point on, your operating system authenticates you to another network or server, which can authenticate you to yet another network and server, and so forth.

Encryption and Firewalls

The next two categories of technical safeguards in Figure 12-3 are encryption and firewalls. They were described in Chapter 6, on pages 128–129, respectively. We will not repeat that discussion here. Just realize that they are very important technical safeguards.

Malware Protection

The next technical safeguard in our list in Figure 12-3 is malware. The term **malware** has several definitions. Here we will use the broadest one: *malware* is viruses, worms, Trojan horses, spyware, and adware. We discussed viruses, worms, and Trojan horses in Chapter 4 (pages 82–85); you should review that material now if you have forgotten their definitions.

Spyware and Adware

Spyware programs are installed on the user's computer without the user's knowledge or permission. Spyware resides in the background and, unknown to the user, observes the user's actions and keystrokes, monitors computer activity, and reports the user's activities to sponsoring organizations. Some malicious spyware captures keystrokes to obtain user names, passwords, account numbers, and other sensitive information. Other spyware supports marketing analyses, observing what users do, Web sites visited, products examined and purchased, and so forth.

   Adware is similar to spyware in that it is installed without the user's permission and it also resides in the background and observes user behavior. Most adware is benign in that it does not perform malicious acts or steal data. It does, however, watch user activity and produce pop-up ads. Adware can also change the user's default window or modify search results and switch the user's search engine. For the most part, it is just annoying, but users should be concerned any time they have unknown programs on their computers that perform unrequested functions.

   Figure 12-4 lists some of the symptoms of adware and spyware. Sometimes these symptoms develop slowly over time as more malware components are installed. Should these symptoms occur on your computer, remove the spyware or adware using anti-malware programs.

Malware Safeguards

Fortunately, it is possible to avoid most malware using the following malware safeguards:

1. *Install antivirus and antispyware programs on your computer.* Your IT department will have a list of recommended (perhaps required) programs for this purpose. If you choose a program for yourself, choose one from a reputable vendor. Check reviews of anti-malware software on the Web before purchasing.
2. *Set up your anti-malware programs to scan your computer frequently.* You should scan your computer at least once a week and possibly more. When you detect malware code, use the anti-malware software to remove it. If the code cannot be removed, contact your IT department or anti-malware vendor.

- Slow system start up
- Sluggish system performance
- Many pop-up advertisements
- Suspicious browser homepage changes
- Suspicious changes to the taskbar and other system interfaces
- Unusual hard-disk activity

Figure 12-4
Spyware and Adware Symptoms

3. *Update malware definitions.* **Malware definitions**—patterns that exist in malware code—should be downloaded frequently. Anti-malware vendors update these definitions continuously, and you should install these updates as they become available.

4. *Open email attachments only from known sources.* Also, even when opening attachments from known sources, do so with great care. According to professor and security expert Ray Panko, about 90 percent of all viruses are spread by email attachments.[2] This statistic is not surprising, because most organizations are protected by firewalls. With a properly configured firewall, email is the only outside-initiated traffic that can reach user computers.

   Most anti-malware programs check email attachments for malware code. However, all users should form the habit of *never* opening an email attachment from an unknown source. Also, if you receive an unexpected email from a known source or an email from a known source that has a suspicious subject, odd spelling, or poor grammar, do not open the attachment without first verifying with the known source that the attachment is legitimate.

5. *Promptly install software updates from legitimate sources.* Unfortunately, all programs are chock full of security holes; vendors are fixing them as rapidly as they are discovered, but the practice is inexact. Install patches to the operating system and application programs promptly.

6. *Browse only in reputable Internet neighborhoods.* It is possible for some malware to install itself when you do nothing more than open a Web page. Don't go there!

Malware Is a Serious Problem

America Online (AOL) and the National Cyber Security Alliance conducted a malware study using Internet users in 2004. They asked the users a series of questions and then, with the users' permission, scanned the users' computers to determine how accurately the users understood malware problems on their own computers. This fascinating study can be found online at *staysafeonline.info/news/safety_study_v04.pdf.*

Figure 12-5 shows a few important results from this study. Among the users, 6 percent thought they had a virus, but 18 percent actually did. Further, half of those surveyed did not know if they had a virus. Of those computers having viruses, an average of 2.4 viruses were found, and the maximum number of viruses found on a single computer was 213!

When asked how often they update their antivirus definitions, 71 percent of the users reported that they had done so within the last week. Actually, only one-third of the users had updated their definitions that recently.

Figure 12-5 shows similar results for spyware. The average user computer had 93 spyware components. The maximum number found on a computer was 1,059. Note that only 5 percent of the users had given permission for the spyware to be installed.

Although the problem of malware will never be eradicated, you can reduce its size by following the six numbered safeguards listed in the previous subsection. You should take these actions as a habit, and you should ensure that employees you manage take them as well.

---

[2]Ray Panko, *Corporate Computer and Network Security* (Prentice Hall, 2004), p. 165.

Question	User Response	Scan Results
Do you have a virus on your computer?	Yes: 6%	Yes: 19%
	No: 44%	No: 81%
	Don't know: 50%	
Average (maximum) number of viruses on infected computer		2.4 (213)
How often do you update your antivirus software?	Last week: 71%	Last week: 33%
	Last month: 12%	Last month: 34%
	Last 6 months: 5%	Last 6 months: 6%
	Longer than 6 months: 12%	Longer than 6 months: 12%
Do you think you have spyware or adware on your computer?	Yes: 53%	Yes: 80%
	No: 47%	No: 20%
Average (maximum) number of spyware/adware components on computer		93 (1,059)
Did you give permission to someone to install these components on your computer?	Yes: 5% No: 95%	

Figure 12-5
Malware Survey Results

Source: AOL/NCSA Online Safety Study, October 2004, *staysafeonline.info/news/ safety_study_v04.pdf* (assessed March 2005).

Design for Secure Applications

The final technical safeguard in Figure 12-3 concerns the design of applications. As a future IS user, you will not design programs yourself. However, you should ensure that any information system developed for you and your department includes security as one of the application requirements.

Q4 How Can Data Safeguards Protect Against Security Threats?

Data safeguards protect databases and other organizational data. Two organizational units are responsible for data safeguards. **Data administration** refers to an organization-wide function that is in charge of developing data policies and enforcing data standards. Data administration is a staff function to the CIO as discussed in Chapter 11.

Database administration refers to a function that pertains to a particular database. The ERP, CRM, and MRP databases each has a database administration function. Database administration ensures that procedures exist to ensure orderly multiuser processing of the database, to control changes to the database structure, and to protect the database.

Both data and database administration are involved in establishing the data safeguards in Figure 12-6. First, data administration should define data policies such as, "We will not share identifying customer data with any other organization" and the like. Then, data administration and database administration(s) work together to specify user data rights and responsibilities. Third, those rights should be enforced by user accounts that are authenticated at least by passwords.

Figure 12-6
Data Safeguards

- Define data policies
- Data rights and responsibilities
- Rights enforced by user accounts authenticated by passwords
- Data encryption
- Backup and recovery procedures
- Physical security

The organization should protect sensitive data by storing it in encrypted form. Such encryption uses one or more keys in ways similar to that described for data communication encryption. One potential problem with stored data, however, is that the key might be lost or that disgruntled or terminated employees might destroy it. Because of this possibility, when data are encrypted, a trusted party should have a copy of the encryption key. This safety procedure is sometimes called **key escrow**.

Another data safeguard is to periodically create backup copies of database contents. The organization should store at least some of these backups off premises, possibly in a remote location. Additionally, IT personnel should periodically practice recovery to ensure that the backups are valid and that effective recovery procedures exist. Do not assume that just because a backup is made, the database is protected.

Physical security is another data safeguard. The computers that run the DBMS and all devices that store database data should reside in locked, controlled-access facilities. If not, they are subject not only to theft, but also to damage. For better security, the organization should keep a log showing who entered the facility, when, and for what purpose.

In some cases, organizations contract with other companies to manage their databases. If so, all of the safeguards in Figure 12-6 should be part of the service contract. Also, the contract should give the owners of the data permission to inspect the premises of the database operator and to interview its personnel on a reasonable schedule.

Q5 How Can Human Safeguards Protect Against Security Threats?

Human safeguards involve the people and procedure components of information systems. In general, human safeguards result when authorized users follow appropriate procedures for system use and recovery. Restricting access to authorized users requires effective authentication methods and careful user account management. In addition, appropriate security procedures must be designed as part of every information system, and users should be trained on the importance and use of those procedures. In this section, we will consider the development of human safeguards first for employees and then for nonemployee personnel.

Human Safeguards for Employees

Figure 12-7 lists security considerations for employees. The first is position definitions.

Position Definitions

Effective human safeguards begin with definitions of job tasks and responsibilities. In general, job descriptions should provide a separation of duties and authorities. For example, no single individual should be allowed both to approve expenses and write checks. Instead, one person should approve expenses, another pay them, and a third should account for the payment. Similarly, in inventory, no single person should be allowed to authorize an inventory withdrawal and also to remove the items from inventory.

Given appropriate job descriptions, user accounts should be defined to give users the *least possible privilege* needed to perform their jobs. For example,

- Position definition
  - Separate duties and authorities.
  - Determine least privilege.
  - Document position sensitivity.

- Hiring and screening

"Where did you last work?"

- Dissemination and enforcement (responsibility, accountability, compliance)

"Lets talk security..."

- Termination
  - Friendly

"Congratulations on your new job"

  - Unfriendly

"We've closed your accounts. Goodbye"

Figure 12-7
Security Policy for In-House Staff

users whose job description does not include modifying data should be given accounts with read-only privilege. Similarly, user accounts should prohibit users from accessing data their job description does not require. Because of the problem of semantic security (Chapter Extension 15, "Reporting Systems and OLAP," on page 493), even access to seemingly innocuous data may need to be limited.

Finally, the security sensitivity should be documented for each position. Some jobs involve highly sensitive data (e.g., employee compensation, salesperson quotas, and proprietary marketing or technical data). Other positions involve no sensitive data. Documenting *position sensitivity* enables security personnel to prioritize their activities in accordance with the possible risk and loss.

Hiring and Screening

Security considerations should be part of the hiring process. Of course, if the position involves no sensitive data and no access to information systems, then screening for information systems security purposes will be minimal. When hiring for high-sensitivity positions, however, extensive interviews, references, and background investigations are appropriate. Note, too, that security screening applies not only to new employees, but also to employees who are promoted into sensitive positions.

Dissemination and Enforcement

Employees cannot be expected to follow security policies and procedures that they do not know about. Therefore, employees need to be made aware of the security policies, procedures, and responsibilities they will have.

Employee security training begins during new-employee training, with the explanation of general security policies and procedures. That general training must be amplified in accordance with the position's sensitivity and responsibilities. Promoted employees should receive security training that is appropriate to their new positions. The company should not provide user accounts and passwords until employees have completed required security training.

Enforcement consists of three interdependent factors: responsibility, accountability, and compliance. First, the company should clearly define the security *responsibilities* of each position. The design of the security program should be such that employees can be held *accountable* for security violations. Procedures should exist so that when critical data are lost, it is possible to determine how the loss occurred and who is accountable. Finally, the security program should encourage security *compliance*. Employee activities should regularly be monitored for compliance, and management should specify disciplinary action to be taken in light of noncompliance.

Management attitude is crucial: Employee compliance is greater when management demonstrates, both in word and deed, a serious concern for security. If managers write passwords on staff bulletin boards, shout passwords down hallways, or ignore physical security procedures, then employee security attitudes and employee security compliance will suffer. Note, too, that effective security is a continuing management responsibility. Regular reminders about security are essential.

Termination

Companies also must establish security policies and procedures for the termination of employees. Most employee terminations are friendly, and occur as the result of promotion, retirement, or when the employee resigns to take another position. Standard human resources policies should ensure that system administrators receive notification in advance of the employee's last day, so that they can remove accounts and passwords. The need to recover keys for encrypted data and any other special security requirements should be part of the employee's out-processing.

Unfriendly termination is more difficult because employees may be tempted to take malicious or harmful actions. In such a case, system administrators may need to remove user accounts and passwords prior to notifying the employee of his or her termination. Other actions may be needed to protect the company's information assets. A terminated sales employee, for example, may attempt to take the company's confidential customer and sales-prospect data for future use at another company. The terminating employer should take steps to protect those data prior to the termination.

The human resources department should be aware of the importance of giving IS administrators early notification of employee termination. No blanket policy exists; the information systems department must assess each case on an individual basis.

Human safeguards are even more important for employees who manage the security system, as discussed in the *Guide* on pages 287a–287b.

Human Safeguards for Nonemployee Personnel

Business requirements may necessitate opening information systems to nonemployee personnel—temporary personnel, vendors, partner personnel (employees of business partners), and the public. Although temporary personnel can be screened, to reduce costs, the screening will be abbreviated from that for employees. In most cases, companies cannot screen either vendor or partner personnel. Of course, public users cannot be screened at all. Similar limitations pertain to security training and compliance testing.

In the case of temporary, vendor, and partner personnel, the contracts that govern the activity should call for security measures appropriate to the sensitivity of the data and IS resources involved. Companies should require vendors and partners to perform appropriate screening and security training. The contract should also mention specific security responsibilities that are particular to the work to be performed. Companies should provide accounts and passwords with least privilege and remove those accounts as soon as possible.

The situation differs with public users of Web sites and other openly accessible information systems. It is exceedingly difficult and expensive to hold public users accountable for security violations. In general, the best safeguard from threats from public users is to *harden* the Web site or other facility against attack as much as possible. **Hardening** a site means to take extraordinary measures to reduce a system's vulnerability. Hardened sites use special versions of the operating system, and they lock down or eliminate operating systems features and functions that are not required by the application. Hardening is actually a technical safeguard, but we mention it here as the most important safeguard against public users.

Finally, note that the business relationship with the public, and with some partners, differs from that with temporary personnel and vendors. The public and some partners use the information system to receive a benefit. Consequently, safeguards need to protect such users from internal company security problems. A disgruntled employee who maliciously changes prices on a Web site potentially damages both public users and business partners. As one experienced IT manager put it, "Rather than protecting ourselves from them, we need to protect them from us."

Account Administration

The third human safeguard is account administration. The administration of user accounts, passwords, and help-desk policies and procedures are important components of the security system.

Account Management

Account management concerns the creation of new user accounts, the modification of existing account permissions, and the removal of unneeded accounts. Information system administrators perform all of these tasks, but account users have the responsibility to notify the administrators of the need for these actions. The IT department should create standard procedures for this purpose. As a future user, you can improve your relationship with IS personnel by providing early and timely notification of the need for account changes.

The existence of accounts that are no longer necessary is a serious security threat. IS administrators cannot know when an account should be removed; it is up to users and managers to give such notification.

Password Management

Passwords are the primary means of authentication. They are important not just for access to the user's computer, but also for authentication to other networks and servers to which the user may have access. Because of the importance of passwords, the National Institute of Standards and Technology (NIST) recommends that employees be required to sign statements similar to that shown in Figure 12-8 (page 288).

Metasecurity

Recall from Chapter 5 that metadata is data about data. In a similar vein, metasecurity is security about security. In other words, it asks the question, "How do we secure the security system?"

Consider an obvious problem: What is a secure way to store a file of accounts and passwords? Such files must exist, otherwise operating systems would be unable to authenticate users. But, how should one store such a file? It cannot be stored as plaintext, because anyone who reads the file gains unlimited access to the computer, the network, and other assets. So, it must be stored in encrypted form, but how? And who should know the encryption key?

Consider another problem. Suppose you work at the help desk at Vanguard Funds, and part of your job is to reset user passwords when users forget them. Clearly, this is an essential job that needs to be done, but what keeps you from resetting the passwords of accounts held by elderly people who never look at their statements? What keeps you from accessing those accounts with your reset password and moving funds to the accounts of your friends?

The accounting profession has dealt with some of these problems for decades and has developed a set of procedures and standards known as *accounting controls*. In general, these controls involve procedures that provide checks and balances, independent reviews of activity logs, control of critical assets, and so forth. Properly designed and implemented, such controls will catch the help-desk representative performing unauthorized account transfers. But many computer network threats are new, proper safeguards are under development, and some threats are not yet known.

The safeguards for some problems have unexpected consequences. For example, suppose you give one of your employees the task of finding security flaws in your network and financial applications (an activity called *white-hat hacking*). Assume that your employee finds ways to crack into your system and, say, schedule undetectable, unauthorized shipments of goods from inventory to any address she wants. Your employee reports the flaws, and you fix them. Except, how do you know she reported all the flaws she found?

Further, when she's finished, what do you do with your white-hat hacker? You are afraid to fire her, because, you have no idea what she'll do with the information she has. But what job can she safely perform now that she knows the holes in your security system? Do you want her, ever again, to have an account and password in your corporate computer network? Even if you fix all the problems she reports, which is doubtful, you suspect that she can always find more.

Or consider Microsoft's problem. If you were a computer criminal, where is the ultimate place to lodge a Trojan horse or trapdoor? In Windows code. Microsoft hires hundreds of people to write its operating system; people who work all over the world. Of course, Microsoft performs background screening on everyone it can, but did it get a complete and accurate background report on every Windows programmer in India, France, Ireland, China, and so on? Microsoft uses careful procedures for controlling what code gets into its products, but even still, somebody at Microsoft must lose sleep over the possibilities.

Ironically, the answers for many metasecurity problems lie in openness. Encryption experts generally agree that any encryption algorithm that relies on secrecy is ultimately doomed, because the secret will get out. Secrecy with encryption must lie only with the (temporary) keys that are used, and not with a secret method. Thus, encryption algorithms are published openly, and anyone with a mathematical bent is encouraged to find (and report) flaws. An algorithm is safe to deploy only when thousands of people have tested and retested it. WEP (see Chapter Extension 23 on page 585) was unwisely deployed before it was tested, and thousands upon thousands of wireless networks are vulnerable as a result.

Clearly, hardware and software are only part of the problem. Metasecurity extends to the data, procedures, and people components as well. It's a fascinating field, one that is continually developing, and one of great importance. It would make an interesting career choice—but be careful what you learn!

DISCUSSION QUESTIONS

1. Explain the term *metasecurity*. Describe two metasecurity problems not mentioned in this guide.

2. Explain the control problem that exists when personnel can reset customer passwords. Describe a way to reduce this threat using an audit log and at least two independent employees.

3. Describe the dilemma posed by an in-house hacker. Describe the problem of using an outside company for hacking. If you were asked to manage a project to test your computer network security, would you use in-house or outsourced personnel? Why?

4. A typical corporate computer has software from Microsoft, SAP, Siebel, Oracle, and possibly dozens of smaller vendors. How do users know that none of the software from these companies contains a Trojan horse?

5. Explain why part of the security solution lies in openness. Describe how openness applies to accounting controls like the one you designed in your answer to question 2. Explain the danger of procedural controls that rely on secrecy.

Figure 12-8
Sample Account
Acknowledgment Form

Source: National Institute of Standards and
Technology, *Introduction to Computer Security: The
NIST Handbook*, Publication 800–812, p. 114.

I hereby acknowledge personal receipt of the system password(s) associated with the user IDs listed below. I understand that I am responsible for protecting the password(s), will comply with all applicable system security standards, and will not divulge my password(s) to any person. I further understand that I must report to the Information Systems Security Officer any problem I encounter in the use of the password(s) or when I have reason to believe that the private nature of my password(s) has been compromised.

When an account is created, users should immediately change the password they are given to a password of their own. In fact, well-constructed systems require the user to change the password on first use.

Additionally, users should change passwords frequently thereafter. Some systems will require a password change every three months or perhaps more frequently. Users grumble at the nuisance of making such changes, but frequent password changes reduce not only the risk of password loss, but also the extent of damage if an existing password is compromised.

Some users create two passwords and switch back and forth between those two. This strategy results in poor security, and some password systems do not allow the user to reuse recently used passwords. Again, users may view this policy as a nuisance, but it is important.

Help-Desk Policies

In the past, help desks have been a serious security risk. A user who had forgotten his password would call the help desk and plead for the help-desk representative to tell him his password or to reset the password to something else. "I can't get this report out without it!" was (and is) a common lament.

The problem for help-desk representatives is, of course, that they have no way of determining that they are talking with the true user and not someone spoofing a true user. But, they are in a bind: If they do not help in some way, the help desk is perceived to be the "unhelpful desk."

To resolve such problems, many systems give the help-desk representative a means of authenticating the user. Typically, the help-desk information system has answers to questions that only the true user would know, such as the user's birthplace, mother's maiden name, or last four digits of an important account number. Usually, when a password is changed, notification of that change is sent to the user in an email. Email, as you learned, is sent as plaintext, however, so the new password itself ought not to be emailed. If you ever receive notification that your password was reset when you did not request such a reset, immediately contact IT security. Someone has compromised your account.

All such help-desk measures reduce the strength of the security system, and, if the employee's position is sufficiently sensitive, they may create too large a vulnerability. In such a case, the user may just be out of luck. The account will be deleted, and the user must repeat the account-application process.

Systems Procedures

Figure 12-9 shows a grid of procedure types—normal operation, backup, and recovery. Procedures of each type should exist for each information system. For example, the order-entry system will have procedures of each of these types, as will the Web storefront, the inventory system, and so forth. The definition and use of standard-

	System users	Operations personnel
Normal operation	Use the system to perform job tasks, with security appropriate to sensitivity.	Operate data center equipment, manage networks, run Web servers, and do related operational tasks.
Backup	Prepare for loss of system functionality.	Back up Web site resources, databases, administrative data, account and password data, and other data.
Recovery	Accomplish job tasks during failure. Know tasks to do during system recovery.	Recover systems from backed up data. Perform role of help desk during recovery.

Figure 12-9
System Procedures

ized procedures reduces the likelihood of computer crime and other malicious activity by insiders. It also ensures that the system's security policy is enforced.

Procedures exist for both users and operations personnel. For each type of user, the company should develop procedures for normal, backup, and recovery operations. As a future user, you will be primarily concerned with user procedures. Normal-use procedures should provide safeguards appropriate to the sensitivity of the information system.

Backup procedures concern the creation of backup data to be used in the event of failure. Whereas operations personnel have the responsibility for backing up system databases and other systems data, departmental personnel have the need to back up data on their own computers. Good questions to ponder are, "What would happen if I lost my computer (or PDA) tomorrow?" "What would happen if someone dropped my computer during an airport security inspection?" "What would happen if my computer were stolen?" Employees should ensure that they back up critical business data on their computers. The IT department may help in this effort by designing backup procedures and making backup facilities available.

Finally, systems analysts should develop procedures for system recovery. First, how will the department manage its affairs when a critical system is unavailable? Customers will want to order, and manufacturing will want to remove items from inventory even though a critical information system is unavailable. How will the department respond? Once the system is returned to service, how will records of business activities during the outage be entered into the system? How will service be resumed? The system developers should ask and answer these questions and others like them and develop procedures accordingly.

Security Monitoring

Security monitoring is the last of the human safeguards we will consider. Important monitoring functions are activity log analyses, security testing, and investigating and learning from security incidents.

Many information system programs produce *activity logs*. Firewalls produce logs of their activities, including lists of all dropped packets, infiltration attempts, and unauthorized access attempts from within the firewall. DBMS products produce logs of successful and failed log-ins. Web servers produce voluminous logs of Web activities. The operating systems in personal computers can produce logs of log-ins and firewall activities.

None of these logs adds any value to an organization unless someone looks at them. Accordingly, an important security function is to analyze these logs for threat patterns, successful and unsuccessful attacks, and evidence of security vulnerabilities.

Additionally, companies should test their security programs. Both in-house personnel and outside security consultants should conduct such testing.

Another important monitoring function is to investigate security incidents. How did the problem occur? Have safeguards been created to prevent a recurrence of such problems? Does the incident indicate vulnerabilities in other portions of the security system? What else can be learned from the incident?

Security systems reside in a dynamic environment. Organization structures change. Companies are acquired or sold; mergers occur. New systems require new security measures. New technology changes the security landscape, and new threats arise. Security personnel must constantly monitor the situation and determine if the existing security policy and safeguards are adequate. If changes are needed, security personnel need to take appropriate action.

Security, like quality, is an ongoing process. There is no final state that represents a secure system or company. Instead, companies must monitor security on a continuing basis.

Q6 What Is Necessary for Disaster Preparedness?

A disaster is a substantial loss of computing infrastructure caused by acts of nature, crime, or terrorist activity. As stated several times, the best way to solve a problem is not to have it. The best safeguard against a disaster is appropriate location. If possible, place computing centers, Web farms, and other computer facilities in locations not prone to floods, earthquakes, hurricanes, tornados, or avalanches. Even in those locations, place infrastructure in unobtrusive buildings, basements, backrooms, and similar locations well within the physical perimeter of the organization. Also, locate computing infrastructure in fire-resistant buildings designed to house expensive and critical equipment.

However, sometimes business requirements necessitate locating the computing infrastructure in undesirable locations. Also, even at a good location, disasters do occur. Therefore, some businesses prepare backup processing centers in locations geographically removed from the primary processing site.

Figure 12-10 lists major disaster preparedness tasks. After choosing a safe location for the computing infrastructure, the organization should identify all mission-critical applications. These are applications without which the organization cannot carry on and which, if lost for any period of time, could cause the organization's failure. The next step is to identify all resources necessary to run

Figure 12-10
Disaster Preparedness Guidelines

- Locate infrastructure in safe location.
- Identify mission-critical systems.
- Identify resources needed to run those systems.
- Prepare remote backup facilities.
- Train and rehearse.

those systems. Such resources include computers, operating systems, application programs, databases, administrative data, procedure documentation, and trained personnel.

Next, the organization creates backups for the critical resources at the remote processing center. So-called **hot sites** are remote processing centers run by commercial disaster-recovery services. For a monthly fee, they provide all the equipment needed to continue operations following a disaster. **Cold sites**, in contrast, provide office space, but customers themselves provide and install the equipment needed to continue operations.

Once the organization has backups in place, it must train and rehearse cutover of operations from the primary center to the backup. Periodic refresher rehearsals are mandatory.

Preparing a backup facility is very expensive; however, the costs of establishing and maintaining that facility are a form of insurance. Senior management must make the decision to prepare such a facility, by balancing the risks, benefits, and costs.

Q7 How Should Organizations Respond to Security Incidents?

The last component of a security plan that we will consider is incident response. Figure 12-11 lists the major factors. First, every organization should have an incident-response plan as part of the security program. No organization should wait until some asset has been lost or compromised before deciding what to do. The plan should include how employees are to respond to security problems, whom they should contact, the reports they should make, and steps they can take to reduce further loss.

Consider, for example, a virus. An incident-response plan will stipulate what an employee should do when he notices the virus. It should specify whom to contact and what to do. It may stipulate that the employee should turn off his computer and physically disconnect from the network. The plan should also indicate what users with wireless computers should do.

The plan should provide centralized reporting of all security incidents. Such reporting will enable an organization to determine if it is under systematic attack or whether an incident is isolated. Centralized reporting also allows the organization to learn about security threats, take consistent actions in response, and apply specialized expertise to all security problems.

When an incident does occur, speed is of the essence. Viruses and worms can spread very quickly across an organization's networks, and a fast response will help to mitigate the consequences. Because of the need for speed, preparation pays. The incident-response plan should identify critical personnel and their off-hours contact information. These personnel should be trained on where to go and what to do when they get there. Without adequate preparation, there is substantial risk that the actions of well-meaning people will make the problem worse. Also, the rumor mill will be alive with all sorts of nutty ideas about what to do. A cadre of well-informed, trained personnel will serve to dampen such rumors.

Finally, organizations should periodically practice incident response. Without such practice, personnel will be poorly informed on the response plan, and the plan itself may have flaws that only become apparent during a drill.

Figure 12-11
Factors in Incident Response

- Have plan in place
- Centralized reporting
- Specific responses
  - Speed
  - Preparation pays
  - Don't make problem worse
- Practice!

The Final, Final Word

Congratulations! You've made it through the entire book. With this knowledge you are well prepared to be an effective user of information systems. And with work and imagination, you can be much more than that. Many interesting opportunities are available to those who can apply information in innovative ways. Your professor has done what she can do, and the rest, as they say, is up to you.

I believe that, today, computer communications and data storage are free—or so close to free that the cost is not worth mentioning. What are the consequences? I do not know, and my nearly 40 years in the IT business make me wary of predictions that extend beyond next year. But I know that free communication and data storage will cause fundamental changes in the business environment. When a company like Getty Images (page 61) can produce its product at zero marginal cost, something's fundamentally different. Further, Getty Images is not the only such business; consider YouTube.

I suspect the rate of technology development will slow in the next five years. Businesses are still digesting the technology that already exists. According to Harry Dent, technology waves always occur in pairs.[3] The first phase is wild exuberance, in which new technology is invented, its capabilities flushed out, and its characteristics understood. That first phase always results in overbuilding, but it sets the stage for the second phase in which surviving companies and entrepreneurs purchase the overbuilt infrastructure for pennies on the dollar and use it for new business purposes.

The automotive industry, for example, proceeded in two stages. The irrational exuberance phase culminated in a technology crash; General Motors' stock fell 75 percent from 1919 to 1921. However, that exuberance led to the development of the highway system, the development of the petroleum industry, and a complete change in the conduct of commerce in the United States. Every one of those consequences created opportunities for business people alert to the changing business environment.

I believe we are poised today to see a similar second stage in the adoption of information technology. Businesses are configuring themselves to take advantage of the new opportunities. Dell builds computers to order and pays for the components days after the customer has paid Dell for the equipment. I use my new computer before Dell pays the supplier for the monitor.

Fiber-optic cable will come to my home (and yours) when telecom companies buy today's dark fiber for pennies on the dollar and light it up. With fiber-optic cable to my house, goodbye video store! Hello DK Enterprises—Internet broadcaster of my music library and sailing photos.

In 2005, bloggers stunned the mainstream media (MSM) with their commentary. Rathergate is old news. A new age is coming to news as bloggers demolish the MSM monopoly and obliterate MSM news control. The

[3]Harry Dent, *The Next Great Bubble Boom* (New York: The Free Press, 2004).

readership of newspapers has fallen consistently for more than a decade; newsprint cannot last in an era of free data communications.

So as you finish your business degree, stay alert for new technology-based opportunities. Watch for the second wave and catch it. If you found this course interesting, take more IS classes. Enroll in a database class or a systems development class, even if you don't want to be an IS major. If you're technically oriented, take a data communications class or a security class. If you enjoy this material, become an IS major. If you want to program a computer, great, but if you do not, then don't. There are tremendous opportunities for nonprogrammers in the IS industry. Look for novel applications of IS technology to the emerging business environment. Hundreds of them abound! Find them and have fun!

DISCUSSION QUESTION

How will you further your career with what you've learned in this class? Give that question serious thought, and write a memo to yourself to read from time to time as your career progresses.

How does the knowledge in this chapter help you at DSI?

You can use the knowledge in this chapter at DSI in two ways. First, you can use it personally; you can act to limit DSI's exposure, and your own exposure, to security threats. First and foremost, you can create a strong password (page 13) and behave in a way to protect that password. If you work for longer than three months at DSI, you also should change your password.

Second, being aware of the problems in Figure 12-1, you can follow appropriate data procedures, even if no DSI manager knows to state them. You can choose not to store sensitive data on your computer. If you have a portable computer, you can limit the data it contains to the absolute minimum you need when away from the office. You can also use all reasonable means to protect that computer from theft.

If you receive phishing attacks at work, you know not to respond to them, and you know to report any such attack at work to DSI's IT manager. You know to report any other suspicious activity as well.

With regard to helping the DSI organization with its security, as discussed at the end of Chapter 11, you are in a bind. You might send a copy of Figures 12-1 and 12-2 to your boss or to the IT manager and explain that you've learned about these issues in your MIS class. You might say something like, "I don't know if these issues are important to DSI or not, but I thought I'd raise them."

Later in your career, if you manage your own department, you can use the guidelines in Figure 12-7 to establish and maintain appropriate human safeguards in your department. Security issues are important. To you as a future manager, Figure 12-7 is one of the most important figures in this text!

That's it! You've reached the end of this text. Take a moment to reflect on how you will use what you will learn, as described in the *Guide* on pages 291a–291b.

Active ? Review

Use this Active Review to verify that you understand the material in the chapter. You can read the entire chapter and then perform the tasks in this review, or you can read the material for just one question and perform the tasks in this review for that question before moving on to the next one.

Q1 What are the sources and types of security threats?

Explain the difference among security threats, threat sources, and threat types. Give one example of a security threat for each cell in the grid in Figure 12-1. Describe a phishing attack. Explain the threat of phishing to individuals. Explain the threat of phishing to company and product brands.

Q2 What are the elements of a security program?

Define *technical, data,* and *human safeguards.* Show how these safeguards relate to the five components of an information system.

Q3 How can technical safeguards protect against security threats?

List five technical safeguards. Define *identification* and *authentication.* Describe three types of authentication. Define *malware,* and name five types of malware. Describe six ways to protect against malware. Summarize why malware is a serious problem.

Q4 How can data safeguards protect against security threats?

Define *data administration* and *database administration,* and explain their difference. List data safeguards.

Q5 How can human safeguards protect against security threats?

Summarize human safeguards for each activity in Figure 12-7. Summarize safeguards that pertain to nonemployee personnel. Describe three dimensions of safeguards for account administration. Explain how system procedures can serve as human safeguards. Describe security monitoring techniques.

Q6 What is necessary for disaster preparedness?

Define *disaster.* List major considerations for disaster preparedness. Explain the difference between a hot site and a cold site.

Q7 How should organizations respond to security incidents?

Summarize the actions that an organization should take when dealing with a security incident.

How does the knowledge in this chapter help you at DSI?

Describe the personal ways you can use security safeguards at DSI. List the appropriate data procedures you should follow at DSI, even if no manager tells you to do so.

Key Terms and Concepts

Adware 281
Authentication 279
Biometric authentication 280
Cold site 291
Data administration 283
Database administration 283
Data safeguards 283
Denial of service (DOS) 277
Drive-by sniffer 275
Email spoofing 275
Hacking 277

Hardening 287
Hot site 291
Human safeguards 284
Identification 279
IP spoofing 275
Key escrow 284
Malware 281
Malware definitions 282
Personal identification number (PIN) 280
Phishing 275

Pretexting 275
Security threat 274
Smart cards 280
Sniffing 275
Spoofing 275
Spyware 281
Technical safeguards 279
Unauthorized data disclosure 275
Usurpation 277

Using Your Knowledge

1. Search online to find the cheapest way possible to purchase your own credit 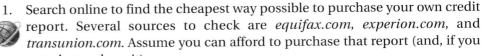 report. Several sources to check are *equifax.com, experion.com,* and *transunion.com.* Assume you can afford to purchase that report (and, if you can, do purchase it).
   a. You should review your credit report for obvious errors. However, other checks are appropriate. Search the Web for guidance on how best to review your credit records. Summarize what you learn.
   b. What actions should you take if you find errors in your credit report?
   c. Define *identity theft.* Search the Web and determine the best course of action if someone thinks he has been the victim of identity theft.

2. Suppose you lose your company laptop at an airport. What should you do? Does it matter what data is stored on your disk drive? If the computer contained sensitive or proprietary data, are you necessarily in trouble? Under what circumstances should you now focus on updating your resume?

3. Suppose you alert your boss to the security threats in Figure 12-1 and to the safeguards in Figure 12-2. Suppose he says, "Very interesting. Tell me more." In preparing for the meeting, you decide to create a list of talking points.
   a. Write a brief explanation of each threat in Figure 12-1.
   b. Explain how the five components relate to safeguards.
   c. Describe two to three technical, two to three data, and two to three human safeguards.
   d. Write a brief description on the safeguards in Figure 12-7.
   e. List security procedures that pertain to you, a temporary employee.
   f. List procedures that your department should have with regard to disaster planning.

4. Dee's consultant was given permission to install software on a server inside Emerson's network. Suppose he had been a computer criminal.
   a. Using Figure 12-1 as a guide, what might he have done?
   b. Suppose he maliciously deleted critical CRM data. What could Emerson do?
   c. Explain how Figure 12-11 pertains to this situation.
   d. In this circumstance, what is likely to happen to Dee? To the manager of the IT department? To the employee who authorized access to the consultant?

5. Suppose you need to terminate an employee who works in your department. Summarize security protections you must take. How would you behave differently if this termination were a friendly one?

6. Suppose DSI is located in a hurricane zone and that it has been given 36 hours warning that a serious, category 4 hurricane is headed its way.
   a. List all the information systems assets that are in danger.
   b. For each asset in your list in a, describe an appropriate safeguard.
   c. Suppose DSI has done little disaster preparedness planning. Summarize what you would do in that 36-hour period.
   d. Suppose DSI has a disaster preparedness plan. Summarize what you would do in that 36-hour period.
   e. Compare your answers to c and d. In your own words, state the advantages of a disaster preparedness plan.

Case Study 12

Antiphishing Tactics at More Than 50 Companies

Read about phishing in *MIS in Use 12* (page 276), if you have not done so already.

In February 2005, Fraudwatch International posted phishing examples for over 50 companies on its Web site at *fraudwatchinternational.com/internetfraud/phishing/examples*. This list is a who's who of major, legitimate financial institutions, e-commerce retailers, and software companies. It includes Amazon.com, eBay, Microsoft/MSN, Yahoo!, Wells Fargo, Washington Mutual, and many other large firms, worldwide. All of these companies have suffered phishing attacks, and the list is by no means complete.

Several characteristics of phishing make it difficult to eliminate. First, attacks often are indirect. Organizations do not know that their name, brand, and graphics are being used to deceive their own customers until someone reports the attack. Second, it is difficult to gauge the size of the attack, and thus it is difficult to calibrate a response. Notifying every customer will alarm the customer base and create a negative brand impression. If the attack is limited, such a warning may not be justified, but who knows if the worst of the attack is yet to come?

Third, according to the Financial Services Technology Consortium, phishing is seldom perpetrated by a single individual, but is perpetrated by organized criminal enterprises. These crime organizations hire technical specialist contractors to phish, but these contractors give the results to the organization, which quickly disseminates them to criminals throughout the world.

Phishing is an attack on an organization's brand, which can be worth millions, even billions, of dollars. The phishing attack is clothed in the brand image, using the brand's familiar graphics. After the attack, in the mind of the customer the brand may be paired with deception, problems, and financial loss. These are not the emotions that any marketer wants paired with its brand.

Additionally, the financial consequence of each incident may be small to the spoofed organization, and so the organization may not be moved to respond. It is only in the aggregate that the tangible and intangible costs mount. Consequently, the cost/benefit ratio of helping a single customer is high. Yet, there does not seem to be any way to resolve the problem except one by one.

Finally, enforcement and punishment of phishers is exceedingly difficult. It is easy for phishers to operate in countries where such activity is tolerated. Also, the victims of a given attack potentially are spread worldwide. Who is available to punish the phishers?

Questions

1. Suppose that you work for Barclays, PayPal, Visa, or any other major organization that is vulnerable to phishing. (It will be easier to answer this question if you choose an organization for which you are a customer.) Using the information in this chapter, write a single-page memo that describes the phishing threat to your company and explains why the threat is difficult for the company to address.

2. List possible actions, if any, that your company can take to eliminate the phishing threat.

3. List possible actions that your company can take to mitigate the consequences of the phishing threat.

4. Phishing is an industry-wide problem. How can organizations better solve the problem or mitigate its consequences by working together?

5. Write a specific policy that you think your organization should take concerning phishing. (Include a program policy, an issue-specific policy, and a system-specific policy in your recommendation.)

6. Suppose you manage a customer help desk. Describe a procedure for the help-desk employees to take when a customer reports a phishing attack.

7. Describe the elements of a phishing incident-reporting system for your company.

Emerson Pharmaceuticals and Dorset-Stratford Interiors, Chapter 12

GOALS

Use Dee's blog and Dorset-Stratford Interiors (DSI) to:

✳ Explore security management by considering security vulnerabilities at DSI.

✳ Consider Emerson's decisions during the development of Dee's blog in light of security risk management.

BACKGROUND

1. This chapter uses the DSI case to provide a broad view of security management. We survey security threats and safeguards and ask if those safeguards are likely to exist at DSI.

2. The wrap-up for the DSI case at the end of this chapter discusses how the intern can exercise effective individual security, even if that function is poorly managed at DSI. It also has suggestions for how a manager can use Figure 12-7.

3. Chapter 11 identified the risk that Emerson took when allowing Dee's consultant to have access to servers inside the corporate network. Chapter 12 does not consider Emerson, but I think that issue should be addressed here, nonetheless.

4. Was it a serious security threat to allow the consultant into the Emerson network? It depends on how much Emerson trusted the consultant. Emerson, after all, has employees who access the network every day. It trusts them. Should Emerson have placed so much trust in a consultant whom they didn't know? I introduced Dee to the consultant, and Dee knew me, so perhaps that counted for something. Still, I was surprised when they allowed the consultant in. Perhaps the data on the servers that he could access did not contain critical data.

5. Dee's blog is a good example of organizational politics in action. She went up her management chain as far as she had to go to find a senior person who could force IT to allow her consultant into the network. Was that a good thing? Not from the standpoint of strong network security.

HOW TO GET THE STUDENTS INVOLVED

1. First consider security threats to DSI. I use Figure 12-1 and go around the classroom, asking each student to give me examples of threats to DSI:

   a. **Give the class an example of a threat to DSI that involves human error and results in unauthorized data disclosure.**

   b. **How serious is this threat?**

   Continue a and b for each threat in Figure 12-1, until it is clear that the students understand this figure. Some of the categories can be done together.

2. Now consider security safeguards at DSI, again, going around the room:

   a. **Give me an example of a security safeguard for each threat in the grid in Figure 12-1.**

   b. **Is your safeguard a technical, data, or human safeguard?**

   c. **Is this the best safeguard for that threat?**

3. Prioritize security threats. (Chapter Extension 22 considers risk management, and you might want to assign it here.)

   a. **Assume the following:**

   • **DSI has a firewall and employees are given user IDs and passwords.**

   • **Employees are given access to anti-virus programs, but no one ensures those programs are used.**

   • **Backups are made once a week, and once a month the backups are stored off-site.**

   b. **Given our discussion, what do you think are the top five security threats to DSI?**

   c. **For each threat in b, what would be an appropriate safeguard?**

   d. **To do risk management, an organization should consider the cost of a security problem and multiply that cost by the likelihood of that problem. The result is the expected loss. Examine the top five security threats for DSI from item b. Which of those threats seems the most likely?**

   e. **How would you guess the five threats from item b rank in order of expected loss?**

4. Suppose you manage the purchasing department at DSI.

   a. **What actions can you take as an individual to protect yourself?**

b. What guidance would you give your employees about how they can protect themselves and the department?

c. Given a one-man IT department and absent any serious attention to security from DSI's owners, what else could you do to protect your department's data?

d. Suppose you believe that no one is backing up your data. What action could you take? If no one will pay attention to the need for backup, would it be wise to back up the data yourself and store it at home?

5. The chapter did not consider the security problem at Emerson, but let's pick up that question, anyway:

a. What did Dee do that caused a security threat to Emerson?

b. How serious was this threat? Give three examples of problems the consultant could have caused.

c. How could Emerson have reduced the likelihood of a problem?

d. Do you think it was a wise decision for Emerson to allow the consultant inside the network? What would have happened had he not been allowed inside the network?

e. Dee's consultant is a very reputable and honest professional. No problem occurred, and the consultant even suggested to Emerson a few ways that their security could be improved. Given this result, was Emerson's decision a good one? Why or why not?

BOTTOM LINE

* Information systems security management is most important. Every business professional has a responsibility for security, even if the organization, like DSI, pays little attention to security.

* As a future manager, understand you have important security responsibilities, even if no one tells you that you do.

Using the Ethics Guide: Metasecurity (page 287a)

GOALS

✳ Sensitize students to problems of securing security.

✳ Emphasize the importance of managers' responsibilities for controls over the security system.

BACKGROUND AND PRESENTATION STRATEGIES

The problem of storing passwords is a technical security problem and is presented only to introduce the idea of metasecurity; it is not the concern of future business managers. The remaining three issues in this guide are relevant to future managers, however.

First, considering accounting controls, most such controls have a strong procedural component. The payables system, for example, is set up so that one person authorizes a payment, a second person generates the check (or uses an information system that causes the check to be created), and a third person accounts for the payment. That separation of duties and authorities is crucial to effective control.

Future managers need to understand the reason and validity of such procedural controls, and they need to manage accordingly. The security of such systems lies in the hands of the managers on the front line.

This knowledge is especially true for managers who work at help desks that have privileges to reset or override passwords or that provide other computer account services. Typically, security administration systems create logs that show summary data, such as how many passwords were reset, which accounts were reset, whether an appropriate notification was sent to the customer, and so forth. If the control requires that the help-desk manager review or reconcile these totals against other data, the manager should take such reconciliation very seriously.

Here, we consider the management of a white-hat hacker employee. The two crucial questions about managing such an employee are: How do you know you learned all of the problems, and what do you do with that person next?

Unlike a consultant, an employee has a continuing need for an account and password in your organization's network. But that person is situated to take advantage of any problems that she did not reveal.

As the guide points out, given that person's expertise, do you want her to have access to your network?

I think the guide overdraws this issue in a way that we can use for class discussion:

➤ **All major software vendors, including Microsoft, Oracle, SAP, Siebel, and others, are obvious targets for security attacks. Every one of those companies has a staff of in-house hackers and other security experts who have the knowledge and access to create havoc in their networks. What do you think these companies do to prevent this?**

➤ **What extra precautions can you take when you hire and manage employees like white-hat hackers?**

Some possibilities: Perform substantial background checks; require such employees to sign specially written employee contracts; regularly investigate the employees' lifestyle and spending habits; require periodic lie-detector tests; perform unannounced security audits of the employees' computers and accounts.

➤ **Those measures are fine for sophisticated software companies. But what about a company like DSI? It won't have the expertise, employees, or resources to perform, for example, an unannounced computer and account audit.**

Even if the IT department were properly staffed, DSI may be too small to have an employee dedicated to white-hat testing, but it may have one or two employees who have knowledge to steal data and create other problems. The company should perform extensive background checks on employees who work with information systems that control assets, and possibly have those employees sign specially worded employee contracts. It's a trade-off, however. A heavy-handed security policy with underlying assumptions of suspicion conflicts with DSI's friendly and open culture. For good or ill, DSI is unlikely to do much about this issue.

The students may not understand how openness can improve security. One good example concerns the separation of duties and authorities. If everyone is trained that managers review logs of their activity, if everyone knows that random checks are made by calling persons whose accounts have been modified, if everyone is trained on such procedures and understands the need for them, security will improve. By the way, when such procedures are presented as standard business practice for a well-managed company, then no one needs to feel that they are under suspicion or that they aren't trusted.

In a related vein, if employees understand all the capabilities that their passwords give them, they will be more likely to safeguard them. If, for example, the employee's account and password provide unlimited access to the employee's salary, benefit, and other personal data, and if every employee is aware of that fact, password management will improve.

 ## SUGGESTED RESPONSES FOR DISCUSSION QUESTIONS

1. Metasecurity is security about security. Two additional examples:

    ➤ **Where and how do you store the list of known holes in your security system? Who can contribute to this list? Who has access to this list?**

    ➤ **Where and how do you store the procedures for conducting a security audit of the computer files and user accounts of in-house security personnel? Who has access to these procedures? Who writes these procedures? Who performs the computer audit of the person who manages computer audits? Who performs the computer audit of that person?**

2. Personnel can grant themselves unauthorized access to customer accounts. To reduce this threat: Use software that automatically generates a log of all password changes. Assign responsibility for reviewing that log to a manager. Assign responsibility for reviewing the managers' review to a manager outside of the help-desk's management chain.

3. Using an outside white-hat hacker involves a stranger and a strange organization, but it eliminates the problem of managing the in-house person. Using an inside white-hat hacker involves a known employee, but that employee will require special management due to his or her knowledge. The hiring decision depends, in large measure, on how large the

organization is. For all but the largest, hire the outside person, but be very careful! Large organizations will have a large IS department to address this issue.

    An interesting side question:

    ➤ **Who provides security testing when the computer infrastructure has been outsourced?**

    ➤ **What special security considerations apply to outsourcing?**

4. No one knows, not even the vendors, whether their software contains a Trojan horse. This possibility reinforces the need to apply patches to vendor software when they are announced. Vendors seldom announce all the problems they've fixed in a patch. It could be that the patch involves removing some suspicious code. In general, the larger the installed base, the more likely that security problems have been identified and fixed. Systems with only a few users are vulnerable to unknown internal problems.

5. See the comments on openness in the Guidelines. In short, if everyone knows what should be happening, it will be harder for exceptions to security procedures to go unnoticed. Procedural controls that rely on secrecy assume that the secret will be kept secret; such controls lose their effectiveness if the secret is lost. As Benjamin Franklin wrote in *Poor Richard's Almanac*, "Three people can keep a secret, as long as two of them are dead."

WRAP UP

➤ **As a manager, you may have control responsibilities for the security system. If so, take those responsibilities seriously. They are important!**

➤ **Securing security is a challenging, interesting, difficult, and important problem. It could make a great career!**

Using the Guide: The Final, Final Word *(page 291a)*

GOAL

* Inspire the students to use what they have learned to find, create, and manage innovative applications of IS technology.

BACKGROUND AND PRESENTATION STRATEGIES

The best is yet to come!

It's tempting to look at Microsoft and Bill Gates, Oracle and Larry Ellison, or Dell and Michael Dell and think, "All the good opportunities are gone." But, the great news is, *it's not true*. Rather, the *great* opportunities are in front of us.

Although I'm sure that many fortunes are yet to be made by companies that develop, market, and sell technology products, I think most of the great opportunities involve innovative applications of the technology that already exists or that others will develop.

The second-wave phenomenon identified by Harry Dent makes sense to me. Although his predictions of a 30,000 Dow-Jones average by 2010 seem over the top (not cited in the guide, but see his book referenced in the footnote), his analysis about the second wave, the application of technology use, seems sensible to me.

Getty Images (GYI) is an excellent example of success through innovative application of IS and IT. The company has harnessed database technology to create a system that produces images at near zero marginal cost. YouTube was purchased by Google for $1.62 billion after just over a year of operations! That is less time than it took to write this textbook!

Getty Images and YouTube are not the last companies to find innovative applications of technology. Many, many more such opportunities exist, and our students are positioned to take advantage of them.

Even students who are uninterested in entrepreneurial opportunities can apply their knowledge to find innovative ways to accomplish the organization's competitive advantage.

Applications of IS, no how matter how clever or how innovative, must reinforce the organization's competitive strategy.

I do not think we can overemphasize the importance of the opportunities for nearly free data storage and data communications. Here are some consequences:

➤ **Numerous cities are sponsoring projects to provide fiber-optic cable to the home.**

➤ **Wireless networks are everywhere—city parks, public buildings, coffee shops, etc.**

➤ **The entertainment, computer, and data communications industries are reinforcing one another.**

➤ **Blogs have revolutionized mainstream media and, in the process, are changing the dynamics of politics.**

➤ **Podcasting provides a podium for everyone and enables listeners to consume the products on their own time and in their own, very flexible space.**

➤ **Cheap storage and data communications, along with standards like XML, will have a major, possibly revolutionary, impact on interorganizational activities like supply chain management.**

➤ **What do you think are some consequences of these changes?**

➤ **What are some opportunities for innovation within a company?**

➤ **Even those of you who aren't interested in innovative applications of IS and IT can think about innovative ways of NOT using IS and IT. For example, wireless, podcasting, and cell phones make it impossible to get off the grid.**

➤ **What opportunities does that fact create for recreation? For travel? For tourism? For employee counseling? Other?**

 SUGGESTED RESPONSES FOR DISCUSSION QUESTION

I think this is a very important exercise, and I assign it for substantial credit.

This exercise asks students to:

* Take business seriously.

* Take their goal of becoming a business professional seriously.

* Take the knowledge they have learned from this class seriously.

* Merge those interests together into a document that can be useful to them during the early years of their careers.

I caution the students to write this memo using as specific language as they can. They should write it expecting that they will evaluate themselves on it in a few years. The more specific the memo is, the easier it will be to perform the evaluation.

I have the students email me their memos, and I take a lot of time grading them. If the student is seriously engaged in the assignment, I sometimes ask for several revisions and amplifications.

In many ways, this question, this memo, is our bottom line. What have the students learned from the class that will help them further their careers as business professionals?

There are so many possibilities—and that's the beauty of teaching this class. This exercise can be useful to anyone who takes their goal of becoming a business professional seriously.

WRAP UP

➤ **The best is yet to come!**

➤ **What that best is, what happens next, will be in large measure up to you!**

➤ **Prosper, do good work, and have fun!**

PART 4 The International Dimension

International IT Development and Management

Study Questions

Q1 What characteristics make international IT management challenging?

Q2 Why is international information systems development difficult?

Q3 What are the challenges of international project management?

Q4 What are the challenges of international IT management?

Q5 How does the international dimension affect computer security risk management?

Q6 What challenges exist for investigating international computer crime?

The International Dimension

Q1 What Characteristics Make International IT Management Challenging?

Size and complexity make international IT management challenging. International information systems are larger and more complex. Projects to develop them are larger and more complicated to manage. International IT departments are bigger and comprised of people from many cultures with many different native languages. International organizations have more IS and IT assets, and those assets are exposed to more risk and greater uncertainty. Security incidents are more complicated to investigate.

We will consider each of these impacts in more detail in the following questions. The bottom line, however, is size and complication.

Q2 Why Is International Information Systems Development Difficult?

Before considering this question, realize that the factors that affect international information systems development are more challenging than those that affect international software development. If the *system* is truly international, if many people from many different countries will be using the system, then the development project is exceedingly complicated. For example, consider the effort required for a multinational company like 3M to create an integrated, worldwide CRM. Such a project is massive!

On the other hand, creating localized software (one or more programs that are available in different human-language versions) is challenging, but not nearly as daunting. As stated in the International Dimension for Part 2, localizing a program is a matter of designing it to accept program menus, messages, and

help text from external files and of translating those files. Of course, different character sets, different sorting orders, different currency symbols, and other complications must be accounted for, but these challenges are surmountable with good software design and development.

Think about the five components of an information system. Running hardware in different countries is not a problem, and localizing software is manageable. Databases pose some problems, namely determining the language, currency, and units of measure used to record data, but these problems are surmountable, however, when we consider procedures.

An international system is used by people who live and work in cultures that are vastly different from one another. The way that customers are treated in Japan differs substantially from the way that customers are treated in Spain, which differs substantially from the way that customers are treated in the United States. The procedures for using a CRM will be correspondingly different.

Consider the phases of the SDLC. During systems definition, we are supposed to determine the purpose and scope of the system. As you know by now, information systems should facilitate the organization's competitive strategy by supporting business processes. But what if the underlying processes differ? Again, customer support in Japan and customer support in Spain may involve completely different processes and activities.

Even if the purpose and scope can be defined in some unified way, how are requirements to be determined? Again, if the underlying business processes differ, then the specific requirements for the information system will differ. Managing requirements for a system in one culture is difficult, but managing requirements for international systems can be many times more difficult.

There are two responses to such challenges: either define a set of standard business processes, or develop alternative versions of the system that support different processes in different countries. Both responses are problematic. The first response requires conversion of the organization to different work processes, and as you learned in Chapter 7, such conversion can be exceedingly difficult. People resist change, and they will do so with vehemence if the change violates cultural norms.

The second response is easier to implement, but creates system design challenges. It also means that, in truth, there is not one system, but many.

In spite of the problems, both responses are used. For example, SAP, Oracle, and other ERP vendors define standard business processes via the inherent procedures in their software products. Many organizations attempt to enforce those standard procedures. When it becomes organizationally infeasible to do so, organizations develop exceptions to those inherent procedures and develop programs to handle the exceptions. This choice means high maintenance expense as explained in Chapter Extension 10, "Cross-Functional Systems," on page 439.

Q3 What Are the Challenges of International Project Management?

Managing a global information systems development project is difficult because of project size and complexity. Requirements are complex, many resources are required, and numerous people are involved. Team members speak different languages, live in different cultures, work in different time zones, and seldom meet face-to-face.

One way to understand how these factors impact global project management is to consider each of the knowledge areas in the *PMBOK® Guide*, as discussed in Chapter Extension 18, "Large-Scale Systems Development," on page 529. Figure ID4-1 summarizes challenges for each knowledge area. Project integration

Figure ID4-1
Challenges for International IS Project Management

Knowledge Areas	Challenge
Project integration	Complex integration of results from distributed work groups. Management of dependencies of tasks from physically and culturally different workgroups.
Scope (requirements)	Need to support multiple versions of underlying business processes. Possibly substantial differences in requirements and procedures.
Time	Development rates vary among cultures and countries.
Cost	Cost of development varies widely among countries. Two members performing the same work in different countries may be paid substantially different rates. Moving work among teams may dramatically change costs.
Quality	Quality standards vary among cultures. Different expectations of quality may result in an inconsistent system.
Human resources	Worker expectations differ. Compensation, rewards, work conditions vary widely.
Communications	Geographic, language, and cultural distance among team members impedes effective communication.
Risk	Development risk is higher. Easy to lose control.
Procurement	Complications of international trade.

is more difficult because international development projects require the complex integration of results from distributed work groups. Also, task dependencies can span teams working in different countries, increasing the difficulty of task management.

The scope and requirements definition for international IS is more difficult for the reasons discussed in Q2. Time management is more difficult because teams in different cultures and countries work at different rates. Some cultures have a 35-hour workweek, and some have a 60-hour workweek. Some cultures expect six-week vacations, and some expect two. Some cultures thrive on efficiency of labor, and other cultures thrive on considerate working relationships. There is no standard rate of development for an international project.

In terms of cost, different countries and cultures pay vastly different labor rates. Using critical path analysis, managers may choose to move a task from one team to another. Doing so, however, may substantially increase costs. Thus, management may choose to accept a delay rather than move work to an available (but more expensive) team. The complex trade-offs that exist between time and cost become even more complex for international projects.

Quality and human resources are also more complicated for international projects. Quality standards

vary among countries. The IT industry in some nations, like India, has invested heavily in development techniques that increase program quality. Other nations, like the United States, have been less willing to invest in quality. In any case, the integration of programs of varying quality results in an inconsistent system.

Worker expectations vary among cultures and nations. Compensation, rewards, and worker conditions vary, and these differences can lead to misunderstandings, poor morale, and project delays.

Because of these factors, effective team communication is exceedingly important for international projects, but because of language and culture differences and geographic separation, such communication is difficult. Effective communication is also more expensive. Consider, for example, just the additional expense of maintaining a team portal in three or four languages.

If you consider all of the factors in Figure ID4-1, it is easy to understand why project risk is high for international IS development projects. So many things can go wrong. Project integration is complex; requirements are difficult to determine; cost, time, and quality are difficult to manage; worker conditions vary widely; and communication is difficult. Finally, project procurement is complicated by the normal challenges of international commerce.

Q4 What Are the Challenges of International IT Management?

Chapter 11 defined the four primary responsibilities of the IT department: plan, operate, develop, and protect information systems and IT infrastructure. Each of these responsibilities becomes more challenging for international IT organizations.

Regarding planning, the principal task is to align IT and IS resources with the organization's competitive strategy. The task does not change character for international companies; it just becomes more complex and difficult. Multinational organizations and operations are complicated, and the business processes that support their competitive strategies tend also to be complicated. Further, changes in global economic factors can mean dramatic changes in processes and necessitate changes in IS and IT support. Technology adoption can also cause remarkable change. The increasing use of cell phones in the Third World, for example, changes the requirements for local information systems. The rising price of oil will also change international business processes. So, planning tasks for international IT are larger and more complex.

Three factors create challenges for international IT operations. First, conducting operations in different countries, cultures, and languages adds complexity. Go to the Web site of any multinational corporation, say *www.mmm.com or www.dell.com,* and you'll be asked to click on the country in which you reside. When you click, you are likely to be directed to a Web server running in some other country. Those Web servers need to be managed consistently, even though they are oper-ated by people living in different cultures and speaking different languages.

The second operational challenge of international IS is the integration of similar, but different systems. Consider inventory. A multinational corporation might have dozens of different inventory systems in use throughout the world. To enable the movement of goods, many of these systems need to be coordinated and integrated.

Or consider customer support that operates from three different support centers in three different countries. Each support center may have its own information system, but the data among those systems will need to be exported or otherwise shared. If not, then a customer who contacts one center will be unknown by the others.

The third complication for operations is outsourcing. Many organizations have chosen to outsource customer support, training, logistics, and other backroom activities. International outsourcing is particularly advantageous for customer support and other functions that must be operational 24/7. Amazon.com, for example, operates customer service centers in the United States, India, and Ireland. Many companies outsource logistics to United Parcel Service (UPS), because doing so offers comprehensive, worldwide shipping and logistical support. The organization's information systems usually need to be integrated with outsource vendors' information systems, and this may need to be done for different systems, all over the world. The challenges for the development of international information systems were addressed in questions Q1 and Q2.

International IS/IT outsourcing is not without controversy, however. It is one thing to shift a job making tennis shoes to Singapore, or even to hire customer support representatives in India. But there was consternation and wringing of hands when IBM announced that it was shifting nearly 5,000 computer-programming jobs to India. Some perceive the moving of such high-tech, high-skill jobs overseas as a threat to U.S. technology leadership. Others say it is just economic factors guiding jobs to places where they are most efficiently performed.

The fourth IT department responsibility is protecting IS and IT infrastructure. We consider that function in the next question.

Q5 How Does the International Dimension Affect Computer Security Risk Management?

Computer security risk management is more difficult and complicated for international information systems. First, IT assets are subject to more threats. Infrastructure will be located in sites all over the world, and those sites differ in the threats to which they are exposed. Some will be subject to political threats, others to the threat of civil unrest, others to terrorists, and still others will be subject to threats of natural disasters of every conceivable type. Place your data center in Kansas, and it's subject to tornados. Place your data center internationally, and it's potentially subject to typhoons/hurricanes, earthquakes, floods, volcanic eruption, or mudslides. And don't forget epidemics that will affect the data center employees.

Second, the likelihood of a threat is more difficult to estimate for international systems. What is the likelihood that the death of Fidel Castro will cause civil unrest and threaten your data center in Havana? How does an organization assess that risk? What is the likelihood that a computer programmer in India will insert a Trojan horse into code that she writes on an outsourcing contract?

In addition to risk, international information systems are subject to far greater uncertainty. As discussed in Chapter Extension 22, "Managing Computer Security Risk" (page 579), uncertainty reflects likelihood that something that "we don't know we don't know" will cause an adverse outcome. Because of the multitudinous cultures, religions, nations, beliefs, political views, and crazy people in the world, uncertainty about risks to IS and IT infrastructure is high. Again, if you place your data center in Kansas, you have some idea of the magnitude of the uncertainty to which you are exposed, even if you don't know exactly what it is. Place a server in a country on every continent of the world, and you have no idea of the potential risks to which they are exposed.

Regarding safeguards, technical and data safeguards do not change for international information systems. Because of greater complexity there may be a need for more safeguards or for more complex ones, but the technical and data safeguards described in Chapter 12 all work for international systems. Human safeguards are another matter. For example, can an organization depend on the control of separation of duties and authorities in a culture for which graft is an accepted norm? Or, what is the utility of a personal reference in a culture in which it is considered exceedingly rude to talk about someone when they are not present? Because of these differences, human safeguards need to be chosen and evaluated on a culture-by-culture basis.

In short, risk management for both international information systems and IT infrastructure is more complicated, more difficult, and subject to greater uncertainty.

Q6 What Challenges Exist for Investigating Global Computer Crime?

Unfortunately, international computer crime is common. Web sites operated in African countries phish for data in the United States. A scam in the United States steals data from a U.S. corporation and sells that data to an illegal operation in South America. Someone kidnaps a U.S. citizen in a foreign country and sends email to relatives in the United States. The email service provider is located in a Mideastern country. In all of these cases, critical evidence is stored in computers located on foreign soil.

With rare exceptions, such as embassies, nations have sovereignty within their borders. A U.S. criminal investigator can obtain evidence only with the consent of the country in which the evidence lies. Most nations have laws, agreements, and treaties for cooperating in criminal investigations, but the formal process for obtaining permission to search is slow and cumbersome. Further, some nations will not cooperate.

For situations in which speed is of the essence, when the data is likely to be moved soon or deleted, the G8 group of nations has developed a 24-hour *point-of-contact system*. This system, which is used by more than 30 nations, requires each country to staff an office that can speed the processing of permission for evidence gathering. For the countries that participate, the system gives international crime investigators a single point of contact.

In some cases, evidence-gathering is facilitated by informal arrangements among individuals in security agencies and organizations. A U.S. investigator may not have permission to search or obtain evidence, but his or her counterpart in another country may be authorized to do so. Informal arrangements are sometimes made, but the law regarding the admissibility of such evidence in court is complicated.

A final consideration is that the U.S. Fourth Amendment may apply in complex ways to searches outside the United States.

The law for gathering evidence for computer crimes in the United States is complicated, and it becomes even more so for international investigations. As stated in Chapter Extension 24, "Computer Crime and Forensics," on page 593, organizations that suspect they have been the victims of a computer crime, especially international computer crime, should seek legal counsel.

Active ? Review

Use this Active Review to verify that you understand the material in the International Dimension. You can read the entire mini chapter and then perform the tasks in this review, or you can read the material for just one question and perform the tasks in this review for that question before moving on to the next one.

Q1 What characteristics make international IT management challenging?

State the two characteristics that make international IT management challenging. Explain how those factors pertain to IS development, IT management, and risk management.

Q2 Why is international information systems development difficult?

Explain the difference between international systems development and international software development. Using the five-component framework, explain why international systems development is more difficult. Describe difficulties that arise during the systems definition and requirements phases during the development of an international IS. Describe two responses to these difficulties, and explain why both are problematic. Give an example of how each is used.

Q3 What are the challenges of international project management?

State two words that characterize the difficulty of international project management. Explain how each of the knowledge areas in Figure ID4-1 are more complicated for international projects. Give an example of one complication for each knowledge area.

Q4 What are the challenges of international IT management?

State the four responsibilities for IT departments. Explain how each of these responsibilities is more challenging for international IT organizations. Describe three factors that create challenges for international IT operations.

Q5 How does the international dimension affect computer security risk management?

Explain why international IT assets are subject to more threats. Give three examples. Explain why the likelihood of international threats is more difficult to determine. Describe uncertainty and explain why it is higher for international IT organizations. Explain how technical, data, and human safeguards differ for international IT organizations. Give two examples of problematic international human safeguards.

Q6 What challenges exist for investigating international computer crime?

Give two examples of international computer crime. Explain the constraints U.S. investigators face when gathering evidence in foreign countries. Explain the role of the 24-hour point-of-contact system. Describe how informal arrangements can facilitate evidence-gathering in foreign countries. State the recommended action for organizations that believe they are the victim of international computer crime.

PART 4 review

Consider Your Net Worth

1. Assume you have graduated and are working in your chosen field of study: sales, marketing, finance, general management, or IT. Suppose that you learn there is a systems development project underway and suppose you decide to volunteer for the project. You do so because you know that it will give you a chance to relate to your boss in a new way and because you will be able to network with others in your organization. (If you are majoring in IT, answer the questions below assuming you are a junior member of the team.)

a. If the project is being developed using the SDLC, summarize your possible role(s). What tasks might you be asked to perform? How will your knowledge of the SDLC help you? How can your knowledge of the SDLC give you a competitive advantage?

To answer parts b, c, and d, you will need to read Chapter Extension 19, "Alternative Development Techniques" (page 545).

b. If the project is being developed using RAD, explain how your answers to the questions in a above will change.

c. If the project is being developed using OOD, explain how your answers to the questions in a above will change.

d. If the project is being developed using XP, explain how your answers to the questions in a above will change.

e. Suppose that you learn that a new information systems project is being proposed and suppose you do *not* volunteer to be a user representative to the team. What is the opportunity cost of your decision?

2. Examine the grid outline of the *PMBOK® Guide* in Figure CE18-3 (page 533).

a. Explain, in general terms, how each of the knowledge areas in that grid pertains to information systems projects.

b. Explain how each of the knowledge areas in that grid pertains to any large project.

c. Suppose that one of your classes requires you to complete a large team project. Explain how you could use that grid as a template for team planning. Explain how you could use that grid to document effective teamwork to your instructor. Do you see any disadvantages of planning your project using that grid? If so, state them.

3. Suppose you have just taken over the management of a department that has just begun to use a new information system. Assume that information system has not been reliable and is difficult to use. It is so difficult, in fact, that the employees in your new department ridicule the new system.

a. Summarize your management problem.

b. Suppose you decide to investigate the origin of the problems before you do anything. Describe what you might want to learn.

c. Suppose you learn that many of the problems your department is experiencing are due to the fact that your predecessor did not take the task of specifying requirements seriously. What do you do with that knowledge?

d. Describe three alternatives for approaching the IT department with these complaints. Which of these three is the most professional? Which of these three is most likely to improve the situation?

e. Describe three alternatives for handling the situation with your department. Which do you think is most likely to generate confidence in you among your team? Which is most likely to improve the situation?

4. Assume that you have just taken over the management of a department that depends on a particular information system to do its work. You ask your employees to show you the procedures for departmental operations in case of system failure, and you learn there are none.

a. What do you suppose will happen if the system fails?

b. Suppose you conduct an informal risk management of the situation and conclude no such procedures are necessary. Speculate on the characteristics of the situation that would cause you to form this conclusion.

c. If, on the basis of your informal risk management assessment, you conclude that such procedures are necessary, how would you proceed? Would you involve the IT department? Why or why not?

d. Assume you decide to involve the IT department. Describe whom you would want to meet and what you would communicate when you did meet him or her.

5. Turn to the Chapter Overview on pages xii–xiii and reflect on what you've learned from this text.

a. Which chapter or chapter extension was the most interesting to you?

b. How can you use your answer to question a to guide your career choice, or what you do within the career you've already chosen?

c. Which chapter or chapter extension do you believe will be the most helpful to you in your career? Explain your answer.

d. Which chapter or chapter extension do you believe will be the least helpful to you in your career? Explain your answer.

6. Summarize the ways that you believe the knowledge you have gained about MIS will be helpful to you in your career. Give specific examples using at least five chapters or chapter extensions.

7. Suppose that you work for a company in an internship in your chosen field of study. Write a memo to your boss requesting that your employer pay the tuition for this class. In your memo, explain how the knowledge you have learned in this class pertains to your work.

Career Assignments

 1. Use your favorite Web search engine to search for the term *systems analyst job opportunities*. Click on four or five of the links you find interesting and answer the following questions.

  a. Describe educational requirements for this job.

  b. Describe the qualifications necessary to obtain such a job.

  c. Describe internships and part-time jobs you could take to prepare for this job.

  d. Summarize the employment prospects for this job.

  e. Are you interested in this job? Explain why or why not.

 2. Answer question 1, but search for the term *PQA test engineer job opportunities*.

 3. Answer question 1, but search for the term *computer support representative job opportunities*.

 4. Search the Web for the term *IT employment trends*. Visit some of the sites that your search reveals. Also, the site *roberthalftechnology.com* often has recent survey data, as does *cio.com*. Use the information you find to answer the following questions.

  a. What is the outlook for IT/IS employment in the next three years? In the next 10 years?

  b. What jobs are projected to have the highest demand?

  c. Identify a job in which you might be interested. What is the projected demand for that job?

  d. Are there differences in job prospects in different geographic regions? Describe how you could improve your job prospects by moving.

  e. Are there differences in job prospects in different industries? Which industries are projected to have the most growth in IT/IS jobs? Which will have the least?

 5. The Web site iNFOSYSSEC (*www.infosyssec.net/ infosyssec/jobsec1.htm*) is an Internet security resource for IS security professionals. Search that site for security management jobs in the United States. Find five different jobs that are currently available.

  a. Describe, in general terms, the responsibilities of security management jobs.

b. Describe qualifications that you think successful candidates would need for these jobs.

c. What courses could you take at your university to prepare yourself for one of these jobs?

d. Describe internships or other activities in which you could engage to prepare yourself for one of these jobs.

 6. The Information Systems Audit and Control Association maintains a Web site at *www.isaca.org*. Visit this site and answer the following questions.

a. What is the purpose of this organization?

b. What are the CISA and CISM examinations? Why would an auditor or accountant or other non-IS professional seek one of these certificates? What value would such a certificate add?

c. Click on the Students and Educators tab on this site. What benefit would you gain from joining this organization?

d. What courses does this organization recommend for systems auditing and systems management?

e. Navigate this site, both the Students and Educators section as well as the overall site. Based on the information presented, what skills and abilities does someone need to become an effective information systems auditor? An effective information systems manager?

f. Search the Web for job opportunities for CISA- or CISM-qualified professionals. Characterize the employment prospects for such professionals.

 7. Search the Web for the term *security jobs hacking*.

a. What is a white-hat hacker? What qualifications does someone need to become a white-hat hacker?

b. What courses or other experience does someone need to become a white-hat hacker?

c. Characterize the employment prospects for white-hat hackers.

d. Would you want to be a white-hat hacker? Why or why not? What are the risks of such a job, as described in this chapter and also as described in articles you find on the Web?

Application Exercises

1. Suppose you are given the task of keeping track of the number of labor hours invested in meetings for systems development projects. Assume your company uses the traditional SDLC and that each phase requires two types of meetings: *Working meetings* involve users, systems analysts, programmers, and PQA test engineers. *Review meetings* involve all of those people, plus level-1 and level-2 managers of both user departments and the IT department.

a. Construct a spreadsheet that computes the total labor hours invested in each phase of a project. When a meeting occurs, assume you enter the project phase, the meeting type, the start time, the end time, and the number of each type of personnel attending. Your spreadsheet should calculate the number of labor hours and should add the meeting's hours to the totals for that phase and for the project overall.

b. Change your spreadsheet to include a budget of the number of labor hours for each type of employee for each phase. In your spreadsheet, show the difference between the number of hours budgeted and the number actually consumed.

c. Change your spreadsheet to include the budgeted cost and actual cost of labor. Assume that you enter, once, the average labor cost for each type of employee.

 2. Use Access to develop a failure-tracking database application. For each failure, your application should record the following:

FailureNumber (Use an Access autonumber data type.)

DateReported

FailureDescription

ReportedBy (the name of the PQA engineer reporting the failure)

FixedBy (the name of the programmer who is assigned to fix the failure)

DateFailureFixed

FixDescription

DateFixVerified

VerifiedBy (the name of the PQA engineer verifying the fix)

a. Create a FAILURE table, a PQA ENGINEER table, and a PROGRAMMER table. The last two tables should have *Name* (assume names are unique in each table) and *Email* columns. Add other appropriate columns to each table.

b. Create one or more forms that can be used to report a failure, to report a failure fix, and to report a failure verification. Create the form(s) so that the user can just pull down the name of a PQA engineer or programmer from the appropriate table to fill in the *ReportedBy, FixedBy,* and *VerifiedBy* fields.

c. Construct a report that shows all failures sorted by reporting PQA engineer and then by *DateReported.*

d. Construct a report that shows only fixed and verified failures

e. Construct a report that shows only fixed but unverified failures.

 3. Suppose you work for a small manufacturer of industrial-handling equipment, such as conveyor belts, wheeled carts, dollies, and so on. Assume your company employs 80 people in standard functions, such as product design, manufacturing, sales, and marketing. You work in accounting and have been asked to recommend three outsource vendors to manage the employees' 401(k) retirement plans. Use the Web to answer the following questions.

a. Explain what a 401(k) retirement plan is.

b. List three vendors that outsource such plans.

c. Summarize the product offerings from each of the vendors in your answer to part b.

d. Compare the costs of each of the products in your answer to part c.

e. Based on the data you have, summarize the advantages and disadvantages of each of the alternatives in your answer to part d. Make and state assumptions, if necessary.

4. Suppose you manage a department of 20 employees and you wish to build an information system to track their computers, the software that resides on those computers, and the licenses for each software product. Assume that employees can have more than one computer and that each computer has multiple software products. Each product has a single license. The license can be either a *site license* (meaning your organization paid for everyone in the company to be able to use that program) or the license is a purchase order number and date for the order that paid for the license.

a. Design a spreadsheet for keeping track of the employees, computers, and licenses. Insert sample data for three employees and at least five computers with typical software.

b. Design a database for keeping track of the employees, computers, and licenses. Assume your database has an EMPLOYEE table, a COMPUTER table, and a SOFTWARE_LICENSE table. Place appropriate columns in these tables and construct the relationship. Insert sample data for three employees, five computers, and multiple software licenses per computer.

c. Compare the spreadsheet and database solutions to this problem. Which is easier to set up? Which is easier to maintain?

d. Use whichever of your solutions you prefer for producing the following two reports:

  • A list of employees and their computers, sorted by employee.

  • A list of software products, the computers on which they reside, and the employees assigned those computers, sorted by software product name.

5. Assume you have been given the task of compiling evaluations that your company's purchasing agents make of their vendors. Each month, every purchasing agent evaluates all of the vendors that he or she has worked with in the past month on three factors: price, quality, and responsiveness. Assume the ratings are from 1 to 5, with 5 being the best. Because your company has hundreds of vendors and dozens of purchasing agents, you decide to use Access to compile the results.

a. Create a database with three tables: VENDOR (*VendorNumber, Name, Contact*), PURCHASER (*EmpNumber, Name, Email*), and RATING (*EmpNumber, VendorNumber, Month, Year, PriceRating, QualityRating, ResponsivenessRating*). Assume *VendorNumber* and *EmpNumber* are the keys of VENDOR and PURCHASER, respectively. Decide what you think is the appropriate key for RATING.

b. Create appropriate relationships using Tools/Relationships.

c. Using the table view of each table, enter sample data for vendors, employees, and ratings.

d. Create a query that shows the names of all vendors and their average scores.

e. Create a query that shows the names of all employees and their averages scores. *Hint:* In this and in question f, you will need to use the Group By function in your query.

f. Create a parameterized query that you can use to obtain the minimum, maximum, and average ratings on each criterion for a particular vendor. Assume you will enter *VendorName* as the parameter.

6. Develop a spreadsheet model of the cost of a virus attack in an organization that has three types of computers: employee workstations, data servers, and Web servers. Assume the number of computers affected by the virus depends on the severity of the virus. For the purposes of your model, assume that there are three levels of virus severity: *Low-severity* incidents affect fewer than 30 percent of the user workstations and none of the data or Web servers. *Medium-severity* incidents affect up to 70 percent of the user workstations, up to half of the Web servers, and none of the data servers. *High-severity* incidents can affect all organizational computers.

Assume 50 percent of the incidents are low severity, 30 percent are medium severity, and 20 percent are high severity.

Assume employees can remove viruses from workstations themselves, but that specially trained technicians are required to repair the servers. The time to eliminate a virus from an infected computer depends on the computer type. Let the time to remove the virus from each type be inputs to your model. Assume that when users eliminate the virus themselves, they are unproductive for twice the time required for the removal. Let the average employee hourly labor cost be an input to your model. Let the average cost of a technician also be an input to your model. Finally, let the total number of user computers, data servers, and Web servers be inputs to your model.

Run your simulation 10 times. Use the same inputs for each run, but draw a random number (assume a uniform distribution for all random numbers) to determine the severity type. Then, draw random numbers to determine the percentage of computers of each type affected, using the constraints stated previously. For example, if the attack is of medium severity, draw a random number between 0 and 70 to indicate the percentage of infected user workstations, and a random number between 0 and 50 to indicate the percentage of infected Web servers.

For each run, calculate the total of lost employee hours, the total dollar cost of lost employee labor hours, the total hours of technicians to fix the servers, and the total cost of technician labor. Finally, compute the total overall cost. Show the results of each run. Show the average costs and hours for the 10 runs.

PART 4 CASE 4-1

The Need for Technical Feasibility

The U.S, Internal Revenue Service (IRS) Business Systems Modernization (BSM) project has been a multiyear attempt to replace the existing tax-processing information systems with systems based on modern technology. Review pages 8 and 18 for a discussion of the underlying need, problems, and suggested problem solutions.

The subsystem that has generated the most controversy and been the cause of the most serious delays is the Customer Account Data Engine (CADE). CADE is an expert system that uses a database of business rules. Unlike most databases that contain facts and figures like CustomerName, Email, Balance, and so forth, the CADE database contains expert-system business rules, which are statements about how an organization conducts its business. In the context of the IRS, this database contains rules about tax laws and the processing of tax forms. An example of such a rule is:

Rule 10:

> IF the amount on line 7 of Form 1040EZ is greater than zero,
> THEN invoke Rule 15.

With a rule-based approach, the IRS need only develop programs that access the database and follow the rules. No other programs need to be developed.

Rule-based systems differ substantially from traditional application programs. Using traditional technology, the developers interview the users, determine what the business rules are, and then write computer code that operates in accordance with the rules. The disadvantage of such traditional programming is that only technically trained programmers can decipher the rules in the program code. Also, only trained programmers can add, change, or delete rules.

The advantage of rule-based systems like CADE is that the business rules are stored in the database and can be read, added, changed, or deleted by personnel with business knowledge but little computer training. Hence, in theory, CADE is more adaptable to changing requirements than a system written with traditional programming languages.

Unfortunately, the technical feasibility of using a rule-based system for a problem as large and complex as IRS tax processing is unknown. It appears, at least from public records, that no one ever tried to estimate that feasibility. The result has been a string of schedule delays and cost overruns. The first CADE release, which processes only the simplest individual tax returns (those using IRS Form 1040EZ), was to be completed by January 2002. It was delayed once until August 2003, and then delayed again to September 2004. At that point, a limited version of this first release was demonstrated.

The database for these simple returns has some 1,200 business rules, but no reliable estimate has yet been developed for the number of rules required for the full system. The lack of an estimate is particularly serious because some experts believe the difficulty and complexity of creating rules increases geometrically with the number of rules. Meanwhile, $33 million was invested in 2003, and another $84 million was spent in 2004.

Given the history of problems, the IRS hired the Software Engineering Institute (SEI) of Carnegie Mellon University to conduct an independent audit of the project. SEI verified that no one knows with any certainty how many business rules will eventually be required. Additionally, according to the SEI report,

> We believe that harvesting the business rules, not coding them, will drive the cost and schedule of future CADE releases. By harvesting, we mean capturing, adjudicating, and cataloging the rules. CADE has invested many resources exploring rules engines, but few resources exploring the rules themselves. The IRS needs to understand and document their business rules as well as the rules' complicated interactions. Some of the delays that have already plagued CADE are a direct result of an imperfect understanding of the business rules. This situation will only grow as the number and complexity of the implemented rules increases.

According to the SEI testimony, without reliable estimates of the number of business rules,

> No one knows how long rule harvesting will take, how many people will be required, the background, training and experience of the people required, or how much it will cost. Based on anecdotal information presented to us, we believe the time will be measured in years and cost will be measured in the tens of millions of dollars.
>
> Until sound, supported cost and schedule estimates for rule harvesting are available, future CADE plans and schedules are only tentative and likely subject to delays and missed milestones.

Sources: U.S. House, Committee on Ways and Means, Subcommittee on Oversight, Statement of M. Steven Palmquist, Chief Engineer for Civil and Intelligence Agencies, Acquisition Support Program, Software Engineering Institute, Carnegie Mellon University, Pittsburgh, Pennsylvania, February 12, 2004; and *treas.gov/irsob/documents/special_report1203.pdf* (accessed June 2005).

Questions

1. Ignoring developments that have occurred since this case was written, what statement can be made about the technical feasibility, cost feasibility, and schedule feasibility of this project?

2. Use your imagination to try to understand how this situation came about. The IRS selected a team of contractors to develop the information systems that would support the modernization effort. Those contractors proposed a rule-based system, but apparently no one asked whether such a system would work on a problem this large. How could that occur? Suppose you were a non-IT manager at the IRS. Would you know to ask? Suppose you were a senior manager at one of the contractors. Would you know to ask? If you did ask and your technical people said, "No problem," what would you do?

3. Suppose you are a senior IRS manager. In defense of your management, you say, "We hired reputable contractors who had extensive experience developing large and complicated systems. When they told us that a rule-based approach was the way to go, we agreed. Should we be required to second-guess the experts?" Comment on that statement. Do you believe it? Do you think it's a justification?

4. Does it seem remarkable that, according to the SEI review, no one has yet considered the time, cost, and difficulty of harvesting the rules? Clearly, the need to allocate time and labor to that problem was visible from the start of

the project. How do you think such an oversight occurred? What are the consequences of that oversight?

5. Suppose it turns out that a rule-based system is infeasible for processing more complicated tax returns. What alternatives are available to the IRS? As a taxpayer, which do you recommend?

6. Google "IRS CADE problems" and read three or four articles and reports on recent developments. Comment on any recent information that sheds light on your answers to questions 1 through 5. What strategy for solving this problem does the IRS seem to be following? How likely is that strategy to succeed?

C A S E   4 - 2

ChoicePoint

Read the ChoicePoint case in MIS in Use CE24 (page 599), if you have not done so already.
ChoicePoint offers a wide array of data products for industries, businesses, and consumers. ChoicePoint's homepage states, "ChoicePoint is the nation's leading provider of identification and credential verification services." Figure PC4-2-1 shows

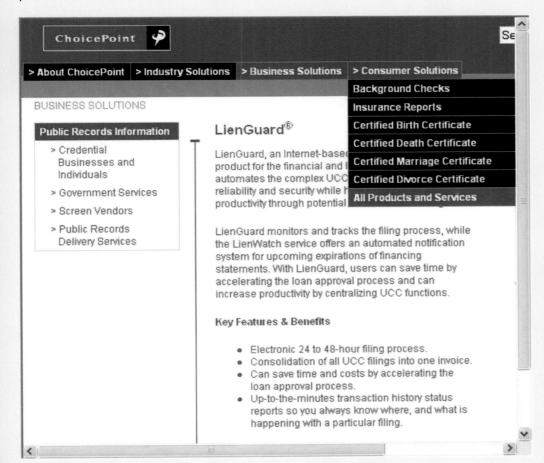

Figure PC4-2-1
ChoicePoint Consumer Services

Source: Used with permission of ChoicePoint.com.

Figure PC4-2-2
Ordering a Birth Certificate
via a ChoicePoint Partner

Source: Used with permission of
ChoicePoint.com.

just the Consumer Solutions from ChoicePoint's Web site at *choicepoint.com* as of February 2006. ChoicePoint provides some of these services directly; partners and data providers offer other of these services by links at the ChoicePoint site.

For example, a user who clicks on Certified Birth Certificate in Figure PC4-2-1 will be asked to provide a state. ChoicePoint then links to other data providers to process the request. Figure PC4-2-2 shows the link activated for obtaining the birth certificate for someone in Denver, Colorado.

Notice the red type in the form in Figure PC4-2-2. Apparently, Colorado law restricts access to birth certificates to those who have a "direct and tangible" interest. It would seem unlikely that this Web site enforces this law. The law and this language possibly exist to provide a basis for legal action when fraudulent use of a birth certificate occurs.

As a data utility, ChoicePoint maintains relationships with many different entities. It obtains its data from both public and private sources. It then sells access to this data to its customers. Much of the data, by the way, can be obtained directly from the data vendor. ChoicePoint adds value by providing a centralized access point for many data needs. In addition to data sources and customers, ChoicePoint maintains relationships with partners like the City of Denver Vital Records shown in Figure PC4-2-2. Finally, ChoicePoint also has relationships to the subjects on which it maintains data.

Questions

1. As discussed in *MIS in Use CE24* (page 599), ChoicePoint exposed itself to considerable expense, many problems, and a possible loss of brand confidence because it notified the Los Angeles Police Department, cooperated in the investigation, and notified the individuals whose records had been compromised. It could have buried the theft and possibly avoided any responsibility. Comment on the ethical issues and ChoicePoint's response. Did ChoicePoint choose wisely? Consider that question from the viewpoint of customers, law enforcement personnel, investors, and management.

2. Given ChoicePoint's experience, what is the likely action of similar companies whose records are compromised in this way? Given your answer, do you think federal regulation and additional laws are required? What other steps could be taken to ensure that data vendors notify people harmed by data theft?

 3. Visit *www.choicepoint.com*. Summarize the products that ChoicePoint provides. What seems to be the central theme of this business?

4. Review the security policy material in this chapter and reflect on an appropriate program policy for ChoicePoint. Describe why ChoicePoint needs a security policy and who and what should be governed by such a policy. Consider not only employees, but also data subjects, customers, data sources, and partners.

5. Suppose that ChoicePoint decides to establish a formal security policy on the issue of inappropriate release of personal data. Summarize the issues that ChoicePoint should address.

Information Systems for Collaboration

Q1 What Is Collaboration?

Collaboration occurs when two or more people work together toward a common goal, result, or product. Collaboration can be as simple as two people working together to set up a computer or as complex as all of the thousands of employees at Microsoft, worldwide, working together to increase the share price of their stock. Teams use information systems to facilitate collaboration. Because collaboration is such a broad term, though, it will be helpful to characterize it before we address its use in IS.

Figure CE1-1 shows two dimensions of collaboration. *People* and *skills* appear in the columns, and the project nature is shown in rows. The people on a collaborative team can practice one or a few skills, or they can practice many different skills. The project can consist of a single product or of many different products. For example, in the top-left cell, software development teams have a few skills (e.g., a programmer, systems analyst, test

Study Questions

Q1 What is collaboration?

Q2 How do teams use IS to communicate?

Q3 How do teams use IS to share resources?

Q4 How do teams use IS to manage projects?

Q5 How do different types of IS relate to different kinds of collaboration?

People ⬇

	One or a Few Skills	Many Skills	
Single Work Product **Projects** ➡	• Software development • Architecture	• Aircraft design • Building construction	Project Management Focus on: • Scheduling • Configuration management • Concurrent work control
Many Work Products	• Portfolio management • National sales	Organizations: • Boeing • Vanguard	Project Management Focus on: • Results • Competitions • Plans and quotas
	Team Management Focus on: • Standards • Training • Skill sharing • Knowledge management	Team Management Focus on: • Coordination and mutual appreciation • Interdependence • Mutual goals and individual needs • Organizational heroes	

Figure CE1-1
Two Dimensions of Collaboration

engineer), and everyone on the team works to produce a single product, the software. Or in the top-right cell, a team of many professionals (e.g., market analysts, engineers, drafts people, manufacturing specialists) can work together to produce a single thing, the design of an airplane.

In the second row, a team with a few skills can work together to produce many different products. At Vanguard, for example, portfolio managers all use financial analysis skills to manage different portfolios. Similarly, salespeople on a national sales team use sales skills to sell to different customers. Finally, in the lower-right cell, a group having many different skills can produce many different products. Here, the collaboration usually occurs at a very high level. For example, everyone at Vanguard works together to accomplish the goals of the entire organization.

We can use this model to understand how different teams use different IS types. Before we do that, we first will survey how teams use information systems to facilitate communication, shared resources, and project management.

Q2 How Do Teams Use IS to Communicate?

In order to accomplish a common goal, teams need to communicate. They use information systems to facilitate written, verbal, and meeting communications.

One could argue that some of these systems represent IT more than IS. When you pick up the phone, for example, are you using an IS (with the five components) or just a piece of IT? Most would argue in the case of the phone that it is just IT. But a personalized Web portal truly does represent an IS. So to emphasize the importance of people and procedures, we will use the term *information system* throughout the chapter extension. In truth, in some cases, calling the resource an IS is a bit of an exaggeration.

What Information Systems Support Written Communications?

Types of IS that support written communications are:

- Email/IM (instant messaging).
- Blogs (*www.DrudgeReport.com*).
- Wikis (*www.wikipedia.com*).
- Team Portals (*www.Microsoft.com/Office/Sharepoint*).

You know what **email** and **IM** are. By now, from Dee's story, you know what a **blog** is. (If you do not, check out *www.DrudgeReport.com*. You can also find employee blogs for companies in which you have an interest.) A **wiki** (pronounced "we-key") is a common-knowledge base that is maintained by its users. Wikis are processed on Web sites that allow users to add, remove, and edit content. The most famous is the general encyclopedia *www.wikipedia.com*. Figure CE1-2 shows the wikipedia entry that defines wikis. Many teams maintain their own wikis as a way of storing and publishing the group's knowledge. Your university most likely has a Web portal that publishes information about current events, the university's calendars, a directory of faculty and students, links to academic programs, and so forth.

A **team portal** is a Web site that publishes information about the team's activities. The portal might contain group schedules, calendars, access to important Web pages or Web sites, and access to information systems important to the

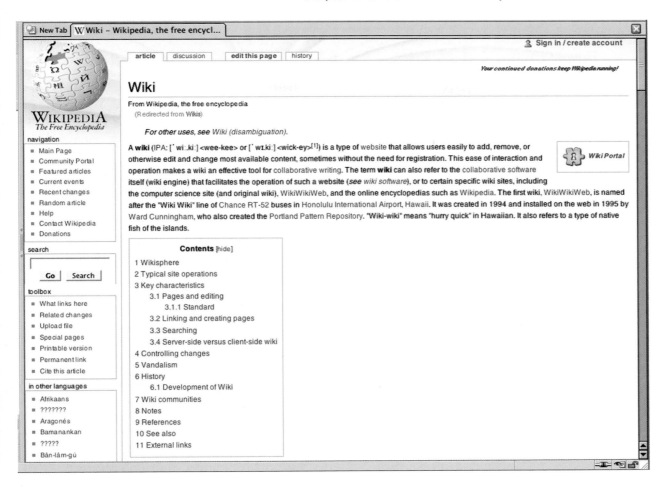

Figure CE1-2
A Wikipedia Entry

group. A sales team might support a portal that includes access to an information system that queries and reports on current sales results. Microsoft Office includes a product called SharePoint that makes it easy for groups to establish team portals.

What Information Systems Support Verbal Communications?

Types of IS that support verbal communications are:

- Phone/VOIP.
- Podcasts.

You certainly know about the phone. **VOIP**, or **Voice over IP**, provides telephone communication over the Internet. VOIP (pronounced "voyp") can be considerably cheaper than a long-distance phone call. Because all VOIP traffic is digital, it can be saved and later sent as attachments to email or other written documents. It can also be transformed into podcasts.

A **podcast** is a digital file that can be downloaded and played. Most podcasts are verbal, though video podcasts are increasing in popularity. You can find an example of both an audio and video podcast of the author of this book describing podcasts at *www.prenhall.com/Kroenke*. Figure CE1-3 (page 320) shows a Web site that offers numerous sports podcasts. Both audio and video podcasts are easy to produce and require only modest equipment investment.

What Information Systems Support Meeting Communications?

A third way that information systems facilitate collaborative communication concerns meetings. Types of IS that support meetings are:

- Conference calls.
- Video conferencing/Net Meeting.
- WebEx.
- Webcasts.

You probably know about conference calls, in which several people are connected in one phone call. **Video conferencing** is just a conference call with video cameras. **Net Meeting** is a proprietary Microsoft product that uses Windows and the Internet to produce a video conference. Figure CE1-4 shows the screen of a user who is participating in a Net Meeting. **WebEx** is a moderated conference call. The attendees dial in for audio on a conference call line and point their browsers to a Web site controlled by the moderator. All of the attendees on the call see the same screen display. The moderator runs the meeting and navigates in a controlled way through the Web site that is displayed. WebEx's are frequently used for conference-based sales calls.

Finally, a **Webcast** is a broadcast over the Internet of the proceedings of, typically, a large conference or meeting. Apple Computer is famous for its elaborate meetings that announce new products. While perhaps 2,000–3,000 people attend the announcement in person, tens or even hundreds of thousands more tune in to the Webcast of the meeting. Figure CE1-5 shows Steve Jobs in the middle of a Webcast presentation.

Figure CE1-4
Net Meeting Graphic

Figure CE1-5
Steve Jobs in a Webcast

Any or all of these techniques can be used to facilitate communication among a collaborative group. By the way, because of the availability of these communication media, it is possible for some people to form **virtual teams**. Such a team is one in which the team members reside in different geographic locations. In some cases, the virtual team members never meet in person.

Q3 How Do Teams Use IS to Share Resources?

Collaborative teams need to share resources. The resource might be something like a drawing or a design, or it could be knowledge of how to do something. Teams use three types of information systems for this purpose:

- Configuration management systems
- Workflow control systems
- Knowledge management systems

What Is Configuration Management?

When people work together to produce the same work product, it is possible for one person's work to interfere with another's. For example, suppose a group of architects work together on the same building. Without control, two architects can unknowingly obtain the same drawing, make changes to that drawing, and return it to the shared drawing database. In this case, one of the architect's changes will be lost.

In addition to control, with a shared work product, it is important to track who made what changes and when. At some point, someone may question the need for a change in the product, or someone may believe that his or her changes have been lost. Or someone may simply want to know what changes exist in what version(s) of the team's shared product.

The term **configuration management** refers to a management process that controls and tracks changes to a shared work product, such as a design, a document, a building, and so on. Configuration management is a *process* and requires an information system with all five components. Team members must follow configuration procedures for checking out and checking in documents, for making changes, and when using the configuration management information system appropriately.

If the configuration management process fails (or, worse, is nonexistent), it is possible to lose control of the shared product. Such loss of control can become a disaster and is an exceedingly poor reflection on team management. Regaining control of the work product is disruptive, time-consuming, and expensive. Truly, the best way to solve such a problem is *not to have it in the first place*. Hence, teams spend considerable time and effort to maintain configuration control.

Many teams use **version management** programs to control the configuration of documents, designs, and other electronic versions of products. For example, software development teams may use software such as CVS (*www.CVS.com*) or Subversion (*www.subversion.com*) to control versions of software code, test plans, and product documentation. Each team member uses the software to check out a resource. The system notes that the item is checked out when anyone else checks out that item. In some projects, only one person at a time can check out an item. When the work is finished, the team member checks the item back into the system and records notes or remarks about what was done. No one can check in any resource that he or she did not already check out. The history of every item in the shared resource can thus be determined at any time. Figure CE1-6 shows the screen a user would employ to check out a document.

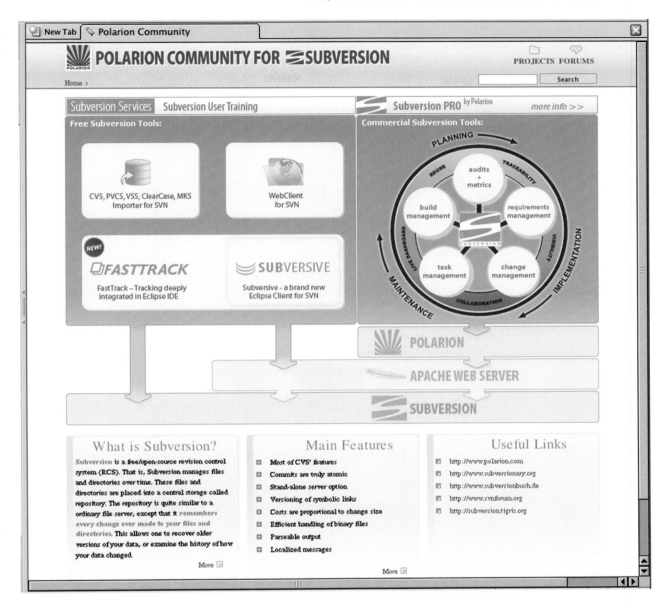

Figure CE1-6
Home Page for Subversion

What Is Workflow Control?

In addition to work-product control, some collaborative teams use **workflow control** systems to monitor the execution of the team's processes. Such systems ensure that appropriate actions are taken at appropriate times and prohibit the skipping of steps or tasks. A county government, for example, would use a workflow control system to control the issuance of building permits—a process that consists of numerous steps that need to be executed by different departments in a particular order. For example, if the project does not use public sewers, then the Health Department needs to approve a septic permit. If the property is located in an environmentally sensitive location, an environmental permit may be needed. There might be a rule that states the environmental permit cannot be issued until the septic permit is issued, and so forth.

A workflow control system ensures that the work team takes all steps in the proper order, and that all intermediate work products are produced as required.

What Is Knowledge Management?

Knowledge management (KM) is a third type of resource-sharing system. Often, especially on teams that involve employees performing the same tasks (portfolio managers, for example), one employee will know how to do something that other employees need to know. KM systems store and facilitate the sharing of such knowledge. See Chapter Extension 3, "Knowledge Management and Expert Systems," on page 335 for more information.

Q4 How Do Teams Use IS to Manage Projects?

Coordination of team activities is critical for the success of collaborative projects. We discuss project management in greater detail in Chapter Extension 18, "Large-Scale Systems Development," on page 529. Here, we will briefly describe three information systems used to facilitate project management:

- Team portals to share plans, calendars, and schedules
- Project management systems (Microsoft Project)
- Issues/results databases (failure-tracking databases)

Team members can share plans, calendars, and schedules using a team portal as described previously. For example, Microsoft provides features for such sharing in Outlook and also in Office Sharepoint.

The scheduling of tasks, equipment, and other resources can and usually does have *dependencies* (activities that depend on other activities). For example, in the construction of a new home, electricians cannot install the wiring before the walls are constructed. **Project management** software like Microsoft Project and other similar software is used to produce charts like the one shown in Figure CE1-7.

Figure CE1-7
A Typical Gantt Chart

Activity	September			October			
	14	21	28	5	12	19	26
Scheduling				8 ★			
Designing							
Ordering							
Delivering materials							
Machining components							
Assembling							
Inspecting							
Shipping							

Symbols:

⌐ Scheduled start and activity   ★ Review date   ⊠ Time not available (because of machine maintenance, material shortages, and so on)

⌐ Scheduled end of activity   ■ Completed work

This example, known as a **Gantt chart**, depicts tasks and dependencies, and it shows schedules. As tasks are finished, the charts are updated; the consequence of early or late tasks on the final delivery date can readily be determined. Many other charts are possible, as described in Chapter Extension 18, "Large-Scale Systems Development," on page 529.

In addition to project management systems, some teams develop **databases** to track important issues or results. In a software development project, for example, a database system is used to keep track of known failures, the employee who reported each failure, the employee charged with fixing the failure, and the current status of each fix. (See Chapter 10 for more about failure tracking.) The variety of database applications is extensive: A customer-support group could keep a database on unresolved customer problems, and a litigation team might use a database system to track trial evidence.

Q5 How Do the Different Types of IS Relate to Different Kinds of Collaboration?

Figure CE1-8 shows the relationships of collaborative information systems to different types of collaborative teams. In the first column, you can see that for teams of employees having one or a few skills, the focus of the IS is on knowledge bases, podcasts, and other forms of communication and knowledge sharing. In the second column, for teams having employees with many different skills, the focus is on Web sites, team portals, and other means of assessing the rich set of resources and activities in which the team engages.

Consider the rows of this table. For teams producing a single work product, the focus is on systems for project management, including systems for planning, scheduling, controlling, and integrating independent work. Information systems for teams that produce different work products focus on results, quotas, blogs, and systems to support competitive contests.

Figure CE1-8 is merely a guideline and a framework for organizing your knowledge. Any collaborative team can use any of the information systems described in this chapter extension. Those shown in Figure CE1-8 are simply the most likely.

	One or a Few Skills	Many Skills	
Single Work Product	• Software development • Architecture	• Aircraft design • Building construction	Project management systems Version management tools Workflow systems Resource sharing systems Issues databases
Many Work Products	• Portfolio management • National sales	Organizations: • Boeing • Vanguard	Results databases Quota systems Blogs Group email
	Knowledge bases Podcasts Net Meetings IM	Web sites Team portals Wikis Webcasts	

Figure CE1-8
Relationships of Collaborative Information Systems to Collaborative Teams

Active ? Review

Use this Active Review to verify that you understand the material in the chapter extension. You can read the entire extension and then perform the tasks in this review, or you can read the material for just one question and perform the tasks in this review for that question before moving on to the next one.

Q1 What is collaboration?

Define *collaboration*. Explain the four types of collaborative work in Figure CE1-1. Give an example, other than one in this figure, of each type.

Q2 How do teams use IS to communicate?

Describe information systems used for written communication. Describe those used for verbal communication. Describe those used for meetings. Explain why the term *information system* is a bit of a stretch in some cases and why *information technology* might be a better term.

Q3 How do teams use IS to share resources?

Describe the purpose and basic features and functions of configuration management, workflow control, and knowledge management systems. Give an example, other than one in this book, of the use of each.

Q4 How do teams use IS to manage projects?

Describe the purpose and basic features and functions of team portals, project management, and issues/results databases. Give an example, other than one in this book, of the use of each.

Q5 How do different types of IS relate to different kinds of collaboration?

Specify three appropriate information systems for each of the examples you developed in your review of Q1. For each category, explain which of the three you think will provide the greatest benefit.

Key Terms and Concepts

Blog 318
Collaboration 317
Configuration management 322
Databases 325
Email 318
Gantt chart 324
IM (instant message) 318

Knowledge management (KM) 324
Net Meeting 320
Podcast 319
Project management 324
Team portal 318
Version management 322
Video conferencing 320

Virtual team 321
Voice over IP (VOIP) 319
Webcast 320
WebEx 320
Wiki 318
Workflow control 323

Using Your Knowledge

1. Suppose you have just taken over management of a group of stockbrokers, who are paid on commission. Assume the performance of the group members is very uneven: Some are brokers who earn substantial commissions, and some earn little at all. Group morale is low. Describe information systems that the group could use to improve its performance. Describe information systems that it could use to improve morale.

2. Suppose you are a public relations executive and part of a product manage-
    ment team for a line of consumer products that sells $300 million annually.
    You are frustrated that you never seem to know what is going on in the group.
    You're not paranoid, but it does seem that you are often the last person in the
    group to learn of other team members' activities. You mention this to one of
    your colleagues, and she feels the same way herself. What kind of informa-
    tion systems could you use to improve this situation? Can you create this sys-
    tem on your own? If not, how would you proceed? Write a memo to your boss
    describing what you think could be done.

3. Suppose you are a production manager for a company that constructs small
    office buildings. Your company has its own employees, and it also works with
    many different subcontractors. What role do you see for a team portal at this
    company? Would there be one portal for the whole company, or one for each
    project? What criteria would you use to answer that question? What content
    would you put on a team portal? If you were asked to cost-justify the team
    portal, how would you respond?

4. Consider your MIS class as a collaborative team. In terms of Figure CE1-1,
    what sort of a team is it? Does your class use Blackboard or Web CT? In terms
    of the systems discussed in this chapter, what kind of system is Blackboard?
    (If your class does not use such products, check out the features and func-
    tions at *www.Blackboard.com*.) Name three other information systems that
    your class uses or could use to facilitate collaboration.

Chapter Extension 2

Chapter 2 provides the background for this Extension.

Information Systems and Decision Making

Chapters 2 and 3 described how information systems support business processes and how organizations use such systems to implement organizational strategy. This chapter extension presents a third perspective: how information systems support decision making.

Decision making in organizations is varied and complex, and so before discussing the role of information systems in support of decision making, we need to investigate the characteristics and dimensions of decision making itself.

Q1 How Do Decisions Vary by Level?

As shown in Figure CE2-1, decisions occur at three levels in organizations: *operational*, *managerial*, and *strategic*. The types of decisions vary depending on the level. **Operational decisions** concern day-to-day activities. Typical operational decisions are: How many widgets should we order from vendor A? Should we extend credit to vendor B? Which invoices should we pay today? Information systems that support operational decision making are called **transaction processing systems (TPS)**.

Managerial decisions concern the allocation and utilization of resources. Typical managerial decisions are: How much should we budget for computer hardware and programs for department A next year? How many engineers should we assign to project B? How many square feet of warehouse space do we need for the coming year? Information systems that support managerial decision making are called **management information systems (MIS)**. (Notice that the term *MIS* can be used in two ways: broadly, to mean the subjects in this entire book, and narrowly, to mean information systems that support managerial-level decision making. Context will make the meaning of the term clear.)

Strategic decisions concern broader-scope, organizational issues. Typical decisions at the strategic level are: Should we start a new product line? Should we open a centralized warehouse in Tennessee? Should we acquire company A? Information systems that support strategic decision making are called **executive information systems (EIS)**. An example is shown in Figure CE2-2 (page 330).

Notice that, in general, the decision timeframe increases as we move from operational to managerial to strategic decisions. Operational decisions normally involve actions in the short term: What should we do today or this week? Managerial decisions involve longer timeframes: What is appropriate for the

Study Questions

Q1 How do decisions vary by level?

Q2 What is the difference between structured and unstructured decisions?

Q3 How do decision level and decision process relate?

Q4 What is the difference between automation and augmentation?

Q5 How does IS support decision steps?

Video

- Decision Level
  - Operational
  - Managerial
  - Strategic
- Decision Process
  - Structured
  - Unstructured

Figure CE2-1
Decision-Making Dimensions

Figure CE2-2
Executive Information System
(EIS)

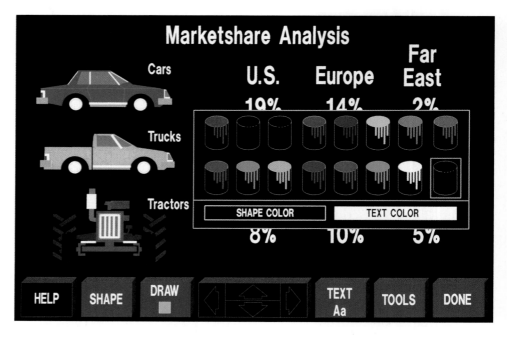

Figure CE2-2
Executive Information System
(EIS)

next quarter or year? Strategic decisions involve the long term; their consequences are not realized for years.

Q2 What Is the Difference Between Structured and Unstructured Decisions?

Figure CE2-3 shows levels of information systems with two decision processes: *structured* and *unstructured*. These terms refer to the method by which the decision is to be made, not to the nature of the underlying problem. A **structured decision** is one for which there is an understood and accepted method for making the decision. A formula for computing the reorder quantity of an item in inventory is an example of a structured decision process. A standard method for allocating furniture and equipment to employees is another structured decision process.

An **unstructured decision** process is one for which there is no agreed-on decision-making method. Predicting the future direction of the economy or the

Figure CE2-3
Relationship of Decision Level
and Decision Process

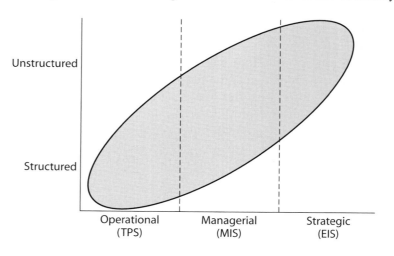

stock market is a famous example. The prediction method varies from person to person; it is neither standardized nor broadly accepted. (As one wit put it, "If you laid all the economists in the world end to end, they still would not reach a conclusion.") Another example of an unstructured decision process is assessing how well suited an employee is for performing a particular job. Managers vary in the manner in which they make such assessments.

Again, keep in mind that the terms *structured* and *unstructured* refer to the decision process, not to the underlying subject. Weather forecasting is a structured decision because the process used to make the decision is standardized among forecasters. Weather itself, however, is an unstructured phenomenon, as tornadoes and hurricanes demonstrate every year.

Q3 How Do Decision Level and Decision Process Relate?

The decision type and decision process are loosely related. As shown by the gray oval in Figure CE2-3, decisions at the operational level tend to be structured, and decisions at the strategic level tend to be unstructured. Managerial decisions tend to be both structured and unstructured.

We use the words *tend to be* because there are exceptions to the relationship illustrated in Figure CE2-3. Some operational decisions are unstructured (e.g., "How many taxicab drivers do we need on the night before the homecoming game?"), and some strategic decisions can be structured (e.g., "How should we assign sales quotas for a new product?"). In general, however, the relationship shown in Figure CE2-3 holds.

Q4 What Is the Difference Between Automation and Augmentation?

Figure CE2-4 contrasts two types of information system. **Automated information systems** are those in which the hardware and software components do most of the work. An information system that computes the quantity of items to order for inventory is an example of an automated system. Humans start the software and use the results, but hardware and software do most of the work.

Augmentation information systems are those in which humans do the bulk of the work. The information system exists to augment, support, or supplement the work done by people. An information system that uses email, instant messaging, and videoconferencing to assist the decision of whether to buy a competing company is an augmentation system. In contrast to the order-quantity computation system, the users look for support rather than answers.

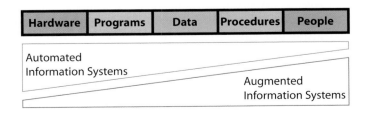

Figure CE2-4
Automated Versus Augmented
Information Systems

Figure CE2-5
How Decision Level, Decision
Type, and IS Type Are Related

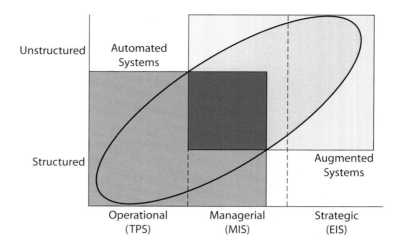

Figure CE2-5
How Decision Level, Decision
Type, and IS Type Are Related

Figure CE2-5 shows the relationship between the decision type and the IS type. In general, structured decisions can be supported by automated information systems, and they are generally applied at the operational and managerial levels of decision making. In contrast, unstructured decisions are supported by augmentation information systems, and they are generally applied at the managerial and strategic levels.

At this point, you may be wondering, "Why does all this matter?" One of the goals of this class is to help you become a better consumer of information systems and information technology. When you think about a new information system, you will be a better IT consumer if you ask yourself, "What is the nature of the underlying decision process?" If you can identify the type of process, you will know what type of information system may be helpful. Additionally, you will know not to invest in automated information systems for unstructured problems or in augmentation information systems for structured problems. This point may seem obvious, but organizations have wasted millions of dollars by not understanding the basic relationships shown in Figure CE2-5.

Q5 How Does IS Support Decision Steps?

Another way to examine the relationship between information systems and decision making is to consider how an information system is used during the steps of the decision-making process. The first two columns of Figure CE2-6 show the typical steps in the decision-making process: intelligence gathering, formulation of alternatives, choice, implementation, and review. During **intelligence gathering**, the decision makers determine what is to be decided, what the criteria for the decision will be, and what data are available. **Alternatives formulation** is the stage in which decision makers lay out various alternatives. They analyze the alternatives and select one during the **choice step**, and then they implement the decision in the **implementation step**. Finally, the organization reviews the results of the decision. The **review step** may lead to another decision and another iteration through the decision process.

As summarized in the right column of Figure CE2-6, each of these decision-making steps needs a different type of information system. During intelligence gathering, email and videoconferencing facilitate communication among the

Decision Step	Description	Examples of Possible Information Systems
Intelligence gathering	• What is to be decided? • What are the decision criteria? • Obtain relevant data	• Communications applications (email, video-conferencing, word processing, presentation) • Query and reporting systems • Data analysis applications
Alternatives formulation	• What are the choices?	• Communications applications
Choice	• Analyze choices against criteria using data • Select alternative	• Spreadsheets • Financial modeling • Other modeling
Implementation	• Make it so!	• Communications applications
Review	• Evaluate results of decision; if necessary, repeat process to correct and adapt	• Communications • Query and reporting • Spreadsheets and other analysis

decision makers. Also, during the first phase, decision makers use query and reporting systems as well as other types of data analysis applications to obtain relevant data. Decision makers use email and videoconferencing systems for communication during the alternatives-formulation step. During the choice step, analysis applications such as spreadsheets and financial and other modeling applications help decision makers to analyze alternatives. The implementation stage again involves the use of communications applications, and all types of information systems can be used during review.

Figure CE2-6
Decision-Making Steps

Active ? Review

Use this Active Review to verify that you understand the material in the chapter extension. You can read the entire extension and then perform the tasks in this review, or you can read the material for just one question and perform the tasks in this review for that question before moving on to the next one.

Q1 How do decisions vary by level?
Describe the differences among operational, managerial, and strategic decision making. Give an example, other than one in this book, of each. Explain how TPS, MIS, and EIS relate to these levels. Describe two different meanings for the term MIS.

Q2 What is the difference between structured and unstructured decisions?
Describe the difference between a structured decision and an unstructured decision. Explain why these terms do not rely on the underlying problem, but rather pertain to the process used.

Q3 How do decision level and decision process relate?
Explain the gray oval in Figure CE2-3.

Q4 What is the difference between automation and augmentation?
Describe the difference between an automated system and an augmentation system. Explain which components do the work for each. Give an example of automated and augmented versions of a customer service application. Describe the practical application to you of the information illustrated in Figure CE2-5.

Q5 How does IS support decision steps?
List and describe the steps in a decision process. Give an example of an information system that supports each step.

Key Terms and Concepts

Alternatives formulation step 332
Augmentation information system 331
Automated information system 331
Choice step 332
Executive information system (EIS) 329

Implementation step 332
Intelligence gathering step 332
Management information system (MIS) 329
Managerial decision 329
Operational decision 329
Review step 332

Strategic decision 329
Structured decision 330
Transaction processing system (TPS) 329
Unstructured decision 330

Using Your Knowledge

Singing Valley Resort is a top-end (rooms cost from $400 to $2,500 per night), 50-unit resort located high in the mountains of Colorado. Singing Valley prides itself on its beautiful location, its relaxing setting, and its superb service. The resort's restaurant is highly rated and has an extensive list of exceptional wines. The well-heeled clients are accustomed to the highest levels of service.

1. Give an example of three different operational decisions that Singing Valley personnel make each day. Describe an information system that could be used to facilitate those decisions.

2. Give an example of three different managerial decisions that Singing Valley managers make each week. Describe an information system that could be used to facilitate those decisions.

3. Give an example of three different strategic decisions that Singing Valley's owners might make in a year. Describe an information system for each.

4. Which of the decisions in your answers to questions 1–3 are structured? Which, if any, are unstructured?

5. Give an example of an automated system that would support one of the decisions in your answer to question 1. Describe work performed by each component of the information system.

6. Give an example of an augmentation system that would support one of the decisions in your answer to question 1. Describe work performed by each component of the information system.

7. Show how Figure CE2-5 applies to your answers to questions 1–6.

8. List the decision steps for one of the decisions in your answer to question 1. List the decision steps for one of the decisions in your answer to question 3. Compare the use of information systems to support each of the decision steps for these two decisions.

Chapter Extension 3

Chapter 3 provides the background for this Extension.

Knowledge Management and Expert Systems

Q1 What Are the Benefits of Knowledge Management?

Study Questions

Q1 What are the benefits of knowledge management?

Q2 What are content management systems?

Q3 What are the challenges of content management?

Q4 How do humans share knowledge via collaboration?

Q5 What are expert systems?

Knowledge management (KM) is the process of creating value from intellectual capital and sharing that knowledge with employees, managers, suppliers, customers, and others who need that capital. Although KM is supported by IS technology, KM is not technology. It is a *process* supported by the five components of an information system. Its emphasis is on people, their knowledge, and effective means for sharing that knowledge with others.

The benefits of KM accrue by managing and delivering organizational knowledge so as to enable employees and others to work smarter. Santosus and Surmacz cite the following as the primary benefits of KM:

1. KM fosters innovation by encouraging the free flow of ideas.
2. KM improves customer service by streamlining response time.
3. KM boosts revenues by getting products and services to market faster.
4. KM enhances employee retention rates by recognizing the value of employees' knowledge and rewarding them for it.
5. KM streamlines operations and reduces costs by eliminating redundant or unnecessary processes.[1]

In addition, KM preserves organizational memory by capturing and storing the lessons learned and best practices of key employees.

Before proceeding, realize that the term *organizational knowledge* is misleading. Organizations are inanimate, and they cannot have knowledge. The *people* in organizations possess and need knowledge. Today, people can share their knowledge in three different ways.

First, humans can share knowledge via books, papers, memos, Web pages, and other documents. Organizational information systems that store, manage, and deliver documents are called *content management systems*. Second, with the advent of modern communications technology, people can share their knowledge via *collaborative KM systems*. Finally, in addition to content management

---

[1]Megan Santosus and John Surmacz, "The ABCs of Knowledge Management," *CIO Magazine*, May 23, 2001, *cio.com/research/knowledge/edit/kmabcs.html* (accessed July 2005).

and collaboration, people can also share knowledge via *expert systems*. Such systems codify human knowledge into rules and process those rules to give advice or guidance. We will consider each type of KM system in the remainder of this chapter extension.

Q2 What Are Content Management Systems?

Content management systems are information systems that track organizational documents, Web pages, graphics, and related materials. Such systems differ from operational document systems in that they do not directly support business operations. An insurance company, for example, scans every document it receives and stores those documents as part of its client-processing application. This is not an example of a KM system because it is part of an operational, transaction-processing application. KM content management systems are not concerned with operational documents. Instead, they are concerned with the creation, management, and delivery of documents that exist for the purpose of imparting knowledge.

The largest collection of documents ever assembled exists on the Internet, and the world's best-known document search engine is Google. When you search for a term, or "Google it," you are tapping into the world's largest content management system. This system, however, was not designed for a particular KM purpose; it just emerged. Here, we are concerned with content management systems that are created and used by organizations for a specific KM purpose.

Typical users of content management systems are companies that sell complicated products and want to share their knowledge of those products with employees and customers. Someone at Toyota, for example, knows how to change the timing belt on the four-cylinder 2007 Toyota Camry. Toyota wants to share that knowledge with car owners, mechanics, and Toyota employees. Cisco wants to share with network administrators its knowledge about how to determine if a Cisco router is malfunctioning. Microsoft wants to share with the data miners of the world its knowledge about how to use its Data Transformation Services product to move data from an Oracle database into Excel.

The basic functions of content management systems are documents. Usually, the authoring of documents is considered to be outside the domain of the content manager. Documents arise from some source, and the goal of the content management system is to manage and deliver them. Documents and other resources have been prepared using Word, FrontPage, Acrobat, or some other document product. The only requirement that content managers place on document authoring is that the document has been created in a standardized format.

Q3 What Are the Challenges of Content Management?

Content management functions are, however, exceedingly complicated. First, most content databases are huge; some have thousands of individual documents, pages, and graphics. Figure CE3-1 shows the scale of the content management problem at Microsoft.com. Although the size of the content store is

- 110GB of content
- 3.2 million files
- Content created/changed 24/7 at a rate of 5GB per day
- 1,100 databases
- Multiple languages
- 125 million unique users per month
- 999 million page views per month

Figure CE3-1
Document Management at Microsoft.com (as of December 2003)

Source: Microsoft.com/backstage/inside.htm (accessed February 2004). ©2003 Microsoft Corporation. All rights reserved.

impressive (10GB is equivalent to 110 pickup trucks of books), the more critical number is the amount of new or changed content per day: 5GB. This means that roughly 5 percent of the content of Microsoft.com changes *every day*.

Another complication for content management systems is that documents do not exist in isolation from each other. Documents may refer to one another or multiple documents may refer to the same product or procedure. When one of them changes, others must change as well. Some content management systems keep linkages among documents so that content dependencies can be known and used to maintain document consistency.

A third complication is that document contents are perishable. Documents become obsolete and need to be altered, removed, or replaced. Consider, for example, what happens when a new product is announced. The document in Figure CE3-2 was first written before Microsoft Reporting Services was available to the public. It was written to build the business case for the product. Once the product became available, however, the description in this document needed to be changed. As shown here, the second paragraph states that the product is now available. As originally written, however, that paragraph stated that the product would be available soon. The day that Reporting Services shipped, every document that referenced that product on Microsoft.com had to be checked and possibly revised or removed.

Finally, consider the content management problem for multinational companies. Microsoft publishes Microsoft.com in over 40 languages. In fact, at Microsoft.com, English is just another language. Every document, in whatever language it was authored, must be translated into all languages before it can be published on Microsoft.com. Figure CE3-3 (page 338) shows the Chinese version of the article in Figure CE3-2.

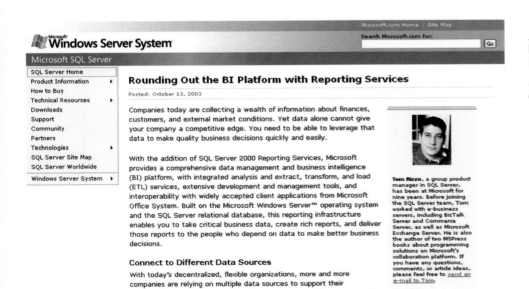

Figure CE3-2
Reporting Services: United States

Source: Used with permission of Tom Rizzo of Microsoft Corporation.

Figure CE3-3
Reporting Services: China

Source: Used with permission of Tom Rizzo of Microsoft Corporation.

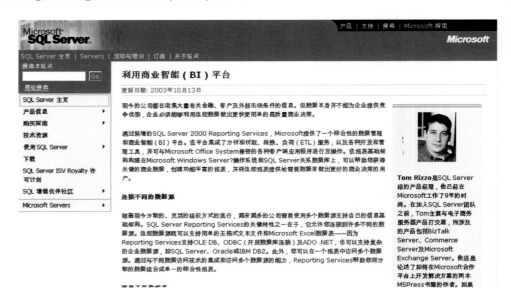

Users cannot pull content if they do not know it exists. So the content must be arranged and indexed, and a facility for searching the content devised. Here, however, organizations get a break, at least for their publicly accessible content.

As stated, the world's largest and most popular search engine is Google. Google searches through all public sites of all organizations. This means that Google is usually the fastest and easiest way to find a document. This often is true even within an organization. It may be easier, for example, for a General Motors employee to find a General Motors document using Google than using an in-house search engine. Google will have crawled through the General Motors site and will have indexed all documents using its superior technology.

Documents that reside behind a corporate firewall, however, are not publicly accessible and will not be reachable by Google or other search engines. Organizations must index their own proprietary documents and provide their own search capability for them.

One last consideration concerns the formatting of documents when they are delivered. Web browsers and other programs can readily format content expressed in HTML, PDF, or another standard format. Also, XML documents (see Chapter Extension 13) often contain their own formatting rules that browsers can interpret. The content management system will have to determine an appropriate format for content expressed in other ways.

Q4 How Do Humans Share Knowledge via Collaboration?

KM systems are concerned with the sharing not only of content, as just described, but also with the sharing of knowledge among humans. How can one person share knowledge with another? How can one person learn of another person's great idea?

Nothing is more frustrating for a manager to contemplate than the situation in which one employee struggles with a problem that another employee knows how to solve easily. Similarly, it would be frustrating to learn of a customer who returns a large order because the customer couldn't perform a basic operation with the product that many employees (and other customers) can readily perform.

Knowledge Management Alternatives

A variety of different information systems can be used to facilitate the sharing of human knowledge. In this section, we will consider several of the major alternatives.

Portals, Discussion Groups, and Email

Consider the following story:

> Around the holidays in 2000, a Giant Eagle deli manager thought of a way to display the seafood delicacy that proved irresistible to harried shoppers, accounting for an extra $200 in one-week sales. But uncertain of his strategy, he first posted the idea on the KnowAsis portal. Other deli managers ribbed him a bit, but one tried the idea in his store and saw a similar boost in sales. The total payoff to the company, for this one tiny chunk of information, was about $20,000 in increased sales in the two stores. The company estimates that if it had implemented the display idea across all its stores during this period, the payoff might have been $350,000. Previously, "there was no tradition of sharing ideas in the store environment," says Jack Flanagan, executive vice president of Giant Eagle business systems.[2]

An employee may have a good idea, a novel approach, or a better way to solve a problem, and KM systems allow that employee to share that knowledge with others. Notice in this example that the employee shared the idea gratuitously; no one asked him about how to arrange the seafood delicacy, the employee just posted the good idea on the team **portal**. It was up to other managers and employees to pull that knowledge down from the portal.

Discussion groups are another form of organizational KM. They allow employees or customers to post questions and queries seeking solutions to problems they have. Oracle, IBM, PeopleSoft, and other vendors support product discussion groups where users can post questions and where employees, vendors, and other users can answer them. Later, the organization can edit and summarize the questions from such discussion groups into **frequently asked questions (FAQs)**, another form of knowledge-sharing.

Basic email can also be used for knowledge-sharing, especially if email lists have been constructed with KM in mind. For example, an email list of all product-quality engineers, across all plants, across the organization, can facilitate communication among those employees.

Blogs and Podcasts

Recall that Dee, the protagonist of Chapters 1 through 6, used a **blog** as a knowledge-sharing device. She used the blog to publish sales materials and PowerPoint presentations and to describe sales techniques. She wanted to promote vicarious learning

[2]Lauren Gibbons Paul, "Why Three Heads Are Better Than One," *CIO Magazine*, December 1, 2003, *cio.com/archive/20103/km.html* (accessed July 2005).

by publishing successful techniques created by the salespeople themselves. And, as the sales rolled in, she wanted to motivate the team by publishing the latest sales data on her site.

Both video and audio **podcasts** can be used to share knowledge as well. An expert in, say, database design can publish a podcast on a particular design problem—for example, the representation of N:M relationships in the relational model. (See Chapter Extensions 5, "Database Design," on page 359 for a description of this problem and a method for solving it.) Expert salespeople can describe the secrets to their sales success in an audio podcast; similarly, experts in particular manufacturing techniques, such as welding stainless steel, can demonstrate in a video podcast how to perform that operation.

Both blogs and podcasts can be effective forms of knowledge sharing, but their characteristics are different. Whereas a blog is open-ended, can take many formats, and address many dimensions of a situation, podcasts are usually short and focused on a particular problem. A blog can be an effective way of publishing podcasts.

Resistance to Knowledge Sharing

Two human factors inhibit knowledge-sharing. The first is that employees can be reluctant to exhibit their ignorance. Out of fear of appearing incompetent, employees may not post their queries on bulletin boards or use email groups. Such reluctance can sometimes be reduced by the attitude and posture of the managers of such groups. One strategy for employees in this situation is to use email lists to identify a smaller group of people who have an interest in a specific problem. Members of that smaller group can then discuss the issue in a less-inhibiting forum.

The other inhibiting human factor is employee competition. "Look," says the top salesperson. "I earn a substantial bonus from being the top salesperson. Why would I want to share my sales techniques with others? I'd just be strengthening the competition." This understandable perspective may not be changeable. A KM application may be ill-suited to a competitive group. Or, the company may be able to restructure rewards and incentives to foster sharing of ideas among employees (e.g., giving a bonus to the group that develops the best idea).

Even in situations where there is no direct competition, employees may be reluctant to share ideas out of shyness, fear of ridicule, or inertia. In these cases, a strong management endorsement for knowledge-sharing can be effective, especially if that endorsement is followed by strong positive feedback. As one senior manager said, "There is nothing wrong with praise or cash, and especially cash."

Q5 What Are Expert Systems?

Expert systems, the last form of KM we will consider, are rule-based systems that encode human knowledge in the form of **IF/THEN rules**. Figure CE3-4 shows an example of a few rules that could be part of a medical expert system for diagnosing heart disease. In this set of rules, the system examines various factors for heart disease and computes a *CardiacRiskFactor*. Depending on the

```
Other rules here...

IF CardiacRiskFactor = 'Null' THEN Set CardiacRiskFactor = 0
IF PatientSex = 'Male' THEN Add 3 to CardiacRiskFactor
IF PatientAge >55 THEN Add 2 to CardiacRiskFactor
IF FamilyHeartHistory = 'True' THEN Add 5 to CardiacRiskFactor
IF CholesterolScore = 'Problematic' THEN Add 4 to CardiacRiskFactor
IF BloodPressure = 'Problematic' THEN Add 3 to CardiacRiskFactor
If CardiacRiskFactor = 'Male' THEN Add 3 to CardiacRiskFactor
IF PatientSex = 'Male' THEN Add 3 to CardiacRiskFactor
IF CardiacRiskFactor >15 THEN Set EchoCardiagramTest = 'Schedule'

Other rules here...
```

Figure CE3-4
Example of IF/THEN Rules

value of that risk factor, other variables are given values. Unlike this example, an operational expert system may consist of hundreds, if not thousands, of rules. The set of rules shown here may need to be processed many times because it is possible that *CardiacRiskFactor* is used on the IF side of a rule occurring before these rules.

The programs that process a set of rules are called **expert systems shells**. Typically, the shell processes rules until no value changes. At that point, the values of all the variables are reported as results.

To create the system of rules, the development team interviews human experts in the domain of interest. The rules in Figure CE3-4 would have been obtained by interviewing cardiologists who are known to be particularly adept at diagnosing cardiac disease. Such a system encodes the knowledge of those highly skilled experts and makes it available to less-skilled or less-knowledgeable professionals.

Many expert systems were created in the late 1980s and early 1990s, and some of them have been successful. They suffer from three major disadvantages, however. First, they are difficult and expensive to develop. They require many labor hours from both experts in the domain under study and designers of expert systems. This expense is compounded by the high opportunity cost of tying up domain experts. Such experts are normally some of the most sought-after employees in an organization.

Second, expert systems are difficult to maintain. Because of the nature of rule-based systems, the introduction of a new rule in the middle of hundreds of others can have unexpected consequences. A small change can cause very different outcomes. Unfortunately, such side effects cannot be predicted or eliminated. They are the nature of complex rule-based systems.

Finally, expert systems were unable to live up to the high expectations set by their name. Initially, proponents of expert systems hoped to be able to duplicate the performance of highly trained experts, like doctors. It turned out, however, that no expert system has the same diagnostic ability as knowledgeable, skilled, and experienced doctors. Even when expert systems were developed that came close in ability, changes in medical technology required constant changing of the expert system, and the problems caused by unexpected consequences made such changes very expensive.

Today, however, there are successful, less ambitious expert systems. Typically these systems address more restricted problems than duplicating a doctor's diagnostic ability. One example, discussed in *MIS in Use CE3* on page 342, is a system at Washington University Medical School.

Expert Systems for Pharmacies

The Medical Informatics group at Washington University School of Medicine in St. Louis, Missouri, develops innovative and effective information systems to support decision making in medicine. The group has developed several expert systems that are used as a safety net to screen the decisions of doctors and other medical professionals. These systems help to achieve the hospital's goal of state-of-the-art, error-free care.

Medical researchers developed early expert systems to support and in some cases to replace med-

ical decision making. MYCIN was an expert system developed in the early 1970s for the purpose of diagnosing certain infectious diseases. Physicians never routinely used MYCIN, but researchers used its expert system framework as the basis for many other medical systems. For one reason or another, however, none of those systems has seen extensive use.

In contrast, the systems developed at Washington University are routinely used, in real time, every day. One of the systems, DoseChecker, verifies appropriate dosages on prescriptions issued in the hospital. Another application, PharmADE, ensures that patients are not prescribed drugs that have harmful interactions. The pharmacy order entry system invokes these applications as a prescription is entered. If either system detects a problem with the prescription, it generates an alert like the sample shown in Figure 1.

A pharmacist screens an alert before sending it to the doctor. If the pharmacist disagrees with the alert, it is discarded. If the pharmacist agrees there is a problem with either the dosage or a harmful drug interaction, he or she sends the alert to the doctor. The doctor can then alter the prescription or override the alert. If the doctor does not respond, the system will

Pharmacy Clinical Decision Support
Version 2.0

Developed by The Division of Medical Informatics at Washington University School of Medicine for the Department of Pharmacy at Barnes Jewish Hospital.

Figure 1
Alert from Pharmacy Clinical Decision Support System

Data as of: Mar 10 2000 4:40 AM   Alert #: 13104   Satellite: CHNE

Patient Name	Registration	Age	Sex	Weight(kg)	Height(in)	IBW(kg)	Location
SAMPLE,PATIENT	9999999	22	F	114	0	0	528

Creatinine Clearance Lab Results (last 3):

Collection Date	Serum Creatinine	Creatinine Clearance
Mar 9 2000 9:55 PM	7.1	14

DoseChecker Recommendations and Thoughts:

Order	Start Date	Drug Name	Route	Dose	Frequency
295	Mar 10 2000 12:00 AM	MEPERIDINE INJ 25MG	IV	25 MG	Q4H
Recommended Dose/Frequency:				0.0 MG	PER DAY
Comments:	0 <= CrCl < 20. Mependine should not be used for more than 48 hours or at doses > 600 mg per day in patients with renal or CNS disease. Serious consideration should be given to using an alternative analgesic in this patient population.				

escalate the alert to higher levels until the potential problem is resolved.

Neither DoseChecker nor PharmADE attempts to replace the decision making of medical professionals. Rather, they operate behind the scenes, as a reliable assistant helping to provide error-free care.

Apparently, the systems work. According to the Informatics Web site, "Over a 6 month period at a 1,400 bed teaching hospital, the system [DoseChecker] screened 57,404 orders and detected 3,638 potential dosing errors." Furthermore, since the hospital implemented the system, the number of alerts has fallen by 50 percent, indicating that the prescribing process has been improved because of the feedback provided by the alerts.

Source: The Division of Medical Informatics at Washington University School of Medicine for the Department of Pharmacy at Barnes Jewish Hospital. *informatics.wustl.edu* (accessed January 2005). Used with permission of Medical Informatics at Washington University School of Medicine and BJC Healthcare.

Active ? Review

Use this Active Review to verify that you understand the material in the chapter extension. You can read the entire extension and then perform the tasks in this review, or you can read the material for just one question and perform the tasks in this review for that question before moving on to the next one.

Q1 What are the benefits of knowledge management?

Define *knowledge management*. Explain five key benefits of KM. Briefly describe three types of KM system.

Q2 What are content management systems?

Explain the purpose of a content management system. Describe how the Internet could be considered a content management system. Describe a more typical use of a content management system. Name and describe two functions of content management.

Q3 What are the challenges of content management?

Describe why size, dependencies, currency, and multinational factors make content management difficult. Explain two ways that organizations can index their documents.

Q4 How do humans share knowledge via collaboration?

Describe a need, other than one in this book, for a collaborative KM. Explain how portals, discussion groups, and email can be used for collaborative KM. Explain how FAQs can be used. Explain how blogs and podcasts be used for collaborative KM. Explain the difference in focus of a blog and a podcast. Describe two human factors that inhibit collaborative knowledge sharing.

Q5 What are expert systems?

Define *expert systems*. Explain the meaning of the rules in Figure CE3-4. Explain why a given set of rules might be evaluated more than once. Define *expert system shell*. Sketch the history of expert systems use. Describe three problems in developing and using expert systems. Describe the kinds of expert systems that are successful today.

Key Terms and Concepts

Using Your Knowledge

1. Consider the test bank that students in a fraternity, sorority, or other organization maintain. Is such a test bank an example of a content management system? Is it a computer-based system? Does it need to be computer-based to be considered a content management system? If it is not computer-based, describe advantages of having it be computer-based. What features and functions would you want in such a system? How could such a test bank be indexed? By professor? By class? What other dimensions might be used for indexing?

2. Assume you developed the system in question 1. Is it legal to use such a system? Is it ethical? Assume that your system is unavailable to all students. Is it unfair? How could you apply the skills and knowledge you obtained in developing such a system to your future career?

3. Explain how the challenges for content management systems described in this chapter would apply to the test bank system in your answer to question 1.

4. Explain how you use collaborative knowledge-sharing in your MIS class. Differentiate between techniques that are sponsored by your professor and techniques that you and your classmates have evolved on your own. Are there techniques described in this extension that you do not use? If so, describe how you might use them.

5. Develop the IF/THEN rules for an expert system that determines whether a particular student can enroll in a class. For your system, is there a need for multiple passes through the rule set? How accurate do you think your system would be? Which of the disadvantages of expert systems described in the text apply to this system?

6. Develop the IF/THEN rules for an expert system that selects a term class schedule for a particular student. (*Warning:* This can require a large number of rules.) Assume you can use the system in your answer to question 5 as part of this system. Would your system determine the optimum class schedule for that student, or just a feasible class schedule? In your answer, explain how you define optimum. How accurate do you think your system would be? Which of the disadvantages of expert systems described in the text apply to this system?

Chapter Extension 4

Chapter 4 provides the background for this Extension.

Preparing a Computer Budget

This chapter extension applies the knowledge you gained from Chapters 4 and 6 to the problem of establishing a hardware and software budget. You might ask, "Why do I need such knowledge?" The first question explains why.

Q1 Is $80,000 Enough?

Suppose that you manage the accounts payable department at a company that generates $100 million in sales—say, a manufacturer of fireplaces and related equipment. Assume that you just started the job and that at the end of your second day, your boss sticks her head in your office and announces, "I'm in a rush and have to go, but I wanted to let you know that I put $80,000 in the budget for computers for your department next year. Is that okay? Unfortunately, I've got to know by the day after tomorrow. Thanks."

How do you respond? You have two days to decide. If you agree to $80,000 and it turns out to be insufficient, then sometime next year your department will lack computing resources, and you'll have a management problem. If that happens, you may have to spend over your budget. You know that effective cost control is important to your new company, so you dread overspending. However, if you ask for more than $80,000, you will need to justify why you need it. How do you proceed?

The goal of this chapter extension is to prepare you to ask the right questions so you can respond effectively to your boss's question. We will return to this budget scenario at the end of the chapter extension.

Study Questions

Q1 Is $80,000 enough?

Q2 What process should I use for establishing a budget?

Q3 What hardware do we need?

Q4 What software do we need?

Q5 How do I plan for change?

Q6 What is the role of the IT department?

Q7 Is $80,000 enough? (continued)

Q2 What Process Should I Use for Establishing a Budget?

The steps for preparing a departmental hardware budget are summarized in Figure CE4-1 (page 346). You need first to determine the base requirements. This involves assessing the work your employees perform, creating job categories, and determining the computer workload requirements for each category. In accounts payable, for example, you might determine that you have three categories of workers: administrators, accounts payable specialists, and managers. You further determine that the administrators need hardware and software to access the

Figure CE4-1
A Process for Preparing a
Departmental IT Budget

Determine base requirements:
- The types of workload your employees perform
- The hardware requirements for each type
- The software requirements for each type

Forecast requirement changes during the budget period:
- Changes in the number of employees
- Changes in workload—new job tasks or information systems
- Mandatory changes in hardware or software

Prepare the budget:
- Using guidance from the IT department and accounting, price the hardware and software
- Determine if your department will be charged for networks, servers, communications, or other overhead expenses
- Add overhead charges as necessary

Figure CE4-1
A Process for Preparing a
Departmental IT Budget

company's Web portal, to email, and to perform minimal word processing. The accounts payable specialists need the same capabilities as the administrators, but they also need access to the organization's accounts payable system. Finally, you and other managers need to be able to perform the same work as the specialists, plus you need to process large spreadsheets for preparing budgets. You also need to access the company's payroll and human resources systems.

Once you have identified the job categories and the computer workload requirements for each, you can apply the knowledge from Chapters 4 and 6 and from the rest of this chapter extension to determine hardware and software requirements for each type. You can also use past departmental experience as a guide. If employees complain about computer performance with the equipment they have, you can determine if more is needed. If there are no bottlenecks or performance problems, you know the current equipment will do.

Given the base requirements, the next step is to forecast changes. Will you be adding or losing employees during the year? Will the workload change? Will your department be given new tasks that will necessitate additional hardware or software? Finally, during the year, will your organization mandate changes in hardware or software? Will you be required to upgrade your operating system or applications software? If so, will your budget be charged for those upgrades?

Once you have the base requirements and your change forecasts, you can prepare the budget. The first task is to price the hardware and software. As you will learn in Chapter 11, your IT department will most likely have established standards for hardware and software from which you will select. They will probably have negotiated prices on your behalf. If not, the accounting department can probably help you estimate costs based on their prior experience. You can also learn from the past experience of your own department.

Your organization may have a policy of charging the department's overhead fees for networks, servers, and communications. If so, you will need to add those charges to the budget as well.

Given this general process, we will now consider hardware and software in more depth than we did in Chapters 4 and 6.

Q3 What Hardware Do We Need?

We discussed the basic features and functions of hardware in Chapters 4 and 6. Figure CE4-2 is based on Figure 4-1 with the addition of a column showing typical prices. In this section, we discuss characteristics of the elements in this table in more detail.

Component	Performance Factors	Beneficial for:	Typical 2006 Price
CPU and data bus	• CPU speed • Cache memory • Data bus speed • Data bus width	• Fast processing of data once the data reside in main memory	Laptop: $500 (1GHz) $2,500 (3GHz) Workstation: $300 (1GHz) $3,000 (3GHz)
Main memory	• Size • Speed	• Holding multiple programs at one time • Processing very large amounts of data	$250–$400 per 500 MB
Magnetic disk	• Size • Channel type and speed • Rotational speed • Seek time	• Storing many large programs • Storing many large files • Swapping files in and out of memory	$100–$400 per 40 GB
Optical disk—CD	• Up to 700 MB • CD-ROM • CD-R (recordable) • CD-RW (rewritable)	• Reading CDs • Writable media can be used to back up files	Included with system
Optical disk—DVD	• Up to 4.7 GB • DVD-ROM • DVD-R (recordable) • DVD-RW (rewritable)	• Process both DVDs and CDs • Writable media can be used to back up files	Included to $400 for DVD-RW
Monitor—CRT	• Viewing size • Dot pitch • Optimal resolution • Special memory?	• Small budgets	$100–$500
Monitor—LCD	• Viewing size • Pixel pitch • Optimal resolution • Special memory?	• Crowded workspaces • When brighter, sharper images are needed	$100–$11,000+
Network access	• Wired • Wireless	• Choose to fit organization's network	Included
Printers	• Shared • Personal	• Reports	$200–$5,000+

Figure CE4-2
Hardware Components, Performance Factors, and Prices

Today, most computers are sold as packages to which the buyer can optionally upgrade and add equipment. You might choose a certain base package and add another 512MB of memory or a larger disk. However, if you find that you are adding substantial equipment to a standard package, you are usually better off to back up and begin with a higher grade standard package.

Laptop or Desktop?

To understand the computer buying process, visit *www.dell.com* (or other hardware vendor sites). You first will be given a choice of computer type: laptop or desktop. In general, desktops are cheaper, so unless employees have a need to travel or take their computers to meetings, select desktop. Also, desktops tend to be more reliable than laptops: They are neither bashed around at airport security check-ins nor dropped in the snow on the street. Furthermore, laptop designs force many components into a small shell and can have heat dissipation problems that lead to failure.

When preparing the budget for your department, you need to make the laptop/desktop decision for each job category. Next, you need to select the CPU speed and size of main memory. We consider these components next.

The CPU and Memory

As stated in Chapter 4, a fast CPU and data bus are most useful when processing data that already reside in main memory. Once you download a large spreadsheet, for example, a fast CPU will rapidly perform complicated, formula-based what-if analyses. A fast CPU also is useful for processing large graphics files. If, for example, you are manipulating the brightness of the elements of a large picture, a fast CPU will enable that manipulation to proceed quickly.

If the applications that you or your employees use do not involve millions of calculations or manipulations on data in main memory, then buying the fastest CPU is probably not worthwhile. In fact, a lot of the excitement about CPU speed is just industry "hype." Speed is an easily marketed and understood idea, but for most business processing, having a very fast CPU is often not as important as other factors, such as main memory.

Main Memory

According to the second row of Figure CE4-2, the two key performance factors for main memory are speed and size. Normally, a particular computer make and model is designed to use a given memory type, and the speed for that type is fixed. Once you buy the computer, there is nothing you can do to increase memory *speed*.

You can, however, increase the *amount* of main memory, up to the maximum size of memory that your computer brand and model can hold. In 2006, the maximum amount of memory for new personal computers ranged from 1.5 to 2.0 GB.

By the way, if budget is a consideration, you can sometimes buy memory from third parties more economically than from the computer manufacturer. However, you must make sure that you buy the correct memory type. Installing more memory is easy; low-skill technicians can perform that task, or if no vendor support is available, someone in your IT department can do it.

As shown in Figure CE4-2, installing more memory is beneficial for situations in which you run many different applications at the same time or if you process many large files (several megabytes or more, each). If your computer is constantly swapping files, installing more memory will dramatically improve performance. In truth, memory is cheap and is often the best way to get more performance out of a computer.

The operating system has tools and utilities that measure main memory utilization and file swapping. A computer technician can use these tools to determine, quite easily, whether more memory would be helpful.

Magnetic Disks

As stated in Chapter 4, magnetic and optical disks provide long-term, non-volatile data storage. The types and sizes of such storage devices will affect computer performance. First, understand that data are recorded on magnetic disks in concentric circles (Figure CE4-3). The disks spin inside the disk unit, and as they spin, magnetic spots on the disk are read or written by the *read/write head*.

The time required to read data from a disk depends on two measures: The first measure, called the **rotational delay**, is the time it takes the data to rotate

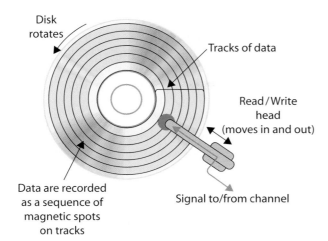

under the read/write head. The second, called **seek time**, is the time it takes the read/write arm to position the head over the correct circle. The faster the disk spins, the shorter the rotational delay. Seek time is determined by the make and model of the disk device.

Once the read/write head is positioned over the correct spot on the disk, data can flow over the channel to or from main memory. Like the data bus, the rate of data transfer depends on the width and speed of the channel. There are a number of different standards for channel characteristics. As of 2006, a common standard is the **ATA-100 (Advanced Technology Attachment) standard**. The number 100 indicates that the maximum transfer rate is 100MB per second.

When you buy a computer, you generally have just a few disk type choices. You may be able to choose one or two different channel standards (e.g., ATA-66 or ATA-100), and you may be able to choose disks with different rotational speeds.

You will always, however, be offered a number of choices in disk size. For most business users, 30GB is more than enough disk space. Large disks are cheap to manufacture, however, and you will be offered disks much larger than this (200GB or more). If you need to store a detailed map of every county in the United States or if you need to store huge downloads from your organization's server computers, then you may need such a large disk. Otherwise, don't fall prey to the hype; buy your employees better monitors or something else, instead.

As stated in Figure CE4-2, you can use a fast disk to compensate, to some extent, for too little memory. Recall that if you have too little memory, your computer will be swapping files in and out; a fast disk will speed this process. You might attempt to compensate with a fast disk if you have installed the maximum memory your computer can take and you still have a swapping problem. In that case, however, you would probably also benefit from a faster processor, and you might just as well buy a new computer.

Optical Disks

There are two kinds of optical disks: compact disks (CDs) and digital versatile disks (DVDs). Both are made of plastic and are coated with a photosensitive material. As stated in Chapter 4, bits are recorded by burning a pit into the photosensitive material using a low-power laser. The presence of a pit causes light to reflect and signifies a one; the absence of reflection signifies a zero. Like magnetic disks, optical disks are nonvolatile; they maintain their contents even when not powered.

The major difference between CDs and DVDs is how they store data; that difference is unimportant to this discussion, however. The *practical* differences between CDs and DVDs are capacity and speed. A typical CD has a maximum capacity of 700MB, whereas a DVD disk can store up to 4.7GB. Additionally, DVD transfer rates are about 10 times faster than those for CDs.

As shown in Figure CE4-3, some optical disks are *read only*; they cannot record data. These disks are abbreviated as **CD-ROM** and **DVD-ROM**. (*ROM* stands for *read-only memory*.) Other optical disks, denoted **CD-R** and **DVD-R**, can record data once. (The *R* stands for *recordable*.) A third group, denoted **CD-RW** and **DVD-RW**, can write data hundreds of times. (The *RW* stands for *rewritable*.)

CDs and DVDs see their greatest use in the entertainment industry for playing music and videos. CDs are used widely in commerce for distributing programs and other large files. Operating systems and programs, such as Windows and Microsoft Office, are distributed and installed from CD, for example. Also, writable media can be used to back up magnetic disk files.

Today, every computer should have at least a CD-ROM for installing programs. Most computers should also have some version of a writable optical disk for backing up data. Beyond those purposes, the major reason for having a CD or DVD is entertainment, and that reason may not be the best use of your organization's resources.

Video Displays

There are two types of video display monitors: CRTs and LCDs. **CRT monitors** use *cathode ray tubes*, the same devices used in traditional TV screens. Because they use a large tube, CRTs are big and bulky, about as deep as they are wide. **LCD monitors** use a different technology called *liquid crystal display* (LCD). With LCD monitors, no tube is required, so they are much slimmer, around 2 inches or so deep.

Both types of monitors display images by illuminating small spots on the screen called **pixels**. Pixels are arranged in a rectangular grid. An inexpensive monitor might display an image 800 pixels wide and 600 pixels high. A higher quality monitor would display a grid of $1,024 \times 768$ pixels, and some display as many as $1,600 \times 1,200$ pixels.

The number of pixels displayed depends not only on the size of the monitor, but also on the design of the mechanism that creates the image. For a CRT monitor, the **dot pitch** of the monitor is the distance between pixels. The smaller the dot pitch, the sharper and brighter the screen image will be. For an LCD monitor, the **pixel pitch** is the distance between pixels on the screen. As with CRT monitors, the smaller the pixel pitch, the sharper and brighter the image will be.

Each monitor has an **optimal resolution**, which is the size of the pixel grid (e.g., $1,024 \times 768$) that will give the best sharpness and clarity. This optimal resolution depends on the size of the screen, the dot or pixel pitch, and other factors. More expensive monitors have higher optimal resolution than others.

Each pixel on the monitor is represented in main memory. If the resolution of the monitor is $1,024 \times 768$, then there will be a table in memory with 1,024 rows and 768 columns. Each cell of this table has a numeric value that represents the color of the pixel that it represents. Programs change the display on the monitor by instructing the operating system to change values in this image table.

The amount of memory used for each cell in the pixel grid depends on the number of colors that each pixel is to display. For a black and white image, the cells can consist of a single bit: zero for white and one for black. To represent 16 colors, each pixel is represented by four bits. (Four bits can hold the numbers from 0 to 15—each number signifies a particular color.) Today, most monitors use a large color palette that necessitates 32 bits for each pixel and allows for 8,589,934,591 colors.

Substantial main memory is needed for this large palette. To represent an image in $1,024 \times 768$ resolution, a total of 3,145,728 bytes of memory ($1,024 \times 768 \times 4$ bytes) is needed. For reasons beyond the scope of this text, sometimes several versions of this pixel table are in memory.

Because these tables occupy a large amount of memory, some computers dedicate a separate memory cache just to the video display. The design of such memory is optimized for video use as well. Such special-purpose video memory is particularly important for multimedia applications where large images change rapidly. It is also important for 3D video in computer games.

For monitors of equivalent quality, the initial cost of CRT monitors is less than that for LCD monitors. LCD monitors have a longer life, however, so they may actually cost less over time. Because of the speed at which technology improvements take place, most people upgrade to a better computer before they ever wear out their monitor, so this extra life may not matter.

The big advantage of LCD monitors is, of course, their smaller footprint, which means they take up less desk space. They are especially desirable when work requires viewing more than one monitor at a time. Stock traders on Wall Street, for example, need three or four monitors, and these monitors are always LCDs.

Network Access

As you learned in Chapter 6, every networked computer must have a network interface card (NIC). NICs support either wired or wireless connections, and the decision about which to choose will be dictated by the type of network your department has. Today, many computers ship with both types of NIC as standard equipment. If not, you'll need to add the proper NIC to the computers you specify. Note, too, that wired computers can be readily upgraded to wireless by the installation of a wireless NIC.

Printers

Printers are available in many different types, sizes, and qualities. The discussion of those options is not within the scope of an MIS book. Visit *www.cnet.com/printers* or other similar Web sites if you want to know more about printer options.

We will be concerned here only with whether you want to share the printer. If you do, there are two options: A printer can be attached to a computer and others can access the printer via that computer, or the printer can be equipped with its own NIC, and users can access it directly. For most purposes, the latter is preferred because it frees up a computer.

Q4 What Software Do We Need?

We discussed the features and functions of software in Chapter 4. Figure CE4-4 (page 352) shows categories of software, the decisions you'll need to make, and approximate prices. Note in the *Price* column that software is sometimes

Category	Decisions to Make	Typical 2006 Prices
Operating system (Windows, Mac OS, Linux)	• Usually determined by organizational policy • May need to select version	• Possibly included with hardware. • Possibly paid for by site license. • Otherwise, $100–$300 for upgrade. • $300–$500 new.
Standard horizontal application, such as Microsoft Office or OpenOffice	• May be determined by organizational policy. • Choose package with components you need: word processing, spreadsheet, presentation, email client, or personal DBMS.	• Usually only the very minimum included with hardware. • Possibly paid for by site license. • Otherwise, $100–$300 for upgrade. • $300–$500 new.
Other horizontal applications	Document creation (Adobe Acrobat), photo processing (Adobe Photoshop, Jasc Paint Shop Pro), illustration (Adobe Illustrator), etc.	• Possibly minimum feature "teaser" versions included with hardware. • Possibly paid for by site license. • Otherwise, $100–$300 for upgrade. • $300–$700 new.
Vertical package software (Goldmine, Act!, AutoCad)	Determined by job category needs.	• Seldom included with hardware. • Possibly paid for by site license. • Otherwise. $100–$300 for upgrade. • $300–$1,500 new.
Vertical applications (CRM, ERP, etc.)	Determined by job category needs.	• Not included with hardware. • Possibly paid for by site license, or a license for a certain number of seats (users). • Otherwise, $500–$1,000 per user or more.

Figure CE4-4
Software Components and Prices

included with the purchase of hardware. Also, the term **site license** means that an organization has purchased a license to equip all of the computers on a site (or possibly across the company at many sites) with certain software. For example, Prentice Hall might negotiate with Microsoft to provide a version of Windows to all of its employees. The cost of a site license is high, but the per-unit is generally much less than the unit retail price. Also, purchasing a site license relieves the organization from tracking which computers have which software and ensuring that all licenses are paid appropriately.

The term **upgrade** means just what it says: Vendors usually do not require their customers to pay the price of *new* software when upgrading from a previous version. For example, Microsoft offers a license to upgrade WindowsXP to Vista for less than the price of a new copy of Vista.

Operating Systems

Organizational policy usually determines the operating system. Although some organizations permit users to run a mixture of operating systems, most standardize on just one. This statement pertains to user computers; many organizations run a different operating system on servers than on user computers. We ignore servers here because you are unlikely to be involved in the decision of a server operating system.

Unless your organization is very small, it likely has an IT department. If so, that department will install the operating system on all new computers and will install upgrades on existing computers as well. In a small organization, you will likely buy a computer from a vendor like Dell that has done the operating system installation for you.

Horizontal Market Software

Most organizations today use Microsoft Office for their standard applications like word processing and spreadsheets. Office licenses are sold in a number of different configurations. Some include just Word and Excel, while others include Word, Excel, PowerPoint, Access, Outlook, and possibly other applications. Your organization may have a site license for a particular version.

OpenOffice is an alternative to Office that is supported by the open-source community and is license-free in most cases. OpenOffice is gaining slowly in popularity, especially in organizations that are very cost-conscious. OpenOffice can process most documents prepared by Office, and the reverse. One exception to this is that OpenOffice does not have personal DBMS that is compatible with Access.

Your employees may require other types of horizontal software. Designers and other document preparers may need software for document preparation, photo processing, desktop publishing, or illustrations. Often vendors of this software provide free teaser versions (products with limited functionality) of their products with new computers. Sometimes these limited versions provide sufficient capability for a given job. In the case of Adobe Acrobat, for example, Adobe makes the Acrobat Reader available license-free. Few organizations need multiple licenses of this type of software, so site licenses for this type are rare.

Vertical Market Software

Examples of vertical market software are contact managers like Goldmine and Act! and engineering software like AutoCad. Such products are almost never included in the price of a new computer. Your organization may have negotiated a site license for such software, or even a restricted site license to provide it to the employees of certain departments.

Licenses for some of this software can be surprisingly expensive, and some small organizations elect to install the software without licenses. **This practice is both illegal and highly unethical.** Some small companies believe they are too small to be worth the cost of a lawsuit and use the software anyway. Such practice is dishonest, disreputable, and entirely reprehensible.

As you will read in Chapter Extension 10, "Cross-Functional Systems: CRM, ERP, and EAI," on page 439, *customer relationship management* (*CRM*) and *enterprise resource planning* (*ERP*) are systems that are used widely throughout an organization and can have hundreds or even thousands of users. The vendors of these products usually charge a license for each user or for a certain number of users (sometimes expressed in **seats**). Your organization might buy a license for, say, up to 500 seats of a particular application. If your department is using any of these systems, you need to check with your IT department to determine what costs apply to you.

Q5 How Do I Plan for Change?

The budgeting method described in this chapter extension is based on the number of employees in each job category in your department. So when thinking about change, the first question is whether there will be changes in the number of employees in each category. If so, you should adjust the budget accordingly.

Figure CE4-5
Issues to Consider When
Planning for Change

- Changes in the number of employees in each category
- Changes in departmental responsibilities
- Merger or aquisition of another department
- Vendor strangle and cram
- Important features in new sofware versions

Next, will there be changes in your departmental responsibilities? Will those changes necessitate defining a new job category with different hardware and software requirements? If so, adjust the budget. Even if no new job category is defined, new responsibilities may require adjustments in the number of employees in existing job categories.

Another source of change is the merger or acquisition of another department. In this case, the best approach is to ensure, as part of the departmental change, that all employees bring their existing computers with them. The employees, who have set up their computers to their needs and tastes, will appreciate that as well. If the new employees will be performing new tasks, they may need new hardware and software, however.

The last source of change arises from vendor **"strangle-and-cram"** marketing. Most vendors will, at some point, stop support for a particular software product. At some point, Microsoft, for example, will stop support for Windows 2000. The company will claim that the software is more than seven years old, has obsolete technology, is requiring inordinate amounts of its resources to maintain, is full of security problems, and so on. When the company ceases support (the strangle), you will be forced to upgrade (the cram). Such decisions are usually announced months or even a year or more in advance, so you will know its coming. Ask your IT department if such a change is on the horizon, and, if so, plan your budget accordingly.

Even if you are not strangled, you may have good reasons for upgrading some of your department's software. If so, adjust your budget. Be aware, however, that newer versions of products can require faster CPUs and more main memory. Vendors will list the minimal required system for their products; such minimums are notoriously understated, however. Check with existing users of the new software to determine what the true hardware requirements are.

Sometimes, you can save money by rotating computers among employees in different job categories. If, for example, you purchase faster computers for employees who run applications necessitating fast performance, you can sometime rotate their old computers to employees in a job category that requires less-powerful computers. Some managers slide computers in this way for years. By doing so, they need to buy new computers only for the group requiring higher performance. It does mean, however, that job categories requiring less computer power never receive a new computer, which can be bothersome to some employees. Anyone who is the youngest of six children will understand the rarity of new clothes!

Figure CE4-5 summarizes the issue to consider when preparing for change.

Q6 What Is the Role of the IT Department?

As you will learn in Chapter 11, the IT department normally provides a help desk or other facility to assist end users. Unknown to most users, however, is that the IT department has many other responsibilities, including maintaining networks and servers, administering databases, planning IT, developing and installing new systems, and so forth. Its responsibilities are compounded because it must do all of this while providing a secure computing environment.

To meet these many responsibilities, most IT departments set standards on the hardware and software that users can employ. In some cases, the IT department will specify a menu of different computer systems, from very powerful computers for, say, high-performance graphics computation, down to less-powerful ones for email and Internet access only. Additionally, the IT department may specify a particular operating system, and particular versions of both horizontal and vertical applications software.

As the manager of an end-user department, you are strongly advised to work within these standards. Even if they seem objectionable, overly restrictive, or excessively costly to you or your employees, you will be better off in the long run by staying within the IT department's guidelines. By following their standards, you will make it easier and cheaper for them to provide high-quality, secure computing service to your department. If you cannot live within those standards, then raise the issue with the IT department manager, but do not work around them.

Q7 Is $80,000 Enough? (continued)

With this chapter as background, we can now return to the question of the $80,000 budget for computers. You need to respond by the end of the next day, and you had scheduled other work that you cannot just drop. So, you must figure out how to respond quickly in the limited time you have.

First, you need to know what the $80,000 is supposed to cover. Is it just for hardware? Is it for both hardware and software? Is it for the PCs that your employees use, or is it for those PCs and also for departmental servers, networks, and other overhead expenses? For our purposes, suppose the $80,000 is for hardware and software for your employees; it does not include servers, networks, or other computing infrastructure.

With those assumptions, you can apply the process in Figure CE4-1. Because the employees in your department will bear the consequences of these decisions, you may decide to involve them in this work. You can ask one or two key employees to specify job categories and the computer resources they believe are necessary for each category. (They can be doing this while you do the other tasks you had planned for tomorrow.)

When addressing this question, you might obtain assistance from the IT or accounting departments. It is possible that either of these departments has already performed hardware/software needs analyses that you can adapt to your situation.

Throughout all of this, you will be asking questions and carefully evaluating answers. Why do we need a new processor for that type of work? Why isn't more main memory sufficient? How do you know? Why do we need such big disks? Do we have the right video monitors? Given the background of this chapter, you should be able to understand the answers to these questions and to generate more questions on your own.

Knowing how to approach the "$80,000 question" will stand you in good stead throughout your business career.

Active ? Review

Use this Active Review to verify that you understand the material in the chapter extension. You can read the entire extension and then perform the tasks in this review, or you can read the material for just one question and perform the tasks in this review for that question before moving on to the next one.

Q1 Is $80,000 enough?

Summarize the task that you have been given. Explain the consequences if you do not budget enough. Explain the consequences if you ask for more budget than you need.

Explain the way that you would proceed. Describe why this task is more difficult and also more important because you are brand new to your job.

Q2 What process should I use for establishing a budget?

List the tasks of the process in Figure CE4-1. Explain the work to be done for each task. Describe why the order of the tasks is important.

Q3 What hardware do we need?

Describe how you would use the table in Figure CE4-2. Explain how this table relates to the process in Figure CE4-1. Ensure you understand each row and column of this table.

Q4 What software do we need?

Describe how you would use the table in Figure CE4-4. Explain how this table relates to the process in Figure CE4-1. Ensure you understand each row and column of this table. Explain the term *site license*. Characterize the behavior of a company that chooses to install software without licenses, assuming they are too small to sue.

Q5 How do I plan for change?

Describe five sources of change in a computer budget. Explain how you would deal with each. Describe one way to save money by rotating computers among employees.

Q6 What is the role of the IT department?

Summarize the responsibilities of the IT department as described in this chapter extension. (You will learn more about these and other responsibilities in Chapter 11.) Describe the importance of standards in light of these responsibilities.

Q7 Is $80,000 enough? (continued)

Describe how you would proceed to answer this question. Show how the process in Figure CE4-1 applies to this situation. Given the little time you have available, explain how you might delegate work to other employees. Explain why you need the knowledge in this chapter extension, even if you are going to delegate the majority of the work.

Key Terms and Concepts

ATA-100 standard 349	DVD-ROM 350	Seats 353
CD-R 350	DVD-RW 350	Seek time 349
CD-ROM 350	LCD monitor 350	Site license 352
CD-RW 350	Optimal resolution 350	Strangle-and-cram 354
CRT monitor 350	Pixel 350	Upgrade 352
Dot pitch 350	Pixel pitch 350	
DVD-R 350	Rotational delay 348	

Using Your Knowledge

1. Because of Moore's Law, computer price/performance data are continually changing. Suppose that you have been given the task of updating the price data in Figure CE4-2. Visit *www.dell.com* and *www.cnet.com*, and any other

site you wish, and verify or change the data in the *Price* column in Figure CE4-2.

2. Software prices also change, but not as dramatically as hardware prices. Nonetheless, visit *www.Amazon.com* or other Web sites and verify the data in Figure CE4-3. For prices on particular products, such as Goldmine, Acrobat, Paint Shop Pro, and so forth, your best strategy might be to Google these products, using the product name and price—thus, Google "Goldmine license prices" or a similar term.

3. Many site licenses are negotiated on a one-on-one basis, and it may be difficult to find the actual price and other terms of a site license for a particular product. Search the Internet, though, for terms like "Windows site license program" or "Acrobat site license program," and determine the terms of the site licenses, even if you cannot obtain the specific price.

4. Why does Adobe provide licenses to Acrobat Reader for free? Do you think a better strategy would be to charge a modest license fee, say $50, for Acrobat Reader? What are the consequences of that action? How can Adobe verify the wisdom of this pricing decision?

5. Create a paper worksheet for preparing a departmental budget. Place job categories on the rows of your worksheet and place hardware items and software items in the columns of your worksheet. Demonstrate the utility of this worksheet by filling it with sample data for three different job categories.

6. Transform your answer to question 5 to an Excel worksheet. Use Excel to compute the total budget. Assume that the user of the worksheet will enter the number of employees in each job category and that this number will be used to compute costs.

7. Regarding the $80,000 question, you, a brand-new employee, have only two days to answer, and you probably had already scheduled meetings for those two days when your boss dropped this in your lap.
   a. Can you complain? Would it be wise to do so?
   b. Often, students will answer this question by specifying a complex, time-consuming, and *totally schedule-infeasible* process. You don't have time for a complex analysis. Still, an answer must be provided, and the answer is important. Explain how you can use delegation.
   c. Do you think your boss already knows the answer to this question? If so, why would she ask you?
   d. Is it possible your boss is using this exercise as a way of learning how you manage? If you think this is possible, how does that realization change your response to this question?
   e. You've been managing your department for only two days. How does the way you respond to this challenge influence the perception that your employees will have of you? Is this an important consideration? Would you consider having a lower-quality answer if it meant a higher-quality process? Is such a trade-off necessary?

Chapter Extension 5

Chapter 5 provides the background for this Extension.

Database Design

In this chapter extension, you will learn about data modeling and how data models are transformed into database designs. You'll also learn the important role that business professionals have in the development of a database application system.

Study Questions

Q1 Who will volunteer?

Q2 How are database application systems developed?

Q3 What are the components of the entity-relationship data model?

Q4 How is a data model transformed into a database design?

Q5 What is the users' role?

Q6 Who will volunteer? (continued)

Q1 Who Will Volunteer?

Suppose you are the manager of fund-raising for a local public television station. Twice a year you conduct fund drives during which the station runs commercials that ask viewers to donate. These drives are important; they provide nearly 40 percent of the station's operating budget.

One of your job functions is to find volunteers to staff the phones during these drives. You need 10 volunteers per night for six nights, or 60 people, twice per year. The volunteers' job is exhausting, and normally a volunteer will work only one night during a drive.

Finding volunteers for each drive is a perpetual headache. Two months before a drive begins, you and your staff start calling potential volunteers. You first call volunteers from prior drives, using a roster that your administrative assistant prepares for each drive. Some volunteers have been helping for years; you'd like to know that information before you call them so that you can tell them how much you appreciate their continuing support. Unfortunately, the roster does not have that data.

Additionally, some volunteers are more effective than others. Some have a particular knack for increasing the callers' donations. Although those data are available, the information is not in a format that you can use when calling for volunteers. You think you could better staff the fund-raising drives if you had that missing information.

You know that you can use a computer database to keep better track of prior volunteers' service and performance, but you are not sure how to proceed. By the end of this chapter extension, when we return to this fund-raising situation, you will know what to do.

Q2 How Are Database Application Systems Developed?

You learned in Chapter 5 that a database application system consists of a database, a DBMS, and one or more database applications. A database application, in turn, consists of forms, reports, queries, and possibly application programs.

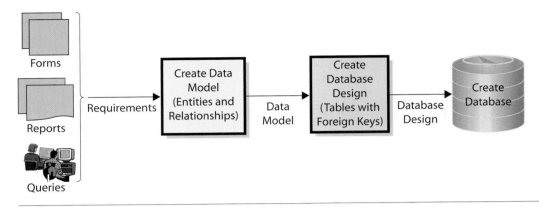

Figure CE5-1
Database Development Process

The question then becomes this one: How are such systems developed? And, even more important to you, what is the users' role? We will address these questions in this chapter extension.

Figure CE5-1 summarizes the database application system development process. First, the developers interview users and develop the requirements for the new system. During this process, the developers analyze existing forms, reports, queries, and other user activities. The requirements for the database are then summarized in something called a **data model**, which is a logical representation of the structure of the data. The data model contains a description of both the data and the relationships among the data. It is akin to a blueprint. Just as building architects create a blueprint before they start construction, so, too, database developers create a data model before they start designing the database.

Once the users have validated and approved the data model, it is transformed into a database design. After that, the design is implemented in a database, and that database is then filled with user data.

You will learn much more about systems development in Chapter 10 and its related extensions. We discuss data modeling here because users have a crucial role in the success of any database development: They must validate and approve the data model. Only the users know what should be in the database.

Consider, for example, a database of students that an advisor uses for his or her advisees. What should be in it? Students? Classes? Records of emails from students? Records of meetings with students? Majors? Student Organizations? Even when we know what themes should be in the database, we must ask, how detailed should the records be? Should the database include campus addresses? Home addresses? Billing addresses?

In fact, there are many possibilities, and the database developers do not and cannot know what to include. They do know, however, that a database must include all the data necessary for the users to perform their jobs. Ideally, it contains that amount of data and no more. So during database development, the developers must rely on the users to tell them what they need in the database. They will rely on the users to check the data model and to verify it for correctness, completeness, and appropriate level of detail. That verification will be your job. We begin with a discussion of the entity-relationship data model—the most common tool to use to construct data models.

Q3 What Are the Components of the Entity-Relationship Data Model?

The most popular technique for creating a data model is the **entity-relationship (E-R) data model**. With it, developers describe the content of a database by defining the things (*entities*) that will be stored in the database and the *relationships* among those entities. A second, less popular tool for data modeling is the **Unified Modeling Language (UML)**. We will not describe that tool here. However, if you learn how to interpret E-R models, with a bit of study, you will be able to understand UML models as well.

Entities

An **entity** is some thing that the users want to track. Examples of entities are *Order, Customer, Salesperson*, and *Item*. Some entities represent a physical object, such as *Item* or *Salesperson*; others represent a logical construct or transaction, such as *Order* or *Contract*. For reasons beyond this discussion, entity names are always singular. We use *Order*, not *Orders*; *Salesperson*, not *Salespersons*.

Entities have **attributes** that describe characteristics of the entity. Example attributes of *Order* are *OrderNumber, OrderDate, SubTotal, Tax, Total*, and so forth. Example attributes of *Salesperson* are *SalespersonName, Email, Phone*, and so forth.

Entities have an **identifier**, which is an attribute (or group of attributes) whose value is associated with one and only one entity instance. For example, *OrderNumber* is an identifier of *Order*, because only one *Order* instance has a given value of *OrderNumber*. For the same reason, *CustomerNumber* is an identifier of *Customer*. If each member of the sales staff has a unique name, then *SalespersonName* is an identifier of *Salesperson*.

Before we continue, consider that last sentence. Is the salesperson's name unique among the sales staff? Both now and in the future? Who decides the answer to such a question? Only the users know whether this is true; the database developers cannot know. This example underlines why it is important for you to be able to interpret data models, because only users like yourself will know for sure.

Figure CE5-2 shows examples of entities for the Student database. Each entity is shown in a rectangle. The name of the entity is just above the rectangle,

Video

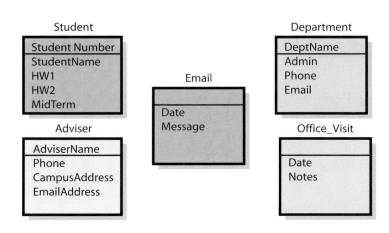

Figure CE5-2
Student Data Model Entities

and the identifier is shown in a section at the top of the entity. Entity attributes are shown in the remainder of the rectangle. In Figure CE5-2, the *Adviser* entity has an identifier called *AdviserName* and the attributes *Phone, CampusAddress,* and *EmailAddress.*

Observe that the entities *Email* and *Office_Visit* do not have an identifier. Unlike *Student* or *Adviser,* the users do not have an attribute that identifies a particular email. We could make one up. For example, we could say that the identifier of *Email* is *EmailNumber,* but if we do so we are not modeling how the users view their world. Instead, we are forcing something onto the users. Be aware of this possibility when you review data models about your business. Do not allow the database developers to create something that is not part of your business world.

Relationships

Entities have **relationships** to each other. An *Order,* for example, has a relationship to a *Customer* entity and also to a *Salesperson* entity. In the Student database, a *Student* has a relationship to an *Adviser,* and an *Adviser* has a relationship to a *Department.*

Figure CE5-3 shows sample *Department, Adviser,* and *Student* entities and their relationships. For simplicity, this figure shows just the identifier of the entities and not the other attributes. For this sample data, *Accounting* has three professors, Jones, Wu, and Lopez, and *Finance* has two professors, Smith and Greene.

The relationship between *Advisers* and *Students* is a bit more complicated, because in this example, an adviser is allowed to advise many students, and a student is allowed to have many advisers. Perhaps this happens because students can have multiple majors. In any case, note that Professor Jones advises students 100 and 400 and that student 100 is advised by both Professors Jones and Smith.

Diagrams like the one in Figure CE5-3 are too cumbersome for use in database design discussions. Instead, database designers use diagrams called **entity-relationship (E-R) diagrams**. Figure CE5-4 shows an E-R diagram for the data in Figure CE5-3. In this figure, all of the entities of one type are represented by a single rectangle. Thus, there are rectangles for the *Department, Adviser,* and *Student* entities. Attributes are shown as before in Figure CE5-2.

Figure CE5-3
Example of Department, Adviser, and Student Entities and Relationships

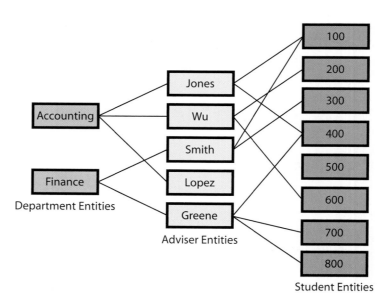

Department Entities

Adviser Entities

Student Entities

Figure CE5-4
Example Relationships—
Version 1

Additionally, a line is used to represent a relationship between two entities. Notice the line between *Department* and *Adviser*, for example. The forked lines on the right side of that line signify that a department may have more than one adviser. The little lines, which are referred to as a **crow's foot**, are shorthand for the multiple lines between *Department* and *Adviser* in Figure CE5-3. Relationships like this one are called **one-to-many (1:N)** relationships because one department can have many advisers.

Now examine the line between *Adviser* and *Student*. Here, a crow's foot appears at each end of the line. This notation signifies that an adviser can be related to many students and that a student can be related to many advisers, which is the situation in Figure CE5-3. Relationships like this one are called **many-to-many (N:M)** relationships, because one adviser can have many students and one student can have many advisers.

Students sometimes find the notation N:M confusing. Interpret the *N* and *M* to mean that a variable number, greater than one, is allowed on each side of the relationship. Such a relationship is not written *N:N*, because that notation would imply that there are the same number of entities on each side of the relationship, which is not necessarily true. *N:M* means that more than one entity is allowed on each side of the relationship and that the number of entities on each side can be different.

Figure CE5-4 is an example of an entity-relationship diagram. Unfortunately, there are several different styles of entity-relationship diagrams. This one is called, not surprisingly, a **crow's-foot diagram** version. You may learn other versions if you take a database management class.

Figure CE5-5 shows the same entities with different assumptions. Here, advisers may advise in more than one department, but a student may have only one adviser, representing a policy that students may not have multiple majors.

Which, if either, of these versions is correct? Only the users know. These alternatives illustrate the kinds of questions you will need to answer when a database designer asks you to check a data model for correctness.

The crow's-foot notation shows the maximum number of entities that can be involved in a relationship. Accordingly, they are called the relationship's **maximum cardinality**. Common examples of maximum cardinality are 1:N, N:M, and 1:1 (not shown).

Another important question is, "What is the minimum number of entities required in the relationship?" Must an adviser have a student to advise, and must a student have an adviser? Constraints on minimum requirements are called **minimum cardinalities**.

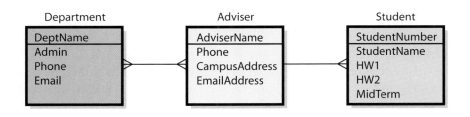

Figure CE5-5
Example Relationships—
Version 2

Figure CE5-6 presents a third version of this E-R diagram that shows both maximum and minimum cardinalities. The vertical bar on a line means that at least one entity of that type is required. The small oval means that the entity is optional; the relationship need not have an entity of that type.

Thus, in Figure CE5-6, a department is not required to have a relationship to any adviser, but an adviser is required to belong to a department. Similarly, an adviser is not required to have a relationship to a student, but a student is required to have a relationship to an adviser. Note, also, that the maximum cardinalities in Figure CE5-6 have been changed so that both are 1:N.

Is the model in Figure CE5-6 a good one? It depends on the rules of the university. Again, only the users know for sure.

Q4 How Is a Data Model Transformed into a Database Design?

Database design is the process of converting a data model into tables, relationships, and data constraints. The database design team transforms entities into tables and expresses relationships by defining foreign keys. Database design is a complicated subject; as with data modeling, it occupies weeks in a database management class. In this section, however, we will introduce two important database design concepts: normalization and the representation of two kinds of relationships. The first concept is a foundation of database design, and the second will help you understand key considerations made during design.

Normalization

Normalization is the process of converting poorly structured tables into two or more well-structured tables. A table is such a simple construct that you may wonder how one could possibly be poorly structured. In truth, there are many ways that tables can be malformed—so many, in fact, that researchers have published hundreds of papers on this topic alone.

Consider the *Employee* table in Figure CE5-7. It lists employee names, hire dates, email addresses, and the name and number of the department in which the employee works. This table seems innocent enough. But consider what happens when the Accounting department changes its name to Accounting and Finance. Because department names are duplicated in this table, every row that has a value of "Accounting" must be changed to "Accounting and Finance."

Data Integrity Problems

Suppose the Accounting name change is correctly made in two rows, but not in the third. The result is shown in Figure CE5-7. This table has what is called a **data integrity problem**: Some rows indicate that the name of Department 100 is

Employee

Name	HireDate	Email	DeptNo	DeptName
Jones	Feb 1, 2002	Jones@ourcompany.com	100	Accounting
Smith	Dec 3, 2004	Smith@ourcompany.com	200	Marketing
Chau	March 7, 2004	Chau@ourcompany.com	100	Accounting
Greene	July 17, 2003	Greene@ourcompany.com	100	Accounting

a. Table Before Update

Employee

Name	HireDate	Email	DeptNo	DeptName
Jones	Feb 1, 2002	Jones@ourcompany.com	100	Accounting and Finance
Smith	Dec 3, 2004	Smith@ourcompany.com	200	Marketing
Chau	March 7, 2004	Chau@ourcompany.com	100	Accounting and Finance
Greene	July 17, 2003	Greene@ourcompany.com	100	Accounting

b. Table with Incomplete Update

Figure CE5-7
A Poorly Designed Employee Table

Accounting and Finance, and another row indicates that the name of Department 100 is Accounting.

This problem is easy to spot in this small table. But consider a table in a large database that has over 300 thousand rows. Once a table that large develops serious data integrity problems, months of labor will be required to remove them.

Data integrity problems are serious. A table that has data integrity problems will produce incorrect and inconsistent information. Users will lose confidence in the information, and the system will develop a poor reputation. Information systems with poor reputations become heavy burdens to the organizations that use them.

Normalizing for Data Integrity

The data integrity problem can occur only if data are duplicated. Because of this, one easy way to eliminate the problem is to eliminate the duplicated data. We can do this by transforming the table in Figure CE5-7 into two tables, as shown in Figure CE5-8. Here, the name of the department is stored just once, therefore no data inconsistencies can occur.

Employee

Name	HireDate	Email	DeptNo
Jones	Feb 1, 2002	Jones@ourcompany.com	100
Smith	Dec 3, 2004	Smith@ourcompany.com	200
Chau	March 7, 2004	Chau@ourcompany.com	100
Greene	July 17, 2003	Greene@ourcompany.com	100

Department

DeptNo	DeptName
100	Accounting
200	Marketing
300	Information Systems

Figure CE5-8
Two Normalized Tables

Of course, to produce an employee report that includes the department name, the two tables in Figure CE5-8 will need to be joined back together. Because such joining of tables is common, DBMS products have been programmed to perform it efficiently, but it still requires work. From this example, you can see a trade-off in database design: Normalized tables eliminate data duplication, but they can be slower to process. Dealing with such trade-offs is an important consideration in database design.

The general goal of normalization is to construct tables such that every table has a *single* topic or theme. In good writing, every paragraph should have a single theme. This is true of databases as well; every table should have a single theme. The problem with the table in Figure CE5-7 is that it has two independent themes: employees and departments. The way to correct the problem is to split the table into two tables, each with its own theme. In this case, we create an *Employee* table and a *Department* table, as shown in Figure CE5-8.

As mentioned, there are dozens of ways that tables can be poorly formed. Database practitioners classify tables into various **normal forms** according to the kinds of problems they have. Transforming a table into a normal form to remove duplicated data and other problems is called *normalizing* the table.[1] Thus, when you hear a database designer say, "Those tables are not normalized," she does not mean that the tables have irregular, not-normal data. Instead, she means that the tables have a format that could cause data integrity problems.

Summary of Normalization

As a future user of databases, you do not need to know the details of normalization. Instead, understand the general principle that every normalized (well-formed) table has one and only one theme. Further, tables that are not normalized are subject to data integrity problems.

Be aware, too, that normalization is just one criterion for evaluating database designs. Because normalized designs can be slower to process, database designers sometimes choose to accept non-normalized tables. The best design depends on the users' requirements.

Representing Relationships

Figure CE5-9 shows the steps involved in transforming a data model into a relational database design. First, the database designer creates a table for each entity. The identifier of the entity becomes the key of the table. Each attribute of the entity becomes a column of the table. Next, the resulting tables are normalized so that each table has a single theme. Once that has been done, the next step is to represent relationship among those tables.

For example, consider the E-R diagram in Figure CE5-10(a). The *Adviser* entity has a 1:N relationship to the *Student* entity. To create the database design, we construct a table for *Adviser* and a second table for *Student*, as shown in

Figure CE5-9
Transforming a Data Model into a Database Design

- Represent each entity with a table
  - Entity identifier becomes table key
  - Entity attributes become table columns
- Normalize tables as necessary
- Represent relationships
  - Use foreign keys
  - Add additional tables for N:M relationships

[1] See David Kroenke, *Database Processing*, 10th ed. (Upper Saddle River, NJ: Prentice Hall, 2006) for more information.

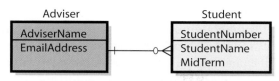

a. 1:N Relationship Between Adviser and Student Entities

Adviser Table—Key is AdviserName

AdviserName	EmailAddress
Jones	Jones@myuniv.edu
Choi	Choi@myuniv.edu
Jackson	Jackson@myuniv.edu

Student Table—Key is StudentNumber

StudentNumber	StudentName	MidTerm
100	Lisa	90
200	Jennie	85
300	Jason	82
400	Terry	95

b. Creating a Table for Each Entity

Adviser Table—Key is AdviserName

AdviserName	Email
Jones	Jones@myuniv.edu
Choi	Choi@myuniv.edu
Jackson	Jackson@myuniv.edu

Foreign Key Column Represents Relationship

Student—Key is StudentNumber

StudentNumber	StudentName	MidTerm	AdviserName
100	Lisa	90	Jackson
200	Jennie	85	Jackson
300	Jason	82	Choi
400	Terry	95	Jackson

c. Using the AdviserName Foreign Key to Represent the 1:N Relationship

Figure CE5-10(b). The key of the *Adviser* table is *AdviserName*, and the key of the *Student* table is *StudentNumber*.

Further, the *EmailAddress* attribute of the *Adviser* entity becomes the *EmailAddress* column of the *Adviser* table, and the *StudentName* and *MidTerm* attributes of the *Student* entity become the *StudentName* and *MidTerm* columns of the *Student* table.

The next task is to represent the relationship. Because we are using the relational model, we know that we must add a foreign key to one of the two tables. The possibilities are: (1) place the foreign key *StudentNumber* in the *Adviser* table or (2) place the foreign key *AdviserName* in the *Student* table.

The correct choice is to place *AdviserName* in the *Student* table, as shown in Figure CE5-10(c). To determine a student's adviser, we just look into the *AdviserName* column of that student's row. To determine the adviser's students, we search the *AdviserName* column in the *Student* table to determine which rows have that adviser's name. If a student changes advisers, we simply change the value in the *AdviserName* column. Changing *Jackson* to *Jones* in the first row, for example, will assign student 100 to Professor Jones.

For this data model, placing *StudentNumber* in *Adviser* would be incorrect. If we were to do that, we could assign only one student to an adviser. There is no place to assign a second adviser.

This strategy for placing foreign keys will not work for all relationships, however. Consider the data model in Figure CE5-11(a); here, there is an N:M relationship between advisers and students. An adviser may have many students, and a student may have multiple advisers (for multiple majors). The strat-

Figure CE5-11
Representing an N:M
Relationship

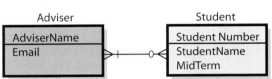

Adviser | Student

Adviser	Student
AdviserName	Student Number
Email	StudentName
	MidTerm

a. N:M Relationship Between Adviser and Student

Adviser—Key is AdviserName

AdviserName	Email
Jones	Jones@myuniv.edu
Choi	Choi@myuniv.edu
Jackson	Jackson@myuniv.edu

No room to place second or third AdviserName

Student—Key is StudentNumber

StudentNumber	StudentName	MidTerm	AdviserName
100	Lisa	90	Jackson
200	Jennie	85	Jackson
300	Jason	82	Choi
400	Terry	95	Jackson

b. Incorrect Representation of N:M Relationship

Adviser—Key is AdviserName

AdviserName	Email
Jones	Jones@myuniv.edu
Choi	Choi@myuniv.edu
Jackson	Jackson@myuniv.edu

Student—Key is StudentNumber

StudentNumber	StudentName	MidTerm
100	Lisa	90
200	Jennie	85
300	Jason	82
400	Terry	95

Adviser_Student_Intersection

AdviserName	StudentNumber
Jackson	100
Jackson	200
Choi	300
Jackson	400
Choi	100
Jones	100

Student 100 has three advisers.

c. Adviser_Student_Intersection Table Represents the N:M Relationship

egy we used for the 1:N data model will not work here. To see why, examine Figure CE5-11(b). If student 100 has more than one adviser, there is no place to record second or subsequent advisers.

It turns out that to represent an N:M relationship, we need to create a third table, as shown in Figure CE5-11(c). The third table has two columns, *AdviserName* and *StudentNumber*. Each row of the table means that the given adviser advises the student with the given number.

As you can imagine, there is a great deal more to database design than we have presented here. Still, this section should give you an idea of the tasks that need to be accomplished to create a database. You should also realize that the database design is a direct consequence of decisions made in the data model. If the data model is wrong, the database design will be wrong as well.

Q5 What Is the Users' Role?

As stated, a database is a model of how the users view their business world. This means that the users are the final judges as to what data the database should contain and how the records in that database should be related to one another.

The easiest time to change the database structure is during the data modeling stage. Changing a relationship from 1:N to N:M in a data model is simply a matter of changing the 1:N notation to N:M. However, once the database has been constructed, loaded with data, and application forms, reports, queries, and application programs created, changing a 1:N relationship to N:M means weeks of work.

You can glean some idea of why this might be true by contrasting Figure CE5-10(c) with Figure CE5-11(c). Suppose that instead of having just a few rows, each table has thousands of rows; in that case, transforming the database from one format to the other involves considerable work. Even worse, however, is that application components will need to be changed as well. For example, if students have at most one adviser, then a single text box can be used to enter *AdviserName*. If students can have multiple advisers, then a multiple-row table will need to be used to enter *AdviserName*, and a program will need to be written to store the values of *AdviserName* into the *Adviser_Student_Intersection* table. There are dozens of other consequences as well, consequences that will translate into wasted labor and wasted expense.

The conclusion from this discussion is that user review of a data model is crucial. When a database is developed for your use, you must carefully review the data model. If you do not understand any aspect of it, you should ask for clarification until you do. The data model must accurately reflect your view of the business. If it does not, the database will be designed incorrectly, and the applications will be difficult to use, if not worthless. Do not proceed unless the data model is accurate.

As a corollary, when asked to review a data model, take that review seriously. Devote the time necessary to perform a thorough review. Any mistakes you miss will come back to haunt you, and by then the cost of correction may be very high with regard to both time and expense. This brief introduction to data modeling shows why databases can be more difficult to develop than spreadsheets. This difficulty causes some people to resist the idea of a database, as discussed in the Chapter 5 *Guide* on pages 105a–105b.

Q6 Who Will Volunteer? (continued)

Knowing what you know now, if you were the manager of fund-raising at the TV station, you would hire a consultant and expect the consultant to interview all of the key users. From those interviews, the consultant would then construct a data model.

You now know that the structure of the database must reflect the way the users think about their activities. If the consultant did not take the time to interview you and your staff or did not construct a data model and ask you to review it, you would know that you are not receiving good service and would take corrective action.

Suppose you found a consultant who interviewed your staff for several hours and then constructed the data model shown in Figure CE5-12. This data model has an entity for *Prospect*, an entity for *Employee*, and three additional entities for *Contact, Phone,* and *Work*. The *Contact* entity records contacts that you or other employees have made with the prospective volunteer. This record is necessary so that you know what has been said to whom. The *Phone* entity is used to record multiple phone numbers for each prospective volunteer, and the *Work* entity records work that the prospect has performed for the station.

After you reviewed and approved this data model, the consultant constructed the database design shown in Figure CE5-13. In this design, table keys are underlined, foreign keys are shown in italics, and columns that are both table and foreign keys are underlined and italicized. Observe that the *Name* column is the table key of *Prospect*, and it is both part of the table key and a foreign key in *Phone, Contact,* and *Work*.

The consultant did not like having the *Name* column used as a key or as part of a key in so many tables. Based on her interviews, she suspected that prospect names are fluid—and that sometimes the same prospect name is recorded in different ways (e.g., sometimes with a middle initial and sometimes without). If that were to happen, phone, contact, and work data could be misallocated to prospect names. Accordingly, the consultant added a new column, *ProspectID* to the prospect table and created the design shown in Figure CE5-14. Values of this

Figure CE5-12
Data Model for Volunteer
Database

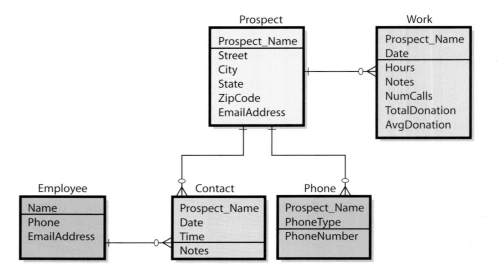

Prospect (<u>Name</u>, Street, City, State, Zip, EmailAddress)
Phone (<u>*Name*</u>, <u>PhoneType</u>, PhoneNumber)
Contact (<u>*Name*</u>, <u>Date</u>, <u>Time</u>, Notes, *EmployeeName*)
Work (<u>*Name*</u>, <u>Date</u>, Notes, NumCalls, TotalDonations)
Employee (<u>EmployeeName</u>, Phone, EmailAddress)

Note:
Underline means table key.
Italics means foreign key.
Underline and italics means both
table and foreign key.

Figure CE5-13
First Table Design for Volunteer
Database

Prospect (<u>*ProspectID*</u>, Name, Street, City, State, Zip, EmailAddress)
Phone (<u>*ProspectID*</u>, <u>PhoneType</u>, PhoneNumber)
Contact (<u>*ProspectID*</u>, <u>Date</u>, Notes, *EmployeeName*)
Work (<u>*ProspectID*</u>, <u>Date</u>, Notes, NumCalls, TotalDonations)
Employee (<u>EmployeeName</u>, Phone, EmailAddress)

Note:
Underline means table key.
Italics means foreign key.
Underline and italics means both
table and foreign key.

Figure CE5-14
Second Table Design for
Volunteer Database

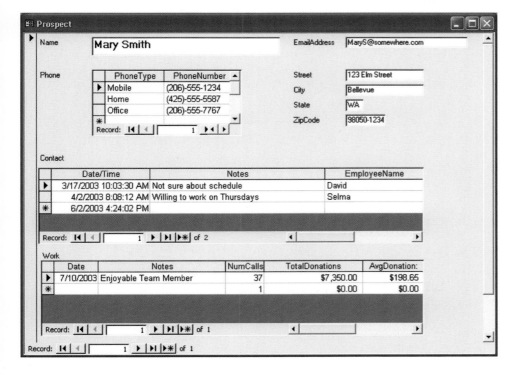

Figure CE5-15
Volunteer Prospect Data-Entry
Form

ID will have no meaning to the users, but the ID will be used to ensure that each prospect obtains a unique record in the Volunteer database. Because this ID has no meaning to the users, the consultant will hide it on forms and reports that users see.

There is one difference between the data model and the table designs. In the data model, the *Work* entity has an attribute, *AvgDonation*, but there is no corresponding *AvgDonation* column in the *Work* table. The consultant decided that there was no need to store this value in the database because it could readily be computed on forms and reports using the values in the *NumCalls* and *TotalDonation* columns.

Once the tables had been designed, the consultant created a Microsoft Access database. She defined the tables in Access, created relationships among the tables, and constructed forms and reports. Figure CE5-15 (page 371) shows the primary data entry form used for the Volunteer database. The top portion of the form has contact data, including multiple phone numbers. It is important to know the type of the phone number so that you and your staff know if you're calling someone at work or another setting. The middle and bottom sections of this form have contact and prior work data. Observe that *AvgDonation* has been computed from the *NumCalls* and *Total Donation* columns.

You were quite pleased with this database application, and you're certain that it helped you to improve the volunteer staffing at the station. Of course, over time, you thought of several new requirements, and you already have changes in mind for next year.

Active ? Review

Use this Active Review to verify that you understand the material in the chapter extension. You can read the entire extension and then perform the tasks in this review, or you can read the material for just one question and perform the tasks in this review for that question before moving on to the next one.

Q1 Who will volunteer?

Summarize the problem that the fund-raising manager must solve. Explain how a database can help solve this problem. Describe the missing information. In your own words, what data must be available to construct the missing information?

Q2 How are database application systems developed?

Name and briefly describe the components of a database application system. Explain the difference between a database application system and a database application program. Using Figure CE5-1 as a guide, describe the major steps in the process of developing a database application system. Explain what role is crucial for users and why that role is so important.

Q3 What are the components of the entity-relationship data model?

Define the terms *entity, attributes*, and *relationship*. Give an example of two entities (other than those in this book) that have a 1:N relationship. Give an example of two entities that have an N:M relationship. Explain the difference between maximum and minimum cardinality. Show two entities having a 1:N relationship in which one is required and one is optional.

Q4 How is a data model transformed into a database design?

Give an example of a data integrity problem. Describe, in general terms, the process of normalization. Explain how normalizing data prevents data integrity problems. Explain the disadvantage of normalized data. Using your examples from Question 3, show how 1:N relationships are expressed in relational database designs. Show how N:M relationships are expressed in relational database designs.

Q5 What is the users' role?

Describe the major role for users in the development of a database application system. Explain what is required to change a 1:N relationship to an N:M relationship during the data modeling stage. Explain what is required to make that same change after the database application systems has been constructed. Describe how this knowledge impacts your behavior when a database application system is being constructed for your use.

Q6 Who will volunteer? (continued)

Examine Figure CE5-12. Describe the maximum and minimum cardinality for each relationship. Justify these cardinalities. Change the relationship between *Prospect* and *Phone* to N:M, and explain what this means. Change the relationship between *Prospect* and *Work* to 1:1, and explain what this means. Explain how each relationship is represented in the design in Figure CE5-14. Show examples of both primary keys and foreign keys in this figure. In *Contact*, determine whether *EmployeeName* is part of a primary key or part of a foreign key.

Explain what problem the consultant foresaw in the use of the *Name* attribute. Explain how that problem was avoided. The consultant added an attribute to the data model that was not part of the users' world. Explain why that attribute will not add unnecessary complication to the users' work experiences.

Key Terms and Concepts

Using Your Knowledge

1. Explain how you could use a spreadsheet to solve the volunteer problem at the television station. What data would you place on each column and row of your spreadsheet? Name each column and row of your spreadsheet. What advantages does a database have over a spreadsheet for this problem? Compare and contrast your spreadsheet solution to the database solution shown in the design in Figure CE5-14 and the data entry form in Figure CE5-15.

2. Suppose you are asked to build a database application for a sports league. Assume that your application is to keep track of teams and equipment that is checked out to teams. Explain the steps that need to be taken to develop this application. Specify entities and their relationships. Build an E-R diagram. Ensure your diagram shows both minimum and maximum cardinalities. Transform your E-R diagram into a relational design.

3. Suppose you are asked to build a database application for a bicycle rental shop. Assume your database is to track customers, bicycles, and rentals. Explain the steps that need to be taken to develop this application. Specify entities and their relationships. Build an entity-relationship diagram. Ensure your diagram shows both minimum and maximum cardinalities. Transform your E-R diagram into a relational design.

4. Assume you work at the television station and are asked to evaluate the data model in Figure CE5-12. Suppose that you want to differentiate between prospects who have worked in the past and those who have never worked, but who are prospects for future work. Say that one of the data modelers tells you, "No problem. We'll know that because any *Prospect* entity that has no relationship to a *Work* entity is a prospect who has never worked." Restate the data modeler's response in your own words. Does this seem like a satisfactory solution? What if you want to keep Prospect data that pertains only to prospects who have worked? (No such attributes are shown in *Prospect* in Figure CE5-12, but say there is an attribute such as *YearFirstVolunteered* or some other attribute that pertains to prospects who have worked in the past.) Show an alternative E-R diagram that would differentiate between prospects who have worked in the past and those who have not. Compare and contrast your alternative to the one shown in Figure CE5-12.

5. Suppose you manage a department that is developing a database application. The IT professionals who are developing the system ask you to identify two employees to evaluate data models. What criteria would you use in selecting those employees? What instructions would you give them? Suppose one of the employees says to you, "I go to those meetings, but I just don't understand what they're talking about." How would you respond? Suppose that you go to one of those meetings and don't understand what they're talking about. What would you do? Describe a role for a prototype in this situation. How would you justify the request for a prototype?

Chapter Extension 6

Chapter 5 provides the background for this Extension.

Using Microsoft Access

In this chapter extension, you will learn fundamental techniques for creating a database and a database application with Microsoft Access.

Q1 How Do I Create Tables?

Before using Access or any other DBMS, you should have created a data model from the users' requirements, and you must transform that data model into a database design. For the purpose of this chapter extension, we will use a portion of the database design created in Chapter Extension 5. Specifically, we will create a database with the following two tables:

PROSPECT (<u>ProspectID</u>, Name, Street, City, State, Zip, EmailAddress)

and

WORK (<u>ProspectID</u>, <u>Date</u>, <u>Hour</u>, NumCalls, TotalDonations)

As in Chapter Extension 5, an underlined attribute is the primary key, and an italicized attribute is a foreign key. Thus, <u>ProspectID</u> is the primary key of PROSPECT, and the combination (ProspectID, Date, Hour) is the primary key of WORK. ProspectID is also a foreign key in WORK.

The data model and database design in Chapter Extension 5 specified that the key of WORK is the combination (ProspectID, Date). Upon review, the users stated that prospects will sometimes work more than one time during the day. For scheduling and other purposes, the users want to record both the date and the hour that someone worked. Accordingly, the database designer added the Hour attribute and made it part of the key of WORK.

The assumption in this design is that each row of WORK represents an hour's work. If a prospect works for consecutive hours, say from 7 to 9 PM, then he or she would have two rows, one with an Hour value of 1900 and a second with an Hour value of 2000. Figure CE6-1 (page 376) further documents the attributes of the design. Sample data for this table are shown in Figure CE6-2 (page 377).

Starting Access

Figure CE6-3 shows the opening screen for Microsoft Access 2003. (If you use another version of Access, your screen will appear differently, but the essentials will be the same.) To create a new database, select Blank database under the New section in the pane on the right-hand side of the screen. It is also possible to create

Study Questions

Q1 How do I create tables?

Q2 How do I create relationships?

Q3 How do I create a data entry form?

Q4 How can I create queries using the query design tool?

Q5 How do I create a report?

a new database from a template, but because we have done our own database design, we need not consider that option. Other choices in this pane are beyond the scope of this extension.

Table	Attribute (Column)	Remarks	Data Type	Example Value
PROSPECT	ProspectID	An identifying number provided by Access when a row is created. The value has no meaning to the user.	AutoNumber	55
PROSPECT	Name	A prospect's name.	Text (50)	Emily Jones
PROSPECT	Street	Prospect's contact street address.	Text (50)	123 West Elm
PROSPECT	City	Prospect's contact city.	Text (40)	Miami
PROSPECT	State	Prospect's contact state.	Text (2)	FL
PROSPECT	Zip	Prospect's contact Zip code.	Text (10)	30210-4567 or 30210
PROSPECT	EmailAddress	Prospect's contact email address.	Text (65)	ExamplePerson@somewhere.com
WORK	ProspectID	Foreign key to PROSPECT. Value provided when relationship is created.	Number (Long Integer)	55
WORK	Date	The date of work.	Date	9/15/2007
WORK	Hour	The hour at which work is started.	Number (Integer)	0800 or 1900 (7 PM)
WORK	NumCalls	The number of calls taken.	Number (Integer)	25
WORK	TotalDonations	The total of donations generated.	Currency	$10,575
WORK	AvgDonations	The average donation.	Currency	To be computed in queries and reports

Figure CE6-1
Attributes of the Database

Example of PROSPECT Data

Prospect ID	Name	Street	City	State	Zip	EmailAddress
1	Carson Wu	123 Elm	Los Angeles	CA	98007	Carson@somewhere.com
2	Emily Jackson	2234 17th	Pasadena	CA	97005	JacksonE@elsewhere.com
3	Peter Lopez	331 Moses Drive	Fullerton	CA	97330	PeterL@ourcompany.com
4	Lynda Dennison	54 Strand	Manhattan Beach	CA	97881	Lynda@somewhere.com
5	Carter Fillmore III	Restricted	Brentwood	CA	98220	Carter@BigBucks.com
6	CJ Greene	77 Sunset Strip	Hollywood	CA	97330	CJ@HollywoodProducers.c
7	Jolisa Jackson	2234 17th	Pasadena	CA	97005	JacksonJ@elsewhere.com

Example of WORK Data

ProspectID	Date	Hour	NumCalls	TotalDonations
3	9/15/2006	1600	17	8755
3	9/15/2006	1700	28	11578
5	9/15/2006	1700	25	15588
5	9/20/2006	1800	37	29887
5	9/10/2007	1700	30	21440
5	9/10/2007	1800	39	37050
6	9/15/2006	1700	33	21445
6	9/16/2006	1700	27)	17558
6	9/10/2007	1700	31	22550
6	9/10/2007	1800	37	36700

Figure CE6-2
Sample Data

Figure CE6-3
Opening Screen for Microsoft
Access 2003

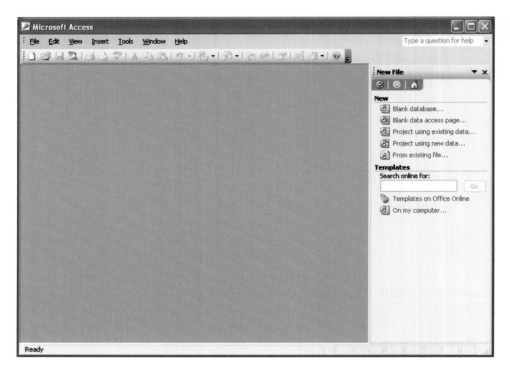

When you select Blank database, Access asks you to provide a file name and location for your new database. Enter the name *Prospect1.mdb* and place it in some convenient directory. Press Enter and you will see the screen shown in Figure CE6-4.

Creating Tables

Because we have created our own database design, we can select Create table in Design view by double-clicking on that entry. When you do this, you will see the screen shown in Figure CE6-5. This screen has two parts. In the upper part, we

Figure CE6-4
Naming the Database

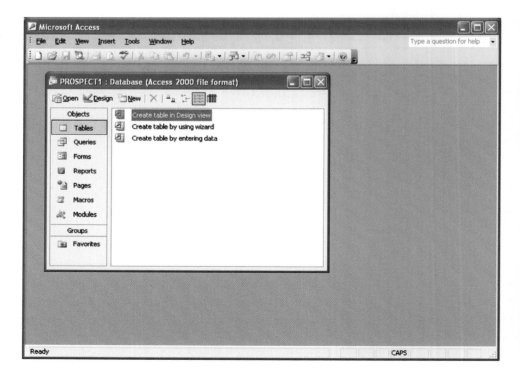

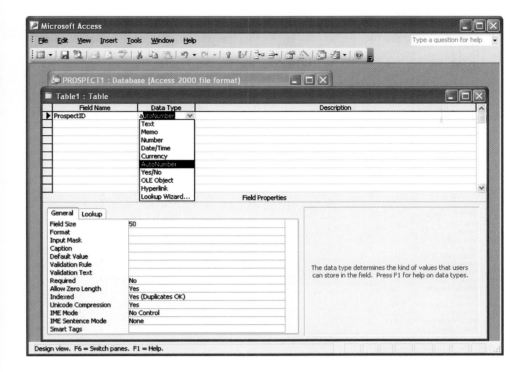

Figure CE6-5
Creating Tables in Access, Step 1

will enter the name of each attribute (called *Fields* by Access) and its *Data Type*. We can optionally enter a Description of that field. The description is used for documentation; as you will see, Access displays any text you enter as help text on forms. In the bottom part of the screen, we set the properties of each field (or attribute, using our term). In Figure CE6-5, the user has entered *ProspectID* and is selecting the Data Type *AutoNumber*.

To create the rest of the table, enter the Field Names and Data Types for our design. Figure CE6-6 shows how to set the length of a Text Data Type. In this figure, the user has set City to Text and then has moved down into the bottom part

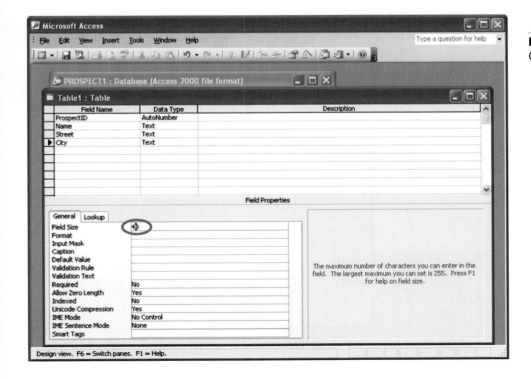

Figure CE6-6
Creating Tables in Access, Step 2

Figure CE6-7
Complete Sample
PROSPECT Table

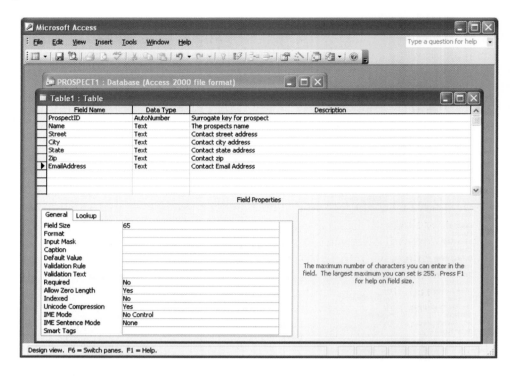

of this form and entered 40 under Field Size. You will do the same thing to set the length of State and Zip. The complete table is shown in Figure CE6-7.

Now we need to declare Prospect as the primary key of this table. To do so, highlight *ProspectID* by clicking on the square just to the left of it and then click on the Key icon (the yellow key a little to the right of the center in the toolbar). At this point, the table definition is complete, and we can save the table. Do so by clicking the Save File icon. Name the table PROSPECT.

Follow similar steps to create the WORK table. The only difference is that you will need to create a key of the three columns (*ProspectID, Date, Hour*). To

Figure CE6-8
Finished PROSPECT and
WORK Tables

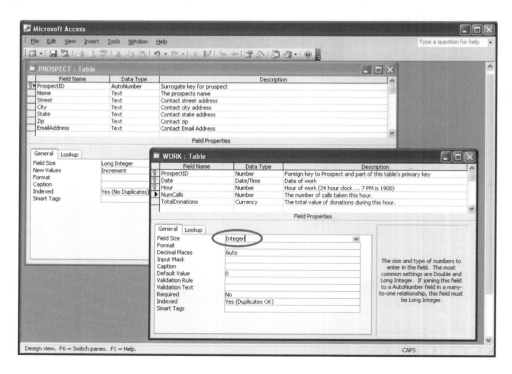

create that key, highlight all three rows by dragging the three squares to the left of the names of *ProspectID, Date,* and *Hour*. Then click the Key icon. The finished tables are shown in Figure CE6-8. This figure also shows how the user created the Data Type Number (Integer) for the *NumCalls* field. This same technique was used to set the Data Type of *ProspectID* (in WORK) to Number (Long Integer) and that of Hour to Number (Integer).

At this point, you can close both tables. You have created your first database!

Q2 How Do I Create Relationships?

After you have created the tables, the next step is to define relationships. To do so, select Tools/Relationships . . . from the Access main menu. The Relationships window will open and the Show Table dialog box will be displayed, as shown in Figure CE6-9. Double-click on both table names, and both tables will be added to the Relationships window. Close the Show Table dialog box.

To create the relationship between these two tables, click on the attribute ProspectID in PROSPECT and drag that attribute on top of the *ProspectID* in WORK. (It is important to drag *ProspectID* from PROSPECT to WORK and not the reverse.) When you do this, the screen shown in Figure CE6-10 (page 382) will appear.

In the dialog box, click Enforce Referential Integrity, click Cascade Update Related Fields, and click Cascade Delete Related Records. The specifics of these actions are beyond the scope of our discussion. Just understand that clicking these options will cause Access to make sure that *ProspectID* values in WORK also exist in PROSPECT. The completed relationship is shown in Figure CE6-11 (page 382). The notation *1 . . . . ∞* at the end of the relationship line means that one row of PROSPECT can be related to an unlimited number (*N*) rows in WORK. Close the Relationships window and save the changes when requested to do so. You now have a database with two tables and a relationship.

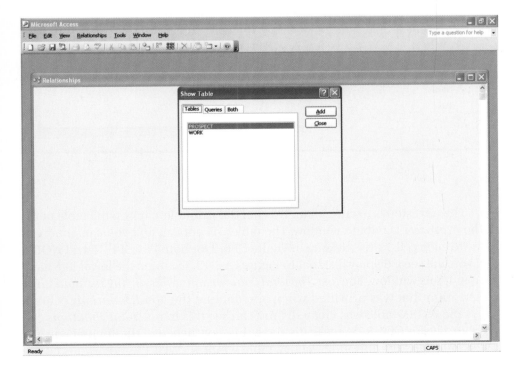

Figure CE6-9
The "Show Table" Dialog Box in Access

Figure CE6-10
Creating a Relationship Between
Two Tables

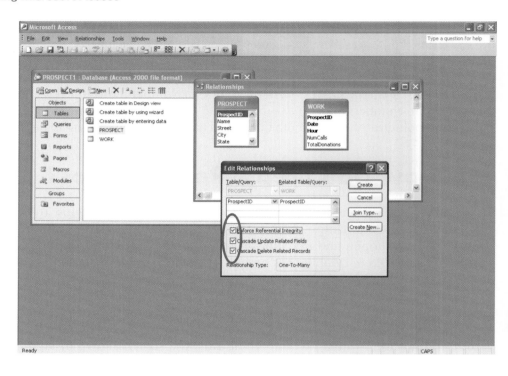

Figure CE6-11
Completed Relationship Between
PROSPECT and WORK Tables

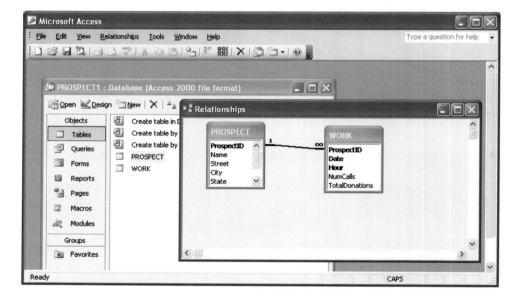

The next step is to enter data. To enter data, double-click on the table name in the *Prospect1* Database window. The table will appear, and you can enter values into each cell. Enter the data in Figure CE6-2 for both PROSPECT and WORK, and you will see a display like that in Figure CE6-12. Examine the lower left-hand corner of this window. The text *The total value of donations during the hour* is the Description that was provided when you defined the *TotalDonations* column when the WORK table was created. (You can see this in the *TotalDonations* column in Figure CE6-8.) Access displays this text because the focus is on the *TotalDonations* column in the active table window (WORK). Move your cursor from field to field and watch this text change.

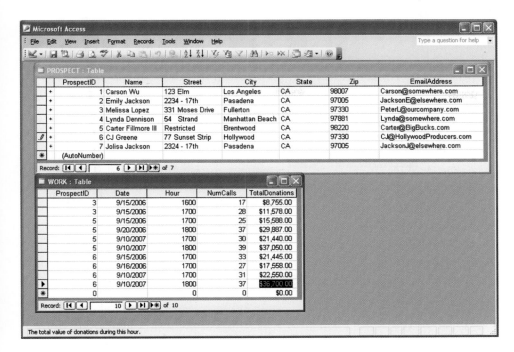

Figure CE6-12
Tables with Data Entered

Q3 How Do I Create a Data Entry Form?

Access provides two alternatives for creating a data entry form. The first is to use the default table display as you did when you entered the data shown in Figure CE6-12. In the PROSPECT table, notice the plus sign on the left. If you click on those plus signs, you will see the PROSPECT rows with their related WORK rows, as shown in Figure CE6-13. This display, while convenient, is limited in its capability.

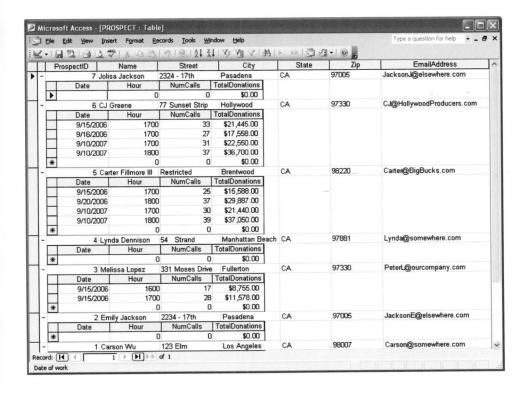

Figure CE6-13
Default Table Display

Figure CE6-14
Selecting the First Table Using
the Form Wizard

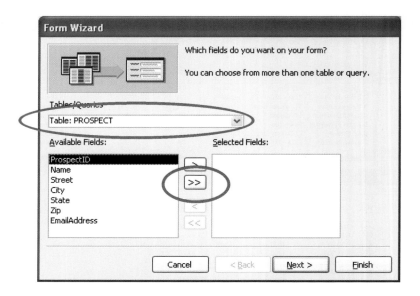

It also does not provide a very pleasing user interface. For more generality and better design, you can use the Access form generator.

To start the form generator, click on Forms in the *Prospect1* Database window. Then double-click on Create form by using Form Wizard. As shown in Figure CE6-14, ensure that the PROSPECT table is highlighted in the Tables/Queries combo box (shown in this figure by the top red oval), and then click the double chevron button (shown in this figure by the lower red oval). All of the columns in the PROSPECT table should appear in the Selected Fields list box.

Next, go back to the Tables/Queries box and select the WORK table. Again, click on the double chevron button. Your screen should appear as shown in Figure CE6-15. Click Finish. (We are skipping over numerous options that Access provides; those options are beyond the scope of this discussion.)

At this point, you should see the data entry form shown in Figure CE6-16. Because you defined the relationship between PROSPECT and WORK, Access will automatically connect each row in PROSPECT with its matching rows in WORK. The first prospect, Jolisa Jackson, has not yet worked, and the form shows no WORK data for her. Click on the right arrow and you will see (in Figure CE6-17) that CJ Greene, the next prospect, has numerous WORK rows related to him.

Figure CE6-15
Selecting the Second Table Using
the Form Wizard

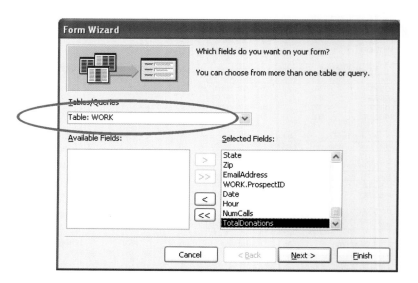

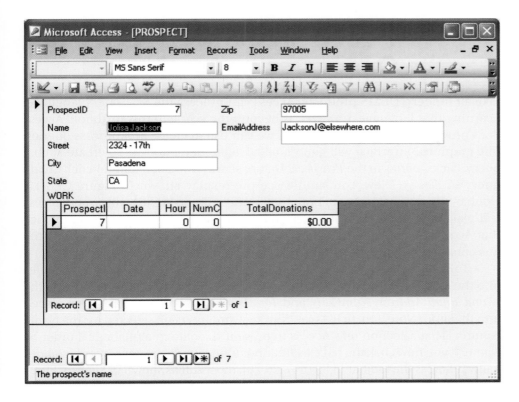

You can add, update, or delete any data in any of these forms. When you do so, Access will make the appropriate changes to the underlying tables.

There are myriads of options for customizing Access forms. You can learn about them if you take a database processing class after you complete this MIS class.

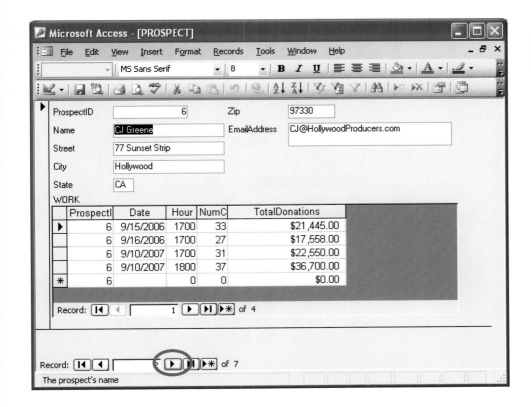

Figure CE6-17
Data Entry Form, CJ Greene

Q4 How Can I Create Queries Using the Query Design Tool?

Like all modern DBMS products, Access can process the SQL query language. Learning that language, however, is beyond the scope of this textbook. Access does provide graphical interface that we can use to create and process queries. The graphical interface will generate SQL statements for us. To create such a query, click Queries in the *Prospect1* Database window. Then double-click Create query in Design View. You should see the display shown in Figure CE6-18. Double-click on the names of both the PROSPECT and WORK tables, and Access will place them into the query design form as shown in Figure CE6-19. Notice that Access remembers the relationship between the two tables (shown by the line connecting *ProspectID* in PROSPECT to the same attribute in WORK.)

To create a query, drag columns out of the PROSPECT and WORK tables into the grid in the lower part of the query definition form. In Figure CE6-20, the *Name, EmailAddress, NumCalls*, and *TotalDonations* columns have been placed into that grid. Note, too, that Ascending keyword has been selected for the Name column. That selection tells Access to present the data in alphabetical order by Name. If you now click the red exclamation point icon in the Access menu (about halfway across the toolbar in Figure CE6-20), the result as shown in Figure CE6-21 will appear. Notice that only PROSPECT rows having a match of *ProspectID* with *ProspectID* in WORK rows are shown. By default, for queries of two (or more) tables, Access (and SQL) show only rows that have value matches in both tables. Save the query under the name *NameAndDonationQuery*.

Queries have many useful purposes. For example, suppose we want to see the average dollar value of donation generated per hour of work. This query, which is just slightly beyond the scope of this chapter extension, can readily be created using either the Access graphical tool or SQL. The reults of such a query are shown in Figure CE6-22. This query processes the

Figure CE6-18
Creating a Query, Step 1

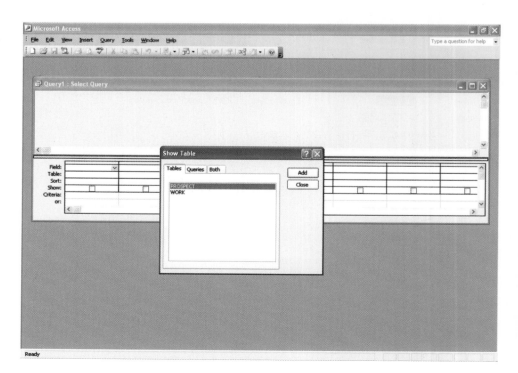

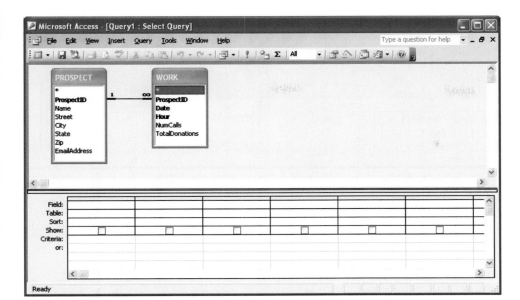

Figure CE6-19
Creating a Query, Step 2

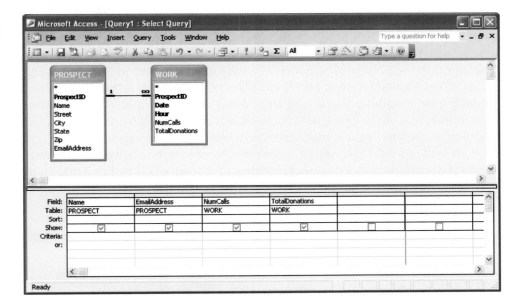

Figure CE6-20
Creating a Query, Step 3

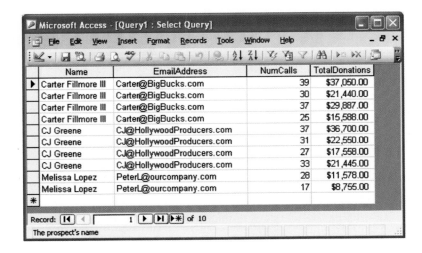

Figure CE6-21
Results of TotalDonations Query

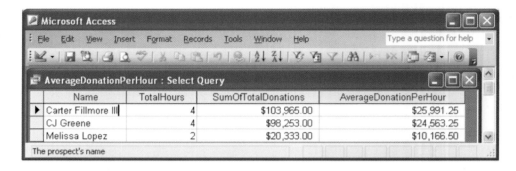

NameAndDonationQuery query just created. Again, if you take a database class, you will learn how to create queries like this and others of even greater complexity (and utility).

Q5 How Do I Create a Report?

The process of creating a report is very similar to that for creating a form. From the *Prospect1* Database window, select Reports and then double-click Create report by using the Wizard. This time, however, we will be more specific in what we want to see. Click Table:PROSPECT in the Table/Queries combo box, highlight *Name*, and click the single chevron (>). You will see the display shown in Figure CE6-23.

Using a similar process, add *EmailAddress*. Then select Table:WORK in the Table/Queries combo box and add *Date, Hour, NumCalls,* and *TotalDonations*. Click Finish and you will see the report shown in Figure CE6-24. Again, we are skipping numerous options that Access provides in creating reports.

We will consider just one of those options now. Suppose we want to show the total donations that a prospect has obtained, in all of his or her work. To do that, open the report in design view by clicking the triangle pencil icon (the small

Figure CE6-23
Selecting a Table to Show in a Report

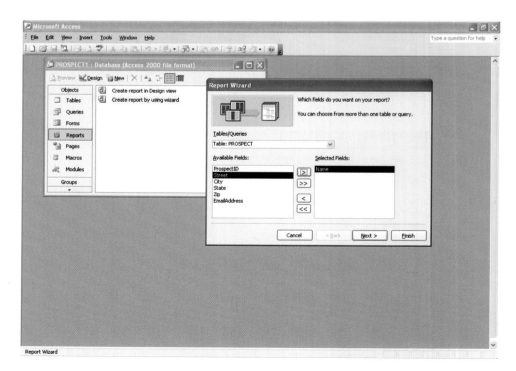

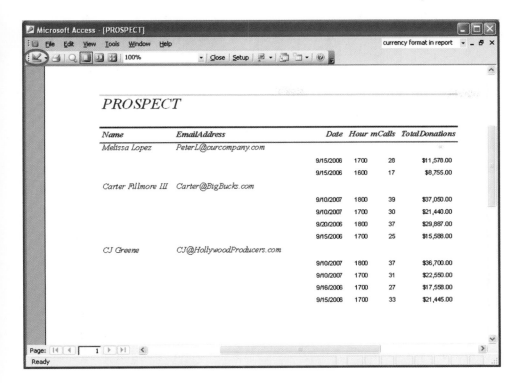

Figure CE6-24
Report on Total Donations, by
Prospect

circle on the left in Figure CE6-27 on page 290) in the left-most position of the
menu bar. Your report will appear as shown in Figure CE6-25. From the View
menu option, click on Sorting and Grouping. In the form that appears (Figure
CE6-26, on page 290), the second element of Group Properties is Group Footer.
Click on No, and change it to Yes as shown in Figure CE6-26. Close this window.

Now click the textbox tool in the Toolbox (the small circle on the left in
Figure CE6-27, on page 290) and drag and drop a toolbox under the rule labeled
ProspectID footer. Your screen should appear as in Figure CE6-27.

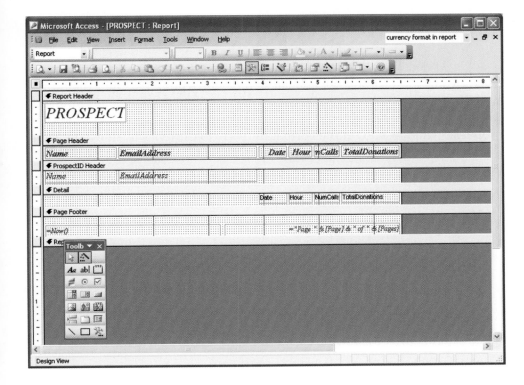

Figure CE6-25
Showing Total Donations
per Prospect, Step 1

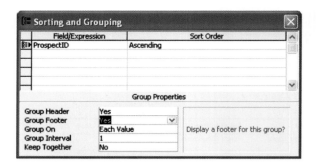

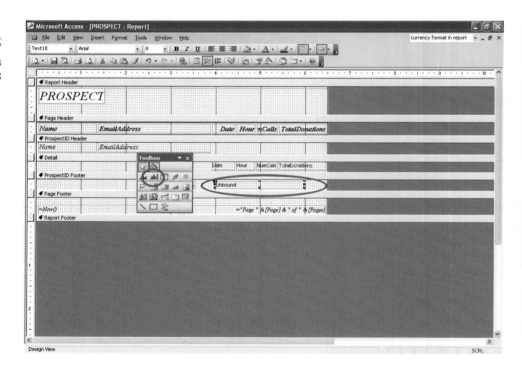

Now select View/Properties from the main Access menu, and the properties for your new text box will appear. In the *Source* property, enter the expression =*sum*(*TotalDonations*). Be sure to omit a space between Total and Donations as shown in Figure CE6-28(a). Now click the Format tab in the properties window and set the Format property to Currency as shown in Figure CE6-28(b). Now click the View icon in the menu bar (in the spot where the trian-

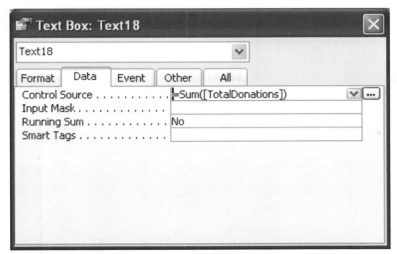

Figure CE6-28
Showing Total Donations
per Prospect, Step 4

a. Set the Control Source to Sum the Donations

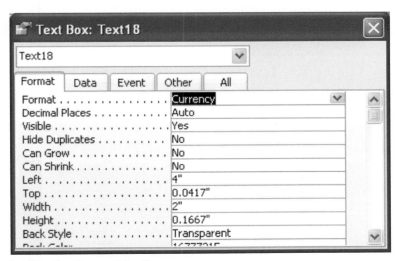

b. Set the Format to Currency

gle and pencil icon was), and your report will appear as shown in Figure CE6-29 (page 392).

The only thing left to do is to go back to the design window (click the triangle and pencil), change the label for the text box from Text18 to Career Donations, and align the new text box. The finished report is shown in Figure CE6-30 (page 392).

Figure CE6-29
Reordered Report, Showing Total Donations History

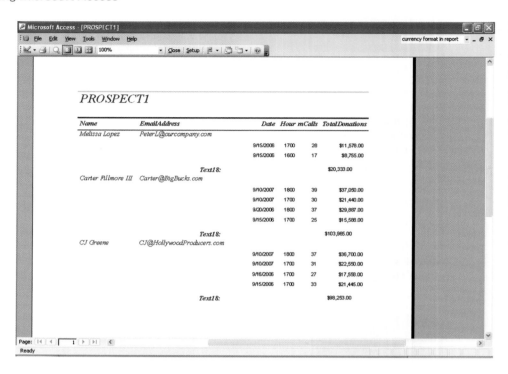

Figure CE6-30
Finished Report

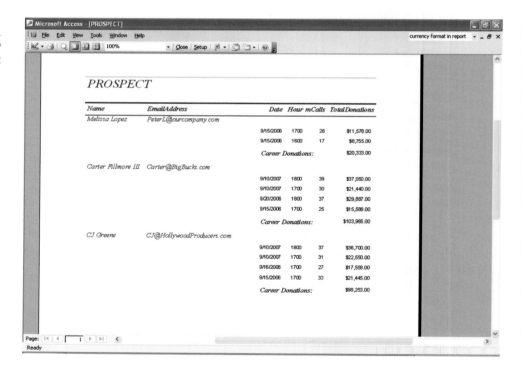

Active ? Review

Use this Active Review to verify that you understand the material in the chapter extension. You can read the entire extension and then perform the tasks in this review, or you can read the material for just one question and perform the tasks in this review for that question before moving on to the next one.

For this active review, assume you are creating a database application having the following two tables:

CUSTOMER (<u>CustomerID</u>, Name, Email)
CONTACT (<u>CustomerID</u>, <u>Date</u>, Subject)

Q1   How do I create tables?

Open Access, create a new database having a name of your choosing. Create the CUSTOMER and CONTACT tables. Assume the following data types:

Attribute (Field)	Data Type
CustomerID (in CUSTOMER)	AutoNumber
Name	Text (50)
Email	Text (75)
CustomerID (in CONTACT)	Number (Long Integer)
Date	Date
Subject	Text (200)

Add Description entries to the Field definitions that you think are appropriate.

Q2   How do I create relationships?

Open the Relationships window and create a relationship from CUSTOMER to CONTACT using the CustomerID attribute. Click all of the check boxes, as before. Enter sample data. Add at least five rows to CUSTOMER and at least seven rows to CONTACT. Ensure that some CUSTOMER rows have no matching CONTACT rows.

Q3   How do I create a data entry form?

Open the default data entry form for the CUSTOMER table. Click on the CUSTOMER rows to display the related CONTACT data. Use the Form Wizard to create a data entry form. Navigate through that form to see that CONTACT rows are correctly connected to CUSTOMER rows.

Q4   How can I create queries using the query design tool?

Create a query that displays *Name, Email, Date*, and *Subject*. Sort the results in alphabetic order of *Name*.

Q5   How do I create a report?

Use the Report Wizard to create a report that has *Name, Email, Date*. and *Subject*. View that report. Add a group total for each CUSTOMER that counts the number of contacts for each customer. Follow the procedure shown for creating career totals except, instead of entering the formula =*Sum*(*TotalDonations*), enter the formula =*Count*(*). Also, you need not set the Format property to Currency. The default Format property will be fine. Label your new text box correctly and position it for a pleasing display.

Using Your Knowledge

1.   Perform all of the tasks in the Active Review.

2.   Answer question 2 at the end of Chapter Extension 5 (page 374). Implement your database design using Access. Create the tables and add sample data. Create a data entry form that shows teams and the equipment they have checked out. Verify that the form correctly processes new checkouts, changes to checkouts, and equipment returns. Create a report that shows each team, the items they have checked out, and the number of items they

have checked out. [Use the *Count*(*) expression as explained in the Active Review.]

3. Answer question 3 at the end of Chapter Extension 5 (page 374). Implement an Access database for the CUSTOMER and RENTAL tables only. Create the tables and add sample data. Create a data entry form that shows customers and all of their rentals (assume customers rent bicycles more than once). Verify that the form correctly processes new rentals, changes to rentals, and rental returns. Create a report that shows each customer, the rentals they have made, and the total rental fee for all of their rentals.

Chapter Extension 7

Chapter 6 provides the background for this Extension.

How the Internet Works

When you send something as simple as an email with an attachment, a true techno-miracle occurs. You are about to learn how. In the process, you will learn important terms like *router*, *IP address*, and *TCP/IP*, and you will see how they relate to make the Internet work.

Q1 How Does Email Travel?

Suppose you are on vacation in Hawaii and you want to send a photo of your amazing surfing skills to a friend in snow-bound Cincinnati, Ohio. You plug your portable computer into your hotel's network, fire up your email program, write the email, attach the photo, and press Send. That's it. In a matter of minutes, your friend will be admiring your surfing antics. Even though you may not know it, a techno-miracle occurred.

Figure CE7-1 (page 396) shows the networks involved in sending your email message and picture. There is a LAN at your hotel, a LAN at your friend's company, and the Internet connects the two. Assume that you sent your message from Computer 3 (C3) at the hotel and that your friend is sitting at Computer 10 (C10) in the company in Ohio.

You know that your email and picture traveled over the Internet, which is a network of networks. But how? A host of problems had to be overcome: Your friend has an Apple computer, and you have a Dell. The two of you use different operating systems and two different email programs. As shown, both you and your friend are connected to LANs, but your hotel's LAN uses wires, and your friend's company's LAN is wireless. Thus, the LANs are of different types and process messages differently.

Furthermore, your message and picture were sent over an optical fiber cable underneath the sea and received by a computer in San Francisco. But, your picture was too big to send in one big chunk, so it was broken into pieces, and the pieces traveled separately. When the pieces (called *packets*) arrived in San Francisco, a device (called a *router*) determined that the best way to get them to your friend was to send them to a router in Los Angeles, which sent the pieces to a router in Denver, which sent them to a router in Cincinnati, which sent them to a company that contracts with your friend's employer to provide Internet access, which sent them to the email server at your friend's company. Meanwhile, your computer determined that one of the pieces got lost along the way, and it automatically resent that piece.

Study Questions

Q1 How does email travel?

Q2 What is a communications protocol?

Q3 What are the functions of the five TCP/IP–OSI layers?

Q4 How does the Internet work?

Q5 How does *www.prenhall.com* become 165.193.123.253?

Video

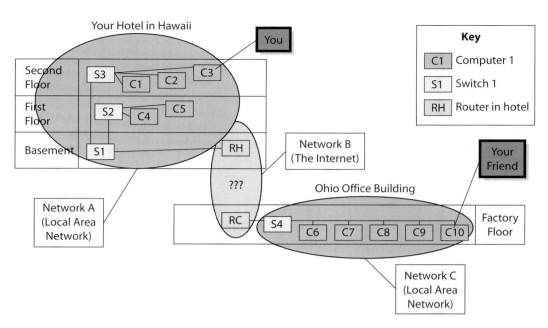

Figure CE7-1
Example Networks

When all of the pieces have been assembled, your friend gets the "You've got mail" indicator on his computer. He looks at your picture and asks, "How does she do that?" What he should be asking is, "How does the Internet do that?"

The key concept is *divide and conquer*. All of the work is divided into categories, and the categories of work are arranged into layers. To understand this further, we must first explain communications protocols.

Q2 What Is a Communications Protocol?

A **protocol** is a standardized means for coordinating an activity between two or more entities. Humans use social protocols. For example, a protocol exists for introducing two people to one another. Another human protocol, illustrated in Figure CE7-2, occurs at the grocery store. This protocol, like all protocols, proceeds through a sequence of ordered steps. If, in response to the clerk's query "Debit or credit," you enter your PIN, you are skipping steps and violating the protocol. The clerk will correct you and ask her question again. Notice, too, that the protocol has a decision branch. If you say, "credit," then the clerk will not ask the question about cash back or ask you to enter your PIN.

Figure CE7-2
Example of a Grocery Store
Protocol

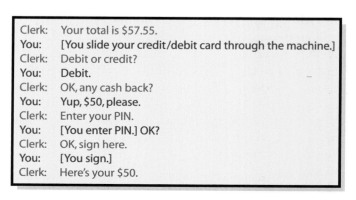

Clerk:	Your total is $57.55.
You:	[You slide your credit/debit card through the machine.]
Clerk:	Debit or credit?
You:	Debit.
Clerk:	OK, any cash back?
You:	Yup, $50, please.
Clerk:	Enter your PIN.
You:	[You enter PIN.] OK?
Clerk:	OK, sign here.
You:	[You sign.]
Clerk:	Here's your $50.

A **communications protocol** is a means for coordinating activity between two or more communicating computers. Two machines must agree on the protocol to use, and they must follow that protocol as they send messages back and forth. Because there is so much to do, communications protocols are broken up into levels or layers.

Q3 What Are the Functions of the Five TCP/IP—OSI Layers?

Several different **layered protocol** schemes, or **protocol architectures**, have been proposed. The **International Organization for Standardization (ISO)** developed the **Reference Model for Open Systems Interconnection (OSI)**, an architecture that has seven layers. Another group, the **Internet Engineering Task Force (IETF)**, developed a four-layer scheme called the **Transmission Control Program/Internet Protocol (TCP/IP) architecture**. For reasons that are beyond our discussion, the Internet uses a five-layer blend of these two architectures called the **TCP/IP—OSI architecture**.

Figure CE7-3 shows the five layers of this hybrid architecture. As shown in the right-most column, the bottom two layers concern the transmission of data within a single network. The next two layers are used for data transmission across an internet (a network of networks, including the Internet). The top layer provides protocols that enable applications to interact.

Layer	Name	Specific Function	Broad Function
5	Application	The application layer governs how two applications work with each other, even if they are from different vendors.	Interoperability of application
4	Transport	Transport layer standards govern aspects of end-to-end communication between two end hosts that are not handled by the internet layer. These standards also allow hosts to work together even if the two computers are from different vendors and have different internal designs.	Transmission across an internet
3	Internet	Internet layer standards govern the transmission of packets across an internet—typically by sending them through several routers along the route. Internet layer standards also govern packet organization, timing constraints, and reliability.	
2	Data Link	Data link layer standards govern the transmission of frames across a single network—typically by sending them through several switches along the data link. Data link layer standards also govern frame organization, timing constraints, and reliability.	Transmission across a single network
1	Physical	Physical layer standards govern transmission between adjacent devices connected by a transmission medium.	

Figure CE7-3
TCP/IP—OSI Architecture

Source: Used by permission from Ray Panko, *Business Data Networks and Telecommunications*, 5th ed. (Upper Saddle River, NJ: Prentice Hall, 2005), p. 92.

Layer 5

Examine the networks in Figure CE7-1 between your hotel in Hawaii and your friend. Unknown to you or your friend, each of your computers contains programs that operate at all five layers of the TCP/IP—OSI architecture. Your email program operates at Layer 5. It generates and receives email (and attachments like your photo) according to one of the standard email protocols defined for Layer 5. Most likely, it uses a protocol called **Simple Mail Transfer Protocol (SMTP)**.

There are many other Layer-5 protocols. **Hypertext Transfer Protocol (HTTP)** is used for the processing of Web pages. When you type the address *www.ibm.com* into your browser, notice that your browser adds the notation *http://.* (Try this, if you've never noticed that it happens.) By filling in these characters, your browser is indicating that it will use the HTTP protocol to communicate with the IBM site.

By the way, the Web and the Internet are not the same thing. The Web, which is a subset of the Internet, consists of sites and users that process the HTTP protocol. The Internet is the communications structure that supports all application-layer protocols, including HTTP, SMTP, and other protocols.

File Transfer Protocol (FTP) is another application-layer protocol. You can use FTP to copy files from one computer to another. In Figure CE7-1, if Computer 1 wants to copy a file from Computer 9, it would use FTP.

Three important terms lurk in this discussion:

1. **Architecture**. An *architecture* is an arrangement of protocol layers in which each layer is given specific tasks to accomplish.
2. **Protocol**. At each layer of the architecture, there are one or more *protocols*. Each protocol is a set of rules that accomplish the tasks assigned to its layer.
3. **Program**. A *program* is a specific computer product that implements a protocol.

So, for example, the TCP/IP—OSI architecture has five layers. At the top level are numerous protocols, including HTTP, SMTP, and FTP. For each of those protocols, there are program products that implement the protocol. Some of the programs that implement the HTTP protocol of the TCP/IP—OSI architecture are called *browsers*. Two common browsers are Netscape Navigator and Microsoft Internet Explorer.

Layer 4

As Figure CE7-4 shows, your email program (which uses SMTP) interacts with another protocol called **Transmission Control Program (TCP)**. TCP operates at Layer 4 of the TCP/IP—OSI architecture. Note that we are using the acronym TCP in two ways: as the name of a Layer-4 *protocol* and as part of the name of the TCP/IP—OSI protocol architecture. In fact, the architecture gets its name because it usually includes the TCP protocol.

TCP performs many important tasks. Your Dell and your friend's Apple have different operating systems that represent data in different ways. Programs in those operating systems that implement the TCP protocol make conversions from one data representation to the other. Also, a TCP program examines your email and picture and breaks lengthy messages (like your picture) into pieces called **segments**. When it does this, it places identifying data at the front of each segment that are akin to the To and From addresses that you would put on a letter for the postal mail.

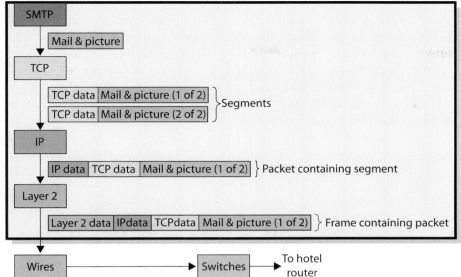

Your computer

Figure CE7-4
TCP/IP—OSI on Your Computer

TCP programs also provide reliability. It was the TCP program on your computer that noticed that one of the pieces did not arrive at your friend's computer, and so it resent that piece.

Your friend's Apple computer also has a program that runs the TCP protocol. It receives the segments from your computer and sends acknowledgments back to your computer when it receives each segment. The TCP program also translates the segments from Windows (Dell) to Macintosh (Apple) format, reassembles the segments into a coherent whole, and makes that assembly available to your friend's email program.

Layer 3

TCP interacts with protocols that operate at Level 3, the next layer down. For the TCP/IP architecture, the layer-3 protocol is the **Internet Protocol (IP)**. The chief purpose of IP is to route messages across an internet. In the case of your email, the IP program on your computer does not know how to reach your friend's computer, but it does know how to start. Namely, it knows to send all of the pieces of your email and picture to a device in your hotel's network called a *router*. In Figure CE7-1, that router is labeled RH. (This is not a brand of router, it is just the label we will put on the hotel's router in this figure.)

To send a segment to RH, the IP layer program on your computer first packages each segment into a **packet**. As shown in Figure CE7-4, it also places IP data in front of the packet, in front of the TCP data. This action is akin to wrapping a letter inside another envelope and placing additional To/From data in the header of the outer envelope.

Routers are special-purpose computers that implement the IP protocol. The router labeled RH examines the destination of your packets and uses the rules of the IP protocol to decide where to send them. RH does not know how to get them all the way to Ohio, but it does know how to get them started on their way. In this case, it decides to send them to another router located in San Francisco. Dozens of other routers on the Internet will eventually cause the packets containing your message and picture to arrive at a router at your friend's employer. We will explain more about this process later in this chapter extension.

Layers 1 and 2

As shown in Figure CE7-1, your hotel uses a LAN to connect the computers in its hotel rooms. (Lucky you—you're staying at an exclusive hotel with just two floors and five rooms.) Basic computer connectivity is accomplished using Layers 1 and 2 of the TCP/IP—OSI architecture. As you learned in Chapter 6, computing devices called **switches** facilitate that data communication. (See Figure CE7-4.)

A program implementing a Layer-2 protocol will package each of your packets into **frames**, which are the containers used at Layers 1 and 2. (Segments go into packets, and packets go into frames.) Then, programs, switches, and other devices cause the pieces of your email and picture to pass from your computer to Switch 3, from Switch 3 to Switch 1, and from Switch 1 to Router RH. (See Figure CE7-1.)

Q4 How Does the Internet Work?

Given this background, we can now explain how your email travels over the networks to reach your friend. This is the most complicated section in this textbook. To understand this material, we will break the discussion into four sections. First, we will consider the addressing of computers and other devices. As you will learn, each computer and device has two addresses, a physical address and a logical one. Next, we will consider how protocols at all five layers of the TCP/IP—OSI model operate to send a request to a Web server within a LAN. Third, we will consider how those same protocols work to send messages across the Internet. Finally, we will wrap up with some details about IP addresses and the domain name system. Be patient, and take your time; you may need to read this section more than once. We begin with addresses.

Network Addresses: MAC and IP

On most networks, and on every internet, two address schemes identify computers and other devices. Programs that implement Layer 2 protocols use *physical addresses*, or *MAC addresses*. Programs that implement Layer 3, 4, and 5 protocols use *logical addresses*, or *IP addresses*. We will consider each type.

Physical Addresses (MAC Addresses)

As stated in Chapter 6, every network device, including your computer, has an NIC for accessing the network. Each NIC is given an address at the factory. That address is the device's **physical address**, or **MAC address**. By agreement among computer manufacturers, such addresses are assigned so that no two NICs will ever have the same MAC address.

MAC addresses are used within networks at Layer 2 of the TCP/IP—OSI model. Physical addresses are only known, shared, and used within a particular network or network segment. For internets, including the Internet, another scheme of addresses must be used. That scheme turned out to be so useful that it is also used within LANs, in addition to MAC addressing.

Logical Addresses (IP Addresses)

Internets, including the Internet, and many private networks use **logical addresses**, which are also called **IP addresses**. You have probably seen IP addresses; they are written as a series of dotted decimals, for example, 192.168.2.28.

IP addresses are not permanently associated with a given hardware device. They can be reassigned to another computer, router, or other device when necessary. To understand one advantage of logical addresses, consider what happens when an organization like IBM changes the device (a router) that receives requests when users type *www.ibm.com*. That name is associated with a particular IP address (as we will explain later in this chapter). If IP addresses were permanent, like MAC addresses, then when IBM upgrades its entry router, all of the users in the world would have to change the IP address associated with *www.ibm.com* to the new address. Instead, with logical IP addresses, a network administrator need only reassign IBM's IP address to the new router.

Public Versus Private IP Addresses

In practice, two kinds of IP addresses exist. **Public IP addresses** are used on the Internet. Such IP addresses are assigned to major institutions in blocks by the **Internet Corporation for Assigned Names and Numbers (ICANN)**. (We'll talk more about ICANN later.) Each IP address is unique across all computers on the Internet. In contrast, **private IP addresses** are used within private networks and internets. They are controlled only by the company that operates the private network or internet.

Dynamic Host Configuration Protocol

Today, in most cases, when you plug your computer into a network (or sign on to a wireless network), a program in Windows or other operating system will search that network for a DHCP server, which is a computer or router that hosts a program called **Dynamic Host Configuration Protocol (DHCP)**. When the program finds such a device, your computer will request a temporary IP address from the DHCP server. That IP address is loaned to you while you are connected to the LAN. When you disconnect, that IP address becomes available, and the DHCP server will reuse it when needed.

Of course, within a private network, administrators can assign private IP addresses manually as well. Often, the strategy within a private network is to manually assign IP addresses to computers that operate Web servers or other shared devices for which it is desirable to have a fixed IP address. Today, most users, however, are assigned IP addresses using DHCP.

Private IP Addresses at the Hawaii Hotel

To make sense of the discussion so far, consider Figure CE7-5, which shows the LAN operated by your hotel in Hawaii. Let's suppose that you occupy the penthouse suite (more good luck!) and that you plug your computer into the network as Computer C3 in Figure CE7-5 (page 402). When you do so, a program in your operating system will search the network for a DHCP server. It turns out that the router labeled RH is such a server. Your computer asks RH for an IP address, and RH assigns one. It will be a number like 192.168.2.28, but for simplicity let's denote your IP address by the symbol IP3.

Using TCP/IP—OSI Protocols within the Hotel

Once you have an IP address, protocol programs on your computer at Layers 3, 4, and 5 can communicate with any other computer in your network. Suppose, for example, that the computer labeled HS is running a Web server that provides information to hotel guests. This Web server is private; the hotel wants only

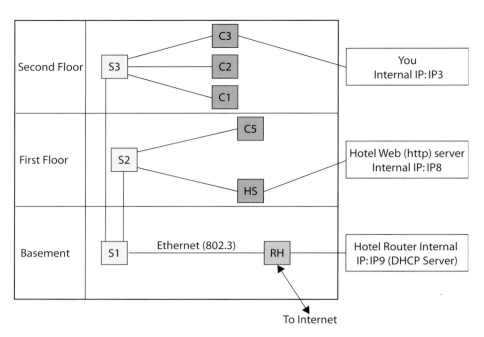

Figure CE7-5
Hotel LAN in Hawaii

guests and others within the hotel to be able to access it. Hence, the server operates only within the LAN.

Suppose the IP address of the server has been assigned by a network administrator; let's denote that address as IP8. The router, RH in Figure CE7-5, also has an IP address. Denote that address as IP9. Now, let's see how all of these addresses are used within the hotel's LAN.

Communications Processing on Your Computer
The hotel provides a brochure in your room that tells you how to sign on to the local Web server by entering a name into your browser. When you follow those instructions, your browser constructs a request for the server and uses the HTTP protocol to send it to HS.

We can follow the action in Figure CE7-6 (page 403). Your browser sends its service request for HS to a program that implements TCP. One function of TCP is to break requests into segments, when necessary. In this case, suppose it breaks the request into two segments. The TCP program adds additional data to the segments. Here we show a header with *IP3 To: IP8*, but other data, and possibly a trailer, are added as well. We will ignore the real headers and trailers to focus on basic concepts.

The TCP program hands the segment(s) to a program that implements IP. As stated, the major function of that IP program is routing. It determines that the only route to IP8 is through the router at RH, whose IP address is IP9. So, the IP program adds the IP9 header and passes the wrapped packet down to a program that implements Ethernet.

The Ethernet program translates the IP address into a MAC address. Ethernet determines that the device at IP9 has a particular MAC address, which will be a long number. Here, for simplicity, we denote that address as RH. Ethernet will wrap the packet into a frame that is addressed to device RH.

When you signed onto the LAN, your Ethernet program learned that the only way it can connect to other computers is via switch S3 (see Figure CE7-5). Accordingly, it sends the frame to S3.

Figure CE7-6
Accessing the (Private) Hotel Web Server

Communications Processing on the Switches

All switches have a table of data called a **switch table**. This table tells the switch where to send traffic to get it to its destination. The table on switch S3 has entries for every other device on the LAN. It knows, for example, that to get a frame to RH, it must send it to switch S1. Accordingly, it sends the frame to S1.

S1 also has a switch table. S1 consults that table and determines that it has a direct connection to RH. Therefore, it sends the frame to RH.

Communications Processing on the Router

When the frame arrives at RH, it has arrived at its destination, and so Ethernet unpacks the frame and sends the contained packet up to IP. IP examines the packet and determines that the packet's destination is IP8. RH, which is a router, has a **routing table** that tells it where to send traffic for IP8. This routing table indicates that IP8 is just one hop away. So, IP changes the destination of the packet to IP8 and passes it back down to Ethernet.

Ethernet determines that the device at IP8 has the MAC address HS. So, it packages the packet into a frame and gives that frame the address HS. It then sends the frame to its switch S1. S1 consults its switch table and sends the frame to S2; S2 sends the frame to HS.

Communications Processing on the Web Server

HS is the destination for the frame, so the Ethernet program unpacks the frame and sends the contained packet to the IP program. IP8 is the destination for the packet, so the IP program strips off the IP header and sends the contained segment up to a program that implements TCP. That program examines the segment and determines that it is the first of two. TCP sends an acknowledgment back to your computer to indicate that it received the first segment. (Of course, the acknowledgment must be routed and switched as well.) TCP waits for the second segment to arrive.

Once both segments have arrived, the TCP program sends the complete request up to the Web server program that processes the HTTP protocol. (Whew!)

To summarize:

- *Switches* work with *frames* at *Layer 2*. They send frames from switch to switch until they arrive at their destination. They use *MAC addresses*.
- *Routers* work with *packets* at *Layer 3*. They send packets from router to router until they arrive at their destination. They use *IP addresses*.

Using TCP/IP—OSI Protocols over the Internet

Finally, we are in position to describe how your email gets from you at the hotel in Hawaii to your friend in the company in Ohio. In fact, you need to know just one more topic to understand the techno-miracle that occurs: how private and public IP addresses are converted.

Network Address Translation

All of the IP addresses described in the prior section were private IP addresses. They are used within the LAN at your hotel. For Internet traffic, however, only public IP addresses can be used. These addresses are assigned in blocks to large companies and organizations like ISPs.

Your hotel has an ISP that it uses to connect to the Internet. That ISP assigned one of its public IP addresses to the router in your hotel. We will denote that IP address as IPx. (Again, it will be a dotted-decimal number, but ignore that right now.)

Therefore, as shown in Figure CE7-7, router RH has two IP addresses: a private one, IP9, and a public one, IPx. All Internet traffic aimed at any computer within the hotel LAN will be sent over the Internet using IP address IPx. The router will receive all packets for all computers at the hotel. When it receives a packet, it determines the internal IP address within the LAN for that computer. It then changes the address in the packet from IPx (the router's IP address) to the internal IP address of a computer in the hotel—the packet's true destination.

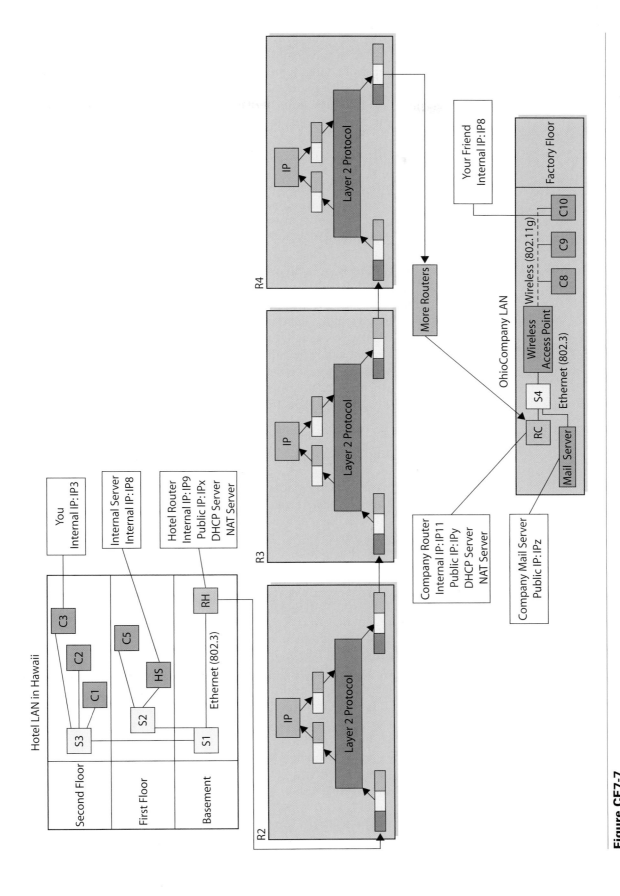

Figure CE7-7
Hawaii Hotel to OhioCompany via Internet

Thus, if the router receives some traffic intended for you, it will change the packets's address from IPx to IP3 and send it to you.[1]

The process of changing public IP addresses into private IP addresses, and the reverse, is called **Network Address Translation (NAT)**. NAT uses a concept called ports. . . . But, let's stop there. We've had enough. If you major in IS, you can learn about NAT. Let's just move on and trust that NAT works.

Your Email (!)

Finally, we can describe how your email gets to your friend in Ohio. You start your email program, and you enter your friend's email address. Suppose that your friend's name is Carter, and his email address is CarterK@OhioCompany.com. Your email program works at the application layer, and it implements SMTP. According to this protocol, your email will be sent to a mail server at the Internet address *OhioCompany.com*.

Your email program will use the domain name system (described later) to obtain the public IP address for the mail server at *OhioCompany.com*. Let's denote that address as IPz.

The message to IPz is then sent to the router RH as follows: Your email program implements SMTP, which sends the message to TCP. There it is broken into segments, and each segment is sent to IP, where they are placed into packets and routed to RH. Then, each packet is sent to your Ethernet program, where it is placed in a frame and sent to switch S3, and then S1, and then the router.

When one of the packets from your email and picture arrives at the router, it implements NAT and replaces your private IP address, IP3, with its public IP address, IPx. Router RH consults its routing table and determines how best to get the packet to IPz. Suppose that it determines that it should send the packet to Internet router R2.

The processing of the packet over the Internet is just the same as described for the hotel in Figure CE7-1. Packets are sent from router to router until they reach the router RC, the gateway router at your friend's company, which sends them to the mail server.

At that server, segments will be unpacked from packets and sent to a TCP program on the mail server that will send an acknowledgment back to your computer. Then TCP will wait for all of the segments in your mail (and picture) to arrive. TCP will then send the entire message and photo attachment to the program that implements SMTP. That program, which operates at Layer 5, will place the message and photo in the mailbox for CarterK.

When your friend checks his mail, the mail program on his computer will use all five layers of the TCP/IP—OSI architecture to send his mail check request to the mail server. His computer, which is also operating behind a router that provides NAT, has the internal IP address IP8. Notice that he has the same IP address as the server HS at your hotel. This duplication will not cause a problem, because these IP addresses are used only in local, private networks. Neither address is used on the public Internet.

Carter's computer connects to the mail server using a wireless protocol, 802.11g, but the essence of his communications to the mail server is the same as that on your hotel LAN. The mail server will send your email and picture to a TCP program on the mail server, from there to an IP program for routing to IP8, and from there to a program that processes Ethernet. Switch S4 will then convert the Ethernet frames into 802.11g frames and send them to your friend's computer.

That's how it works!

---

[1]Believe it or not, we are simplifying here. This description is typical for a SOHO network. A real hotel and company would use devices in addition to the router for DHCP and NAT.

Q5 How Does *www.prenhall.com* Become 165.193.123.253?

IP addresses are useful for computer-to-computer communication, but they are not well suited for human use. I want to be able to enter a name like *www.icann.org* into my browser and not have to remember and enter its public IP address, which is 192.0.34.65. The purpose of the **domain name system (DNS)** is to convert user-friendly names into their IP addresses. Any registered, valid name is called a **domain name**. The process of changing a name into its IP address is called *resolving the domain name*.

This process requires the solution of two problems. First, to be useful, every domain name must be unique, worldwide. To ensure that duplicates do not occur, an agency registers names and records the corresponding IP addresses in a global directory. Second, when the user enters a domain name into his or her browser or other Layer 5 application, there needs to be some way for the application to resolve the domain name. We will consider each problem in turn.

Domain Name Registration

ICANN is a nonprofit organization that is responsible for administering the registration of domain names. ICANN does not register domain names itself; instead, it licenses other organizations to register names. ICANN is also responsible for managing the *domain name resolution system*.

The last letters in any domain name are referred to as the **top-level domain (TLD)**. For example, in the domain name *www.icann.org*, the TLD is *.org*. Similarly, in the domain name *www.ibm.com*, *.com* is the TLD. For non-U.S. domain names, the TLD is often a two-letter abbreviation for the country in which the service resides. For example, a name like *www.somewhere.cn* would be a domain name in China, and *www.somewhere.uk* would be a domain name in the United Kingdom.

Figure CE7-8 (page 408) shows the U.S. top-level domains as of 2007. Some of these TLDs are restricted to particular industries, purposes, or organizations. The TLD *.aero*, for example, is restricted for use by organizations in the air transport industry. Similarly, *.name* is intended for use by individuals, and *.mil* is reserved for use by the U.S. military.

If you want to register a domain name, the first step is to determine the appropriate TLD. You should then visit *icann.org* and determine which agencies ICANN has licensed to register domains for that TLD. Finally, follow the registration process as required by one of those agencies. Again, if the domain name you want is already in use, your registration will be disallowed, and you will need to select another domain name.

Domain Name Resolution

A **uniform resource locator (URL)**, pronounced either by saying the three letters or as "Earl," is a document's address on the Web. URLs begin with a domain name and then are followed by optional data that locates a document within that domain. Thus, in the URL *www.prenhall.com/kroenke*, the domain name is *www.prenhall.com*, and */kroenke* is a directory within that domain.

Domain name resolution is the process of converting a domain name into a public IP address. The process starts from the TLD and works to the left across the URL. As of 2007, ICANN manages 13 special computers called **root servers**

Figure CE7-8
U.S. Top-Level
Domains, 2007

TLD	Introduced	Purpose	Sponsor/Operator
.aero	2001	Air-transport industry	Societe Internationale de Telecommunications Aeronautiques SC (SITA)
.biz	2001	Businesses	
.com	1995	Unrestricted (but intended for commercial registrants)	VeriSign, Inc.
.coop	2001	Cooperatives	DotCooperation, LLC
.edu	1995	U.S. educational institutions	EDUCAUSE
.gov	1995	U.S. government	U.S. General Services Administration
.info	2001	Unrestricted use	Afilias, LLC
.int	1998	Organizations established by international treaties between governments	Internet Assigned Numbers Authority
.mil	1995	U.S. military	U.S. DoD Network Information Center
.museum	2001	Museums	Museum Domain Management Association (MuseDoma)
.name	2001	For registration by individuals	Global Name Registry, LTD
.net	1995	Unrestricted (but intended for network providers, etc.)	VeriSign, Inc.
.org	1995	Unrestricted (but intended for organizations that do not fit elsewhere)	Public Interest Registry; Global Registry Services
.pro	2002	Accountants, lawyers, physicians, and other professionals	RegistryPro, LTD

that are distributed around the world. Each root server maintains a list of IP addresses of servers that resolve each type of TLD.

For example, to resolve the address *www.somewhere.biz*, you would first go to a root server and obtain the IP address of a server that resolves *.biz* domain names. To resolve the address *www.somewhere.com*, you would go to a root server and obtain the IP address of a server that resolves *.com* domain names. In the first case, given the address of the server that resolves *.biz*, you would query that server to determine the IP address of the server that resolves the particular name *somewhere.biz*. Then you would go to that server to determine the IP address of the server that manages *www.somewhere.biz*.

In practice, domain name resolution proceeds more quickly because there are thousands of computers called **domain name resolvers** that store the correspondence of domain names and IP addresses. These resolvers reside at ISPs, at academic institutions, at large companies, at governmental organizations, and so forth. A domain name resolver may even be located on your campus. If so, whenever anyone on your campus resolves a domain name, that resolver will store, or **cache**, the domain name and IP address on a local file. Then, when someone else on campus needs to resolve that same domain name, there is no need to go through the entire resolution process. Instead, the resolver can supply the IP address from the local file.

Of course, domain names and their IP addresses can change. Therefore, from time to time, the domain name resolvers delete old addresses from their lists or refresh old addresses by checking their correctness.

Active ? Review

Use this Active Review to verify that you understand the material in the chapter extension. You can read the entire extension and then perform the tasks in this review, or you can read the material for just one question and perform the tasks in this review for that question before moving on to the next one.

Q1 How does email travel?

Identify the local area networks and the Internet network in Figure CE7-1. Describe some of the problems that must be overcome in sending your email and picture to your friend. Explain why some of your message was broken into sections. Describe the route your message took. Explain what happened when one of the sections was lost.

Q2 What is a communications protocol?

Give an example of a social protocol other than paying at the grocery store. In your own words, describe what a protocol does. Define *communications protocol*.

Q3 What are the functions of the five TCP/IP—OSI layers?

Compare and contrast the terms *communication protocol architecture, communication protocol*, and *program*. Using the example of Firefox (a browser) processing a Web site on the Internet, give an example of each of these. Using Figure CE7-3 as a guide, explain the purpose of each layer of the TCP/IP architecture in layperson's terms. Name the layers used for an internet and the layers used for a LAN. Explain how Figure CE7-4 shows a message being wrapped in packages, packages within packages, and so forth.

Q4 How does the Internet work?

Define the terms *MAC address* and *IP address*. Define the terms *physical address* and *logical address*, and relate them to MAC and IP addresses. Explain which layers of the TCP/IP—OSI architecture use MAC addresses. Explain which use IP addresses. Explain the advantage of being able to transfer an IP address from one device or computer to another.

Compare and contrast a public IP address and a private IP address. State who assigns each type of address. Explain the meaning of the statement,

"Most user computers obtain IP addresses from DHCP servers." Explain the process by which you were granted an IP address at your hotel. Identify the computer that provided that address to you.

Using the network structure in Figure CE7-5, explain the message processing shown in Figure CE7-6. Explain how switches use MAC addresses and switch tables, while the router and the Web server use IP addresses and routing tables. Ensure you understand the differences in each of the rectangles in Figure CE7-6.

Explain why the router in your hotel needs two IP addresses. Explain how it uses IP9 and how it uses IPx. Show an example value for either IP address. Explain why your internal, private IP address must be transformed. Explain why all traffic directed to you from outside of the hotel will be sent to address IPx. Identify the device that translates your IP address into IPx and the reverse. Explain, at a high level, the purpose of network address translation.

Trace the flow of one email from you to your friend in Figure CE7-7. On each line that connects two devices, state whether a MAC or an IP address is used. If it is an IP address, state whether it is an internal or an external IP address. Explain why it is possible that your computer and the computer of your friend can have the same IP address. Compare and contrast segment, packet, and frame.

Q5 How does *www.prenhall.com* become 165.193.123.253?

Explain the meaning of the phrase *resolving a domain name*. Define the term *top-level domain*, and indicate what are the top level domains of *www.prenhall.com*, *www.irs.gov*, and *www.myvalleyInn.uk*. Define *uniform resource locator*. Explain the role of ICANN with regard to domain registration. Summarize the process for registering the domain, *www.mydogspot.info*. Explain ICANN's role with regard to domain name resolution, and describe the purpose of a root server. Summarize the process of resolving the URL *www.mydogspot.info*. Explain why it is likely that the first person to access *www.mydogspot.info* at a major university is likely to wait longer for a response than will subsequent people who access that same site.

Key Terms and Concepts

Architecture 398
Cache 408
Communications protocol 397
Domain name 407
Domain name resolution 407
Domain name resolver 408
Domain name system (DNS) 407
Dynamic Host Configuration
  Protocol (DHCP) 401
File Transfer Protocol (FTP) 398
Frame 400
Hypertext Transfer Protocol (HTTP)
  398
International Organization for
  Standardization (ISO) 397
Internet Corporation for Assigned
  Names and Numbers (ICANN) 401
Internet Engineering Task Force
  (IETF) 397

Internet Protocol (IP) 399
IP address 400
Layered protocols 397
Logical address 400
MAC address 400
Network Address Translation (NAT)
  406
Packet 399
Physical address 400
Private IP address 401
Program (that implements a
  protocol) 398
Protocol 396, 398
Protocol architecture 397
Public IP address 401
Reference Model for Open Systems
  Interconnection (OSI) 397
Root server 407
Routing table 404

Segment 398
Simple Mail Transfer Protocol
  (SMTP) 398
Switch 400
Switch table 403
TCP/IP—OSI (protocol) architecture
  397
Top-level domain (TLD) 407
Transmission Control Program
  (TCP) 398
Uniform resource locator (URL) 407
Transmission Control Program/
  Internet Protocol (TCP/IP)
  architecture 397

Using Your Knowledge

1. Assume you teach your MIS class and that a student comes to your office one day and asks, "Why do I have to learn how the Internet works? Give me three practical applications of this knowledge." How would you respond? Before you answer this question, read and think about the questions that follow.

2. How important do you think the existence of the TCP/IP—OSI protocols and architecture are to the success of the Internet? How did they contribute to the growth of the Internet? In what ways do protocols decrease competition? In what ways do they increase competition? In what ways do protocols stifle innovation? In what ways do they facilitate innovation? Explain how protocol architectures enable many different vendors to create interoperable products. In 2007 and beyond, what other industries might benefit from a similar standard?

3. Search the Internet for four companies that make products for one or more of the five layers of the TCP/IP—OSI architecture. Search for terms introduced in Chapter 6 and in this extension, such as *802.3, 802.11, optical cable, VPN, firewall, switch, ftp,* and others. For each company, name one of their products, explain its function, and describe how that product relates to the TCP/IP—OSI architecture.

4. At one time, it was believed that the world would soon run out of IP addresses. Accordingly, a new protocol called IPv6 was proposed with longer IP addresses that provide many more unique IP addresses. During that same time, however, DHCP and NAT began to see widespread use, and their use dramatically reduced the growth in need for unique IP addresses. Explain why this is so. Suppose you are the director of product planning for a high-tech company, and five years ago, you had been the initiator and principal

proponent for the development of a new line of products based on IPv6. Your product sales have been substantially below your estimates. What do you do now? What product development principle(s) can you extract from this situation? How can you protect your organization from such situations in the future?

5.   The biggest bottleneck in the Internet is the last mile from the ISP to the home. Numerous cities are developing plans and proposals to provide optical cable to the doors of small businesses and homes. When this occurs, applications that require high bandwidth, such as home movies, will become feasible. Explain how companies like Netflix are positioning themselves to pounce on that high bandwidth when it becomes available. Name three other products or services that become feasible when most homes have optical cable at the door. What companies or industries stand to lose from the development of high bandwidth capability? If you worked in one of those companies, how would you respond to this threat? How can you use the knowledge you gained from this question to guide your search for your first job?

Chapter Extension 8

Chapter 6 provides the background for this Extension.

SOHO Networks

Q1 What Are the Components of a SOHO LAN?

Figure CE8-1 shows a portion of a LAN and Internet hardware used by a **small office, home office (SOHO)** company. The messy set of wires, devices, and office paraphernalia illustrates the need for many of the concepts in Chapter 6 and in Chapter Extension 7. The small, flat, black box is a DSL modem that is connected to a telephone line. The DSL modem also connects to the silver, upright box with the small dark gray antenna. That silver box is a **device access router**. Amazingly, that little box contains an Ethernet LAN switch, an 802.11g wireless access point, a router, and a special-purpose computer with programs loaded in firmware. Those firmware programs act as a DHCP server and perform network address translation (NAT). See Chapter Extension 7 for information about DHCP and NAT. Those firmware programs also set up wireless security and to perform administrative tasks.

Note the several UTP cables that connect the device access router to computers and other devices on the LAN. The printer

Study Questions

Q1 What are the components of a SOHO LAN?

Q2 How do I access programs in the device access router?

Q3 How does a SOHO network use DHCP?

Q4 What security options do I have?

Q5 How do I set up a SOHO network?

Figure CE8-1
A SOHO Network

Figure CE8-2
Components of a SOHO
LAN

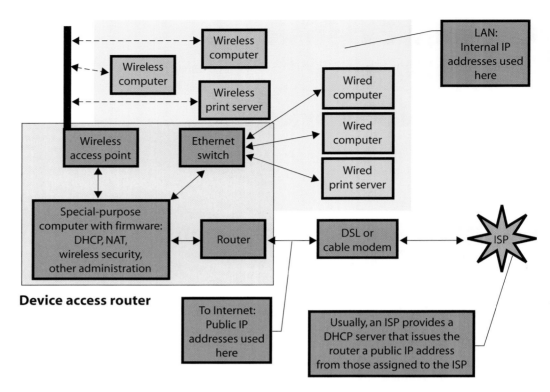

Device access router

(behind the tape dispenser) has a small black box with a gray UTP cable and a small black power line going into it. The black box is an NIC that connects the printer to the LAN via the device access router. This NIC is called a **printer server**, and it, too, contains a special-purpose computer with firmware programs. These programs can be used to set up and administer the printer server and printer. By using the printer server, it is unnecessary to connect the printer to any computer. Any of the users on the LAN can use the printer without turning on a computer to serve the printer. Figure CE8-2 shows a schematic of the contents of the device access router in the context of a typical SOHO LAN.

Q2 How Do I Access Programs in the Device Access Router?

The router in the device access router has two IP addresses. One is a private IP address that is used only within the LAN. Any computer or printer server on the LAN that wishes to send traffic to the router will use the private IP address. The device access router also has a second, public IP address that is provided by the ISP. That address is valid on the public Internet, worldwide. Any outside computer or server that wishes to send traffic to any device on this LAN will use the router's public IP address to do so.

The manufacturer of the device access router assigns the local IP address to the router. That IP address is always stated in the device's documentation. If you cannot locate that documentation, you can Google the brand name and model of your device, and you will most likely be able to find a copy of it. (Of course, if you're setting up your network, you won't have access to the Internet, yet. Go next door, and ask to borrow your neighbor's Internet connection.)

The internal IP address for the device access router in Figure CE8-1 is 192.168.2.1. To contact that router, the network administrator used a browser on

Local Area Network (LAN) Settings

This section displays a summary of settings for your LAN.

Local IP address:	192.168.2.1
Subnet mask:	255.255.255.0
DHCP server:	Enabled
Firewall:	Enabled

DHCP Client List

This section lists the computers and other devices that the base station detects on your network.

IP address	Host name	MAC address
192.168.2.28		0x00c002a5e78a
192.168.2.20		0x000e3589b565
192.168.2.19		0x000cf18e7a55

Base Station Information

Runtime code version:	V1.11.017
Boot code version:	V1.02
LAN MAC address:	00-50-F2-C7-B0-9A
MAC address:	00-01-03-21-AB-98
Serial number:	A240054408

a computer on the LAN and keyed *http://192.168.2.1* in the address field. The router responded with a page that looks like that in Figure CE8-3. We have not discussed *subnet masks* in this text. Other than that, however, you should be able to understand everything in this figure based on the knowledge you gained in Chapter 6 and Chapter Extension 7.

Q3 How Does a SOHO Network Use DHCP?

The device access router provides a DHCP server. When a computer, printer server, or other device wishes to sign on to the network, it contacts the device access router and obtains an internal IP address from it. The DHCP client list in Figure CE8-3 shows the three computers or other devices that asked for an IP address. This list shows the addresses assigned by the device access router, as well as the MAC address of each device. If another device signs on to the LAN, the device access router will issue it an internal IP address and add its MAC address to the list.

The last part of Figure CE8-3 shows data about the base station itself. The LAN MAC address is the MAC address of the Ethernet switch in the device. The MAC address is the MAC address of the router.

A similar scheme is used whenever you sign on to a LAN at your university or at your favorite coffee shop. Your computer will search the neighborhood for a wireless connection (really a wireless access point within a device access router). When it finds one, it will ask for an Internal IP address. The DHCP server in the device access router will issue one. When you sign off, that IP address goes back into the unused set of IP addresses to be reused by another student or customer.

Q4 What Security Options Do I Have?

If you are connecting via wireless to a network at a public place such as your university or a coffee shop, you have no security protection on that LAN. Understand that any unprotected text that you send over a wireless network can easily be intercepted by anyone nearby. Unless you take special precautions—precautions that are rare and seldom taken—all of your email is unprotected text. Your IM conversations are also unprotected, and the URLs of any Web sites you visit are unprotected. Of course, any text that you send using *https* is encrypted and is comparatively safe.

Intercepting wireless traffic is quite easy. Using readily available shareware, your professor or any of your classmates could readily obtain and read the text of any email or IM you send during class. They could also obtain the URL of any Web site you access during class. So, use your computer in the classroom and other public places with care!

The good news is that if you are setting up your own SOHO LAN, you do have a number of security options. The first is called **Wired Equivalent Privacy (WEP)**. The goal of WEP is to provide the same level of security over wireless networks as exists on wired networks. WEP requires that each computer accessing the LAN enter a lengthy key (a long string consisting of digits and the letters *A* through *F*). That string is a symmetric key that is used to encrypt data transmissions on the LAN. Obviously, WEP will not work at a public place because giving the key to every customer who wants to use the LAN would invalidate security.

Unfortunately, WEP was rushed to market before it was sufficiently tested, and it has serious flaws. In response, the IEEE 802.11 committee developed improved wireless standards known as **Wi-Fi Protected Access (WPA)**, and a newer, better version called **WPA2**. Only newer wireless devices can use these techniques.

Another security option for SOHO LANs is **MAC address filtering**. This option will not protect data transmissions from being intercepted, but it will prevent unauthorized users from accessing the device access router and the LAN. To set up MAC address filtering, you first need to obtain the MAC address of every computer and device that you want to allow to sign on to your network. You can obtain the MAC address of NIC devices in a variety of ways. On Windows computers, you can go to the Start menu, select Run, type in the letters **Cmd**, and click OK. You will see a flashing underscore in a black window. Type the letters **Ipconfig** (all one word) and press Enter. Windows will respond with the MAC addresses for all NIC devices on your computer. Select the MAC address that corresponds to the wireless device on that computer. Note, too, that if you employ MAC address filtering, you will need to enter the MAC addresses of all devices on the LAN—and not just the wireless devices.

Once you have the list of MAC addresses, connect to your device access router from your browser using its internal IP address as described. Then find and select the Wireless Security menu on the device's page, and find the entry for MAC Address Filtering. The particular format of the screen varies depending on the product, but it will appear something like that shown in Figure CE8-4. Enter the MAC addresses for all of your devices. Be sure to enter at least one of them correctly, because once you have saved those addresses, if none is correct, you will be locked out of your own LAN!

MAC Filtering   ℹ Help

You can exercise greater control over your network — as well as increase network security — by specifying which Media Access Control (MAC) addresses are allowed to access the base station. Each network adapter on each computer or networked device that connects to the network has a unique MAC address. When MAC filtering is enabled, a computer is allowed to connect to the base station with full access to the Internet and network resources. If the computer uses a wireless connection, you can give it the same access by selecting the **Enable association control** check box.

MAC Address Control

☑ Enable **connection** control and [deny ▾] unspecified MAC addresses to connect:
☑ Enable **association** control and [deny ▾] unspecified MAC addresses to associate:

MAC Address						Allow Connection	Allow Association
00	0C	00	8E	7A	00	☑	☐
00	01	35	21	AB	00	☑	☐
00	0E	03	89	B5	00	☑	☑
00	C0	DA	A5	E7	00	☑	☑
00	50	35	EB	83	00	☑	☑
00	09	03	86	33	00	☑	☑

Figure CE8-4
MAC Address Filtering

Q5 How Do I Set Up a SOHO Network?

Given the knowledge you have gained in Chapter 6 and Chapter Extensions 7 and 8, it should be easy for you to set up a SOHO network. Before doing anything, however, first read the instructions that come with your device access router. It will have specific instructions for tasks to perform and the order in which they should be performed. If you follow those instructions in the proper order, setting up the SOHO LAN should not be difficult.

Most likely, the instructions will call for you to set up cabling correctly before turning on any devices. The reason for this is that your computer and other devices will attempt to obtain IP addresses or take other actions when they are turned on. If the cabling is not present, those attempts will fail, and the devices will go into indeterminate states.

In most cases (not all—see your device access router documentation), you will work upstream from the modem to your computer. If so, you will first turn on the modem and then turn on the device access router. In almost every case, the device access router will communicate via the modem to the ISP in an attempt to contact a DHCP server. If that attempt succeeds, then the modem has a connection to the Internet. At the same time, the Ethernet switch and the wireless access point become live. At that point, turn on your computers and other devices, and they will contact the device access router for an IP address for use within the LAN.

If you have problems, they are most likely in the cabling. Ensure that you have connected all wires to the proper sockets. If you're using a DSL line, you may have a splitter—one side of which is for your phone and the other is for the modem. Make sure the lines are connected to the correct sockets. On the device access router, a particular socket is designated for the line from the modem. Ensure that line is connected to the proper socket. Also, make sure all of the cable connections are fully inserted into their sockets; you will normally hear a click when the connector seats correctly.

After rechecking all of your cabling, turn off the device access router and wait a minute or so. This delay will cause the ISP's DHCP server to terminate its prior connection (if any) with your router. After that delay, power up the modem and then the device access router. Unless you have a defective device (very unlikely if you bought it from a reputable source), if the cabling is correct, and if you follow the instructions that accompany the device access router, you should not have any problems.

Be sure to use MAC address filtering. Without it, anyone who drives by can sign on to your network, and depending on their skill and intent, cause potential harm. At the least, they will be able to freeload on your ISP connection. At the worst, they can invade and damage files on computers on your LAN. You may or may not want to use WEP or WSA. If you do not, then understand that all of your email, IMs, and URLs are readily readable by anyone within receiving distance of your wireless network.

Good luck!

Active ? Review

Use this Active Review to verify that you understand the material in the chapter extension. You can read the entire extension and then perform the tasks in this review, or you can read the material for just one question and perform the tasks in this review for that question before moving on to the next one.

Q1 What are the components of a SOHO LAN?

List the components of a SOHO LAN. List the components of a device access router, and describe the function of each. Explain the purpose and advantage of a printer server.

Q2 How do I access programs in the device access router?

Explain why the device access router has two IP addresses, and explain the role of each. Describe how you can access programs on the device access router. Assume that the internal IP address of your device access router is 192.168.2.8.

Q3 How does a SOHO network use DHCP?

Explain what happens when a computer, printer server, or other LAN device attempts to sign on to a SOHO network like the network described here. Explain the entries in Figure CE8-3. Ignore subnet mask.

Q4 What security options do I have?

Describe the security protection you have when signing on using a wireless connection at your university or in a public coffee shop. Describe the traffic you send that is protected by encryption. Describe the traffic that is not protected. Explain your privacy vulnerability when using a wireless network in class. Explain the purpose of WEP, and describe why it cannot be used for a public network. Explain the problem with WEP. Explain the purposes and limitations of WPA and WPA2. Explain MAC address filtering. Describe one way to obtain the MAC address of NIC devices on your computer. Describe the process of setting up MAC address filtering. Describe the process for enabling MAC address filtering.

Q5 How do I set up a SOHO network?

Describe the first step in setting up a SOHO network. Describe why it is usually important to set up cabling before powering up any devices. Describe the order of powering devices that is most commonly used. Explain the most common source of problems in setting up a SOHO LAN. Explain why it is important to wait a minute or so before restarting your device access router.

Key Terms and Concepts

Cmd 416
Device access router 413
Ipconfig 416

MAC address filtering 416
Printer server 414
SOHO (small office, home office) 413

Wi-Fi Protected Access (WPA and
  WPA2) 416
Wired Equivalent Privacy (WEP) 416

Using Your Knowledge

1. Suppose that you are a consultant and that you share an office suite with two
    other consultants. The suite has three offices, a small lobby, and a utility room.
    All five rooms are on the same level and within close proximity to one another.
    Assume that each of you has a laptop computer and that the three of you want
    to share a fast, black-and-white laser printer and a slower, full-color printer.
    Describe a SOHO LAN that would meet your needs. Assume you have no
    Internet cabling and no authority to install any in your building. What devices
    would each computer or printer require? What other device is necessary?

2. Describe security alternatives that are available to the SOHO LAN in your
    answer to question 1. Explain the advantages and disadvantages of each.
    Which alternatives would you recommend?

3. Assume that one of the consultants for the LAN in question 1 runs Windows
    and when he clicked on the small LAN icon at the bottom of his computer
    screen, the following screen appeared:

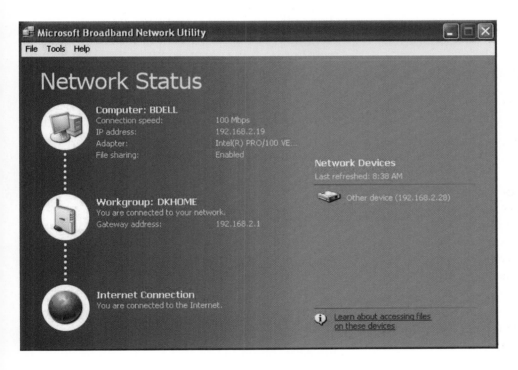

Figure CE8-5

Source: Microsoft product screen shot reprinted with
permission from Microsoft Corporation.

  a. Are the IP addresses in the screen private or public IP addresses?
  b. What computer is located at IP address 192.168.2.19?
  c. What device is located at IP address 192.168.2.1?
  d. What will happen if the user enters *http://192.168.2.1* into her browser?

4. The user did not know what device was located at IP address 192.168.2.28, so she typed *http://192.168.2.28* into her browser and the following screen appeared:

Figure CE8-6

Source: Used with permission of NETGEAR, Inc.

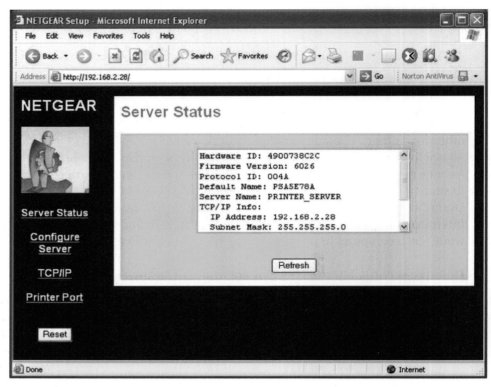

a. What type of device has been assigned to this IP address?
b. Which device created this display?
c. What seems to be the purpose of this display?

5. The user then entered *http://192.168.2.1* into her browser and received back several pages of screens. One of them appeared as follows:

Figure CE8-7

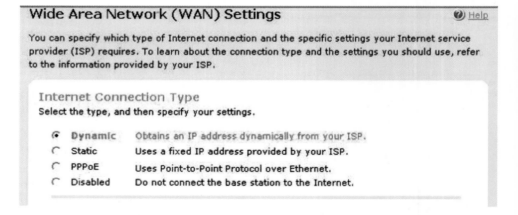

a. Do the data in this display pertain to the Ethernet switch or the router?
b. This screen allows the base station to use DHCP to obtain its public IP address from the ISP. What benefits accrue to the ISP of using DHCP?
c. When would the network administrator *not* use DHCP to connect to the ISP?
d. Under what circumstances would someone use a device access router and not connect it to the Internet?

Chapter Extension 9

Chapter 7 provides the background for this Extension.

Functional Information Systems

Q1 What Is the Difference Between a Functional Application and a Functional System?

A **functional application** is a computer program that provides features and functions necessary to support a particular business activity. As shown in Figure 7-3 (page 161), functional applications map to business activities in the value chain. Accounting applications map to the accounting support activity, and so forth.

A **functional system** is an information system having the five components of all information systems: hardware, software, data, procedures, and people. You can buy hardware, and you can license a functional application. You cannot however buy or license procedures, nor can you buy people who are trained for an organization's specific system(s). Those components of a functional system must be developed in-house. Similarly, while the functional application will have built-in database designs and built-in features for processing and storing data, the data itself must come from you and your organization.

As you read about the functional systems in this extension, keep these differences in mind. The software is just software; by itself, it does nothing. As a manager, it will be your job to ensure that proper procedures are developed and that your employees are trained on the use of those procedures. Keep these differences in mind when developing a new functional system as well. The licensing of the software and the buying of the hardware are the easy parts; integrating those components into an effective system in your organization is more challenging.

Q2 What Are the Functions of Sales and Marketing Information Systems?

The purpose of sales systems is to find prospects and to transform those prospects into customers by selling them something. Sales systems are also used to *manage customers*, which is a euphemism for selling existing cus-

Study Questions

Q1 What is the difference between a functional application and a functional system?

Q2 What are the functions of sales and marketing information systems?

Q3 What are the functions of operations information systems?

Q4 What are the functions of manufacturing information systems?

Q5 What are the functions of human resources information systems?

Q6 What are the functions of accounting information systems?

Q7 What functional systems does DSI use?

tomers more product. Other functional sales systems are used to forecast future sales.

Marketing systems are used most commonly for product and brand management. Companies use such systems to assess the effectiveness of marketing messages, advertising, and promotions, and to determine product demand among various market segments. (Dee's blog, in Parts 1 and 2 of this book, is a marketing system.)

Figure CE9-1 shows specific functions for sales and marketing systems. **Lead generation systems** (also called *prospect generation* systems) include those used to send both postal mailings and email. Web sites are commonly used to generate leads as well. Some Web sites feature just product information; other sites offer to send the prospect white papers or other documents of value in exchange for the prospect's contact information.

Lead tracking systems record lead data and product interests, and keep records of customer contacts. Figure CE9-2 shows a form used by a small company that sells classic 1960s muscle cars (fast cars with large engines and under-designed brakes). The company uses this form for both lead tracking and customer management. (Note that the company uses the term *customer* rather than *lead* or *prospect*.) As you can see, the system maintains customer name and contact data, the customer's product interests, past purchases, and a history of all contacts with the customer.

Figure CE9-1
Functions of Sales and
Marketing Systems

- **Prospect (or lead) generation**
  - Mailings
  - Emailings
  - Web site

- **Lead tracking**
  - Record leads
  - Track product interests
  - Maintain history of contacts

- **Customer management**
  - Maintain customer contact and order history
  - Report credit status
  - Track product interests

- **Sales forecasting**
  - Record individual sales projections
  - Roll up sales projections into district, region, national, and international
  - Track variances over time

- **Product and brand management**
  - Obtain sales results from order processing or receivables systems
  - Compare results to projections
  - Assess promotions, advertising, and sales channels
  - Asses product success in market segments
  - Manage product life cycle

It is not clear from this form whether *Autos Currently Owned* represents autos purchased just from Bainbridge, or autos the customer has purchased from any source. This ambiguity illustrates the need for procedures and employee training. If Bainbridge has five salespeople, and if two salespeople record only autos purchased from Bainbridge while the three other salespeople record autos purchased from any source, the data will be inconsistent. Subsequent reports or analyses based on this data will be hampered by this discrepancy. Again, applications (programs) are not information systems!

Companies use **customer management systems** to obtain additional sales from existing customers. As Figure CE9-1 showed, such systems maintain customer contact and order-history data and track product interests, and some maintain information about the customer's credit status with the organization (not shown in Figure CE9-1). The latter data is used to prevent salespeople from generating orders that the accounts receivable department will later refuse due to poor customer credit.

The most common functional systems in marketing are **product and brand management systems**. With these, records of past sales are imported from order processing or accounts receivable systems and compared to projections and other sales estimates. The company uses the comparisons to assess the effectiveness of promotions and advertising as well as sales channels. It also can use such systems to assess the desirability of the product to different market segments. Finally, the company uses such systems to manage the product through its life cycle. Sales trends may indicate the need for new versions of the product or may help to determine when it is time to remove a product from the market.

In truth, it is impossible to manage a product or a brand without these kinds of information. Without the data, there is no feedback, and anyone's guess is as good as any other's with regard to the effectiveness of the marketing messaging, promotions, advertising, and other marketing activities.

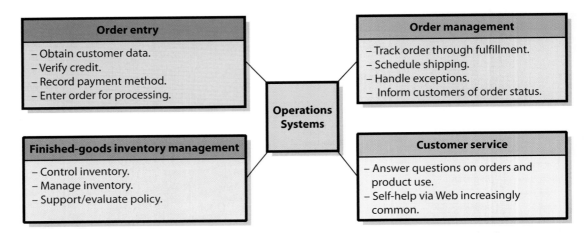

Q3 What Are the Functions of Operations Information Systems?

Operations activities concern the management of finished-goods inventory and the movement of goods from that inventory to the customer. **Operations systems** are especially prominent for nonmanufacturers, such as distributors, wholesalers, and retailers. For manufacturing companies, many, if not all, of the operations functions are merged into manufacturing systems.

Figure CE9-3 lists the principal operations systems. Order entry systems record customer purchases. Typically, an order-entry system obtains customer contact and shipping data, verifies customer credit, validates payment method, and enters the order into a queue for processing. Order management systems track the order through the fulfillment process, arrange for and schedule shipping, and process exceptions, such as out-of-stock products. Order management systems inform customers of order status and scheduled delivery dates.

In nonmanufacturing organizations, operations systems include systems to manage finished-goods inventory. We will not address those systems here; see the discussion of inventory in the discussion of manufacturing systems in the next section. As you read that discussion, just realize that nonmanufacturers do not have raw materials or goods-in-process inventories. They have only finished-goods inventories.

Customer service is the last operations system in Figure CE9-3. Customers call customer service to ask questions about products, order status, and problems and to make complaints. Today, many organizations are placing as much of the customer service function on Web pages as they can. Many organizations allow customers direct access to order status and delivery information. Also, organizations are increasingly providing product-use support via Web systems.

Q4 What Are the Functions of Manufacturing Information Systems?

Manufacturing systems facilitate the production of goods. As shown in Figure CE9-4, manufacturing systems include inventory, planning, scheduling, and manufacturing operations. We begin with inventory.

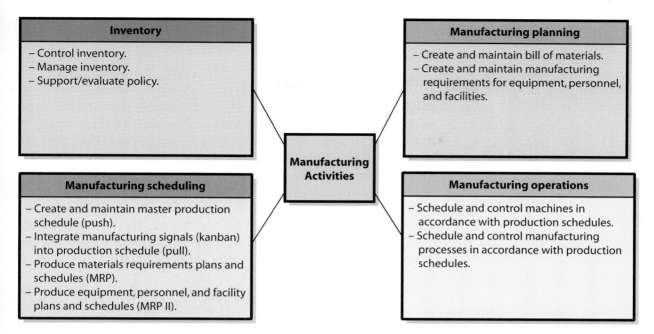

Figure CE9-4
Functions of Manufacturing
Information Systems

Inventory Systems

Information systems support inventory control, management, and policy. In terms of inventory control, inventory applications track goods and materials into, out of, and between inventories. Inventory tracking requires that items be identified by a number. In the least sophisticated systems, employees must enter inventory numbers manually. Today, however, most systems use UPC bar codes (the familiar bar code you find on items at the grocery store) or RFIDs to track items as they move in, around, and out of inventories.

Inventory management applications use past data to compute stocking levels, reorder levels, and reorder quantities in accordance with inventory policy. They also have features for assisting inventory counts and for computing inventory losses from those counts and from inventory-processing data.

With regard to inventory policy, there are two schools of thought in modern operations management. Some companies view inventories primarily as assets. In this view, large inventories are beneficial. Their cost is justified because large inventories minimize disruptions in operations or sales due to outages. Large finished-goods inventories increase sales by offering greater product selection and availability to the customer.

Other companies, such as Dell, view inventories primarily as liabilities. In this view, companies seek to keep inventories as small as possible and to eliminate them completely if possible. The ultimate expression of this view is demonstrated in the **just-in-time (JIT) inventory policy**. This policy seeks to have production inputs (both raw materials and work-in-process) delivered to the manufacturing site just as they are needed. By scheduling delivery of inputs in this way, companies are able to reduce inventories to a minimum.

Still others use both philosophies: Wal-Mart, for example, has large inventories in its stores, but minimizes all other inventories in its warehouses and distribution centers.

Inventory applications help an organization implement its particular philosophy and determine the appropriate balance between inventory cost and item availability, given that philosophy. Features include computing the inventory's return on investment (ROI), reports on the effectiveness of current inventory policy, and some means of evaluating alternative inventory policies by performing what-if analyses.

Manufacturing Planning Systems

In order to plan materials for manufacturing, it is first necessary to record the components of the manufactured items. A **bill of materials (BOM)** is a list of the materials that comprise a product. This list is more complicated than it might sound, because the materials that comprise a product can be subassemblies that need to be manufactured. Thus, the BOM is a list of materials, and materials within materials, and materials within materials within materials, and so forth.

In addition to the BOM, if the manufacturing application schedules equipment, people, and facilities, then a record of those resources for each manufactured product is required as well. The company may augment the BOM to show labor and equipment requirements or it may create a separate nonmaterial requirements file.

Figure CE9-5 shows a sample BOM for a child's red wagon having four components: handle bar, wagon body, front-wheel assembly, and rear-wheel assembly. Three of these have the subcomponent parts shown. Of course, each of these subcomponents could have sub-subcomponents, and so forth, but these are not shown. Altogether, the BOM shows all of the parts needed to make the wagon and the relationships of those parts to each other.

Manufacturing-Scheduling Systems

Companies use three philosophies to create a manufacturing schedule. One is to generate a **master production schedule (MPS)**, which is a plan for producing products. To create the MPS, the company analyzes past sales levels and makes

Figure CE9-5
Bill of Materials Example

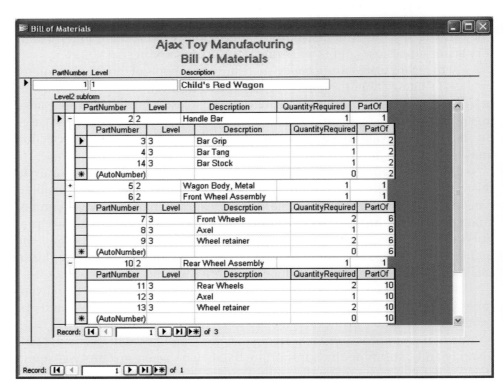

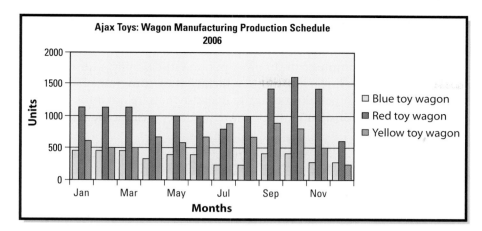

Figure CE9-6
Sample Manufacturing Plan

estimates of future sales. As noted in Chapter 7, this process is called a **push manufacturing process**, because the company pushes the products into sales (and customers) according to the MPS.

Figure CE9-6 shows a manufacturing schedule for wagon production at a toy company. This plan includes three colors of wagons and shows subtle production increases prior to the summer months and prior to the holiday season. Again, the company obtains these production levels by analyzing past sales. The MPS for an actual manufacturer would, of course, be more complicated.

A second philosophy is not to use a preplanned, forecasted schedule, but rather to plan manufacturing in response to signals from customers or downstream production processes that products or components are currently needed. The Japanese word *kanban*, which means "card," is sometimes used to refer to the signal to build something. Manufacturing processes that respond to kanbans must be more flexible than those that are MPS based. A process based on such signals is sometimes called a **pull manufacturing process**, because the products are pulled through manufacturing by demand.

Finally, a third philosophy is a combination of the two. The company creates an MPS and plans manufacturing according to the MPS, but it uses kanban-like signals to modify the schedule. For example, if the company receives signals that indicate increased customer demand, it might add an extra production shift for a while in order to build inventory to meet the increased demand. This combination approach requires sophisticated information systems for implementation.

Two acronyms are common in the manufacturing domain: **Materials requirements planning (MRP)** is an information system that plans the need for materials and inventories of materials used in the manufacturing process. MRP does not include the planning of personnel, equipment, or facilities requirements.

Manufacturing resource planning (MRP II) is a follow-up to MRP that includes the planning of materials, personnel, and machinery. MRP II supports many linkages across the organization, including linkages with sales and marketing via the development of a master production schedule. MRP II also includes the capability to perform what-if analyses on variances in schedules, raw materials availabilities, personnel, and other resources.[1]

---

[1]To add even more complication to this subject, some in the operations management field use the terms *MRP Type I* and *MRP Type II* instead of *MRP* and *MRPII*. MRP Type I refers to material requirements planning; MRP Type II refers to manufacturing resource planning. When used in this way, the different interpretations of the letters *MRP* are ignored, as if *MRP* were not an acronym. Unfortunately, such sets of confusing terminology cannot be avoided in a growing field.

Manufacturing Operations

A fourth category of IS in manufacturing is the control of machinery and production processes. Computer programs operate lathes, mills, and robots, and even entire production lines. In a modern facility, these programs have linkages to the manufacturing-scheduling systems. Because they are not information systems in the sense we consider in this text, we will not consider them further.

Q5 What Are the Functions of Human Resources Information Systems?

Human resources systems support recruit, compensation, assessment, development and training, and planning. The first-era human resources (HR) applications did little more than compute payroll. Modern HR applications concern all dimensions of HR activity, as listed in Figure CE9-7.

Depending on the size and sophistication of the company, recruiting methods may be simple or very complex. In a small company, posting a job may be a simple task requiring one or two approvals. In a larger, more formal organization, posting a new job may involve multiple levels of approval requiring use of tightly controlled and standardized procedures.

Compensation includes payroll for both salaried employees and hourly employees. It may also include pay to consultants and permanent, but nonemployee, workers, such as contractors and consultants. Compensation means not only pay, but also the processing and tracking of vacation, sick leave, and health care and other benefits. Compensation activities also support retirement plans, company stock purchases, and stock options and grants. They can also include transferring employee contribution payments to organizations like the United Way and others.

Figure CE9-7
Functions of
Human Resources
Information
Systems

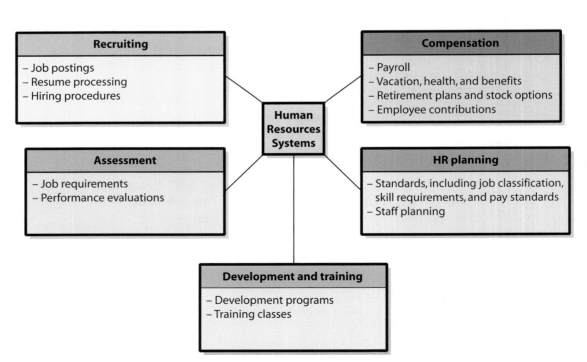

Employee assessment includes the publication of standard job and skill descriptions as well as support for employee performance evaluations. Such support may include systems that allow employees to create self-evaluations as well as evaluation of peers and subordinates. Employee assessment is used for the basis of compensation increases as well as promotion.

Development and training activities vary widely from firm to firm. Some organizations define career paths formally, with specific jobs, skills, experience, and training requirements. HR systems have features and functions to support the publication of these paths. Some HR applications track training classes, instructors, and students.

Finally, HR applications must support planning functions. These include the creation and publication of organizational standards job classifications and compensation ranges for those classifications. Planning also includes determining future requirements for employees by level, experience, skill, and other factors.

Q6 What Are the Functions of Accounting Information Systems?

Typical **accounting systems** are listed in Figure CE9-8. You know what a general ledger is from your accounting classes. Financial reporting applications use the general ledger data to produce financial statement and other reports for management, investors, and federal reporting agencies like the Securities and Exchange Commission (SEC).

Figure CE9-8
Functions of Accounting
Information Systems

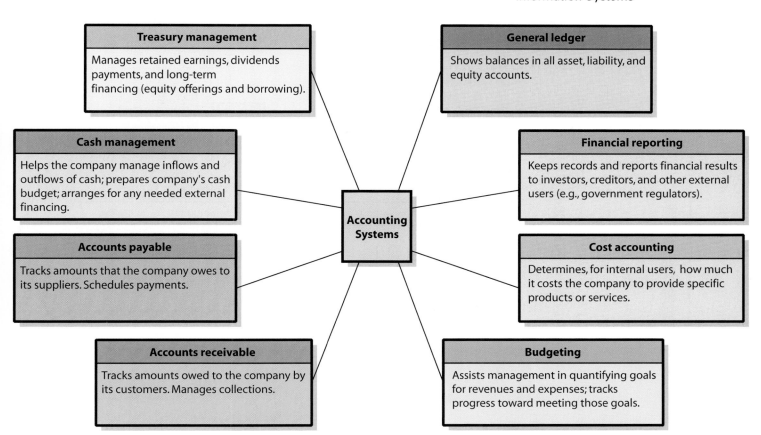

Treasury management
Manages retained earnings, dividends payments, and long-term financing (equity offerings and borrowing).

General ledger
Shows balances in all asset, liability, and equity accounts.

Cash management
Helps the company manage inflows and outflows of cash; prepares company's cash budget; arranges for any needed external financing.

Financial reporting
Keeps records and reports financial results to investors, creditors, and other external users (e.g., government regulators).

Accounts payable
Tracks amounts that the company owes to its suppliers. Schedules payments.

Cost accounting
Determines, for internal users, how much it costs the company to provide specific products or services.

Accounting Systems

Accounts receivable
Tracks amounts owed to the company by its customers. Manages collections.

Budgeting
Assists management in quantifying goals for revenues and expenses; tracks progress toward meeting those goals.

Cost-accounting applications determine the marginal cost and relative profitability of products and product families. Budgeting applications allocate and schedule revenues and expenses and compare actual financial results to the plan.

Accounts receivable includes not just recording receivables and the payments against receivables, but also account aging and collections management. Accounts payable systems include features to reconcile payments against purchases and to schedule payments according to the organization's payment policy.

Cash management is the process of scheduling payments and receivables and planning the use of cash so as to balance the organization's cash needs against cash availability. Other financial management applications concern checking and other account reconciliation as well as managing electronic funds transfer throughout the organization. Finally, treasury applications concern the management and investment of the organization's cash, as well as the payment of cash dividends.

Q7 What Functional Systems Does DSI Use?

DSI differs from many manufacturers in that it produces a few, highly customized, very expensive products per year. The company has selected and tailored its functional information systems accordingly. Figure CE9-9 shows how DSI's functional systems relate to the adjusted Porter model. Figure CE9-10 illustrates DSI's primary business processes.

Sales and Marketing Information Systems

Few of the functions of sales and marketing systems in Figure CE9-1 pertain to DSI. Regarding lead generation, the company does have a Web site, but it is not a

Figure CE9-9
Principal Functional Systems
and the Value Chain at DSI

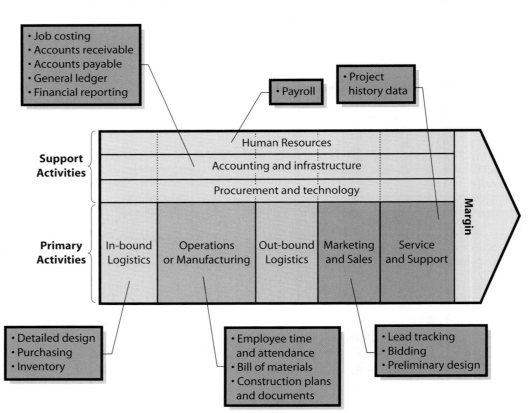

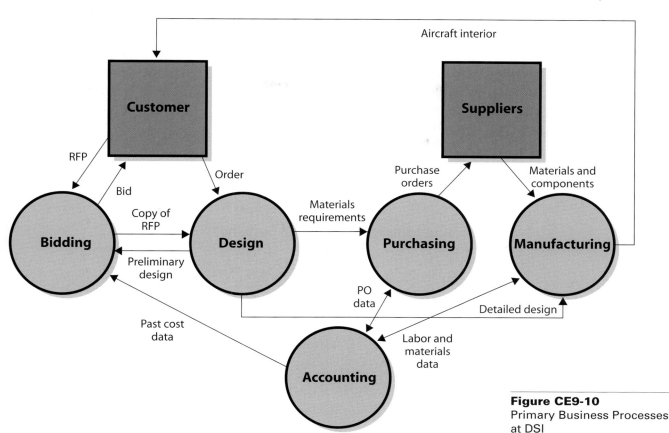

Figure CE9-10
Primary Business Processes at DSI

primary source of leads. Instead, its leads come from public requests for proposals from governmental organizations, from word-of-mouth, or from personal networking by Eleanor Dorset and, to a lesser extent, John Stratford. Given the complexity of DSI's corporate and governmental customers, it does use a lead tracking system. The system helps Ms. Dorset and her sales department track customers, customer employees and their roles, and customer contacts.

A large portion of DSI's business comes from existing customers, primarily corporations and governments, but the company does not have the classic customer-management process. Unlike salespeople at, say, the muscle car dealer in Figure CE9-2, the nature of DSI's product precludes generating sales by telling existing customers that it's time to buy a new airplane. DSI can hardly send an email to a senior Chinese government official saying, in essence, "Hi, we hope you're enjoying your new airplane interior. Would you like to buy another?"

Furthermore, DSI has relatively few existing customers to track. Given the size of its hangar, the company can work on just three airplanes at once and typically has three active customers. In a year, DSI has five or six customers, total. Given this small number of customers, DSI does not see the need for a customer management system. Neither does it see the need for sales forecasting systems, nor for classic product or brand management systems.

Instead, the primary sales and marketing system at DSI is **bidding**. Some customers approach DSI with a plan and even a detailed interior design. Other customers have no plan at all, and DSI works with them to determine their requirements. Once those requirements are known, DSI prepares a preliminary design.

Either way, given the preliminary design, most customers ask for a fixed bid. (Some very wealthy individuals are willing to accept a time-and-materials contract, but they are the exception.) Corporations and governmental agencies often ask for a sealed, competitive bid. In preparing the bids, DSI relies heavily on past experience. Those involved in the bidding access their accounting system, which uses the software product Sage MAS 90 (*www.bestsoftware.com/mas90*). This system provides past project-cost data, and DSI bidders use that data from projects similar to the one being bid. They scale that data as necessary and adjust it for specific system differences, such as the need for different interior equipment. Because DSI specializes in the Boeing 737, past data are usually pertinent, and the company is able to prepare very accurate bids.

As stated, most bids are fixed-price, and bid computation and preparation are serious matters. As a small company, an $8 million bid on a project that actually costs $10 million would mean disaster.

In-bound Logistics Information Systems

DSI uses two primary information systems for in-bound logistics. Engineers create detailed designs and process those designs to create material requirements documents. For this purpose, they use *AutoCad*, a popular design product used by engineers and architects worldwide. AutoCad can transform designs into BOM and *item lists*. Figure CE9-11 shows a typical AutoCad design screen.

Engineers use the BOM and item lists to prepare materials requirements documents, from which Purchasing generates purchase orders for vendors. One material requirements document can generate many different purchase orders, to different vendors. When goods arrive, they are placed in raw materials inventory. Both purchasing and inventory systems are processed by the Sage MAS 90 software.

In-bound logistics involves information systems across organizations. You can read more about such systems in Chapter 8.

Manufacturing Information Systems

DSI uses information systems to track employee time and attendance and to allocate labor hours to specific projects. When employees clock in with their time cards, they must sign in to a project by entering a valid project code. If an

Figure CE9-11
AutoCad Screen Image

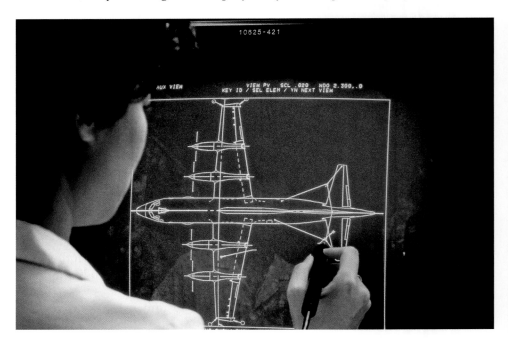

employee changes work from one airplane to another during the day, he or she clocks out of the first project and onto the second. *WinStar*, a time-and-attendance software product, manages the time card data. All WinStar data are input to the MAS 90 accounting system for job costing.

DSI uses a number of other software products to facilitate manufacturing. It uses AutoCad and other vertical-market software products for preparing bills of materials, construction drawings, and construction documents. MAS 90 software maintains raw materials inventory, and it allocates material costs to specific projects as well. Using these systems, DSI can determine the total cost and labor of any project at any point in time and know if projects are exceeding their budgets.

For the purposes of tracking and controlling tools and tool equipment, DSI supplements MAS 90 with a software product called *CribWare*, a product that can be used for checking tools and equipment out to employees (*www.appcim.com/cribware*).

Out-bound Logistics

DSI has a simple and elegant out-bound logistics system as shown in Figure CE9-12.

Service and Support Information Systems

DSI differentiates on quality, and one aspect of that quality is taking good care of its customers. Because the company has few customers, it can tailor service to the particular needs of each customer. This is especially important given the expectations of some of DSI's wealthy clientele.

Figure CE9-12
The Shipping Department at DSI

DSI keeps all designs, drawings, many construction documents, and all cost data on all of its projects. If, in the future, a customer or agent for the customer needs drawings or data about any aspect of any project, DSI can provide them. Also, any time any customers experience a problem with DSI's equipment on an airplane, the company does everything it can to assist, including flying a team of employees with parts, drawings, and documents to any customer location, worldwide.

Many drawings and documents are stored in electronic form, and DSI must ensure that it always has the correct software and version of software for processing those electronic files. Not having the correct software can be a problem for files that are 10 or 15 years old.

Human Resources and Accounting Information Systems

DSI uses the MAS 90 software for payroll and accounting functions. As a small company, DSI does not use automated HR systems other than payroll.

DSI makes extensive use of the core accounting facilities in the MAS 90 system, including general ledger, accounts payable, accounts receivable, project cost accounting, general ledger, and financial reporting.

Software Products Used

Ms. Dorset and Mr. Stratford state emphatically that they are in the aircraft-interior construction business, and not in the software development business. Accordingly, they develop no software. As the preceding discussion indicates, they use only licensed products for software components of all their functional systems. Figure CD9-13 summarizes the software DSI uses.

Figure CE9-13
Summary of Software Products Used by DSI for Primary Business Activities

- **Sales and marketing**
  - Sage MAS 90 (job cost data)
  - Microsoft Excel
- **In-bound logistics**
  - Autocad (design and BOM)
  - Sage MAS 90 (purchasing, inventory)
- **Manufacturing**
  - Autocad (construction documents)
  - WinStar (time and attendance)
  - Cribware (tool tracking)
- **Out-bound logistics**
  - Wild blue yonder…
- **Service and support**
  - Past data using all software above
- **Human resources**
  - Sage MAS 90 (Payroll)
- **Accounting**
  - Sage MAS 90 (job costing, receivables, payables, general ledger, financial reporting)

Active ? Review

Use this Active Review to verify that you understand the material in the chapter extension. You can read the entire extension and then perform the tasks in this review, or you can read the material for just one question and perform the tasks in this review for that question before moving on to the next one.

Q1 What is the difference between a functional application and a functional system?

Use the five-component model to explain the difference between a functional application and a functional system. Explain why this distinction is important to you as a future manager.

Q2 What are the functions of sales and marketing information systems?

List the functional categories of sales and marketing information systems and describe primary functions for each.

Q3 What are the functions of operations information systems?

List the functional categories of operations information systems and describe primary functions for each.

Q4 What are the functions of manufacturing information systems?

List the functional categories of manufacturing information systems and describe primary functions for each. Explain just-in-time inventory policy. Describe a bill of materials and give a brief example. Describe push manufacturing and explain the role of the MPS. Describe pull manufacturing systems and explain the term *kanban*. Decode the acronyms *MRP* and *MRP II*, and explain the functions of each.

Q5 What are the functions of human resources information systems?

List the functional categories of human resource information systems and describe primary functions for each.

Q6 What are the functions of accounting information systems?

List the functional categories of accounting information systems and describe primary functions for each.

Q7 What functional systems does DSI use?

Using Figure CE9-9 as a guide, explain the major functional information systems DSI uses. Explain the business processes documented in Figure CE9-10; be sure to explain each activity and arrow.

Key Terms and Concepts

Accounting information systems 429

Accounts payable information systems 429f

Accounts receivable information systems 429f

Assessment information systems 428f

Bidding information systems 431

Bill of materials (BOM) 426

Budgeting information systems 429f

Cash management information systems 429f

Compensation information systems 428f

Cost accounting information systems 429f

Customer management systems 423

Development and training information systems 428f

Financial reporting information systems 429f

Functional application 421

Functional system 421

General ledger information systems 429f

HR planning information systems 428f

Human resources systems 428

Inventory systems 425f

Just-in-time (JIT) inventory policy 425

Lead generation systems 422

Lead tracking systems 422

Manufacturing information systems 424

Manufacturing resource planning (MRP II) 427

Master production schedule (MPS) 426

Materials requirements planning (MRP) 427

Operations systems 424

Product and brand management systems 423

Using Your Knowledge

1. DSI's manufacturing systems vary substantially from those described in Q4 of this extension. Answer the following questions to assess whether DSI has made a mistake.
   a. Does DSI have a push or pull manufacturing philosophy?
   b. Does it need an MPS? Why or why not?
   c. The text says nothing about DSI endorsing just-in-time inventory policy. Do you think JIT has a place in DSI's organization? Why do you think nothing was indicated about JIT?
   d. What characteristics of DSI's products and market cause it to operate differently than described in Q4?
   e. Describe a business that would be more likely than DSI to use the ideas and concepts discussed under Q4.

2. Suppose you work for a manufacturer that makes and sells baseballs, basketballs, footballs, and volleyballs. Assume you have two sales channels: sport equipment distributors (who sell, in turn, to retailers) and sports organizations, such as the NFL, the NBA, and the baseball leagues. You also sell to major organizations such as city school and state university systems.
   a. Compare and contrast your business to DSI's. Base your analysis on the revised Porter value chain model (like that shown in Figure CE9-9).
   b. Draw a diagram of your business processes similar to that shown in Figure CE9-10.
   c. How will sales and marketing information systems at your company vary from those at DSI?
   d. How will manufacturing information systems at your company vary from those at DSI?
   e. How will service and support information systems at your company vary from those at DSI?
   f. How will HR information systems at your company vary from those at DSI?
   g. How will finance and accounting information systems at your company vary from those at DSI?
   h. What conclusions do you draw from this exercise?

3. Suppose you work for a distributor of home construction materials. You carry windows, doors, hardware, finished wood products, and other materials necessary for home construction. Assume you sell to retail lumberyards and hardware stores, to major chains (like Home Depot and Lowe's) and directly to major home contractors.
   a. Describe what you think are likely business processes in each activity in the revised Porter value chain model in Figure CE9-9.
   b. Draw a diagram of your business processes similar to that shown in Figure CE9-10.
   c. Describe the features of two information systems you could use for sales and marketing.

    d. Describe the features of two information systems you could use for operations.

    e. Describe the features of two information systems you could use for service and support.

    f. Describe the features of two information systems you could use for human resources.

    g. Describe the features of two information systems you could use for accounting.

    h. In what major ways do the business processes and information systems vary between a distributor like yours and a manufacturer like DSI and like the manufacturer described in question 2?

4. The text claims that DSI's out-bound logistics system is the airport. This clearly is an exaggeration. Even if its products do fly away, there must be considerable testing and verification to ensure the aircraft's interior systems perform to specification and that all systems operate correctly.

    a. Describe an information system that could be used to track tests, verification, and systems operation.

    b. Would your system be likely to use a spreadsheet or a database? Explain your answer.

    c. In what ways could the data produced by your information system create information that would benefit DSI? What business processes are likely to benefit, and why?

    d. Write a memo to Mr. Stratford recommending your system. As you write your memo, keep in mind Ms. Dorset's statement on page 155, the one on the opening page of Part 3.

Chapter Extension 10

Chapter 7 provides the background for this Extension.

Cross-Functional Systems: CRM, ERP, and EAI

Q1 What Is the Importance of Inherent Processes?

As computer networks became prevalent in the 1990s, systems developers realized that networks provided a means to do more than simply automate functional applications. As technologists pondered the question, "What, exactly, do networks enable?" Porter's work on value chains became popular. Systems developers began to wonder how they could develop information systems that would integrate several, or many, different areas in an entire value chain. Using another of Porter's concepts, they sought to design information systems that would support linkages across departments and activities. This thinking became the foundation of a movement called **business process design** or sometimes *business process redesign*. The central idea is that organizations should not automate or improve existing functional systems. Rather they should create new, more efficient business processes that integrate the activities of all departments involved in a value chain.

Thus, in the early 1990s, some organizations began to design new cross-departmental business processes. The goal was to take advantage of as many activity linkages as possible. For example, a cross-departmental customer management process integrates all interactions with the customer, from prospect, through initial order, through repeat orders, including customer support, credit, and accounts receivable.

Study Questions

Q1 What is the importance of inherent processes?

Q2 What are the characteristics of customer relationship management (CRM) systems?

Q3 What are the characteristics of enterprise resource planning (ERP) systems?

Q4 How is an ERP system implemented?

Q5 What are the characteristics of enterprise application integration (EAI) systems?

Challenges of Business Process Design

Unfortunately, process design projects are expensive and difficult. Highly trained systems analysts interview key personnel from many departments and document the existing system as well as one or more system alternatives. Managers review the results of the analysts' activity, usually many times, and attempt to develop new, improved processes. Then new information systems are developed to implement those new business processes. All of this takes time, and meanwhile, the underlying processes are changing, which means the process design may need to be redesigned before the project is completed.

Once these difficulties have been overcome and the new integrated systems designed, an even greater challenge arises: Employees resist change. People do not want to work in new ways, they do not want to see their department reorganized or abolished, and they do not want to work for someone new. Even if the system can be implemented over this resistance, some people will continue to resist. All of these difficulties translate into labor hours, which translate into costs. Thus, business process design is very expensive.

Even worse, the ultimate outcome is uncertain. An organization that embarks on a business process design project does not know ahead of time how effective the ultimate outcome will be.

Some businesses were successful in their process design activities, but many others failed. In some cases, millions of dollars were spent on projects that ultimately were abandoned. The idea of designing business processes for greater integration was floundering when it received a boost from an unexpected source: integrated application vendors.

Benefits of Inherent Processes

Many early business process design projects failed because they were tailor-made. They were custom-fit to a particular organization, and so just one company bore the cost of the design effort. In the mid-1990s, a number of successful software vendors began to market premade integrated applications, with built-in processes. Such processes saved hundreds of hours of design work.

When an organization acquires, say, a business application from Oracle or SAP, the processes for using the software are built-in or **inherent processes**. In most cases, the organization must conform its activities to those processes. If the software is designed well, the inherent processes will effectively integrate activities across departments. These prebuilt processes will save the organization the substantial, sometimes staggering, costs of designing new processes itself.

Figure CE10-1 shows an example of an inherent process in a software product called **SAP R/3**, a product licensed by SAP. When an organization licenses this product, SAP provides hundreds of diagrams just like this one. These diagrams show the business processes that must be created in order to effectively use the software.

This diagram shows the flow and logic of one set of inherent processes. In the top lines, if the purchase requisition does not exist and if the request for quotation (RFQ) is to be created, then the purchasing department creates an RFQ and sends it to potential vendors. You can read through the rest of this sample diagram to obtain the gist of this process snippet.

To some, when an organization licenses cross-departmental software, the primary benefit is not the software, but the inherent processes for using the software. Licensing an integrated application not only saves the organization the time, expense, and agony of process design, it also enables the organization to benefit immediately from tried and tested cross-departmental processes.

Of course, there is a disadvantage. The inherent processes may be very different from existing processes and thus require the organization to change substantially. Such change will be disruptive to ongoing operations and very disturbing to employees. The *Guide* on pages 441a–441b discusses the effects of organizational change in more detail.

Three cross-functional application categories have emerged: CRM, ERP, and EAI. We consider these categories next.

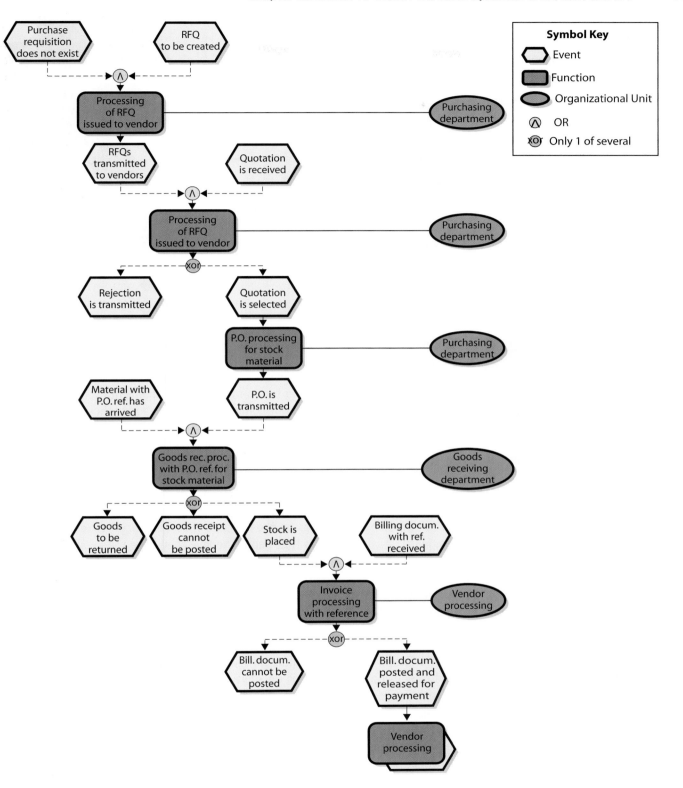

Figure CE10-1
Example of SAP R/3 Ordering
Process

Source: Thomas A. Curran, Andrew Ladd, Dennis Ladd, *SAP R/3 Reporting and E-Business Intelligence*, 1st ed., © 2000. Reprinted by permission of Pearson Education, Inc., Upper Saddle River, NJ.

Thinking About Change

New information systems, especially those that cross departmental boundaries, require employees to change. Employees may do their jobs differently, they may be assigned to a new job or a new boss or a new department, and they will probably work with new people. At the very least, they will certainly use new information systems forms, reports, and other features. Many organizations have found that implementing such change is the most difficult part of IS implementation.

Because organizational change is a common problem, a change management industry has emerged to help organizations deal with it. Change management is a blend of business, engineering, sociology, and psychology that strives to understand the dynamics of organizational change and to develop and communicate theories, methods, and techniques that enable successful organizational change.

According to Adel Aladwani (2001), the top obstacle to successful change is employee resistance. Employees resist change for several reasons. For one, change requires adapting to a new situation or system, and, for a while, all changes make work harder, not easier. Unless employees understand the need for change, they will be unwilling to devote the extra energy and work required.

To be willing to change, employees need to understand the importance of and need for the new system or project. The CEO or other senior manager needs to sponsor the new system. The sponsor should explain the rationale for the system at the onset and throughout the project. Many managers, when reviewing their projects after implementation, say that they did not communicate the need for the new system frequently enough. Experience shows that employees want to hear about the necessity for change from two people: the CEO and their immediate boss.

Another reason that employees resist change is fear of the unknown. Recent motivational research focuses on the concept of self-efficacy. Self-efficacy means that people believe they have the knowledge and skills necessary to be successful at their jobs. When employees feel that way, they not only are happier, but they also work better. Self-efficacy breeds success: When employees feel confident, they bring more of their natural abilities to the problems they face.

Change, however, threatens self-efficacy. When change is underway, people ask questions like, "Will I understand how to use the new system?" "Will I be as successful with it as I was in the past?" "Will I be asked to do things I don't know how to do?" Just having such questions impairs one's ability to work.

Because change is threatening, organizations need to take steps to increase employees' sense of self-efficacy. These steps must go beyond explaining the need for the system. Employees need to be shown how the new system will improve their work situation. They need to be trained on new procedures. If possible, employees should be given opportunities to gain confidence in the new system and in their ability to use it. They also need to see others, either employees in their own organization or other organizations, achieve positive outcomes from the new system. Some organizations find that creating networks or alliances of employees helps to reduce the stress of the change.

In a recent study, Siebel Systems identified a number of key factors in successful change management. Of those factors, two emerged as most important: bosses' behavior and communication. Employees respond to how the boss responds. If their boss supports the change, not just with words, but also with his or her attitude and actions, then employees are more likely to accept the change. Also, frequent two-way communication is important. Management frequently needs to explain the rationale and importance of the change, and employees need frequent opportunities to express their thoughts and feelings about the change.

Employees tend to support what they create. When employees are given an opportunity to participate in the change and to express their thoughts about the change (how it could be improved and so forth), they have a stake in the change and are more likely to support it.

Sources: Adel Aladwani, "Change Management Strategies for Successful ERP Implementation," *Business Process Management Journal*, vol. 7, no. 3, 2001, page 266; Siebel Systems, "Applied Change Management: A Key Ingredient for CRM Success," Siebel eBusiness, June 2003, *www.siebel.com/ resource-library/reg-resource.shtm* (accessed June 2005); Tom Werner, "Change Management and E-Learning," *www.brandon-hall.com* (accessed September 2004).

DISCUSSION QUESTIONS

Imagine that your university announces that next semester students will be required to use a new information system to enroll in classes.

1. What is your first feeling (not thought) on hearing that news?

2. What would you like the university administration to communicate to you about the change?

3. Explain the term *self-efficacy* in relation to this change. What could the university do to increase your sense of self-efficacy?

4. Suppose a good friend tries the new system and says, "Hey, it's much better than the old one. Very easy to use." How does that affect your feelings about the change? What if your friend says, "It's terrible, such a hassle." How does that affect your feelings?

5. Given your answer to question 4, what programs could the university develop to reduce resistance to the change?

6. What might your professors say about the change that would cause you to feel better about it? What might your professors say that would cause you to feel worse about it?

7. In this situation, which is more powerful, the opinions of your good friend or the opinion of your professor? Explain your response. In business, which would be more important, your co-workers' opinions or your boss's?

Q2 What Are the Characteristics of Customer Relationship Management (CRM) Systems?

Customer relationship management (CRM) systems support the business processes of attracting, selling, managing, delivering, and supporting customers. As shown in Figure 7-7 (page 168), CRM systems support all of the direct value chain activities that involve the customer.

The difference between CRM systems and traditional functional applications is that CRM addresses all activities and events that touch the customer and provides a single repository for data about all customer interactions. With functional systems, data about customers are sprinkled in databases all over the organization. Some customer data exist in customer management databases, some in order entry databases, some in customer service databases, and so forth. CRM systems store all customer data in one place and make it possible to access all data about the customer.

By the way, some CRM systems include activities that occur at the customer's site. Such systems support linkages between two organizations and are discussed in Chapter 8 in the context of supply chain management.

Figure CE10-2 shows four phases of the **customer life cycle**: marketing, customer acquisition, relationship management, and loss/churn. Marketing sends messages to the target market to attract customer prospects. When prospects order, they become customers who need to be supported. Additionally, resell processes increase the value of existing customers. Inevitably, over time the organization loses customers. When this occurs, win-back processes categorize customers according to value and attempt to win back high-value customers.

Figure CE10-2
The Customer Life Cycle

Source: Douglas MacLachlan, University of Washington.

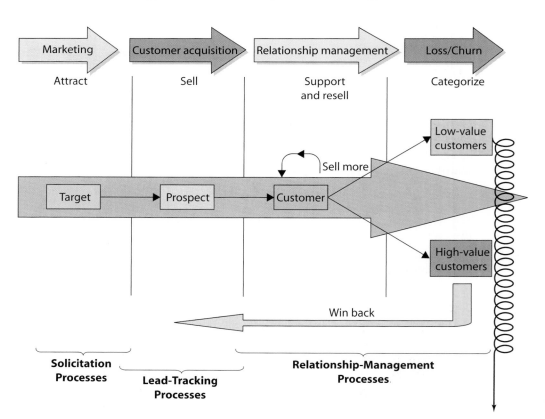

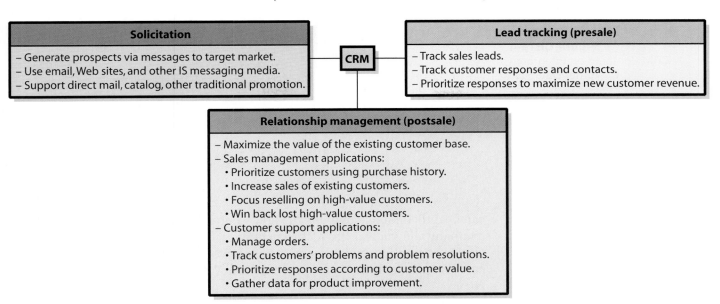

Solicitation
– Generate prospects via messages to target market. – Use email, Web sites, and other IS messaging media. – Support direct mail, catalog, other traditional promotion.

CRM

Lead tracking (presale)
– Track sales leads. – Track customer responses and contacts. – Prioritize responses to maximize new customer revenue.

Relationship management (postsale)

– Maximize the value of the existing customer base.
– Sales management applications:
  • Prioritize customers using purchase history.
  • Increase sales of existing customers.
  • Focus reselling on high-value customers.
  • Win back lost high-value customers.
– Customer support applications:
  • Manage orders.
  • Track customers' problems and problem resolutions.
  • Prioritize responses according to customer value.
  • Gather data for product improvement.

Figure CE10-3
CRM Components

Figure CE10-3 shows the major components of a CRM system. Notice there are components for each stage of the customer life cycle. Information systems that support solicitation include email applications and organizational Web sites. Additionally, some information systems support traditional direct mail, catalog, and other solicitations.

The organizational Web site is an increasingly important solicitation tool. Web addresses are easy to promote (and remember), and once a target prospect is on the site, product descriptions, use cases, success stories, and other solicitation materials can be provided easily. Further, the cost of distributing these materials via the Web is substantially less than the cost of creating and distributing printed materials. Many Web sites require customer name and contact information before releasing high-value promotional materials. That contact information then feeds lead-tracking applications.

The purpose of lead-tracking, or presale, applications is to turn prospects into customers. Such applications track sales leads and record customer responses and contacts. Most of these applications enable the sales department to prioritize contacts so as to focus on high-potential prospects.

Lead tracking is particularly important when multiple salespeople call on the same customer. Often salespeople may join forces to work out a strategy for sales calls and follow-ups. If nothing else, consolidated lead tracking can keep sales personnel from duplicating efforts and from interfering with one another.

With the first order, a prospect becomes a customer and is a candidate for relationship management applications. The purpose of relationship management applications is to maximize the value of the existing customer base. As Figure CE10-3 shows, two types of applications are used. Sales management applications support sales to existing customers. They have features to prioritize customers according to their purchase history. Salespeople can increase sales to existing customers by focusing on customers who have already made large purchases, by focusing on large organizations that have the potential to make large purchases, or both. The goal of such applications is to ensure that sales management has sufficient information to prioritize and allocate sales time and effort.

Sales management applications also have features to prioritize lost customers, to determine which of those are high-value lost customers, and to help the sales team to develop a strategy to win those customers back. Surprisingly, it

Figure CE10-4
CRM Centered on Integrated
Customer Database

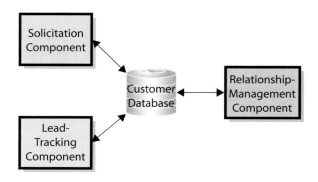

can be difficult for a company to know when it has lost a customer. A telephone company will know it has lost a customer when the customer cancels the service, but an online retailer many not know when it has lost a customer. In such a case, only an analysis of past purchase history can indicate that the customer is gone.

Of course, it is cheaper to keep an existing customer than to acquire a new customer or win back a lost one. Accordingly, another important component to relationship management is customer support. Order management applications help the customer to determine the status of an order, how and when it was shipped, the status of returns, and so forth. Additionally, other customer support applications track customer problems and resolutions and ensure that customers need not repeat their problem history to each new support representative.

Integrated CRM applications store data in a single database, as shown in Figure CE10-4. Because all customer data reside in one location, CRM processes can be linked to one another. For example, customer service activities can be linked to customer purchase records. In this way, both sales and marketing know the status of customer satisfaction, both on an individual customer basis for future sales calls and also collectively for analyzing customers' overall satisfaction. Also, many customer support applications prioritize customers in order to avoid giving $10,000 worth of support to a customer with a lifetime value of $500. Finally, customer support has an important linkage to product marketing and development; it knows more than any other group what customers are doing with the product and what problems they are having with it.

Q3 What Are the Characteristics of Enterprise Resource Planning (ERP) Systems?

Enterprise resource planning (ERP) systems support all of the primary business processes as well as the human resource and accounting support processes. Contrast Figure 7-7 with Figure 7-8 (page 168) to see how ERP differs from CRM. ERP systems are truly enterprisewide.

ERP is an outgrowth of MRP II, and the primary ERP users are manufacturing companies. The first and most successful vendor of ERP software is SAP (SAP AG Corp., headquartered in Germany). More than 12 million people use SAP in over 100,000 SAP installations worldwide (*sap.com/company*, accessed November 2007).

Thus far, ERP represents the ultimate in cross-departmental process systems. ERP integrates sales, order, inventory, manufacturing, and customer service activities. ERP systems provide software, predesigned databases, proce-dures, and job descriptions for organization-wide process integration.

Before continuing, be aware that some companies misapply the term *ERP* to their systems. It is a hot topic, and there is no truth-in-ERP-advertising group to ensure that all of the vendors that claim ERP capability have anything remotely similar to what we describe here. Again, let the buyer beware.

ERP Characteristics

Figure CE10-5 lists the major ERP characteristics. First, as stated, ERP takes a cross-functional, process view of the entire organization. With ERP, the entire organization is considered a collection of interrelated activities.

Second, true ERP is a formal approach that is based on documented, tested business models. ERP applications include a comprehensive set of inherent processes for all organizational activities. SAP defines this set as the **process blueprint** and documents each process with diagrams that use a set of standard-ized symbols. The process diagram in Figure CE10-1 is a SAP process diagram.

Because ERP is based on formally defined procedures, organizations must adapt their processing to the ERP blueprint. If they do not, the system cannot operate effectively, or even correctly. In some cases, it is possible to adapt ERP software to procedures that are different from the blueprint, but such adaptation is expensive and often problematic.

As stated, with isolated systems, each application has it own database. This separation makes it difficult for authorized users to readily obtain all of the per-tinent information about customers, products, and so forth. With ERP systems, organizational data are processed in a centralized database. Such centralization makes it easy for authorized users to obtain needed information from a single source.

Once an organization has implemented an ERP system, it can achieve large benefits. However, as shown in Figure CE10-5, the process of moving from separated, functional applications to an ERP system is difficult, fraught with challenge, and can be slow. In particular, changing organizational procedures

- Provides cross-functional, process view of organization

- Has a formal approach based on formal business models

- Maintains data in centralized database

- Offers large benefits but is difficult, fraught with challenges, and can be slow to implement

- Often VERY expensive

Figure CE10-5
Characteristics of ERP

Figure CE10-6
Potential Benefits of ERP

- Efficient business processes
- Inventory reduction
- Lead-time reduction
- Improved customer service
- Greater, real-time insight into organization
- Higher profitability

has proved to be a great challenge for many organizations, and in some cases was even a pitfall that prevented successful ERP implementation. Finally, the switch to an ERP system is very costly—not only because of the need for new hardware and software, but also due to the costs of developing new procedures, training employees, converting data, and other developmental expenses.

Benefits of ERP

Figure CE10-6 summarizes the major benefits of ERP. First, the processes in the business blueprint have been tried and tested over hundreds of organizations. The processes are effective and often very efficient. Organizations that convert to ERP do not need to reinvent business processes. Rather, they gain the benefit of processes that have already been proved successful.

By taking an organization-wide view, many organizations find they can reduce their inventory, sometimes dramatically. With better planning, it is not necessary to maintain large buffer stocks. Additionally, items remain in inventory for shorter periods of time, sometimes no longer than a few hours or a day.

Another advantage is that ERP helps organizations reduce lead times. Because of the more efficient processes and better information, organizations can respond more quickly to process new orders or changes in existing orders. This means they can deliver goods to customers faster. In some cases, ERP-based companies can receive payments on orders shipped before they pay for the raw materials used in the parts on the order.

As discussed earlier, data inconsistency problems are not an issue because all ERP data are stored in an integrated database. Further, because all data about a customer, order, part, or other entity reside in one place, the data are readily accessible. This means that organizations can provide better information about orders, products, and customer status to their customers. All of this results not only in better, but also less costly, customer service. Integrated databases also make companywide data readily accessible and result in greater, real-time visibility, thus allowing a peek into the status of the organization.

Finally, ERP-based organizations often find that they can produce and sell the same products at lower costs due to smaller inventories, reduced lead times, and cheaper customer support. The bottom-line result is higher profitability. The trick, however, is getting there. Despite the clear benefits of inherent processes and ERP, there may be an unintended consequence. See the *Guide* on pages 447a–447b to consider the risk.

Q4 How Is an ERP System Implemented?

Figure CE10-7 summarizes the major tasks in the implementation of an ERP system. The first task is to model the current business processes. Managers and analysts then compare these processes to the ERP blueprint processes and note

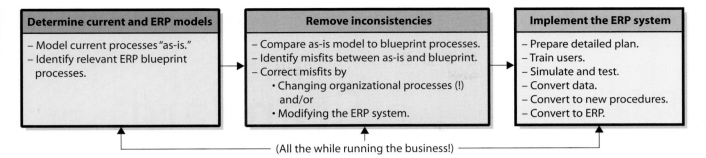

Determine current and ERP models	Remove inconsistencies	Implement the ERP system

– Model current processes "as-is."
– Identify relevant ERP blueprint processes.
	– Compare as-is model to blueprint processes.
	– Identify misfits between as-is and blueprint.
	– Correct misfits by
	  • Changing organizational processes (!) and/or
	  • Modifying the ERP system.
		– Prepare detailed plan.
		– Train users.
		– Simulate and test.
		– Convert data.
		– Convert to new procedures.
		– Convert to ERP.

——————— (All the while running the business!) ———————

Figure CE10-7
ERP Implementation

the differences. The company then must find ways to eliminate the differences, either by changing the existing business process to match the ERP process or by altering the ERP system.

Modeling the current business processes is a difficult and time-consuming task. Trained and skilled analysts are needed to observe, investigate, and document current practices. Often, existing procedures are not documented and are known only by those who perform them. Many meetings, interviews, and observations can be necessary to tease out and document these procedures. This activity is crucial because the organization must understand what procedural changes will be necessary before converting to the new system.

To appreciate the magnitude of these tasks, consider that the SAP blueprint contains over a thousand process models. Organizations that are adopting ERP must review those models and determine which ones are appropriate to them. Then, they compare the ERP models to the models developed based on their current practices. Inevitably, some current-practice models are incomplete, vague, or inaccurate, so the team must repeat the existing process models. In some cases, it is impossible to reconcile any existing system against the blueprint model. If so, the team must adapt, cope, and define new procedures, often to the confusion of current employees.

Once the differences between as-is processes and the blueprint have been reconciled, the next step is to implement the system. Before implementation starts, however, users must be trained on the new processes, procedures, and use of the ERP system features and function. Additionally, the company needs to conduct a simulation test of the new system to identify problems. Then, the organization must convert its data, procedures, and personnel to the new ERP system. All of this happens while the business continues to run on the old system.

As explained in Chapter 10, plunging the organization into the new system is an invitation to disaster. Instead, a thorough and well-planned test of the new system is necessary, followed by a careful rollout to the new system. Realize, too, that while the new ERP system is being installed, normal business activity continues. Somehow the employees of the organization must continue to run the company while the rollout is underway. It is a difficult and challenging time for any organization that undergoes this process.

Implementing an ERP system is not for the faint of heart. Because so much organizational change is required, all ERP projects must have the full support of the CEO and executive staff. Because ERP processes cross departmental boundaries, no single departmental manager has the authority to force an ERP implementation. Instead, full support for the task must come from the top of the organization. Even with such support, there is bound to be second-guessing and griping, as was shown in the *Guide* on pages 167a–167b in Chapter 7.

ERP and the Standard, Standard Blueprint

Designing business processes is difficult, time consuming, and very expensive. Highly trained experts conduct seemingly countless interviews with users and domain experts to determine business requirements. Then, even more experts join those people, and together this team invests thousands of labor hours to design, develop, and implement effective business processes that meet those requirements. All of this is a very high-risk activity that is prone to failure. And it all must be done before IS development can even begin.

ERP vendors, such as SAP, have invested millions of labor hours into the business blueprints that underlie their ERP solutions. These blueprints consist of hundreds or thousands of different business processes. Examples are processes for hiring employees, processes for acquiring fixed assets, processes for acquiring consumable goods, and processes for custom "one-off" (a unique product with a unique design) manufacturing, to name just a few.

Additionally, ERP vendors have implemented their business processes in hundreds of organizations. In so doing, they have been forced to customize their standard blueprint for use in particular industries. For example, SAP has a distribution-business blueprint that is customized for the auto parts industry, for the

electronics industry, and for the aircraft industry. Hundreds of other customized solutions exist as well.

Even better, the ERP vendors have developed software solutions that fit their business-process blueprints. In theory, no software development is required at all if the organization can adapt to the standard blueprint of the ERP vendor.

As described in this chapter, when an organization implements an ERP solution, it first determines any differences that exist between its business processes and the standard blueprint. Then, the organization must remove that difference, which can be done in one of two ways: It changes business processes to fit the standard blueprint. Or, the ERP vendor or a consultant modifies the standard blueprint (and software solution that matches that blueprint) to fit the unique requirements.

In practice, such variations from the standard blueprint are rare. They are difficult and expensive to implement, and they require the using organization to maintain the variations from the standard as new versions of the ERP software are developed. Consequently, most organizations choose to modify their processes to meet the blueprint, rather than the other way around. Although such process changes also are difficult to implement, once the organization has converted to the standard blueprint, they no longer need to support a "variation."

So from a standpoint of cost, effort, risk, and avoidance of future problems, there is a huge incentive for organizations to adapt to the standard ERP blueprint.

Initially, SAP was the only true ERP vendor, but other companies have developed and acquired ERP

solutions as well. Because of competitive pressure across the software industry, all of these products are beginning to have the same sets of features and functions. ERP solutions are becoming a commodity.

All of this is fine as far as it goes, but it introduces a nagging question: If, over time, every organization tends to implement the standard ERP blueprint, and if, over time, every software company develops essentially the same ERP features and functions, then won't every business come to look just like every other business? How will organizations gain a competitive advantage if they all use the same business processes?

If every auto parts distributor uses the same business processes, based on the same software, are they not all clones of one another? How will a company distinguish itself? How will innovation occur? Even if one parts distributor does successfully innovate a business process that gives it a competitive advantage, will the ERP vendors be conduits to transfer that innovation to competitors? Does the use of "commoditized" standard blueprints mean that no company can sustain a competitive advantage?

DISCUSSION QUESTIONS

1. In your own words, explain why an organization might choose to change its processes to fit the standard blueprint. What advantages does it accrue by doing so?

2. Explain how competitive pressure among software vendors will cause the ERP solutions to become commodities. What does this mean to the ERP software industry?

3. If two businesses use exactly the same processes and exactly the same software, can they be different in any way at all? Explain why or why not.

4. Explain the statement that an ERP software vendor can be a conduit to transfer innovation. What are the consequences to the innovating company? To the software company? To the industry? To the economy?

5. In theory, such standardization might be possible, but worldwide there are so many different business models, cultures, people, values, and competitive pressures, can any two businesses ever be exactly alike?

Q5 What Are the Characteristics of Enterprise Application Integration (EAI) Systems?

ERP systems are not for every organization. For example, some nonmanufacturing companies find the manufacturing orientation of ERP inappropriate. Even for manufacturing companies, some find the process of converting from their current system to an ERP system too daunting. Others are quite satisfied with their MRP systems and do not wish to change them.

Companies for which ERP is inappropriate still have the problems of isolated systems, however, and some choose to use **enterprise application integration (EAI)** to solve those problems. EAI integrates existing systems by providing layers of software that connect applications together. EAI does the following:

- It connects system "islands" via a new layer of software/system.
- It enables existing applications to communicate and share data.
- It provides integrated information.
- It leverages existing systems—leaving legacy/functional applications as is, but providing an integration layer over the top.
- It enables a gradual move to ERP.

The layers of EAI software shown in Figure CE10-8 enable existing applications to communicate with each other and to share data. For example, EAI software can be configured to automatically make the data conversion required in Figure 7-6 (page 167). When the CRM applications send data to the MRP system, for example, the CRM system sends its data to an EAI software program. That EAI program makes the conversion and then sends the converted data to the ERP system. The reverse action is taken to send data back from the ERP to the CRM.

Although there is no centralized EAI database, the EAI software keeps files of metadata that describe where data are located. Users can access the EAI system to find the data they need. In some cases, the EAI system provides services that provide a "virtual integrated database" for the user to process.

The major benefit of EAI is that it enables organizations to use existing applications while eliminating many of the serious problems of isolated systems. Converting to an EAI system is not nearly as disruptive as converting to ERP, and it provides many of the benefits of ERP. Some organizations develop EAI applications as a steppingstone to complete ERP systems.

Figure CE10-8
Enterprise Application Integration
(EAI) Architecture

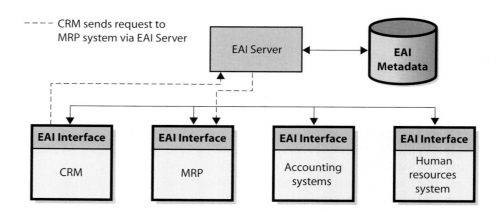

Active ? Review

Use this Active Review to verify that you understand the material in the chapter extension. You can read the entire extension and then perform the tasks in this review, or you can read the material for just one question and perform the tasks in this review for that question before moving on to the next one.

Q1 What is the importance of inherent processes?

Describe the role of networks and Porter's value chain model in the development of cross-functional applications. Summarize the challenges of business process design. Explain how licensed software and inherent processes eliminated those challenges but introduced another challenge. Explain the statement that the primary benefit of licensing cross-departmental software is not the software.

Q2 What are the characteristics of customer relationship management (CRM) systems?

Define *customer relationship management systems*. Using Figure CE10-2 as a guide, describe the customer life cycle. Explain how CRM systems support each phase of this cycle. Summarize the major components of a CRM system. Explain the importance of a single database of customer data.

Q3 What are the characteristics of enterprise resource planning (ERP) systems?

Define *enterprise resource planning systems*. Using the value chain model, differentiate between CRM and ERP systems. Summarize the characteristics of ERP systems. Define *process blueprint*. Explain the benefit of a single ERP database. Summarize the difficulties of moving from functional systems to ERP systems. List the benefits of ERP.

Q4 How is an ERP system implemented?

List the three major stages of an ERP implementation. Describe the tasks in each. Explain why ERP conversions are such a large project. Explain the difficulties of converting to an ERP system while continuing normal business operations. Describe why the conversion to an ERP system requires the full support of the CEO and executive staff

Q5 What are the characteristics of enterprise application integration (EAI) systems?

Describe why ERP is not appropriate for some organizations. Define *EAI*. Describe a situation in which EAI may be a better solution than ERP. List the major functions of an EAI system. Describe how metadata enables EAI software to make data conversions. Explain the term *virtual integrated database*. Describe the major benefit of EAI.

Key Terms and Concepts

Business process design 439
Customer life cycle 442
Customer relationship management
  (CRM) system 442

Enterprise application integration
  (EAI) 448
Enterprise resource planning (ERP)
  system 444

Inherent processes 440
Process blueprint 445
SAP R/3 440

Using Your Knowledge

1. Suppose that your university decides to streamline the process by which students enroll in classes. The university commissions a "blue-ribbon" panel to determine the optimal means to enroll students in classes. Describe what you think is the ideal composition of members of this panel. Describe the work that this panel would need to accomplish. How would the panel deal

with opposition to its plans? What, in general, would need to be done in order to make the transition from the existing system to a new system?

2. Suppose that your university decides to streamline the process by which students enroll in classes. After deliberation among deans and senior administrators, the university decides to license a software package that performs course enrollments. That software, of course, has inherent processes. Compare and contrast this situation to that in question 1. In what ways is the situation in question 1 both more ideal and more risky? In what ways does licensing software reduce the risk, confusion, and speed of conversion? For the situation in question 1, what happens when an important user says, "We need to have feature *X*?" When licensing software, what happens when an important user says, "We need to have feature *X*" and the software does not have that feature? If you were an IT developer, which situation would you prefer?

 3. Search the Web for the term *customer relationship management software*. Find the most elaborate CRM software that you can. Find the simplest CRM software that you can. Describe the differences in these two packages. Are you surprised that two such different software products could both be called CRM? What does this tell you when researching software products?

4. Oracle Corporation licenses CRM software, and it also licenses the DBMS product Oracle. Not all of Oracle's CRM versions require the Oracle DBMS, but clearly Oracle Corporation has an incentive to make the Oracle DBMS versions the best. Similarly, Microsoft Corporation licenses CRM software, and it also licenses the DBMS product SQL Server. As with Oracle Corporation, not all of its CRM versions require SQL Server, but clearly Microsoft has an incentive to make the SQL Server versions the best. Converting from one DBMS to another requires considerable work, measured in labor years or even labor decades. What would you recommend if the Oracle CRM product best meets your organization's needs, but your organization uses SQL Server? What questions do you need to ask? How will you utilize the answers to make your recommendation?

 5. Search the Web for the terms *ERP cases* and *ERP disasters*. Are there common threads in the cases and disasters you find? List the major challenges of converting to ERP systems. Under what conditions would you not recommend an ERP system, even though your organization could benefit from ERP?

6. Explain the differences between ERP and EAI. Under what conditions would an organization choose EAI?

7. Read the section "Q7. What Functional Systems Does DSI Use?" starting on page 430 (in Chapter Extension 9). Do you think DSI would benefit from a CRM system? Explain why or why not. Do you think DSI could benefit from an ERP system? What would be the advantages to DSI of using ERP? Do you think the advantages of ERP would be worth the agony of the conversion to DSI? Describe additional data you might need to better answer that question.

you be the Guide

Using the Guide: Thinking About Change *(page 441a)*

GOALS

* Explain, demonstrate, or illustrate that humans resist change.

* Suggest ways that managers can reduce employee resistance to change.

BACKGROUND AND PRESENTATION STRATEGIES

Humans resist change. Whether from fear, anxiety, extra work, or loss of self-efficacy, humans do not like to change. One way to bring home the resistance to change is to play a hoax on the students.

HOAX PRESENTATION (*Alternatively, use the nonhoax presentation that follows.*)

The hoax: Start your presentation by reading the following *fake memo from the Dean*:

> *Starting this term, all students will be required to perform 100 hours of community service as part of their graduation requirement. The College of Business will provide a list of organizations that the students can serve. Students, especially seniors, are encouraged to visit their adviser as soon as possible to plan their community service. Advisers have been given special training to help students adapt to this change. See your adviser as soon as possible.*

(Possibly have a colleague read the memo as a special announcement.)

Now, to continue the hoax, ask questions like:

➤ **Can I answer any questions about this important new program?**

➤ **Are there any seniors in the class? You will need to get started right away!**

➤ **I can see that this program will place a burden on you. But it seems like an excellent idea. How many of you have done public service before?**

➤ **Has anyone heard whether past public service will count?**

Attempt to develop an emotional outrage, a belief that this just cannot be, and so forth. At some point, *reveal the hoax.*

➤ **How did you feel about this change?**

➤ **What did you think about this change?**

➤ **What if this were your job, and the issue was that your department had been broken up and you now worked for someone new?**

NONHOAX PRESENTATION (*Skip if you used the hoax.*) Suppose a business issues the following statement:

> *Because of efficiencies brought about by our new ERP system, your department has been abolished. You have been assigned to a new department. Your new boss is Ms. Jones, and you should see her immediately to learn your new job responsibilities.*

Some questions to ask the students:

➤ **As an employee, what is your first response?**

➤ **How likely are you, as an employee, to support the new program?**

➤ **How does the concept of self-efficacy apply to this situation?**

➤ **Consider two alternative statements from your boss:**

* **"I don't know why they did this. I think it's stupid. They're just trying to reduce costs and the whole program will cause a mess for years."**

* **"These new changes are important in order to compete internationally. If we don't make changes like this, unemployment will be rampant. I know this is awkward, but in the long run, this change will benefit the health of our organization and increase opportunities for the future."**

➤ **Explain the impact of your boss's statement on your attitude.**

 SUGGESTED RESPONSES FOR DISCUSSION QUESTIONS

Note: If you used the hoax, base these questions on the hoax situation. If not, use the new information system example in the questions.

1. Likely first feelings are fear, anger, resentment, frustration. All negative responses. Good questions to ask:

   ➤ **What do you fear?**

   ➤ **What are you angry about?**

   ➤ **Suppose the new system will actually make your life easier. Will you still feel negatively? Why?**

2. According to the text, the communication should include not just why the change is necessary, but also how the students will be able to succeed with it—how it will make life easier *for the student* and how the student will have self-efficacy (see question 3).

Suppose the university says (adapt if you used the hoax):

➤ **This system will reduce administrative costs.**

➤ **This system will reduce administrative costs and enable a reduction in tuition.**

➤ **This system will make registration easier for you.**

➤ **What if the university says nothing at all?**

Which of these statements is most reassuring and helpful? Why?

3. Examples of self-efficacy are:

- "Will I be able to get the classes I want?"
- "How long will it take me?"
- "How long will it take me to learn the system?"

Another form of self-efficacy is the loss of the utility of knowledge.

- "I know how to manipulate the existing system to get what I want. Now, all that knowledge will be wasted."

The university could increase self-efficacy with training and examples of how easy the system will be to use. It could also provide testimonials from students who have used the new system.

4. In general, friends' opinions matter very much. However, people also adjust those opinions based on what they think of the friend: "Oh, she's an engineer; of course it will be easy for her" or "If he can do it, then so can I." Peer opinions are very important, but they are also hard to manage, and their consequences are difficult to predict. As stated in question 3, testimonials can be effective means for instituting change.

5. A resistance-reducing program could be a pilot program of students using the system. Then, have those students become coaches to others. Or, the university's Web site could post testimonials of the ease of use of the new system, and so on. All such efforts should be aimed at increasing student self-efficacy.

6. If the professor is viewed as a part of the administration, that is, as a paid voice for the administration, nothing positive the professor says will be trusted. Certainly, though, no matter how the professor is viewed, any negative statements the professor makes will have a seriously deleterious impact on student attitudes.

The parallel between students/professors and employees/managers may not be strong. Employees and managers are "all in it together" in a way that students and professors are not. The department manager works with the employees 40+ hours per week. The employees' frustrations will quickly become the manager's frustrations. Students and professors are more isolated from one another.

7. The students are likely to have some interesting comments here. If they feel unthreatened, they may reveal how they view professors, which could lead to some interesting discussion quite apart from the topic of this guide.

In my opinion, it depends on what they think of their professor/boss and what they think of their fellow students/coworkers. If the professor/boss seems trustworthy, that person's opinion probably means more than the student's/coworker's.

Opinions vary, though. It will be interesting to see what your students say.

WRAP UP

List the five components of an information system: hardware, software, data, procedures, and people. Remind the students that these components are *listed in increasing order of difficulty of change*. Changing procedures and altering the organization, altering job descriptions, and creating new reporting structures can be incredibly difficult, as we have seen.

Self-efficacy is the key. Ask the students to summarize actions that management can take to offset the consequences of procedural and people (organizational and reporting to) changes.

you be the Guide

Using the Guide: ERP and the Standard, Standard Blueprint
(page 447a)

GOALS

* Reinforce the importance of inherent processes in ERP and other licensed software and the expense and challenges of variances from those processes.

* Introduce possible longer-range consequences of adapting to vendors' inherent processes.

* Demonstrate an example of long-range thinking.

BACKGROUND AND PRESENTATION STRATEGIES

Warning: Before using this guide, ensure the students understand what an ERP system is and how much it integrates the organization's activities. It may be a good idea to start with a review of ERP systems.

Are organizations that enforce the standard ERP blueprint for their industry condemning themselves to industry-wide uniformity?

I don't know if this problem is real or not. But, in theory, as ERP packages become commodities (and we do know that competitive software products always becomes a commodity), then every business will be run just like every other business. If that is the case, then how will one business gain a competitive advantage? Possibly, the company that executes the ERP processes most efficiently becomes the leader, but that is a difference in scale more than a difference in kind.

Even more worrisome, once ERP systems are solidly integrated into the organization, *will they stifle creativity?* Employees already complain that they are forced to do silly things because the "software requires them to." Will the software mean that it is a waste of time to develop improved ways of doing business, because the improved way is incompatible with the "always-enforced" ERP way?

I posed this question to a PeopleSoft (now Oracle) salesperson who said the answer lay with business intelligence applications of the data generated by the ERP system. "Organizations can gain a competitive advantage," he said, "*by reporting and mining the data* that we generate in their databases."

Is that answer credible? If the information created by the business intelligence system can be applied in the context of the existing ERP or other system, then his answer may have merit. But what if the information created indicates the need for a change to a system that cannot be changed because of the structure of an existing ERP system?

Side effect: When an organization requests a feature change in the ERP system, that action may mean that every other customer of that vendor, and ultimately the entire industry, will have that change. *Thus, the competitive advantage will be unsustainable.*

What to do? No organization today that can benefit from ERP would choose not to implement it. But, having done so, has the organization entered a *conformity trap*?

SUGGESTED RESPONSES FOR DISCUSSION QUESTIONS

1. The vendors would say that customers should adapt because the standard blueprint, the inherent processes, are the "best-of-class solutions." They also know that variances are expensive and difficult to maintain. Life for the vendor and for the IT department is a lot easier if the company converts to the standard process.

   ➤ **What does the organization lose by converting to the standard blueprint?**

   ➤ **What are the costs of that conversion? (Also consider nonmonetary costs.)**

2. Ask the marketing students what causes products to become commodities. Software is no different. (*This point, by the way, opens the door to talk about careers in software sales, marketing, and support. These are great, high-paying jobs, and this class is the first step toward one.*)

   The process: No vendor can allow another vendor to have a competitive advantage, so they all copy the features and functions from one another. Ultimately, like cans of tomatoes on the grocery shelf, they all look the same.

3. This is the key question, and I don't know a definite answer. The answer may come down to the issue of whether they can be better in the execution of the inherent processes in the software.

   ➤ **If a company executes the standard blueprint better than its competitors, will that give it a competitive advantage?**

   ➤ **Is it possible for a company to engage in a differentiation strategy if all companies use the same inherent processes?**

➤ **Consider Lowe's and Home Depot. They have the same business processes. What will make one better than the other? If they're both using the same ERP package, the differentiation won't be in IS innovation.**

There is no obvious nor easy answer.

4. Such transfer of innovation happens when a company has an exception to the ERP system for which it asks the ERP vendor to program supporting software. If the exception represents an improved process, the ERP vendor can put it into its new software versions. Voila! The ERP vendor has been a conduit of innovation from one company to an industry.

   Ultimately, this phenomenon is beneficial to the industry and the economy. That may be small consolation to the company that cannot maintain its competitive advantage. Then again, innovation should be a continuous process. As Rudyard Kipling wrote,

   > "They copied all they could follow, but they couldn't copy my mind,
   >
   > And I left 'em sweating and stealing a year and a half behind."

   (*The Mary Gloster*, 1894)

5. It is probably not possible for two companies ever to be completely alike, but they may be close enough to make sustainable competitive advantages difficult, if not impossible. Example: Lowe's versus Home Depot.

One way to teach this is to play devil's advocate (or, depending on your views, an honest critic). Say something like:

➤ **This essay is much ado about nothing. It has no real issue; the points it makes are hair-splitting, unrealistic, theoretical, and vapid. We're wasting our time.**

See how the students respond. If they take an opposing position, continue in this vein. If they don't, ask them if they think they've wasted their time by considering this essay. To me, thinking about something that might be important and concluding that it is not important is hardly a waste of time.

WRAP UP

➤ **From time to time, it's worth thinking about the long-range consequences of technology trends. In this case, we find that adapting to industry-wide inherent processes may create competitive advantages but—at least for interdepartmental processes—those advantages may not be sustainable.**

➤ **By the way, most medium to large-scale companies have a person called the CTO, or chief technology officer. You'll learn more about that person in Chapter 11. One of the key roles of that person is to think about the longer-range consequences of technology use. The job of CTO is fascinating, and it is one that some of you might want to consider.**

Chapter Extension 11

Chapter 8 provides the background for this Extension.

E-Commerce

Q1 What Is E-Commerce?

E-commerce is the buying and selling of goods and services over public and private computer networks. Notice that this definition restricts e-commerce to buying and selling transactions. Checking the weather at *yahoo.com* is not e-commerce, but buying a weather service subscription that is paid for and delivered over the Internet is.

Figure CE11-1 lists the different categories of e-commerce companies. The U.S. Census Bureau, which publishes statistics on e-commerce activity, defines **merchant companies** as those that take title to the goods they sell. They buy goods and resell them. It defines **nonmerchant companies** as those that arrange for the purchase and sale of goods without ever owning or taking title to those goods. Regarding services, merchant companies sell services that they provide; nonmerchant companies sell services provided by others. We will consider merchants and nonmerchants separately in the following sections.

Study Questions

Q1 What is e-commerce?

Q2 How does e-commerce improve market efficiency?

Q3 What economic factors disfavor e-commerce?

Q4 What Web technology is used for e-commerce?

Q5 What is three-tier architecture?

E-Commerce Merchant Companies

There are three main types of merchant companies: those that sell directly to consumers, those that sell to companies, and those that sell to government. Each uses slightly different information systems in the course of doing business. **Business-to-consumer (B2C)** e-commerce concerns sales between a supplier and a retail customer (the consumer). A typical information system for B2C provides a Web-based application or **Web storefront** by which customers enter and manage their orders. Amazon.com, REI.com, and LLBean.com are examples of companies that use B2C information systems.[1]

Merchant companies
– Business-to-consumer (B2C)
– Business-to-business (B2B)
– Business-to-government (B2G)

Nonmerchant companies
– Auctions
– Clearinghouses
– Exchanges

Figure CE11-1
E-Commerce Categories

---

[1]Strictly speaking, B2C is not commerce between two organizations. However, because it is commerce between two independently owned entities (the retailer and the consumer), we include it in this chapter.

Figure CE11-2
Example of Use of B2B, B2G,
and B2C

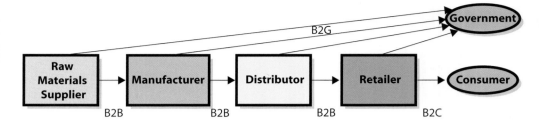

Figure CE11-2
Example of Use of B2B, B2G,
and B2C

The term **business-to-business (B2B)** e-commerce refers to sales between companies. As Figure CE11-2 shows, raw materials suppliers use B2B systems to sell to manufacturers, manufacturers use B2B systems to sell to distributors, and distributors uses B2B systems to sell to retailers.

Business-to-government (B2G) refers to sales between companies and governmental organizations. As Figure CE11-2 shows, a manufacturer that uses an e-commerce site to sell computer hardware to the U.S. Department of State is engaging in B2G commerce. Suppliers, distributors, and retailers can sell to the government as well.

B2C applications first captured the attention of mail-order and related businesses. However, companies in all sectors of the economy soon realized the enormous potential of B2B and B2G. The number of companies engaged in B2B and B2G commerce now far exceeds those engaging in B2C commerce.

Furthermore, today's B2B and B2G applications implement just a small portion of their potential capability. Their full utilization is some years away. Although most experts agree that these applications involve some sort of integration of CRM and supplier relationship management (SRM) systems, the nature of that integration is not well understood and is still being developed. Consequently, you can expect further progress and development in B2B and B2G applications during your career. Later in this chapter extension, we will discuss some problems of B2B and the technology used to solve those problems.

Nonmerchant E-Commerce

The most common nonmerchant e-commerce companies are auctions and clearinghouses. **E-commerce auctions** match buyers and sellers by using an e-commerce version of a standard auction. This e-commerce application enables the auction company to offer goods for sale and to support a competitive-bidding process. The best-known auction company is eBay, but many other auction companies exist; many serve particular industries. *MIS in Use CE11* describes a B2B e-commerce site for the steel industry.

Clearinghouses provide goods and services at a stated price and they arrange for the delivery of the goods, but they never take title. One division of Amazon.com, for example, operates as a nonmerchant clearinghouse and sells books owned by others. As a clearinghouse, Amazon.com matches the seller and the buyer and then takes payment from the buyer and transfers the payment to the seller, minus a commission. Figure CE11-3 shows a typical Amazon.com listing for selling books that it does not own.

Other examples of clearinghouse businesses are **electronic exchanges** that match buyers and sellers; the business process is similar to that of a stock exchange. Sellers offer goods at a given price through the electronic exchange, and buyers make offers to purchase over the same exchange. Price matches result in transactions from which the exchange takes a commission. Priceline.com is an example of an exchange used by consumers.

Steel Spider

Steel Spider (*www.steelspider.com*) is a nonmerchant Web site that helps steel suppliers promote their companies, generate sales leads, and sell steel. It helps buyers locate and purchase steel. Sellers pay a fee to advertise their steel products and sponsor invitational steel auctions on Steel Spider. Buyers participate without charge.

Suppliers make dozens of different types and formats of steel. Buyers search Steel Spider for the type and format of steel they require. If the steel they need is not currently available, buyers can register their ongoing needs with the site. A software agent, named Boris, on the Steel Spider site watches new supplier listings and notifies registered buyers when steel of the desired type and format becomes available. Another feature allows a buyer to describe an immediate need and Steel Spider transmits a notification of that need to its existing suppliers who can contact the buyer directly if they desire.

Steel Spider also provides a platform for invitational auctions. Suppliers schedule an auction with the site and specify date, time, and length of the sale. They also provide a description of the steel to be sold, the minimum acceptable bid, and the minimum bid increment. Additionally, the supplier provides a list of the email addresses of buyers who are allowed to bid. Steel Spider then conducts the auction for these terms. The auction process is similar to that on a public auction site like eBay. The major differences are that the seller pays a fixed fee per auction and that bidders must be preapproved by the seller.

Source: steelspider.com (accessed May 2005). Used with permission of Mountain Hawk Corporation.

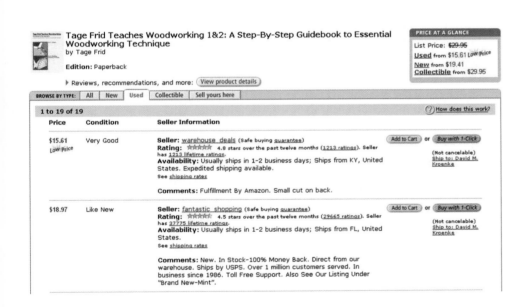

Figure CE11-3
Amazon Clearinghouse Sales

Source: © 2005 Amazon.com, Inc. All Rights Reserved.

Q2 How Does E-Commerce Improve Market Efficiency?

The debate continues among business observers as to whether e-commerce is something new or if it is just a technology extension to existing business practice. During the dot-com heyday in 1999–2000, some claimed that e-commerce

was ushering in a new era and a "new economy." Although experts differ as to whether a "new economy" was created, all agree that e-commerce does lead to greater market efficiency.

For one, e-commerce leads to **disintermediation**, which is the elimination of middle layers in the supply chain. You can buy a flat-screen LCD HDTV from a typical electronics store or you can use e-commerce to buy it from the manufacturer. If you take the latter route, you eliminate the distributor, the retailer, and possibly more. The product is shipped directly from the manufacturer's finished goods inventory to you. You eliminate the distributor's and retailer's inventory carrying costs, and you eliminate shipping overhead and handling activity. Because the distributor and associated inventories have become unnecessary waste, disintermediation increases market efficiency.

E-commerce also improves the flow of price information. As a consumer, you can go to any number of Web sites that offer product price comparisons. You can search for the HDTV you want and sort the results by price and vendor reputation. You can find vendors that avoid your state sales tax or that omit or reduce shipping charges. The improved distribution of information about price and terms enables you to pay the lowest possible cost and serves ultimately to remove inefficient vendors. The market as a whole becomes more efficient.

From the seller's side, e-commerce produces information about **price elasticity** that has not been available before. Price elasticity measures the amount that demand rises or falls with changes in price. Using an auction, a company can learn not just what the top price for an item is, but also learn the second, third, and other prices from the losing bids. In this way, the company can determine the shape of the price elasticity curve.

Similarly, e-commerce companies can learn price elasticity directly from experiments on customers. For example, in one experiment, Amazon.com created three groups of similar books. It raised the price of one group 10 percent, lowered the price of the second group 10 percent, and left the price of the third group unchanged. Customers provided feedback to these changes by deciding whether to buy books at the offered prices. Amazon.com measured the total revenue (quantity times price) of each group and took the action (raise, lower, or maintain prices) on all books that maximized revenue. Amazon.com repeated the process until it reached the point at which the indicated action was to maintain current prices.

Managing prices by direct interaction with the customer yields better information than managing prices by watching competitors' pricing. By experimenting with customers, companies learn how customers have internalized competitors' pricing, advertising, and messaging. It might be that customers do not know about a competitor's lower prices, in which case there is no need for a price reduction. Or, it may be that the competitor is using a price that, if lowered, would increase demand sufficiently to increase total revenue. Figure CE11-4 summarizes e-commerce market consequences.

Figure CE11-4
E-Commerce Market
Consequences

Greater market efficiency	Knowledge of price elasticity
– Disintermediation – Increased information on price and terms	– Losing-bidder auction prices – Price experimentation – More accurate information obtained directly from customer

Q3 What Economic Factors Disfavor E-Commerce?

Although there are tremendous advantages and opportunities for many organizations to engage in e-commerce, the economics of some industries may disfavor e-commerce activity. Companies need to consider the following economic factors:

- Channel conflict
- Price conflict
- Logistics expense
- Customer service expense

Figure CE11-2 (page 452) shows a manufacturer selling directly to a government agency. Before engaging in such e-commerce, the manufacturer must consider each of the economic factors just listed. First, what *channel conflict* will develop? Suppose the manufacturer is a computer maker that is selling directly, B2G, to the State Department. When the manufacturer begins to sell goods B2G that State Department employees previously purchased from a retailer down the street, that retailer will resent the competition and may drop the manufacturer. If the value of the lost sales is greater than the value of the B2G sales, e-commerce is not a good solution, at least not on that basis.

Furthermore, when a business engages in e-commerce it may also cause *price conflict* with its traditional channels. Because of disintermediation, the manufacturer may be able to offer a lower price and still make a profit. However, as soon as the manufacturer offers the lower price, existing channels will object. Even if the manufacturer and the retailer are not competing for the same customers, the retailer still will not want a lower price to be readily known via the Web.

Also, the existing distribution and retailing partners do provide value; they are not just a cost. Without them, the manufacturer will have the increased *logistic expense* of entering and processing orders in small quantities. If the expense of processing a 1-unit order is the same as that for processing a 12-unit order (which it might be), the average logistic expense per item will be much higher for goods sold via e-commerce.

Similarly, *customer service* expenses are likely to increase for manufacturers that use e-commerce to sell directly to consumers. The manufacturer will be required to provide service to less-sophisticated users and on a one-by-one basis. For example, instead of explaining to a single sales professional that the recent shipment of 100 Gizmo 3.0s requires a new bracket, the manufacturer will need to explain that 100 times to less knowledgeable, frustrated customers. Such service requires more training and more expense.

All four economic factors are important for organizations to consider when they contemplate e-commerce sales.

Q4 What Web Technology Is Used for E-Commerce?

As stated, e-commerce is the buying and selling of products and services over public and private networks. Most B2C commerce conducted over the World Wide Web (WWW) uses Web storefronts supported by commerce servers. A

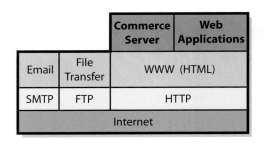

Figure CE11-5
Internet Protocols and Uses

commerce server is a computer that operates Web-based programs that display products, support online ordering, record and process payments, and interface with inventory-management applications. If you are involved in managing your company's e-commerce activity, you will need to understand how commerce servers work. However, first we need to discuss the structure and components of the World Wide Web.

Several prominent Internet protocols are shown in Figure CE11-5. **Simple Mail Transport Protocol (SMTP)** is used for email; **File Transfer Protocol (FTP)** is used to exchange files. Those protocols are important for email and file transfer, but for e-commerce and Web applications, most sites generate HTML and transmit it using **Hypertext Transfer Protocol (HTTP)**. See Chapter Extension 7 for more information about these protocols.

Web Pages and Hypertext Markup Language

HTTP is used to exchange **Web pages** over the Internet. Such pages are documents encoded in a language called **Hypertext Markup Language (HTML)**. This language defines the structure and layout of Web pages. An HTML **tag** is a notation used to define a data element for display or other purposes. A typical tag is:

```
<h2>Price of Item</h2>
```

Notice that tags are enclosed in < > (called *angle brackets*) and that they occur in pairs. The start of this tag is indicated by <h2>, and the end of the tag is indicated by </h2>. The words between the tags are the value of the tag. This HTML tag means to place the words "Price of Item" on a Web page in the style of a level-two heading. The creator of the Web page will define the style (font size, color, and so forth) for such headings and other tags.

Web pages include **hyperlinks**, which are pointers to other Web pages. A hyperlink contains the Uniform Resource Locator (URL—see Chapter Extension 7, page 407), which shows the Web page that will open when the user clicks the hyperlink. The URL can reference a page on the server that generated the page containing the hyperlink or it can reference a page on another server.

Figure CE11-6 shows a simple HTML document. The document has a heading that provides metadata about the page and a body that contains the content. The tag <h1> means to format the indicated text as a level-one heading; <h2> means a level-two heading. The tag <a> defines a hyperlink. This tag has an **attribute**, which is a variable used to provide properties about a tag. Not all tags have attributes, but many do. Each attribute has a standard name. The attribute for a hyperlink is *href*, and its value indicates which Web page is to be displayed when the user clicks the link. Here, the page *www.prenhall.com/kroenke* is to be

```
<html>

<head>
<meta http-equiv="Content-Language" content="en-us">
<meta http-equiv="Content-Type" content="text/html; charset=windows-1252">
<title>Example HTML Document</title>
</head>

<body>
<h1 align="center"><font color="#FF00FF">Experiencing MIS</font></h1>
<h2> </h2>
<h2> </h2>
<h2 align="left"><font color="#0000FF"><i>Example HTML Document</h1></i></font></h2></i>

<p> </p>
<p>Click here for textbook Web site:  <a href="http://www.prenhall.com/kroenke">Web
Site Link</a></p>

</body>

</html>
```

Figure CE11-6
Sample HTML Document

returned when the user clicks the hyperlink. Figure CE11-7 shows this page as rendered by Internet Explorer.

HTML documents are transmitted by **Web servers** and are consumed by (used by) **browsers**. A Web server is a program that processes the HTTP protocol and transmits Web pages on demand. When you type *http://ibm.com*, you are issuing a request via HTTP for the server at the domain name *ibm.com* to send you its default Web page. The two most popular Web server programs are Apache, commonly used on Linux, and IIS (Internet Information Server), a component of Windows XP Professional and other Windows products.

A browser is a program that processes the HTTP protocol; it receives, displays, and processes HTML documents. Browsers also transmit user responses and requests. Common browsers are Internet Explorer, Netscape Navigator, and Mozilla's Firefox. By the way, some HTML documents contain snippets of program code. That code is sent from the Web server to the user's browser and is processed by the browser on the user's computer.

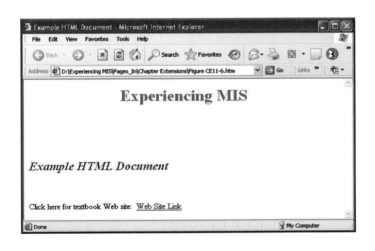

Figure CE11-7
HTML Document in Figure CE11-6, Rendered Using Internet Explorer

Source: Microsoft product screen shot reprinted with permission from Microsoft Corporation.

Q5 What Is Three-Tier Architecture?

Most commerce server applications use what is called **three-tier architecture**. The tiers refer to three different classes of computers. The **user tier** consists of computers that have browsers that request and process Web pages. The **server tier** consists of computers that run Web servers and in the process generate Web pages in response to requests from browsers. Web servers also process application programs. In Figure CE11-8, the server computers are running both a commerce server and other applications.

To ensure acceptable performance, commercial Web sites usually are supported by several or even many Web server computers. A facility that runs multiple Web servers is sometimes called a **Web farm**. Work is distributed among the computers in a Web farm so as to minimize customer delays. The coordination among multiple Web server computers is a fantastic dance, but, alas, we do not have space to tell that story here. Just imagine the coordination that must occur as you add items to an online order when, to improve performance, different Web servers receive and process each addition to your order.

The third tier is the **database tier**. The computer at this tier receives and processes SQL requests to retrieve and store data (see Chapter 5, page 100). Figure CE11-8 shows only one computer at the database tier. Although multicomputer database tiers exist, such tiers are less common than multicomputer server tiers.

An Active Example

To see an application of this discussion, go to your favorite Web site, place something in a shopping cart, and consider Figure CE11-8 as you do so. When you enter an address into your browser, the browser sends a request for the default site page to the server at that address. A Web server on a computer in a Web farm somewhere processes your request and sends back the default page.

As you click that Web page and others to find products you want, a commerce server on a computer in the Web farm accesses one or more databases to fill the pages with data for the products you want. The commerce server creates pages according to your selections and sends the results back to your browser. Again, different computers on the server tier may process your series of requests and must constantly communicate about your activities.

In Figure CE11-9a, the user has navigated through climbing equipment at REI.com to find a particular item. To produce this page, the commerce server

Figure CE11-8
Three-Tier Architecture

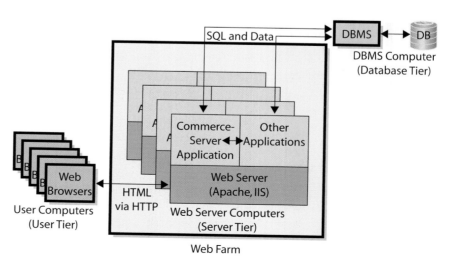

Figure CE11-9a
Sample of Commerce Server
Pages: Product-Offer Page

Source: Used with permission of REI.

Figure CE11-9b
Shopping-Cart Page

Source: Used with permission of REI.

accessed a database to obtain the product picture, price, special terms (a 5 percent discount for buying six or more), product information, and related products.

The user placed six items in her basket, and you can see the response in Figure CE11-9(b). Again, trace the action in Figure CE11-8 and imagine what occurred to produce the second page. Notice that the discount was applied correctly.

When the customer checks out, other commerce server programs will be called to process payments, schedule inventory processing, and arrange for shipping. Most likely the commerce server interfaces with CRM applications for processing the order. Truly, this is an amazing capability!

Active **?** Review

Use this Active Review to verify that you understand the material in the chapter extension. You can read the entire extension and then perform the tasks in this review, or you can read the material for just one question and perform the tasks in this review for that question before moving on to the next one.

Q1 What is e-commerce?

Define *e-commerce*. Define *B2C*, *B2B*, *B2G*. Distinguish among auctions, clearinghouses, and exchanges.

Q2 How does e-commerce improve market efficiency?

Define and explain *disintermediation*, and give an example other than one in this text. Explain how e-commerce improves the flow of price information. Define *price elasticity*, and explain how e-commerce companies can estimate it.

Q3 What economic factors disfavor e-commerce?

Name four factors that disfavor e-commerce. Explain the impact of each factor.

Q4 What Web technology is used for e-commerce?

Define *commerce servers*, *Web pages*, and *HTML*. Explain the purpose of SMTP, FTP, and HTTP. Define *tag*, *hyperlink*, *attribute*, and *Web server*. Explain the purpose of a browser and cite two example products.

Q5 What is three-tier architecture?

Name the three tiers of three-tier architecture and explain the purpose of each. Explain the term *Web farm*. Describe what is happening behind the scenes when the user processes the Web pages shown in Figures CE11-9a and CE11-9b.

Key Terms and Concepts

Attribute 456
Business-to-business (B2B) 452
Business-to-consumer (B2C) 451
Business-to-government (B2G) 452
Browser 457
Clearinghouse 453
Commerce server 456
Database tier 458
Disintermediation 454
E-commerce 451
E-commerce auction 452

Electronic exchanges 453
File Transfer Protocol (FTP) 456
Hypertext Transfer Protocol (HTTP) 456
Hyperlink 456
Hypertext Markup Language (HTML) 456
Merchant company 451
Nonmerchant company 451
Price elasticity 454
Server tier 458

Simple Mail Transfer Protocol (SMTP) 456
Tag 456
Three-tier architecture 458
User tier 458
Web farm 458
Web page 456
Web server 457
Web storefront 451

Using Your Knowledge

1. Suppose you are the manufacturer of high-end consumer kitchen appliances, and you are about to bring out a line of mixers that will make an existing model obsolete. Assume you have 500 mixers of that existing model in finished goods inventory. Describe three different strategies for using e-commerce to unload that inventory.

2. Traditionally, publisher sales representatives have been paid a commission on the sale of textbooks for the colleges and universities on which they call. However, many students today buy their textbooks from online vendors, such as Amazon.com, and it is not possible to allocate the sale of a book via an online vendor to a particular university. Explain the challenges this situation presents to publishers' sales management. What course of action do you recommend?

3. With e-commerce technology, it is possible for textbook publishers to sell textbooks directly to students. Explain how the term *disintermediation* applies to this situation. Discuss how the four factors that disfavor e-commerce apply to direct sales of textbooks. No large publisher is selling direct to students, so apparently the factors that disfavor direct sales to students are overriding. Major publishers like Prentice Hall and McGraw-Hill sell many more nontextbooks than they sell textbooks. Explain the power that this fact gives to the existing sales channels. How do you expect textbooks will be sold in 10 years? In 20 years?

4. Go to *www.Amazon.com*, and explain the activity that occurs at each tier to produce the result you see. Now search for the book *Gone with the Wind*, and select a hardbound version of this title. Explain the activity that occurs at each tier to produce the result that you now see. Explain how the data under the heading "Buyers Who Bought This Item Also Bought" could have been determined. Do you think the books listed there are actually purchased with *Gone with the Wind*? Does anything prevent Amazon.com from listing any book at all in this category? What books might it want to place in this list?

5. On December 14, 2005, Amazon.com processed an average of 41 line-items per second for a 24-hour period. Amazon claims that 99 percent of these items were delivered on time. Clearly, this capability requires a sophisticated and high-performance e-commerce capability. At the time, Amazon.com had over 3,000 servers, worldwide. The scale of this e-commerce system is impressive, but consider additional value chain activities. Comment on what the ability to process so many orders, worldwide, says about in-bound logistics, operations, out-bound logistics, and service activities. What information systems both within Amazon.com and from Amazon.com across to its vendors must exist to support such an enormous volume?

Chapter Extension 12

Chapter 8 provides the background for this Extension.

Supply Chain Management

Q1 What Is a Supply Chain?

A **supply chain** is a network of organizations and facilities that transforms raw materials into products delivered to customers. Figure CE12-1 shows a generic supply chain. Customers order from retailers, who, in turn, order from distributors, who, in turn, order from manufacturers, who, in turn, order from suppliers. In addition to the organizations shown here, the supply chain also includes transportation companies, warehouses, and inventories and some means for transmitting messages and information among the organizations involved.

Because of disintermediation, not every supply chain has all of these organizations. Dell, for example, sells directly to the customer. Both the distributor and retailer organizations are omitted from its supply chain. In other supply chains, manufacturers sell directly to retailers and omit the distribution level.

The term *chain* is misleading. *Chain* implies that each organization is connected to just one company up (toward the supplier) and down (toward the customer) the chain. That is not the case. Instead, at each level, an organization can work with many organizations both up and down the supply chain. Thus, a supply chain is a network.

To understand the operation of a supply chain, consider Figure CE12-2 (page 464). Suppose you decide to take up cross-country skiing. You go to REI (either by visiting one of its stores or its Web site) and purchase skis, bindings, boots, and poles. To fill your order, REI removes those items from its inventory of goods.

Study Questions

Q1 What is a supply chain?

Q2 What factors affect supply chain performance?

Q3 How does supply chain profitability differ from organizational profitability?

Q4 What is the bullwhip effect?

Q5 What are the functions of supplier relationship management?

Q6 How do information systems affect supply chain performance?

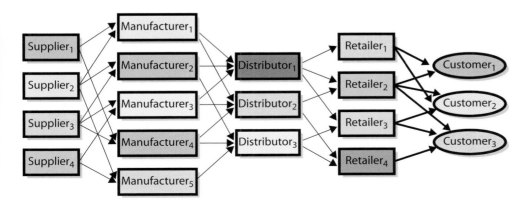

Figure CE12-1
Supply Chain Relationships

Figure CE12-2
Supply Chain Example

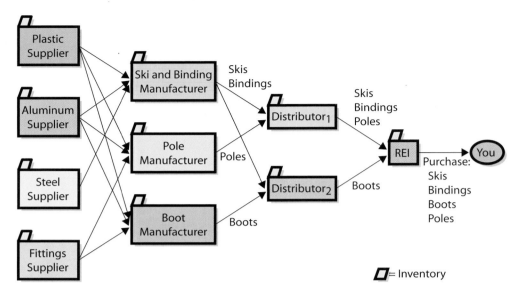

Those goods have been purchased, in turn, from distributors. According to Figure CE12-2, REI purchases the skis, bindings, and poles from one distributor and boots from a second. The distributors, in turn, purchase the required items from the manufacturers, which, in turn, buy raw materials from their suppliers.

The only source of revenue in a supply chain is the customer. In the REI example, you spend your money on the ski equipment. From that point all the way back up the supply chain to the raw material suppliers, there is no further injection of cash. The money you spend on the ski equipment is passed back up the supply chain as payments for goods or raw materials. Again, the customer is the only source of revenue.

Q2 What Factors Affect Supply Chain Performance?

Four major factors, or *drivers*, affect supply chain performance: facilities, inventory, transportation, and information.[1] Figure CE12-3 lists these drivers of supply chain performance. We will summarize the first three factors in this text and focus our attention on the fourth factor, information. (You can learn in detail about the first three factors in operations management classes.)

As Figure CE12-3 indicates, *facilities* concern the location, size, and operations methodology of the places where products are fabricated, assembled, or stored. The optimal design of facilities is a complicated subject. For example, given all of REI's stores and its e-commerce site, where should it locate its warehouses? How large should they be? How should items be stored and retrieved from the inventories? If one considers facilities for the entire supply chain, these decisions become even more complicated.

Inventory includes all of the materials in the supply chain, including raw materials, in-process work, and finished goods. Each company in Figure CE12-2 maintains one or more inventories. When you and others purchase items from REI, its inventory is reduced, and at some point REI reorders from its distribu-

[1]Sunil Chopra and Peter Meindl, *Supply Chain Management* (Upper Saddle River, NJ: Prentice Hall, 2004), pp. 51–53.

- **Facilities**
  – Location, size, operations methodology

- **Inventory**
  – Size, inventory management

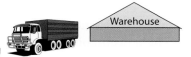

- **Transportation**
  – In-house/outsourced, mode, routing

- **Information**
  – Purpose, availability, means

Figure CE12-3
Drivers of Supply Chain
Performance

tors. The distributors, in turn, maintain their inventories, and at some point they reorder from the manufacturers, and so forth.

Managing an inventory requires balancing between availability and cost. Inventory managers can increase product availability by increasing inventory size. Doing so, however, increases the cost of the inventory and, thus, reduces the company's profitability. However, decreasing the size of the inventory increases the odds that an item will be unavailable for purchase. If that happens, the customer may order from a different source, which will reduce the company's revenue and profit. Inventory management is always a balance between availability and cost.

Inventory management decisions include not only the size of the inventory, but also the frequency with which items are reordered and the size of reorders. For example, assume that REI determines that it needs an inventory of 1,000 boots per month. It can order the full 1,000 at the start of the month or it can order 250 four times per month. Decisions like this and other inventory management decisions have a major impact on supply chain performance.

Transportation, the third driver in Figure CE12-3, concerns the movement of materials in the supply chain. Some organizations have their own transportation facilities; others use outsourced vendors such as Roadway, UPS, and FedEx; still others use a combination. The transportation mode (such as surface versus air) influences both speed and cost. Routing decisions affect how goods are moved from stage to stage throughout the supply chain.

The fourth driver, *information*, is the factor that most concerns us. Information influences supply chain performance by affecting the ways that organizations in the supply chain request, respond, and inform one another. Figure CE12-3 lists three factors of information: purpose, availability, and means. The *purpose* of the information can be transactional, such as orders and order returns, or it can be informational, such as the sharing of inventory and customer order data. *Availability* refers to the ways in which organizations share their information; that is, which organizations have access to which information and when. Finally, *means* refers to the methods by which the information is transmitted. EDI and XML are two means discussed later in this chapter extension.

We will expand on the role of information in the supply chain throughout this chapter extension. For now, however, we consider two of the ways that information can affect supply chain performance: supply chain profitability and the bullwhip effect.

Q3 How Does Supply Chain Profitability Differ from Organizational Profitability?

Each of the organizations in Figures CE12-1 and CE12-2 is an independent company, with its own goals and objectives. Each has a competitive strategy that may differ from the competitive strategies of the other organizations in the supply chain. Left alone, each organization will maximize its own profit, regardless of the consequences of its actions on the profitability of the others.

Supply chain profitability is the difference between the sum of the revenue generated by the supply chain and the sum of the costs that all organizations in the supply chain incur to obtain that revenue. In general, the maximum profit to the supply chain *will not* occur if each organization in the supply chain maximizes its own profits in isolation. Usually, the profitability of the supply chain increases if one or more of the organizations operates at less than its own maximum profitability.

To see why this is so, consider your purchase of the ski equipment from REI. Assume that you purchase either the complete package of skis, bindings, boots, and poles or you purchase nothing. If you cannot obtain boots, for example, the utility of skis, bindings, and poles is nil. In this situation, an outage of boots causes a loss of revenue not just for the boots, but also for the entire ski package.

According to Figure CE12-2, REI buys boots from distributor 2 and the rest of the package from distributor 1. If boots are unavailable, distributor 2 loses the revenue of selling boots, but does not suffer any of the revenue loss from the nonsale of skis, bindings, and poles. Thus, distributor 2 will carry an inventory of boots that is optimized considering only the loss of boot revenue—not considering the loss of revenue for the entire package. In this case, the profitability to the supply chain will increase if distributor 2 carries an inventory of boots that is larger than optimal for it.

In theory, the way to solve this problem is to use some form of transfer payment to induce distributor 2 to carry a larger boot inventory. For example, REI could pay distributor 2 a premium for the sale of boots in packages and recover a portion of this premium from distributor 1, who would recover a portion of it from the manufacturers, and so forth, up the supply chain. In truth, such a solution is difficult to implement, as illustrated in the *Guide* on pages 467a–467b. For higher-priced items or for items with very high volume, there can be an economic benefit for creating an information system to identify such a situation. If the dynamic is long-lasting, it will be worthwhile to negotiate the transfer-payment agreements. All of this requires a comprehensive supply-chain-wide information system, as you will see.

Q4 What Is the Bullwhip Effect?

The **bullwhip effect** is a phenomenon in which the variability in the size and timing of orders increases at each stage up the supply chain, from customer to supplier (in Figure CE12-2, from *You* all the way back to the suppliers). Figure CE12-4 summarizes the situation. In a famous study,[2] the bullwhip effect was observed in Procter & Gamble's supply chain for diapers.

[2]Hau L. Lee, V. Padmanabhan, and S. Whang, "The Bullwhip Effect in Supply Chains," *Sloan Management Review*, Spring 1997, pp. 93–102.

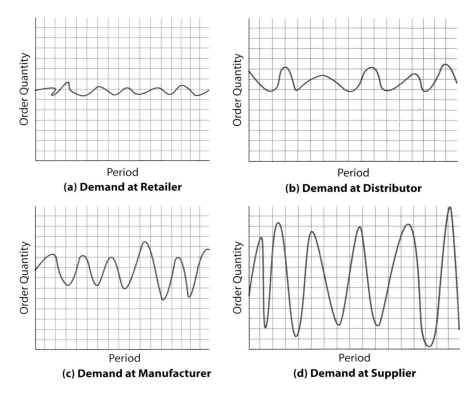

Figure CE12-4
The Bullwhip Effect

(a) Demand at Retailer

(b) Demand at Distributor

(c) Demand at Manufacturer

(d) Demand at Supplier

As you can imagine, except for random variation, diaper demand is constant. Diaper use is not seasonal; the requirement for diapers doesn't change with fashion or anything else. The number of babies determines diaper demand, and that number is constant or possibly slowly changing.

Retailers do not order from the distributor with the sale of every diaper package. The retailer waits until the diaper inventory falls below a certain level, called the *reorder quantity*. Then the retailer orders a supply of diapers, perhaps ordering a few more than it expects to sell to ensure that it does not have an outage.

The distributor receives the retailer's orders and follows the same process. It waits until its supply falls below the reorder quantity, and then it reorders from the manufacturer, with perhaps an increased amount to prevent outages. The manufacturer, in turn, uses a similar process with the raw-materials suppliers.

Because of the nature of this process, small changes in demand at the retailer are amplified at each stage of the supply chain. As shown in Figure CE12-4, those small changes become quite large variations on the supplier end.

The bullwhip effect is a natural dynamic that occurs because of the multistage nature of the supply chain. It is not related to erratic consumer demand, as the study of diapers indicated. You may have seen a similar effect while driving on the freeway. One car slows down, the car just behind it slows down a bit more abruptly, which causes the third card in line to slow down even more abruptly, and so forth, until the thirtieth car or so is slamming on its brakes.

The large fluctuations of the bullwhip effect force distributors, manufacturers, and suppliers to carry larger inventories than should be necessary to meet the real consumer demand. Thus, the bullwhip effect reduces the overall profitability of the supply chain.

One way to eliminate the bullwhip effect is to give all participants in the supply chain access to consumer-demand information from the retailer. Each organization can plan its inventory or manufacturing based on the true demand (the demand from the only party that introduces money into the system) and not

The Lawyer's Full-Employment Act

"I don't think this supply chain profitability thing is likely to work the way it's described here. It sounds like some head-in-the-clouds idea dreamed up by economists.

"First of all, how many products does REI sell? Thousands. And how many distributors does it have? Dozens. How would the company ever know that outages on boots were limiting sales of ski packages? It's got 40-some stores, all over the United States; a Web storefront; and telephone sales. How would REI ever know about patterns like that?

"But for the sake of argument, let's say it did know. Then what? Suppose REI figured out that every time it runs out of ski boots, on average it loses some number of ski-package sales. Pick any number—say, one out of five. And say that REI makes $200 profit on a ski package. So every time it runs out of ski boots, let's say it loses $40 in profit.

"Knowing that, REI decides to pay a premium to the boot distributor to carry a larger-than-normal inventory of boots. First of all, you wonder why REI doesn't just carry that inventory itself. But anyway, somehow it is going to make a payment to the distributor to carry more boot inventory. All of that, of course, supposes that the distributor is managing inventory that closely, which it probably isn't. Anyway, now REI is going to recoup that payment from the ski, binding, and pole distributor. How—with a check?

"Let's just abandon all sense of reason and say, 'OK, that's what they're going to do.' Now REI has to negotiate an agreement among at least three companies, and probably more if you include the manufacturers. Know what it's like to negotiate an agreement among multiple companies? It takes forever. Just setting up the meetings is tough because everyone's busy, and then the discussions start! And every time you add another company, the required time doubles, at least.

"But let's suppose that somehow REI does get an agreement. Then what happens? The parties take it to the lawyers. And what may have started as a simple, 1-page agreement becomes a booklet, maybe 20 or 30 pages. Of course none of the people who are trying to get the agreement know 'legalese,' so they have to take it to *their lawyers*, and voilà, you've an ego contest among lawyers and law firms. All of this not only delays the project, but now you're running up the price tag. Those lawyers are expensive.

"By the time you get all of this done, it's no longer ski season, and you're not selling any ski equipment. By the time next year rolls around, you're working with different distributors. It just won't work."

DISCUSSION QUESTIONS

1. Do you agree that it is unlikely that REI will know that outages of ski boots are limiting sales of ski packages? Describe three different ways the company could find out.

2. Products vary in the contribution that they make to profit. Explain how organizations could use profitability to choose which products they intend to examine for supply chain profitability.

3. Why do you think REI might choose not to carry a larger inventory of ski boots rather than asking the distributor to do so? Under what circumstances would it make sense for REI to carry the larger inventory itself?

4. Suppose REI wants the distributor to carry a larger inventory. Other than sending the distributor a check, how could REI induce the distributor to do so?

5. What steps could these companies take to reduce the time, labor, and expense required to obtain an agreement that would increase supply chain profitability?

on the observed demand from the next organization up the supply chain. Of course, an *interorganizational information system* is necessary to share such data.

Q5 What Are the Functions of Supplier Relationship Management?

Figure CE12-5 shows the three fundamental information systems involved in supply chain management: supplier relationship management (SRM), inventory, and customer relationship management (CRM). Note that a manufacturer may also have manufacturing applications such as MRP, MRP II, or ERP systems. We discussed all of these applications except SRM in Chapter Extensions 9 and 10. We discuss it here.

Supplier relationship management (SRM) is a business process for managing all contacts between an organization and its suppliers. The term *supplier* in *supplier relationship management* is broader than the use of the term *supplier* in Figures CE12-1 and CE12-2. In those figures, the term refers to the supplier of raw materials and assemblies to a manufacturer. *Supplier* in SRM is used generically: It refers to *any organization* that sells something to the organization that has the SRM application. Thus, in this generic sense, a manufacturer is a supplier to a distributor.

SRM is an integrated system in the same sense of CRM and MRP. With regard to Porter's model, an SRM supports both the in-bound logistics primary activity and the procurement support activity. Considering business processes, SRM applications support three basic processes: source, purchase, and settle, as summarized in Figure CE12-6.

Considering sourcing, the organization needs to find possible vendors of needed supplies, materials, or services; to assess the vendors that it does find; to negotiate terms and conditions; and to formalize those terms and conditions in a procurement contract. SRM software is especially relevant to finding and assessing vendors. Some SRM applications have features to search for product sources and to find evaluations of vendors and products. You see something akin to this functionality when you search for electronics products on a site such as *cnet.com*. There, you can readily determine which vendors provide which products, and you can also obtain evaluations of products and vendors. Similar capabilities are built into SRM packages.

Once the company has identified vendors and has procurement contracts in place, the next stage is to procure the goods. The SRM application requests

Figure CE12-5
B2B in One Section of the Supply Chain

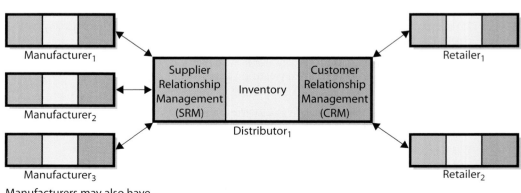

Manufacturers may also have
MRP, MRP II, or ERP applications.

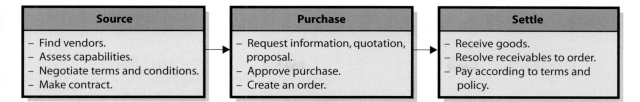

Source	Purchase	Settle
– Find vendors. – Assess capabilities. – Negotiate terms and conditions. – Make contract.	– Request information, quotation, proposal. – Approve purchase. – Create an order.	– Receive goods. – Resolve receivables to order. – Pay according to terms and policy.

Figure CE12-6
Summary of SRM Processes

information, quotations, and proposals from would-be suppliers. The company then can use the SRM to manage the approval workflow in order to approve the purchase and issue the order.

The third major SRM activity is to settle. Here, the accounting department reconciles the receipt of the goods or services against the purchase documents and schedules the vendor payment. The payment portion of the SRM typically connects to the cash management subsystem in the financial management application.

Some SRM packages include features to support procurement auctions. Generally, companies use auctions to obtain large amounts of materials, energy, or other consumables. In these procurement auctions, an organization indicates its desire to purchase a product or service and invites would-be sellers to submit bids. Typically, the low bid wins the auction. Organizational auctions can attract a large number of vendors and often result in substantial cost savings.

Q6 How Do Information Systems Affect Supply Chain Performance?

Information systems have had an exceedingly positive impact on supply chain performance. CRM, SRM, and less-integrated functional systems such as e-commerce sales systems have dramatically reduced the costs of buying and selling. Sourcing, buying, and settling have all become faster, easier, more effective, and less costly.

Furthermore, the presence of information systems has expanded supply chain **speed**, which is the dollar value of goods exchanged in a given period of time. Without information systems, Amazon.com would not have been able to process an average of 41 items per second for 24 hours on December 14, 2005. And, without information systems, it would not have been able to deliver 99 percent of those items on time.

As shown in Figure CE12-7, a third factor is that information systems have enabled both suppliers and customers to reduce the size of their inventories and, thus, reduce their inventory costs. This reduction is possible because the speed and efficiency provided by information systems enables processing of small orders, quickly.

Information systems also improve delivery scheduling. Using information systems, suppliers can deliver materials and components at the time and in the

* Reduce costs of buying and selling.
* Increase supply chain speed.
* Reduce size and cost of inventories.
* Improve delivery scheduling—enable JIT.
* Fix bullwhip effect.
* Do not optimize supply chain profitability.

Figure CE12-7
Benefits of Information Systems on Supply Chain Performance

sequence needed. Such delivery enables just-in-time inventory, and it allows manufacturers to reduce raw materials inventory size as well as the handling of raw materials.

Information systems have the capability to eliminate the bullwhip effect, though doing so requires retailers to be willing to share sales data with the entire supply chain. As discussed in the *Ethics Guide* in Chapter 8 (pages 187a–187b), such sharing entails some risk, and many retailers refuse to release such data. Part of the problem is that the benefit of releasing such data accrues to the supply chain and not to the retailer. While there is some possibility that eliminating the bullwhip effect will reduce prices, many retailers view it only as a *potential* possibility. In their view, it is more likely that the savings will be kept by upstream companies.

This doubt brings us to the last factor in Figure CE-12-7. Information systems do not optimize supply chain profitability. They benefit the companies that actively participate in a particular information system, but as noted, maximizing individual company profitability does not necessarily maximize supply chain profitability. Perhaps some system of transfer payments will someday be worked out, but not during my career, and I doubt during yours either.

Active ? Review

Use this Active Review to verify that you understand the material in the chapter extension. You can read the entire extension and then perform the tasks in this review, or you can read the material for just one question and perform the tasks in this review for that question before moving on to the next one.

Q1 What is a supply chain?

Define *supply chain*. Explain how disintermediation affects supply chain structure. Explain why the term *chain* is misleading. Give an example of a supply chain different from the one in Figure CE12-2.

Q2 What factors influence supply chain performance?

Name the four factors that influence supply chain performance. Briefly explain each.

Q3 How does supply chain profitability differ from organizational profitability?

Explain the difference between supply chain profitability and organizational profitability. Give an example that demonstrates why maximizing organizational profitability does not necessarily lead to the maximization of supply chain profitability. Explain how, in theory, these two can be made the same.

Q4 What is the bullwhip effect?

Define the *bullwhip effect*, and explain how it occurs. Describe why the bullwhip effect is undesirable. Explain how information systems can eliminate this effect.

Q5 What are the functions of supplier relationship management?

Define *supplier relationship management (SRM)*. Explain the relationship of SRM, inventory, and CRM. List and explain the major functions of SRM.

Q6 How do information systems affect supply chain performance?

List the ways in which information systems affect supply chain performance. Define *speed* as it pertains to supply chains. Explain why information systems cannot, today, maximize supply chain profit.

Key Terms and Concepts

Bullwhip effect 466

Speed 469

Supplier relationship management

(SRM) 468

Supply chain 463

Supply chain profitability 466

Using Your Knowledge

1. Search the Web for the term *supplier relationship management software.* Identify two software products from two different vendors. Choose one product that is vended by a major software company, such as Oracle or SAP. Choose another product that is vended by a lesser known, smaller company.
   a. Compare the features of each product to the functions shown in Figure CE12-6. Are any functions missing? Does either product have functions in addition to those in the list in Figure CE12-6?
   b. Attempt to determine the license fee for each product. If you are successful, state the fee. If you are unsuccessful, state the reasons why you think the vendor might not make its fees public.
   c. Most likely one or both of these sites will offer white papers that describe the use of their product and case studies that showcase their product in use. Download a white paper or case study. You may have to provide your contact data before you can download. To save the follow-up salesperson's time (unless you want to talk to him or her about career prospects selling that software), be certain to specify that you are a student. Summarize the white paper or case study.

2. Consider the supply chain in which DSI is a part.
   a. Diagram this supply chain. Use Figure CE12-2 as an example.
   b. Explain how the four factors described in Q2 affect this supply chain's performance. Describe how these factors affect DSI's profitability.
   c. Do you think the bullwhip effect is a problem for this supply chain? Why or why not?
   d. Explain how DSI can use an SRM system. What benefits would accrue to DSI for using such a system?
   e. Explain how the benefits of information systems listed in Figure CE12-7 apply to DSI.

3. Consider the supply chain for Amazon.com. Assume that Amazon.com buys books directly from publishers and also buys from book distributors. Ignore used book sales.
   a. Diagram this supply chain. Use Figure CE12-2 as an example. Because shippers are so important to Amazon.com, include them in your diagram.
   b. Explain how the four factors described in Q2 affect this supply chain's performance. Describe how these factors affect Amazon.com's profitability.
   c. Do you think the bullwhip effect is a problem for this supply chain? Why or why not?
   d. Explain how Amazon.com can use an SRM system. What benefits would accrue to Amazon.com for using such a system?
   e. Explain how the benefits of information systems listed in Figure CE12-7 apply to Amazon.com.

4. Consider the supply chain for a grocery store chain. Assume the chain buys dry goods from distributors, but buys meat, fish, poultry, produce, and dairy

goods directly from suppliers. Assume that it sells magazines and certain snack foods on a consignment basis.

a. Diagram this supply chain. Use Figure CE12-2 as an example.

b. Explain how the four factors described in Q2 affect this supply chain's performance. Describe how these factors affect the grocery store chain's profitability.

c. Do you think the bullwhip effect is a problem for this supply chain? Why or why not?

 d. Search the Web to find an SRM (or equivalent) application that is specifically designed for operations like grocery store chains. Explain the major features and functions of that system. Describe benefits that would accrue to the chain by using such a system.

e. Suppose the grocery store chain has developed its own in-house SRM application software. Explain the advantages and disadvantages of in-house versus commercial SRM software. Consider maintenance costs for the in-house software and license fees for the commercial software. What problems would you expect if the chain decided to switch from its in-house system to a commercially available system?

f. Explain how the benefits of information systems listed in Figure CE12-7 apply to Amazon.com.

Using the Guide: The Lawyer's Full-Employment Act (page 467a)

GOALS

✱ Understand the difference between supply chain profit and individual company profit.

✱ Investigate the feasibility of maximizing supply chain profit.

✱ Teach some of the inhibitors to obtaining interorganizational agreements.

BACKGROUND AND PRESENTATION STRATEGIES

The primary purpose of this guide is to *underline the difference between supply chain profit and individual company profit*:

- Supply chain profit is the difference between revenue paid by the consumers (the only source of cash) and the costs incurred by all the companies in the supply chain.

- Individual company profit is the difference between revenue received by the company and that company's costs.

Supply chain profit is *not maximized when each company maximizes its own profit*. Instead, as in the example of the ski boots and ski packages, supply chain profit will be greater if some of the companies operate at other-than-maximal profit for them. For any company to do that, that company needs to be compensated by other members of the supply chain— at least as much as the forgone profit, but likely even more as an inducement.

In practice, as our contrarian points out, pragmatic issues may make this issue moot. His important points:

- Difficulty (impossibility?) in determining which items need to be managed from a supply chain, rather than individual company, basis.

- Difficulty negotiating contract terms.

- Difficulty getting lawyers to approve.

- Time delays make agreement schedule infeasible.

If it is (or ever becomes) possible to determine how to maximize supply chain profits, that computation *will rely heavily on interorganizational information systems*. Information is the key to determining how to maximize

supply chain profit—no other driver (facility, inventory, or transportation) can accomplish that task.

Even if supply chain profit maximization is not feasible today, it is an important goal for the future. Perhaps future supply-chain-wide use of Web services (see Chapter Extension 13) will enable supply chains to be managed from the standpoint of supply-chain-wide profitability.

Nothing so facilitates interorganizational activity as a well-written contract that clearly specifies the responsibilities and obligations of each party. A clearly worded contract simplifies life for everyone, and the benefits continue for years. Furthermore, every organization that needs its day in court is thankful for competent legal representation. It's hard to remember that, though, when you've negotiated the deal, the opportunity awaits (or is passing), and the only thing holding up progress is groups of lawyers wrangling over seemingly innocent terminology!

 SUGGESTED RESPONSES FOR DISCUSSION QUESTIONS

1. It might be difficult to compute the effect that the boot outage is having, or to know other than anecdotally, but experienced salespeople probably know some of the major patterns. Three possible ways to learn this effect is to ask salespeople, to survey customers, or to compute it by comparing sales of individual items versus sales of packages. (Note: *This question sets up the discussion of market-basket analysis* in Chapter Extension 14.)

2. To choose which products to examine for supply chain profitability, organizations could constrain the analysis of purchasing patterns to high-margin items. Look carefully at which items tend to be purchased with high-margin items. Ask customers and salespeople if the absence of those companion items constrains the purchase of the high-margin item.

   This answer has a problem, however. First, ask the students:

   ➤ **Do you see a problem of constraining the analysis to high-margin items?**

   The companies in the supply chain are concerned with total margin, not individual-item margin. If it turns out that, because of higher volume, REI earns more total margin on packages of dehydrated corn, peas, and a spoon than it earns on sales of ski packages, then the analysis should examine corn-package sales before ski-package sales. Even though the margin on a ski package might be $40 and the margin on a package of corn, peas, and a spoon might be $1, volume differences can make the sale of corn packages contribute more to the total margin.

3. Ostensibly, the distributor is selling to more vendors than just REI. If the distributor carries the larger inventory, it can balance REI's needs against its other customers' needs. The total profit for the supply chain that includes both REI and its competitors will be higher.

   In practice, REI probably doesn't consider total supply chain management, including its competitors. It may want the distributor to carry the larger inventory just to save its (REI's) inventory costs. REI would carry the larger inventory if the cost of doing so was compensated by greater sales of ski packages and if the distributor would not agree to do so (or if it was too difficult to induce the distributor to do so).

4. Several alternative inducements are to threaten to take one's business elsewhere; to threaten to buy directly from the manufacturer; and to negotiate penalties for out-of-stock situations.

5. They could negotiate a blanket agreement that would pertain to all members of the supply chain and would pertain to a large group of goods. The terminology of the blanket agreement would be negotiated once, approved by attorneys of all the involved firms, and be used over and over. Such an agreement would need to be drawn carefully, however, to avoid restraint of trade concerns and the appearance of collusion or a trust. The lawyers really do need to be involved on this one!

WRAP UP

➤ **Supply chain profitability is an interesting concept, but it may only be a concept, at least right now. It may be difficult to take practical action to take advantage of the additional profits that companies could make by optimizing supply chain profit over individual company profit.**

➤ **If it ever becomes possible to have a pragmatic solution to the supply chain profitability problem, that solution will involve information systems. Stay tuned!**

Chapter Extension 13

Chapter 8 provides the background for this Extension.

Information Technology for Data Exchange: EDI and XML

Q1 What Technologies Are Used for Data Exchange?

Web commerce-server applications are useful for B2C, but they are not sufficient for B2B needs. In general, organizations need to exchange data and messages in more general and flexible ways than they can do with commerce servers. From the discussion in Chapter 8, you know they may need to exchange orders, order confirmations, requests for quotations, item inventory status data, accounts payable and accounts receivable data, and a myriad of other types of data and documents.

Figure CE13-1 summarizes alternatives for exchanging data. The most basic are telephone calls and documents exchanged via fax or postal mail. Another alternative is to exchange data and documents via email. None of these requires information technology beyond what you already know.

The next three alternatives do involve additional technology. *Electronic Data Interchange* (*EDI*) is a standard for exchanging documents from machine to machine, electronically. In the past, EDI was used over point-to-point or value-added networks. Recently, EDI systems have been developed that use the Internet as well. Another alternative is *extensible markup language* (*XML*), a standard that offers advantages over EDI and that most believe will eventually replace EDI. We will discuss both EDI and XML in this chapter extension.

In addition to sharing documents, some SCM application programs interact directly with each other. In the past, two organizations needed to design a proprietary system developed specifically to meet this need. More recently, a set of standards called *XML Web services* has been developed that many organizations

Study Questions

Q1 What technologies are used for data exchange?

Q2 How does EDI facilitate data exchange?

Q3 How does XML facilitate data exchange?

Q4 How are proprietary distributed applications used in the supply chain?

Q5 How are XML Web service applications used in supply chains?

Message and Data Exchange	Application Interaction
– Telephone – Paper (fax, postal mail) – Email – Electronic Data Interchange (EDI) – EDI over Internet – eXtensible Markup Language (XML)	– Proprietary applications – XML Web services

Figure CE13-1
Alternatives for Interorganizational Message and Data Exchange

use for interprogram communication. We will discuss this topic later in the chapter.

Q2 How Does EDI Facilitate Data Exchange?

Electronic Data Interchange (EDI) is a standard of formats for common business documents. To understand the need for EDI, consider the supply chain in Figure CE12-1 (page 463), and suppose that there are 5 distributors and 10 manufacturers. Further, suppose that each distributor wants to send orders electronically to all of the manufacturers. Because the transmissions are electronic, the distributors and manufacturers must agree on a format for the orders. This format will include how many data fields will be sent, in what order they will be sent, how many characters will be sent in each data field, and so forth. This is not difficult work; it merely requires a common design for the order transmissions.

However, if each distributor designs a *different* electronic order format for each manufacturer, then a total of 5 times 10, or 50, different formats must be designed. When you consider that the companies may wish to exchange not only orders, but also requests for quotations, order confirmations, order shipping notices, and so forth, you can see that the distributors and manufacturers would have to develop thousands of different document formats.

This work is needlessly repetitive. None of these companies considers the design of such forms to be a proprietary secret; these designs are just necessary clerical work. To reduce this clerical workload, more than 30 years ago, companies began to define standard formats for the electronic transmission of documents.

The EDI X12 Standard

In the United States, the X12 Committee of the American National Standards Institute (ANSI) manages EDI standards. Today, the **EDI X12 standard** includes hundreds of documents. They have standard names like EDI 850 (purchase order), EDI 856 (advance ship notices), and EDI 810 (electronic invoice).

An EDI document definition consists of a set of segments, each of which has a defined set of fields. Figure CE13-2 shows a segment of the EDI 850 (purchase order) standard that specifies the items that are being ordered. There is one segment of this type for each item on the order. For this example, the segment is named PO1, and each of the data fields within that segment is named PO1*xx*, as in PO101, PO102, and so forth. Each data element has a number, a description (name), and attributes, including whether the data element is required, the type of data that should be used for that data element, and the required number and maximum number of characters written in the form *nn/mm*, where *nn* is the required number of characters and *mm* is the maximum number.

You do not need to memorize the information in Figure CE13-2; instead, just use that figure to appreciate the nature of EDI standards. Understand the amount of detailed work that must go into the development of such formats and why companies decided they needed standards for them. Without standards, specifications like those in Figure CE13-2 need to be negotiated for each trading partner.

Segment: PO1–Baseline item data
Usage: Mandatory
Max Use: 99
Purpose: To specify basic and most frequently used line item data

Segment Number	Data Element	Name	Attributes
PO101	350	Assigned Identification *Purchase Order Line Number*	M AN 1/11
PO102	330	Quantity Ordered	X R 1/7
PO103	355	Unit or Basis for Measurement *Code*	M ID 2/2
PO104	212	Unit Price *Three Decimal Places*	X R 1/9
PO106	235	Product ID Qualifier *UI – UPC Consumer Package Code* *UP – UPC Consumer Package Code*	M ID 2/2
PO107	234	Product ID *UPC Code*	M AN 12
Etc.			

Other EDI Standards

Unfortunately, the X12 standard is not the only EDI standard. A second standard, called the **EDIFACT standard**, is used internationally. A third standard, called the **HIPAA standard**, is used for medical records. Because of the existence of multiple standards, when two organizations today wish to exchange documents electronically, they must first agree on which standard they will use.

One further complication is that the standards do not stand still. With usage, organizations find a need to make adjustments to the standards. Thus, there are various versions of each of the X12, EDIFACT, and HIPAA standards. So to exchange documents, two companies need to agree on the standard and the version of the standard that they will use. From that point on, however, the companies can exchange documents without further configuration work.

Q3 How Does XML Facilitate Data Exchange?

At this point, you may be asking a burning question—namely, why not use HTML for document interchange? Why mess around with EDI or anything else when the greatest success story in modern history involves the sharing of Web pages over the Internet? Why not use HTML to create purchase orders, price quotations, or other business documents? They could then be transmitted using HTTP, just as Web pages are.

In fact, organizations have used HTML to share documents. However, doing so presents several problems. We will first summarize those problems and then describe a successor markup language called XML that overcomes them.

Problems with HTML

Three problems with HTML are:

1. HTML tags have no consistent meaning.
2. HTML has a fixed number of tags.
3. HTML mixes format, content, and structure.

The first problem is that tags are used inconsistently. For example, in standard use, heading tags should be arranged in outline format. The highest-level heading tag should be an h1; within h1, there should be one or more h2 tags; and within the h2 tags, there should be h3 tags; and so forth, for as many heading levels as the author of a document wants.

Unfortunately, there is no feature of HTML that forces consistent use. An h2 tag can appear anywhere—above an h1 heading, below an h4 heading, or anyplace else. An h2 tag can represent a level-two heading, but it can also be used just to obtain a particular type of formatting. If I want the words *Prices guaranteed until Jan. 1, 2008* to appear in the formatting of a level-two heading, I can code:

```
<h2>Prices guaranteed until Jan. 1, 2008</h2>
```

This statement is not intended to be a level-two heading, but it will be given the font size, weight, and color that such headings have.

The possibility of tag misuse means that we cannot depend on tags to infer the document's structure. An h2 tag may not be a heading at all. This limitation means that organizations cannot use HTML tags to reliably exchange documents.

A second problem with HTML is that it defines a fixed set of tags. If two businesses want to define a new tag, say <PriceQuotation>, there is no way in HTML for them to define it. HTML documents are limited to the predefined tags.

The third problem with HTML is that HTML mixes the structure, formatting, and content of a document. Consider the following line of HTML code:

```
<h2 align="center"><font color="#FF00FF">Price of
Item</font></h2>
```

This heading mixes the structure (h2) with the formatting (alignment and color) with the content (Price of Item). Such mixing makes HTML difficult to work with. Ideally, the structure, format, and content should be separate.

Importance of XML

To overcome the problems in HTML, the computer industry designed a new markup language called the **eXtensible markup language (XML)**. XML is the product of a committee that worked under the auspices of the **World Wide Web**

Consortium (W3C), a body that sponsors the development and dissemination of Web standards. By the way, W3C publishes excellent tutorials, and you can find an XML tutorial on its Web site, *www3c.org*.

XML provides a superior means for organizations to exchange documents. It solves the problems mentioned for HTML, and it has become a significant standard for computer processing. For example, all Microsoft Office 2003 products can save their documents in XML format. XML is also a key part of standards for Web services, and it is particularly important for supply chain management, as you will see.

Application of XML to the Supply Chain

XML has the potential to improve, sometimes drastically, the efficiency of supply chain processes and activities. To understand how, consider REI and its relationship to its distributors. Suppose REI wants to transmit counts of inventory items to all of its suppliers. To do so, REI designs an XML document for sending the item counts. (For now, think of an XML document as a sequence of tags and data, like HTML documents.) Once it has designed the document, REI records the structure of that document in what is called an **XML schema**. Such a schema is just another XML document, but one that records the structure (or schema) of the first (item count) document. Call that schema the item count schema.

Next, REI prepares inventory count documents according to its design. Before sending those documents to its distributors, REI double-checks that the documents are valid by comparing them to the schema. Fortunately, there are hundreds of readily available programs that can validate an XML document against its schema. For example, both Internet Explorer and Netscape Navigator can validate any XML document. This validation feature means significant cost savings because no human labor is required to check documents.

Before sending item count documents to the distributors, REI shares the item count schema with them, possibly by publishing it on a Web site that the distributors have permission to access. When a distributor receives an inventory count document from REI, it uses the published schema to validate the received document. In this way, the distributors ensure that they receive correct and complete documents and that no part of the document has been lost in transmission. Again, this automated process saves labor because it frees the distributors from manually validating the correctness of the documents they receive. This automated validation can mean enormous labor savings.

Using XML in an Industry

Now broaden this idea from two businesses to an entire industry. Suppose, for example, that the real estate industry agrees on an XML schema document for property listings. Every real estate company that can produce data in the format of the schema can then exchange listings with every other such real estate company. Given the schema, each company can ensure that it is transmitting and receiving valid documents.

Figure CE13-3 (page 478) lists some XML-standards work that is underway in various industries.

Industry	Example of XML Standards
Accounting	American Institute of Certified Public Accountants (AICPA): Extensible Financial Reporting Markup Language
Automotive	Society of Automotive Engineers (SAE): XML for the Automotive Industry—SAE J2008
Banking	Financial Services Technology Consortium (FSTC): Bank Internet Payment System (BIPS)
Human Resources	HR-XML Consortium
Insurance	ACORD: Property and Casualty
Real Estate	OpenMLS: Real Estate Listing Management System
Workflow	Internet Engineering Task Force (IETF): Simple Workflow Access Protocol (SWAP)

Q4 How Are Proprietary Distributed Applications Used in the Supply Chain?

Companies can use EDI and XML to exchange documents, but what if two organizations want their computer programs to interact? What if a company wants its SRM application program to connect directly to a supplier's CRM application? Neither the EDI nor the XML standard, by itself, supports such activity.

The process of a program on one computer accessing programs on a second computer is called **distributed computing**. Several different techniques are used. Two important ones are the use of proprietary applications and Web services. Consider proprietary first.

Proprietary means that the solution is unique to and is owned by the organizations that develop and pay for the distributed systems. It is a one-of-a-kind solution. To develop a proprietary design, teams of developers from the companies involved work together using a development process like that described in Chapter 10. The teams determine application requirements, develop a design, and write and test programs according to that design. Such projects are distinguished from other development projects only in the requirement for remote processing.

Consider an example. Suppose the companies in a supply chain decide they want to eliminate the bullwhip effect (see Chapter Extension 12, page 466). To do this, the retailers in the supply chain must share sales data with all companies up the chain. Accordingly, the companies in the supply chain organize a development team consisting of IT personnel from all of the major companies.

The joint development team designs this application to use a particular communications capability, particular operating systems, and particular distributed computing techniques. A major portion of the development effort is in selecting which communications technologies, operating systems, and distributed techniques are to be used and how program code will use those techniques. (By the way, whenever you participate in meetings of this, or any, sort with employees of other companies, you must be careful about what you say. See the

Guide on pages 479a–479b for some practical guidelines on interorganizational information exchange.)

An alternative proprietary method is for one company to develop all of the necessary programs itself and then to install some of its programs on another company's computers. In the past, some manufacturers developed order-entry programs that they installed on their customers' computers. These programs call directly into the manufacturer's CRM application. The customers only need to install the programs that the manufacturer provides.

Of course, this process is much simpler to describe than it is to do. Inevitably, there are differences on the customers' computers that the manufacturer did not expect, and so the manufacturer has to make special-purpose program versions for different distributors. Sometimes this happens dozens of times, resulting in a software-configuration management nightmare for the manufacturer.

Proprietary solutions are difficult and expensive to develop and operate. If they provide sufficient business value, the return on investment can make them worthwhile. Even so, considerable management time and attention is necessary. Because of the difficulty, expense, and time involved in developing such solutions, many organizations today are beginning to use another technology that uses a different strategy—XML Web services. We consider it next.

Q5 How Are XML Web Service Applications Used in Supply Chains?

XML Web services, sometimes called simply *Web services*, are a set of standards that facilitate distributed computing using Internet technology. Web services are the latest and greatest tool for application interaction, and they will be important in the early years of your career. Every major software vendor has products that support Web services. For example, Microsoft provides .Net development tools, and IBM provides J2EE development tools. Because of the standards, applications developed by these different tools will work together without a problem.

Fundamental Web Services Concepts

The goal of Web services is to provide a standardized way for programs to access one another remotely, without the need to develop proprietary solutions. Because they are standardized worldwide, they are immediately accessible. Right now, for example, without a meeting or even a conversation, you can access Amazon.com and use Web services standards to write your own personal front-end to Amazon.com's catalog. (To learn more, see *www.amazon.com/webservices.*) There is no need for developer meetings to create designs for interprogram communication. Everything necessary is already part of the Web services standards.

A number of important standards have been defined to make Web services possible, but a discussion of those standards is beyond the scope of this book. In general, these standards enable programs on one computer to obtain a **service description** that details what programs exist on another computer and how to communicate with those programs.

Once the service user has the service description, it uses the information it contains to invoke the service. In the case of Amazon.com, a service user can invoke the Amazon.com service to find a particular book, to find a set of books, or to provide additional Amazon.com catalog information. Remarkably, it

Interorganizational Information Exchange

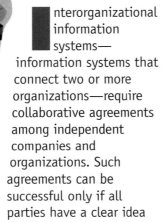

Interorganizational information systems—information systems that connect two or more organizations—require collaborative agreements among independent companies and organizations. Such agreements can be successful only if all parties have a clear idea of the goals, benefits, costs, and risks of working together. The creation of collaborative agreements requires many joint meetings in which the parties make their goals and objectives clear and decide how best to share information and other resources.

During your career, you may be asked to participate in such meetings. You should understand a few basic guidelines before participating.

First, when you meet with employees of another company, realize that you must apply stronger limits on your conversation than when you meet with employees in your own firm. For all you know, the company you are meeting with may become your strongest competitor. In general, you should assume that whatever you say to an employee of another company could be general knowledge in your industry the next day.

Of course, the goal of such meetings is to develop a collaborative relationship, and you cannot accomplish that goal without saying something. The best strategy, however, is to reveal exactly what you must reveal and no more.

Before you meet with another company, you and your team should have a clear and common understanding of the purpose of the meeting. Your team needs to agree beforehand on the topics that are to be addressed and those that are to be avoided. Relationships often develop in stages: Two companies meet, establish one level of understanding, meet again with another level of understanding, and so forth, feeling one another out on the way to some type of relationship.

You may be asked to sign a nondisclosure agreement. Such agreements are contracts that stipulate the responsibilities of each party in protecting the other's proprietary information. Such agreements vary in length; some are a page long and some are 30 pages long. You need to understand the policy of your organization with regard to such agreements before the meeting starts. Sometimes, companies exchange their standard nondisclosure agreements before the meeting so that the respective legal departments can review and approve the agreements ahead of time.

In your remarks, stick to the purpose of the meeting. Avoid conversations about your company or about third parties that do not relate to the meeting topic. You never know the agenda of the other party; you never know what other companies they are meeting; and you never know what other information about your company they may want.

Realize that a meeting isn't over until it's over. The meeting is still underway in the hallway waiting for the elevator. It's still underway at lunch. And it's still underway as you share a cab to the airport. By the way, the only two topics in an elevator should be the weather and the number of the floor you want. Don't embarrass yourself or the employees of the other company by discussing in a public place anything other than the weather.

All of these suggestions may seem paranoid, but even paranoid companies have competitors. There is simply no reason, other than carelessness or stupidity, to discuss topics with another company that do not relate to the matter at hand. Your company will assume enough risk just setting up the interorganizational system. Don't add to that risk by making gratuitous comments about your or any other company.

DISCUSSION QUESTIONS

1. Suppose you are asked to attend a meeting with your suppliers to discuss the sharing of your sales data. You have no idea as to the specific purpose of the meeting, why you were invited, or what will be expected of you. What should you do?

2. Suppose you flew 1,500 miles for a meeting, and at the start of the meeting, the other company asks you to sign a nondisclosure statement. You knew nothing about the need to sign such an agreement. What do you do?

3. Some companies have an open, democratic style with lots of collaboration and open discussion. Others are closed and authoritarian, and employees wait to be told what to do. Describe what will happen when employees from two such companies meet. What can be done to improve the situation?

4. Suppose during lunch, an employee of another company asks you, "What are you all doing about XML Web services?" Assume that this topic has little to do with the purpose of your meeting. You think about it and decide that it doesn't seem too risky to respond, so you say, "Not much." What information have you conveyed by this statement? What is a better way to respond to the question?

5. Suppose you are in a joint meeting, and you are asked, "So who else are you working with on this problem?" Describe guidelines you could use in deciding how to answer this question.

6. Explain the statement, "A meeting isn't over until it's over." How might this statement pertain to other meetings—say, a job interview?

appears to the service user that all of the Amazon.com programs are actually on the service user's computer. If you were the service user, it would be as if you had Amazon.com's catalog programs (and database) on your own machine.

All Web service data are transmitted in XML documents. These documents have XML schemas defined, and all program components of the XML Web services architecture can automatically validate them.

Web Services and the Supply Chain

Web services have the potential to simplify the automation of supply chain interactions. Any organization in the supply chain can develop Web services and publish those services to other organizations in the supply chain. Developers in those other organizations can access the service description and write programs that call the Web services.

Consider an example: Suppose that, to reduce the bullwhip effect, a retailer develops a Web service to share its CRM sales data with companies in the supply chain. Other companies in the supply chain, such as distributors and manufacturers, consume this service to plan their inventory and production activities. As Figure CE13-4 shows, the retailer publishes a service description and makes that description available to distributors and manufacturers. Developers in those companies write programs according to the Web service description.

To obtain sales data, the Web service programs of the distributor or manufacturer create a service request. Those Web service programs transmit that request to the service provider at the retailer's computer. The message goes to the retailer and is processed by the Web service programs. Those programs call the CRM application to read data in the CRM database. They then format a response in an XML document and send the response to the service consumer (the distributor or manufacturer).

Because of the standards, no joint development meetings or other coordination activities are required among the organizations to enable the use of these Web services. The developers are all working on the same page, so to speak. They all use the same Web services standards.

Web services not only provide cost savings for the development of interorganizational IS, but they also drastically reduce the time required to achieve

Figure CE13-4
Example of Web Services for Sharing Sales Data

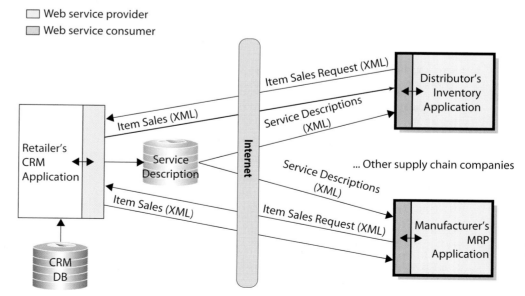

operational capability. Furthermore, the use of Web services provides tremendous flexibility. A manufacturer, for example, can combine Web services from several different companies into a single application. The manufacturer can also readily change and adapt those combinations to meet new business requirements.

Active ? Review

Use this Active Review to verify that you understand the material in the chapter extension. You can read the entire extension and then perform the tasks in this review, or you can read the material for just one question and perform the tasks in this review for that question before moving on to the next one.

Q1 What technologies are used for data exchange?

Summarize the technologies used to facilitate data exchange. Explain the difference between message exchange and application interaction.

Q2 How does EDI facilitate data exchange?

Define *EDI*, and explain its advantages for a supply chain. Describe the EDI X12 standard. In general terms, describe the structure of an EDI document as specified by this standard. Name two other EDI standards.

Q3 How does XML facilitate data exchange?

Explain how HTML can be used to exchange documents. Summarize the problems of using HTML for this purpose. Define *XML*. Define *XML schema*, and explain document validation. Describe how the use of XML schemas saves labor. Describe how the real estate industry can use XML to its advantage. Name two other industries that are using XML.

Q4 How are proprietary distributed applications used in the supply chain?

Define *distributed computing*, and name two distributed computing alternatives. Summarize two alternatives for developing a proprietary distributed computing supply chain application. Describe the disadvantages of proprietary distributed applications.

Q5 How are XML Web service applications used in supply chains?

Define *XML Web services*. Describe the goal of XML Web services. Explain the advantage of standardization. Explain how you could use Web services to incorporate Amazon.com's Web site into your application. Define *service description*. Describe the use of XML in Web service applications. Explain how XML Web services could be used to reduce the bullwhip effect. Explain the flows of data and information in Figure CE13-4.

Key Terms and Concepts

Distributed computing 478
EDI X12 standard 474
EDIFACT standard 475
Electronic Data Interchange (EDI) 474

eXtensible Markup Language (XML) 476
HIPAA standard 475
Service description 479

World Wide Web Consortium (W3C) 476–477
XML schema 477
XML Web services 479
Service description 479

Using Your Knowledge

1. This chapter extension contends that over time, XML Web services will replace EDI. Search the Web for evidence that either supports or contradicts this contention. Do you find applications that are being converted from EDI

to Web services? Are EDI vendors adding Web services applications to their product suites? On a site for a vendor like SAP, do you see more evidence of EDI or of Web services features and functions?

 2. Search the Web for case histories on the use of Web services and supply chain management. You can start by searching for the terms *supply chain* and *Web services*. See where that takes you. Find an article about a major company's use of Web services in the supply chain. Summarize the experience of that company.

3. Amazon.com makes it exceedingly easy for developers to use its Web services. Why do you think Amazon.com does that? What competitive advantage does it receive? Describe another B2C business, in another industry, that might achieve similar benefits by developing an easily used Web service.

4. Consider the importance of standards for the Internet.
   a. How would the Web be different if multiple standards competed with HTTP and HTML? What would be lost? What needless expense would be incurred?
   b. Visit *www.w3c.org* and *www.xml.org*. Describe the importance of these sites for developing and maintaining standards. Who participates in these activities? Who pays for these people's time?
   c. According to this chapter extension, both Microsoft and IBM have developed products that support the XML Web services standard. What incentive do they have to support such a standard? Are they better off to support the standard or to develop their own proprietary standard. Why or why not?
   d. According to Bill Gates, XML is the *lingua franca* of the Internet. What is a *lingua franca*? Why do you think he believes this statement? Why do you think he made this statement? Why does the Internet need a *lingua franca*?
   e. Suppose someone tells you that standards reduce creativity. How would you respond? Is it possible that standards also increase creativity? How could such a paradoxical statement be true?

you be the Guide

Using the Guide: Interorganizational Information Exchange (page 479a)

GOALS

* Help students become better business professionals by teaching them proper etiquette at intercompany meetings.

* Forewarn the students of common blunders that can occur when meeting with personnel from other companies.

BACKGROUND AND PRESENTATION STRATEGIES

Supply chain and other interorganizational information systems require meetings between people from different companies. In such meetings, communication behaviors should be more limited than when meeting with personnel from your own company.

Intercompany meetings usually begin with everyone going around the table and introducing him- or herself. The students should anticipate that first activity and *prepare an introduction ahead of time.* Once they have a title like Senior VP of International Sales, they won't have to say much. However, while they are still in junior positions, they need to find a way to positively introduce themselves without appearing conceited. They need to steer between:

➤ **"Hello, my name is XXX. I'm a very junior employee, and I can't imagine why anyone would want me in this meeting."**

and

➤ **"Hello, my name is XXX, and I invented the Internet. You are so fortunate that I'm here."**
   Because a personal introduction is such a common communication requirement, I have my students practice it on me and the class. Each class session, I ask two or three students to introduce themselves. (Actually, I start this practice in the second or third lecture, but it's especially relevant to intercompany meetings where a strong first impression is important.)

Nondisclosure statements are common, at least in the high-tech industry. Employees should *know their company's policy about signing such agreements* long before they schedule their travel. See question 2 for a suggestion about how to handle surprise requests for signing such agreements.

It is so important, especially for people in junior positions, to *know the purpose of the meeting* and to understand *what can and cannot be communicated.* Once something inappropriate has been said, there is no way to take it back. Again, the best way to solve a problem is not to have it at all.

A good guideline is to exchange only that information that needs to be exchanged and no more. Even innocuous statements can be revealing. For social chat, focus on the weather, sporting events, local attractions, antics of your children, or the leading article in today's *Wall Street Journal* (unless it relates to the matter at hand).

A meeting isn't over until it's over. I learned that lesson the hard way. In the heyday of the PC industry between 1985 and 1995, Stuart Alsop was an important columnist and industry pundit for *PCWeek, PC Magazine,* and other such magazines. For several years, he published his own industry newsletter. Alsop's behavior was so unassuming, almost bumbling, that you'd let your guard down. At least I did. And, of course, he was "dumb like a fox." I probably had four or five meetings with him during those years, and in every one I found myself revealing information that I had no intention of revealing. Even worse, after the first meeting, I even knew what he was doing. In that first meeting, he suggested that we get out of the office for some fresh air and walk around the building. Sure enough, in that relaxed and informal atmosphere, I was blathering on and on, as if I was talking to a fellow manager in our company, about what I hoped we'd accomplish in the next year or so. When news of our plans appeared in his next newsletter, our CEO had a serious discussion with me, beginning with a question relating to my IQ. *The meeting isn't over until it's over!*

Corollary to the above: Be especially vigilant at meals.

➤ **When you all go out to lunch, watch what you say in the car, at the restaurant, and on the drive back. You're not having lunch with your family. You're having it with a potential partner, but one who is also meeting with your competitors, the press, and who knows whom else. This person may become your competitor someday.**

➤ **There is no need to make an issue of it in front of the person. Just be aware of the need for care.**

➤ **Stick to the agenda of the meeting. Know what is supposed to be accomplished. Think through ahead of time what you need to communicate and communicate only that.**

➤ **Be *exceedingly careful if alcohol is served* at the meal. If you like to drink, do it some other time with your friends. These people are professional associates, not your friends. Don't mix your personal and professional lives.**

? SUGGESTED RESPONSES FOR DISCUSSION QUESTIONS

1. Find out what you need to know to function effectively. Get answers to all those questions. What is the purpose of this meeting? Why are you being invited? Ask your manager or someone to help you.

   ➤ **If you're not sure of your role, keep quiet until you are sure. As you rise to higher levels of management, you will have experience to extemporize. Don't start that way, however. You need experience.**

2. When I am caught by surprise by a request to sign a nondisclosure and I have any doubt about whether I want to sign one, I say something like:

   ➤ **I didn't realize we were going to be exchanging confidential information. For now, why don't we just keep our conversation to the nonconfidential aspects of our business together? I'll take your nondisclosure form home with me and let our lawyers OK it. If we need to discuss confidential information in future meetings, we can sign then. OK?**

   If that doesn't work, then, depending on the policy of my company, I may need to fax the form to our attorneys for immediate review, reschedule the meeting, or sign the form.

3. These are very odd and awkward meetings, full of long silences and awkward pauses. (By the way, there is nothing wrong with silence—and it's not for you, as a junior staff member, to fill awkward pauses, anyway.) The key is to know the purpose of the meeting and to stick with that agenda. If you're with the more open company, beware. Just do your business and go home.

   When personnel from another company act odd, there may be something going on. Maybe they've already decided to go with another partner, maybe they have lost interest in the project, maybe they're about to be acquired by your number one competitor. Any of this may have occurred, but they may not have been able to cancel the meeting without revealing what is going on.

4. Don't talk about company business that is not related to the purpose of the meeting. By replying, "Not much," you've said something—maybe that your company is behind the times. A better response would be:

   ➤ **"I don't work in that area, and I wouldn't be able to give you a good answer. How about those Red Sox?"**

5. Answer only if the question is pertinent to the purpose of the meeting and within the scope of what your team has agreed to reveal. Otherwise, duck the question with a response like:

   ➤ **"We're here to work with you, and we're excited to be doing so."**

   A more aggressive—and not recommended response—is:

   ➤ **"Who, besides yourselves, would you recommend?"**

6. The job interview starts with the initial phone call or email, and it isn't over until you've either been hired or not. Every interaction you have with an employee of your future employer is part of your job interview. If someone picks you up at the airport or hotel, the interview begins when you first meet. It's going on while having breakfast, standing in line for a taxi, waiting for the elevator, combing your hair in the bathroom, or walking down the hall to the coffee room. Everything you say is part of the job interview.

WRAP UP

➤ **Business is a social activity. It is in our nature to communicate with one another, and most of us want to appear friendly, or at least not rude. All of that is fine.**

➤ **But always keep in mind, especially when meeting with employees from another company, that you are talking with business associates, not friends. If you say something revealing, you cannot take it back.**

➤ **Stick to the agenda!**

Chapter Extension 14

Chapter 9 provides the background for this Extension.

Database Marketing

Q1 What Is a Database Marketing Opportunity?

Database marketing is the application of business intelligence systems to the planning and execution of marketing programs. The term is broader than it sounds. Databases are a key component of database marketing, but, as you'll see, data-mining techniques are also very important. To understand the need for database marketing, consider the following scenario:

> Mary Keeling owns and operates Carbon Creek Gardens, a retailer of trees, garden plants, perennial and annual flowers, and bulbs. "The Gardens," as her customers call it, also sells bags of soil, fertilizer, small garden tools, and garden sculptures. Mary started the business 10 years ago when she bought a section of land that, because of water drainage, was unsuited for residential development. With hard work and perseverance, Mary has created a warm and inviting environment with a unique and carefully selected inventory of plants. The Gardens has become a favorite nursery for serious gardeners in her community.

> "The problem," she says, "is that I've grown so large, I've lost track of my customers. The other day, I ran into Tootsie Swan at the grocery store, and I realized I hadn't seen her in ages. I said something like, 'Hi, Tootsie, I haven't seen you for a while,' and that statement unleashed an angry torrent from her. It turns out that she'd been in over a year ago and wanted to return a plant. One of my part-time employees waited on her and had apparently insulted her or at least didn't give her the service she wanted. So she decided not to come back to the Gardens.

> "Tootsie was one of my best customers. I'd lost her, and I didn't even know it! That really frustrates me. Is it inevitable that as I get bigger, I lose track of my customers? I don't think so. Somehow, I have to find out when regular customers aren't coming around. Had I known Tootsie had stopped shopping with us, I'd have called her to see what was going on. I need customers like her.

> "I've got all sorts of data in my sales database. It seems like the information I need is in there, but how do it get it out?"

> Mary needs database marketing.

Study Questions

Q1 What is a database marketing opportunity?

Q2 How does RFM analysis classify customers?

Q3 How does market-basket analysis identify cross-selling opportunities?

Q4 How do decision trees identify market segments?

Q2 How Does RFM Analysis Classify Customers?

RFM analysis is a way of analyzing and ranking customers according to their purchasing patterns.[1] It is a simple technique that considers how *recently* (R) a customer has ordered, how *frequently* (F) a customer orders, and how much *money* (M) the customer spends per order. We consider this technique here because it is a useful analysis that can be readily implemented.

To produce an RFM score, the program first sorts customer purchase records by the date of their most recent (R) purchase. In a common form of this analysis, the program then divides the customers into five groups and gives customers in each group a score of 1 to 5. Thus, the 20 percent of the customers having the most recent orders are given an **R score** of 1, the 20 percent of the customers having the next most recent orders are given an R score of 2, and so forth, down to the last 20 percent, who are given an R score of 5.

The program then re-sorts the customers on the basis of how frequently they order. The 20 percent of the customers who order most frequently are given an **F score** of 1, the next 20 percent of most frequently ordering customers are given a score of 2, and so forth, down to the least frequently ordering customers, who are given an F score of 5.

Finally, the program sorts the customers again according to the amount spent on their orders. The 20 percent who have ordered the most expensive items are given an **M score** of 1, the next 20 percent are given an M score of 2, and so forth, down to the 20 percent who spend the least, who are given an M score of 5.

Figure CE14-1 shows sample RFM data. The first customer, Ajax, has ordered recently and orders frequently. The company's M score of 3 indicates, however, that it does not order the most expensive goods. From these scores, the sales team members can surmise that Ajax is a good and regular customer but that they should attempt to up-sell more expensive goods to Ajax.

The second customer in Figure CE14-1 could be a problem. Bloominghams has not ordered in some time, but when it did order in the past, it ordered frequently, and its orders were of the highest monetary value. This data suggests that Bloominghams may have taken its business to another vendor. Someone from the sales team should contact this customer immediately.

No one on the sales team should be talking to the third customer, Caruthers. This company has not ordered for some time; it did not order frequently; and when it did order, it bought the least-expensive items, and not many of them. The sales team should not waste any time on this customer; if Caruthers goes to the competition, the loss would be minimal.

The last customer, Davidson, is right in the middle. Davidson is an OK customer, but probably no one in sales should spend much time with it. Perhaps sales can set up an automated contact system or use the Davidson account as a training exercise for an eager departmental assistant or intern.

A reporting system can generate the RFM data and deliver it in many ways. For example, a report of RFM scores for all customers can be pushed to the vice president of sales; reports with scores for particular regions can be pushed to regional sales managers; and reports of scores for particular accounts can be pushed to the account salespeople. All of this reporting can be automated.

Customer	RFM Score		
Ajax	1	1	3
Bloominghams	5	1	1
Caruthers	5	4	5
Davidson	3	3	3

Figure CE14-1
Example of RFM Score Data

[1] Arthur Middleton Hughes, "Boosting Response with RFM," *Marketing Tools*, May 1996. See also *www.dbmarketing.com*.

Q3 How Does Market-Basket Analysis Identify Cross-Selling Opportunities?

Suppose you run a dive shop, and one day, you realize that one of your salespeople is much better at up-selling to your customers. Any of your sales associates can fill a customer's order, but this one salesperson is especially good at selling customers items *in addition to* those for which they ask. One day, you ask him how he does it.

"It's simple," he says. "I just ask myself what is the next product they would want to buy. If someone buys a dive computer, I don't try to sell her fins. If she's buying a dive computer, she's already a diver and she already has fins. But, these dive computer displays are hard to read. A better mask makes it easier to read the display and get the full benefit from the dive computer."

A **market-basket analysis** is a data-mining technique for determining sales patterns. A market-basket analysis shows the products that customers tend to buy together. In marketing transactions, the fact that customers who buy product *X* also buy product *Y* creates a **cross-selling** opportunity. That is, "If they're buying *X*, sell them *Y*" or "If they're buying *Y*, sell them *X*."

Figure CE14-2 shows hypothetical sales data of 1,000 items at a dive shop. The first row of numbers under each column is the total number of times an item was sold. For example, the 270 in the first row of *Mask* means that 270 of the 1,000 items were masks. The 120 under *Dive Computer* means that 120 of the 1,000 purchased items were dive computers.

We can use the numbers in the first row to estimate the probability that a customer will purchase an item. Because 270 of the 1,000 items were masks, we can estimate the probability that a customer will buy a mask to be 270/1,000, or .27.

In market-basket terminology, **support** is the probability that two items will be purchased together. To estimate that probability, we examine sales transactions and count the number of times that two items occurred in the same transaction. For the data in Figure CE14-2, fins and masks appeared together 150 times, and thus the support for fins and a mask is 150/1,000, or .15. Similarly, the

1,000 Items	Mask	Tank	Fins	Weights	Dive Computer
	270	200	280	130	120
Mask	20	20	150	20	50
Tank	20	80	40	30	30
Fins	150	40	10	60	20
Weights	20	30	60	10	10
Dive computer	50	30	20	10	5
No additional product	10	—	—	—	5

Support = P (A & B)   Example: P (Fins & Mask) = 150/1,000 = .15

Confidence = P (A | B)   Example: P (Fins | Mask) = 150/270 = .5556

Lift = P (A | B)/P (A)   Example: P (Fins | Mask)/P (Fins) = .5556/.28 = 1.98

   Note: P(Mask | Fins)/P (Mask) = (150/280)/.27 = 1.98

Figure CE14-2
Market-Basket Example

support for fins and weights is 60/1,000, or .06, and the support for fins along with a second pair of fins is 10/1,000, or .01.

These data are interesting by themselves, but we can refine the analysis by taking another step and considering additional probabilities. For example, what proportion of the customers who bought a mask also bought fins? Masks were purchased 270 times, and of those individuals who bought masks, 150 also bought fins. Thus, given that a customer bought a mask, we can estimate the probability that he or she will buy fins to be 150/270, or .5556. In market-basket terminology such a conditional probability estimate is called the **confidence**.

Reflect on the meaning of this confidence value. The likelihood of someone walking in the door and buying fins is 280/1,000, or .28. But the likelihood of someone buying fins, given that he or she bought a mask, is .5556. Thus, if someone buys a mask, the likelihood that he or she will also buy fins almost doubles, from .28 to .5556. Thus, all sales personnel should be trained to try to sell fins to anyone buying a mask.

Now consider dive computers and fins. Of the 1,000 items sold, fins were sold 280 times, so the probability that someone walks into the store and buys fins is .28. But of the 120 purchases of dive computers, only 20 appeared with fins. So the likelihood of someone buying fins, given he or she bought a dive computer, is 20/120 or .1666. Thus, when someone buys a dive computer, the likelihood that she will also buy fins falls from .28 to .1666.

The ratio of confidence to the base probability of buying an item is called **lift**. Lift shows how much the base probability increases or decreases when other products are purchased. The lift of fins and a mask is the confidence of fins given a mask, divided by the base probability of fins. In Figure CE14-2, the lift of fins and a mask is .5556/.28, or 1.98. Thus, the likelihood that people buy fins when they buy a mask almost doubles. Surprisingly, it turns out that the lift of fins and a mask is the same as the lift of a mask and fins. Both are 1.98.

We need to be careful here, though, because this analysis only shows shopping carts with two items. We cannot say from this data what the likelihood is that customers, given that they bought a mask, will buy both weights and fins. To assess that probability, we need to analyze shopping carts with three items. This statement illustrates, once again, that we need to know what problem we're solving before we start to build the information system to mine the data. The problem definition will help us decide if we need to analyze three-item, four-item, or some other sized shopping cart.

Many organizations are benefiting from market-basket analysis today. You can expect that this technique will become a standard CRM analysis during your career.

By the way, one famous market-basket analysis shows a high correlation of the purchase of beer and diapers.[2] That correlation was strongest on Thursdays. Interviews indicated that customers were buying goods for the weekend, goods which included both beer and diapers.

Q4 How Do Decision Trees Identify Market Segments?

A **decision tree** is a hierarchical arrangement of criteria that predict a classification or a value. Here, we will consider decision trees that predict classifications. Decision-tree analyses are an unsupervised data-mining technique: The analyst

---

[2]Michael J. A. Berry and Gordon Linoff, *Data Mining Techniques for Marketing, Sales, and Customer Support* (New York: John Wiley, 1997).

sets up the computer program and provides the data to analyze, and the decision-tree program produces the tree.

A Decision Tree for Student Performance

The basic idea of a decision tree is to select attributes that are most useful for classifying entities on some criterion. Suppose, for example, that we want to classify students according to the grades they earn in the MIS class. To create a decision tree, we first gather data about grades and attributes of students in past classes.

We then input that data into the decision-tree program. The program analyzes all of the attributes and selects an attribute that creates the most disparate groups. The logic is that the more different the groups, the better the classification will be. For example, if every student who lived off campus earned a grade higher than 3.0 and if every student who lived on campus earned a grade lower than 3.0, then the program would use the variable *live-off-campus* or *live-on-campus* to classify students. In this unrealistic example, the program would be a perfect classifier, because each group is pure, with no misclassifications.

More realistically, consider Figure CE14-3, which shows a hypothetical decision-tree analysis of MIS class grades. Again, assume we are classifying students depending on whether their GPA was greater than 3.0 or less than or equal to 3.0.

The decision-tree tool that created this tree examined student's characteristics, such as their class (junior or senior), their major, their employment, their age, their club affiliations, and other student characteristics. It then used values of those characteristics to create groups that were as different as possible on the classification GPA above or below 3.0.

For the results shown here, the decision-tree program determined that the best first criterion is whether the students are juniors or seniors. In this

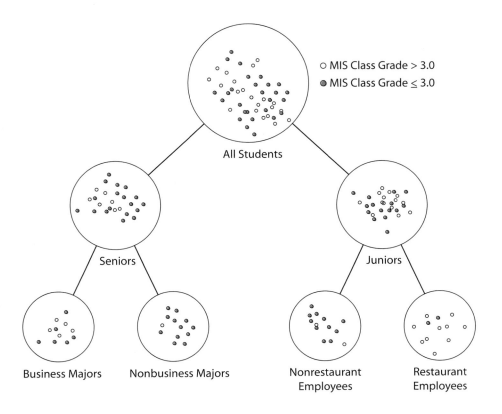

○ MIS Class Grade > 3.0
● MIS Class Grade ≤ 3.0

All Students

Seniors

Juniors

Business Majors

Nonbusiness Majors

Nonrestaurant Employees

Restaurant Employees

Figure CE14-3
GPAs of Students from Past MIS Class (Hypothetical Data)

case, the classification was imperfect, as shown by the fact that neither of the senior nor the junior groups consisted only of students with GPAs above or below 3.0. Still, it did create groups that were less mixed than in the *All Students* group.

Next, the program examined other criteria to further subdivide *Seniors* and *Juniors* so as to create even more pure groups. The program divided the senior group into subgroups: those who are business majors and those who are not. The program's analysis of the junior data, however, determined that the difference between majors is not significant. Instead, the best classifier (the one that generated the most different groups) is whether the junior worked in a restaurant.

Examining this data, we see that junior restaurant employees do well in the class, but junior nonrestaurant employees and senior nonbusiness majors do poorly. Performance in the other senior group is mixed. (Remember, these data are hypothetical.)

A decision tree like the one in Figure CE14-3 can be transformed into a set of decision rules having the format, **If . . . then**. Decision rules for this example are:

- If student is a junior and works in a restaurant, then predict grade ≥ 3.0.
- If student is a senior and is a nonbusiness major, then predict grade < 3.0.
- If student is a junior and does not work in a restaurant, then predict grade < 3.0.
- If student is a senior and is a business major, then make no prediction.[3]

As stated, decision-tree algorithms create groups that are as pure as possible, or stated otherwise, as different from each other as possible. The algorithms use several metrics for measuring difference among groups. Further explanation of those techniques is beyond the scope of this text. For now, just be sure to understand that maximum difference among groups is used as the criterion for constructing the decision tree.

There are many problems with classification schemes, especially schemes that classify people. The *Ethics Guide* on pages 489a–489b examines some of them.

Let's now apply the decision-tree technique to a business situation.

A Decision Tree for Loan Evaluation

A common business application of decision trees is to classify loans by likelihood of default. Organizations analyze data from past loans to produce a decision tree that can be converted to loan-decision rules. A financial institution could use such a tree to assess the default risk on a new loan. Sometimes, too, financial institutions sell a group of loans (called a loan portfolio) to one another. The results of a decision-tree program can be used to evaluate the risk in a given portfolio.

Figure CE14-4 shows an example provided by Insightful Corporation, a vendor of business intelligence tools. This example was generated using its Insightful Miner product. This tool examined data from 3,485 loans. Of those loans, 72 percent had no default and 28 percent did default. To perform the analysis, the decision-tree tool examined values of six different loan characteristics.

---

[3]Do not confuse these If/Then rules with those in expert systems. These rules are developed as a result of data-mining via decision-tree analysis. Typically, there are 10 or 12 such rules. Expert-systems rules are created by interviewing human experts. Typically, there are hundreds or even thousands of them.

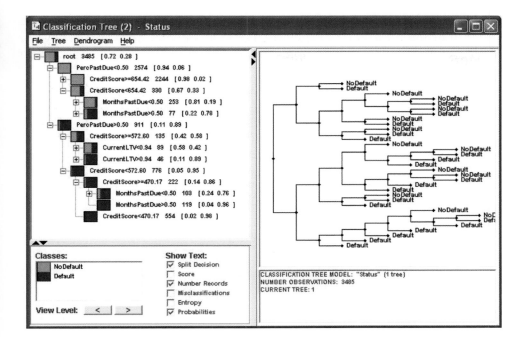

Figure CE14-4
Credit Score Decision Tree

Source: Used with permission of Insightful Corporation. Copyright © 1999–2005 Insightful Corporation. All Rights Reserved.

In this example, the decision-tree program determined that the percentage of the loan that is past due (*PercPastDue*) is the best first criterion. Reading Figure CE14-4, you can see that of the 2,574 loans with a *PercPastDue* value of .5 or less (more than half paid off), 94 percent were not in default. Hence, any loan that is more than half paid off has little risk of default.

Reading down several lines in this tree, 911 loans had a value of *PercPastDue* greater than .5; of those loans, 89 percent were in default.

These two major categories are then further subdivided into three classifications: *CreditScore* is a creditworthiness score obtained from a credit agency; *MonthsPastDue* is the number of months since a payment; and *CurrentLTV* is the current ratio of outstanding balance of the loan to the value of the loan's collateral.

With a decision tree like this, the financial institution can structure a marketing program for "instant approval" refinancing. For example, from Figure CE14-4, the bank can deduce the following rules:

- If the loan is more than half paid, then accept the loan.
- If the loan is less than half paid and
  - If *CreditScore* is greater than 572.6 and
    - If *CurrentLTV* is less than .94, then accept the loan.
- Otherwise, reject the loan.

These rules identify loans the bank will approve, and they also specify characteristics that identify a particular market segment. On the basis of this analysis, the bank can structure a marketing campaign to appeal to that segment.

We have shown here how decision trees can identify a market segment, but realize that they can be used for numerous other classification and prediction problems as well. They are easy to understand and—even better—easy to implement using decision rules. They also can work with many types of variables, and they deal well with missing values. Organizations can use decision trees by themselves or combine them with other techniques. In some cases, organizations use decision trees to select variables that are then used by other types of data-mining tools.

The Ethics of Classification

Classification is a useful human skill. Imagine walking into your favorite clothing store and seeing all of the clothes piled together on a center table. T-shirts, pants, and socks intermingle, with the sizes mixed up. Retail stores organized like this would not survive, nor would distributors or manufacturers who managed their inventories this way. Sorting and classifying are necessary, important, and essential activities. But those activities can also be dangerous.

Serious ethical issues arise when we classify people. What makes someone a good or bad "prospect"? If we're talking about classifying customers in order to prioritize our sales calls, then the ethical issue may not be too serious. What about classifying applicants for college? As long as there are more applicants than positions, some sort of classification and selection process must be done. But what kind?

Suppose a university collects data on the demographics and the performance of all of its students. The admissions committee then processes these data using a decision-tree data-mining program. Assume the analysis is conducted properly and the tool uses statistically valid measures to obtain statistically valid results. Thus, the following resulting decision tree accurately represents and explains variances found in the data; no human judgment (or prejudice) was involved.

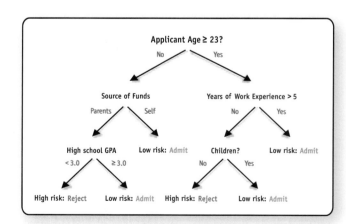

DISCUSSION QUESTIONS

1. Explain what conditions in the data could have caused this particular structure to emerge. For example, what conditions may have existed for self-funding students under the age of 23 to be classified as low risk? Explain how you think the three other branches in this tree may have come about.

2. Consider this tree from the standpoint of:

   a. A 23-year-old woman whose job experience is three years as a successful Wall Street financial analyst.

   b. A 28-year-old gay male with four years' job experience who has no children and pays his own college education.

   c. The university fund-raising committee that wants to raise money from parent donations.

   d. A student who was seriously ill while attending a top-notch high school but managed to graduate with a GPA of 2.9 by working independently on her classes from her hospital room.

3. Suppose you work in admissions and your university's public relations department asks you to meet with the local press for an article it is preparing regarding your admittance policy. How do you prepare for the press meeting?

4. Would your answer to question 3 change if you work at a private rather than public institution? Would it change if you work at a small liberal arts college rather than a large engineering-oriented university?

5. What conclusions do you make regarding the use of decision trees for categorizing student applicants?

6. What conclusions do you make regarding the use of decision trees for categorizing prospects in general?

Active ? Review

Use this Active Review to verify that you understand the material in the chapter extension. You can read the entire extension and then perform the tasks in this review, or you can read the material for just one question and perform the tasks in this review for that question before moving on to the next one.

Q1 What is a database marketing opportunity?

Define *database marketing*. Explain why the term is a misnomer. Give an example of the need for database marketing other than ones described in this chapter extension.

Q2 How does RFM analysis classify customers?

Explain the meaning of *R*, *F*, and *M scores*. Describe how each score is computed. State the action(s) that should be taken for customers having the following RFM scores: [1, 1, 3], [5, 4, 5], [2, 2, 2], [3, 1, 1], [1, 3, 1], and [1, 1, 1].

Q3 How does market-basket analysis identify cross-selling opportunities?

Define *cross-selling*. Define *support, confidence,* and *lift*. In Figure CE14-2, state the probability that someone walks into the store and buys fins. Compute the support for fins and a dive computer. Explain what it means if the value of lift is greater than 1. Explain what it means if the value of lift is less than 1. Compute the lift for fins and a dive computer.

Q4 How do decision trees identify market segments?

Define *decision tree*, and explain the basic idea of decision trees. For the hypothetical data in Figure CE14-3, state the grade you would predict for senior, nonbusiness students. State the grade you would predict for junior, restaurant employees. State the grade you would predict for senior, business majors. Explain how a decision tree was used to identify a desirable market segment for loan refinancing.

Key Terms and Concepts

Confidence 486	F score 484	Market-basket analysis 485
Cross-selling 485	If/then rule 488	R score 484
Database marketing 483	Lift 486	RFM analysis 484
Decision tree 486	M score 484	Support 485

Using Your Knowledge

1. Of the three database marketing techniques described in this chapter, which best solves the problem at Carbon Creek Gardens? Explain how Mary could have used that technique to identify Tootsie as a lost customer.

2. Describe a use for RFM analysis other than one discussed in this chapter extension. What business problem are you addressing? Assume a competitive strategy for the organization using your system. State that strategy and explain how the solution to your problem contributes to your organization's competitive strategy.

3. Describe an application for market-basket analysis other than for a dive shop. Explain how you would use the knowledge that two products have a lift

of 7. Explain how you would use the knowledge that two products have a lift of .003. Explain how you would use the knowledge that two products have a lift of 1.004.

4. Describe an application for decision-tree analysis for customer service and support at a computer vendor like Dell. Assume your decision-tree analysis considered customer name, company, number of employees at that company, job title, and number and type of computer systems purchased. How could you use the results of your analysis to classify the knowledge and experience of your customers? How could you use those results to structure the buying experience for each of those customers? What other uses can you think of for the results of this decision-tree analysis?

5. Read the Home Depot case on page 211. Explain how you could adapt the RFM analysis technique to classify models of washers and dryers. How would the RFM analysis help you quickly identify poorly selling products? Suppose you performed an RFM analysis for sales in each geographic region. Explain how you would use the results.

you be the Guide

Using the Ethics Guide: The Ethics of Classification (page 489a)

GOAL

* Explore difficult ethical issues about using decision trees for classifying people.

BACKGROUND AND PRESENTATION STRATEGIES

Classification, especially the classification of people, poses many ethical problems. But, organizations must classify; they must decide which students to admit, which people to promote, or which people to deny loans. *It has to be done.*

Decision trees are a classification scheme that analyzes data to create the most dissimilar groups. As such, it is *free of human bias.* The analysis is performed, and the data speak for themselves.

Thus, even though the results of such an analysis may be *unpopular,* such as the example in the guide, these results come directly from the data. The data are speaking for themselves. No subjective human judgment entered into this analysis, and the results *should be less biased* than when using human categorizers.

However, *not all decision trees are equally valid.* Like all statistics techniques, decision tree analyses vary in the degree of fit. Some data analyses have clear separation of groups—the criteria really do split the data. For others, the split is less clear, even murky. However, the analysis software will show the criteria, even if they are weak. Unless the analysts know to investigate standard errors, confidence intervals, and related measures, they will not be able to discriminate a strong classification scheme from a weak one. From the data presented, we have no idea of how strong this decision tree analysis was.

However, the results of a decision tree analysis may tend to reinforce negative social stereotypes and may be organizationally, legally, and socially infeasible.

? SUGGESTED RESPONSES FOR DISCUSSION QUESTIONS

1. This question has no correct answer. Often, the students' answers are fascinating. Sometimes, the students become angry, even though they know this is

an example, and I need to remind them that this is only an example.

2. None of these people will like this scheme. The people in a, b, and d would be furious. You might let students role-play and speak for each of them. By the way, what relevance is the sexual preference of the person in b? It will have been more difficult for him to have children by 28 than it would have been for a straight man. He might prevail in a discrimination suit against the university.

   The university fund-raising committee in c won't like this scheme because it is biased toward students who are paying their own way. There may be many students under age 23 with a high school GPA under 3.0 who have parents who would be pleased to donate, but not if their children aren't admitted.

3. Would anyone want that job? What will happen if the press finds out about the person in 2(d)? It will be a public relations nightmare.

   One teaching possibility: *Conduct a mock press interview in class.* Divide the students into two groups—one group of university admissions personnel who must defend this scheme and a second group of press reporters. Conduct the interview. If the class is large, bring three to five members of each group to the front of the class and conduct the interview in front of the class.

Cues for the University Personnel:

➤ **Our analysis is based on reliable data about the success of past students.**

➤ **We provided no human input to obtain these results. We are only responding to what the data tell us.**

➤ **We used the best, most up-to-date statistical techniques.**

➤ **We will review this policy each year and rerun our analysis when appropriate.**

Questions from the Press:

➤ **We hear you are operating a harsh and inhumane computer-based system for school admissions. Is this true?**

➤ **Are you actually turning away people because they were sick in high school?**

➤ **Please describe the scheme you use.**

➤ **We've heard of a discrimination suit from one of the rejected students. Does the system, in fact, discriminate against gay people?**

   Good luck!

4. Private institutions may have some leeway that public institutions don't. I doubt there would be much difference depending on the type of school. The students may have other opinions.

5. You might also ask:

   ➤ **Does the answer depend on the statistical strength of the results?**

   I think that any university using decision trees would at least have to (a) ensure their tree was defensible to the public, (b) provide human review to overrule the classification for exceptional situations, and (c) ensure the results are *statistically* valid.

6. Ensure that the results are statistically strong. Be sure that the results are publicly defensible. Consult corporate legal about the risk of antidiscriminatory practices and other legal risks.

WRAP UP

To wrap up, I say that many different opinions are possible with regard to the use of decision trees, but that each business professional should take the time to consider what his or her own opinions are. Here are some questions that help the students form their own opinions. The answers depend on each students' perspective and values.

➤ **Do individuals who are classified by an automated process have a right to know this is being done? For example, when applying for a loan, does the applicant have a right to know that the approval or rejection notification is made by an automated process and not by a human?**

➤ **Are decision tree classification schemes more appropriate for single events, such as a loan approval, than they are for life-changing events, such as college admissions?**

➤ **Can decision trees be used to advantage to eliminate situations that have substantial human bias?**

➤ **Should decision trees be used when they reinforce negative social stereotypes? Does it matter if the data strongly support the negative social stereotype?**

➤ **Can techniques like decision trees offer an organization an easy way to hide its social bias? What if the organization chooses to use analyses that have results that reinforce their biases, but ignore analyses the do not reinforce them? Isn't this just a smokescreen to hide behind?**

Chapter Extension 15

Chapter 9 provides the background for this Extension.

Reporting Systems and OLAP

Q1 How Do Reporting Systems Create Information?

The purpose of a **reporting system** is to create meaningful information from disparate data sources and to deliver that information to the proper user on a timely basis. Before we describe the components of a reporting system, first consider how reporting operations can be used to construct meaningful information.

Chapter 1 defined the difference between data and information. Data are recorded facts or figures; information is knowledge derived from data. Alternatively, information is data presented in a meaningful context. Reporting systems generate information from data as a result of four operations:

1. Filtering data
2. Sorting data
3. Grouping data
4. Making simple calculations on the data

Study Questions

Q1 How do reporting systems create information?

Q2 What are the components and characteristics of reporting systems?

Q3 How are reports authored, managed, and delivered?

Q4 How are OLAP reports dynamic?

To illustrate the use of these operations, consider Figure CE15-1 (page 494), which shows a portion of a file of raw data on the price of the NDX.X, an index fund of 100 stocks traded on the NASDAQ stock exchange. As shown, the data consist of the trading date, the opening price, the closing price, and the volume of shares traded. Figure CE15-1 is a simple list of data. As it stands, this list shows little information.

Information can be constructed from these data, however, by applying the four reporting operations listed earlier. Specifically, suppose you believe the up/down direction of the price on this index fund depends on the day of the week. To assess your belief, you create a report on the trading data for 2006. In your report, you *filter* the trading data to obtain data for trades in 2006. Then you *compute* the change in closing price from day to day. You then *group* the data by day of week, and finally, you *sort* the results according to the order of the days in the week.

Figure CE15-2 (page 494) shows the result of these operations. Indeed, in 2006, on average, NDX.X traded up on Monday, Tuesday, and Thursday, and

Figure CE15-1
Trade Data for NDX.X
(NASDAQ 100)

TDate	Open	Close	Volume
2006-08-27	1305.98	1318.93...	13497300.0
2006-08-26	1298.23	1309.05	13828600.0
2006-08-25	1302.5	1306.64...	11178400.0
2006-08-22	1338.19...	1304.54	17052000.0
2006-08-21	1309.56...	1314.65...	17224700.0
2006-08-20	1289.43...	1299.73	15067600.0
2006-08-19	1291.37...	1299.69...	17243900.0
2006-08-18	1258.18...	1284.80...	14763100.0
2006-08-15	1250.45	1253.63...	7039500.0
2006-08-14	1241.17...	1251.90...	13115700.0
2006-08-13	1247.55...	1240.37...	14492000.0
2006-08-12	1227.5	1240.7	13298400.0
2006-08-11	1209.35...	1223.14...	12037800.0
2006-08-08	1223.66...	1207.28	13363300.0
2006-08-07	1214.89...	1217.17...	16380400.0
2006-08-06	1221.99	1215.13...	18622700.0
2006-08-05	1263.79	1229.72	17433800.0
2006-08-04	1263.62...	1267.38...	15734100.0
2006-08-01	1274.61...	1264.33...	14840400.0
2006-07-31	1278.29	1276.94...	18584700.0
2006-07-30	1276.57...	1263.78	15137600.0
2006-07-29	1284.24	1275.17...	17038000.0
2006-07-28	1281.5	1280.53	15358200.0
2006-07-25	1252.62...	1278.30...	15879800.0

down on Wednesday and Friday.[1] To restate, Figure CE15-1 shows data; Figure CE15-2 shows information.

The construction of such reports is not particularly difficult. (Figure CE15-2 was generated using SQL, the database processing language you learned about in Chapter 5. Programmers can create reasonably complex data transformations using simple statements in this language.)

In the remainder of this section, we look at various aspects of reporting systems—including components and functions of these systems—and some examples.

Figure CE15-2
Report Based on Trade Data in
Figure CE15-1

Day of Week	2006 AverageChangeInClosePrice
Monday	3.77
Tuesday	4.41
Wednesday	−1.70
Thursday	5.71
Friday	−2.48

[1]Wait! Before you rush off to trade on this pattern, realize that this is just one year's data. This pattern did not hold in other years. Most analysts believe that day-of-week is a poor indicator of market direction. Although the report produces the information, the insight (and action) is up to the human interpreter of the information.

Q2 What Are the Components and Characteristics of Reporting Systems?

Figure CE15-3 shows the major components of a reporting system. Data from disparate data sources are read and combined, using filtering, sorting, grouping, and simple calculating, to produce information. Figure CE15-3 combines data from an Oracle database, a SQL Server database, and other nondatabase data. Some data are generated within the organization, other data are obtained from public sources, and still other data may be purchased from data utilities.

A reporting system maintains a database of reporting metadata. The metadata describe reports, users, groups, roles, events, and other entities involved in the reporting activity. The reporting system uses the metadata to prepare and deliver reports to the proper users on a timely basis.

As shown in Figure CE15-3, organizations can prepare reports in a variety of formats. Figure CE15-4 (page 496) lists report characteristics by type, media, and mode, which we discuss next.

Report Type

In terms of **report type**, reports can be *static* or *dynamic*. **Static reports** are prepared once from the underlying data, and they do not change. A report of past year's sales, for example, is a static report. Other reports are **dynamic**; at the time of creation, the reporting system reads the most current data and generates the report using that fresh data. A report on sales today and a report on current stock prices are both dynamic reports.

Query reports are prepared in response to data entered by users. Google provides a handy example of a query report: You enter the keywords you want to

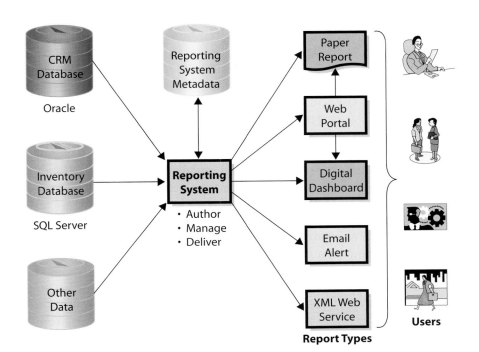

Figure CE15-3
Components of a Reporting System

Type	Media	Mode
Static	Paper and PDF file	Push
Dynamic	Computer screen via application	Pull
Query	Web site	
Online Analytical Processing (OLAP)	Digital dashboard	
	Alerts, via email or cell phone	
	Export to Excel, Quicken, TurboTax, QuickBooks, or other application	
	XML Web service	

search on, and the reporting system within Google searches its database and generates a response that is particular to your query. Within an organization, a query report could be generated to show current inventory levels. The user enters item numbers, and the reporting system responds with inventory levels of those items at various stores and warehouses.

Online analytical processing (OLAP) is a fourth type of report. OLAP reports allow the user to dynamically change the report grouping structures. An OLAP reporting application is illustrated later in this chapter extension.

Report Media

Today, reports are delivered via many different **report media** or channels. Some reports are printed on paper, and others are created in a format like PDF whereby they can be printed or viewed electronically. Other reports are delivered to computer screens. Applications for CRM and ERP systems, for example, include dozens of different reports that users view online. Additionally, companies sometimes place reports on internal corporate Web sites for employees to access. For example, an organization might place a report of its latest sales on the sales department's Web site or a report on customers serviced on the customer service department's Web site.

Another report medium is a **digital dashboard**, which is an electronic display that is customized for a particular user. Vendors like Yahoo! and MSN provide common examples. Users of these services can define content they want—say, a local weather forecast, a list of stock prices, or a list of news sources—and the vendor constructs the display customized for each user. Figure CE15-5 shows an example.

Other dashboards are particular to an organization. Executives at a manufacturing organization, for example, might have a dashboard that shows up-to-the-minute production and sales activities.

Alerts are another form of report. Users can declare that they wish to receive notification of events, say, via email or on their cell phones. Of course, some cell phones are capable of displaying Web pages, and digital dashboards can be delivered to them as well.

Some reports are exported from the report generator to another program such as Excel, Quicken, QuickBooks, and so forth. For example, application programs at many banks can export customer checking account transactions into Excel, Quicken, or Money.

Figure CE15-5
Digital Dashboard Example

Finally, reports can be published via a Web service. The Web service produces the report in response to requests from the service-consuming application, as discussed in Chapter Extension 13. This style of reporting is particularly useful for interorganizational information systems like supply chain management.

Report Mode

The final report characteristic in Figure CE15-4 is the **report mode**. Organizations send a **push report** to users according to a preset schedule. Users receive the report without any activity on their part. In contrast, users must request a **pull report**. To obtain a pull report, a user goes to a Web portal or digital dashboard and clicks a link or button to cause the reporting system to produce and deliver the report.

Q3 How Are Reports Authored, Managed, and Delivered?

In the middle of Figure CE15-3, under the drawing of the reporting system, three functions of a reporting system are listed: author, manage, and deliver. Consider each.

Report Authoring

Authoring a report involves connecting to data sources, creating the report structure, and formatting the report. Figures CE15-6 and CE15-7 (page 498) show the use of a Microsoft developer tool called VisualStudio.Net for authoring a report. In Figure CE15-6, the developer has already specified a database that contains the NASDAQ trading data and has just entered a SQL statement, shown in the lower-center portion of this display, to generate this report.

In Figure CE15-7, the report author is creating the format of the report by specifying the headings and format of the data items. In a more complicated report, the author would specify sorting and grouping of data items, as well as page headers and footers. The developer sets values for item properties using the property list in the right-hand side of the display in Figure CE15-7.

Figure CE15-6
Connecting to a Report Data
Source Using VisualStudio.Net

Source: Microsoft product screen shot reprinted with
permission from Microsoft Corporation.

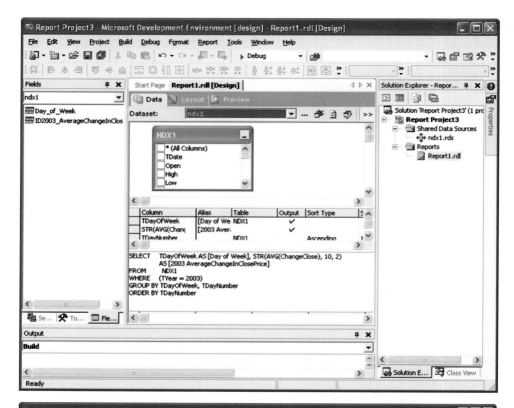

Figure CE15-7
Formatting a Report Using
VisualStudio.Net

Source: Microsoft product screen shot reprinted with
permission from Microsoft Corporation.

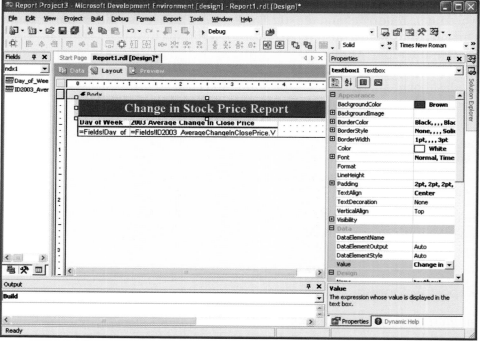

Report Management

The purpose of *report management* is to define who receives what reports, when, and by what means. Most report-management systems allow the report administrator to define user accounts and user groups and to assign particular users to particular groups. For example, all of the salespeople would be assigned to the sales group, all of the executives assigned to the executive group, and so forth. All of these data are stored in the reporting system's metadata shown in Figure CE15-3 (page 495).

Reports that have been created using the report-authoring system are assigned to groups and users. Assigning reports to groups saves the administrator work: When a report is created, changed, or removed, the administrator need only change the report assignments to the group. All of the users in the group will inherit the changes.

As stated, the report-management metadata indicate which format of this report is to be sent to which user. The metadata also indicate what channel is to be used and whether the report is to be pushed or pulled. If the report is to be pushed, the administrator declares whether the report is to be generated on a regular schedule or as an alert.

Report Delivery

The *report-delivery* function of a reporting system pushes reports or allows them to be pulled according to report-management metadata. Reports can be delivered via an email server, via a Web site, via XML Web services, or by other program-specific means. The report-delivery system uses the operating system and other program security components to ensure that only authorized users receive authorized reports. It also ensures that push reports are produced at appropriate times.

For query reports, the report-delivery system serves as an intermediary between the user and the report generator. It receives user query data, such as the item numbers in an inventory query, passes the query data to the report generator, receives the resulting report, and delivers the report to the user.

For a discussion of security issues relating to reporting systems, see the *Guide* on pages 499a–499b.

Q4 How Are OLAP Reports Dynamic?

Online analytical processing (OLAP) provides the ability to sum, count, average, and perform other simple arithmetic operations on groups of data. The remarkable characteristic of OLAP reports is that their format is dynamic. The viewer of the report can change the report's structure—hence the term *online*.

An OLAP report has measures and dimensions. A **measure** is the data item of interest. It is the item that is to be summed or averaged or otherwise processed in the OLAP report. Total sales, average sales, and average cost are examples of measures. A **dimension** is a characteristic of a measure. Purchase date, customer type, customer location, and sales region are all examples of dimensions.

Figure CE15-8 shows a typical OLAP report. Here, the measure is *Store Sales Net*, and the dimensions are *Product Family* and *Store Type*. This report shows how net store sales vary by product family and store type. Stores of type *Supermarket*, for example, sold a net of $36,189 worth of nonconsumable goods.

Figure CE15-8
OLAP Product Family by Store Type

	A	B	C	D	E	F	G
1							
2							
3	Store Sales Net	Store Type ▼					
4	Product Family ▼	Deluxe Supermarket	Gourmet Supermarket	Mid-Size Grocery	Small Grocery	Supermarket	Grand Total
5	Drink	$8,119.05	$2,392.83	$1,409.50	$685.89	$16,751.71	$29,358.98
6	Food	$70,276.11	$20,026.18	$10,392.19	$6,109.72	$138,960.67	$245,764.87
7	Nonconsumable	$18,884.24	$5,064.79	$2,813.73	$1,534.90	$36,189.40	$64,487.05
8	Grand Total	$97,279.40	$27,483.80	$14,615.42	$8,330.51	$191,901.77	$339,610.90

Semantic Security

Security is a very difficult problem—and it gets worse every year. Not only do we have cheaper, faster computers (remember Moore's Law). We also have more data; more systems for reporting and querying that data; and easier, faster, and broader communication. All of these combine to increase the chances that we inadvertently divulge private or proprietary information.

Physical security is hard enough: How do we know that the person (or program) that signs on as Megan Cho really is Megan Cho? We use passwords, but files of passwords can be stolen. Setting that issue aside, we need to know that Megan Cho's permissions are set appropriately. Suppose Megan works in the HR department, so she has access to personal and private data of other employees. We need to design the reporting system so that Megan can access all of the data she needs to do her job, and no more.

Also, the report-delivery system must be secure. A reporting server is an obvious and juicy target for any would-be intruder. Someone can break in and change access permissions. Or a hacker could pose as someone else to obtain reports. Reporting servers help the authorized user, resulting in faster access to more information. But without proper security, reporting

servers also ease the intrusion task for unauthorized users.

All of these issues relate to physical security. Another dimension to security is equally serious and far more problematic: semantic security. **Semantic security** concerns the unintended release of protected information through the release of a combination of reports or documents that are independently not protected.

Take an example from class. Suppose I assign a group project, and I post a list of groups and the names of students assigned to each group. Later, after the assignments have been completed and graded, I post a list of grades on the Web site. Because of university privacy policy, I cannot post the grades by student name or identifier; so instead, I post the grades for each group. If you want to get the grades for each student, all you have to do is combine the list from Lecture 5 with the list from Lecture 10. You might say that the release of grades in this example does no real harm—after all, it is a list of grades from one assignment.

But go back to Megan Cho in HR. Suppose Megan evaluates the employee compensation program. The COO believes that salary offers have been inconsistent over time and that they vary too widely by department. Accordingly, the COO authorizes Megan to receive a report that lists *SalaryOfferAmount* and *OfferDate*, and a second report that lists *Department* and *AverageSalary*.

Those reports are relevant to Cho's task and seem innocuous enough. But Megan realizes that she could use the information they contain to determine individual salaries—information she does not have and is not authorized to receive. She proceeds as follows.

Like all employees, Megan has access to the employee directory on the Web portal. Using the directory, she can obtain a list of employees in each department, and using the facilities of her ever-so-helpful report-authoring system, she combines that list with the department and average-salary report. Now she has a list of the names of employees in a group and the average salary for that group.

Megan's employer likes to welcome new employees to the company. Accordingly, each week, the company publishes an article about new employees who have been hired. The article makes pleasant comments about each person and encourages employees to meet and greet them.

Megan, however, has other ideas. Because the report is published on the Web portal, she can obtain an electronic copy of it. It's an Acrobat report, and using Acrobat's handy Search feature, she soon has a list of employees and the week they were hired.

She now examines the report she received for her study, the one that has *SalaryOfferAmount* and the offer date, and she does some interpretation. During the week of July 21, three offers were extended: one for $35,000, one for $53,000, and one for $110,000. She also notices from the "New Employees" report that a director of marketing programs, a product test engineer, and a receptionist were hired that same week. It's unlikely that they paid the receptionist $110,000; that sounds more like the director of marketing programs. So she now "knows" (infers) that person's salary.

Next, going back to the department report and using the employee directory, she sees that the marketing director is in the marketing programs department. There are just three people in that department, and their average salary is $105,000. Doing the arithmetic, she now knows that the average salary for the other two people is $102,500. If she can find the hire week for one of those other two people, she can find

out both the second and third person's salaries.

You get the idea. Megan was given just two reports to do her job. Yet she combined the information in those reports with publicly available information and is able to deduce salaries, for at least some employees. These salaries are much more than she is supposed to know. This is a semantic security problem.

DISCUSSION QUESTIONS

1. In your own words, explain the difference between physical security and semantic security.

2. Why do reporting systems increase the risk of semantic security problems?

3. What can an organization do to protect itself against accidental losses due to semantic security problems?

4. What legal responsibility does an organization have to protect against semantic security problems?

5. Suppose semantic security problems are inevitable. Do you see an opportunity for new products from insurance companies? If so, describe such an insurance product. If not, explain why not.

Store Sales Net								
			Store Type ▸					
Product Family ▸	Store ▸	Store State ▸	Deluxe Supermarket	Gourmet Supermarket	Mid-Size Grocery	Small Grocery	Supermarket	Grand Total
Drink	USA	CA		$2,392.83		$227.38	$5,920.76	$8,540.97
		OR	$4,438.49				$2,862.45	$7,300.94
		WA	$3,680.56		$1,409.50	$458.51	$7,968.50	$13,517.07
	USA Total		$8,119.05	$2,392.83	$1,409.50	$685.89	$16,751.71	$29,358.98
Drink Total			$8,119.05	$2,392.83	$1,409.50	$685.89	$16,751.71	$29,358.98
Food	USA	CA		$20,026.18		$1,960.53	$47,226.11	$69,212.82
		OR	$37,778.35				$23,818.87	$61,597.22
		WA	$32,497.76		$10,392.19	$4,149.19	$67,915.69	$114,954.83
	USA Total		$70,276.11	$20,026.18	$10,392.19	$6,109.72	$138,960.67	$245,764.87
Food Total			$70,276.11	$20,026.18	$10,392.19	$6,109.72	$138,960.67	$245,764.87
Nonconsumable	USA	CA		$5,064.79		$474.35	$12,344.49	$17,883.63
		OR	$10,177.89				$6,428.53	$16,606.41
		WA	$8,706.36		$2,813.73	$1,060.54	$17,416.38	$29,997.01
	USA Total		$18,884.24	$5,064.79	$2,813.73	$1,534.90	$36,189.40	$64,487.05
Nonconsumable Total			$18,884.24	$5,064.79	$2,813.73	$1,534.90	$36,189.40	$64,487.05
Grand Total			$97,279.40	$27,483.80	$14,615.42	$8,330.51	$191,901.77	$339,610.90

Figure CE15-9

OLAP Product Family and Store Location by Store Type

A presentation of a measure with associated dimensions like that in Figure CE15-8 is often called an **OLAP cube**, or sometimes simply a *cube*. The reason for this term is that some products show these displays using three axes, like a cube in geometry. The origin of the term is unimportant here, however. Just know that an *OLAP cube* and an *OLAP report* are the same thing.

The OLAP report in Figure CE15-8 was generated by SQL Server Analysis Services and is displayed in an Excel pivot table. The data were taken from a sample instructional database, called Food Mart, that is provided with SQL Server. It is possible to display OLAP cubes in many ways besides with Excel. Some third-party vendors provide more extensive graphical displays. For more information about such products, check for OLAP vendors and products at the Data Warehousing Review at *www.dwreview.com/OLAP/ index.html*. Note, too, that OLAP reports can be delivered just like any of the other reports described for report management systems.

As stated earlier, the distinguishing characteristic of an OLAP report is that the user can alter the format of the report. Figure CE15-9 (page 500) shows such an alteration. Here, the user added another dimension, *store country and state*, to the horizontal display. Product-family sales are now broken out by the location of the stores. Observe that the sample data include only stores in the United States and only in the western states of California, Oregon, and Washington.

With an OLAP report, it is possible to **drill down** into the data. This term means to further divide the data into more detail. In Figure CE15-10 (page 502), for example, the user has drilled down into the stores located in California; the OLAP report now shows sales data for the four cities in California that have stores.

Notice another difference between Figures CE15-9 and CE15-10. The user has not only drilled down, but she has also changed the order of the dimensions. Figure CE15-9 shows *Product Family* and then store location within *Product Family*. Figure CE15-10 shows store location and then *Product Family* within store location.

Both displays are valid and useful, depending on the user's perspective. A product manager might like to see product families first and then store location data. A sales manager might like to see store locations first and then product data. OLAP reports provide both perspectives, and the user can switch between them while viewing the report.

Unfortunately, all of this flexibility comes at a cost. If the database is large, doing the necessary calculating, grouping, and sorting for such dynamic displays will require substantial computing power. Although standard, commercial DBMS products do have the features and functions required to create OLAP reports, they are not designed for such work. They are designed, instead, to provide rapid response to transaction processing applications such as order entry or manufacturing operations.

Accordingly, special-purpose products called **OLAP servers** have been developed to perform OLAP analysis. As shown in Figure CE15-11 (page 503), an OLAP server reads data from an operational database, performs preliminary calculations, and stores the results of those calculations in an OLAP database. Several different schemes are used for this storage, but the particulars of those schemes are beyond this discussion. (Databases that are structured to support OLAP processing are called **dimensional databases**.) Normally, for performance and security reasons, the OLAP server and the DBMS run on separate computers.

MIS in Use CE15 (page 503) discusses the successful implementation of OLAP to improve the productivity of business intelligence analysts.

					Store Type ▼				
Store Sales Net									
Store Country ▼	Store Sta ▼	Store City	Product Family ▼	Deluxe Super	Gourmet Supermarket	Mid-Size Grocery	Small Grocery	Supermarket	Grand Total
USA	CA	Beverly Hills	Drink		$2,392.83				$2,392.83
			Food		$20,026.18				$20,026.18
			Nonconsumable		$5,064.79				$5,064.79
		Beverly Hills Total			$27,483.80				$27,483.80
		Los Angeles	Drink					$2,870.33	$2,870.33
			Food					$23,598.28	$23,598.28
			Nonconsumable					$6,305.14	$6,305.14
		Los Angeles Total						$32,773.74	$32,773.74
		San Diego	Drink					$3,050.43	$3,050.43
			Food					$23,627.83	$23,627.83
			Nonconsumable					$6,039.34	$6,039.34
		San Diego Total						$32,717.61	$32,717.61
		San Francisco	Drink				$227.38		$227.38
			Food				$1,960.53		$1,960.53
			Nonconsumable				$474.35		$474.35
		San Francisco Total					$2,662.26		$2,662.26
	CA Total				$27,483.80		$2,662.26	$65,491.35	$95,637.41
	OR		Drink	$4,438.49				$2,862.45	$7,300.94
			Food	$37,778.35				$23,818.87	$61,597.22
			Nonconsumable	$10,177.89				$6,428.53	$16,606.41
	OR Total			$52,394.72				$33,109.85	$85,504.57
	WA		Drink	$3,680.56		$1,409.50	$458.51	$7,968.50	$13,517.07
			Food	$32,497.76		$10,392.19	$4,149.19	$67,915.69	$114,954.83
			Nonconsumable	$8,706.36		$2,813.73	$1,060.54	$17,416.38	$29,997.01
	WA Total			$44,884.68		$14,615.42	$5,668.24	$93,300.57	$158,468.91
USA Total				$97,279.40	$27,483.80	$14,615.42	$8,330.51	$191,901.77	$339,610.90
Grand Total				$97,279.40	$27,483.80	$14,615.42	$8,330.51	$191,901.77	$339,610.90

Figure CE15-10

OLAP Product Family and Store Location by Store Type

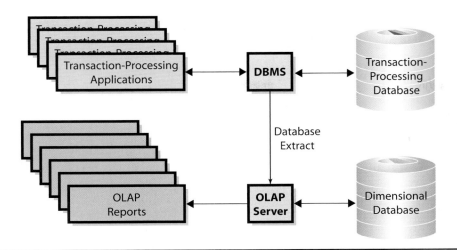

Figure CE15-11
Role of OLAP Server and Dimensional Database

CE15

Business Intelligence at Avnet, Inc.

In 2004, Avnet, Inc., generated over $10 billion in revenue by selling a wide array of electronics products and services to more than 100,000 companies in 68 countries. Avnet, based in Phoenix, Arizona, operates several divisions and sells many product lines. It operates as a wholesale distributor of electronic components, and it adapts some of those components to the needs of large enterprises. It also creates, markets, and sells special-purpose embedded computing systems. Given its size and breadth, Avnet is a key player in the electronics supply chain.

Avnet accelerated its growth by acquiring more than 30 different companies over the past 10 years. As a result, according to Steve Slatzer, Avnet's director of strategic finance, "We had growing pains." Integrating the disparate information systems of these acquired companies while supporting strong growth in sales transactions caused accounting and financial reporting nightmares.

Between 1997 and 2001, Avnet had developed OLAP applications that enabled financial man-

agers to drill down into the financial data, depending on their unique requirements. Unfortunately, as the company grew, the OLAP applications slowed considerably. Updates to the structure of the OLAP cubes required so much time that the OLAP-based financial reporting application was unreliable.

To respond to these challenges, the company decided to redesign its business intelligence systems. Because some divisions of Avnet were using SAP for operational processing, the company decided to acquire the add-on SAP product called Business Information Warehouse (SAP BW). SAP BW not only provided better OLAP performance and reliability, but also eased the data integration task.

Today, Avnet has used SAP BW to integrate not only the SAP data sources but also data from the non-SAP legacy systems used by companies Avnet acquired. According to Slatzer,

> Now that we can pull information from all our data sources into one place, we can create a very rich reporting environment. It lets users drill down to all kinds of underlying detail—detail that wouldn't have been visible with the old system . . . For example, they can drill from the general ledger into the fixed-asset system, in order to see what fixed assets are currently assigned to a particular location.

With the new system, users do not need to switch back and forth between different information systems with different user interfaces, become familiar with different data presentations, or worry about getting data from one system to another. Instead, they can focus their efforts on analyzing results, which is both what they are paid to do and also what they want to do.

Sources: www.avnet.com (accessed January 2005); www.sap.com (accessed January 2005).

Active ? Review

Use this Active Review to verify that you understand the material in the chapter extension. You can read the entire extension and then perform the tasks in this review, or you can read the material for just one question and perform the tasks in this review for that question before moving on to the next one.

Q1 How do reporting systems create information?

Describe the purpose of a reporting system. Give two definitions of *information*. Name four basic reporting operations. Using Figures CE15-1 and CE15-2, explain the difference between data and information.

Q2 What are the components and characteristics of reporting systems?

Describe the role of each of the components in Figure CE15-3. Explain what reporting metadata describes. Name four types of report and give an example of each. Name seven different report media. Explain the difference between push and pull reports.

Q3 How are reports authored, managed, and delivered?

Name the three functions of report authoring. Explain the purpose of report management. Describe the role of metadata for report management. Describe the report-delivery function. Explain the role of report delivery for security and for query reports.

Q4 How are OLAP reports dynamic?

Describe the basic operation of an OLAP report. Define *measure*, and give an example. Define *dimension*, and give at least two examples. Using hypothetical data and using Figure CE15-8 as a guide, show how your measure and dimensions would appear in an OLAP report. Show how the structure of the report changes if you switch the two dimensions. Using your sample data, explain why OLAP reports are considered more dynamic than standard reports. Describe the circumstances under which an OLAP server is required.

Key Terms and Concepts

Alert 496
Digital dashboard 496
Dimension 499
Dimensional database 501
Drill down 501
Dynamic report 495
Measure 499

Online analytical processing (OLAP) 499
OLAP cube 501
OLAP server 501
Pull report 497
Push report 497
Query report 495

Report media 496
Report mode 497
Report type 495
Reporting system 493
Semantic security 499a
Static report 495

Using Your Knowledge

1. Suppose you manage a production line at DSI, and at the end of each month, you would like information about the people who have worked for you and the number of hours they have spent on a project (like a particular airplane interior) and on a task with a project (such as install forward bulkhead). Using Figure CE15-4 as a guide, describe the type, media, and mode of the report you want.

2. Same question as question 1 except assume that you want to be able to obtain the report at any time, not just at the end of the month, and that you want to specify the reporting period for the report.

3. Read the Home Depot case on page 211. Explain how you could use OLAP to understand sales trends. Assume you have the same data as indicated in that case (total sales data for each brand and model, for each store, for each month, and store city and state). What measure(s) would be appropriate? What dimensions would be appropriate? Sketch the structure of two different OLAP views of this data. Use hypothetical data. Does this report help you with the problem of identifying losing models? Why or why not? As a buyer, what is the chief value of this report to you?

4. Dee Clark, the marketing manager at Emerson Pharmaceuticals, wants to place an OLAP report on her blog. Assume each salesperson reports to a district manager, each district manager reports to one of seven regional managers, and the regional managers report to the vice president of sales. Further assume that Emerson reports the total sales for each product family for each salesperson for each month.
   a. Define the measure and dimensions of an OLAP cube for this situation.
   b. Using hypothetical data, show how the cube would appear if the dimensions are organized by Region, Territory, and Product Family, in that order.
   c. Using hypothetical data, show how the cube would appear if the dimensions are organized by Product Family, Region, and Territory, in that order.
   d. Under what conditions would a salesperson (who is accessing this report on Dee's blog) be interested in the display in question b?
   e. Under what conditions would a salesperson be interested in the display in question c?
   f. Would it be important for Dee to disallow reporting the sales by salesperson? Explain your answer.

Chapter Extension 15

be the Guide

Using the Guide: Semantic Security (page 499a)

GOALS

* Discuss the trade-off between information availability and security.

* Introduce, explain, and discuss ways to respond to *semantic security*.

BACKGROUND AND PRESENTATION STRATEGIES

This guide briefly discusses physical security and mentions some of its problems, especially authorization. We will address authorization in Chapter 12, thus here I recommended focusing on the second theme: *semantic security*.

Semantic security is the "unintended release of protected information through the release of a combination of reports or documents that individually do not contain protected information."

In this guide, Megan was able to combine data in reports that she receives for her job with data in a combination of public documents to infer at least one employee's salary, and possibly several others. She is not supposed to have this information. The fact that both the new-employee report and the employee newsletter were *delivered electronically* greatly simplified her task. This fact enabled her to readily search those documents.

In truth, this problem has existed for as long as records have been kept. It is becoming a larger factor today because more reports are being produced, and those reports are being produced *in readily searchable form.* Thus, more data can be searched faster.

The critical question is: *What can be done about it?* Who has the time to consider every possible inference from combinations of every available document? Who has the ability to make every possible inference? No one.

We consider those issues in the following questions.

SUGGESTED RESPONSES FOR DISCUSSION QUESTIONS

1. *Physical security* ensures that only authorized users can take authorized actions at appropriate times.

Semantic security concerns information that is inadvertently released via a combination of information that is obtained via authorized methods. Questions to ask:

➤ **Did Megan break into any security system?**

(No.)

➤ **Did Megan violate any corporate policy?**

(No.)

➤ **Was she able to obtain, through her efforts, information she was not authorized to have?**

(Yes.)

2. Reporting systems increase the risk because they deliver information in formats that are readily searched electronically.

➤ **Should (or even can) anything be done to make electronic documents not searchable?**

(No.)

➤ **So, do we stop producing electronic reports?**

(Obviously not, but this leads to question 3.)

3. This is a tough question to answer. Organizations need to understand that combinations of documents can give away sensitive data. With that awareness, managers need to manage with the expectation that some confidential data will ultimately be released. We just don't know what or when.

➤ **Is there a way for organizations to eliminate this possibility?**

It is difficult to imagine that there is a way. Even investigating the possibilities would be incredibly expensive.

➤ **How would you know if you found all the possibilities?**

➤ **If you know your organization is subject to a threat, what can you do?**

One answer: While hoping that confidential data stays that way, manage as if it won't. See the Wrap Up discussion. Also, the next two questions provide some guidance.

4. Organizations have a responsibility to comply with privacy law. Federal organizations must comply with the Privacy Act of 1974. Medical offices must comply with HIPAA. The Gramm-Leach-Bliley (GLB) Act requires financial institutions to protect their clients' data. (See the "Ethics Guide" in Chapter Extension 22, page 581a, for more information.)

Most of these laws require basic accounting controls for security. They do not address semantic security. However, I believe lawyers will require corporations to take reasonable and prudent steps to avoid obvious semantic security problems.

5. Most business insurance policies contain clauses that cover some liability for semantic security lapses. There might be an opportunity for a new type of policy that addresses such risks. It seems doubtful, but for enough money you can get someone to insure anything. These are good questions for students to ask their insurance-course professor.

WRAP UP

It is not possible to protect against all semantic security problems. Too much information is published, and the world is full of clever, curious people.

➤ **Given this fact, what can we do?**

Where possible, *design business programs for transparency*. Insofar as possible, design business programs *assuming sensitive data will become known*.

In the encryption discipline, it has long been recognized that any security technique that relies on a secret algorithm will *eventually be breached*. The technique must assume that the algorithm is in the public domain; secrecy is provided by the keys that are used with the technique.

Another point relates to salaries, a sensitive topic for most people:

➤ **Suppose you manage a department in which salaries are to be kept confidential. Are they?**

➤ **Knowing that salaries may not always be confidential, what do you do if there's a serious salary imbalance in your department?**

You can hope it never becomes public; you can try to correct it by raising someone's salary; you can prepare yourself for the lower-paid employee to come angrily in your door some day. There's no way around it, you're exposed to a risk.

For a second example, if it is important that the number of employees and the revenue of a given division remain confidential, then do all you can to keep that data confidential. But, expect that reporters, business analysts, stock pickers, and many others will be able to infer that data. *Do not construct a business plan that relies on such secrecy*. Someone will find a way to discover the information.

Chapter Extension 16

Chapter 9 provides the background for this Extension.

Information Systems and Counterterrorism

Q1 What Is the Goal of Counterterrorism Intelligence?

In broad terms, the goal of **counterterrorism intelligence** is to produce information that can be used to prevent terrorist attacks. But how is this to be done? What information is useful and potentially obtainable?

Figure CE16-1 shows stages in the terrorism process. Most counterterrorism professionals believe that it is quite difficult to prevent events by focusing solely on the operational phase of this process. Absent other information, law enforcement is unlikely to catch a terrorist stepping on the bus with a bomb.

Instead, counterterrorism intelligence focuses on the entire process. It seeks evidence of recruiting, training, planning, and then operations (deployment). There is a terrorist supply chain. The goal of counterterrorism intelligence is to discover evidence of that supply chain sufficient to allow preemptive action against its components.

Q2 How Does Synthesis Produce Information?

Chapter 1 defined *information* in several ways. Two of those definitions are: (1) Information is data presented in a meaningful context; and (2) information is a difference that makes a difference. Much of the time, we produce information via **analysis**, which simply means to break something up into its constituent parts. For example, in a study of employee salaries, we might divide the organization into departments and compute the average salary per department. Or we might group the employees according to skill code and compute the average for

Study Questions

Q1 What is the goal of counterterrorism intelligence?

Q2 How does synthesis produce information?

Q3 What are the characteristics of counterterrorism intelligence decision making?

Q4 How do information systems facilitate intelligence collaboration?

Q5 How do data connections synthesize?

Q6 How is data mining used in counterterrorism intelligence?

Q7 What are the social and legal implications of counterterrorism intelligence?

Figure CE16-1
Stages in the Terrorism Process

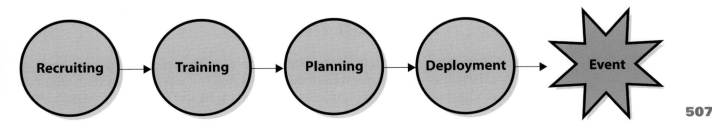

Figure CE16-2
Synthesis Produces Information

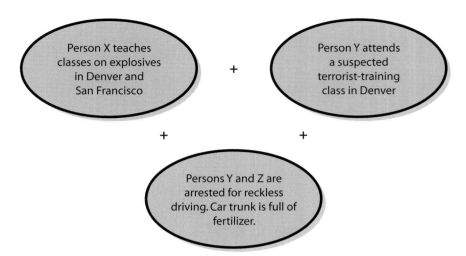

each group. In either example, we are producing data in a meaningful context (the average salary per department or skill code), or we are seeking a difference that makes a difference (average salaries that are out of line with each other).

While it is less common in business, we can also produce information via **synthesis**, which means to construct a larger entity out of its constituent parts. Chemists talk of synthesizing compounds by combining elements or smaller compounds. In information systems, we can talk of synthesizing information by combining data.

In counterterrorism intelligence, most information is produced via synthesis. Consider Figure CE16-2. Each of the three ovals contains the report of an isolated event. By themselves, they contain little information. However, if we bring all three statements together—if we *synthesize* them—we construct a pattern that contains information. The fertilizer in the truck becomes far more important both if we know that the driver, Person Y, attended a terrorism class in Denver and if we know that Denver is the site at which classes on explosives have been taught.

Before continuing, note that all data in this chapter extension are hypothetical. None of the events described here are known to have occurred. Furthermore, the data models presented in this chapter extension are hypothetical as well.

By synthesizing these facts into a pattern, we create information: We present data in a meaningful context, or we find a difference (the fertilizer) that makes a difference (the background of the driver).

Synthesis is the primary operation in the construction of counterterrorism intelligence. It is so important that, for the purpose of producing intelligence, relationships are often more important than facts. Knowing how Person X relates to Person Y and how Person Y relates to Person Z can be far more important than knowing any of their phone numbers or their eye colors.

Q3 What Are the Characteristics of Counterterrorism Intelligence Decision Making?

As discussed in Chapter Extension 2, decision processes can be structured or unstructured. A **structured decision process** follows a known path that can readily be documented. An example of a structured decision is: "Which ship-

> • **Structured decision:**
>   Process follows a known path that can readily be documented. Example: "Which shipper should we use for this order?"
> • **Unstructured decision:**
>   Process evolves step-by-step. Often don't know next step until you observe result of current step. Example: "How can we fix the gas turbine?"

Figure CE16-3
Decision Processes

per should we use for this order?" We can write a procedure for making that decision. The procedure might consider the weight of the package, how perishable the contents are, where the customer is located, and the day of the week. Whatever the procedure is, it is known and can be documented ahead of time.

An **unstructured decision process** evolves as each step in the decision process is taken. Often, the complete process is known only *after* the final decision has been made. For example, suppose a gas turbine fails for an unknown reason. The repair team proceeds step-by-step until the problem source is discovered. Once we have determined the cause, we can explain how we reached that decision. Had someone asked us ahead of time how we would make that determination (decision), we would have been unable to give an accurate description. Figure CE16-3 summarizes these differences.

As explained in question Q2 of this chapter extension, the information that informs a decision can be created by analysis or by synthesis, called **decision modes** in Figure CE16-4. The top part of that figure shows *analysis* of the elements of an item-purchasing decision. Using the analytic mode, we break the problem up into constituent parts and address each part separately. When we create information using *synthesis*, we build a pattern or a picture. As shown in the second part of Figure CE16-4, when meteorologists forecast weather, they synthesize a pattern of the wind flows and air masses that will affect the location of the forecast.

Figure CE16-5 combines decision process and decision mode. Deciding whether to order more product is structured and analytic. Forecasting weather is structured (the weather forecasting process is known and can be documented) and synthetic. Diagnosing the gas turbine problem is unstructured but analytic. We break the decision into steps and don't know the next step to take until we see the result of the current step.

Counterterrorism intelligence falls in the fourth quadrant; it is unstructured and synthetic. The process for deciding whether to take preemptive action

> • **Analytic: Break decision into components**
>   Should we order more Product X?
>   – How much did we sell last quarter?
>   – How much did we sell a year ago?
>   – What is the cost of the product?
>   – What is the inventory storage cost?
>   – What is the cost of a lost sale?
> • **Synthetic: Build a pattern or picture**
>   Should we forecast rain for Spokane tomorrow?
>   – What wind is the North Pacific High generating at 47 degrees north?
>   – How fast is the thermal low moving out of California?
>   – What is the latitude and breadth of the jet stream at 500 mb?
>   – How strong are the anabatic winds over the Cascades?

Figure CE16-4
Analysis Versus Synthesis
Decision Modes

Figure CE16-5
Decision Process and Mode

Source: Used by permission of the ATS Corporation.
www.IntelligentDiscovery.com

	Analytic	**Synthetic**
Structured	Should we order more Product X?	Should we forecast rain for Spokane tomorrow?
Unstructured	How can we fix the gas turbine?	Should we take pre-emptive action against Person Y as a terrorist?

Relationships are often more important than data

Process evolves step-by-step

Intelligence Process

against Person Y is not known ahead of time because it depends on what information is discovered about Person Y. We don't know the next step to take until we have a result on the current step. After observing Person Y's behavior, it might be necessary to tap his phone. The process depends on events and information. At the same time, the intelligence process produces information by synthesis. Facts are brought together to form patterns; during the formation of these patterns, relationships are often more important than the data itself.

Q4 How Do Information Systems Facilitate Intelligence Collaboration?

As we learned in the 9/11 congressional hearings, in the intelligence community, the right hand seldom knows what the left hand is doing (or has discovered). This lack of collaboration is particularly harmful for counterterrorism intelligence because intelligence is built by synthesis. If the three facts in Figure CE16-2 are known by three different entities, none of which collaborate, none of them can create the appropriate pattern.

The lack of collaboration is caused by political, historical, and technological factors. The political factors concern the infighting and competition that occur among rival government agencies. The historical factors concern the practice among intelligence activities to reduce risk by separating duties and authorities. One person studies Subject A and a second studies Subject B, but they are not allowed to talk about their subjects to each other. Indeed, they often do not know of each other's existence.

The third problem is technological, and that is the problem that concerns information systems. Assuming the political and historical impediments have been overcome, what technology can be used to facilitate synthesis? What technology can be used to bring all of the relevant facts together?

As you learned in Chapter 7, customer relationship management (CRM) systems address this same problem: How can we bring all of the customer data together? The answer for CRM was to build a customer database. The answer for intelligence collaboration is the same: build a database that is shared among the relevant intelligence analysts.

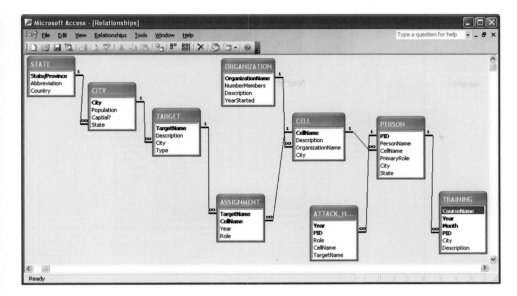

Figure CE16-6
Hypothetical Database for Storing
Intelligence Results

Figure CE16-6 shows the structure of a hypothetical counterterrorism database. Each rectangle in this figure represents a table in a relational database. The black lines connecting the rectangles are relationships. The *OrganizationName* in the CELL table matches the *OrganizationName* in the ORGANIZATION table.

Placing intelligence data into a database does facilitate collaboration, but there is a problem. Relational databases succeed for applications in which the requirements are known and stable. For instance, Amazon.com has a process for selling books, and the requirements for processing the customer-sales database are known ahead of time and are stable. Amazon.com does not change its selling process for each customer.

As discussed, the intelligence process is unstructured; each situation is different, and the process for addressing each situation varies. This means that predefined relationships like those shown in Figure CE16-6 are seldom adequate. Intelligence analysts require more flexibility than predefined relationships allow.

While it is possible to create additional, new relationships, they must be predefined to a developer. However, the intelligence decision process is unstructured; the analyst often does not know the next question to ask until he or she has an answer to the current question. Hence, creating more relationships as the analysis proceeds is infeasible. Another technique must be used: data connections.

Q5 How Do Data Connections Synthesize?

A **data connection** is a match of data values. If two people have the same phone number, they have a data connection. Or if two people have the same last name, they have a data connection. Data connections need not be predefined, and, in fact, seldom are. Also, data connections can be meaningful or meaningless. Two people who happen to have the same first name and the same birth date have a strong data connection, but that connection is likely meaningless. On the other hand, two people who have the same telephone number have a data connection that is likely significant.

Consider data connections among values of City. The red circles in Figure CE16-7 show that City is located in our sample database in five different tables. *City* is used, however, as the key for just one predefined relationship (TARGET to CITY).

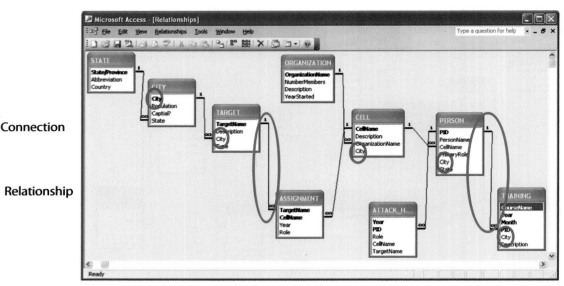

Hypothetical model

Key:

◯ Connection

⬭ Relationship

Figure CE16-7
Difference Between Connections
and Relationships

Now suppose an analyst wants to know of all of the entities connected to the city San Francisco (again, all data are hypothetical). Standard techniques for processing a relational database will not work because that connection is not predefined. It could be found by writing special-purpose SQL code, but the analyst does not have the necessary skill, nor does he or she have permission to process *ad hoc* queries against that database. And because the process is unstructured, the analyst does not know ahead of time whether this connection will be worth the cost of hiring someone to create it.

Processing data connections requires technology other than the relational model. One feasible way to process data connections is to export the relational data to a data warehouse DBMS designed to process data connections. Figure CE16-8 shows the display produced by a DBMS based on the **contiguous connection model (CCM)**, a data model purpose-built for processing connections.

The particulars of that model are beyond the scope of this text,[1] but consider the display in Figure CE16-8. The CCM data warehouse DBMS processed the data, found all of the connections to the *City* value San Francisco, and displayed them in the form of a hierarchy. The database had facts about San Francisco, such as it has a population of one million and is located in California. This hypothetical data also shows connections of other entities to San Francisco. There is a terrorist cell named Strong Soldiers Primary (reminder: all data are hypothetical) located in San Francisco. Three persons (*PID* stands for *person identifier*) are linked to that cell. Additionally, two people are known to live in San Francisco. Three targets are located in San Francisco, and some event occurred in San Francisco in 2001. (The user of this display could click on 2001 to learn more about that event.)

This display shows all of the connections in the database to the *City* value of San Francisco. Those connections synthesize a pattern and produce information. For example, this display shows that the person "7787" is assigned to a cell in San Francisco, but 7787 is the only member of the cell who does not live in San Francisco. It will be up to the analyst to determine if this difference makes a difference.

---

[1]For information about CCM, go to *www.IntelligentDiscovery.com*.

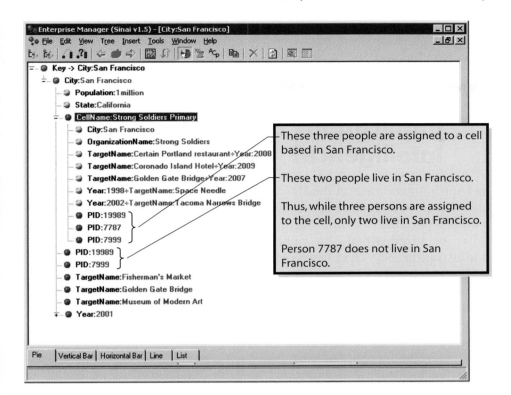

Figure CE16-8
Using Connections: Information
as a Difference That Makes a
Difference

Source: Used by permission of the ATS Corporation.
www.IntelligentDiscovery.com

Q6 How Is Data Mining Used in Counterterrorism Intelligence?

The connection processing just illustrated fails the definition for data mining given in Chapter 9. Namely, it does not involve sophisticated mathematical processing. So it would be more accurate to call connection processing a form of reporting.

Data-mining techniques are used for counterterrorism intelligence, however. The most common is **text mining**, in which large bodies of documents are searched for keywords and keyword patterns. In Figure CE16-9, an analyst has searched for the keywords *bomb* and *terrorist group* and found the (hypothetical) news report shown. The analyst reads and extracts relevant data from that document and stores that data in an intelligence database.

Figure CE16-9
Pattern Population

Source: Used by permission of the ATS Corporation.
www.IntelligentDiscovery.com

Source document

Constructed Pattern

Hypothetical pattern and data

Intelligence organizations do far more sophisticated text and other data mining than keyword search, however. Should you work for such an organization, you undoubtedly will learn more.

Q7 What Are the Legal and Social Implications of Counterterrorism Intelligence?

The Fourth Amendment of the U.S. Constitution gives citizens protection from unreasonable search and seizure. However, the interpretation of that amendment as it pertains to counterterrorism is complex and evolving. In 2006, an uproar occurred when the public learned that the National Security Administration (NSA) had been examining phone records of U.S. citizens to identify persons who had been calling known terrorists. NSA had no warrant and limited government oversight. Many citizens believed the federal government had invaded the privacy of those whose phone records had been examined.

Others disagreed. They concluded that such a search was not unreasonable, at least as long as the government went no further with the records of individuals who had not made suspect calls. Their reasoning was that protecting citizens from terrorism is a legitimate government function, and having the government data mine on phone numbers is not an invasion of privacy.

Part of the confusion is that it is unclear, even to legal scholars, what body of law is applicable to terrorist acts. If I were to break into an Air Force base and steal a guard's pistol, that would be a criminal act, and I would be tried under civilian criminal law. I would have the benefit of the doubt, the right to a trial by jury, and so forth. However, if I were to break into that same Air Force base and steal a nuclear weapon, that act would seriously compromise national security and would be considered an *act of war*. I could be shot on sight, without benefit of doubt, without trial by jury, and without other protections of criminal law.

There is no bright line, however, to demark the domain of criminal law and the domain of national security. Many events fall in between. Is attempting to bomb a public monument a criminal act or an act of war? The answer determines not only which set of laws pertains, but also what is a reasonable search. Clearly, more intrusion is deemed acceptable when investigating an act of war.

A further complication is that intelligence agencies do not always know ahead of time what type of event they are investigating. They are attempting to uncover a terrorist supply line, but they cannot know ahead of time whether the terrorists are planning a bank robbery (criminal) or a nerve gas attack (act of war). Without knowing the event-type ahead of time, they cannot know which search rules pertain.

These problems are especially serious because of the power and comprehensiveness of data mining, connection processing, and related technologies. For example, if you were to search public news for people who have met with known terrorists, your search would quickly produce Condoleezza Rice, the U.S. Secretary of State. No one suspects her of being a terrorist, but her name would appear. Even worse, if your search were to find people who have met someone who has met with known terrorists, your search would produce everyone whom Rice has met, likely including every member of Congress.

Now consider the position of the data miner. By policy, he or she is not allowed to keep records of public officials. Also by policy, he or she is not allowed to produce names of public figures in lists of suspected terrorists. But the only way to know *not* to produce a name is to have a database of the names not to produce (which, in this example, would include Dr. Rice). The first policy, however, prohibits the keeping of such a database.

Another irony concerns intelligence quality. It is highly desirable to find the identity of real terrorists and highly undesirable to make false accusations. As stated, intelligence processes create information by synthesis, and all other things equal, the more complete the synthesis, the more accurate the intelligence. However, creating large databases of very large social patterns can readily become a serious violation of privacy.

These are difficult questions requiring trade-offs, and answers and guidelines can emerge only from serious and informed public discourse. As a citizen, pay attention to the national debate on these issues, and speak up!

Active ? Review

Use this Active Review to verify that you understand the material in the chapter extension. You can read the entire extension and then perform the tasks in this review, or you can read the material for just one question and perform the tasks in this review for that question before moving on to the next one.

Q1 What is the goal of counterterrorism intelligence?

Describe the goal of counterterrorism intelligence.

Q2 How does synthesis produce information?

In your own words, explain the difference between analysis and synthesis. Give an example (other than the one in this chapter extension) of information produced by analysis and of information produced by synthesis.

Q3 What are the characteristics of counterterrorism intelligence decision making?

Define *structured* and *unstructured decision processes*. Give an example (other than one in this chapter extension), of each. Define *analytic* and *synthetic* modes. Give an example (other than one in this chapter extension), of each of the four categories of decision process and mode shown in Figure CE16-5. Explain why the intelligence gathering process is in the fourth quadrant.

Q4 How do information systems facilitate intelligence collaboration?

Name and describe three factors that inhibit collaboration among intelligence analysts. Explain why a database is useful for intelligence collabora-

tion. Explain the limitation of a relational database for this problem. Explain how the requirements for processing an intelligence database differ from those for processing a customer-sales database at Amazon.com.

Q5 How do data connections synthesize?

Define *data connection*, and explain how data it differs from relationships. Give two examples of data connections (other than ones in this chapter extension). Explain why it is not practical to process data connections using a relational database. Describe the connections shown in Figure CE16-8.

Q6 How is data mining used in counterterrorism intelligence?

Explain why connection processing is not data mining. Name the most common form of data mining in the intelligence community. Explain the process illustrated in Figure CE16-9.

Q7 What are the social and legal implications of counterterrorism intelligence?

State the provision for privacy granted by the Fourth Amendment. Describe the cause of the uproar regarding the NSA. Describe the differences between criminal law and national security law as explained in this chapter extension. Describe why it is difficult to know which body of law pertains to terrorist events. Describe how the unstructured nature of intelligence decision making complicates this issue. Explain how the power and comprehensiveness of data mining complicate intelligence activities. Describe the dilemma of not producing the names of public figures in intelligence reports. Explain the irony that concerns intelligence quality.

Key Terms and Concepts

Analysis 507
Contiguous connection model
  (CCM) 512
Counterterrorism intelligence 507

Data connection 511
Decision mode 509
Structured decision process 508
Synthesis 508

Text mining 513
Unstructured decision process 509

Using Your Knowledge

1. Give five examples of meaningful data connections and five examples of meaningless data connections. Suppose someone says that because meaningless data connections are always a possibility, data connections should not be used for synthesizing information. How would you respond? Is it possible that someone could be wrongly accused of an act because of the processing of meaningless connections? Is this possibility new because of information systems, or has it existed for some time? How does the presence of information systems alter the likelihood of false accusations due to false data connections?

2. Suppose you are testing a data connection tool, and you need sample data for the test. You decide to use your organization's employee telephone directory because it is readily available. During the test, you accidentally discover that a manager and one of the manager's employees have the same home telephone number, but they are not married or known to be in a relationship. Further, suppose your organization has a policy of nonfraternization of employees. What do you do?

3. Suppose you have a tool for processing data connections that you can use on student registration data. Suppose that data includes student name, school address, home address, phone numbers, email addresses, major, and classes taken (without grade). Describe five different data connections that you could make with this data. Do any of those violate student privacy? If so, why?

4. Do you think the NSA should be allowed to search telephone records to determine who has called the phones of known terrorists? If so, do you think there should be government oversight, and what type of oversight should there be? If not, explain why not.

5. Do you think the NSA or any other agency should be allowed to search bank records to determine who has made deposits to accounts of known terrorists? Should any agency be allowed to search bank records to determine who has received payments from accounts of known terrorists?

 6. Search the Web to find statements from your U.S. senators or congressperson about the NSA phone number search, or about any other related search or limit on the activities of intelligence agencies. Summarize the views you find. Explain why you agree or disagree with those views.

Chapter Extension 17

Chapter 10 provides the background for this Extension.

Small-Scale Systems Development

Q1 How Does Systems Development Vary According to Project Scale?

The SDLC discussed in Chapter 10 can be applied to projects of any scale, but the nature and character of the work performed varies considerably. For example, for a small project, a yacht broker having three salespeople can use the SDLC to develop a shared prospect-tracking database. For a large project, a major insurance company can use the SDLC to develop a system to sell insurance policies over its Web site. While the same SDLC phrases apply to these two situations, the specific tasks vary widely.

Figure CE17-1 (page 518) summarizes the differences in small- and large-project characteristics. Small-scale projects have relatively simple requirements. The yacht broker needs to decide what prospect data is to be stored and how it is to be accessed and updated. The insurance company needs to determine requirements for selling to existing versus new customers, the type of insurance to be sold, risk and policy premium calculations, the preparation of legal documents, payments and links to accounts receivable, and so forth. Most small-scale projects involve just one or a few business processes. Large-scale projects usually touch and involve many different business processes.

Small-scale projects seldom have professional IT support. A small business like the yacht broker cannot afford to employ IT personnel. Typically, consultants, working on a part-time basis, provide IT support to small projects. Even in a large organization such as Emerson Pharmaceuticals, a small project like Dee's blog may have little IT support.

On the other hand, large-scale projects always involve IT professionals, and those professionals usually possess many different skills and expertise. A large-scale project will have project managers, systems analysts, network administrators, programmers, database designers, PQA professionals, and trainers and user support personnel.

Small- and large-scale projects also vary in duration. The yacht broker can develop the system within several months, whereas the insurance company may require a year or more to implement the Web-based policy sales system.

Study Questions

Q1 How does systems development vary according to project scale?

Q2 What is a typical small-scale project?

Q3 How does the systems definition phase apply to BBB?

Q4 How does the requirements phase apply to BBB?

Q5 How do design and implementation phases apply to BBB?

Q6 How does the maintenance phase apply to BBB?

Q7 What can you learn from the BBB case?

Figure CE17-1
Systems Development
Characteristics

Small-Scale Systems Development	Large-Scale Systems Development
Simple requirements	Complex requirements
Few processes affected	Many processes affected
Little IT expertise	IT personnel with diverse backgrounds
Short development interval	Long development interval
Limited budget	Large budget
Informal/loose	Formal/structured
Inexperienced, often naïve	Experienced, sometimes cynical
Operations support by users	Professional operations support
Security lax	Security important and managed
Backup and recovery lax	Backup and recovery planned and managed

Because of the differences in complexity, personnel, and duration, projects vary in budget as well. Small-scale projects typically have a limited budget; sometimes the budget is unrealistically limited due to the naïveté of business owners or to the company's limited cash. The budget of a large-scale project will be sizable; it must be so to support the personnel and duration of a complex project. Budgeting of large-scale projects is difficult, and sometimes even very large budgets are inadequate. The IRS case in Chapter 1 is a good example.

Small-scale projects tend to be informal and loose. Few users are involved, the progress of the project is easy to review, and a limited budget is involved. Large-scale projects are formal and structured. As you can learn in Chapter Extension 18, "Large-Scale Systems Development," formal project management is the key to success.

Small-scale projects usually involve inexperienced personnel who can be naïve. The yacht brokers, for example, specialize in selling yachts. They know little about development processes like the SDLC and probably do not even distinguish between a computer program and an information system. Sometimes, the users are like lambs headed for fleecing. Large-scale projects are staffed by personnel with considerable experience and many battle scars. They have seen projects go awry, be delivered late, and have costs well over budgets. Like the estimator in the *Guide* in Chapter 10 (page 249a), development personnel sometimes become cynical. Managers and business users who have been burned before can also be cynical.

After the system has been installed, small-scale projects are usually operated by the users themselves. The yacht brokers will turn on the network equipment, start the server, and initiate the project management system. Large-scale projects will be supported by professional operations personnel. Such personnel will be trained on formal operations procedures.

Small-scale and large-scale projects also differ regarding security, backup, and recovery. In a small-scale project, little attention is paid to either. Given limited IT experience, the yacht brokers probably won't consider the possibility of someone stealing their data, nor will they worry about loss of data due to fire or natural disaster. On the other hand, the professional IT personnel on a large-scale project will devote considerable time and energy to security, backup, and recovery. IT professionals at the insurance company will consider security threats and develop safeguards against those threats. They will also ensure that the systems are backed up in such a way that they can be recovered in the event of destruction from fire or natural disaster.

In the future, when you are involved in a systems development project, keep these differences in mind. On a small-scale project, the knowledge you gain from this class should help you compensate for the project's limited experience and naïveté. On a large-scale project, this knowledge will help you understand the reason for the project's formal process and enable you to better participate as a team member.

Q2 What Is a Typical Small-Scale Project?

Baker, Barker, and Bickel met in June 2007 at a convention of resort owners and tourism operators. They sat next to each other by chance while waiting for a presentation, and after introducing themselves and laughing at the odd sound of their three names, they were surprised to learn that they managed similar businesses. Wilma Baker lives in Santa Fe, New Mexico, and specializes in renting homes and apartments to visitors to Santa Fe. Jerry Barker lives in Whistler Village, British Columbia, and specializes in renting condos to skiers and other visitors to the Whistler/Blackcomb Resort. Chris Bickel lives in Chatham, Massachusetts, and specializes in renting homes and condos to vacationers to Cape Cod.

The three agreed to have lunch after the presentation. During lunch, they shared frustrations about the difficulty of obtaining new customers. As the conversation developed, they began to wonder if there was some way to combine forces (i.e., they were seeking a competitive advantage from an alliance). So they decided to skip the next day's presentations and meet to discuss ways to form an alliance. Ideas they wanted to discuss further were sharing customer data, developing a joint reservation service, and exchanging property listings.

As they talked, it became clear they had no interest in merging their businesses; each wanted to stay independent. They also discovered they were all very concerned, paranoid even, about protecting their existing customer bases from poaching. Still, the conflict wasn't as bad as it first seemed. Barker's business was primarily the ski trade, and winter was his busiest season; Bickel's business was mostly Cape Cod vacations, and she was busiest during the summer. Baker's high season was the summer and fall. So it appeared that there was enough difference in their high seasons that they would not necessarily cannibalize their businesses by selling the others' offerings to their own customers.

The question then became how to proceed. Given their desire to protect their own customers, they did not want to develop a common customer database. The best idea seemed to be to share data about properties. That way, they could keep control of their customers but still have an opportunity to sell time at the others' properties.

They discussed several alternatives. Each could develop her or his own property database, and the three could then share those databases over the Internet. Or they could develop a centralized property database that they would all use. Or they could find some other way to share property listings.

Baker, Barker, and Bickel (BBB) need the systems development process. While they do not have the time, interest, or expertise to rigidly apply each phase of the SDLC, they need that process to guide their thinking and actions and to assess progress. They need to take the time to perform systems definition well. If they decide the proposed project is feasible, they need to understand and document their requirements. If the system requires custom application development of any sort, BBB will need to hire outside expertise. Even if not, the partners need to consider each of the five components as they design and implement their system. Finally, they need to prepare to maintain their system, even if that maintenance is informal. We will consider each of these phases in subsequent questions.

Q3 How Does the Systems Definition Phase Apply to BBB?

The systems definition phase is very important for the BBB partners. They have developed an innovative idea for growing their businesses, but they do not know if they have a common understanding of what it means to share properties, nor do they know if a system to implement that understanding is feasible. They will save themselves considerable time and money if they carefully follow the four steps in Figure CE17-2 (these steps are from Figure 10-3, page 240).

First, what does it mean to share property data, and how elaborate of a system do they want? A wide range of possibilities exists. They could agree on a system as simple as emailing one another from time to time, describing the properties they have available. Or they could build a BBB Web site on which each agency advertises its best properties. The Web site might be public, or it could be protected via a VPN for BBB personnel only. They could each share their own databases over the Web, or they could build a common database.

Another consideration is to define the properties they want to share. Do they want to share only properties having a particular range of rental rates? Do they want to share only the top-quality properties? Or do they want to share all properties? They need to ask and answer these questions as part of their definition of system scope.

Compensation is another issue. How will the agency that offers the property listing be compensated by the agency that rents that listing? They need to negotiate a business relationship. Given that, they must decide if they want their information system to compute compensation or to generate payments.

Once they know the goals of the system, they can assess feasibility. Unless they choose an elaborate system or unless they are up against a tight calendar deadline, the project is probably schedule-feasible. It is probably also technically feasible; they do not propose any capability that is not already widely used on the Internet. If they have gotten this far in their discussions, the new system is likely organizationally feasible. Were it not, one of the Bs would have dropped out of the project.

Figure CE17-2
Systems Definition for BBB

Task	Application to BBB
Define system goals and scope	Understand how the agencies want to share properties and how elaborate a system they want. Determine the range of properties they want to share. Determine compensation plan.
Assess cost, schedule, technical, and operational feasibility	Assess four feasibilty dimensions. Possibly reevaluate system goals and scope.
Form project team	Determine who will build the system and how they will be paid.
Plan project	Plan personnel and tasks for the requirements, design, and implementation phases. Consider maintenance needs.

Cost feasibility will be most important to BBB, and it will be difficult for the three partners to assess themselves. Unless they have chosen a very simple system, such as emailing listings to one another, they will need to bring in outside expertise to help them estimate costs of the new system.

If they decide the system is cost-infeasible, they may choose to revisit the system goals and scope. This is an example of the nonwaterfall nature of an actual implementation of the SDLC. Given cost-infeasibility, BBB might choose to back up to an early task to define a less ambitious version of the system. They then would assess the feasibility of that alternate system.

Assuming they can define an acceptable, feasible system, they next need to form a project team and to plan the project. They need to negotiate up-front who will do what and who will pay for what. Clear statements of responsibility and compensation at the onset will avoid later surprises and conflict.

For a small-scale project like this, systems definition is critical. Without it, BBB will flounder and waste time and money. This stage is also one in which nonexpert users and managers can play the leading role.

Q4 How Does the Requirements Phase Apply to BBB?

The tasks for the BBB partners in the requirements phase depend on the type of system they develop. If they plan only to exchange email attachments with listing data, then very little needs to be done. On the other hand, if they decide to develop a shared Web-accessible database, considerable work will need to be done.

Let's suppose that BBB decides on an alternative between these extremes. Suppose the three of them choose to create a private property-listing Web site. The site needs to be restricted to BBB personnel because it includes not only property data but also confidential data like the size of discounts and fees to be paid for listing the property.

Figure CE17-3 shows the tasks for requirements analysis (tasks from Figure 10-4, page 243) as they apply to the BBB Web site system. The system will involve two user roles: users who access the site for the purpose of finding listings to rent, and users who add/update/remove listings from the site. These may be the same or different people. BBB should most likely interview users from all three agencies.

Task	Application to BBB
Conduct user interviews	Interview personnel who will be using the property listings as well as personnel who will post listing data.
Evaluate existing systems	Compare and contrast current methods for renting properties.
Determine new forms, reports, and queries	Mock-up forms for property listings as well as forms for adding, updating, and removing listings.
Identify application features and functions	Specify procedures for renting a listing and removing dates of availability.
Consider security	Need VPN access to limit site to BBB personnel. Describe actions to take when an employee leaves one of the BBB offices.
Create data model	None.
Consider all five components	Whose Web server will support the site? What applications need to be written? How will the data be input? What procedures are needed? What user training will be required?

Figure CE17-3
Requirements Analysis for BBB

Figure CE17-4
Mock-up of Reservation
Request Form

Baker, Barker, & Bickel

Reservations Query Form

Start Date:

End Date:

Number Bedrooms: ⊙ 1 ⊙ 2 ⊙ 3 ⊙ 4

Maximum Daily Rate:

Figure CE17-4
Mock-up of Reservation
Request Form

There is no comparable existing system, but the development team should review the current procedures for renting properties at each agency. This review may reveal additional requirements. It can also expose possible conflicts between agency procedures and the procedures of the new system.

Another task is to create mock-ups or **prototypes** of forms for finding available listings and for updating listing data. Figure CE17-4 shows a simple form mock-up. You can find more about the use of prototypes in Chapter Extension 19, "Alternative Development Techniques."

We need to know more about the actual BBB system to know whether application programs are required. If the system includes features to search the site for available listings (as the form in Figure CE17-4 implies), then an application program will be necessary to perform the search. On the other hand, if the system is designed to be a simple online catalog of listings, then users can use their browsers to search the site themselves. If programs are required, the specific features and functions of those programs should be identified here.

Because BBB wants the Web site to be private, some form of VPN or other secure access must be specified. Also, a procedure needs to be created to revoke access privileges from employees who leave a BBB agency. We assume that the new system does not require a database, so no data model needs to be created. As a final check, the development team should think about each of the five components of an information system and ensure that requirements have been specified for each component. Typical questions are shown in the last row of Figure CE17-3.

The *Guide* on pages 523a–523b discusses the need to have accurate requirements as a starting point, whether you are doing small-scale development or large-scale development—or whether you are aiming toward a goal of any sort.

Q5 How Do Design and Implementation Phases Apply to BBB?

Most likely, the BBB partners will need to bring in an outside IT consultant to help them design and implement their new system. They should ensure the consultant considers each of the five components of the information system as each pertains to design and implementation. Figure 10-8 (page 247) provides a framework for assessing progress and performance.

To create a shared, private Web site, the BBB partners will need to identify hardware to host the Web site. Most likely, BBB will contract with an independent Web-hosting service to provide that site. They must select a vendor that has the expertise necessary to set up the VPN. User computers will already have VPN software as part of Windows, so no additional user software should be needed for the VPN.

The Web site will need Web server software to support the site. BBB may or may not need to supplement the basic services of the Web server with application programs. If they are required, those programs will be designed and written at this time. Since we assume there is no database for the site, each agency will simply upload HTML pages that provide a listing of their available properties. Users of the Web site will not need any additional software; they will just need their browsers. BBB employees who add, modify, or remove listings from their site will need an HTML editor such as FrontPage to create the pages.

BBB, like most small businesses, should strive to use off-the-shelf software as much as possible. During design, BBB or its vendors or consultants should search the Web for existing property-rental software. If there is a package that is close to BBB's needs, they will normally be far better off to license that software than to attempt to build it themselves. On the other hand, if BBB can support this new system using only browsers and HTML editors, they may not need additional software. Most small businesses should avoid extensive custom software development. It is too difficult to manage, and the outcome is risky.

BBB will probably define three types of users: property-listing users, property-listing updaters, and system administrators. The property-listing users will employ the Web site to identify properties to rent. Property-listing updaters will add, modify, and remove property listings. System administrators will maintain the VPN access list and ensure the site is backed up on a regular basis.

Considering procedures, property-listing users will need little training. They will need to learn how to sign on to the VPN and how to use their browsers to locate listings. Those who modify the listings will need procedures for adding, updating, and removing listing data. Finally, the administrators will need to add and remove user names from the VPN access list as personnel come and go. Someone needs to ensure that the site is backed up. BBB should also ensure that the Web site vendor has backup and recovery procedures in case of natural disaster at its site.

Next, the BBB partners should determine the conversion method of the new system. While some version of either pilot or phased conversion could work, the new system can easily be run in parallel with existing property listing activities. Thus, BBB could implement the new system, and if it fails to work or has other problems, each agency can continue to rent properties using the nonshared systems that it currently uses until the new system is fixed. So the likely best choice for conversion will be to run the new system in parallel with existing systems.

Q6 How Does the Maintenance Phase Apply to BBB?

As you learned in Chapter 10, for information systems, the term *maintenance* means either to *fix the system* to make it do what it was supposed to do in the first place, or to *adapt the system* to changes in requirements. Regarding fixing the

Aim for
What
You Want

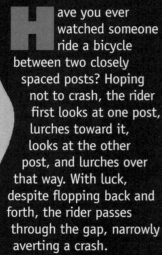

Have you ever watched someone ride a bicycle between two closely spaced posts? Hoping not to crash, the rider first looks at one post, lurches toward it, looks at the other post, and lurches over that way. With luck, despite flopping back and forth, the rider passes through the gap, narrowly averting a crash.

Race-car drivers know how to avoid all that lurching. They advise, "Always put your eyes where you want to go. Don't look at the other cars. Look where you want to go, look at the spot between the other cars." Try it the next time you ride a bicycle through a narrow gap. Stare at a spot in the middle of the gap, between the posts, and 5 or 10 feet beyond them. Fixing your attention where you want to go, you'll ride straight to that spot, moving smoothly between the posts. It works.

Why does this strategy work? Possibly, the anatomy of our brains is such that we unconsciously bring about what we focus on. Although consciously we may be thinking, "This is what I *don't* want to happen," somehow the *don't* part of that statement doesn't reach our subconscious. Focusing on the post, we crash into it.

Rather than focusing on what you want to avoid, focus on what you want and where you want to go. These simple ideas work well in business, too. Put your attention on the desired outcome, and manage your efforts to that outcome.

Of course, to use this strategy, you have to know what you want. And therein lies the rub. You want a great job. OK, but what sort of great job? What specific tasks and responsibilities do you want? Do you want to manage people? Money? Projects? Maybe you want to be a financial analyst. If so, what kinds of analysis do you want to do? In what industry? Focus on the details of the job you want, and it will be easier to obtain. Any job recruiter will agree.

Suppose you say, "I just don't know. I know I should know, but I don't." As soon as you make those statements, you're focusing on the post and not on the job you want. Instead, focus on what you can do to determine the job you want. Or just pick a job that's close to what you want and start focusing on it. That strategy will take you out of the mire of self-criticism.

What does this discussion have to do with IS? Requirements. What do you want the new system to do? Without accurate requirements, the system cannot be built. You need to know what you want before you or anyone else can build it. Furthermore, you need consistent requirements. If one part of the team focuses on one set of requirements and another part of the team focuses on a different, inconsistent set, the result will be chaos, or worse.

As a future user, your most important systems development task is to manage your requirements. Are they complete? Consistent? Does the development team understand them? Is the team focused on them?

Do you have a system for tracking requirements? Are your requirements prioritized? Do you have a way of tracking deferred requirements? Do you meet regularly with developers to ensure that everyone understands the same set of requirements and is working toward the same goal?

Perhaps the project is too big for all the requirements to be known. In that case, build the system incrementally. You may want to move the risk forward. If so, focus on defining the requirements for the most uncertain part of the project. Define that aspect and accomplish that part of the system.

Put your attention where you want to go.

DISCUSSION QUESTIONS

1. On a stretch of remote highway, a car slides off the road in a snowstorm. A power line runs along the highway. A driver in a car behind stares incredulously as the car steers off the road and straight into the only pole within 1,000 feet. (A true story.) What happened? Why did the driver not slide into the 500 feet of open space on either side of the pole?

2. "Baloney, this is just psycho-babble. It may work for race-car drivers, but race-car driving takes different skills than job hunting." Do you agree or disagree with this statement? Why or why not?

3. Consider the following statement made by a retired senior manager: "As a general rule, I think you find in your employees whatever you look for. If you think they're lazy and incompetent, that's what you'll find. If you think they're bright, motivated, and want to do good work, you'll find that as well." How does this statement relate to the race-car driver's strategy? Do you agree or disagree with it?

4. In your own words, describe how the race-car driver's strategy applies to systems development. What are some of the posts to be avoided? Where should users place their attention? Where should developers place their attention? Where should management place its attention?

system, BBB should ensure that its contracts with outside vendors specify an acceptable level of system performance. The contract should specify that vendors are not finished until that performance level is reached. Because BBB has little expertise, checking the references and choosing high-quality vendors is the best way for it to control system quality.

Because the agency owners perceive this system as a first step, it is likely to be adapted considerably over time. They may find the new system does not contribute sufficiently to their businesses to justify the effort, and the adaptation will be to stop the project. On the other extreme, they may find the new system generates considerable new business, and they will want to expand it to a shared, online property database. They may find the new arrangement works so well that they want to merge their agencies into a single partnership. One of the agencies may decide to drop out and the other two agencies will carry on. Perhaps several more agencies will join their system.

Neither they nor we can know ahead of time how this will turn out. This system is only a first step.

Q7   What Can You Learn from the BBB Case?

Sometime during your career, you are likely to participate in the development of an information system. If you work in medium-to-large organizations, the development project will be staffed and managed by IT professionals. However, if you work for a small company or for a workgroup in a large company that, like Dee Clark, cannot obtain IT support, you need to know how to proceed.

In my experience, when a small business contemplates an information system, it is like a deer in headlights: frozen by the possibility. The organization's managers have some idea of what they want to do, they know they do not know what they need to know, and they worry about wasting money or getting involved in projects they cannot afford to finish. As one small businessman once asked me, "I want to build a prospect database, but how do I proceed? Run an ad in the newspaper under *P* for *programmer*?"

If this should happen to you, use the knowledge you have gained in this chapter extension. Use the SDLC as a guide. You need not slavishly perform each task as described here, and some tasks may not be appropriate to your situation, but be guided by the SDLC. Begin with *systems definition*. Spend time describing the scope of the system, think about alternatives, and always keep in mind that you will need to build a system having the five components, not just computer programs. Once you have identified a possible system, take the time to *investigate feasibility*. Careful attention to this phase can save you considerable time, effort, and money.

If you decide to proceed, realize that you need to *specify requirements*, *design*, and *implement*. The ways in which you do that will vary according to the system and according to the work methods of vendors you hire. They may choose to modify the SDLC using some of the alternative techniques described in Chapter Extension 19, "Alternative Development Techniques." If the vendors know what they are doing, this can be better than using the SDLC in many cases.

Also, keep in mind that *you and your employees are in charge of requirements*. You decide what you need. Realize, too, that if you keep changing your mind, the expense of the project will skyrocket, and the quality of the final system will suffer. If you do not know your requirements well, tell your vendor. In that case, build prototypes and proceed cautiously.

The resulting system should help you accomplish your goals and objectives. It likely will not be perfect, but it should be good enough to more than justify its costs and the efforts to construct it. Expect that the day you implement the new system, someone will want some new feature. That's typical. Keep a master list of the requests for change, and plan to adapt the system at some future point. And don't forget to back up your files (or ensure that someone else does)!

Active ? Review

Use this Active Review to verify that you understand the material in the chapter extension. You can read the entire extension and then perform the tasks in this review, or you can read the material for just one question and perform the tasks in this review for that question before moving on to the next one.

Q1 How does systems development vary according to project scale?

Explain how the SDLC applies differently to small-scale and large-scale projects. Use Figure CE17-1 as a guide.

Q2 What is a typical small-scale project?

Summarize the situation at BBB. Describe the goals the three people want to accomplish. Explain why they do not wish to share customer data. Describe the information system they wish to build. Explain why BBB needs the SDLC.

Q3 How does the systems definition phase apply to BBB?

Name four major tasks for the systems definition phase. Describe the work that BBB needs to perform for each task. Name four dimensions of feasibility, and state which is likely to be of concern to BBB. Explain why system definition is crucial to BBB.

Q4 How does the requirements phase apply to BBB?

Describe three different systems that BBB could build. Identify the system that they did choose, and

explain why they wish to use a VPN. Describe the role for the VPN. (See page 130 in Chapter 6 if you have forgotten what a VPN is.) Explain the requirements work that BBB needs to perform. Use Figure CE17-3 as a guide. Define *prototype*, and explain its use.

Q5 How do design and implementation phases apply to BBB?

Using the five-component framework as a guide, explain the tasks that need to be performed for the design and implementation of the BBB system. Identify tasks that BBB can perform and tasks that must be performed by outside vendors. Describe the conversion method that BBB will use.

Q6 How does the maintenance phase apply to BBB?

Name the two activities of the maintenance phase. Explain how BBB should structure its contracts with regard to maintenance. Describe three different possible future adaptations for this system.

Q7 What can you learn from the BBB case?

Describe the situations in which you are most likely to need the knowledge in this chapter extension. Summarize the concerns of many small businesses when they think of building a new information system. Describe how you can use the SDLC. Summarize the ways you would use knowledge of each phase of the SDLC. State what you can expect the day you implement a new system.

Key Terms and Concepts

Prototype 522

Using Your Knowledge

1. Reflect on the experience of Dee Clark at Emerson Pharmaceuticals. Dee did not use (or even know about) the SDLC. Cast her project into the SDLC framework. What work should she have done at each phase? What value would the SDLC have contributed to her project? Why do you think she was successful, in spite of her lack of knowledge?

2. Suppose you are the commissioner of a city softball league consisting of 16 teams, and each team has a roster of up to 15 players. Teams also have two to three coaches. Assume you want to create a database application to record the name of each team and the names of the players and coaches. The league provides materials and some equipment to each team. You'd also like your database application to track the checkout of those materials and equipment.
    a. Describe why the SDLC would be useful for this project.
    b. Explain the activities that you would take for each phase of the project.
    c. Plan the specific tasks you would take for the systems definition phase.

3. Suppose you are the director of a summer camp for middle-school children. Assume the camp has fallen on hard times, the facilities have been poorly maintained, and attendance at the camp has been dwindling. You have been hired to turn the situation around. A number of well-to-do families have contributed funds to supplement the city's budget and have constituted a board of directors to provide guidance over the use of those funds. You have been directed to use the funds to (1) repair facilities as necessary, (2) promote the camp, and (3) improve the efficiency and effectiveness of the camp's operation.
    a. Describe how you could use information systems to facilitate each of your three goals.
    b. Choose one of the information systems you identified in question a, and describe why the SDLC would be useful for this project.
    c. Explain the activities that you would take for each phase of the project.
    d. Plan the specific task you would take for the systems definition phase.

4. Suppose you sell yachts for a small yacht broker. Your company specializes in selling yachts in the $150,000 to $500,000 range. You are the regional dealer for a manufacturer of yachts in this category, and you also sell used boats. Although the management of the company has stated that customers are to be assigned to particular salespeople, you know that this arrangement is fluid, and sometimes it is not clear either to the salespeople or the customers which customer is assigned to which salesperson. Furthermore, you would like to maintain a database of customer boat preferences (make, model, length) so that when the brokerage takes a listing on a new boat, you can query a database of your customers to determine who might be interested in that new listing.

    You have thought about developing your own personal database, and you know that it would help you identify which of your customers are interested in particular boats. Your own personal database would not, however, help to clarify which customers belong to which salespeople. You also do not want to pay for the development of a new system out of your own pocket.

You decide to approach the partners of the yacht brokerage about creating an information system to track customers and prospects.

a. Describe the characteristics of such an information system.

b. Explain how you can use the SDLC to summarize the process you believe the brokerage could take to develop this system.

c. Plan the specific tasks you would take for the systems definition phase for this project.

d. Suppose one of the partners says to you, "How much will it cost?" How do you respond?

you be the Guide

Using the Guide: Aim for What You Want (page 523a)

GOALS

* Teach students to focus on what they want and not on what they fear.

* Apply the "focus on what you want" strategy to systems development.

BACKGROUND AND PRESENTATION STRATEGIES

In Chapter 2, we discussed the idea that, although people cannot change their IQ, they can improve the way they use the IQ they have. This guide is a perfect example of one such technique.

Focus on what you want, not on what you fear. The nature of our minds seems to be that we get whatever we focus on. If we focus on limitations, we'll find our limitations. As Richard Bach wrote in *Jonathan Livingston Seagull* (Avon, 1976), "Focus on your limitations and, sure enough, they're yours."

Sometimes *students become curmudgeons* with me about this guide.

"Oh, come on, this is just the 'power of positive thinking.' You sound like my mother!"

Here are some possible responses:

➤ **Maybe so, but it works. Try it on your bicycle—go ride between two posts and see which strategy works better. Staring at the posts or staring at the space between the posts. And don't forget your helmet!**

➤ **Next time you have a meeting with a group of students, focus on the positive aspects of the other students. Focus on the ideas they're producing, the things you're learning from them, the enjoyable time you're spending. Tell your fellow students that their comments are insightful and interesting (when they are, that is). Contrast this with the results you get from a meeting in which everyone doubts and criticizes everyone else.**

➤ **Or, try this strategy on me. Consider the different results you'll get from me by using one of these two statements:**

* **Professor XXX, I think the BBB case is really interesting. Tell me how you think they should**

address feasibility. I have a problem like that right now!

* **This systems development stuff is really boring. Do I have to learn it? Will it be on the exam?**

Students should be applying this strategy to their job search right now. They need to know what job they want and how they are going to get it. There are hundreds of jobs out there. Some will be perfect, setting the student up for a great career, or at least for an interesting and fruitful first job. Others will be a bad fit and provide little more than a paycheck. The students need to be thinking, NOW, about which jobs they want.

➤ **Here's an assignment for you tonight: Write a paragraph that describes the job you want after graduation. Don't think about your limitations, don't wonder how you're going to get that job. Just think as hard as you can about what you want, and describe that job. Be realistic (you're not going to be the CEO of 3M), but be aggressive in what you want.**

How does all this relate to systems development? Requirements!!! No one can build a system if they don't know what that system is supposed to do. Classical SDLC and RAD have a formal requirements phase, with documented requirements and user reviews. UP has use cases, and XP integrates users into the process. In all cases, it is a matter of focusing the team on building what is wanted.

Case Study 10 ("Slow Learners, or What?") works well with this guide. That case study addresses failures caused by a lack of user involvement in requirements. You might combine this guide with a discussion of that case.

In short, for over 30 years, studies have consistently shown that a lack of user involvement and poor requirements are the leading causes of information systems failures. Our students, once they become business professionals, need to know how to help the development team focus on what is wanted!

 SUGGESTED RESPONSES FOR DISCUSSION QUESTIONS

1. The driver was focused on the power pole. Had the driver focused on the space between the poles, the accident would have been most unlikely. "Gosh, I hope I don't hit that pole" somehow becomes, "Hit the pole." It's as if our bodies only hear *hit the pole* during a time of stress.

2. Use this question to bring forth objections from the students. Some ideas for dealing with resistance to

this idea appear under the curmudgeon point in the Background discussion.

3. There is no single secret to effectively managing every employee in every situation. If there were, there wouldn't be courses on management and miles of books on "effective people management." People are so different; their talents, hopes, and goals vary so much; and every project presents different challenges.

However, as a general rule, I know of no better guide to good management than realizing that *you're likely to find what you look for*. If you expect your employees to be lazy and undependable, you will eventually find evidence to support your expectation, even in the best employees. However, if you expect your employees to be interested in their work, to be motivated, to want to excel, to want to accomplish their job goals, then you will find evidence to support those characteristics as well. My experience managing software development projects is that when a project has a culture of wanting to excel, any employees who do not have that attitude will leave the project.

(This applies to students as well. I find the supply of maturity rises to meet the expectation. When I expect my students to be responsible, to take assignments seriously, to do their homework, to act like the business professionals they say they want to become, then they tend to act that way. Not always, but almost. And, if nothing else, my high expectation raises the level of professionalism at least a bit. Focus your thinking on a classroom full of interested, motivated students who are asking interesting questions and with whom you're having fun. You'll get it!)

4. Use the BBB case. BBB should focus on the result they want, which is greater revenue by being able to rent one another's properties. Given that focus, they should deal with problems that crop up as nuisances to be eliminated. Deal with the problem and get back to the primary focus: increased revenue.

Such a focus will mean that the team does not get bogged down in alternatives that won't lead to increased revenue. If an email with an attachment enables them to achieve their goals, they need do nothing more. If, however, a more sophisticated system will help them achieve greater revenue, then they should build that system.

Possible systems development "posts" to avoid:

- Lack of clear communication of requirements/ needs (among BBB and in general)
- Lack of knowledge of systems development processes
- Focus on problems rather than solutions to those problems
- Starting with too elaborate a system
- Becoming distracted from the system's goals

Everyone should place their attention on the BBB system's goals: increase revenue by renting one another's properties.

WRAP UP

➤ **Ironically, this simple idea, *focus on what you want, focus on the space between the posts,* is among the most important ideas you'll learn in this class.**

➤ **It pertains to systems development, and it pertains to your wider life as well.**

➤ **The trick is to remember it: *Focus on what you want.***

Chapter Extension 18

Chapter 10 provides the background for this Extension.

Large-Scale Systems Development

Q1 What Characterizes Large-Scale Information Systems Development Projects?

Large-scale IS development projects are, well . . . big. The information systems they create have many functions and features. They necessitate the creation of large, complex computer programs. They process databases with hundreds of tables, dozens and possibly hundreds of relationships, and terabytes of data. Large-scale systems affect many business processes and support hundreds, possibly thousands, of concurrent users.

Because they are so big, large-scale systems require a large development team, 50 to 100 or more systems analysts, programmers, PQA engineers, and managers. To add further complexity, large-scale systems are often simultaneously developed at multiple sites. A project might involve teams in the United States, India, China, and other countries. Additionally, the development of large-scale systems can involve integrating products and services from different companies. In these development projects, some companies provide licensed software, others provide particular expertise such as database design, and others provide development labor. Large-scale systems are frequently localized for different languages (see "The International Dimension," Part 2, page 138). Finally, large-scale systems development requires extended development intervals, sometimes as long as five or six years. Figure CE18-1 (page 530) summarizes the characteristics of large-scale systems.

The IRS example in Chapter 1 is a good example of a large-scale project. The IRS employs more than 100,000 people in 1,000 different sites and processes over 200 million tax returns a year. In 1995, it set out to modernize the information systems for processing tax returns. Today, more than 10 years and several billion dollars later, it still is not finished with that project.

Closer to home, consider Emerson Pharmaceuticals. Dee's blog was small-scale, but Emerson has embarked on a large-scale project as well. For the past three years, Emerson has

Study Questions

Q1 What characterizes large-scale information systems development projects?

Q2 What are the trade-offs in requirements, cost, and time?

Q3 What is the *PMBOK®* *Guide* for project management?

Q4 How does a work-breakdown structure drive project management?

Q5 What is the biggest challenge for planning a large-scale systems development project?

Q6 What are the biggest challenges for managing a large-scale systems development project?

Q7 What is the single most important task for users on a large-scale systems development project?

Figure CE18-1
Characteristics of Large-Scale
Systems Development Projects

- Many features and functions
- Large, complex computer programs
- Databases with hundreds of tables, dozens of relationships, and terabytes of data
- Affect many business processes
- Support hundreds or thousands of concurrent users
- Large development team
- Multiple sites
- International development
- Integration of work from several companies
- Localization necessary
- Extended development intervals

been developing an information system to modernize the ordering of its products from hospitals and large clinics. The existing system is a thick-client system that requires the installation of software on the customers' computers. To improve security and to reduce administration costs for its customers, Emerson is constructing a thin-client, Web browser version of its order-entry system. Emerson elected, however, to do far more than just convert to thin-client. It also drastically changed the way it receives and processes order data and added many new features and functions to its system. Because the system will be used throughout North America, Emerson localized it for English, Spanish, and French speakers. Emerson created a development team of more than 75 people for this project and hired several contractors to support the project as well. The first customer capability is to be delivered within the next six months. We will use this system to illustrate large-scale systems development in this chapter extension.

Q2 What Are the Trade-offs in Requirements, Cost, and Time?

Large-scale systems development projects require the balancing of three critical drivers: **requirements (scope)**,[1] **cost**, and **time**. To understand this balancing challenge, consider the construction of something relatively simple—say, a piece of jewelry like a necklace or the deck on the side of a house. The more elaborate the necklace or the deck, the more time it will take. The less elaborate, the less time it will take. Further, if we embellish the necklace with diamonds and precious gems, it will cost more. Similarly, if we construct the deck from old crates it will be cheaper than if we construct it of clear-grained, prime Port Orford cedar.

We can summarize this situation as shown in Figure CE18-2. We can *trade off* requirements against time and against cost. If we make the necklace simpler, it will take less time. If we eliminate the diamonds and gems, it will be cheaper. The same **trade-offs** exist in the construction of anything: houses, airplane interiors, buildings, ships, furniture, *and* information systems.

The relationship between time and cost is more complicated. Normally, we can reduce time by increasing cost *only to a point*. For example, we can reduce the time it takes to produce a deck by hiring more laborers. At some point, how-

---

[1]When we speak of information systems, we usually refer to the characteristics of the system to be constructed as *requirements*. The discipline of project management refers to those characteristics as project *scope*. If you read literature from the Project Management Institute, for example, it will use the term *scope* in the same sense that we use *requirements*. For the purposes of this chapter extension, consider *scope* and *requirements* to be the same.

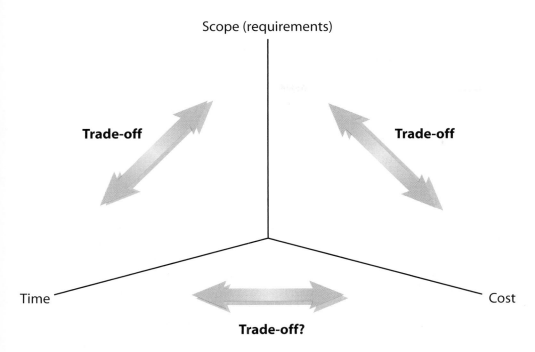

Scope (requirements)

Trade-off

Trade-off

Time

Cost

Trade-off?

Figure CE18-2
Primary Drivers of Systems Development

ever, there will be so many laborers working on the deck that they will get in one another's way, and the time to finish the deck will actually increase. Thus, at some point, adding more people creates **diseconomies of scale** (recall Brooks's Law in Chapter 10).

In some projects, we can reduce costs by increasing time. If, for example, we are required to pay laborers time-and-a-half for overtime, we can reduce costs by eliminating overtime. If finishing the deck—by, say, Friday—requires overtime, then it may be cheaper to avoid overtime by completing the deck sometime next week. This trade-off is not always true, however. Extending the project interval means that we need to pay labor and overhead for a longer period. Adding more time can increase cost.

Consider how these trade-offs pertain to information systems. We specify a set of requirements for the new information system, and we schedule labor over a period of time. Suppose the initial schedule indicates the system will be finished in three years. If business requirements necessitate the project be finished in two years, we must shorten the schedule. We can proceed in two ways: reduce the requirements or add labor. For the former, we eliminate functions and features. For the latter, we hire more staff or contract with other vendors for development services. Deciding which course to take will be difficult and risky.

Furthermore, in most projects, we cannot make these decisions once and for all. We begin with a plan, called the **baseline**. It stipulates the tasks to be accomplished, the labor and other resources assigned to those tasks, and the schedule for completion. However, nothing ever goes according to plan, and the larger the project and the longer the development interval, the more things will violate the plan. Critical people may leave the company; a hurricane may destroy an office; the company may have a bad quarter and freeze hiring just as the project is staffing up; technology will change; competitors may do something that makes the project more (or less) important; or the company may be sold and new management may change requirements and priorities. When these events occur, project managers must reassess the trade-offs between requirements, cost, and time. It is a balancing act undertaken in the presence of continual change, and substantial risk and uncertainty.

Q3 What Is the *PMBOK*® *Guide* for Project Management?

Many methods exist for developing information systems. Chapter 10 described the systems development life cycle (SDLC), the workhorse of the industry for years. Chapter Extension 19, "Alternative Development Techniques," describes three other methods for developing systems and programs. These techniques stipulate phases and processes for constructing information systems, but they do not address the management of projects, particularly large-scale projects. The systems definition phase of the SDLC, for example, stipulates that the project should be planned, but it does not indicate how. It stipulates that components need to be designed, but it does not address the management of the design activity, nor the communications among employees, groups, and sites. And so forth.

Large-scale projects need formalized project management. While Dee can get by with informal meetings with her consultant, Emerson cannot deliver its new thin-client ordering system that way. Over the years, people have proposed dozens of different project management processes. In recent years, the process promulgated by the **Project Management Institute (PMI)** has achieved prominence. PMI is an international organization focused on disseminating best practices in project management. Both the American National Standards Institute (ANSI) and International Standards Organization (ISO) have endorsed PMI's work.

PMI publishes project management documents and offers project management training. It also offers the **Project Management Professional (PMP)** certification. Professionals who have 4,500 hours of project work experience can earn the certification by passing PMI's examination. Once you have the required work experience, the PMP is a worthwhile certification for any professional involved in project management work of any type. (The PMP certification pertains to project management in general and not only to information systems project management. See *www.pmi.org* for more information.)

Since its origin in 1969, PMI has evaluated many project management concepts and techniques and brought the best of them together under the umbrella of a document entitled *Project Management Body of Knowledge* (*PMBOK*®) *Guide*. This document contains what many believe are the best project management processes, practices, and techniques. The document does not describe the details of each practice or technique, but instead it identifies practices that are known to be effective for different situations and briefly describes their use. Versions of this document are denoted by the year in which they are published. The current version is *PMBOK*® *Guide 2004*.

PMBOK® *Guide 2004* is organized according to the grid in Figure CE18-3, which shows five *process groups* and nine *knowledge areas*. The process groups refer to different stages in the life of a project; the nine knowledge areas refer to factors to be managed throughout the life of the project.

You can surmise the meanings of the process groups from their titles. The knowledge areas provide an excellent summary of project management dimensions. *Project integration* refers to the management of the overall project and the construction of the final product. We have already discussed the trade-offs among *scope* (*requirements*), *time*, and *cost*. *Quality* management refers to quality assurance; for an IS project, it concerns planning and managing the product quality-assurance function.

The nature of *human resources* management is clear from its name. *Communications* management concerns the methods, media, and schedules for

Project Management Processes

Knowledge Areas	Initiating	Planning	Executing	Monitoring and Controlling	Closing
Project integration					
Scope (requirements)					
Time					
Cost					
Quality					
Human resources					
Communications					
Risk					
Procurement					

Figure CE18-3
Structure of the
PMBOK® Guide 2004

communicating with the project's sponsors, within the team itself, and with others having an interest in the progress of the project. The decision to use a team Web portal, for example, would be part of communications management. Risk is inherent in all projects and especially so for projects that involve new technology or the innovative application of existing technology. The purpose of *risk* management is to ensure that managers understand project risks and balance risk factors—or that they take other appropriate action to mitigate unwanted outcomes. Finally, *procurement* management concerns contracts with outside vendors for services, materials, and outsourcing of functions.

Consider the elements in Figure CE18-3 as an inventory of management issues that large-scale information systems development projects must address. The *PMBOK® 2004 Guide* specifies practices, documents, techniques, and methods to be used for most of the cells of the grid in Figure CE18-3. For specific guidance on particular practices for process groups or knowledge areas, see the *PMBOK® Guide 2004*. (If you are interested, you can download excerpts from the *PMBOK® 2004 Guide* from *www.PMI.org*.) The particular contents of each cell are beyond the scope of this text; to learn more, take a project management class.

Q4 How Does a Work-Breakdown Structure Drive Project Management?

The key strategy for large-scale systems development—and, indeed, the key strategy for any project—is to divide and conquer. Break up large tasks into smaller tasks and continue breaking up the tasks until they are small enough to manage, thus enabling you to estimate time and costs. Each task should culminate in one or more **deliverables**. Examples of deliverables are documents, designs, prototypes, data models, database designs, working data entry screens, and the like. Without a deliverable, it is impossible to know if the task was accomplished.

A **work-breakdown structure (WBS)** is a hierarchy of the tasks required to complete a project. The WBS for a large project is huge; it might entail hundreds or even thousands of tasks. Figure CE18-4 shows the WBS for the system definition phase of the Emerson thin-client order-entry system. The overall task, *System definition*, is divided into *Define goals and scope, Assess feasibility, Plan project,* and *Form project team.* Each of those tasks is broken into smaller tasks, until the work has been divided into small tasks that can be managed and estimated.

Note, by the way, that the term *scope* is being used here in two different ways. As used in this WBS example, *scope* means to define the system boundaries, which is the sense in which it is used in the SDLC. As noted in Q3, scope for the *PMBOK® Guide* means to define the requirements. That use of scope does not appear in Figure CE18-4.

Once the project is decomposed into small tasks, the next step is to define task dependencies and to estimate task durations. Regarding dependencies, some tasks must begin at the same time, some tasks must end at the same time, and some tasks cannot start until other tasks have finished. Task dependencies are normally input to planning software such as Microsoft Project. Figure CE18-5 shows the WBS as input to Microsoft Project, with task dependencies and dura-

Figure CE18-4
Sample Work Breakdown
Structure for the Definition Phase
of the Emerson Thin-Client Order-
Entry System

System definition
1.1	Define goals and scope	
1.1.1	Define goals
1.1.2	Define system boundaries
1.1.3	Review results
1.1.4	Document results
1.2	Assess feasibility
1.2.1	Cost
1.2.2	Schedule
1.2.3	Technical
1.2.4	Organizational
1.2.5	Document feasibility
1.2.6	Management review and go/no go decision
1.3	Plan project
1.3.1	Establish milestones
1.3.2	Create WBS
1.3.2.1	Levels 1 and 2
1.3.2.2	Levels 3+
1.3.3	Document WBS
1.3.3.1	Create WBS baseline
1.3.3.2	Input to Project
1.3.4	Determine resource requirements
1.3.4.1	Personnel
1.3.4.2	Computing
1.3.4.3	Office space
1.3.4.4	Travel and Meeting Expense
1.3.5	Management review
1.3.5.1	Prepare presentation
1.3.5.2	Prepare background documents
1.3.5.3	Give presentation
1.3.5.4	Incorporate feedback into plan
1.3.5.5	Approve project
1.4	Form project team
1.4.1	Meet with HR
1.4.2	Meet with IT Director
1.4.3	Develop job descriptions
1.4.4	Meet with available personnel
1.4.5	Hire personnel

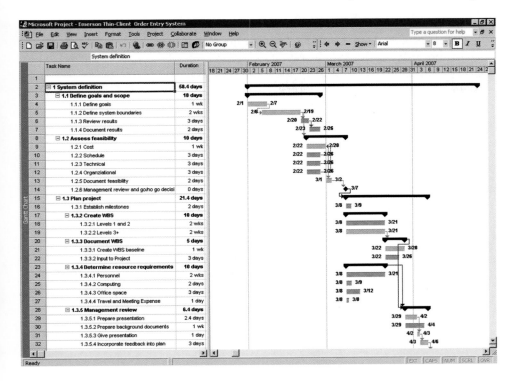

Figure CE18-5
Gantt Chart of WBS for Definition Phase of the Emerson Thin-Client System

tions defined. The display on the right, called a **Gantt chart**, shows tasks, dates, and dependencies.

The user has entered all of the tasks from the WBS and assigned each task a duration. She has also specified task dependencies, although the means she used are beyond our discussion. The two red arrows emerging from task 5, *Define system boundaries*, indicate that neither the *Review results* task nor the *Assess feasibility task* can begin until *Define system boundaries* is completed. Other task dependencies are also shown; you can learn about them in a project management class.

The **critical path** is the sequence of activities that determine the earliest date by which the project can be completed. Reflect for a moment on that statement: The earliest date is the date determined by considering the *longest path* through the network of activities. Paying attention to task dependencies, the planner will compress the tasks as much as possible. Those tasks that cannot be further compressed lie on the critical path. Microsoft Project and other project planning applications can readily identify critical path tasks.

Figure CE18-5 shows the tasks on the critical path in red. Consider the first part of the WBS. The project planner specified that task 5 cannot begin until two days before task 4 starts. (That's the meaning of the red arrow emerging from task 4.) Neither task 6 nor task 9 can begin until task 5 completes. Task 9 will take longer than tasks 6 and 7, and so task 9 and not tasks 6 or 7 are on the critical path. Thus, the critical path to this point is tasks 4, 5, and 9. You can trace the critical path through the rest of the WBS by following the tasks shown in red.

Using Microsoft Project or similar products, it is possible to assign personnel to tasks and to stipulate the percentage of time that each person devotes to a task. Figure CE18-6 shows a Gantt chart for which this has been done. The notation means that Eleanore works only 25 percent of the time on task 4; Lynda and Richard work full time. Additionally, one can assign costs to personnel and compute a labor budget for each task and for the WBS overall. One can assign resources to tasks and use Microsoft Project to detect and prevent two tasks from using the same resources. Resource costs can be assigned and summed as well.

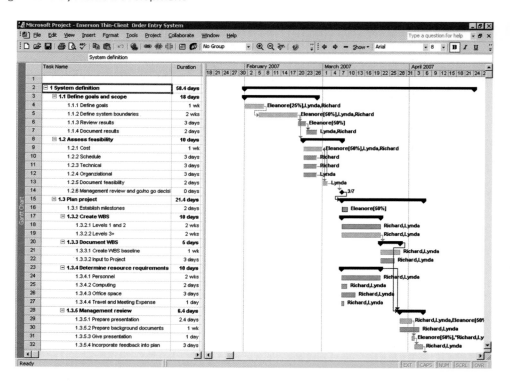

Managers can use the critical path to perform **critical path analysis**. First, note that if a task is on the critical path and if that task runs late, the project will be late. Hence, tasks on the critical path cannot be allowed to run late if the project is to be delivered on time. Second, tasks not on the critical path can run late to the point at which they would become part of the critical path. Hence, up to a point, resources can be taken from noncritical path tasks to shorten tasks on the critical path. Using critical path analysis, managers can move resources among tasks so as to compress the schedule.

So far, we have discussed the role of the WBS for planning. It can be used for monitoring as well. The final WBS plan is denoted the **baseline WBS**. This baseline shows the planned tasks, dependencies, durations, and resource assignments. As the project proceeds, project managers can input actual dates, labor hours, and resource costs. At any point in time, Microsoft Project can report whether the project is ahead or behind schedule, and how the actual project costs compare to baseline costs.

As you can see, the WBS provides invaluable project management information. In fact, it is the single most important management tool for large-scale projects.

Q5 What Is the Biggest Challenge for Planning a Large-Scale Systems Development Project?

The biggest challenge in planning large-scale systems is scheduling. How long does it take to develop a large data model? How long does it take to adapt that data model to the users' satisfaction? How long does it take to develop a computer program to process orders if that program uses XML Web services and no one on the team knows how to develop a Web service program?

Fred Brooks defined software as logical poetry. It is pure thought-stuff. Some years ago, when I pressed a seasoned software developer for a schedule, he responded by asking me, "What would Shakespeare have said if someone asked him how long it would take him to write *Hamlet*? " Another common rejoinder is, "What would a fisherman say if you ask him how long will it take to catch three fish? He doesn't know, and neither do I."

No company should know better how to estimate software schedules than Microsoft. It has more experience developing software than any other company; is loaded with smart, even brilliant developers; can draw from enormous financial resources; and has strong incentives to schedule projects accurately. However, Microsoft's latest operating system, Vista, was delivered two years late. It was supposed to take three years, and it took five. That's a 67 percent schedule overrun from the largest software developer in the world, on what is arguably the world's most important computer program. And this is not just one project that ran awry. SQL Server 2005 barely made it into 2005. Office 2003 was late, and so on.

Part of the problem is that errors accumulate. If scheduling a single task is difficult, then scheduling a large-scale project becomes a nightmare. Suppose you have a WBS with thousands of tasks, and any one of those tasks can be 67 percent over schedule. It is impossible to do any credible planning. The term *critical path* loses meaning when there is that much doubt about task duration. In that setting, every task has some chance of being on the critical path.

Organizations take three approaches to this challenge. The first is never to develop software in-house. Instead, they license software from vendors. For example, few companies choose to develop their own ERP or CRM software. ERP or CRM systems still have the substantial schedule risks of adapting procedures and training personnel, but those risks are much smaller than the schedule risks of developing complex software and databases.

But what if no suitable software exists? In that case, companies take one of two remaining approaches. They can admit the impossibility of systems development scheduling and plan accordingly. They abandon the SDLC and decide to invest a certain level of resource into a project, manage it as best they can, and take the schedule that results. Only loose commitments are made regarding the completion date and final system functionality. Project sponsors dislike this approach because they feel they are signing a blank check. But sometimes it is just a matter of admitting the reality that exists: "We don't know, and it's worse to pretend that we do." Chapter Extension 19, "Alternative Development Techniques," describes three techniques that can be used in this way.

The third approach is to attempt to schedule the development project in spite of all the difficulties. Several different estimation techniques can be used. If the project is similar to a past project, the schedule data from that past project can be used for planning. When such similar past projects exist, this technique can produce quality schedule estimates. If there is no such past project, managers can estimate the number of **lines of code** that will need to be written. Then they can use industry or company averages to estimate the time required. Another technique is to estimate the **function points** in a program, use each function point to determine the number of lines of code, and use that number to estimate schedules. A function point is simply a feature or function of the new program. Updating a customer record is an example. For more information on the use of lines of code and function points for software scheduling, go to *http://sunset.usc.edu/research/Cocomo II/CocoomO_main.html*. Of course, lines of code and function point techniques estimate schedules only for software components. The schedules for creating databases and the other system components must be estimated using other techniques.

During your career, be aware of the challenges and difficulties of scheduling large-scale information systems development. As a user or manager, do not take schedules as guarantees. Plan for schedule slippage, and if it does *not* occur, be pleasantly surprised.

Q6 What Are the Biggest Challenges for Managing a Large-Scale Systems Development Project?

The challenges of managing large-scale systems development projects arise from four different factors:

1. Coordination
2. Diseconomies of scale
3. Configuration control
4. Unexpected events

Large-scale projects are usually organized into a variety of development groups that work independently. Coordinating the work of these independent groups can be difficult, particularly if the groups reside in different geographic locations or different countries. An accurate and complete WBS facilitates coordination, but no project ever proceeds exactly in accordance with the WBS. Delays occur, and unknown or unexpected dependencies develop among tasks.

The coordination problem is increased because software is only thought-stuff. When constructing a new house, electricians install wiring in the walls as they exist; it is impossible to do otherwise. No electrician can install wiring in the wall as designed six months ago, before a change. In software, such physical constraints do not exist. It is entirely possible for a team to develop a set of application programs to process a database using an obsolete database design. When the database design was changed, all involved parties should have been notified, but this may not have occurred. Wasted hours, increased cost, and poor morale are the result.

As mentioned in Chapter 10, another problem is diseconomies of scale. Adding more people to a project increases coordination requirements. The number of possible interactions among team members rises exponentially with the number of team members. Ultimately, no matter how well-managed a project is, diseconomies of scale will set in. According to Brooks's Law, adding more people to a late software project makes it later.

As the project proceeds, controlling the configuration of the work product becomes difficult. Consider requirements, for example. The development team produces an initial statement of requirements. Meetings with users produce an adjusted set of requirements. Suppose an event then occurs that necessitates a change to requirements. After deliberation, assume the team decides to ignore a large portion of the requirements changes resulting from the event. At this point, there are four different versions of the requirements. If the changes to requirements are not carefully managed, changes from the four versions will be mixed up, and confusion and disorder will result. No one will know which requirements are the correct, current requirements.

Similar problems occur with designs, program code, database data, and other system components. The term **configuration control** refers to a set of management policies, practices, and tools that developers use to maintain control over the project's resources. Such resources include documents, schedules, designs, program code, test suites, and any other shared resource needed to complete the project. Configuration control is vital; a loss of control over a project's configuration is so expensive and disruptive that it can result in termination for senior project managers.

The last major challenge to large-scale project management is unexpected events. The larger and longer the project, the greater the chance of disruption due to an unanticipated event. Critical people can change companies; even whole teams have been known to pack up and join a competitor. The organization can be acquired, and new management may have different priorities. Congress can change applicable law; Sarbanes-Oxley is a good example of a law that affected not only financial systems, but also other systems whose resources were taken to comply with the new law. Natural disasters like hurricanes can destroy offices or, if not that, significantly impact employees' lives.

Because software is thought-stuff, team morale is crucial. I once managed two strong-headed software developers who engaged in a heated argument over the design of a program feature. The argument ended when one threw a chair at the other. The rest of the team divided its loyalties between the two developers, and work came to a standstill as subgroups sneered and argued with one another when they met in hallways or at the coffee pot. How do you schedule that event in your WBS? As a project manager, you never know what strange event is heading your way. Such unanticipated events make project management challenging, but also incredibly fascinating!

Q7 What Is the Single Most Important Task for Users on a Large-Scale Systems Development Project?

Taking responsibility for requirements is the single most important task you, a future user or manager of users, can perform for a large-scale development project. Taking responsibility goes beyond participating in requirements meetings and stating your opinion on how things should work. Taking responsibility means understanding that the information system is built for your business function and managing requirements accordingly. As the *Guide* on pages 539a–539b discusses, user involvement from start to finish is crucial to systems development success.

"There are no IT projects," says Kaiser-Permanente CIO Cliff Dodd. Rather, he says, "Some business projects have an IT component."[2] Mr. Dodd is right. Information systems exist to help organizations achieve their goals and objectives. Information systems exist to facilitate business processes and to improve decision making. Every information system is simply a part of some larger business project.

When investigating the problems in the IRS modernization program, the IRS Oversight Board stated, "The IRS business units must take direct leadership

---

[2]Quoted in Steve Ulfelder, "How to Talk to Business," *www.Computerworld.com*, March 13, 2006 (accessed August 2006).

Dealing with Uncertainty

In the mid-1970s, I worked as a database disaster repairman. As an independent consultant, I was called by organizations that licensed the then-new database management systems but had little idea of what to do with them.

One of my memorable clients had converted the company's billing system from an older-technology system to the new world of database processing. Unfortunately, after it cut off the old system, serious flaws were found in the new one, and from mid-November to mid-January, the company was unable to send a bill. Of course, customers who do not receive bills do not pay, and my client had a substantial cash flow problem. Even worse, some of its customers used a calendar-year tax basis and wanted to pay their bills prior to the end of the year. When those customers called to find the amount they owed, accounts receivable clerks had to say, "Well, we don't know. The data's in our computer, but we can't get it out." That was when the company called me for database disaster repair.

The immediate cause of the problem was that the client used the plunge conversion technique. But looking deeper, I asked, "How did that organization find itself with a new billing system so full of failures?"

In this organization, management had little idea about how to communicate with IT, and the IT personnel had no experience in dealing with senior management. They talked past one another.

Fortunately, this client was, in most other respects, a well-managed company. Senior management only needed to learn to manage its IS projects with the same discipline as it managed other departments. So once we had patched the billing system together to solve the cash flow problem, the management team began work on implementing policies and procedures to instill the following principles:

- Business users, not IS, would take responsibility for the success of new systems.
- Users would actively work with IS personnel throughout systems development, especially during the requirements phase.
- Users would take an active role in project planning, project management, and project reviews.
- No development phase would be considered complete until the work was reviewed and approved by user representatives and management.
- Users would actively test the new system.
- All future systems would be developed in small increments.

I cannot claim that all future development projects at this company proceeded smoothly after the users began to practice these principles. In fact, many users were slow to take on their new responsibilities; in some cases, the users resented the time they were

asked to invest in the new practices. Also, some were uncomfortable in these new roles. They wanted to work in their business specialty and not be asked to participate in IS projects about which they knew little. Still others did not take their responsibilities seriously; they would come to meetings ill-prepared, would not fully engage in the process, or would approve work they did not understand.

However, after that billing disaster, the members of senior management understood what needed to be done. They made these practices a priority, and over time user resistance was mostly overcome. When it was not overcome, it was clear to senior management where the true problem lay.

DISCUSSION QUESTIONS

1. In general terms, describe how the billing system might have been implemented using pilot conversion. Describe how it might have been implemented using parallel conversion.

2. If you were the billing system project manager, what factors would you consider when deciding the style of conversion to use?

3. If the billing system had been converted using either pilot or parallel, what would have happened?

4. Explain in your own words the benefits that would accrue using the new principles.

5. Summarize the reasons that users resisted these new principles. What could be done to overcome that resistance?

6. Suppose you work in a company where users have little to no active involvement in systems development. Describe likely consequences of this situation. Describe five actions you could take to correct this situation.

and ownership of the Modernization program and its projects. In particular this must include defining the scope of each project, preparing realistic and attainable business cases, and controlling scope changes throughout each project's life cycle."[3]

Users cannot be passive recipients of the IT department's services. Instead, users are responsible for ensuring that requirements are complete and accurate. Users must ask only for what they need and must avoid creating requirements that cannot possibly be constructed within the available budget. Because users may not know what is difficult or unrealistic, requirements definition can occur only through an extended conversation among the users and the development team.

Once the requirements are known, the development team will create a project WBS and will initiate management activities for each of the nine knowledge areas in Figure CE18-3. It will staff positions, and it will begin design and, later, implementation work on the stated requirements. If users subsequently change their minds about what is needed, considerable rework and waste will occur. **Requirements creep** is the process by which users agree to one set of requirements, then add a bit more ("It won't take too much extra work"), then add a bit more, and so forth. Over time, the requirements creep so much that they describe a completely new project. But the development team is left with the budget and plan of the original project.

Users must take responsibility for managing requirements changes and for avoiding requirements creep. Some requirements change is inevitable; but if changes become extensive, if requirements creep cannot be avoided, start a new project. Don't try to turn a doghouse into a skyscraper, one small change at a time. In that course of action, disaster is the only outcome.

A final part of the users' responsibility for requirements concerns *testing*. You and those who work for you may be asked to help in several different ways. You may be asked to specify testing criteria. If so, you need to help define testable conditions that determine whether or not a feature or function is complete and operational. Testing may occur in several stages during the project. For example, you may be asked to test design components; evaluating a data model is a good example. Or you may be asked to provide sample data and sample scenarios for program and systems testing. You may be asked to participate in the testing of beta versions. Because only the users can know if a feature works correctly, testing is part of requirements management.

Once more: Taking responsibility for system requirements is the single most important ask you can perform on a large-scale development project!

---

[3]IRS Oversight Board, "Independent Analysis of IRS Business Systems Modernization Special Report," *www.irsoversightboard.treas.gov* (accessed August 2006).

Active ? Review

Use this Active Review to verify that you understand the material in the chapter extension. You can read the entire extension and then perform the tasks in this review, or you can read the material for just one question and perform the tasks in this review for that question before moving on to the next one.

Q1 What characterizes large-scale information systems development projects?

Summarize the characteristics of large-scale information systems development projects. Explain why these characteristics make large-scale projects hard to manage. Give two examples of large-scale systems development projects.

Q2 What are the trade-offs in requirements, cost, and time?

Describe two meanings for the term *scope*. Describe how requirements affect cost and time. Describe the trade-offs that exist between requirements and time. Explain the trade-offs that exist between time and cost. Describe circumstances in which increasing cost reduces time. Explain circumstances in which increasing cost increases time. Describe circumstance in which time extensions reduce costs.

Q3 What is the *PMBOK® Guide* for project management?

Describe the difference between development processes like the SDLC and project management. Summarize the activities of the PMI. Describe the contents of the *PMBOK® Guide 2004*. Name the five process groups and the nine knowledge areas. Briefly explain the focus of each management area. Explain how you can use Figure CE18-3.

Q4 How does a work-breakdown structure drive project management?

State the key strategy for large-scale systems development. Explain why each task needs to produce one or more deliverables. Define *work-breakdown structure*, and give an example. In Figure CE18-4, explain the numeric notation under task 1.3. Define *Gantt chart* and describe its contents. Explain how task dependencies influence project work. Define *critical path analysis*, and using your own words, explain what it means. Describe two ways managers can use critical path analysis. Summarize how the WBS can be used to estimate costs. Define *baseline WBS*, and explain how the baseline can be used to monitor a project.

Q5 What is the biggest challenge for planning a large-scale systems development project?

Name the biggest challenge for large-scale systems development planning. Explain why this is so. Describe how the logical-poetry nature of software development affects scheduling. Summarize the three approaches that organizations can take to the systems development scheduling challenge. Describe two ways of estimating time to write computer programs. Describe how you can use the knowledge you have about systems development scheduling.

Q6 What are the biggest challenges for managing a large-scale systems development project?

Name four factors that create challenges for managing large-scale systems development. Give an example of each factor. Define *configuration control*.

Q7 What is the single most important task for users on a large-scale systems development project?

State and describe the single most important task for users on a large-scale systems development project. Explain why, as Mr. Dodd put it, there are no IT projects. Summarize user responsibilities for managing requirements. Define *requirements creep*. Describe the action that should occur if requirements creep cannot be stopped. Summarize the users' role for systems testing.

Key Terms and Concepts

Baseline 531
Baseline WBS 536
Configuration control 538
Cost 530
Critical path 535
Critical path analysis 536
Deliverable 533
Diseconomies of scale 531
Function point (estimating technique) 537

Gantt chart 535
Lines of code (estimating technique) 537
Project Management Institute (PMI) 532
Project management professional (PMP) 532

Requirements 530
Requirements creep 540
Scope (two meanings) 530
Time 530
Trade-off 530
Work-breakdown structure (WBS) 534

Using Your Knowledge

1. Consider two projects: one to upgrade the tracking system for the tool crib at DSI, and the second to upgrade the reservations system for United Airlines. Explain how the general characteristics of these two systems development projects differ.

2. Consider the project at DSI to use RFID devices to determine where to place received components into raw materials inventory. Explain the trade-offs that can be made between requirements, cost, and schedule. For a given set of requirements, explain how cost and schedule can be traded off.

3. With regard to Emerson Pharmaceuticals' project to upgrade to a thin-client order-entry system, briefly explain how you think project management must address each of the knowledge areas shown in Figure CE18-3. For each activity, describe one or two issues that could arise and the major management activities that will need to be undertaken. Make assumptions as necessary.

4. Consider the process of an election campaign—say, a campaign to elect one of your fellow students for the position of student government president (or similar office at your university).
   a. Develop a WBS for the election campaign.
   b. Explain how knowledge of the critical path could help you plan the campaign.
   c. Explain two ways you can use critical path analysis for planning the campaign.
   d. Explain how you can use critical path analysis for executing and monitoring the campaign progress.
   e. If you have access to Microsoft Project (or other planning software):
      i. Input your WPS to Project.
      ii. Assign durations to tasks in your project.
      iii. Specify task dependencies.
      iv. Identify the critical path.

5. Suppose you have a computer virus that is so severe you must reformat your hard drive.
   a. Develop a WBS for the process for recovering your computer.
   b. Estimate the time it will take you to perform each task.

    c.   Neither lines of code nor function point estimation pertains to this task. Explain one other way you can improve the quality of your estimate.

    d.   Suppose you suspect that your estimate for the time of recovery could be low by as much as 200 percent. How could you use this knowledge?

    e.   Suppose you are the manager of the shipping department at Emerson Pharmaceuticals. Assume Emerson is planning the project to build the new thin-client order-entry application. What observations or conclusions from your answers to questions a through d could you apply to planning for your department at Emerson?

6.   Suppose you are the manager of the shipping department at Emerson during the order-entry project. Assume you conclude that the requirements are not complete.

    a.   What outcome do you project?

    b.   What can you do?

    c.   Give an example of requirements creep for this project.

    d.   How could you determine if requirements creep were a problem for this project?

    e.   If requirements creep is a problem, what could you do?

7.   What is the single most important task for users on a large-scale systems development project? Do you agree? Why or why not? Why must requirements emerge as a result of a conversation between users and IT professionals?

you be the Guide

Using the Guide: Dealing with Uncertainty (page 539a)

GOALS

✳ Reinforce the dangers of the plunge style of implementation.

✳ Introduce principles of effective IS management.

BACKGROUND AND PRESENTATION STRATEGIES

System conversion of critical business functions like billing is important and usually difficult. Regardless of the style of implementation, problems usually occur. Pilot and piecemeal conversion reduce the risk, but they still demand careful attention—from both users and developers. Parallel implementation is expensive and requires users to perform double duty. If parallel implementation is used, the plan should include hiring additional, temporary personnel to ease the users' workload.

The story recounted in this guide occurred around 1980. I hope that the plunge conversion of a critical system like billing would be rare today. I suppose, though, that in smaller companies, it still must occur.

At the time of the billing system disaster, this company had about $70 million in sales. Its credit was excellent, and borrowing money for the cash flow crisis was thankfully not a problem. Interest rates were high then, however, and borrowing was expensive.

The person in charge of the company's IT department had been promoted from within. He was in over his head. I worked with him for a year or so after this billing system disaster; the company wanted him to succeed. Ultimately, however, the job required him to grow faster than he could. He left the company and took a job managing computer operations at another company. That job was a better fit for his skills. The company then hired a more senior and experienced person as its IS director.

The billing disaster caught the attention of the CEO. Up until then, he'd not paid too much attention to his information systems. Until the billing system, the company's information systems were primarily calculating systems (see Figure 7-1) and had been managed with a light touch by the CFO. The billing system changed the CEO's posture.

At the time of the disaster, the attitude of the entire company mirrored that of the CEO. No one knew exactly what the IS department did, and as long as they got their paychecks on time, they didn't much care. Once the CEO decided that users need to be more closely involved, once he understood and believed the criticality of user involvement in information systems, he embarked on a program to get the users involved.

As stated in the guide, employee attitudes did not change overnight, however. To facilitate a change in attitude, he asked me to conduct a series of meetings with key users in headquarters and other major offices, explaining the importance of user involvement in information systems development and use.

You might forewarn your students about how difficult it can be to choose to actively participate in systems requirements:

- It's easy to de-prioritize requirement meetings because the new system is usually months away, and you'll have jobs that need to be done today.

- The new system may involve discussions about technology that you find tedious and boring.

- The systems development personnel may not be terribly skilled at communicating with you.

- Meetings may require lots of preparation.

- Possibly none of your managers will see the importance of your involvement and will not reinforce your activities.

- You may know that you'll be long gone into a new position or new job by the time the system comes along.

- Users may differ with each other and with you. Meetings can become tedious.

All these factors can make it difficult for you to participate. It's still *very important* for you to do so, however.

Over time, user resistance was overcome, at least for most user managers. The next system the company developed was an order entry and production scheduling system. It had active user involvement, and though that process, too, had problems, that system's development was a vast improvement over the billing system.

See Case Study 10. Even today, active user management of requirements is a serious problem. We have 30 years' experience with this phenomenon, and yet it still continues. Why? I hope someone will someday do research that will lead us out of this continuing, unsolved problem. It's a puzzle.

 SUGGESTED RESPONSES FOR DISCUSSION QUESTIONS

1. Pilot conversion: Implement for one product line, for a set of a few customers, or for one production plant. Parallel conversion: Run both the old billing system and the new one at the same time. Reconcile the two systems.

2. Risk, cost, and disruption of business activities would be good factors to consider. It's a balancing of trade-offs.

3. It would have become obvious that the system was not finished and was not ready for use. For piecemeal conversion, the damage would have been limited to a section of the business, and the company would have needed to borrow less money, or possibly none at all. Damage to the company's reputation by not being able to send bills would have been limited to a few customers. In the case of parallel conversion, no customers would have been impacted at all, and there would have been no need to borrow money.

4. The ultimate result is better information systems: information systems that meet user requirements; information systems that are easy to use; information systems with appropriate security. I think, too, that ultimately, it results in lower cost. Although the cost of development may be higher because of the cost of users' labor in creating such systems, over the long haul, an information system that meets user needs and is easy to use will result in less operations labor, and if the system is in use long enough, will recoup the greater initial investment.

5. Users resisted because the system required more work from them. They had to devote time and attention to the new system. Also, they could no longer sit on the sidelines and criticize whatever result

occurred. They also became partly responsible for the new system. If the system did not meet user needs, they would be held accountable for the failure by their peers. In this particular company, however, the major form of resistance was from the extra work.

Some of the factors in this company were senior management's posture that user involvement and user training were going to be required. Consistency was also important; when users balked at attending meetings, senior management made it clear that attendance at such meetings was required. When users came to meetings ill-prepared, senior management objected.

6. Systems for which users have little active involvement will not meet users' needs; they will be difficult to use; they will constantly be "in development." Users will be frustrated and unproductive. They will hold the IS department responsible for the systems failures.

What the student could do depends on his or her job description and management level in the organization. Apply the five principles stated in the middle of the guide in a way that is appropriate for that job and level.

➤ **Tell me a job you'd like to have, and how you could use the principles in this guide to change the situation.**

WRAP UP

➤ **Unless the system has an inconsequential impact on operations, do not take the plunge. (And why develop a system that has an inconsequential impact?)**

➤ **Active user involvement is key! As a future manager and business professional, take the principles in the middle of this guide seriously.**

➤ **The bottom, bottom line:** *Users are ultimately responsible for the quality of the information systems they have!*

Chapter Extension 19

Chapter 10 provides the background for this Extension.

Alternative Development Techniques

Q1 Why Is Rapid Application Development Rapid?

James Martin, one of the pioneers in information systems, popularized the term *rapid application development* in the title of his 1991 book. The basic idea of **rapid application development (RAD)** is to break up the design and implementation phases of the SDLC into smaller chunks and to design and implement those chunks using as much computer assistance as possible. Figure CE19-1 shows the process Martin envisioned.

Like SDLC, RAD has a requirements phase, but it interweaves the design and implementation phases. That is, developers design, implement, and fix a piece of the new system until the users are satisfied with that piece. Then developers move on to design, implement, and fix another section of the system, and so forth, until the entire system has been developed in pieces. This process, sometimes called **incremental development**, reduces development challenges by using a divide-and-conquer strategy.

The RAD requirements analysis can be less detailed and less complete than with SDLC, because the users are actively involved during design and implementation. In effect, during the design/implement/fix process, the users provide detailed requirements in context.

The main RAD characteristics are listed on the next page:

Study Questions

Q1 Why is rapid application development rapid?

Q2 What is object-oriented development?

Q3 What are the phases and principles of the unified process?

Q4 What is extreme about extreme programming?

Q5 How do development techniques compare?

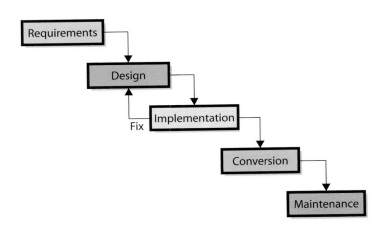

Figure CE19-1
Martin's RAD Process

1. The design/implement/fix development process
2. Continuous user involvement throughout
3. Extensive use of prototypes
4. Joint application design
5. Use of CASE tools

With RAD, users are actively involved throughout the development process and become key members of the development team. Having users as part of the team not only increases the accuracy and completeness of the requirements, but it also promotes a better environment for conversion. The new system will be installed not by strangers, but rather with the active participation of involved users.

We discuss the final three RAD characteristics below.

Prototypes

Another RAD characteristic is the use of prototypes. A **prototype** is a mock-up of an aspect of the new system. A prototype could be a mock-up of a form, report, query, or other element of the user interface. Figure CE19-2 shows a prototype of a data entry form for the Baker, Barker, and Bickel property rental system. This particular form was generated using Microsoft Access, which developers frequently use as a prototyping tool.

Prototypes vary in functionality and utility. Some prototypes are just visual mock-ups of eventual system components. Others are working prototypes from which users can activate some of the system's features. Furthermore, some prototypes are just demonstrations—they are designed to be thrown away. Other prototypes are kept and evolve into the final form, report, or other system component.

Prototypes help users evaluate requirements because they show actual data in context. A user reviewing the form in Figure CE19-2, for example, might realize that the system should sort the data in the grid by *StartDate*. This requirement would be difficult to know or specify without the prototype.

Prototypes also can provide an opportunity for users to test the user interface. The user can employ the form in Figure CE19-2 to enter, modify, or delete data.

Prototypes are more understandable than data models. For example, the prototype in Figure CE19-3 illustrates that each customer has many rentals, and it implies that each rental has at most one customer. It also shows that the same

Figure CE19-2
Example of Prototype Form

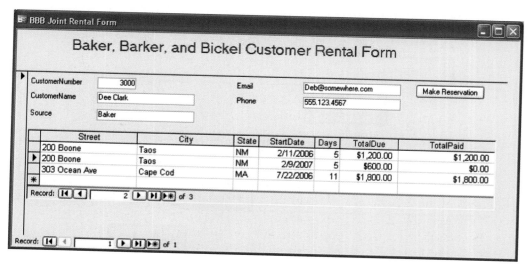

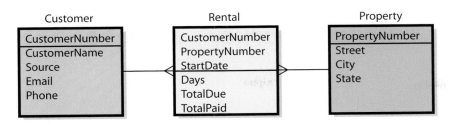

Customer | Rental | Property

Customer	Rental	Property
CustomerNumber	CustomerNumber	PropertyNumber
CustomerName	PropertyNumber	Street
Source	StartDate	City
Email	Days	State
Phone	TotalDue	
	TotalPaid	

Figure CE19-3
Data of Prototype Form in
Figure CE19-2

customer can rent the same property on different dates. We can show the same facts using a data model, as shown in Figure CE19-3, but the form prototype is easier for users to understand.

Unfortunately, prototypes can imply that the application is more complete than it actually is. For example, the form in Figure CE19-2 is only a mock-up. If you click the *Make Reservation* button, nothing happens. The program code that will actually create the reservation does not yet exist. Because writing this code may take three or four or more times more effort than generating the mock-up, the users on the team will believe the system is closer to being done than it is.

Prototypes are very useful as communication devices between users and developers. As long as the developers limit the users' expectations, prototypes are helpful tools.

Joint Application Design

Joint application design (JAD) is another key element of RAD. The term *joint* is used because a *team* of users, developers, and PQA personnel conducts design activities. Prior to 1990, only professional developers participated in design, and the idea of including users and PQA personnel was radical. JAD came about because developers wanted to incorporate feedback and testing earlier in the development process. Ultimately, developers decided that the best place to get feedback was during design creation.

A **JAD session** is a design meeting of short duration, perhaps an afternoon or a day or two at most. During the session, attendees develop the design of a particular component of the system. The goal is to keep the scope of the component small enough that the design can be completed in a short period.

Organizations vary in the degree of structure given to JAD sessions. Some organizations have strict guidelines for both the JAD process and for the documents created both before and after the JAD sessions. Other organizations are less formal in process and documentation. If you are invited as a user to a JAD session, learn the rules and expectations ahead of time. Also, devote time and attention to the meeting; such meetings are important.

CASE and Visual Development Tools

CASE stands for **computer-assisted software engineering** or **computer-assisted systems engineering**, depending on who is using the term. The first meaning focuses on program development; the second focuses on development of systems having the five components. You will encounter both meanings.

For either meaning, the basic idea is to use a computer system, called a **CASE tool**, to help develop computer programs or systems. CASE tools vary in their features and functions. Some such tools address the entire systems development process from requirements to maintenance; others address just the design and implementation phases. Either way, most CASE tools have a **repository**,

Figure CE19-4a
Visual Web Page
Development

Baker, Barker, & Bickel

Reservations Query Form

Start Date: [   ]

End Date: [   ]

Number Bedrooms: ⦿ 1 ⦿ 2 ⦿ 3 ⦿ 4

Maximum Daily Rate: [   ]

which is a database that contains documents, data, prototypes, and program code for the software or system under development.

Most CASE products have tools for creating prototypes, and many have **code generators**, which are programs that generate application code for commonly performed tasks. The idea is to improve developer productivity by having the tool generate as much code as possible. The developer can then add code for application-specific features.

To give you an idea of how a code generator works, examine Figure CE19-4, which illustrates the use of Microsoft FrontPage, a product used to generate Web pages. FrontPage is not a CASE tool, but because it has code generation capabilities, we will use it for illustration.

In Figure CE19-4a, the developer has created a Web page with text, labels, and data entry boxes. The developer can resize elements on the page, move them

Figure CE19-4b
Code Behind Visual Web Page

```
<meta name="ProgID" contents="FrontPage.Editor.Document">
<title>IS300 - Classes</title>
<meta name="MicroSoft Border" content="1">
<link rel="File-List" href="Figure%206-13_files/filelist.xml">
</head>
<body>
<h1 align="center"><font face="Comic Sans MS" size="7">Baker, Barker, &amp; Bickle</font></h1>
<p align="center"><b><font face="Comic Sans MS" size="5" color="#FF0000">
Reservations Query Form<font></b></p>
<blockquote>
<p align="left"><b><font face="Comic Sans MS" color="#ff0000" size="5">     </font> </b></p>
<p align="left"><b><font face="Comic Sans MS" size="5" color="#0000FF">
Start Date:              </font></b>
<input type="text" name="T1" size="20"></p>
    <p align="left"><b><font face="Comic Sans MS" size="5" color="#0000FF">End
    Date:                 
    </font></b><input type="text" name="T1" size="20"><b><font face="Comic Sans MS" size="5"color="#0000FF">   
    </font></b></p>
    <p align="left"><b><font face="Comic Sans MS" size="5" color="#0000FF">
    Number Bedrooms:       </font>
    <font face="Comic Sans MS"><font size="5" color="#008000">
    <input type="radio" Value="V1" checked name="R1"> 1 </font>
    <font size="5" color="#008000">
    <input type="radio" Value="V1" checked name="R1"> 2
    <input type="radio" Value="V1" checked name="R1"> 3
    <input type="radio" Value="V1" checked name="R1"> 4 </font></font></b></p>
    <p align="left"><!--[if gte vml 1]><v:rect id="_x0000_s1027"
  alt="" style='position:absolute;left:3.75pt;top:8.25pt;width:663.75pt;
  height:347.25pt;z-index:-1' strokecolor="#930" strokeweight="3pt"/><![endif]--><![if !vml]><span
style='mso-ignore:vglayout;position:absolute;z-index:-1;left:3px;top:9px;
width:899px;height:467px'><img width=889 height=467
src="Figure%206-13_files/image001.gif" v:shapes="_x0000_s1027"></span><![endif]>
<b><font face="Comic Sans MS" size="5" color="#0000FF">Maximum
  Daily Rate:</font></b></p>
</blockquote>

</body>

</html>
```

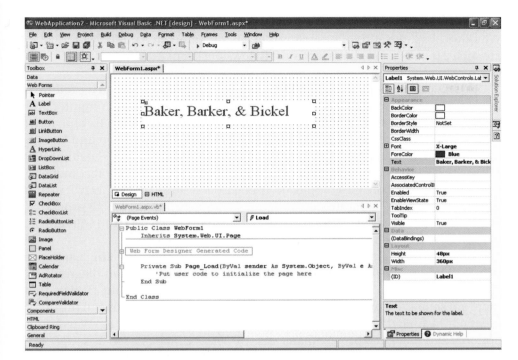

Figure CE19-5
Visual Programming Tool Example

around, change colors, and so forth, all using the graphical tools and symbols. Behind the scenes, FrontPage is generating code in HTML, a language used by browsers to define Web pages. Figure CE19-4b shows the code that corresponds to Figure CE19-4a.

As you can imagine, using the graphical facilities in Figure CE19-4a is much easier than writing the code in Figure CE19-4b. Code generators in CASE tools provide similar functionality. They can do more than just write code for forms and reports, however. Some CASE tools, for example, generate code for common actions like reading, inserting, updating, and deleting rows of tables in a relational database.

Visual development tools also are used in RAD projects to improve developer productivity. Figure CE19-5 shows the use of Microsoft's Visual Studio.Net. The window in the bottom center has program code for processing the form shown in the top center. The code was written by Visual Studio.Net. The developer starts with that code as a skeleton and adds features and functions to it.

By the way, even though we are introducing visual development tools here, in the discussion of RAD, do not be misled into thinking that such tools are used only in RAD projects. They are used for software development projects of all types.

Q2 What Is Object-Oriented Development?

Another development technique arose from the discipline of object-oriented programming, and it is called **object-oriented development (OOD)**. As you will see, OOD has a number of characteristics in common with RAD, but it extends those concepts as well. OOD use began after RAD in the early to mid-1990s.

OOD arose in response to the judgment that there is too much freedom in computer programming. Fred Brooks, author of *The Mythical Man-Month*, wrote that computer programs are logical poetry. Just as there are a myriad of ways to write poetry, so, too, there are a myriad of ways to write computer programs.

Unlike poetry, however, programs must work together. A large system like Windows has thousands of programs that work together in a unified way. To create such a product, programmers must follow consistent practices; if they do not, chaos results.

OOD develops programs using the techniques of **object-oriented programming (OOP)**, which is a discipline for designing and writing computer programs. Programs developed using OOP are easier and cheaper to fix and adapt than those developed using traditional techniques. For this reason and various others, almost every software vendor today writes programs using OOP. Microsoft Windows and Office, for example, are written using OOP techniques.

Developers of business applications have been slower to adopt OOP, in part because they must integrate new programs with existing, non-OOP programs. Still, OOP sees increased use for business applications each year and will soon be the standard for such applications, too.

A series of diagramming techniques called the **Unified Modeling Language (UML)** facilitates OOP development. UML has dozens of different diagrams for all phases of system development. In fact, one complaint about UML is that there are so many diagrams that projects bog down in diagramming to the detriment of finishing the system. UML proponents argue that use of the diagrams is optional and that good project managers will select which ones to use.

UML itself does not require or promote any particular development process. There is, however, one methodology, called the **unified process (UP)**, which was designed for use with UML. We will summarize that process here. Be aware, however, that UML and UP are just examples of OOD diagrams and processes. Your organization may use different techniques. Also note that although UP is primarily a process for developing computer programs and not information systems, the ideas of UP can be broadened to include development of systems having the five components.

Q3 What Are the Phases and Principles of the Unified Process?

Figure CE19-6 shows the basic UP phases. Three of the five phases are similar to phases in the SDLC:

1. The *inception* phase is similar to the first part of the SDLC definition phase.
2. The *transition* phase is similar to the conversion phase in SDLC implementation.
3. The *maintenance* phase is similar to maintenance in the SDLC.

The remaining two phases—*elaboration* and *construction*—are very different from SDLC, as you will see.

Elaboration Phase

During the **elaboration phase**, developers construct and test the framework and architecture of the new system. The result is a working system with basic capabilities. Elaboration includes requirements determination, design, programming, and testing.

With UML and UP, developers express requirements in the form of *use cases*. A **use case** is simply a description of an application of the new system.

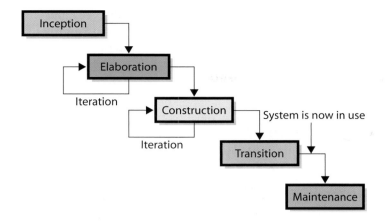

Figure CE19-7 shows a sample use case for the BBB property reservation system. As shown, a use case consists of one or more scenarios that describe how the system will be used. The main success scenario describes how the system is used to create the desired outcome. This is the so-called *happy scenario*. Alternative scenarios describe other situations. They can be other versions of success or scenarios for different cases of failure.

Use cases drive the elaboration iterations. For example, in one iteration, developers would implement scenario 1 in the use case in Figure CE19-7. With subsequent iterations, they would implement other scenarios. Each iteration terminates with a functioning, tested system. Developers will not implement all of the use cases or use-case scenarios in an iteration, but those that they do implement will work.

According to the UP, the elaboration phase addresses the aspects of the system that have the most risk and uncertainty. Developers save the creation of features and functions for which there is little risk for the construction phase.

In today's world, security is an important source of system requirements. Developers need to address security needs, regardless of the style of development

---

Baker Reserves Barker or Bickel Property

Main success scenario:
1. Customer calls Baker and wants to make a reservation in Barker or Bickel's territory. Customer states needs. Baker agent queries system for properties meeting those needs. Customer states dates desired. Agent checks availability for those dates. Property is available. Agent states prices and customer agrees to terms. Agent takes credit card information. Agent sends notification to the relevant Barker or Bickel and confirmation to customer.

Alternative scenarios:
2. Property is found and dates are available. Customer wants to think about it. Agent sends more information to customer and holds property reservation for 48 hours.

3. Property is found, and dates are available. Customer says price is too high.
   a. Agent seeks another property.
   b. Agent asks customer for budget and seeks price change from external agent at Barker or Bickel.
      (1) Price change is OK and customer accepts terms.
      (2) Price change is not OK. Agent seeks another property.

4. Property is found and dates are not available.
   a. Agent seeks another property.
   b. Customer changes dates required.

used. For the SDLC and RAD, developers obtain security requirements during requirements analysis. For UP, developers normally would address security during the elaboration phase.

Construction Phase

During the UP **construction phase**, developers design, implement, and test the easier, lower-risk features and functions that were not addressed during elaboration. Just as with the elaboration phase, construction consists of multiple iterations, each of which ends with a tested, working version of the system. Once developers have constructed all features and functions, the system is ready for deployment.

As noted earlier, the last two UP phases, transition and maintenance, are similar to phases in the SDLC, and we will not consider them further.

At this point in the chapter, we have studied three different development processes—the SDLC process, RAD, and UP. Do companies choose one process for use with all of their IT projects? Some do, but others do not. *MIS in Use CE19* discusses how Sears, Roebuck and Company found itself using a variety of development processes and the steps the company took to standardize on a single process.

UP Principles

Figure CE19-8 summarizes the principles that underlie the UP. We have already discussed the first five. Considering the sixth principle, UP continuously involves users throughout the development process. Because the elaboration and construction phases proceed in iterations, and because users provide requirements for each iteration, there is a continuous need for user involvement. In addition, users provide test criteria and may even perform incremental testing.

One of the dangers of incremental development is that the project is never finished. Users add more requirements in each iteration, and so there is always a need for additional work. Continual iterations are less likely if the users are paying for the system (as they would be at BBB) or if they need the system to solve a troublesome problem. But there is always the chance that different user groups will insist on different sets of requirements. To keep the project from spinning out of control and to ensure that the system does eventually finish, the project team managers must prioritize requirements and have a process for deferring some requirements when necessary.

Similar comments apply to managing changes. As developers complete iterations, the users may want to change aspects of the system that have already been developed. Some changes are unavoidable and should be expected. If

Figure CE19-8
UP Principles

Source: Adapted from Craig Larman, Applying UML and Patterns: An Introduction to Object-Oriented Analysis and Design and the Unified Process, 2nd Edition. Adapted by permission of Pearson Education, Inc., Upper Saddle River, NJ.

1. Develop incrementally.
2. State requirements with use cases.
3. Address high-risk functions early.
4. Build cohesive architecture early.
5. Test and verify quality early and often.
6. Involve users continuously.
7. Manage requirements.
8. Manage change requests.

Sears Standardizes Development

Sears, Roebuck and Company sells home merchandise, apparel, and auto products throughout the United States and Canada. Sears operates 2,300 retail outlets and sells over the Web at *sears.com* and *www.landsend.com*. It also offers products through a variety of specialty catalogs. Additionally, Sears operates the largest home-product repair service in the United States, making more than 14 million service calls per year.

Sears employs over 1,000 IT professionals who were using a variety of different system development methodologies, including SDLC, RAD, and versions of UP. This variety of different development methodologies resulted in systems having inconsistent quality and timeliness. According to John Morrison, IT methodology consultant at Sears,

> One of our central challenges was the use of multiple methodologies throughout IT. Associates

were interpreting these methodologies in different ways. . . . [A]t the start of every project, the team had to establish roles for the project, decide which artifacts were going to be used. . . . [W]ithout a consistent, repeatable methodology, you have no way to pass on the process knowledge you've acquired.

To solve this problem, Sears created a single, consistent, enterprisewide development process. This process is backed by software development tools licensed from IBM and based on a version of the unified process called the Rational Unified Process (RUP)® Methodology. These tools provide Sears' developers the ability to manage requirements, development documentation, defects and testing results, and changes to requirements. RUP was chosen as the standard because teams within Sears had obtained success using it on isolated projects.

The results so far have been encouraging. IT personnel are more effective because they need to learn only one development process. Furthermore, the improved management of development projects has reduced the costs related to system defects and failures by 20 percent. The IT department expects further cost savings as developers gain more experience with the methods and tools.

Source: "Sears Builds Enterprise-wide Solution Delivery Framework," *306.ibm.com/ software/success/cssdb.nsf/CS/MGER-5S3N9N?OpenDocument&Site=software* (accessed June 2005).

---

developers and the organization allow too many changes, however, the system can go into paralysis and never move forward.

Most successful UP projects prioritize change requests and implement them in accordance with that priority. To ensure that requests are not lost or duplicated, developers use some sort of change-tracking database system.

Q4 What Is Extreme About Extreme Programming?

Another alternative development technique is **extreme programming (XP),** which is an emerging technique for developing computer programs. It is not useful for developing large systems that require new business processes and procedures. Organizations have used it successfully, however, in developing application programs.

Extreme programming represents the ultimate in iterative development. Programmers create only features and functions of the new program that they can complete in two weeks or less. If many programmers are working on the project, each person's work must be done in such a way that all of the individual work can be combined and assembled at the end of that period. Users and PQA professionals test the developed code continuously throughout the process.

In addition to this extremely iterative style, XP is distinguished by three key characteristics: (1) It is customer centric, (2) it uses just-in-time design, and (3) it involves paired programming.

Customer-Centric Nature

With XP, the customer or user of the new program is a critical part of the development team. The customer works full time on the project and consults closely with programmers and test engineers. The customer actively and personally defines requirements for the development team, fleshing out requirement details as they are needed by the programmers. The customer also helps testing personnel develop test plans and automated tests as well as performs application testing on a regular and recurring basis.

JIT Design

As discussed in Chapter Extension 9, "Functional Information Systems," the acronym JIT means *just-in-time*. The **JIT design** of XP means that programmers defer program design until the last possible moment. Programmers create the minimal design they need to accomplish the requirements of the current iteration— and nothing more. Unlike other development techniques, developers prepare no overarching program design until the code to be written requires it.

As the project proceeds and as an existing design becomes unworkable, the development team discards that design and creates a new design. (The new design might be more or less complex than the discarded one, depending on the nature of the developing system.) Developers then alter existing programs as necessary to conform to the new design. Such a design technique means that developers will change and adapt programs dozens of times during the development process. Although this reprogramming may be expensive, the JIT design process means that the final programs will be as simple as possible.

Paired Programming

Paired programming is the most unconventional characteristic of XP. With it, two programmers work together, side-by-side, on the very same computer. They look over each other's shoulders, and they continuously communicate as they program on that single machine. According to XP proponents, studies show that two programmers working in this way can do at least as much work as two programmers working separately, and the resulting program code has fewer errors and is more easily maintained.[1] According to the same source, 90

---

[1]Ron Jeffries, "What Is Extreme Programming?" *XP Magazine*, November 11, 2001. *www.xprogramming.com/ xpmag/shatisex.htm#pair* (accessed May 2005).

percent of programmers who have tried paired programming for three weeks or more prefer it.

At each iteration of the project, one of the programmers moves to a different team. In this way, many different programmers see the same code. Over time, the jointly developed code attains a consistent look and feel. Also, the project never becomes dependent on one programmer for his or her specialized expertise. Many programmers know many different sections of code.

Extreme programming is not suited for every project or for every organization, but it does offer at least the promise of advantages over traditional programming methods.

Q5 How Do Development Techniques Compare?

Figure CE19-9 compares the SDLC and the three alternative techniques described in this chapter extension. Both the SDLC and RAD address information *systems* consisting of the five components. OOD with UP and XP are primarily concerned with the development of computer *programs*. Software development vendors, such as Microsoft or Oracle, are more likely to use the latter two techniques. Companies that are developing organizational information systems—say, an inventory or order-entry system—are more likely to use the SDLC and RAD.

You should be familiar with each of these techniques because you may be asked to participate as a user or customer of one of these systems. If so, take that responsibility seriously.

Figure CE19-9
Comparison of Development Techniques

Development Methodology	Scope	Advantages	Disadvantages
SDLC	All five components	• Comprehensive. • Addresses both business and technical issues. • Tried and tested.	• Requirements analysis may lead to analysis paralysis. • Waterfall nature unrealistic.
RAD	All five components	• Iterative nature reduces risk. • JAD improves design. • Use of prototypes and CASE tools increases productivity.	• Requirements analysis may lead to analysis paralysis. • Less suited to very large projects.
OOD with UP	Primarily object-oriented programs	• Use cases are effective requirements documents. • Risk moved forward to elaboration phase. • Each iteration terminates with a working system.	• Less useful for business systems development than for program development. • Danger of sinking into elaboration black hole.
Extreme Programming	Programs	• Customer (user) is always involved. • Paired programming improves quality and reduces risk. • Most useful when requirements evolve with systems development.	• Focus is on programming. • JIT design can require wasteful redesign. • Less useful when system involves many users having different, possibly conflicting requirements.

Active **?** Review

Use this Active Review to verify that you understand the material in the chapter extension. You can read the entire extension and then perform the tasks in this review, or you can read the material for just one question and perform the tasks in this review for that question before moving on to the next one.

Q1 Why is rapid application development rapid?

State the basic idea of RAD. Name the phases of the RAD process, and explain the unusual relationship of the design and implementation phases. Define the term *incremental development*. List five characteristics of RAD. Give an example of a prototype, and explain why prototypes are useful. Explain how a prototype can be used to illustrate a data model. State the disadvantage of prototypes. Describe joint application design. Give two meanings for CASE, and explain the purpose of a code generator. Describe the advantage of visual development tools.

Q2 What is object-oriented development?

Explain the statement, "There is too much freedom in computer programming." Describe the disadvantage of too much freedom. Describe how OOP-developed programs compare to programs using traditional techniques. Explain why developers of business applications have been slower to adopt OOP than developers of systems like Windows. Define *UML*, and state one complaint about it.

Q3 What are the phases and principles of the unified process?

Explain the purpose of the UP. Name the phases of the UP, and compare those phases to the SDLC phases. Describe the purpose and tasks in the elaboration and construction phases. Explain which features and functions are developed in each phase. Explain the role of a use case. State eight UP principles.

Q4 What is extreme about extreme programming?

Describe the purpose and role of extreme programming. Explain the iterative nature of XP. Name and explain three distinguishing characteristics of XP. Define *JIT design*, and explain why it might be considered extreme. Describe the disadvantage of JIT design. Describe paired programming and explain its advantages.

Q5 How do development techniques compare?

Compare and contrast the scope, advantages, and disadvantages of the SDLC, RAD, OOD with UP, and XP.

Key Terms and Concepts

Using Your Knowledge

1. Reread question 1 of Chapter 10.
   a. Develop a plan for this project using RAD.
   b. Compare your plan in a to a plan using the SDLC.

    c.   Explain how OOD with UP might be used in this project

    d.   Explain how XP might be used in this project.

2.   Reread question 2 of Chapter 10.

    a.   Develop a plan for this project using RAD.

    b.   Compare your plan in a above to a plan using the SDLC.

    c.   Explain how OOD with UP might be used in this project

    d.   Explain how XP might be used in this project.

3.   Reread question 4 of Chapter 10.

    a.   Develop a plan for this project using RAD.

    b.   Compare your plan in a above to a plan using the SDLC.

    c.   Explain how OOD with UP might be used in this project.

    d.   Explain how XP might be used in this project.

4.   Consider Figure CE19-3, and suppose a single rental can relate to many properties. This would happen if, for example, a group reserved a set of properties under a single reservation.

    a.   Change the data model in Figure CE19-3 to reflect this situation.

    b.   Explain the changes needed to the prototype form in Figure CE19-2.

    c.   Sketch a prototype form that shows properties and their rentals.

    d.   Summarize the utility of prototypes for illustrating data models.

Chapter Extension 20

Chapter 11 provides the background for this Extension.

Outsourcing

Q1 What Is Outsourcing?

Outsourcing is the process of hiring another organization to perform a service. Just about any business activity in the value chain can be outsourced, from marketing and sales, to logistics, manufacturing, or customer service. Support functions, such as accounting and HR, can be outsourced as well. In this chapter extension, we will focus on the outsourcing of IS and IT services, but realize that companies also outsource most other business activities.

The outsourced vendor can be domestic or international. Some companies choose to outsource overseas because labor is cheaper and to take advantage of time differences. International outsourcing is addressed in "Part 4 International Dimension," on page 298.

Peter Drucker, the father of modern management theory, is reputed to have said, "Your back room is someone else's front room." For example, in most companies, the employee cafeteria is a "back room"; running the cafeteria is not an essential service. Neither Emerson Pharmaceuticals nor DSI wants to be known for the quality of its employee cafeteria. Using Drucker's sentiment, both companies would be better off hiring a company that specializes in food service. That company *does* want to be known for the quality (or low cost, depending on its competitive strategy) of its food.

Because food service is that company's "front room," it will be better able to provide a given quality of food at an appropriate price. Hiring that company frees Emerson and DSI management from thinking about the cafeteria at all. Food quality, chef scheduling, silverware acquisition, kitchen cleanliness, waste disposal, and so on will be the concern of the outsource company. Emerson management can focus on the manufacture and sale of pharmaceuticals, and DSI can focus on manufacturing head-of-state airplane interiors.

Study Questions

Q1 What is outsourcing?

Q2 Why do organizations outsource IS and IT services?

Q3 What are popular outsourcing alternatives?

Q4 What are the risks of outsourcing?

Q2 Why Do Organizations Outsource IS and IT?

Many companies today have chosen to outsource portions of their information systems activities. Figure CE20-1 (page 560) lists popular reasons for doing so. Consider each major group of reasons.

Figure CE20-1
Popular Reasons for Outsourcing
IS Services

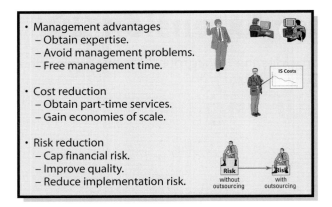

Management Advantages

First, outsourcing can be an easy way to gain expertise. Suppose, for example, that an organization wants to upgrade its thousands of user computers on a cost-effective basis. To do so, the organization would need to develop expertise in automated software installation, unattended installations, remote support, and other measures that can be used to improve the efficiency of software management. Developing such expertise is expensive, and it is not in the company's strategic direction. Efficient installation of software to thousands of computers is not in the "front room." Consequently, the organization might choose to hire a specialist company to perform this service.

Another reason for outsourcing is to avoid management problems. Suppose DSI wants to develop Web services so as to share its inventory data with its suppliers. How can DSI hire the appropriate staff? It doesn't even know if it needs a C++ programmer or an HTML programmer. Even if the company could find and hire the right staff people, how would it manage them? How does DSI create a good work environment for a C++ programmer, when it doesn't even know what such a person does? Consequently, DSI may hire an outside firm to develop and maintain the Web service just to avoid having to address such management problems.

Similarly, some companies choose to outsource to save management time and attention. Suppose Emerson does substantial business over the Web and needs a large Web farm to process the workload. Even if the company knows how to manage a Web farm, acquiring the appropriate computers, installing the necessary software, tuning the software for better performance, and hiring and managing the staff will all require significant management time.

Note, too, that the management time required is not just that of the direct manager of the activity. It is also time from more senior managers who approve the purchase and hiring requisitions for that activity. And those senior managers will need to devote the time necessary to understand enough about Web farms to approve or reject the requisitions. Outsourcing saves both direct and indirect management time.

Cost Reduction

Other common reasons for choosing to outsource concern cost reductions. With outsourcing, organizations can obtain part-time services. An office of 25 attorneys does not need a full-time network administrator. It does need network administration, but only in small amounts. By outsourcing that function, the office of attorneys can obtain network administration in the small amounts needed.

Hewitt Associates, Inc.

Hewitt Associates is an Illinois-based company that provides outsourcing services, primarily for HR. The company, founded in 1940, initially provided employee benefits administration. Over the years, it expanded to offer products and services for HR administration, health care, payroll, and retirement programs. Hewitt employs more than 19,000 people in 35 countries, and revenues in 2004 exceeded $2.2 billion.

Most of Hewitt's customers are large. According to Steve Unterberger, HR outsourcing technology leader at Hewitt, "We focus, specialize, on large employer markets, which we define to be 15,000 to 20,000 employees and higher, all the way up to 150,000, 250,000 employees." Unterberger claims these companies choose Hewitt because it can provide HR systems at less cost and with a higher level of service than companies can do for themselves. Further, outsourcing requires no capital investment.

The demand for HR outsourcing grew dramatically in the last half of 2004. Unterberger believes demand accelerated due to Hewitt's growing reputation: "There are enough success stories for the really early adopter clients, so those who typically sit on the sidelines have talked to those folks, have gotten success stories and are now ready to engage, not as bleeding edge but more of the mainstream and leading edge."

The typical sales cycle is from 3 to 12 months, and during that period, Unterberger says prospective customers need to be reassured on three key factors. First, they want a commitment for a significant percentage reduction in current costs. Prospects need to know that they will not be "nickel-and-dimed or surprised." Second, they need to believe that Hewitt can provide HR services that will be effective within their particular company culture. Large clients like those of Hewitt are unique, and they need to understand how Hewitt's HR services will work for them. Third, prospective customers want to know that outsourcing will provide new expertise and improved service. According to Unterberger, "You don't just put new shirts on the same old people."

One major challenge is that the people who contract with Hewitt are the very people whose jobs will be most changed. Says Unterberger, "It's a very complicated chain of interaction to get the full benefit of these services deployed. It takes a while. It takes some persistence. It takes some good communication skills and good communication programs."

When interviewed in January 2005, Unterberger projected a bright future: "We'll see more fence-sitters getting into the market. The trend we have now—which I call surf's up—will continue. The waves are going to ride pretty high for the next 12 to 18 months. I don't think this is an abnormal spike. More and more people in the mainstream are getting into this."

Source: Originally published at *www.EcommerceTimes.com/sotry/39468.html.* Reproduced with permission of *E-Commerce Times*® and ECT News Network. Copyright 2005 ECT News Network. All rights reserved.

Another benefit of outsourcing is to gain economies of scale. If 25 organizations develop their own payroll applications in-house, then when the tax law changes, 25 different groups will have to learn the new law, change their software to meet the law, test the changes, and write the documentation explaining the changes. However, if those same 25 organizations outsource to the same payroll vendor, then that vendor can make all of the adjustments once, and the cost of the change can be amortized over all of them (thus lowering the cost that the vendor can charge).

Risk Reduction

Another reason for outsourcing is to reduce risk. First, outsourcing can cap financial risk. In a typical outsourcing contract, the outsource vendor will agree to provide, say, computer workstations with certain software connected via a particular network. Typically, each new workstation will have a fixed cost, say, $3,500 per station. The company's management team members may believe that there is a good chance that they can provide workstations at a lower unit cost, but there is also the chance that they'll get in over their heads and have a disaster. If so, the cost per computer could be much higher than $3,500. Outsourcing caps that financial risk and leads to greater budgetary stability.

Second, outsourcing can reduce risk by ensuring a certain level of quality, or avoiding the risk of having substandard quality. A company that specializes in food service knows what to do to provide a certain level of quality. It has the expertise to ensure, for example, that only healthy food is served. So, too, a company that specializes in, say, Web-server hosting knows what to do to provide a certain level of service for a given workload.

Note that there is no guarantee that outsourcing will provide a certain level of quality or quality better than could be achieved in-house. Emerson might get lucky and hire a great chef. So, too, it might get lucky and hire the world's best Web farm manager. But, in general, a professional outsourcing firm knows what to do to avoid giving everyone food poisoning or to avoid two days of downtime on the Web servers. And if that minimum level of quality is not provided, it is easier to hire another vendor than it is to fire and rehire internal staff.

Finally, organizations choose to outsource IS in order to reduce implementation risk. Hiring an outside vendor reduces the risk of picking the wrong hardware or the wrong software, using the wrong network protocol, or implementing tax law changes incorrectly. Outsourcing gathers all of these risks into the risk of choosing the right vendor. Once the company has chosen the vendor, further risk management is up to that vendor. *MIS in Use CE20* (page 561) illustrates the services of one particular outsource vendor, Hewitt Associates.

However, not everyone agrees on the desirability of outsourcing, as described in the *Guide* on pages 563a–563b.

Q3 What Are Popular Outsourcing Alternatives?

Organizations have found hundreds of different ways to outsource information systems and portions of information systems. Figure CE20-2 organizes the major categories of alternatives according to information systems components.

Some organizations outsource the acquisition and operation of computer hardware. Electronic Data Systems (EDS) has been successful for more than 20 years as an outsource vendor of hardware infrastructure. Figure CE20-2 shows another alternative, outsourcing the computers in a Web farm.

Figure CE20-2
IS/IT Outsourcing Alternatives

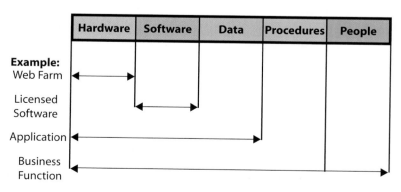

Acquiring licensed software, as discussed in Chapters 3 and 10, is a form of outsourcing. Rather than develop the software in-house, an organization licenses it from another vendor. Such licensing allows the software vendor to amortize the cost of software maintenance over all of the users, thus reducing that cost for all users.

Another possible outsourcing alternative is to outsource an entire system. PeopleSoft attained prominence by outsourcing the entire payroll function. In such a solution, as the arrow in Figure CE20-2 implies, the vendor provides hardware, software, data, and some procedures. The company needs to provide only employee and work information; the payroll outsource vendor does the rest.

A Web storefront is another form of application outsourcing. Amazon.com, for example, provides a Web storefront for product vendors and distributors who choose not to develop their own Web presence. In this case, rather than pay a fixed fee for the storefront service, the product vendors and distributors pay Amazon.com a portion of the revenue generated. Such Web-service hosting has become a major profit center for Amazon.com.

Finally, some organizations choose to outsource an entire business function. For years, many companies have outsourced to travel agencies the function of arranging for employee travel. Some of these outsource vendors even operate offices within the company facilities. More recently, companies have been outsourcing even larger and more important functions. In 2005, for example, Marriott International chose Hewitt Associates to handle its HR needs for the next seven years. Such agreements are much broader than outsourcing IS, but information systems are key components of the applications that are outsourced.

Q4 What Are the Risks of Outsourcing?

With so many advantages and with so many different outsourcing alternatives, you may wonder why any company has any in-house IS/IT functions. In fact, outsourcing presents significant risks, as listed in Figure CE20-3.

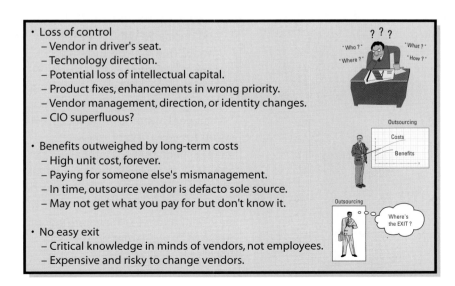

- Loss of control
  - Vendor in driver's seat.
  - Technology direction.
  - Potential loss of intellectual capital.
  - Product fixes, enhancements in wrong priority.
  - Vendor management, direction, or identity changes.
  - CIO superfluous?

- Benefits outweighed by long-term costs
  - High unit cost, forever.
  - Paying for someone else's mismanagement.
  - In time, outsource vendor is defacto sole source.
  - May not get what you pay for but don't know it.

- No easy exit
  - Critical knowledge in minds of vendors, not employees.
  - Expensive and risky to change vendors.

Figure CE20-3
Outsourcing Risks

Is Outsourcing Fool's Gold?

"People are kidding themselves. It sounds so good—just pay a fixed, known amount to some vendor, and all your problems go away. Everyone has the computers they need, the network never goes down, and you never have to endure another horrible meeting about network protocols, HTTPs, and the latest worm. You're off into information systems nirvana. . . .

"Except it doesn't work that way. You trade one set of problems for another. Consider the outsourcing of computer infrastructure. What's the first thing the outsource vendor does? It hires all of the employees who were doing the work for you. Remember that lazy, incompetent network administrator that the company had—the one who never seemed to get anything done? Well, he's baaaaack, as an employee of your outsource company. Only this time, he has an excuse, 'Company policy won't allow me to do it that way.'

"So the outsourcers get their first-level employees by hiring the ones you had. Of course, the outsourcer says it will provide management oversight, and if the employees don't work out, they'll be gone. What you're really outsourcing is middle-level management of the same IT personnel you had. But there's no way of knowing whether the managers they supply are any better than the ones you had.

"Also, you think you had bureaucratic problems before? Every vendor has a set of forms, procedures, committees, reports, and other management 'tools.' They will tell you that you have to do things according to the standard blueprint. They have to say that because if they allowed every company to be different, they'd never be able to gain any leverage themselves, and they'd never be profitable.

"So now you're paying a premium for the services of your former employees, who are now managed by strangers who are paid by the outsource vendor, who evaluates those managers on how well they follow the outsource vendor's profit-generating procedures. How quickly can they turn your operation into a clone of all their other clients? Do you really want to do that?

"Suppose you figure all this out and decide to get out of it. Now what? How do you undo an outsource agreement? All the critical knowledge is in the minds of the outsource vendor's employees, who have no incentive to work for you. In fact, their employment contract probably prohibits it. So now you have to take an existing operation within your own company, hire employees to staff that function, and relearn everything you ought to have learned in the first place.

"Gimme a break. Outsourcing is fool's gold, an expensive leap away from responsibility. It's like saying, 'We can't figure out how to manage an important function in our company, so you do it!' You can't get away from IS problems by hiring someone else to manage them for you. At least you care about *your* bottom line."

DISCUSSION QUESTIONS

1. Hiring an organization's existing IS staff is common practice when starting a new outsourcing arrangement. What are the advantages of this practice to the outsource vendor? What are the advantages to the organization?

2. Suppose you work for an outsource vendor. How do you respond to the charge that your managers care only about how they appear to their employer (the outsource vendor), not how they actually perform for the organization?

3. Consider the statement, "We can't figure out how to manage an important function in our company, so you do it!" Do you agree with the sentiment of this statement? If this is true, is it necessarily bad? Why or why not?

4. Explain how it is possible for an outsource vendor to achieve economies of scale that are not possible for the hiring organization. Does this phenomenon justify outsourcing? Why or why not?

5. In what ways is outsourcing IS infrastructure like outsourcing the company cafeteria? In what ways is it different? What general conclusions can you make about infrastructure outsourcing?

Loss of Control

The first risk of outsourcing is a loss of control. Outsourcing puts the vendor in the driver's seat. Each outsource vendor has methods and procedures for its service. Your organization and employees will have to conform to those procedures. For example, a hardware infrastructure vendor will have standard forms and procedures for requesting a computer, for recording and processing a computer problem, or for providing routine maintenance on computers. Once the vendor is in charge, your employees must conform.

When outsourcing the cafeteria, employees have only those food choices that the vendor cooks. Similarly, when obtaining computer hardware and services, the employees will need to take what the vendor supports. Employees who want equipment that is not on the vendor's list will be out of luck.

The outsource vendor chooses the technology that it wants to implement. If the vendor, for some reason, is slow to pick up on a significant new technology, then the hiring organization will be slow to attain benefits from that technology. An organization can find itself at a competitive disadvantage because it cannot offer the same IS services as its competitors.

Another concern is a potential loss of intellectual capital. The company may need to reveal proprietary trade secrets, methods, or procedures to the outsource vendor's employees. As part of its normal operations, that vendor may move employees to competing organizations, and the company may lose intellectual capital as that happens. The loss may not be intellectual theft; it may simply be that the vendor's employees learned to work in a new and better way at your company, and then they take that learning to your competitor.

Similarly, all software has failures and problems. Quality vendors track those failures and problems and fix them according to a set of priorities. When a company outsources a system, it no longer has control over prioritizing those fixes. Such control belongs to the vendor. A fix that may be critical to an organization may be of low priority to the outsource vendor.

Other problems are that the outsource vendor may change management, adopt a different strategic direction, or be acquired. When any of those changes occurs, priorities may change, and an outsource vendor that was a good choice at one time may be a bad fit after it changes direction. It can be difficult and expensive to change an outsource vendor when this occurs.

The final loss-of-control risk is that the company's CIO can become superfluous. When users need a critical service that is outsourced, the CIO must turn to the vendor for a response. In time, users learn that it is quicker to deal directly with the outsource vendor, and the CIO is soon out of the communication loop. At that point, the vendor has essentially replaced the CIO, who has become a figurehead. However, employees of the outsource vendor work for a different company, with a bias toward their employer. Critical managers will not share the same goals and objectives as the rest of the management team. Biased, bad decisions can result.

Benefits Outweighed by Long-Term Costs

The initial benefits of outsourcing can appear huge. A cap on financial exposure, a reduction of management time and attention, and freedom from many management and staffing problems are all possible. (Most likely, outsource vendors promise these very benefits.) Outsourcing can appear too good to be true.

In fact, it *can* be too good to be true. For one, although a fixed cost does indeed cap exposure, it also removes the benefits of economies of scale. If the Web storefront takes off—and suddenly the organization needs 200 servers instead of 20—the using organization will pay 200 times the fixed cost of supporting one server. It is likely, however, that because of economies of scale, the costs of supporting 200 servers are far less than 10 times the costs of supporting 20 servers.

Also, the outsource vendor may change its pricing strategy over time. Initially, an organization obtains a competitive bid from several outsource vendors. However, as the winning vendor learns more about the business and as relationships develop between the organization's employees and those of the vendor, it becomes difficult for other firms to compete for subsequent contracts. The vendor becomes the *de facto* sole source and, with little competitive pressure, may increase its prices.

Another problem is that an organization can find itself paying for another organization's mismanagement, with little recourse. Over time, if the outsource vendor is mismanaged or suffers setbacks in other arenas, costs will increase. When this occurs, an outsourcing arrangement that initially made sense no longer makes sense. But the cost and risk of switching to another vendor are high.

Don Gray, Dee's consultant, who also specializes in managing off-shore development projects, warns that a common problem (at least for off-shore projects) is the vendor's lack of management expertise: "If you contracted for 200 hours of programmer time, you will probably get that time. What you may not get, however, is the expertise required to manage that time well."[1] By choosing to employ an outsource vendor, the organization loses all visibility into the management effectiveness of the outsource vendor. The organization contracting with the outsource vendor may be paying for gross inefficiency and may not know it. Ultimately, such a situation will result in a competitive disadvantage with organizations that are not subsidizing such inefficiency.

No Easy Exit

The final category of outsourcing risk concerns ending the agreement. There is no easy exit. For one, the outsource vendor's employees have gained significant knowledge of the company. They know the server requirements in customer support, they know the patterns of usage, and they know the best procedures for downloading operational data into the data warehouse. Consequently, lack of knowledge will make it difficult to bring the outsourced service back in-house.

Also, because the vendor has become so tightly integrated into the business, parting company can be exceedingly risky. Closing down the employee cafeteria for a few weeks while finding another food vendor would be unpopular, but employees would survive. Shutting down the enterprise network for a few weeks would be impossible; the business would not survive. Because of such risk, the company must invest considerable work, duplication of effort, management time, and expense to change to another vendor. In truth, choosing an outsource vendor can be a one-way street.

---

[1]Don Gray, conversation with author, May 2003.

Active ? Review

Use this Active Review to verify that you understand the material in the chapter extension. You can read the entire extension and then perform the tasks in this review, or you can read the material for just one question and perform the tasks in this review for that question before moving on to the next one.

Q1   What is outsourcing?

Define *outsourcing*. Explain the implications of Drucker's statement, "Your back room is someone else's front room." Give an example of an outsourcing opportunity at your university.

Q2   Why do organizations outsource IS and IT services?

Name three categories of advantages of outsourcing. Describe two to three specific advantages of each.

Q3   What are popular outsourcing alternatives?

Explain how you can use the five components to organize outsourcing alternatives. Explain how the outsourcing of Web farms, licensed software, applications, and business functions pertains to the five components.

Q4   What are the risks of outsourcing?

Explain how outsourcing results in a loss of control. Describe why the long-term costs of outsourcing may outweigh the short-term benefits. Explain why there is no easy exit from outsourcing, and describe some of the challenges of ending an outsourcing agreement.

Key Terms and Concepts

Outsourcing 559

Using Your Knowledge

1. Consider the following statement: "In many ways, choosing an outsource vendor is a one-way street." Explain what this statement means. Do you agree with this statement? Why or why not?

2. Consider outsourcing of the following business functions:
   - Employee cafeteria
   - General ledger accounting
   - Corporate IT infrastructure (networks, servers, and infrastructure applications such as email)

   a. Compare the benefits of outsourcing for each business function.
   b. Compare the risks of outsourcing for each business function.
   c. Do you believe the decision to outsource is easier for some of these functions than for others? Why or why not?

3. Read the Marriott International case at the end of Chapter 11 (page 270).
   a. List the advantages of outsourcing the HR function.
   b. List the risks of outsourcing the HR function.
   c. How did outsourcing HR reduce the risk in developing OneSystem?

d. Think of all of the systems and IT infrastructure that a company like Marriott has. List five or six information systems that Marriott is likely to have, and list two or three items of IT infrastructure it is likely to need. Consider your two lists as the elements of a portfolio. Explain how outsourcing can be used to balance the risk in the total portfolio. Explain the advantages and disadvantages of outsourcing to the same or different vendors.

4. Suppose you are offered two jobs as a systems analyst. One is for a sizable, quality company like Marriott, and you will work on its in-house information systems. The second job is to work for a quality outsourcing company like EDS (*www.EDS.com*). What do you expect your professional life would be like for the two different jobs? Which job do you think is more secure? Which job do you think has greater career prospects? Can you imagine that one job would be more fulfilling than the other? If so, which one? Assuming pay and benefits were equal, which job would you choose? Reflect on your answers to these questions. If you manage a group that directly interfaces with outsourcing personnel, would you treat the outsourcing personnel different from your own? Why or why not?

Using the Guide: Is Outsourcing Fool's Gold? (page 563a)

GOAL

* Investigate advantages and disadvantages of computer infrastructure outsourcing.

BACKGROUND AND PRESENTATION STRATEGIES

Here is a real-world case that you might use as an opening narrative:

When I worked for Wall Data in the mid-1990s, senior management gave up managing the firm's computing infrastructure and hired EDS to take over the IS function. From my perspective (a business-unit manager for an off-site development group), I didn't think the service was much better—but it wasn't worse—and senior management of the company no longer needed to devote so much of its time and attention to infrastructure management.

Prior to the change to EDS, our group, which was remote from headquarters, was supported by an individual who never seemed to be able to get anything done. Whenever I had a problem, it seemed to me that he had an excuse, but no fix. I'll never forget my shock and dismay when, after the switch to EDS, I rounded the corner in the hallway one morning, only to run into that same person, wearing an EDS shirt!

In fairness to the employee, and in fairness to EDS, his performance did improve. He wasn't much better at fixing problems on the spot, but the EDS reporting systems required him to keep better track of open problems, and eventually someone from his new management team would insist that he find a solution. Problem reports did not disappear into a black hole as they had prior to EDS involvement.

As an aside, I can't imagine a worse client for an outsourcing vendor than a company of professional software developers! Developers aren't prone to keeping their machines in the "standard configuration." They add all sorts of bells and whistles to their machines, and they're good at hiding it, too. Making additions to their computers tends to make the developers happy, and a happy developer is a more productive developer, so I'd look the other way unless the changes were particularly egregious.

I wasn't involved in the contract negotiation or the justification of the switch to EDS. I suspect it was quite expensive—certainly more expensive than the prior internal IS had been. But if you compute the opportunity cost of lost labor from the regular network failures that we'd had, and if you consider the savings in management time that resulted, it may have been more than worth it.

The contrarian makes an excellent point about conflicting management goals. During crunch time, we stressed our computing infrastructure just when we needed the highest reliability. The development team commonly put in 80-hour work weeks. It was a management challenge when we watched the outsourcing vendor's employees leave in the middle of a problem because they were not authorized to work overtime. We were exhausted from our long hours, the network was inhibiting our progress, and we needed a solution. Such events were rare, but they are memorable. They also made it difficult to convince developers of the need to keep their machines in the "standard configuration."

From this anecdotal experience from a single data point, I'd say that outsourcing computer infrastructure removes the highs and the lows from internal support. Although we didn't have heroic support during crunch time, we stopped having infrastructure disasters, too. The support provided by EDS middle management gave us reliability, if not immediate solutions.

By the way, an outsourcing vendor has an advantage that an in-house staff never has. *The outsource vendor can say no.* It is difficult for in-house staff to say no, especially to senior management. So the in-house staff finds itself supporting all sorts of "special situations" that an outsource vendor avoids. "It's not in the contract. Would you like to negotiate an out-of-scope change?" puts a severe damper on special requests.

 SUGGESTED RESPONSES FOR DISCUSSION QUESTIONS

1. Advantages to the vendor: reduced recruitment costs; quicker staffing; and reduced training time, because existing employees know much of the computing infrastructure. Advantages to the customer: no downtime while vendor hires personnel, working relationships already established, less customer time for training new personnel.

2. Good question for the students:

   ➤ **If you worked for EDS, how would you respond to a customer's complaint, "You care only about the EDS bottom line"?**

I think the response has to be that the vendor's bottom line and the customer's bottom line are inextricably related. In the long run, the vendor succeeds only if the customer succeeds. Also, part of the evaluation of vendor employees' performance is customer satisfaction.

3. This statement need not be true. It could be that the company knows how to manage the infrastructure but finds the management opportunity cost to be too high. But, it probably is true for many outsourcing situations. It doesn't seem necessarily bad—if you say it about the company cafeteria, it seems innocuous enough, and, at bottom, how is outsourcing the cafeteria fundamentally different from outsourcing the computer infrastructure? See question 5.

4. Economies of scale are the key for outsourcing vendors' success. When an outsourcing vendor develops a system for problem recording, tracking, and resolution, it can amortize the cost of that system over all its clients. A single company must pay for the development of such a system by itself.

   Consider, too, the use of new technology. An outsourcing vendor can dedicate personnel to learning new technology and developing the means of utilizing the technology for its customers. It then amortizes the cost of that technology assessment and development over all its clients.

   An outsourcing vendor can also afford to train specialists in particular problems and to make those specialists available on an as-needed basis to all its clients. An outsourcing vendor can afford to pay someone to know, for example, all the dials and knobs and options on a Cisco router of a particular type and to understand how that router works with certain types of ACLs in particular firewalls. Such specialized knowledge is not available to a single company. Again, the cost of that specialized expertise is amortized over all clients.

5. I think the cafeteria is more separable than the computing infrastructure. It would be relatively easy to change the cafeteria vendor—just move one group out and another one in. Also, in most cases, the cafeteria could be closed for a period of time, if necessary. Employees can eat elsewhere.

The computing infrastructure is akin to the nervous system of the organization. Outsourcing personnel are integrated into the organization, removing them will be more problematic than removing cafeteria personnel. Also, the computing infrastructure is required—the organization cannot close it down for a period of time while it's being repaired.

Because of the difficulty and expense of recovering from a mistaken vendor choice, I believe there is considerably more risk when choosing a computer infrastructure outsource firm than when considering someone to run the cafeteria.

WRAP UP

➤ **Outsourcing computer infrastructure has both advantages and disadvantages.**

➤ **What are two advantages?**

(Figure CE20-1 has a list of possibilities.)

➤ **What are two disadvantages?**

(Figure CE20-3 has a list of possibilities.)

➤ **Suppose you're working as a department manager and you learn that your company has decided to outsource its computing infrastructure. In a weekly meeting, one of your employees asks you what you think about that. How do you respond?**

The answer depends on what I know: If I've been informed about the reasons for the change, then I explain those reasons. If this is a surprise to me, I would say I don't know anything about it, but will learn more and pass along information as I obtain it. I'd also say something positive about the company.

Chapter Extension 21

Chapter 11 provides the background for this Extension.

Financing and Accounting for IT Projects

Q1 What Are the Costs in a Typical IT Budget?

In most of this book, we have discussed IT projects without considering costs. Alas, everything costs something, and IT and IS are no exception. Figure CE21-1 lists the costs that appear in a typical IT budget. There is some overlap in categories. For example, operations costs might include personnel costs to operate the system. Often, direct labor costs are placed with the costs of the project, and indirect labor costs (such as management and staff functions like data administration) are included in the personnel category.

Deployment and systems development costs refer to the costs of creating new systems. *Deployment costs* are those required to set up systems having little custom development. The cost of installing an email system would be a deployment cost. *Systems development costs* are the costs to create new information systems that require either custom software or substantial work in the other four components of an information system.

As you will learn in your accounting classes, some of these costs will be capitalized and the expense recorded as depreciation against that capital expense. Expensive hardware and large systems development projects often fall into that category.

In most organizations, the IT budget is developed by incremental change. The manager of the department examines last year's expenses and creates the budget by determining incremental changes from last year's results. New projects will require cost estimation, as discussed in Chapter Extension 18, "Large-Scale Systems Development."

Study Questions

Q1 What are the costs in a typical IT budget?

Q2 Who pays IT costs?

Q3 What are tangible and intangible costs and benefits?

Q4 How are IT projects evaluated?

Q5 How is total cost of ownership used to compare alternatives?

Q6 What cost/benefit techniques are used to evaluate IT projects?

Q7 What factors complicate the financing and accounting for IT projects?

- Hardware
- Software license fees
- Operations
- Maintenance
- Personnel
- Training
- Deployment and systems development
- Procurement
- Backup, recovery, and disaster preparedness

Figure CE21-1
Costs in a Typical IT Budget

Q2 Who Pays IT Costs?

Who pays IT costs depends on the size of the organization and its accounting systems and philosophy. In small organizations, IT costs are just accumulated, and no attempt is made to assign those costs to departments or users. In that case, IT costs are just an overhead expense. In larger organizations with more sophisticated accounting, IT costs are allocated to the users. The allocation is sometimes called a **chargeback** expense. Figure CE21-2 shows the consequences of three different chargeback schemes.

Assume in this example that the annual cost of operating and maintaining a network is $24,000 (including possible depreciation expense). The simplest way of allocating costs is to share it equally among the three departments. In that case, each department would be charged $8,000. A more sophisticated scheme is to allocate costs on the basis of the number of employees in a department. As shown in the figure, Sales, having the largest department, will pay the largest share of network expenses. Still a third chargeback scheme is to allocate network expenses on the basis of the number of computers in a department. In that case, Engineering would pay the largest share of the network expenses.

A still more sophisticated scheme (not shown) is to allocate costs based on the number of IP packets sent across the network. To compute a cost per packet, the budgeter would divide the $24,000 by the number of packets sent across the network. Suppose that result is $.05 for every 10,000 packets. The accounting department would use the number of packets sent by each department to compute the department's share of the network expense. Similar allocations would be made for all of the IT expenses listed in Figure CE21-1.

Detailed allocation schemes like cost per packet are expensive to operate. The accounting department faces a trade-off between accuracy of allocation and cost of administration. How much detail is needed? The more detail, the more accurate the financial statements will be, and the easier it will be for managers to monitor and control their employees' use of computer resources. But at some level of allocation detail, the costs of administration and accounting overwhelm the advantages.

The bottom line for you, a future manager, is to understand how IT costs are allocated to your department and manage accordingly. Furthermore, if you

Figure CE21-2
Allocating Network Costs

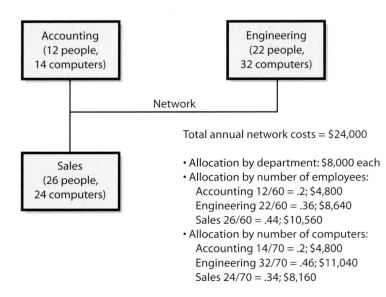

don't believe the allocation scheme is fair, speak up. The scheme may not be fair. For the system in Figure CE21-2, it might be that Engineering sends 95 percent of the traffic over the network. If so, you, as a manager of the Sales department, ought not to be charged $8,000 or more of the expense.

Q3 What Are Tangible and Intangible Costs and Benefits?

Decisions on whether to develop new information systems and decisions among system alternatives for any new or altered system are made on the relationship of costs and benefits. Unfortunately, for most IT/IS projects, many costs and benefits are intangible.

Figure CE21-3 shows typical costs and benefits, both tangible and intangible. Tangible costs and benefits are directly measurable in dollar terms. The costs of computer hardware and the costs of software licenses are easily determined. Similarly, labor savings, material savings, and service cost savings are also easily calculated.

Intangible costs and benefits are difficult, if not impossible, to fix with a dollar value. What is the cost of management time to address the need for a system? What is the cost of lost user time, lost opportunities, and customer bad will? The items have a cost; that is certain. But what is it? Similarly, what is the dollar value of improved morale, more information, or customer goodwill?

Dee's blog is a great example of a system whose benefits are intangible. What is the value of providing more information to the sales force? At some level, that value is increased sales, but how would we determine how much of a sales increase is due to her blog? Or suppose the true value is the prevention of lost sales. How would we ever know that? Dee could claim she had prevented $250,000 in lost sales, but how would she document that?

Beware of systems in which the majority of the costs are tangible and the majority of the benefits are intangible. During your career, you will undoubtedly see proposed projects like one I once saw that had $1.2 million in tangible costs, $650,000 in tangible benefits, and $27.8 million in intangible benefits. (Intangible costs were not considered.) On its face, such a proposal lacks credibility. As a manager, you know you'll pay the costs, you just don't know if you'll ever see the benefits. If you ever propose a project with ratios like that, be ready for considerable (and appropriate) close questioning, scrutiny, and doubt.

	Cost	Benefit
Tangible	Computer hardware Software license fees IT Department personnel WAN and ISP communications fees	Labor savings Material savings Service-cost savings
Intangible	Management reviews Lost user time Lost opportunities Customer badwill	Improved morale More information Customer goodwill

Figure CE21-3
Example of Tangible and Intangible Costs and Benefits

Q4 How Are IT Proposals Evaluated?

The means of evaluating IT proposals depend on the nature and size of the project. Some IT projects provide mandatory organizational infrastructure. Almost every business today needs some sort of network, an email system, and a Web site. For any of those systems, the question is not, "What is the ratio of costs and benefits?" Like employee bathrooms, those systems are required. The analysis for such required systems is simple: just choose the cheapest alternative that will do the job. However, the decision makers need to ensure that they consider the *total cost of ownership* of the system over the system's lifetime, and not just the most apparent costs.

Other systems are small and cheap enough that managers can make the commitment using a back-of-the-envelope assessment. Dee's blog is a good example. The costs are small ($5,000 plus some allocation of server time plus incidentals). Dee's manager can estimate that the costs are less than, say, $10,000 all tolled. The benefits are all intangible: better information to the sales force, better sales force morale because it feels greater support from headquarters, more confident sales reps, and so forth. Trying to estimate these benefits would be expensive and possibly fruitless. So Dee's manager can make that decision in a few minutes, once he understands what she wants to do.

Figure CE21-4 summarizes IT project evaluation techniques. We just described back-of-the-envelope. We will now consider the other four techniques in the next two study questions.

Q5 How Is Total Cost of Ownership Used to Compare Alternatives?

As stated, most businesses make the decision among alternatives for mandatory systems by choosing the cheapest alternative that will do the job. However, this analysis needs to consider the **total cost of ownership (TCO)**, which is the sum of all the costs of the system, for the life of the system.

Figure CE21-4
IT Project Evaluation Techniques

Method	Purpose	Description
Informal, back-of-the- envelope	Quick decision on low-cost systems.	Estimate costs and benefits informally.
Total cost of ownership (TCO)	Compare alternatives for mandatory projects.	Estimate lifetime costs, choose alternative with lowest cost.
Payback	Use costs and benefits to choose among alternative projects.	Determine the length of time required for benefits to offset costs.
Net present value (NPV)	Use costs and benefits to choose among alternative projects.	Consider the discounted value of future costs and benefits. Compute net present value.
Return on investment (ROI)	Use costs and benefits to choose among alternative projects.	Compute the ROI; best to use discounted future costs and benefits.

A good example of the utility of TCO concerns the choice of server operating system. Two viable options are Linux and Microsoft Windows Server. Linux was produced by the open-source community and is license-free; Windows Server is produced by Microsoft and carries a hefty license fee, measured in thousands of dollars (depending on factors beyond the scope of this discussion). So on the surface, Linux appears to be cheaper than Windows Server.

However, as Microsoft is forever preaching, license fees are not the only cost. Microsoft claims that if all of the costs in Figure CE21-1 are considered in the decision, Windows server is actually 10 to 15 percent cheaper than Linux. If you want to read the latest rationale for this, go to *www.Microsoft.com* and search for *Total Cost of Ownership*.

Not to pick on Microsoft, consider DBMS license fees. A DBMS is mandatory in most organizations, so it is amenable to TCO analysis. The open-source product MySQL is license-free; MySQL would appear to be cheaper than a commercial, license-bearing product like Oracle. Go to *www.Oracle.com* and search for *Total Cost of Ownership* to see how Oracle documents that its product has lower TCO than MySQL.

Most of the TCO analyses that favor license-bearing products do so on the basis of higher training and maintenance costs. Both Microsoft and Oracle provide substantial documentation, training, advice on best practices, and so forth, "for free." Open-source software does not provide the same degree of support. Companies like IBM have included Linux and MySQL support and training as part of their services. However, Microsoft and Oracle argue, you are then paying IBM for that service and support, and after you add that cost, the TCO of the Microsoft or Oracle is lower. What an incredibly fascinating business!

Q6 What Cost/Benefit Techniques Are Used to Evaluate IT Projects?

As shown in the last three rows of Figure CE21-4, there are three common cost/benefit techniques: payback analysis, net present value, and return on investment (ROI). To illustrate these techniques, consider the example project shown in Figure CE21-5.

Period	Benefit (Cost)	Remarks
Initial	$(100,000)	Systems development cost is $100,000.
Year 1	(25,000)	Customer confusion elimination of benefits, lost sales.
Year 2	0	Costs and benefits balance each other.
Year 3	25,000	Benefits begin to show.
Year 4	75,000	Strong benefits.
Year 5	75,000	Strong benefits.
Year 6	50,000	Benefits beginning to fade as system ages.
Year 7	25,000	Reduced benefits.
Year 8	0	Costs and benefits again equal.

Figure CE21-5
Example of CRM Project

Suppose we are considering a new CRM system and have planned one alternative for a project that we believe will last eight years. The development and deployment expense of the project is $100,000, and the project delivers the benefits and costs as shown in this figure. Note that costs are denoted by parentheses.

If we use a **payback analysis**, we examine the costs and benefits, and we determine how long it will take for the benefits to pay off the costs. By the end of year 1, the project has a net cost of $125,000. By the end of year 4, $100,000 of the initial amount is paid off. The remaining $25,000 will be paid off in the first four months of year 5 (assuming straight-line accrual of benefits), so the payback period is four years and four months.

We could use this technique to compare this alternative to other alternatives. It does not, however, tell us how good of an investment the proposed system will be. Furthermore, payback analysis assumes that a benefit four years from now has the same value as a cost today, which is not the case. Money has a **time value**: If I have $100,000 today, I can invest it at some interest rate, and I will have something more than $100,000 in four years. Also, if I know I need $100,000 in four years, I can invest something less than that amount today at some interest rate in order to have the $100,000 in four years. So the value of $100,000 in four years is less than that today. How much less depends on the interest rate.

The time value of money is considered in the second cost/benefit technique, **net present value (NPV)**. You will learn about NPV in your financial management classes; for now, we will briefly summarize its use for evaluating IT projects and alternatives. NPV discounts the value of future costs and benefits by some interest rate, called the **discount rate**. This rate is normally the organization's *cost of capital*, which you can think of here as the cost of borrowing money (either from a bank or from other projects at the company).

To apply NPV to the project in Figure CE21-5, we first choose a discount rate—say, 7 percent. Now the cost of $25,000 at the end of year 1 is reduced by 7 percent. The benefit in year 3 is discounted by 7 percent over the three-year period, which turns out to be $1/1.07^3$, which is .816. So, the benefit of year 3 is calculated to be $20,400 and not $25,000. Similar calculations are made on the other benefits in other years.

If we add together all of the discounted costs and benefits for the project in Figure CE21-5, the net of discounted costs and benefits is $156,619. Because this exceeds the investment of $100,000, this project is a good investment.

Is it as good as other, alternative CRM systems? To find out, we compute the NPV of each of the other alternatives. If the intangibles are equivalent among those alternatives, we would normally choose the alternative having the highest NPV.

The third technique for evaluating projects using costs and benefits is to compute the project's **return on investment (ROI)**. Using this technique, we divide the net gain (benefits minus investment) by the investment. Normally, discounted costs and benefits are used for the calculation. For the project in Figure CE21-5, the ROI is 57 percent. Again, we can calculate the ROI for other CRM alternatives as well and choose the one with the highest value.

All three of these techniques consider only tangible costs and benefits. The decision makers will need to factor in intangible costs and benefits as well before making a final decision.

Q7 What Factors Complicate the Financing and Accounting for IT Projects?

Unfortunately, the budgeting and evaluation of IT projects are not nearly as straightforward as this chapter extension has so far implied. First, technology changes fast, so fast that it may be silly even to consider an eight-year project like that in Figure CE21-5. New technology, like XML Web services, may make the CRM system obsolete in four years. Also, as explained in Chapter Extension 18, "Large-Scale Systems Development," the costs of an IT project are very difficult to estimate. Unfortunately, IT projects that are 300 percent or more over their initial cost estimate are not uncommon. Given that imprecision, an NPV analysis, for example, can be pure fiction.

Furthermore, uncertainty is high. As defined in the next chapter extension, **uncertainty** represents the things we don't know we don't know. In 2004, organizations licensed PeopleSoft software because they wanted to work with a smaller company that would support the DBMS product SQL Server. That year, PeopleSoft was acquired by Oracle. Suddenly, the customers were working with a very large company, one that had a very strong preference to move all of the PeopleSoft applications from SQL Server to Oracle. The managers of the companies that originally chose PeopleSoft did not know that they should consider in the cost-benefit analysis the impact of Oracle's acquisition of PeopleSoft.

Finally, intangibles have such an overwhelming impact on systems costs and benefits that performing financial analyses on them may just be a distracting game. Consider system costs in terms of the five components. It is relatively easy to estimate the costs of hardware and software. Data costs are not too hard to estimate, either. But what about people and procedures?

Suppose the CRM system analyzed in Figure CE21-5 will be used by 16,000 people in its eight-year life. Suppose each of those people uses the system for one-fourth of the work day, or 500 hours a year. Using these numbers, we can see that the system will consume eight million human hours in its eight-year life. Now suppose the system turns out to be hard to use and the users are 10 percent less productive than they otherwise could be. That 10 percent means a loss of 800,000 hours, or 100,000 hours per year. If the cost of labor is, say, $30 an hour, then the lost productivity costs $3 million per year, a number that is an order of magnitude larger than any of the numbers in Figure CE21-5.

Thus, choosing the right product for the users turns out to swamp any potential NPV or other analysis. But, determining what is the right set of requirements for the users—and either the benefit of choosing correctly or the cost of choosing incorrectly—are all intangible.

The correct decision may not always be clear, but time and events may force the company to decide. Sometimes, you just don't know the right decision but must choose one course of action. The *Guide* on pages 575a–575b discusses such situations.

We do NPV and other analyses because that's all we have. We base our decisions partly on those analyses and partly on experience guided by intuition. It is very important to know how to perform and interpret NPV and related analyses. It is equally important to know when to ignore them. Welcome to the real world!

What If You Just Don't Know?

What if you have to make a decision and you just don't know which way to go? For complex issues like outsourcing, it can be difficult to know what the right decision is. In many cases, more analysis won't necessarily reduce the uncertainty.

Consider outsourcing as a typical, complex, real-life decision problem. The question is, will outsourcing save your organization money? Will the cap on financial exposure be worth the loss of control? Or is your organization avoiding managing the IS function because you would just like to have the whole IS mess out of your hair?

Suppose the CIO is adamantly opposed to the outsourcing of computer infrastructure. Why is that? He is obviously biased, because such outsourcing will mean a huge cut in his department and a big loss of control for him. It might even mean he loses his job. But is that all there is to it? Or does he have a point? Are the projected savings real? Or are they the result of a paper analysis that misses many of the intangibles? For that matter, does that analysis miss some of the tangibles?

You could do another study; you could commission an independent consultant to examine this situation and make a recommendation. However, is that avoiding the issue yet again? Further, what if there is no time? The network is down for two days for the third time this quarter, and you've got to act. You've got to do something. But what? Take it to the board of directors? No, they don't know. That's just another way of avoiding a tough decision. You've got to decide.

In some ways, higher education does you a disservice. In school, you're taught that a bit more study, another report, or a little more analysis will help you find a better answer. But many decisions don't work that way. There may not be the time or money for another study, or another study may just cloud the issue more. Or maybe it's just not possible to know. What will be the price of IBM stock on January 1, 2010? You just don't know.

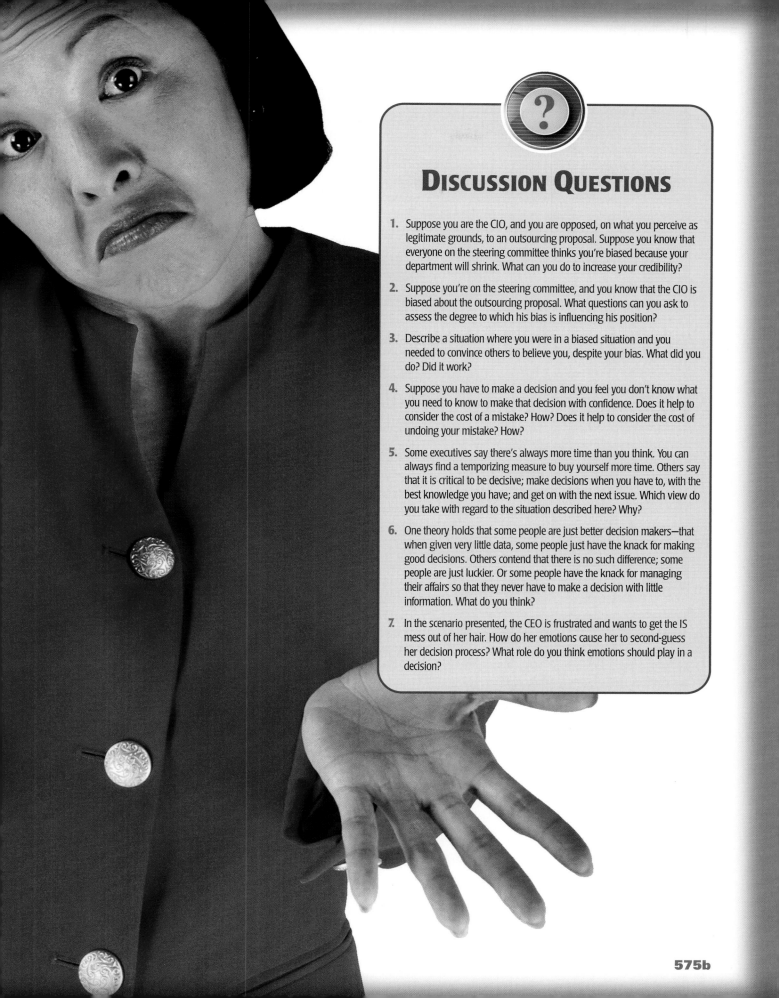

DISCUSSION QUESTIONS

1. Suppose you are the CIO, and you are opposed, on what you perceive as legitimate grounds, to an outsourcing proposal. Suppose you know that everyone on the steering committee thinks you're biased because your department will shrink. What can you do to increase your credibility?

2. Suppose you're on the steering committee, and you know that the CIO is biased about the outsourcing proposal. What questions can you ask to assess the degree to which his bias is influencing his position?

3. Describe a situation where you were in a biased situation and you needed to convince others to believe you, despite your bias. What did you do? Did it work?

4. Suppose you have to make a decision and you feel you don't know what you need to know to make that decision with confidence. Does it help to consider the cost of a mistake? How? Does it help to consider the cost of undoing your mistake? How?

5. Some executives say there's always more time than you think. You can always find a temporizing measure to buy yourself more time. Others say that it is critical to be decisive; make decisions when you have to, with the best knowledge you have; and get on with the next issue. Which view do you take with regard to the situation described here? Why?

6. One theory holds that some people are just better decision makers—that when given very little data, some people just have the knack for making good decisions. Others contend that there is no such difference; some people are just luckier. Or some people have the knack for managing their affairs so that they never have to make a decision with little information. What do you think?

7. In the scenario presented, the CEO is frustrated and wants to get the IS mess out of her hair. How do her emotions cause her to second-guess her decision process? What role do you think emotions should play in a decision?

Active ? Review

Use this Active Review to verify that you understand the material in the chapter extension. You can read the entire extension and then perform the tasks in this review, or you can read the material for just one question and perform the tasks in this review for that question before moving on to the next one.

Q1 What are the costs in a typical IT budget?

List the costs that appear in a typical IT budget. Explain why there may be overlap in some categories. State how the cost of capitalized projects enters the IT budget. Describe how the typical IT budget is prepared.

Q2 Who pays IT costs?

Define *chargeback*. Explain the three methods of network cost allocation shown in Figure CE21-2. Explain how you would justify the per-user charge to the Sales department. Explain how you would justify the per-computer charge to the Engineering department. State the takeaway point for you from this question.

Q3 What are tangible and intangible costs and benefits?

Define *tangible* and *intangible*. Give examples other than the ones in Figure CE21-3 of tangible and intangible costs and benefits. Explain how these terms pertain to Dee's blog. State the dangers of approving a system in which the majority of the costs are tangible and the majority of the benefits are intangible. State the dangers of proposing such a system.

Q4 How are IT projects evaluated?

Explain how required-infrastructure projects are evaluated. Describe the conditions under which a back-of-the envelope analysis is appropriate. Name three techniques that can be used to evaluate projects on the basis of costs and benefits.

Q5 How is total cost of ownership used to compare alternatives?

Define the term *total cost of ownership*. Describe the projects for which TCO is appropriate. Explain how TCO is used by Microsoft and Oracle to justify their license fees. Describe the service that companies like IBM provide for open-source software.

Q6 What cost/benefit techniques are used to evaluate IT projects?

Explain why the payback period for the project in Figure CE21-5 is four years and four months. State what the payback period would be if the expense in year 1 were zero. Explain the disadvantages of using payback analysis. Define *time value of money, net present value*, and *discount rate*. State, in your own words, how NPV analysis works. State how the conclusions of the NPV analysis would change if the initial cost of the project in Figure CE21-5 were $175,000. Define *return on investment*. State what the ROI would be for the project in Figure CE21-5 if the initial cost were $175,000.

Q7 What factors complicate the accounting and financing of IT projects?

Describe the impact of technology on the accounting and financing of IT projects. Define *uncertainty*, and explain how it pertained to the licensers of PeopleSoft products in 2004. Explain how the nature of costs changes among the five components of an information system. Using your own words, describe how intangible costs can swamp an NPV or other financial analysis. Explain why it is still worthwhile to make such analyses. Describe factors besides financial analysis that should guide decisions among IT projects.

Key Terms and Concepts

Chargeback 570
Discount rate 574
Net present value (NPV) 574

Payback analysis 574
Return on investment (ROI) 574
Time value of money 574

Total cost of ownership (TCO) 572
Uncertainty 575

Using Your Knowledge

1. Consider the per-user and per-computer allocations in Figure CE21-2.
   a. Suppose you are the manager of Sales, and the company is proposing to use a per-user cost allocation. Explain how you could argue that such an allocation is unfair.
   b. Suppose you are the manager of Engineering, and the company is proposing to use a per-computer cost allocation. Explain how you could argue that such an allocation is unfair.
   c. Suppose you are the CFO or the person designated to make the allocation method decision. Suppose you have heard the arguments in a and b. How would you proceed?
   d. Suppose you are the manager of Sales, and you win the argument. However, management then reduces your computer budget to the new, lower level. Have you gained anything? If so, what?

2. Why is TCO important to Microsoft and Oracle? In the long run, can they win this argument? Why or why not? What will happen to their advantage when users have become better trained on Linux and Oracle? Given your answer, explain why Microsoft generously provides your university and, in many cases you, license-free software. Is it unethical for your university to accept such software? Is Microsoft's behavior smart or unethical? Why are products from the open-source community, such as OpenOffice, not supported by your university?

3. The Microsoft Excel product in your computer lab (see question 2) can be used to perform NPV analysis. You can also find a simple NPV calculator at *www.investopedia.com* (or Google for others using the term *NPV calculator*).
   a. Enter the data for the project in Figure CE21-5, but change the initial expense to $125,000. Explain the results.
   b. Enter the data for the project in Figure CE21-5, but change the discount rate to 3 percent. Explain the results. Change the discount rate to 15 percent and explain the results. What does this exercise tell you about the role and importance of the discount rate?
   c. Enter the data for the project in Figure CE21-5, and experiment with the discount rate until you make the NPV zero. What is this rate? What does this rate mean?

4. Reread section Q7.
   a. Make the argument that, because of intangibles, NPV for IT projects is nothing more than a numeric smokescreen. Argue that such analyses are not only worthless, they are misleading.
   b. Make the argument that you can fudge the numbers on any IT project to the extent that the project is financially desirable or not, depending on your goal.
   c. Make the argument that intangibles are just that, intangible, and that they, therefore, should not be considered in any IT project. The decision should be made on tangibles alone.
   d. Which of the three arguments do you most believe? State another argument that you feel is more appropriate than any of these.
   e. Extract from your answers to questions a through d your own guiding principles for NPV and related analyses as they pertain to IT projects.

you be the Guide

Using the Guide: What If You Just Don't Know (page 575a)

GOALS

* Sensitize students to problems that cannot be solved by quantitative analysis.

* Discuss the impact of bias and emotions in such decisions.

BACKGROUND AND PRESENTATION STRATEGIES

One of the joys of working in business is the tremendous variety of problems that one encounters and the many different solution strategies that those problems require. Consider some examples:

➤ **If you want to know the financial impact of a 2 percent raise in loan interest rate on the five-year cost of purchasing an item of equipment, do a financial analysis. The quantitative techniques you are learning in your accounting and finance classes will serve you well.**

➤ **But *what about less quantitative decisions*? Or what about decisions for which there is no agreed-on procedure? Marketing is replete with examples of such decisions. For example:**

➤ **How do you select a product name? Say you have created a new XML data store software product. Suppose you hire a name-development consultant who creates a list of the following alternative names: Baton, SmoothSail, and Kenya. How do you *decide which is the best name*?**

➤ **Or, consider strategic marketing. To whom do you sell your new XML data store? To the people who are using relational DBMS products? They will be *invested in the old, relational technology*. Or, do you sell it to people who are exchanging XML documents? They will not be aware of the *need for secure, reliable storage* and won't appreciate your product's features. Which market should you choose?**

➤ **Although you can commission analytical studies, convene focus groups, conduct surveys, and so on, these measures may not appreciably improve the quality of your decision. And often you don't have time.**

➤ **So you must make a subjective decision. But suppose the person who knows the most about the**

situation has a bias, as in the scenario in this guide. The person who knows the most about the IS infrastructure is the person whose budget and responsibilities will be dramatically reduced— maybe even eliminated.

➤ **How do you use the input from such a source when making a subjective decision?**

Some business decisions, like the interest rate computation, are quantitative in nature. Others are very subjective—like choosing the best advertising campaign. (I know you can try them on focus groups, but still, ultimately, it's a subjective decision.) *Outsourcing* is a decision between these two extremes: Parts of the decision are quantitative, but other parts are subjective. The management decision team's decision-making capability is greatly hampered by the clear bias of the person who knows the most about the organization's IS infrastructure.

 SUGGESTED RESPONSES FOR DISCUSSION QUESTIONS

1. First, raise the objection! Tell everyone you know you're biased; tell everyone that you are, of course, concerned about the reduction in your budget and responsibilities. Then, having made your bias clear, make as fact-based a quantitative analysis as you can. Do not be emotional. State the facts in a calm professional manner.

   If you cannot make a solid analysis against the outsourcing proposal, don't try. Be a professional, take your hit, and move on. You may end up with a job with the outsourcing vendor, or you may have to find another company. Or, you may find that you don't mind managing the outsourcing vendor's contract instead of managing IS. But, be a professional about it. Guard your reputation as a businessperson with high integrity; you need it for the long run.

2. In the case of the CIO's bias, look at the quality of the analysis. Is it solidly based on facts, or is it full of difficult-to-prove subjective judgments? Does the CIO appear to be defensive or balanced? This is tough— on everyone. It may be that you just have to discount the CIO's input.

3. The students should have good examples to share. You could start the discussion by asking for examples from academia. Though I have to be careful bringing it up, lest I have a line of students outside my door after the next exam, one example is the student who's arguing for 10 extra points on an exam score.

4. The circumstances are such that you may make a bad decision. You can use the best process available to you and still not have a solid basis for the decision. In this case, do consider the cost of the wrong decision. If the cost is likely to be catastrophic, seek more input; find out what you need to know; strive to find another way to analyze the situation. Use your professional network; talk to others. If the cost of a mistake is modest, it may make sense just to make the decision and move on, preparing as best you can for dealing with a mistake. If the cost of undoing the decision is not great, just make the decision. Or, try to alter the situation so that the cost of undoing it will not be great.

➤ **By the way, it is important to distinguish between a bad decision and a bad result. You can use a superb decision-making process and be unlucky. If so, you'll have a good decision but a bad result. That happens, but it's important to know, for future use, that your decision making was not defective.**

5. My answer to these opinions is that both may be right—it just depends. Usually, there is more time than you think. Usually, you don't have to decide right now, and usually you can take the time for further consideration, more points of view, or additional analysis. But not always!

At the same time, in some situations any decision, even a bad one, will be better than further temporizing. This occurs when the organization is "holding its breath," waiting for a signal about which way to go. In my experience, such situations in business are, thankfully, rare.

With regard to outsourcing, I think the steering committee should listen to the CIO, review the proposals from the outsourcing vendors, do its homework investigating the performance of the outsourcing vendors at other companies that are similar, and make a decision. The only reason I'd wait would be if there is a suspicion, based on the analysis of the vendors' reputations, that none of the vendors is particularly good.

6. To my mind, there is no question that some people are better decision makers with limited data than others. Some people just seem to make a long string of good decisions. Bill Gates is one of them. There were many, perhaps dozens, of young men like Gates who had successful early products and companies. Philippe Kahn (Borland) and Mitch Kapor (Lotus) are two examples. Neither of these two, nor the others, seemed to be able to thread the complexities of the early PC world as well as Gates. Recall that Gates outfinagled IBM when IBM was *the* powerhouse of the industry. Famous stock pickers like Peter Lynch are another example. Lynch would say that he just did his homework, but so did everyone else in that business, and no one had the success he had at Magellan.

I think part of it is that some people have an excellent sense of timing for their decisions. They delay a risky decision until the situation has clarified itself, and then they make the decision. For example, in the late 1980s, Microsoft supported both DOS/Windows and IBM's OS/2. Gates went out on the road, touting OS/2 along with IBM. He pushed both operating systems until the point when it was clear that DOS/Windows would be the winner. Then, when Windows was clearly the winner, he broke from IBM with Windows 95. (Of course, Microsoft heavily influenced that result. Microsoft Office ran only on Windows. OS/2 had few desktop applications, so no one wanted to use it. There was no way that Microsoft was going to put Office on OS/2 unless OS/2 started gaining market share. Had that occurred, Microsoft would have inundated the market with Office for OS/2, which it never had to do.)

7. She'll be concerned that her desire to be rid of the problem will overcome sound business judgment. Regarding the proper role of emotions, I'd say be guided, be informed, by one's emotions. They're pointing you in some direction. But, make the decision on as rational a basis as you can.

WRAP UP

➤ **Not every decision can be analyzed quantitatively. Some require subjective judgment.**

➤ **We've identified a few ways of dealing with difficult decisions. Keep thinking about them. For an exercise, consider this subjective decision:**

➤ **Cast out every thought you've ever had about what job you want. From that blank slate, what job do you want?**

Chapter Extension 22

Chapter 12 provides the background for this Extension.

Managing Computer Security Risk

Q1 What Is Management's Role for Computer Security?

Management has a crucial role in information systems security. Management sets the policy, and only management can balance the costs of a security system against the risk of security threats. The National Institute of Standards and Technology (NIST) published an excellent security handbook that addresses management's responsibility. It is available online at *www.csrc.nist.gov/publications/nistpubs/800-12/handbook.pdf*. We will follow its discussion in this chapter extension.

Figure CE22-1 lists principles of computer security described in the *NIST Handbook*. First, computer security must support the organization's mission. There is no "one size fits all" solution to security problems. Security systems for a diamond mine and security systems for a wheat farm will differ.

According to the second point in Figure CE22-1, when you manage a department, you have a responsibility for information security in that department, even if no one tells you that you do. Do appropriate safeguards exist? Are your employees properly trained? Will your department know how to respond when the computer system fails? If these issues are not addressed in your department, raise the issue to higher levels of management.

Security can be expensive. Therefore, as shown in the third principle of Figure CE22-1, computer security should have an appropriate cost-benefit ratio.

Study Questions

Q1 What is management's role for computer security?

Q2 What are the elements of security policy?

Q3 What is the difference between risk and uncertainty?

Q4 How do managers assess risk?

Q5 Why are risk management decisions difficult?

---

1. Computer security should support the mission of the organization.
2. Computer security is an integral element of sound management.
3. Computer security should be cost-effective.
4. Computer security responsibilities and accountability should be made explicit.
5. System owners have computer security responsibilities outside their own organizations.
6. Computer security requires a comprehensive and integrated approach.
7. Computer security should be periodically reassessed.
8. Computer security is constrained by societal factors.

Figure CE22-1
Principles of Computer Security

Source: National Institute of Standards and Technology, *Introduction to Computer Security: The NIST Handbook*, Publication 800-12, p. 9.

Costs can be direct, such as labor costs, and they can be intangible, such as employee or customer frustration.

According to the fourth principle in Figure CE22-1, security responsibilities and accountabilities must be explicit. General statements like "everyone in the department must adequately safeguard company assets" are worthless. Instead, managers should assign specific tasks to specific people or specific job functions.

Because information systems integrate the processing of many departments, security problems originating in your department can have far-reaching consequences. If one of your employees neglects procedures and enters product prices incorrectly on your Web storefront, the consequences will extend to other departments, other companies, and your customers. Understanding that computer system owners have security responsibilities outside their own departments and organizations is the fifth principle of computer security.

As the sixth principle in Figure CE22-1 implies, there is no magic bullet for security. No single safeguard, such as a firewall or a virus protection program, or increased employee training, will provide effective security. The problems described in Figure 12-1 (page 274) require an integrated security program.

Once a security program is in place, the company cannot simply forget about it. As the seventh principle in Figure CE22-1 indicates, security is a continuing need, and every company must periodically evaluate its security program.

Finally, social factors put some limits on security programs. Employees resent physical searches when arriving at and departing from work. Customers do not want to have their retinas scanned before they can place an order. Computer security conflicts with personal privacy, and a balance may be hard to achieve.

Q2 What Are the Elements of a Security Policy?

As stated, management has two overarching security tasks: defining a security policy and managing computer-security risk. Although management may delegate the specific tasks, it maintains the responsibility for the organization's security and must approve and endorse all such work.

A **security policy** has three elements: The first is a general statement of the organization's *security program*. This statement becomes the foundation for more specific security measures throughout the organization. In this statement, management specifies the goals of the security program and the assets to be protected. This statement also designates a department for managing the organization's security program and documents, in general terms, *how* the organization will ensure enforcement of security programs and policies.

The second security policy element is *issue-specific policy*. For example, management might formulate a policy on personal use of computers at work and email privacy. The organization has the legal right to limit personal use of its computer systems and to inspect personal email for compliance. Employees have a right to know such policies. For another example, management sets security policies to ensure compliance with security privacy law as discussed in the *Ethics Guide* on pages 581a–581b.

The third security policy element is *system-specific policy*, which concerns specific information systems. For example, what customer data from the order entry system will be sold or shared with other organizations? Or, what policies govern the design and operation of systems that process employee data? Companies should address such policies as part of the standard systems development process.

Q3 What Is the Difference Between Risk and Uncertainty?

Management's second overarching security task is risk management. **Risk** is the likelihood of an adverse occurrence. Management cannot manage threats directly, but it *can* manage the likelihood that threats will be successful. Thus, management cannot keep hurricanes from happening, but it can limit the security consequences of a hurricane by creating a backup processing facility at a remote location.

Companies can reduce risks, but always at a cost. It is management's responsibility to decide how much to spend, or stated differently, how much risk to assume.

Unfortunately, risk management takes place in a sea of uncertainty. Uncertainty is different from risk. Risk refers to threats and consequences that we know about. **Uncertainty** refers to the things we don't know that we don't know. For example, an earthquake could devastate a corporate data center on a fault that no one knew about. An employee may have found a way to steal inventory using a hole in the corporate Web site that no expert knew existed. Because of uncertainty, risk management is always approximate.

Q4 How Do Managers Assess Risk?

The first step in risk management is to assess what the threats are, how likely they are to occur, and what the consequences are if they occur. Figure CE22-2 lists factors to consider. First, what are the assets that are to be protected? Examples are computer facilities, programs, and sensitive data. Other assets are less obvious. Phishing threatens an organization's customers as well its trademark and brand. Employee privacy is another asset that can be at risk.

Given the list of assets to be protected, the next action is to assess the threats to which they are exposed. The company should consider all of the threats in Figure 12-1 (page 274); there may be other threats as well.

The third factor in risk assessment is to determine what safeguards are in place to protect company assets from the identified threats. According to the *NIST Handbook*, a **safeguard** is any action, device, procedure, technique, or other measure that reduces a system's vulnerability to a threat.[1] No safeguard is ironclad; there is always a *residual risk* that the safeguard will not protect the assets in all circumstances.

A **vulnerability** is an opening or a weakness in the security system. Some vulnerabilities exist because there are no safeguards or because the existing safeguards are ineffective. Because of residual risk, there is always some residual vulnerability even to assets that are protected by effective safeguards.

Consequences, the fifth factor listed in Figure CE22-2, are the damages that occur when an asset is compromised. Consequences can be tangible or intangible. *Tangible* consequences are those whose financial impact can be measured. The costs of *intangible* consequences, such as the loss of customer goodwill due to an outage, cannot be measured. Normally, when analyzing consequences, companies estimate the costs of tangible consequences and simply list intangible consequences.

1. Assets	5. Consequences
2. Threats	6. Likelihood
3. Safeguards	7. Probable loss
4. Vulnerability	

Figure CE22-2
Risk Assessment

---

[1] *NIST Handbook, www.csrc.nist.gov/publications/nistpubs/800-12/handbook.pdf*, p. 61 (accessed July 2005).

Security

Privacy

Some organizations have legal requirements to protect the customer data they collect and store, but the laws may be more limited than you think. The Gramm-Leach-Bliley (GLB) Act, passed by Congress in 1999, protects consumer financial data stored by financial institutions, which are defined as banks, securities firms, insurance companies, and organizations that provide financial advice, prepare tax returns, and provide similar financial services.

The **Privacy Act of 1974** provides protections to individuals regarding records maintained by the U.S. government, and the privacy provisions of the **Health Insurance Portability and Accountability Act (HIPAA)** of 1996 gives individuals the right to access health data created by doctors and other health-care providers. HIPAA also sets rules and limits on who can read and receive your health information.

The law is stronger in other countries. In Australia, for example, the Privacy Principles of the Australian Privacy Act of 1988 govern not only government and health-care data, but also records maintained by businesses with revenues in excess of AU$3 million.

To understand the importance of the limitations, consider online retailers that routinely store customer credit card data. Do Dell, Amazon.com, the airlines, and other e-commerce businesses have a legal requirement to protect their customers' credit card

data? Apparently not—at least not in the United States. The activities of such organizations are not governed by the GLB, the Privacy Act of 1974, or HIPAA.

Most consumers would say, however, that online retailers have an ethical requirement to protect a customer's credit card and other data, and most online retailers would agree. Or at least the retailers would agree that they have a strong business reason to protect those data. A substantial loss of credit card data by any large online retailer would have detrimental effects on both sales and brand reputation.

Let's bring the discussion closer to home. What requirements does your university have on the data it maintains about you? State law or university policy may govern those records, but no federal law does. Most universities consider it their responsibility to provide public access to graduation records. Anyone can determine when you graduated, your degree, and your major. (Keep this service in mind when you write your résumé.)

Most professors endeavor to publish grades by student number and not by name, and there may be a state law that requires that separation. But what about your work? What about the papers you write, the answers you give on exams? What about the emails you send to your professor? The data are not protected by federal law, and they are probably not protected by state law. If your professor chooses to cite your work in research, she will be subject to copyright law, but not privacy law. What you write is no longer your personal data; it belongs to the academic community. You can ask your professor what she intends to do with your coursework, emails, and office conversations, but none of those data are protected by law.

The bottom line: Be careful with your personal data. Large, reputable organizations are likely to endorse ethical privacy policy and to have strong and effective safeguards to effectuate that policy. But individuals and small organizations may not. If in doubt, ask.

Discussion Questions

1. As stated, when you order from an online retailer, the data you provide is not protected by U.S. privacy law. Does this fact cause you to reconsider setting up an account with a stored credit card number? What is the advantage of storing the credit card number? Do you think the advantage is worth the risk? Are you more willing to take the risk with some companies than with others? Why or why not?

2. Suppose you are the treasurer of a student club, and you store records of club members' payments in a database. In the past, members have disputed payment amounts; therefore, when you receive a payment, you scan an image of the check or credit card invoice and store the scanned image in a database.

   One day, you are using your computer in a local wireless coffee shop and a malicious student breaks into your computer over the wireless network and steals the club database. You know nothing about this until the next day, when a club member complains that a popular student Web site has published the names, bank names, and bank account numbers for everyone who has given you a check.

   What liability do you have in this matter? Could you be classified as a financial institution because you are taking students' money? (You can find the GLB Act at *www.ftc.gov/privacy/glbact.*) If so, what liability do you have? If not, do you have any other liability? Does the coffee shop have a liability?

3. Suppose you are asked to fill out a study questionnaire that requires you to enter identifying data as well as answers to personal questions. You hesitate to provide the data, but the top part of the questionnaire states, "All responses will be strictly confidential." So, you fill out the questionnaire.

   Unfortunately, the person who is conducting the study visits the same wireless coffee shop that you visited (in question 2), and the same malicious student breaks in and steals the study results. Your name and all of your responses appear on that same student Web site. Did the person conducting the study violate a law? Does the confidentiality assurance on the form increase that person's requirement to protect your data? Does your answer change if the person conducting the study is (a) a student, (b) a professor of music, or (c) a professor of computer security?

4. In truth, only a very talented and motivated hacker could steal databases from computers using a public wireless network. Such losses, although possible, are unlikely. However, any email you send or files you download can readily be sniffed at a public wireless facility. Knowing this, describe good practice for computer use at public wireless facilities.

5. Considering your answers to the above questions, state three to five general principles to guide your actions as you disseminate and store data.

The final two factors in risk assessment are likelihood and probable loss. **Likelihood** is the probability that a given asset will be compromised by a given threat, despite the safeguards. **Probable loss** is the "bottom line" of risk assessment. To obtain a measure of probable loss, companies multiply likelihood by the cost of the consequences. Probable loss also includes a statement of intangible consequences.

Q5 Why Are Risk-Management Decisions Difficult?

Given the probable loss from the risk assessment just described, management must decide what to do. In some cases, the decision is easy. Companies can protect some assets by use of inexpensive and easily implemented safeguards. Installing virus protection software is an example. However, some vulnerability is expensive to eliminate, and management must determine if the costs of the safeguard are worth the benefit of probable loss reduction. Such risk-management decisions are difficult because the true effectiveness of the safeguard is seldom known, and the probable loss is subject to uncertainty.

Uncertainty, however, does not absolve management from security responsibility. Management has a fiduciary responsibility to the organization's owners, and managers must make reasonable and prudent decisions in light of available information. They must consider the factors listed in Figure CE22-2 and take cost-effective action to reduce probable losses, despite the uncertainty.

Computer security safeguards are discussed in Chapter 12, starting on page 272.

Active ? Review

Use this Active Review to verify that you understand the material in the chapter extension. You can read the entire extension and then perform the tasks in this review, or you can read the material for just one question and perform the tasks in this review for that question before moving on to the next one.

Q1 What is management's role for computer security?
State management's role for information systems security. List the principles of computer security as described in the *NIST Handbook of Security*. State management's two overarching security tasks.

Q2 What are the elements of security policy?
Name the three elements of a security policy. Explain each. Give an example of two different types of policy.

Q3 What is the difference between risk and uncertainty?
Define *risk*. Define *uncertainty*. Explain why risk can be managed, but uncertainty cannot.

Q4 How do managers assess risk?
Describe three tasks for risk assessment. Define the terms *safeguard, vulnerability, consequences, likelihood*, and *probable loss*. Explain how probable loss is calculated.

Q5 Why are risk management decisions difficult?
Explain why risk management decisions are difficult. Describe management's duties with regard to risk management decisions.

Key Terms and Concepts

Using Your Knowledge

1. Suppose you manage a 10- to 15-person accounts receivable department. Assume your boss has asked you to plan a review of computer security as it affects your department. Write a memo describing your plan, using Figure CE22-1 as a guide.

2. Consider the fifth principle in Figure CE22-1, "System owners have security responsibilities outside their own organizations."
   a. Explain, in your own words, what this statement means.
   b. DSI shares its AutoCad files with its suppliers. Explain how this principle affects DSI's responsibilities.
   c. DSI's suppliers receive and possibly store DSI's AutoCad files. Explain how this principle affects the suppliers' responsibilities.
   d. In the event that someone steals one of the designs that DSI has shared with a supplier, what is likely to happen? Assume it is not clear how the design was stolen.

3. From a risk-management perspective, consider the decision to allow Dee's consultant to install software within the Emerson network.
   a. State how Emerson management could assess each of the factors in Figure CE22-2 to make a risk-management decision.
   b. Emerson did not make a risk assessment of this decision. If it had, and if the consultant had caused damaged, would Emerson's management's position be any different? Why or why not?
   c. Dee's consultant was not a computer criminal, and he took no action that caused Emerson any harm. Given this outcome, would Emerson have been wasting management time to perform a risk-management decision? Why or why not?

Using the Ethics Guide: Security Privacy (page 581a)

GOALS

✱ Understand the legal requirements, ethical considerations, and business consequences of data acquisition, storage, and dissemination.

✱ Help students formulate personal principles with regard to data acquisition, storage, and dissemination.

BACKGROUND AND PRESENTATION STRATEGIES

Throughout this text, we've discussed three categories of criteria for evaluating business actions and employee behavior:

- Legal
- Ethical
- Good business practice

We can clearly see the differences in these criteria with regard to data security. A doctor's office that does not create systems to comply with HIPAA is violating the law. An e-commerce business that collects customer data and sells it to spammers is behaving unethically (at least according to the accepted principles of behavior of most business professionals). An e-commerce business that is lackadaisical about securing its customer data is engaging in poor business practices.

Business professionals need to be worried, much more so than they are, about unsecured wireless networks. Depending on the business, not securing a wireless network could be illegal, unethical, and poor business practice!

Recently, while stopped in a bad traffic jam in my car, I turned on my notebook computer to obtain a phone number. I was on the freeway in the middle of a residential neighborhood, and my laptop found three wireless networks, only one of which was secure. Later that week, while parked in a small tourist town on vacation, I turned on my notebook and found four wireless networks, *none* of which was protected! I'm wondering, "Why does anyone even bother to buy Internet access anymore?" One could just set up shop in his or her car!

Wireless security is changing rapidly; but as of this writing, one effective (not ironclad, but effective) technique for securing a wireless network is MAC address filtering. See Q4 in Chapter Extension 8 for instructions. Briefly: Access the management firmware of the wireless access point (the product documentation always shows how to do this). Check MAC address filtering, and enter the MAC address of every device that is allowed to connect to the LAN. Any device that is not in the list will not be able to connect to the access point.

Careful, here, though! Make sure to enter those addresses correctly—otherwise you won't be able to reconnect to the access point, and you'll have to call the vendor's help desk to learn how to recover.

On Windows, to obtain the computer's MAC address, open a command window (Click *Start, Run, cmd*), and execute the program *Ipconfig*. It will return your computer's MAC address. For printer drivers and other devices, the product's documentation should include the MAC address.

➤ **MAC address filtering is easy to do. Not doing it is poor business practice, possibly unethical, and maybe even illegal!**

Two guidelines that apply the principle, "The best way to solve a problem is not to have it" are:

➤ **Resist providing sensitive data.**

➤ **Don't collect data you don't need.**

I have become very aggressive in not divulging personal data. At least 95 percent of the time, when I challenge someone as to why they need some piece of personal data, they respond, "Oh, don't bother—we don't have to have it." I recommend a similar strategy to my students.

When someone says, "All answers are strictly confidential," consider the source. If that statement comes from the university computer security staff, I believe they understand what they are claiming to provide and will take every professional effort to comply with that statement. If it is made by a team of undergraduates with majors that predispose me to believe they know little of computer security, then I suspect they may not know what they are claiming to provide. Furthermore, in the event of a security system failure, the university has a deep enough pocket to provide compensation for damages. It would be difficult to obtain compensation from a group of undergraduates.

➤ **Don't provide data to sources with questionable data security!**

SUGGESTED RESPONSES FOR DISCUSSION QUESTIONS

1. The advantage of an account is you don't have to enter credit card data every time you buy. The problem is that your credit card data is stored on at least one of their disks, and hence it is vulnerable to theft. (The order entry software may also store your credit card data for a one-time purchase, but that storage should be temporary.)

   I recommend four general principles:

   ➤ **Never set up an account with a vendor unless you know that vendor has substantial financial assets (Amazon.com versus Mom-and-Pop Plant Sales).**

   ➤ **Set up accounts only with companies with which you do enough business that the time-savings benefits of the account justify the risk of a security problem.**

   ➤ **Send credit card data only to organizations that are using SSL/TLS (https).**

   ➤ **Never send your Social Security number, driver's license number, or any password to anyone.**

   (Caveat: Maybe it would be OK to send your SSN to the IRS? The alternative is paying by mail, but is that any more secure? The IRS stores your SSN, regardless of how you pay. A good question.)

2. You probably do have some liability in this instance, but unless you have substantial personal assets, it's probably not worth anyone's time to sue you. Your club or university may have liability, however. I doubt anyone could claim that you are a financial institution, but there may be other liability. The possible liability of the coffee shop is interesting. I suspect there is some language somewhere that limits its liability. These are questions to explore with a business law professor because the relevant case law is evolving.

   As a practical matter, whenever you collect any sort of confidential computer-sensible data, don't store it on the notebook computer you carry around campus or use for wireless access. Store it on a memory stick and when you're not using that data lock the memory stick up at home—or at the club offices. Take the memory stick out only when you need the data for a meeting, and don't sign on to a wireless network while you're using it.

3. Use the three categories of criteria: Collecting sensitive data and not protecting it is *poor business practice*, even if you provide no confidentiality statement. Collecting data and not protecting becomes *unethical* if you do provide a confidentiality statement.

As to the *legality*, I am not an attorney, but I don't believe this event violates any commonly enacted law. However, you may have violated an implied contract between you and the responder. If your statement does constitute a contract, you are expected to do what a reasonable and prudent person would do to protect that data. If you do not take such precautions, you are in violation of the contract and could be held financially accountable.

The three different backgrounds alter what the reasonable and prudent person would be expected to do. The student would have the least responsibility, because of his or her assumed immaturity and inexperience. The professor of music would have greater responsibilities because his or her position as a professor would imply greater experience and world knowledge. The professor of computer security would have a very high level of expectation of behavior for protecting that data.

4. I think the following is the very best guideline for email:

   ➤ **Never send an email, from anywhere, unless you would be pleased to see it published on the front page of the *New York Times* or your local newspaper the next day. If you'd be embarrassed, likely to be sued, or likely to go to jail were that email published, don't send it. Don't write it, either.**

5. One possible list of general principles for storing and disseminating data:

   ➤ **Don't disseminate data when you can avoid it.**

   ➤ **Don't collect data when you can avoid it.**

   ➤ **When you do collect sensitive data, keep it on removable devices and minimize the exposure of those devices to security threats. (This guideline is appropriate for an individual; obviously a business has other requirements.)**

   ➤ **Never generate an email that you'd regret seeing on the front page of the *New York Times*.**

   ➤ **Secure your personal/home/SOHO wireless networks.**

WRAP UP

➤ **As a business professional, you have the responsibility to consider the legality, the ethics, and the wisdom when you request, store, or disseminate data. The more knowledge and experience you have, the greater that responsibility is.**

➤ **Think about this and develop your own code of behavior. Then, follow that code. Prevent problems before they occur!**

Chapter Extension 23

Chapter 12 provides the background for this Extension.

SSL/TLS and https

Q1 How Does SSL/TLS Use Encryption?

We described some **encryption** techniques in Chapter 6 (page 128). To review, senders use a key to encrypt a plaintext message and then send the encrypted message to a recipient, who then uses a key to decrypt the message. See Figure CE23-1 (page 586).

With **symmetric encryption**, both parties use the same key. With **asymmetric encryption**, the parties use two keys, one that is public and one that is private. A message encoded with one of the keys can be decoded with the other key. Asymmetric encryption is slower than symmetric encryption, but it is easier to implement over a network.

Secure Sockets Layer (SSL) is a protocol that uses both asymmetric and symmetric encryption. SSL is a protocol layer that works between Levels 4 (transport) and 5 (application) of the TCP—OSI protocol architecture. With SSL, asymmetric encryption transmits a symmetric key. Both parties then use that key for symmetric encryption for the balance of that session.

Netscape originally developed SSL. After a brief skirmish in the marketplace, Microsoft endorsed its use and included it in Internet Explorer and other products. SSL version 1.0 had problems, most of which were removed in version 3.0, which is the version Microsoft endorsed. A later version, with more problems fixed, was renamed **Transport Layer Security (TLS)**.

Using SSL/TLS, the client verifies that it is communicating with the true Web site, and not with a site that is spoofing the true Web site. However, to ease the burden on users, the opposite is not done. Web sites seldom verify the true identity of users. Hence, programs can spoof legitimate users and fool Web sites. Because the consequences affect the Web site and not the client, such spoofing has no effect on the consumer. It is a problem that Web sites must address, however.

Study Questions

Q1 How does SSL/TLS use encryption?

Q2 What prevents spoofing of the public key?

Q3 How do digital signatures detect text alteration?

Q4 How are digital certificates used to obtain public keys?

Q5 Why not send confidential data via email?

Q6 Why is https the only practical secure transmission on public wireless networks?

Q2 What Prevents Spoofing of the Public Key?

What prevents spoofing of the public key? So far, nothing. Here and in Chapter 6, we glibly passed by this difficult question. To summarize this situation, when your browser initiates an https session, it uses SSL/TLS to provide security. You

Figure CE23-1
Components of SSL/TLS

Technique	How it works	Characteristics
Symmetric encryption	Sender and receiver transmit message using the same key.	Fast, but difficult to get the same key to both parties.
Asymmetric encryption	Sender and receiver transmit message using two keys, one public and one private. Message encrypted with one of the keys can be decrypted with the other.	Public key can be openly transmitted, but needs certificate authority (see below). Slower than symmetric.
SSL/TLS (https)	Works between Levels 4 and 5 of the TCP—OSI architecture. Sender uses public/private key to transmit symmetric key, which both parties use for symmetric encryption—for a limited, brief period.	Used by most Internet applications. A useful and workable hybrid of symmetric and asymmetric.
Digital signatures	Sender hashes message, and uses private key to "sign" a message digest, creating digital signature; sender transmits plaintext message and digital signature. Receiver rehashes the plaintext message and decrypts the digital signature with the public key. If the message digests match, receiver knows that message has not been altered.	Ingenious technique for ensuring plaintext has not been altered.
Digital certificates	A trusted third party, the certificate authority (CA), supplies the public key and a digital certificate. Receiver decrypts message with public key (from CA), signed with CA's digital signature.	Eliminates spoofing of public keys. Requires browser to have CA's public key.

and the party you are attempting to communicate with need to share a key for symmetric encryption, and you exchange that key using asymmetric encryption. But to use asymmetric encryption, you need the public key of the site you are attempting to communicate with. We might naïvely say, "Just ask for it." If you want to contact *www.Vanguard.com*, just ask Vanguard's server for its public key.

The problem is that nothing prevents a third party from intercepting that communication and substituting the third party's public key for Vanguard's. If that were to happen, all of your communications would be secure with the third party—who will be able to obtain all of the confidential data you send.

So we need some means to verify that we are truly communicating with Vanguard and not someone spoofing Vanguard. As you will see, SSL/TLS uses digital certificates for that purpose. Before you can understand such certificates, however, you must first learn how digital signatures are used to detect text alternation. We consider that topic next.

Q3 How Do Digital Signatures Detect Text Alteration?

Because encryption slows processing, most messages are sent over the Internet as plaintext. This means it is possible for someone to intercept your email and change your message unbeknownst to you. For example, suppose a purchasing agent sends an email to one of its vendors with the message, "Please deliver shipment 1000 to our Oakdale facility." Because email is protected, it is possible for a third party to intercept the email, remove the words *our Oakdale facility*, substitute its own address, and send the message on to its destination.

Digital signatures ensure that plaintext messages are received without alterations. Figure CE23-2 summarizes their use. The plaintext message is first *hashed*. **Hashing** is a method of mathematically manipulating the message to create a string of bits that characterize the message. The bit string, called the **message digest**, has a specified, fixed length, regardless of the length of the plaintext. According to one popular standard, message digests are 160 bits long.

Hashing is a one-way process. Any message can be hashed to produce a message digest, but the message digest cannot be unhashed to produce the original message.

Hashing techniques are designed so that if someone changes any part of a message, rehashing the changed message will create a different message digest. For example, the email message with the words *our Oakdale facility* and the same message but with the interceptor's address will generate two different message digests.

Authentication programs use message digests to ensure that plaintext messages have not been altered. The idea is to create a message digest for the original message and to send the message and the message digest to the receiver. The receiver hashes the message it received and compares the resulting message

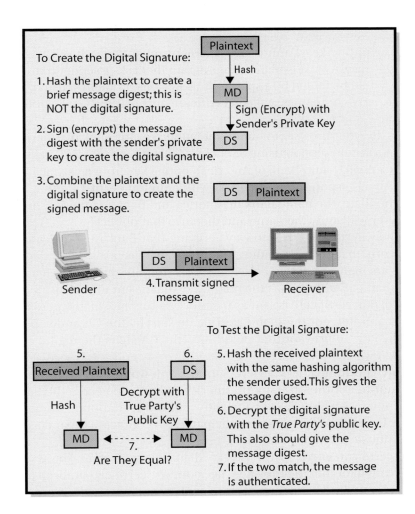

Figure CE23-2
Digital Signatures for Message Authentication

Source: Ray Panko, *Corporate Computer and Network Security*, 1st Edition, © 2004. Reprinted by permission of Pearson Education, Inc., Upper Saddle River, NJ.

To Create the Digital Signature:

1. Hash the plaintext to create a brief message digest; this is NOT the digital signature.

2. Sign (encrypt) the message digest with the sender's private key to create the digital signature.

3. Combine the plaintext and the digital signature to create the signed message.

4. Transmit signed message.

Sender

Receiver

To Test the Digital Signature:

5. Hash the received plaintext with the same hashing algorithm the sender used. This gives the message digest.

6. Decrypt the digital signature with the *True Party's* public key. This also should give the message digest.

7. If the two match, the message is authenticated.

Are They Equal?

digest to the message digest that was sent with the message. If the two message digests are the same, then the receiver knows that the message was not altered. If they are different, then the message was altered.

For this technique to work, the original message digest must be protected when it is transmitted. Accordingly, as Figure CE23-2 shows, the message digest (MD in this figure) is encrypted using the sender's private key. The result is called the message's digital signature. Applying one's private key to the message digest is called *signing* the message. As shown in step 4 of Figure CE23-2, the system sends the signed message to the receiver.

The receiver hashes the plaintext message that arrived to produce a message digest for the received message. It then decrypts the digital signature with the sender's public key (called the **true party's** public key, in this figure) and compares the message digest for the received message with the original message digest. If they are the same, then the message was not altered. If the message digests differ, then the receiver knows that someone altered the message somewhere along the line.

Only one problem remains: How does the receiver obtain the true party's public key? As stated, the receiver cannot ask the sender for its public key, because the sender could be spoofing.

Q4 How Are Digital Certificates Used to Obtain Public Keys?

When using public keys, a message recipient must know that it has the true party's public key. As just explained, a program that asks a sender to transmit its public key could be fooled by a spoofer. To solve this problem, trusted, independent third-party companies, called **certificate authorities (CAs)**, supply public keys.

Thus, for your browser to obtain the public key for Bank of America, either to conduct a secure session using SSL/TLS or to authenticate a digital signature, your browser will obtain Bank of America's public key from a certificate authority. The CA will respond to the request with a **digital certificate** that contains, among other data, the name Bank of America and Bank of America's public key. Your browser will verify the name and then use that public key.

By the way, the CA is in no way verifying that Bank of America is a legitimate concern, that it is law-abiding, that it has paid its taxes, that its accounting standards are high, or anything else. The CA is simplify verifying that a company known as Bank of America has the public key that it sent to your browser.

The digital certificate is sent as plaintext, so there is still the possibility that an entity can intercept the digital certificate sent by the CA and substitute its own public key. To prevent that possibility, the CA signs the digital certificate with its digital signature.

Before continuing, let's review. Suppose you want to transfer money from one account to another at Bank of America. When you access the bank's Web server, it initiates an SSL/TLS session with your browser. Your browser needs the public key for Bank of America to participate, so it contacts a CA and asks for the digital certificate for Bank of America.

The certificate arrives with the CA's digital signature. Your browser hashes the certificate to obtain the message digest for the certificate it received. It then uses the CA's public key to decrypt the signature and obtain the message digest for the certificate that the CA transmitted. If the two message digests match, your browser can rely on the fact that it has the true public key for Bank of America.

Except . . . See if you can find the flaw in what we have described so far before you continue reading.

The flaw is that your browser needs the CA's public key to authenticate the digital certificate. Your browser cannot ask for that public key from the CA because someone could be spoofing the CA. Your browser could obtain the CA's public key by requesting a digital certificate for the first CA from a second CA, but the problem still remains. Your browser would then need to contact a third CA to obtain a digital certificate for the second CA. And so it goes. Meanwhile, you're thinking it would be easier to walk down to the bank.

The infinite regress halts because browsers contain the public keys for the common CAs in their program code. As long as you receive your browser from a reputable source, you can rely on the public keys it uses when authenticating digital certificates from the CAs it uses.

Q5 Why Not Send Confidential Data via Email?

The SSL/TLS protocol lies between Layers 4 and 5 of the TCP/IP—OSI architecture. This means that any Layer 5 protocol can use SSL/TLS. Layer 5 protocols are the application layer and include http, ftp (for file transfer), and SMTP and other email protocols. The version of http that uses SSL/TLS is called https. Thus, anytime you see //https in your browser's address field, you know you are using SSL/TLS, and that your transmissions are secure. You can send account numbers, credit card numbers, and so forth. (At least you know the transmission is secure. Whether or not you actually want the party on the other end to have your account number, credit card or other personal data is a separate question!) The https protocol is commonly used.

There are also versions of ftp and email that can use SSL/TLS. In the case of email, however, *SSL/TLS is almost never used*. Thus, as a general rule, never send sensitive, confidential, or proprietary data via email. That statement means never send it as part of an email message, and never send it as an attachment to an email. You will frequently be asked to send such data via email; it happens all the time. Don't do it! If you want to share that data, call the party on the telephone and provide it verbally.

By the way, you can digitally sign email messages. If you do so, you can be assured that the contents of your email have not been altered. You have no protection from sniffing, however.

Q6 Why Is https the Only Practical Secure Transmission on Public Wireless Networks?

For a wired network, a potential intruder must obtain physical access to the network. For a wireless network, however, no direct connection is needed. Drive-by sniffers can walk or drive around business or residential neighborhoods with a wireless computer and locate dozens, or even hundreds, of wireless networks. The wireless network will broadcast whether or not it is protected. If not, the sniffer can use it to obtain free access to the Internet or to connect to LANs that are connected to the access point.

In 2004, in a short ride through the Back Bay section of Boston, Massachusetts, a security consultant found 2,676 wireless connections, most of which were residential. Of those, almost half were unprotected.[1] Anyone with a wireless device could have connected to those unprotected access points and tapped into the Internet for free or taken more disruptive actions.

It is possible to protect wireless networks. Businesses with sophisticated communications equipment use elaborate techniques—techniques that require the support of highly trained communications specialists. Common protections use VPNs and special security servers.

For the less-sophisticated SOHO market, wireless networks are less secure. The IEEE 802.11 Committee, the group that develops and maintains wireless standards, first developed a wireless security standard called **Wired Equivalent Privacy (WEP)**. Unfortunately, WEP was insufficiently tested before it was deployed, and it has serious flaws. In response, the IEEE 802.11 committee developed improved wireless security standards known as **Wi-Fi Protected Access (WPA)** and a newer, better version, called **WPA2**. Unfortunately, only newer wireless devices can use these techniques.

Wireless security technology is changing rapidly. By the time you read this, even-newer security standards will have been developed. Search the Internet for the term *wireless network security* to learn about the latest standards. In the meantime, on any wireless network you use, make sure you enable the highest level of security that you can and be aware that, at present, especially on SOHO networks, wireless networks are not nearly as secure as wired networks.

Warning: Any plaintext you send over a public wireless network can be read using readily available software. For example, in a classroom with a wireless network, all normal email and IM messages can be read by others. Only data you send via https is protected when you are using a public wireless network.

---

[1] Bruce Mohl, "Tap into Neighbors' Wi-Fi? Why Not, Some Say," *Boston Globe*, July 4, 2004, *www.boston.com/business/technology/articles/2004/07/04/tap_into_neighbors_wifi_why_not_some_say?pg=1* (accessed July 2005).

Active ? Review

Use this Active Review to verify that you understand the material in the chapter extension. You can read the entire extension and then perform the tasks in this review, or you can read the material for just one question and perform the tasks in this review for that question before moving on to the next one.

Q1 How does SSL/TLS use encryption?

Define *encryption, symmetric encryption*, and *asymmetric encryption*. Explain how SSL/TLS uses encryption. Define *SSL* and *TLS*. Explain the consequences of users verifying Web sites but Web sites not verifying users.

Q2 What prevents spoofing of the public key?

Describe the role of the public key in the SSL/TLS protocol. Explain how the public key of a site could be spoofed, and discuss the consequences of that spoofing.

Q3 How do digital signatures detect text alteration?

Define *hashing, message digest*, and *digital signature*. Using Figure CE23-2 as a guide, explain how digital signatures work. Explain how messages that have been altered can be detected.

Q4 How are digital certificates used to obtain public keys?

Define *certificate authority*. Explain how certificate authorities are used to prevent spoofing. Describe the assertion that a CA makes when it issues a digital certificate. Explain why the public key of the CA must be hard-coded into a browser.

Q5 Why not send confidential data via email?

Name three protocols that could use SSL/TLS. Name one that does not usually use SSL/TLS. Describe the consequences of its not using SSL/TLS. Explain the protection that you can obtain if you digitally sign your emails.

Q6 Why is https the only practical secure transmission on public wireless networks?

Explain the security problem of wireless networks. Define *WEP*, and explain its drawback. Define *WPA*. Describe the level of security protection available at most public wireless networks.

Key Terms and Concepts

Asymmetric encryption 585
Certificate authority (CA) 588
Digital certificate 588
Digital signature 587
Encryption 585
Hashing 587
Message digest 587
Secure Sockets Layer (SSL) 585
Symmetric encryption 585
Transport Layer Security (TLS) 585
True party 588
Wi-Fi Protected Access (WPA) 590
Wired equivalent privacy (WEP) 590
WPA2 590

Using Your Knowledge

1. Suppose you work in a doctor's office and you notice that medical personnel frequently send confidential patient information via regular email. You mentioned this to the office manager and explain the security risks. She asks you to prepare a memo for her to present to the managing doctors. Write that memo. See HIPPA (page 518a) for additional information about this situation.

2. Suppose you are applying for a job with a company for which you really want to work. That company asks you to prepare an application and send that

application as an email attachment. Assume the application includes personal and private data.

   a. What do you do?
   b. What do you conclude from this situation about the HR department at this company? What do you conclude about the company?
   c. Apply the concept of risk management (page 581) as it pertains to this situation.
   d. Assume you decide to notify the company that it is violating the privacy of job applicants. How would you proceed?

3. Ask three or more fellow students, friends, or co-workers about their computer activities at public wireless hot spots. Specifically, ask:

   a. How frequently do they use computers on a public wireless net?
   b. Do they know the difference between http and https?
   c. What applications do they typically use? Email? Web browsing (http)? E-commerce (https)? Instant messaging?
   d. Do they know which of these activities are secure and which are not secure?
   e. What general conclusions can you make from your small survey?
   f. Write a one-page memo recommending computing practices on a public wireless net.

4. Imagine that you are sitting in a classroom with a wireless network and that you have the software and skills to read every other student's unprotected communications (all communications other than https).

   a. What information might you obtain?
   b. What does your answer to question a tell you about your own computer use in class?
   c. Apply the concept of risk management (page 581) to this situation.

Chapter Extension 24

Chapter 12 provides the background for this Extension.

Computer Crime and Forensics

Q1 What Are the Three Types of Computer Crime?

Prosecutors, accountants, and security experts use the term **computer crime** for three types of activity as summarized in Figure CE24-1. The first type includes crimes committed *using a computer*. Such crimes include theft of financial assets, phishing, child pornography, and any other crime in which a computer system plays a role in perpetrating the crime. Second, computer crime refers to crimes committed *against a computer*. This category includes viruses, unauthorized access, and theft of proprietary data. It also includes the theft of computer equipment. Finally, computer crime refers to crimes in which a computer was *used to store data that can be used as evidence*. Examples are address books, emails, and databases of criminal activity. A database containing records of drug shipments is an example of the latter.

Computer crime differs from terrorism because it is a criminal act. As explained in Chapter Extension 16, "Information Systems and Counterterrorism," terrorism is an act of war, and terrorist acts do not fall under criminal law. The rules of evidence and the boundaries of allowed search and seizure differ between computer crime and terrorism. Furthermore, those who work in the field of computer crime seek evidence of crimes that have already occurred. Those who work to counter terrorism seek evidence of crimes that have not yet occurred.

Study Questions

Q1 What are the three types of computer crime?

Q2 What is the extent of computer crime?

Q3 How can computer crime be prevented?

Q4 What laws pertain to governmental search of computers?

Q5 What is computer forensics?

Q6 How should organizations respond to a suspected computer crime?

- **Using computer system**
  - Theft of financial assets, credit cards, money laundering
  - Phishing
  - Child pornography
  - ID theft
- **Against a computer system**
  - Viruses
  - Unauthorized access
  - Theft of proprietary data
  - Theft of equipment
- **Storing evidence on a computer system**
  - Address books
  - Emails
  - Databases of activities

Figure CE24-1
Examples of Computer Crime

Q2 What Is the Extent of Computer Crime?

We don't know the extent of computer crime. Unfortunately, there is no national census of computer crime. We can only rely on surveys taken of sample organizations. One of the oldest and most respected surveys is the one conducted by the Federal Bureau of Investigation and the Computer Security Institute (known as the FBI/CSI survey).

The FBI/CSI survey has been conducted since 1995, and the organizations involved in the survey are balanced among for-profit and not-for-profit businesses and governmental agencies. They are also balanced for size of organization, from small to very large. You can obtain a copy of the most recent survey from the site *www.gocsi.com.*

The 2006 survey addressed computer crime that occurred in 2005 among 616 different organizations. According to the survey, the total loss due to computer crime among these organizations was $52.5 billion. However, for fear of adverse public relations, privacy, or other reasons, many organizations will not report computer crimes they have experienced. In the 2006 survey, in fact, only 313 organizations were willing (or able) to report the size of their loss. Keep in mind this number reflects only the losses of the companies in the survey; we have no idea of the total losses of *all* companies. We can say that there was *at least* $52 billion of loss due to computer crime, but the actual number is likely many, many times larger.

Figure CE24-2 lists the top four categories of computer crime. Notice the survey reports the percentage of incidents using the full 616 respondents, but the size of loss is just that attributed to the 313 respondents who reported their losses.

The top four losses were virus attacks, unauthorized access, laptop theft, and theft of proprietary data. *Unauthorized access* is unfortunately a very broad term that includes attacks and infiltration of computer systems as well as misuse of computer systems by employees. Employees who make personal airline reservations from their computers against organizational policy are included in this category.

However, guard your laptop! Nearly 50 percent of the companies reported theft of laptops or other mobile computer equipment, and a total of $6.6 billion of such devices were lost. The final category was losses due to theft of proprietary data. Such losses must have been huge; only 9 percent of the respondents reported such theft, but the total of such losses was $6 billion.

It is not clear from the survey results how much of the loss of proprietary data was due to data lost on stolen laptops. However, every six months or so the

Figure CE24-2
Computer Crime, 2006 FBI/CSI Survey

Source: Data from 2006 CSI/FBI Computer Crime and Security Survey www.gocsi.com (accessed August 2006).

Source	Percent Attacked in Prior 6 Months (of 616 respondents)	Total Loss (313 respondents)
Viruses	52 percent	$15.6 billion
Unauthorized access	32 percent	$10.6 billion
Theft of laptop or mobile device	47 percent	$6.6 billion
Theft of proprietary data	9 percent	$6.0 billion

press reports another incident in which individual identities were exposed to risk when some employee lost his or her laptop containing proprietary data. As a business professional, make it your practice not to carry out of your office on a laptop any data that you do not need. In general, store proprietary data on servers or removable devices that do not travel with you. If you are required to carry proprietary data on your laptop, outside of your offices, then guard that data appropriately. Assume your laptop is a case containing rare gems; in fact, the data it contains may be worth more than a case of rare gems!

Q3 How Can Computer Crime Be Prevented?

Computer crime can be prevented using the techniques described in Chapter 12 and in Chapter Extension 22, "Managing Computer Security Risk." In short, organizations need to develop a security plan, and they need to manage their security risk. Risk management entails listing the assets that are threatened, determining threats against those assets, and developing appropriate safeguards against those threats. As stated in Chapter Extension 22, management must consider the value of the assets, the likelihood of threats, and the cost of safeguards. In some cases, it is uneconomic to create safeguards, and management chooses to accept the risk of loss.

Computer crime prevention apparently works. According to the 2006 FBI/CSI survey, except for laptop theft, the number of incidents has been in steady decline for the past five years. The survey attributes this decline to the substantial increase in security expenditures among small- and medium-sized companies. (By the way, 80 percent of the respondents stated that they use some form of financial analysis, like NPV or ROI, to justify their security spending. You can learn about the use of such techniques in Chapter Extension 21, "Financing and Accounting for IT Projects.")

Q4 What Laws Pertain to Governmental Search of Computers?

The body of law pertaining to the governmental search for evidence of computer crime is exceedingly complicated. Accordingly, the first step for any organization that believes it has been the victim of a computer crime should be to contact legal counsel.

The Fourth Amendment of the U.S. Constitution protects citizens against illegal search or seizure by the government. When organizations wish to prosecute computer criminals, the actions of government investigators and their agents must not violate accepted precedents concerning such search. Further, actions of the employer can also be limited. The law is complicated, in and of itself, but it becomes even more so when considering that digital evidence may reside on computer systems geographically far removed from the crime.

To briefly summarize the principles, the Fourth Amendment prevents a government agent from searching computer files if the person who uses that computer has a reasonable expectation of privacy. For example, if you use your personal computer in your own room, and do not allow your roommate or others to access that computer, you have a reasonable expectation of privacy. However, if you share the computer with others, you may give up that expectation of privacy. If so, investigators can search your computer disk without a warrant.

A more likely case is that you send sensitive information to another person, say, via an email. Sending the email to your ISP and other organizations that transmit the email does not violate your expectation of privacy. However, once your email has been received, you most likely have given up the expectation of privacy. Unless your correspondent is your attorney, your doctor, or your clergyman, the law presumes that you give up your right to privacy by sharing the information with someone else. As Benjamin Franklin said, "Three people can keep a secret as long as two of them are dead."

However, if you are preparing information for publication, then your material may be protected by the First Amendment (the right to free speech). That limitation may not sound relevant to most businesses, but placing material on a Web site is considered publication. Thus, employees who work on the company Web site may have protections that go beyond the Fourth Amendment. Again, the law around such evidence is complicated!

In most cases, your employer can consent to the warrantless search of your computer files at work, and in some cases, even a co-worker can consent to such a search. This means if you are suspected of a computer crime, investigators can search your work computer without a warrant. If a co-worker believes you are viewing child pornography, for example, investigators can search your computer without a warrant.

Furthermore, employees of governmental organizations have even less protection (because the government is not just the government; it is also their employer). In some cases, all computer data for government employees is considered searchable without a warrant. Again, however, the law is complicated.

This brief survey provides two take-home messages. First, as an employee, assume that any computer data you process can be searched not only by your employer but also, without a warrant, by governmental employees and agents. You may have protections, but if so, they are limited. Second, as a manager or employer, if you believe your organization is the victim of a computer crime, and if you want to preserve the possibility of prosecuting the suspect, then your first call should be to your organization's legal staff.[1]

Q5 What Is Computer Forensics?

Forensics is defined as the use of science to obtain data for use by the legal system. **Computer forensics** is defined as the identification, collection, examination, and preservation of digitally recorded data. The goals of computer forensics are to help investigators determine what happened, learn how to prevent similar future incidents, catch the perpetrator, and gather evidence for trial.

Computer forensics is complicated because it is easy to damage data while attempting to identify and collect it. For example, with most operating systems, deleted data is not truly deleted. When you delete a file, the operating system de-allocates the space the file occupies on disk and adds that space to

---

[1]For more information about this topic, see *Searching and Seizing Computers and Obtaining Electronic Evidence in Criminal Investigations*, U.S. Department of Justice, July 2002.

a list of free disk space. The data still reside on the disk in the de-allocated space. Software tools exist for reading de-allocated space, and such tools are understandably useful for recovering evidence. They must, however, be used with care. Because the operating system places the de-allocated space on a list of available space, the operating system will use that space when it needs disk space for other tasks. In fact, the act of turning on the computer can cause the operating system to over-write that space. So, when a computer has been seized that may include evidence in deleted file space, the investigators will need to proceed with great caution. This is especially so because different operating systems treat deleted space and other critical elements differently.

Furthermore, data can be hidden in many file locations, and if the computer is on a network, data can be hidden in many locations on the network. Files can be disguised by name and by type. Few criminals would name a database *MyDrugShipments.mdb*. It might instead be named something like *win32SysParam* to make it appear to be part of the operating system. The disguise can be made stronger by placing the file in a Windows directory. File types can also deceive. A file with a .jpg extension is normally an image file. However, it could, in fact, be an Access database. Simply searching for the Access file extension, .mdb will not necessarily reveal all of the Access databases on the disk.

Steganography is an even stronger hiding method. **Steganography** is the hiding of messages by encoding them in innocent-looking files. The following sentence is a simple example of text steganography: *Most Investment Strategies invested sequentially cancel ordinary office liabilities.* This sentence encodes the message *MIS is cool.*

Some steganography techniques hide messages in inessential overhead data. It is possible, for example, to hide messages in the Formats and Styles of a Word document. The most dramatic, examples, however, hide messages in pictures and audio files. As discussed in Chapter Extension 4, "Preparing a Computer Budget," most displays today represent the color of each pixel by a string of 32 bits. However, it is possible to change one or two of those bits without substantially degrading the image. Those bits can be used to carry a message or another image.

Figure CE24-3 (page 598) shows an example in which the entire first chapter of *The Hunting of the Snark* has been encoded in a .jpg image. The original picture in Figure CE24-3(a) appears to be only slightly distorted after the chapter has been hidden in it. Similar techniques can be used to hide text, images, or audio messages in innocent sounding audio files. The added message will sound like background static when the audio is played.

Steganography detection is difficult. Programs for finding steganographically modified files exist, but they are not effective. Detection and decoding of such images is today a forensics research topic.

Computer forensics is fascinating, but it is a poor first job. You need years of experience as a network administrator, systems programmer, or other highly technical computer professional before you can qualify. If you have an interest in such a career, begin with more mundane technical aspirations.

By the way, some people include auditors and account examiners in the category of computer forensics. Certainly such professionals provide a key role in complicated crimes, such as the accounting fraud at Enron, but their expertise lies in accounting and auditing and not in computer technology. Hence, it seems a stretch to group their activities into computer forensics.

Figure CE24-3
Steganography Example

a. The Unmodified Original Picture

b. The Picture with the Entire Book Chapter Embedded

Q6 How Should Organizations Respond to a Suspected Computer Crime?

Organizations should respond to a suspected computer crime as they would any other security incident. As stated in Chapter 12, the first step is to develop an incident response plan. That plan should address all types of security incidents, including computer crime, and should be created long before any suspected incident.

The specific actions to take depend on the nature of the crime and the goals of the organization. If there is no intent to prosecute and no need to preserve

The ChoicePoint Attack

ChoicePoint, a Georgia-based corporation, provides risk-management and fraud-prevention data. Traditionally, ChoicePoint provided motor vehicle reports, claims histories, and similar data to the automobile insurance industry; in recent years, it broadened its customer base to include general business and government agencies. Today, it also offers data for volunteer and job-applicant screening and data to assist in the location of missing children. ChoicePoint has over 4,000 employees, and its 2004 revenue was $918 million.

In the fall of 2004, ChoicePoint was the victim of a fraudulent spoofing attack in which unauthorized individuals posed as legitimate customers and obtained personal data on more than 145,000 individuals. According to the company's Web site:

> These criminals were able to pass our customer authentication due-diligence processes by using stolen identities to create and produce the documents needed to appear legitimate. As small business customers of ChoicePoint, these fraudsters accessed products that contained basic telephone directory-type data (name and address information) as well as a combination of Social Security numbers and/or driver's license numbers and, at times, abbreviated credit reports. They were also able to obtain other public record information including, but not limited to bankruptcies, liens, and judgments; professional licenses; and real property data.

ChoicePoint became aware of the problem in November 2004, when it noticed unusual processing activity on some accounts in Los Angeles. Accordingly, the company contacted the Los Angeles Police Department, which requested that ChoicePoint not reveal the activity until the department could conduct an investigation. In January, the LAPD notified ChoicePoint that it could contact the customers whose data had been compromised.

This crime is an example of a failure of authentication and not a network break-in. ChoicePoint's firewalls and other safeguards were not overcome. Instead, the criminals spoofed legitimate businesses. The infiltrators obtained valid California business licenses, and until their unusual processing activity was detected, appeared to be legitimate users.

In response to this problem, ChoicePoint established a hotline for customers whose data were compromised to call for assistance. They also purchased a credit report for each of these people and paid for a one-year credit-report-monitoring service. In February 2005, attorneys initiated a class-action lawsuit for all 145,000 customers with an initial loss claim of $75,000 each. At the same time, the U.S. Senate announced that it would conduct an investigation.

Ironically, ChoicePoint exposed itself to a public relations nightmare, considerable expense, a class-action lawsuit, a Senate investigation, and a 20 percent drop in its share price because it contacted the police and cooperated in the attempt to apprehend the criminals. When ChoicePoint noticed the unusual account activity, had it simply shut down data access for the illegitimate businesses, no one would have known. Of course, the 145,000 customers whose identities had been compromised would have unknowingly been subject to identity theft, but it is unlikely that such thefts could have been tracked back to ChoicePoint.

Source: www.choicepoint.com/news/statement_0205_1.html#sub1 (accessed February 2005). Used with permission of ChoicePoint.com.

---

evidence, then the general strategy is to contain, eradicate, and recover. This strategy is appropriate for events like a virus attack.

If there is intent to prosecute, or if the full nature of the attack is not evident, it might be necessary to allow the attack to continue so as to gather evidence. In the ChoicePoint attack discussed in *MIS in Use CE24*, the Los Angeles Police Department asked ChoicePoint not to reveal the strategy until it could conduct an investigation. That delay, of course, subjected ChoicePoint to greater liability, but it had to balance that liability against the need to learn the full nature of the attack.

If during your career you suspect a computer crime, follow the guidelines in your organization's incident response plan. If there is no such plan, contact the CIO or other designated person. If you are unsure of what to do, contact a senior manager or your organization's lawyers. Do not proceed on your own! See the *Ethics Guide* on page 99a for a related story.

Active ? Review

Use this Active Review to verify that you understand the material in the chapter extension. You can read the entire extension and then perform the tasks in this review, or you can read the material for just one question and perform the tasks in this review for that question before moving on to the next one.

Q1 What are the three types of computer crime?

Name three types of computer crime and give two examples of each. Explain the differences between computer crime and terrorism.

Q2 What is the extent of computer crime?

Describe the respondents in the FBI/CSI survey of computer crime. State the total losses reported by this survey, and explain why the true losses due to computer crime are likely to be much greater. Explain why some organizations choose not to report computer crime loss. Name the four types of attack that generated the greatest loss. Explain why the term *unauthorized access* is vague. State guidelines for protecting laptop computers and the data they contain.

Q3 How can computer crime be prevented?

Summarize the ways in which organizations can prevent computer crime. Describe how risk management pertains to computer crime prevention. Summarize the evidence that indicates computer crime prevention seems to be working.

Q4 What laws pertain to governmental search of computers?

State the first step for any organization that believes it has been the victim of a computer crime. Explain the meaning of the term *reasonable expectation of privacy*, and state how it applies to the governmental search of computer systems. Describe how your sending a message to someone affects your presumed expectation of privacy. Name three exceptions to this effect. Describe how the preparation of materials for a Web site may have additional protections. Summarize the restrictions on governmental searches of work computers. State the two take-home messages from the discussion of this question.

Q5 What is computer forensics?

Define *computer forensics*. Give an example of how it would be easy to damage data while attempting to identify and collect it. Explain two ways of disguising the contents of a file. Define *steganography*, and give a simple text example. Describe, in general terms, how images can be hidden in other images. Explain why computer forensics is a poor first job. Explain why auditors and account examiners are not considered computer forensic experts, at least according to this text.

Q6 How should organizations respond to a suspected computer crime?

Summarize the ways that organizations should respond to computer crime. State the three verbs that define the strategy for responding to computer crime when there is no intent to prosecute. Describe circumstances in which this strategy may not be used. Explain what you should do if, as a business professional, you suspect a computer crime.

Key Terms and Concepts

Computer crime 593   Computer forensics 596   Steganography 597

Using Your Knowledge

1. Consider Dee's forcing Emerson's IT department to allow her consultant to install software on their internal network.
   a. Using Figure CE 24-1 as a guide, give five different examples of criminal acts that her consultant could have taken.
   b. Explain how his being allowed inside the network circumvented IT controls.
   c. What do you conclude from your answers to a and b?
   d. What do you conclude about the vice president of sales who forced the IT department to allow the consultant access?
   e. Suppose senior IT management did not know about this situation. If they learned about it after the fact, what should they do?

2. Consider the IT department at DSI and the fact that the department consists of one person.
   a. Using Figure CE24-1 as a guide, summarize DSI's vulnerability.
   b. Give an example of each of the crimes in Figure CE24-2, and explain how each could happen at DSI.
   c. Suppose that a computer crime is perpetrated at DSI. For each of the crimes in Figure CE24-2, explain how likely it is that DSI will know about the crime.
   d. Explain how steganography could be used to send designs of DSI's interiors without detection. Give a scenario in which this might be done.
   e. Suppose you were not a summer intern at DSI, but rather a senior manager in manufacturing. Given the knowledge you have gained from Chapter 12 and from this chapter extension, what would you do?

3. Suppose you are an employee in each of the following situations. Describe what you would do.
   a. You manage an employee, Jones, whom you suspect of selling proprietary data to the competition.
   b. You have a co-worker, Jones, whom you suspect of selling proprietary data to the competition.
   c. You suspect your boss, Jones, is selling proprietary data to the competition.
   d. How does your right to give consent for a search of Jones' computer vary among a through c?
   e. Suppose that no evidence can be found to substantiate Jones' selling of proprietary data. If it is known that you were the one to start the investigation, explain your position for each one of the three scenarios, a through c.
   f. Suppose that Jones is, indeed, selling proprietary data. How does your answer to question e change?
   g. State your own personal guidelines for reporting suspected computer crime.

GLOSSARY

10/100/1000 Ethernet A type of Ethernet that conforms to the IEEE 802.3 protocol and allows for transmission at a rate of 10, 100, or 1,000 Mbps (megabits per second). 119

Access A popular personal and small workgroup DBMS product from Microsoft. 99

Access control list (ACL) A list that encodes the rules stating which packets are to be allowed through a firewall and which are to be prohibited. 129

Access devices Devices, typically special-purpose computers, that connect network sites. The particular device required depends on the line used and other factors. Sometimes switches and routers are employed, but other types of equipment are needed as well. 124

Access point A point in a wireless network that facilitates communication among wireless devices and serves as a point of interconnection between wireless and wired networks. The AP must be able to process messages according to both the 802.3 and 802.11 standards, because it sends and receives wireless traffic using the 802.11 protocol and communicates with wired networks using the 802.3 protocol. 120

Accounting information systems Systems that support accounting functions, such as budgeting, cash management, accounts payable and receivable, and financial reporting. 161

Accounts payable information systems Accounting information systems that maintain data on amounts owed to suppliers and that schedule those payments. 429f

Accounts receivable information systems Accounting information systems that maintain data on amounts owed to the company by customers and that manage collections. 429f

Accurate information Information that is based on correct and complete data and that has been processed correctly as expected. 25

Activity The part of a business process that transforms resources and information of one type into resources and information of another type; can be manual or automated. 23

Adware Programs installed on the user's computer without the user's knowledge or permission that reside in the background and, unknown to the user, observe the user's actions and keystrokes, modify computer activity, and report the user's activities to sponsoring organizations. Most adware is benign in that it does not perform malicious acts or steal data. It does, however, watch user activity and produce pop-up ads. 281

Agile enterprise An organization that can quickly adapt to changes in the market, industry, product, law, or other significant external factors; the term was coined by Microsoft. 259

Alert A form of report, often requested by recipients, that tells them some piece of usually time-related information, such as notification of the time for a meeting. 496

Alternative formulation step A step in the decision-making process in which decision makers lay out various alternatives. 332

Analog signal A wavy signal. A modem converts the computer's digital data into analog signals that can be transmitted over dial-up Internet connections. 122

Analysis Breaking something into its constituent parts, as a way of producing information; contrasts with *synthesis*. 507

Analysis paralysis When too much time is spent documenting project requirements. 250

Antivirus programs Software that detects and possibly eliminates viruses. 84

Application software Programs that perform a business function. Some application programs are general purpose, such as Excel or Word. Other application programs are specific to a business function, such as accounts payable. 78

Assessment information systems Human resources information systems that maintain data on job requirements and performance evaluations. 428f

Asymmetric digital subscriber lines (ADSL) DSL lines that have different upload and download speeds. 123

Asymmetric encryption An encryption method whereby different keys are used to encode and to decode the message; one key encodes the message, and the other key decodes the message. Symmetric encryption is simpler and much faster than asymmetric encryption. 128, 585

Asynchronous transfer mode (ATM) A protocol that divides data into uniformly sized cells, eliminates the need for protocol conversion, and can process speeds from 1 to 156 Mbps. ATM can support both voice and data communication. 126

ATA-100 standard Within a computer, a standard type of channel connecting the CPU to main memory. The number 100 indicates that the maximum transfer rate is 100MB per second. 349

Attribute (1) A variable that provides properties for an HTML tag. Each attribute has a standard name. For example, the attribute for a hyperlink is *href*, and its value indicates which Web page is to be displayed when the user clicks the link. (2) Characteristics of an entity. Example attributes of *Order* would be *OrderNumber, OrderDate, SubTotal, Tax, Total*, and so forth. Example attributes of *Salesperson* would be *SalespersonName, Email, Phone*, and so forth. 361, 456

Augmentation information system An information system in which humans do the bulk of the work but are assisted by the information system. 331

Authentication The process whereby an information system approves (authenticates) a user by checking the user's password. 279

Automated information system An information system in which the hardware and software components do most of the work. 27, 331

Baseline An initial plan for the development of an IS. 531

Baseline WBS The final work breakdown structure plan that shows the planned tasks, dependencies, durations, and resource assignments of a large-scale development project. 536

Beta testing   The process of allowing future system users to try out the new system on their own. Used to locate program failures just prior to program shipment.   246

Bidding information systems   Sales and marketing information systems that pull together costs and other inputs and present them to potential customers in competitive project bids.   431

Bill of materials (BOM)   A list of the materials that comprise a product.   426

Binary digits   The means by which computers represent data; also called *bits*. A binary digit is either a zero or a one.   72

Biometric authentication   The use of personal physical characteristics, such as fingerprints, facial features, and retinal scans, to authenticate users.   280

Bit   The means by which computers represent data; also called *binary digit*. A bit is either a zero or a one.   72

Blog (Web-log)   An online journal, which uses technology to publish information over the Internet.   3, 318, 339

Broadband   Internet communication lines that have speeds in excess of 256 kbps. DSL and cable modems provide broadband access.   124

Brooks's Law   The famous adage that states: *Adding more people to a late project makes the project later.* Brooks's Law is true not only because a larger staff requires increased coordination, but also because new people need training. The only people who can train the new employees are the existing team members, who are thus taken off productive tasks. The costs of training new people can overwhelm the benefit of their contribution.   237

Browser   A program that processes the HTTP protocol; receives, displays, and processes HTML documents; and transmits responses.   457

Budgeting information systems   Accounting information systems that help management quantify goals for revenues and expenses in the short and long term and that track progress toward those goals.   429f

Bullwhip effect   Phenomenon in which the variability in the size and timing of orders increases at each stage up the supply chain, from customer to supplier.   466

Bus   Means by which the CPU reads instructions and data from main memory and writes data to main memory.   74

Business intelligence (BI) system   A system that provides the right information, to the right user, at the right time. A tool produces the information, but the system ensures that the right information is delivered to the right user at the right time.   199

Business process   A network of activities, resources, facilities, and information that interact to achieve some business function; sometimes called a business system.   22

Business process design   The creation of new, usually cross-departmental business practices during information systems development. With process design, organizations do not create new information systems to automate existing business practices. Rather, they use technology to enable new, more efficient business processes.   439

Business system   Another term for *Business process*.   22

Business-to-business (B2B)   E-commerce sales between companies.   452

Business-to-consumer (B2C)   E-commerce sales between a supplier and a retail customer (the consumer).   451

Business-to-government (B2G)   E-commerce sales between companies and governmental organizations.   452

Byte   (1) A character of data; (2) An 8-bit chunk.   72, 95

Cable modem   A type of modem that provides high-speed data transmission using cable television lines. The cable company installs a fast, high-capacity optical fiber cable to a distribution center in each neighborhood that it serves. At the distribution center, the optical fiber cable connects to regular cable-television cables that run to subscribers' homes or businesses. Cable modems modulate in such a way that their signals do not interfere with TV signals. Like DSL lines, they are always on.   124

Cache   A file on a domain name resolver that stores domain names and IP addresses that have been resolved. Then, when someone else needs to resolve that same domain name, there is no need to go through the entire resolution process. Instead, the resolver can supply the IP address from the local file.   74, 408

Calculation systems   The very first information systems. The goal of such systems was to relieve workers of tedious, repetitive calculations. These systems were labor-saving devices that produced little information.   158

CASE   An acronym for *computer-assisted software engineering* or *computer-assisted systems engineering*. The first meaning focuses on program development; the second focuses on development of systems having the five components. For either meaning, the basic idea is to use a computer application, called a CASE tool, to help develop computer programs or systems.   547

CASE tool   A tool used to help develop computer programs or systems. CASE tools vary in their features and functions. Some such tools address the entire systems development process from requirements to maintenance; others address just the design and implementation phases.   547

Cash management information systems   Accounting information systems that help manage inflows and outflows of cash, prepare a cash budget, and notify management of external financing needs.   429

CD-R   An optical disk that can record data once.   350

CD-ROM   A read-only optical disk.   350

CD-RW   A rewritable optical disk.   350

Central processing unit (CPU)   The CPU selects instructions, processes them, performs arithmetic and logical comparisons, and stores results of operations in memory.   71

Certificate authority (CA)   Trusted, independent third-party company that supplies public keys for encryption.   588

Chargeback   The allocation of IT cost to departmental users.   570

Chief information officer (CIO)   The title of the principal manager of the IT department. Other common titles are *vice president of information services, director of information services,* and, less commonly, *director of computer services*.   261

Chief technology officer (CTO)   The head of the technology group. The CTO sorts through new ideas and products to identify those that are most relevant to the organization. The CTO's job requires deep knowledge of information technology and the ability to envision how new IT will affect the organization over time.   262

Choice step   A step in the decision-making process in which decision makers analyze their alternatives and select one.   332

Clearinghouse   Entity that provides goods and services at a stated price, prices and arranges for the delivery of the goods, but never takes title to the goods.   453

Clickstream data   E-commerce data that describes a customer's clicking behavior. Such data includes everything the customer does at the Web site.   202

Client   A computer that provides word processing, spreadsheets, database access, and usually a network connection.   75

Cluster analysis   An unsupervised data-mining technique whereby statistical techniques are used to identify groups of entities that have similar characteristics. A common use for cluster analysis is to find groups of similar customers in data about customer orders and customer demographics.   206

Code generator   A program that generates application code for commonly performed tasks. The idea is to improve developer productivity by having the tool generate as much code as possible. The developer can then add code for application-specific features.   548

Cold site   A remote processing center that provides office space, but no computer equipment, for use by a company that needs to continue operations after a natural disaster.   291

Collaboration   The situation in which two or more people work together toward a common goal, result, or product; information systems facilitate collaboration.   317

Collaboration systems   Information systems that enable people to work together more effectively.   326

Collaborative KM systems   Information systems that enable people to share their knowledge.   326

Columns   Also called *fields*, or groups of bytes. A database table has multiple columns that are used to represent the attributes of an entity. Examples are *PartNumber*, *EmployeeName*, and *SalesDate*.   95

Commerce server   A computer that operates Web-based programs that display products, support online ordering, record and process payments, and interface with inventory-management applications.   456

Communications protocol   A means for coordinating activity between two or more communicating computers. Two machines must agree on the protocol to use, and they must follow that protocol as they send messages back and forth. Because there is so much to do, communications tasks are broken up into levels, or layers, of protocols.   397

Compensation information systems   Human resources information systems that maintain data on payroll, compensation, such as vacation, health, and retirement benefits, and other employee contributions.   428

Competitive strategy   The strategy an organization chooses as the way it will succeed in its industry. According to Porter, there are four fundamental competitive strategies: cost leadership across an industry or within a particular industry segment, and product differentiation across an industry or within a particular industry segment.   39

Component design phase   The third phase in the SDLC, in which developers determine hardware and software specifications, design the database (if applicable), design procedures, and create job descriptions for users and operations personnel.   244

Computer crime   Broad term used to cover three types of activity: crimes committed using a computer, crimes committed against a computer, and crimes in which a computer is used to store data that can be used as evidence.   593

Computer forensics   The identification, collection, examination, and preservation of digitally recorded data, for use in solving a computer crime.   596

Computer hardware   One of the five fundamental components of an information system.   6

Computer-assisted software engineering (CASE)   A style of program development that uses a tool, called a CASE tool, to help develop computer programs.   547

Computer-assisted systems engineering (CASE)   A style of program development that uses a tool, called a CASE tool, to help develop computer systems.   547

Computer-based information system   An information system that includes a computer.   6

Confidence   In market-basket terminology, the probability estimate that two items will be purchased together.   486

Configuration control   Use by developers of a set of management policies, practices, and tools to maintain control over a project's resources.   538

Configuration management   A management process that controls and tracks changes to a shared work product; team members must follow procedures for checking documents in and out and for making changes to the work product.   322

Consequences   The damages that occur when an asset is compromised; a risk assessment factor.   581

Construction phase   The phase of the unified process (UP) in which developers design, implement, and test the easier, lower-risk features and functions that were not addressed during elaboration.   552

Content management systems   Information systems that track organizational documents, Web pages, graphics, and related materials.   336

Contiguous connection model (CCM)   A data model purpose-built for processing data connections.   512

Contingent liability   A liability that could *possibly*, but not necessarily will, occur. Failure to adequately secure a company's data, for example, could produce a contingent liability.   164

Cost   The dollar amount required to develop an IS from start to finish; one of the critical drivers in large-scale IS development, which typically involves trade-offs with requirements and time.   530

Cost accounting information systems   Accounting information systems that determine for internal users the cost of providing specific products or services.   429

Cost feasibility   One of four dimensions of feasibility.   240

Counterterrorism intelligence   An activity in which the goal is to produce information that can be used to prevent terrorist attacks.   507

Critical path The sequence of activities that determine the earliest date by which a project can be completed; takes into account task dependencies. 535

Critical path analysis The planning and management of the tasks on the critical path. Tasks on the critical path cannot be allowed to run late; those not on the critical path can run late to the point at which they become part of the critical path. 536

Cross-departmental systems The third era of computing systems. In this era, systems are designed not to facilitate the work of a single department or function, but rather to integrate the activities of a complete business process. 159

Cross-functional systems Synonym for *Cross-departmental systems.* 159

Cross-selling The sale of related products; salespeople try to get customers who buy product *X* to also buy product *Y*. 485

Crow's foot A line on an entity-relationship diagram that indicates a 1:N relationship between two entities. 363

Crow's-foot diagram A type of entity-relationship diagram that uses a crow's foot symbol to designate a 1:N relationship. 363

CRT monitors A type of video display monitor that uses *cathode ray tubes,* the same devices used in traditional TV screens. Because they use a large tube, CRTs are big and bulky, and about as deep as they are wide. 350

Curse of dimensionality The more attributes there are, the easier it is to build a data model that fits the sample data but that is worthless as a predictor. 202

Custom-developed software Tailor-made software. 79

Customer life cycle Taken as a whole, the processes of marketing, customer acquisition, relationship management, and loss/churn that must be managed by CRM systems. 442

Customer management systems Sales and marketing information systems that maintain data on customer contact, product interests, order history, and sometimes their credit status. 423

Customer relationship management (CRM) The set of business processes for attracting, selling, managing, and supporting customers. 183

Customer relationship management (CRM) system An information system that maintains data about customers and all their interactions with the organization. 167, 442

Data Recorded facts or figures. One of the five fundamental components of an information system. 6

Data administration A staff function that pertains to *all* of an organization's data assets. Typical data administration tasks are setting data standards, developing data policies, and providing for data security. 283

Data channel Means by which the CPU reads instructions and data from main memory and writes data to main memory. 74

Data connection A match of data values. 511

Data integrity problem In a database, the situation that exists when data items disagree with one another. An example is two different names for the same customer. 364

Data marts Facilities that prepare, store, and manage data for reporting and data mining for specific business functions. 204

Data mining The application of statistical techniques to find patterns and relationships among data and to classify and predict. 205

Data model A logical representation of the data in a database that describes the data and relationships that will be stored in the database. Akin to a blueprint. 360

Data safeguards Steps taken to protect databases and other organizational data, by means of data administration and database administration. 283

Data warehouses Facilities that prepare, store, and manage data specifically for reporting and data mining. 203

Database A self-describing collection of integrated records. 95, 325

Database administration The management, development, operation, and maintenance of the database so as to achieve the organization's objectives. This staff function requires balancing conflicting goals: protecting the database while maximizing its availability for authorized use. In smaller organizations, this function usually is served by a single person. Larger organizations assign several people to an office of database administration. 283

Database application A collection of forms, reports, queries, and application programs that process a database. 102

Database application system Applications, having the standard five components, that make database data more accessible and useful. Users employ a database application that consists of forms, formatted reports, queries, and application programs. Each of these, in turn, calls on the database management system (DBMS) to process the database tables. 99

Database management system (DBMS) A program used to create, process, and administer a database. 99

Database marketing The application of data business intelligence systems to the planning and execution of marketing programs. 483

Database tier In the three-tier architecture, the tier that runs the DBMS and receives and processes SQL requests to retrieve and store data. 458

Data-mining system IS that processes data using sophisticated statistical techniques like regression analysis and decision-tree analysis to find patterns and relationships that cannot be found by simpler operations like sorting, grouping, and averaging. 200

Data-mining tools Tools that use statistical techniques, many of which are sophisticated and mathematically complex, to process data to look for hidden patterns. 200

DB2 A popular, enterprise-class DBMS product from IBM. 99

Decision mode The style—either by *analysis* or by *synthesis*—in which one creates the information that informs a decision. 509

Decision tree A hierarchical arrangement of criteria for classifying customers, items, and other business objects. 486

Deliverable A task that is one of many measurable or observable steps in a development project. 533

Denial of service Security problem in which users are not able to access an IS; can be caused by human errors, natural disaster, or malicious activity. 277

Development and training information systems Human resources information systems that maintain data on development programs and training classes. 428

Device access router A generic term for a communications device that includes an access point, a switch, and a router. Normally the device access router provides DHCP and NAT services. 413

Dial-up modem A modem that performs the conversion between analog and digital in such a way that the signal can be carried on a regular telephone line. 123

Digital certificate A document supplied by a certificate authority (CA) that contains, among other data, an entity's name and public key. 588

Digital dashboard An electronic display that is customized for a particular user. 496

Digital signature Encrypted message that uses *hashing* to ensure that plaintext messages are received without alteration. 587

Digital subscriber line (DSL) DSL uses voice telephone lines with a DSL modem; it operates so that the signals do not interfere with voice telephone service. DSL provides much faster data transmission speeds than dial-up connections. Additionally, DSL is an always-on connection, so there is no need to dial in. 123

Dimension A characteristic of an OLAP measure. Purchase date, customer type, customer location, and sales region are examples of dimensions. 499

Direct installation Sometimes called plunge installation, a type of system conversion in which the organization shuts off the old system and starts the new system. If the new system fails, the organization is in trouble: Nothing can be done until either the new system is fixed or the old system is reinstalled. Because of the risk, organizations should avoid this conversion style if possible. 247

Dirty data Problematic data. Examples are a value of *B* for customer gender and a value of *213* for customer age. Other examples are a value of *999-999-9999* for a U.S. phone number, a part color of *green*, and an email address of *WhyMe@GuessWhoIAM-Hah-Hah.org*. All these values are problematic when data mining. 201

Discount rate The interest rate at which an organization can borrow money; normally, the organization's cost of capital. 574

Discussion groups A form of organizational knowledge management. They allow employees or customers to post questions and queries seeking solutions to problems they have. 339

Diseconomies of scale The added cost that will eventually occur as more people are added to an IS development project. 531

Disintermediation Elimination of one or more middle layers in the supply chain. 454

Distributed computing The process of a program on one computer invoking programs on a second computer. 478

Domain name The registered, human-friendly valid name in the domain name system (DNS). The process of changing a name into its IP address is called *resolving the domain name*. 407

Domain name resolution The process of converting a domain name into a public IP address. 407

Domain name resolvers Computers that facilitate domain name resolution by storing the correspondence of domain names and IP addresses. 408

Domain name system (DNS) A system that converts user-friendly names into their IP addresses. Any registered, valid name is called a domain name. 407

Dot pitch The distance between pixels on a CRT monitor; the smaller the dot pitch, the sharper and brighter the screen image will be. 350

Drill down With an OLAP report, to further divide the data into more detail. 501

Drive-by sniffers People who take computers with wireless connections through an area and search for unprotected wireless networks in an attempt to gain free Internet access or to gather unauthorized data. 275

Drop shipping Process in which a customer buys a product from a vendor, and the vendor has the item shipped directly to the customer from the manufacturer, without it ever entering the vendor's inventory. 187

DSL modem A type of modem. DSL modems operate on the same lines as voice telephones and dial-up modems, but they operate so that their signals do not interfere with voice telephone service. DSL modems provide much faster data transmission speeds than dial-up modems. Additionally, DSL modems always maintain a connection, so there is no need to dial in; the Internet connection is available immediately. 123

DVD-R A digital versatile disk that can record data once. 350

DVD-ROM A read-only digital versatile disk. 350

DVD-RW A rewritable digital versatile disk. 350

Dynamic Host Configuration Protocol (DHCP) A service provided by some communications devices that allocates and deallocates a pool of IP addresses. A device that hosts the DHCP service is called a DHCP server. On request, a DHCP server loans a temporary IP address to a network device like a computer or printer. When the device disconnects, the IP address becomes available, and the DHCP server will reuse it when needed. 401

Dynamic report Report that is generated at the time of request; the reporting system reads the most current data and generates the report using that fresh data. A report on sales today and a report on current stock prices are both dynamic reports. 495

E-commerce The buying and selling of goods and services over public and private computer networks. 181, 451

E-commerce auctions Applications that match buyers and sellers by using an e-commerce version of a standard auction. This e-commerce application enables the auction company to offer goods for sale and to support a competitive bidding process. 452

EDI X12 standard An EDI standard that formally describes hundreds of documents that are commonly exchanged among businesses. 474

EDIFACT standard An EDI standard that formally describes hundreds of documents that are commonly exchanged among businesses. Used internationally. 475

Elaboration phase The phase of the unified process (UP) in which developers construct and test the framework and architecture of the new system. 550

Electronic Data Interchange (EDI) A standard for exchanging documents from machine to machine, electronically. In the past, EDI was used over point-to-point or value-added networks. Recently, EDI systems have been developed that use the Internet as well. 474

Electronic exchanges Sites that facilitate the matching of buyers and sellers; the business process is similar to that of a stock exchange. Sellers offer goods at a given price through the electronic exchange, and buyers make offers to purchase over the same exchange. Price matches result in transactions from which the exchange takes a commission. 453

Email spoofing A synonym for phishing. A technique for obtaining unauthorized data that uses pretexting via email. The *phisher* pretends to be a legitimate company and sends email requests for confidential data, such as account numbers, Social Security numbers, account passwords, and so forth. Phishers direct traffic to their sites under the guise of a legitimate business. 275

Encryption The process of transforming clear text into coded, unintelligible text for secure storage or communication. 128, 585

Encryption algorithms Algorithms used to transform clear text into coded, unintelligible text for secure storage or communication. Commonly used methods are DES, 3DES, and AES. 128

Enterprise application integration (EAI) The integration of existing systems by providing layers of software that connect applications and their data together. 448

Enterprise DBMS A product that processes large organizational and workgroup databases. These products support many users, perhaps thousands, and many different database applications. Such DBMS products support 24/7 operations and can manage databases that span dozens of different magnetic disks with hundreds of gigabytes or more of data. IBM's DB2, Microsoft's SQL Server, and Oracle's Oracle are examples of enterprise DBMS products. 105

Enterprise resource management (ERM) systems Cross-functional, enterprise-wide systems that integrate the primary value-chain activities with the functions of human resources and accounting. 168

Enterprise resource planning (ERP) The integration of all the organization's principal processes. ERP is an outgrowth of MRP II manufacturing systems, and most ERP users are manufacturing companies. 168, 444

Entity In the E-R data model, a representation of some thing that users want to track. Some entities represent a physical object; others represent a logical construct or transaction. 361

Entity-relationship data model (E-R model) Popular technique for creating a data model, in which developers define the things that will be stored and the relationships among them. 361

Entity-relationship (E-R) diagrams A type of diagram used by database designers to document entities and their relationships to each other. 362

Ethernet Another name for the IEEE 802.3 protocol, Ethernet is a network protocol that operates at Layers 1 and 2 of the TCP/IP–OSI architecture. Ethernet, the world's most popular LAN protocol, is used on WANs as well. 119

Exabyte 10^{18} bytes. 198

Executive information system (EIS) An information system that supports strategic decision making. 329

Expert system Knowledge-sharing system that is created by interviewing experts in a given business domain and codifying the rules used by those experts. 201, 340

Expert system shell A program in an expert system that processes a set of rules, typically many times until the values of the variables no longer change, at which point the system reports the results. 341

eXtensible Markup Language (XML) A very important document standard that separates document content, structure, and presentation; eliminates problems in HTML; and offers advantages over EDI. Most believe XML will eventually replace EDI. 476

Extreme programming (XP) An emerging technique for developing computer programs. Programmers create only features and functions of the new program that they can complete in two weeks or less. If many programmers are working on the project, each person's work must be done in such a way that all their work can be combined and assembled at the end of that period. Users and PQA professionals test the developed code continuously through the process. Three key XP characteristics are: (1) it is customer centric, (2) it uses just-in-time design, and (3) it involves paired programming. 553

F score In RFM analysis, a number rating that indicates in which fifth a customer ranks in terms of ordering *frequency*. 484

Facilities Structures used within a business process. 24

Feasibility Whether a project is or is not possible. Feasibility has four dimensions: cost, schedule, technical, and organizational feasibility. The purpose of assessing feasibility is to eliminate any obviously infeasible systems as soon as possible. 240

Fields Also called *columns*, groups of bytes in a database table. A database table has multiple columns that are used to represent the attributes of an entity. Examples are *PartNumber*, *EmployeeName*, and *SalesDate*. 96

File A group of similar rows or records. In a database, sometimes called a *table*. 96

File Transfer Protocol (FTP) A Layer-5 protocol used to copy files from one computer to another. In interorganizational transaction processing, ftp enables users to easily exchange large files. 398, 456

Financial reporting information systems Accounting information systems that record and report financial results to investors, creditors, and other external users. 429

Firewall A computing device located between a firm's internal and external networks that prevents unauthorized access to or from the internal network. A firewall can be a special-purpose computer or it can be a program on a general-purpose computer or on a router. 129

Firmware Computer software that is installed into devices like printers, print services, and various types of communication devices. The software is coded just like other software, but it is installed into special, programmable memory of the printer or other device. 80

Five-component framework The five fundamental components of an information system—computer hardware, software, data, procedures, and people—that are present in every information system, from the simplest to the most complex. 6

Five-forces model Model, proposed by Michael Porter, that assesses industry characteristics and profitability by means of five competitive forces—bargaining power of suppliers, threat of substitution, bargaining power of customers, rivalry among firms, and threat of new entrants. 38

Foreign keys A column or group of columns used to represent relationships. Values of the foreign key match values of the primary key in a different (foreign) table. 97

Form Data entry forms are used to read, insert, modify, and delete database data. 102

Frame Relay A protocol that can process traffic in the range of 56 kbps to 40 Mbps by packaging data into frames. 126

Frames The containers used at Layers 1 and 2 of the TCP/IP–OSI model. A program implementing a Layer-2 protocol packages data into frames. 400

Frequently asked questions (FAQs) A form of knowledge sharing in which the organization edits, prioritizes, and summarizes questions generated from discussion groups. 339

ftp See *File Transfer Protocol*. 185

Function point technique Estimating technique that attempts to schedule a development project by the number of function points in a project, using each function point to determine the number of lines of code and the time for the project. 537

Functional application Software that provides features and functions necessary to support a particular business activity (function). 421

Functional systems The second era of information systems. The goal of such systems was to facilitate the work of a single department or function. Over time, in each functional area, companies added features and functions to encompass more activities and to provide more value and assistance. 159, 421

Gantt chart A project-management chart that shows tasks and their dependencies on each other, and schedules them in an optimal way so as to reduce the time it takes to complete them. 324, 535

General ledger information systems Accounting information systems that maintain balances in all asset, liability, and equity accounts. 429

Gigabyte (GB) 1,024MB. 73

Gramm-Leach-Bliley (GLB) Act Passed by Congress in 1999, this act protects consumer financial data stored by financial institutions, which are defined as banks, securities firms, insurance companies, and organizations that provide financial advice, prepare tax returns, and provide similar financial services. 581a

Granularity The level of detail in data. Customer name and account balance is large granularity data. Customer name, balance, and the order details and payment history of every customer order is smaller granularity. 202

Hacking Occurs when a person gains unauthorized access to a computer system. Although some people hack for the sheer joy of doing it, other hackers invade systems for the malicious purpose of stealing or modifying data. 277

Hardening a site The process of taking extraordinary measures to reduce a system's vulnerability. Hardened sites use special versions of the operating system, and they lock down or eliminate operating systems features and functions that are not required by the application. Hardening is a technical safeguard. 287

Hardware Electronic components and related gadgetry that input, process, output, store, and communicate data according to instructions encoded in computer programs or software. 70

Hashing A method of mathematically manipulating an electronic message to create a string of bits that characterize the message. 587

Health Insurance Portability and Accountability Act (HIPAA) The privacy provisions of this 1996 act give individuals the right to access health data created by doctors and other health-care providers. HIPAA also sets rules and limits on who can read and receive a person's health information. 581a

HIPAA standard An EDI standard that is used for medical records. 475

Horizontal-market application Software that provides capabilities common across all organizations and industries; examples include word processors, graphics programs, spreadsheets, and presentation programs. 78

Hot site A remote processing center, run by a commercial disaster-recovery service, that provides equipment a company would need to continue operations after a natural disaster. 291

HR planning information systems Human resources information systems that maintain data on organizational standards for job classifications and compensation ranges and on future hiring requirements. 428f

HTTPs An indication that a Web browser is using the SSL/TLS protocol to ensure secure communications. 128

Human resources information systems Systems that support recruitment, compensation, evaluation, and development of employees and affiliated personnel. 161, 428

Human safeguards Steps taken to protect against security threats by establishing appropriate procedures for users to follow for system use. 284

Hyperlink A pointer on a Web page to another Web page. A hyperlink contains the URL of the Web page to access when the user clicks the hyperlink. The URL can reference a page on the Web server that generated the page containing the hyperlink, or it can reference a page on another server. 456

Hypertext Markup Language (HTML) A language that defines the structure and layout of Web page content. An

HTML tag is a notation used to define a data element for display or other purposes. 456

Hypertext Transfer Protocol (HTTP) A Layer-5 protocol used to process Web pages. 398, 456

Identification The process whereby an information system identifies a user by requiring the user to sign on with a user name and password. 279

Identifier An attribute (or group of attributes) whose value is associated with one and only one entity instance. 361

IEEE 802.3 protocol This standard, also called *Ethernet*, is a network protocol that operates at Layers 1 and 2 of the TCP/IP–OSI architecture. Ethernet, the world's most popular LAN protocol, is used on WANs as well. 119

If . . . then . . . Format for rules derived from a decision tree (data mining) or by interviewing a human expert (expert systems). 340, 488

Implementation phase The fourth phase in the SDLC, in which developers build and integrate system components, test the system, and convert to the new system. 245

Implementation step A step in the decision-making process in which decision makers implement the alternative they have selected. 332

Incremental development A development process whereby developers design, implement, and fix portions of an application, one-by-one, until the entire program has been developed in pieces. This method reduces development challenges by using a divide-and-conquer strategy. 545

Information (1) Knowledge derived from data, where *data* is defined as recorded facts or figures; (2) Data presented in a meaningful context; (3) Data processed by summing, ordering, averaging, grouping, comparing, or other similar operations; (4) A difference that makes a difference. 24

Information system (IS) A group of components that interact to produce information. 6

Information technology (IT) The products, methods, inventions, and standards that are used for the purpose of producing information. 8

Inherent processes The procedures that must be followed to effectively use licensed software. For example, the processes inherent in MRP systems assume that certain users will take specified actions in a particular order. In most cases, the organization must conform to the processes inherent in the software. 440

Input hardware Hardware devices that attach to a computer; includes keyboards, mouse, document scanners, and bar-code (Universal Product Code) scanners. 71

Instruction set The collection of instructions that a computer can process. 76

Intangible benefit A benefit of an IS for which it is impossible to compute a dollar value. 264

Intelligence-gathering step The first step in the decision-making process in which decision makers determine what is to be decided, what the criteria for selection will be, and what data are available. 332

Internal firewalls A firewall that sits inside the organizational network. 129

International Organization for Standardization (ISO) An international organization that sets worldwide standards.

ISO developed a seven-layer protocol architecture called Open Systems Interconnection (OSI). Portions of that protocol architecture are incorporated into the TCP/IP–OSI hybrid protocol architecture. 397

Internet When spelled with a small i, as in internet, a private network of networks. When spelled with a capital *I*, as Internet, the public internet known as the Internet. 116

Internet Corporation for Assigned Names and Numbers (ICANN) The organization responsible for managing the assignment of public IP addresses and domain names for use on the Internet. Each public IP address is unique across all computers on the Internet. 401

Internet Engineering Task Force (IETF) An organization that specifies standards for use on the Internet. Developed a four-layer scheme called the TCP/IP (Transmission Control Program/Internet Protocol) architecture. TCP/IP is part of the TCP/IP–OSI protocol architecture that is used on the Internet and most internets today. 397

Internet Protocol (IP) A Layer-3 protocol. As the name implies, IP is used on the Internet, but it is used on many other internets as well. The chief purpose of IP is to route packets across an internet. 399

Internet service provider (ISP) An ISP provides users with Internet access. An ISP provides a user with a legitimate Internet address; it serves as the user's gateway to the Internet; and it passes communications back and forth between the user and the Internet. ISPs also pay for the Internet. They collect money from their customers and pay access fees and other charges on the users' behalf. 122

Interorganizational transaction processing IS processing of routine transactions between two or more organizations. 184

Inventory systems Operations systems that help control and manage inventory, and support inventory policy. 425f

IP address A series of dotted decimals in a format like 192.168.2.28 that identifies a unique device on a network or internet. With the IPv4 standard, IP addresses have 32 bits. With the IPv6 standard, IP addresses have 128 bits. Today, IPv4 is more common but will likely be supplanted by IPv6 in the future. With IPv4, the decimal between the dots can never exceed 255. 400

IP spoofing A type of spoofing whereby an intruder uses another site's IP address as if it were that other site. 275

Islands of automation The structure that results when functional applications work independently in isolation from one another. Usually problematic because data is duplicated, integration is difficult, and results can be inconsistent. 159

JAD session A design meeting of short duration, during which attendees develop the design of a particular component of an IS. 547

JIT design A development technique used in extreme programming in which programmers defer program design until the last possible moment; they use a minimal design, and nothing more, to accomplish the requirements of each iteration of the system. 554

Joint application design (JAD)   A key element of rapid application design. A team of users, developers, and PQA personnel conducts design activities during JAD sessions. JAD came about because developers wanted to incorporate feedback and testing earlier in the development process. Ultimately, developers decided that the best place to get feedback was during design creation.   547

Just-barely-sufficient information   Information that meets the purpose for which it is generated, but just barely so.   26

Just-in-time (JIT) inventory policy   A policy that seeks to have production inputs (both raw materials and work-in-process) delivered to the manufacturing site just as they are needed. By scheduling delivery of inputs in this way, companies are able to reduce inventories to a minimum.   425

Key   (1) A column or group of columns that identifies a unique row in a table. (2) A number used to encrypt data. The encryption algorithm applies the key to the original message to produce the coded message. Decoding (decrypting) a message is similar; a key is applied to the coded message to recover the original text.   96, 128

Key escrow   A control procedure whereby a trusted party is given a copy of a key used to encrypt database data.   284

Kilobyte (K)   1,024 bytes.   73

Knowledge management (KM)   The process of creating value from intellectual capital and sharing that knowledge with employees, managers, suppliers, customers, and others who need that capital.   200, 324, 335

Knowledge management system (KMS)   An information system for storing and retrieving organizational knowledge, whether that knowledge is in the form of data, documents, or employee know-how.   200

Layered protocols   Different ways of arranging the layers of communication protocols for transmission of data across networks. TCP/IP is one such layered protocol.   397

LCD monitor   A type of video display monitor that uses a technology called *liquid crystal display*. LCD monitors are flat and require much less space than CRT monitors.   350

Lead-generation systems   Sales and marketing information systems that send mailings (postal or email) for the purpose of generating sales prospects.   422

Lead-tracking systems   Sales and marketing information systems that record data on sales prospects and keep records of customer contacts.   422

License   Agreement that stipulates how a program can be used. Most specify the number of computers on which the program can be installed and sometimes the number of users that can connect to and use the program remotely. Such agreements also stipulate limitations on the liability of the software vendor for the consequences of errors in the software.   78

Lift   In market-basket terminology, the ratio of confidence to the base probability of buying an item. Lift shows how much the base probability changes when other products are purchased. If the lift is greater than 1, the change is positive; if it is less than 1, the change is negative.   486

Likelihood   The probability that a given asset will be compromised by a given threat; a risk assessment factor.   582

Lines of code technique   Estimating technique that attempts to schedule a development project by the number of lines of code developers must write for the project.   537

Linkages   Process interactions across value chains. Linkages are important sources of efficiencies and are readily supported by information systems.   42

Linux   A version of Unix that was developed by the open-source community. The open-source community owns Linux, and there is no fee to use it. Linux is a popular operating system for Web servers.   78

Local area network (LAN)   A network that connects computers that reside in a single geographic location on the premises of the company that operates the LAN. The number of connected computers can range from two to several hundred.   116

Localizing software   The process of making a computer program work in a second language.   138

Logical address   Also called *IP address*, a series of dotted decimals in a format like 192.168.2.28 that identifies a unique device on a network or internet. With the IPv4 standard, IP addresses have 32 bits. IP addresses are called logical addresses because they can be reassigned from one device to another.   400

Lost-update problem   An issue in multi-user database processing, in which two or more users try to make changes to the data but the database cannot make all those changes because it was not designed to process changes from multiple users.   105

M score   In RFM analysis, a number rating that indicates in which fifth a customer ranks in terms of *amount spent* per order.   484

MAC address   Also called *physical address*. A permanent address given to each network interface card (NIC) at the factory. This address enables the device to access the network via a Level-2 protocol. By agreement among computer manufacturers, MAC addresses are assigned in such a way that no two NIC devices will ever have the same MAC address.   117, 400

MAC address filtering   A security device for SOHO LANs that prevents unauthorized users from accessing the device access router and the LAN.   416

Mac OS   An operating system developed by Apple Computer, Inc., for the Macintosh. The current version is Mac OS X. Macintosh computers are used primarily by graphic artists and workers in the arts community. Mac OS was developed for the PowerPC, but as of 2006 will run on Intel processors as well.   77

Macro virus   Virus that attaches itself to a Word, Excel, PowerPoint, or other type of document. When the infected document is opened, the virus places itself in the startup files of the application. After that, the virus infects every file that the application creates or processes.   84

Main memory   A set of cells in which each cell holds a byte of data or instruction; each cell has an address, and the CPU uses the addresses to identify particular data items.   71

Maintenance   In the context of information systems, (1) to fix the system to do what it was supposed to do in the first place or (2) to adapt the system to a change in requirements. 248

Maintenance phase The fifth and final phase in the SDLC, in which developers record requests for changes, including both enhancements and failures, and fix failures by means of patches, service packs, and new releases. 248

Malware Viruses, worms, Trojan horses, spyware, and adware. 281

Malware definitions Patterns that exist in malware code. Anti-malware vendors update these definitions continuously and incorporate them into their products in order to better fight against malware. 282

Management information system (MIS) An information system that helps businesses achieve their goals and objectives. 7, 161, 329

Managerial decision Decision that concerns the allocation and use of resources. 329

Manual information system An information system in which the activity of processing information is done by people, without the use of automated processing. 29

Manufacturing information systems Information systems that support one or more aspects of manufacturing processes, including planning, scheduling, integration with inventory, quality control, and related processes. 161, 424

Manufacturing operation systems Systems that control machinery and production processes.

Manufacturing resource planning (MRP II) A follow-on to MRP that includes the planning of materials, personnel, and machinery. It supports many linkages across the organization, including linkages with sales and marketing via the development of a master production schedule. It also includes the capability to perform what-if analyses on variances in schedules, raw materials availabilities, personnel, and other resources. 427

Many-to-many (N:M) relationship Relationships involving two entity types in which an instance of one type can relate to many instances of the second type, and an instance of the second type can relate to many instances of the first. For example, the relationship between Student and Class is N:M. One student may enroll in many classes and one class may have many students. Contrast with one-to-many relationships. 363

Margin The difference between value and cost. 40

Market-basket analysis A data-mining technique for determining sales patterns. A market-basket analysis shows the products that customers tend to buy together. 200, 485

Master production schedule (MPS) A plan for producing products. To create the MPS, the company analyzes past sales levels and makes estimates of future sales. This process is sometimes called a *push manufacturing process*, because the company pushes the products into sales (and customers) according to the MPS. 426

Materials requirements planning (MRP) An information system that plans the need for materials and inventories of materials used in the manufacturing process. Unlike MRP II, MRP does not include the planning of personnel, equipment, or facilities requirements. 427

Maximum cardinality The maximum number of entities that can be involved in a relationship. Common examples of maximum cardinality are 1:N, N:M, and 1:1. 363

Measure The data item of interest on an OLAP report. It is the item that is to be summed, averaged, or otherwise processed in the OLAP cube. Total sales, average sales, and average cost are examples of measures. 499

Media access control (MAC) address Also called *physical address*. A permanent address given to each network interface card (NIC) at the factory. This address enables the device to access the network via a Level 2 protocol. By agreement among computer manufacturers, MAC addresses are assigned in such a way that no two NIC devices will ever have the same MAC address. 117

Megabyte (MB) 1,024KB. 73

Memory swapping The movement of programs and data into and out of memory. If a computer has insufficient memory for its workload, such swapping will degrade system performance. 74

Merchant companies In e-commerce, companies that take title to the goods they sell. They buy goods and resell them. 451

Message digest A bit string of a specific, fixed length, produced by hashing and used to produce digital signatures. 587

Metadata Data that describe data. 98

Minimum cardinality The minimum number of entities that must be involved in a relationship. 363

Modem Short for *modulator/demodulator*, a modem converts the computer's digital data into signals that can be transmitted over telephone or cable lines. 122

Moore's Law A law, created by Gordon Moore, stating that the number of transistors per square inch on an integrated chip doubles every 18 months. Moore's prediction has proved generally accurate in the 40 years since it was made. Sometimes this law is stated that the performance of a computer doubles every 18 months. While not strictly true, this version gives the gist of the idea. 12

Multi-user processing When multiple users process the database at the same time. 104

MySQL A popular open-source DBMS product that is license-free for most applications. 99

Narrowband Internet communication lines that have transmission speeds of 56 kbps or less. A dial-up modem provides narrowband access. 124

Net Meeting A proprietary Microsoft product that uses Windows and the Internet to produce a video conference. 320

Net present value (NPV) A technique used to evaluate the cost of an IT project, which considers the time value of money. NPV discounts the value of future costs and benefits using the interest rate at which the organization could borrow funds. 574

Network A collection of computers that communicate with one another over transmission lines. 116

Network Address Translation (NAT) The process of changing public IP addresses into private network IP addresses, and the reverse. 406

Network interface card (NIC)   A hardware component on each device on a network (computer, printer, etc.) that connects the device's circuitry to the communications line. The NIC works together with programs in each device to implement Layers 1 and 2 of the TCP/IP–OSI hybrid protocol.   117

Network of leased lines   A WAN connection alternative. Communication lines are leased from telecommunications companies and connected into a network. The lines connect geographically distant sites.   124

Neural networks   A popular supervised data-mining technique used to predict values and make classifications, such as "good prospect" or "poor prospect."   207

Nonmerchant companies   E-commerce companies that arrange for the purchase and sale of goods without ever owning or taking title to those goods.   451

Nonvolatile memory   Memory that preserves data contents even when not powered (e.g., magnetic and optical disks). With such devices, you can turn the computer off and back on, and the contents will be unchanged.   74

Normal forms   A classification of tables according to their characteristics and the kinds of problems they have.   366

Normalization   The process of converting poorly structured tables into two or more well-structured tables.   364

Object-oriented development (OOD)   A systems development methodology that arose from the discipline of object-oriented programming. OOD develops programs using the object-oriented programming (OOP) techniques. Programs developed using OOP are easier to maintain than those developed using traditional techniques.   549

Object-oriented programming (OOP)   A discipline for designing and writing computer programs. Programs developed using OOP are easier and cheaper to maintain than those developed using traditional techniques.   550

Object-relational database   A type of database that stores both OOP objects and relational data. Rarely used in commercial applications.   97

Off-the-shelf software   Software that can be used without having to make any changes.   79

OLAP   See *Online analytical processing.*   499

OLAP cube   A presentation of an OLAP measure with associated dimensions. The reason for this term is that some products show these displays using three axes, like a cube in geometry. Same as OLAP report.   501

OLAP servers   Computer servers running software that performs OLAP analyses. An OLAP server reads data from an operational database, performs preliminary calculations, and stores the results of those calculations in an OLAP database.   501

Onboard NIC   A built in NIC.   117

One-of-a-kind application   Software that is developed for a specific, unique need, usually for a particular company's operations.   79

One-to-many (1:N) relationship   Relationships involving two entity types in which an instance of one type can relate to many instances of the second type, but an instance of the second type can relate to at most one instance of the first. For example, the relationship between Department and Employee is 1:N. A department may relate to many employees, but an employee relates to at most one department.   363

Online analytical processing (OLAP)   A dynamic type of reporting system that provides the ability to sum, count, average, and perform other simple arithmetic operations on groups of data. Such reports are dynamic because users can change the format of the reports while viewing them.   499

Open-source community   A loosely coupled group of programmers who mostly volunteer their time to contribute code to develop and maintain common software. Linux and MySQL are two prominent products developed by such a community.   78

Operations information systems   Systems that maintain data on finished goods inventory and the movements of goods from inventory to the customer.   161, 424

Operating system (OS)   A computer program that controls the computer's resources: It manages the contents of main memory, processes keystrokes and mouse movements, sends signals to the display monitor, reads and writes disk files, and controls the processing of other programs.   74

Operational decisions   Decisions that concern the day-to-day activities of an organization.   329

Optical fiber cable   A type of cable used to connect the computers, printers, switches, and other devices on a LAN. The signals on such cables are light rays, and they are reflected inside the glass core of the optical fiber cable. The core is surrounded by a *cladding* to contain the light signals, and the cladding, in turn, is wrapped with an outer layer to protect it.   118

Optimal resolution   The size of the pixel grid (e.g., 1,024 × 768) on a video display monitor that will give the best sharpness and clarity. This optimal resolution depends on the size of the screen, the dot or pixel pitch, and other factors.   350

Oracle   A popular, enterprise-class DBMS product from Oracle Corporation.   99

Organizational feasibility.   One of four dimensions of feasibility.   240

Output hardware   Hardware that displays the results of the computer's processing. Consists of video displays, printers, audio speakers, overhead projectors, and other special-purpose devices, such as large flatbed plotters.   71

Outsourcing   The process of hiring another organization to perform a service. Outsourcing is done to save costs, to gain expertise, and to free up management time.   559

Packet   A small piece of a an electronic message, that has been divided into chunks, which are sent separately and reassembled at their destination.   399

Packet-filtering firewall   A firewall that examines each packet and determines whether to let the packet pass. To make this decision, it examines the source address, the destination addresses, and other data.   129

Paired programming   The most unconventional characteristic of XP. With it, two programmers work together, side by side, on the very same computer. They look over each other's shoulders, and they continuously communicate as they program on that single machine. According to XP proponents, studies show that two programmers working in this way can do at least as much work as two programmers working separately, and the resulting program code has fewer errors and is more easily maintained.   554

Parallel installation   A type of system conversion in which the new system runs in parallel with the old one for a while. Parallel installation is expensive because the organization incurs the costs of running both systems.   247

Patch   A group of fixes for high-priority failures that can be applied to existing copies of a particular product. Software vendors supply patches to fix security and other critical problems.   84, 248

Payback analysis   A technique used to evaluate the cost of an IT project; totals the costs and benefits of a project and measures the number of years it will take for the benefits to pay off the costs.   574

Payload   The program code of a virus that causes unwanted or hurtful actions, such as deleting programs or data, or even worse, modifying data in ways that are undetected by the user.   82

People   As part of the five-component framework, one of the five fundamental components of an information system; includes those who operate and service the computers, those who maintain the data, those who support the networks, and those who use the system.   6

Perimeter firewall   A firewall that sits outside the organizational network. It is the first device that Internet traffic encounters.   129

Personal DBMS   DBMS products designed for smaller, simpler database applications. Such products are used for personal or small workgroup applications that involve fewer than a 100 users, and normally fewer than 15. Today, Microsoft Access is the only prominent personal DBMS.   106

Personal identification number (PIN)   A form of authentication whereby the user supplies a number that only he or she knows.   280

Petabyte 10^{15} bytes.   198

Phased installation   A type of system conversion in which the new system is installed in pieces across the organization(s). Once a given piece works, then the organization installs and tests another piece of the system, until the entire system has been installed.   247

Phishing   A technique for obtaining unauthorized data that uses pretexting via email. The *phisher* pretends to be a legitimate company and sends an email requesting confidential data, such as account numbers, Social Security numbers, account passwords, and so forth.   275

Physical address   Also called *MAC address*. A permanent address given to each network interface card (NIC) at the factory. This address enables the device to access the network via a Level-2 protocol. By agreement among computer manufacturers, physical addresses are assigned in such a way that no two NIC devices will ever have the same address.   400

Pilot installation   A type of system conversion in which the organization implements the entire system on a limited portion of the business. The advantage of pilot implemen-

tation is that if the system fails, the failure is contained within a limited boundary. This reduces exposure of the business and also protects the new system from developing a negative reputation throughout the organization(s).   247

Pixel pitch   The distance between pixels on the screen of an LCD monitor; the smaller the pixel pitch, the sharper and brighter the image will be.   350

Pixels   Small spots on the screen of a video display monitor arranged in a rectangular grid. The number of pixels displayed depends not only on the size of the monitor, but also on the design of the computer's video card.   350

Plunge installation   Sometimes called direct installation, a type of system conversion in which the organization shuts off the old system and starts the new system. If the new system fails, the organization is in trouble: Nothing can be done until either the new system is fixed or the old system is reinstalled. Because of the risk, organizations should avoid this conversion style if possible.   247

Podcast   A digital file that can be downloaded and played; can be audio or video.   319, 340

Point of presence (POP)   The location at which a line connects to a PSDN network. Think of the POP as the phone number that one dials to connect to the PSDN. Once a site has connected to the PSDN POP, the site obtains access to all other sites connected to the PSDN.   126

Point-to-Point Protocol (PPP)   A Layer-2 protocol used for networks that involve just two computers, hence the term *point-to-point*. PPP is used between a modem and an ISP as well as on some networks of leased lines.   123

Portal   A Web site that publishes information for users; can be public (such as Yahoo!) or private (such as for a company's employees or a specific work team).   339

Porter's five competitive forces model   See *Five-forces model*.   38

Pretexting   A technique for gathering unauthorized information in which someone pretends to be someone else. A common scam involves a telephone caller who pretends to be from a credit card company and claims to be checking the validity of credit card numbers. Phishing is also a form of pretexting.   275

Price elasticity   A measure of the sensitivity in demand to changes in price. It is the ratio of the percentage change in quantity divided by the percentage change in price.   454

Primary activities   In Porter's value chain model, the fundamental activities that create value—inbound logistics, operations, outbound logistics, marketing/sales, and service.   40

Printer server   A network interface card (NIC) that contains a special-purpose computer with firmware programs that enable the computers on a LAN to use a shared printer.   414

Privacy Act of 1974   Federal law that provides protections to individuals regarding records maintained by the U.S. government.   581a

Private IP address   A type of IP address used within private networks and internets. Private IP addresses are assigned and managed by the company that operates the private network or internet.   401

Probable loss   The "bottom line" of risk assessment; consists of consideration of the likelihood of loss multiplied by the consequences.   582

Procedures   Instructions for humans. One of the five fundamental components of an information system.   6

Process blueprint   In an ERP product, a comprehensive set of inherent processes for organizational activities.   445

Process-based systems   The third era of computing systems. In this era, systems are designed not to facilitate the work of a single department or function, but rather to integrate the activities in an entire business process.   159

Product and brand management systems   Marketing information systems that import records of past sales from order processing or accounts receivable systems and compare those data to projections and sales estimates, in order to assess the effectiveness of promotions, advertising, and general success of a product brand.   423

Product quality assurance (PQA)   The testing of a system. PQA personnel usually construct a test plan with the advice and assistance of users. PQA test engineers perform testing, and they also supervise user-test activity. Many PQA professionals are programmers who write automated test programs.   246

Program (that implements a protocol)   A specific computer product that implements a protocol; for example, Netscape Navigator and Microsoft Internet Explorer are two such programs.   398

Project management   Use of software to produce charts (such as Gantt charts) that schedule tasks and resources that are dependent on each other.   324

Project Management Institute (PMI)   International organization focused on disseminating best practices in project management.   532

Project management professional (PMP)   Certification awarded by the Project Management Institute to IT professionals who meet the organization's standards of practice and pass an examination.   532

Protocol   A standardized means for coordinating an activity between two or more entities.   116, 396, 398

Protocol architecture   See *Layered protocols*.   397

Prototype   A mock-up of an aspect of a new system; it could be a mock-up of a form, report, query, or other element of the user interface.   522, 546

Public IP address   An IP address used on the Internet. Such IP addresses are assigned to major institutions in blocks by the Internet Corporation for Assigned Names and Numbers (ICANN). Each IP address is unique across all computers on the Internet.   401

Public key/private key   A special version of asymmetric encryption that is popular on the Internet. With this method, each site has a public key for encoding messages and a private key for decoding them.   128

Public switched data network (PSDN)   A WAN connection alternative. A network of computers and leased lines is developed and maintained by a vendor that leases time on the network to other organizations.   125

Pull manufacturing process   A manufacturing process whereby products are pulled through manufacturing by demand. Items are manufactured in response to signals from customers or other production processes that products or components are needed.

Pull report   A report that the user must request. To obtain a pull report, a user goes to a Web portal or digital dashboard and clicks a link or button to cause the reporting system to produce and deliver the report.   497

Push manufacturing process   A plan for producing products whereby the company analyzes past sales levels, makes estimates of future sales, and creates a master production schedule. Products are produced according to that schedule and pushed into sales (and customers).   427

Push report   Reports sent to users according to a preset schedule. Users receive the report without any activity on their part.   497

Query   A request for data from a database.   103

Query report   Report that is prepared in response to data entered by users.   495

R score   In RFM analysis, a number rating that indicates in which fifth a customer ranks in terms of *most recent* order.   484

Radio frequency identification tags (RFIDs)   A computer chip that transmits data about the container or product to which it is attached. RFID data include not just product numbers, but also data about where the product was made, what the components are, special handling requirements, and, for perishable products, when the contents will expire. RFIDs facilitate inventory tracking by signaling their presence to scanners as they are moved throughout the manufacturing facility.   163

RAM memory   Stands for *random access memory*, which is main memory consisting of cells that hold data or instructions. Each cell has an address that the CPU uses to read or write data. Memory locations can be read or written in any order, hence the term *random access*. RAM memory is almost always volatile.   71

Rapid application development (RAD)   A type of application development pioneered by James Martin. The basic idea is to break up the design and implementation phases of the SDLC into smaller chunks and to design and implement those chunks using as much computer assistance as possible.   545

Records   Also called *rows*, groups of columns in a database table.   96

Recruiting information systems   Human resources information systems that maintain data on job postings, résumé processing, and hiring.   428

Reference Model for Open Systems Interconnection (OSI)   A protocol architecture created by ISO that has seven layers. Portions of the OSI model are incorporated into the TCP/IP–OSI hybrid architecture that is used on the Internet and most internets.   397

Regression analysis   A type of supervised data mining that estimates the values of parameters in a linear equation. Used to determine the relative influence of variables on an outcome and also to predict future values of that outcome.   206

Relation   The more formal name for a database table.   97

Relational database Database that carries its data in the form of tables and that represents relationships using foreign keys. 97

Relationship An association among entities or entity instances in an E-R model or an association among rows of a table in a relational database. 362

Relevant information Information that is appropriate to both the context and the subject. 26

Replicated databases Databases that contain duplicated records. Processing of such databases is complex if users want to be able to update the same items at the same time without experiencing *lost-update problems*. 140

Report A presentation of data in a structured, or meaningful context. 102

Report authoring The function of reporting systems that describes the generation of reports, by means of connecting to data sources, creating the report structure, and formatting the report. 497

Report delivery The function of reporting systems that determines that reports are pushed or pulled, in the right form, and to the right people at the right time. 499

Report management The function of reporting systems that defines who receives what reports, when, and by what means.

Report media In reporting systems, the channels by which reports are delivered, such as in paper form or electronically. 496

Report mode In reporting systems, the categorization of reports into either *push reports* or *pull reports*. 497

Report type In reporting systems, the categorization of reports into either *static* or *dynamic*. 495

Reporting system A system that creates information from disparate data sources and delivers that information to the proper users on a timely basis. 199, 493

Repository A CASE tool database that contains documents, data, prototypes, and program code for the software or system under development. 547

Requirements The characteristics of an information system; one of the critical drivers in large-scale IS development, which typically involves trade-offs with cost and time. 530

Requirements analysis phase The second phase in the SDLC, in which developers conduct user interviews, evaluate existing systems, determine new forms/reports/queries, identify new features and functions, including security, and create the data model. 243f

Requirements creep The process in which users agree to one set of requirements, and then add more over time. 540

Resources Items of value, such as inventory or funds, that are part of a business process. 24

Return on investment (ROI) A technique used to evaluate the cost of an IT project; a percentage rate, calculated as the net gain (benefits minus cost of the investment) divided by the cost of the investment. 574

Review step The final step in the decision-making process, in which decision makers evaluate results of their decision, and if necessary, repeat the process to correct or adapt the decision. 332

RFM analysis A way of analyzing and ranking customers according to the recency, frequency, and monetary value of their purchases. 484

Risk The likelihood of an adverse occurrence. 581

Root servers Special computers that are distributed around the world that maintain a list of IP addresses of servers that resolve each type of top-level domain. 407

Rotational delay On a disk, the time it takes the data to rotate under the read/write head. The faster the disk spins, the shorter the rotational delay. 348

Router A special-purpose computer that moves network traffic from one node on a network to another. 124

Routing table A table of data used by a router to determine where to send a packet that it receives. 404

Rows Also called *records*, groups of columns in a database table. 96

Safeguard Any action, device, procedure, technique, or other measure that reduces a system's vulnerability to a threat. 581

SAP R/3 A software product licensed by German company SAP that integrates business activities into *inherent processes* across an organization. 440

Sarbanes-Oxley Act Law passed by the U.S. Congress in 2002 that governs the reporting requirements of publicly held companies. Among other things, it strengthened requirements for internal controls and management's responsibility for accurate financial reporting. 164

Schedule feasibility One of four dimensions of feasibility. 240

Scope In the discipline of project management, the characteristics needed to be built into an IS; same as the term *requirements*. 530

Seats A measure of a certain number of users of a software product by a company, for licensing purposes. 353

Secure Socket Layer (SSL) A protocol that uses both asymmetric and symmetric encryption. SSL is a protocol layer that works between Levels 4 (transport) and 5 (application) of the TCP–OSI protocol architecture. When SSL is in use, the browser address will begin with https://. The most recent version of SSl is called TLS. 128, 585

Security policy Management's policy for computer security, consisting of a general statement of the organization's security program, issue-specific policy, and system-specific policy. 580

Security threat A problem with the security of an information or the data therein, caused by human error, malicious activity, or natural disasters. 274

Seek time On a disk, the time it takes the read/write arm to position the head over the correct circle. Seek time is determined by the make and model of the disk device. 349

Segments The containers that a TCP uses to carry messages. The TCP program places identifying data at the front and end of each segment that are akin to the To and From addresses that you would put on a letter for the postal mail. 398

Semantic security Concerns the unintended release of protected information through the release of a combination of reports or documents that are independently not protected. 499a

Separation of duties and authorities An internal control that requires that different people be responsible for different portions of activities involving receipt and disbursement of a company's funds. 164

Server A computer that provides some type of service, such as hosting a database, running a blog, publishing a Web site, or selling goods. Server computers are faster, larger, and more powerful than client computers. 75

Server farm A large collection of server computers that coordinates the activities of the servers, usually for commercial purposes. 75

Server tier In the three-tier architecture, the tier that consists of computers that run Web servers to generate Web pages and other data in response to requests from browsers. Web servers also process application programs. 458

Service description With Web services, an XML file that details what programs exist on another computer and how to communicate with those programs. 479

Service pack A large group of fixes that solve low-priority software problems. Users apply service packs in much the same way that they apply patches, except that service packs typically involve fixes to hundreds or thousands of problems. 248

Simple Mail Transfer Protocol (SMTP) A Layer-5 architecture used to send email. Normally used in conjunction with other Layer-5 protocols (POP3, IMAP) for receiving email. 398, 456

Site license A license purchased by an organization to equip all the computers on a site with certain software. 352

Smart card A plastic card similar to a credit card that has a microchip. The microchip, which holds much more data than a magnetic strip, is loaded with identifying data. Normally requires a PIN. 280

Sniffing A technique for intercepting computer communications. With wired networks, sniffing requires a physical connection to the network. With wireless networks, no such connection is required. 275

Software Instructions for computers. One of the five fundamental components of an information system. 6

SOHO (small office, home office) An acronym for small office/home office. 413

Special function cards Cards that can be added to the computer to augment the computer's basic capabilities. 71

Speed The dollar-value rate at which goods are exchanged in a given period of time within a supply chain. 469

Spoofing When someone pretends to be someone else with the intent of obtaining unauthorized data. If you pretend to be your professor, you are spoofing your professor. 275

Spyware Programs installed on the user's computer without the user's knowledge or permission that reside in the background and, unknown to the user, observe the user's actions and keystrokes, modify computer activity, and report the user's activities to sponsoring organizations. Malicious spyware captures keystrokes to obtain user names, passwords, account numbers, and other sensitive information. Other spyware is used for marketing analyses, observing what users do, Web sites visited, products examined and purchased, and so forth. 281

SQL Server A popular enterprise-class DBMS product from Microsoft. 99

Static report Report that is prepared once from the underlying data and that does not change. A report of the past year's sales, for example, is a static report. 495

Steganography The hiding of messages by encoding them in innocent-looking digital files. 597

Storage hardware Hardware that saves data and programs. Magnetic disk is by far the most common storage device, although optical disks, such as CDs and DVDs, also are popular. 71

Strangle-and-cram A marketing strategy that involves a vendor stopping its support for a software product, thus forcing users to purchase a new product. 354

Strategic decision Decision that concerns broader-scope, organizational issues. 329

Strong password A password with the following characteristics: seven or more characters; does not contain the user's user name, real name, or company name; does not contain a complete dictionary word, in any language; is different from the user's previous passwords; and contains both upper- and lowercase letters, numbers, and special characters. 13

Structured decision A type of decision for which there is a formalized and accepted method for making the decision. 330

Structured decision process A decision process that follows a known path, which can be readily documented. 508

Structured Query Language (SQL) An international standard language for processing database data. 100

Supervised data mining A form of data mining in which data miners develop a model prior to the analysis and apply statistical techniques to data to estimate values of the parameters of the model. 206

Supplier relationship management (SRM) A business process for managing all contacts between an organization and its suppliers. 468

Supply chain A network of organizations and facilities that transforms raw materials into products delivered to customers. 463

Supply chain profitability The difference between the sum of the revenue generated by the supply chain and the sum of the costs that all organizations in the supply chain incur to obtain that revenue. 466

Supply chain management (SCM) system An IS that integrates the primary inbound logistics business activity. 183

Support In market-basket terminology, the probability that two items will be purchased together. 485

Support activities In Porter's value chain model, the activities that contribute indirectly to value creation—procurement, technology, human resources, and the firm's infrastructure. 40

Switch A special-purpose computer that receives and transmits data across a network. 117, 400

Switch table A table of data used by switch to determine where to send frames that it receives. 403

Symmetric encryption An encryption method whereby the same key is used to encode and to decode the message. 128, 585

Symmetrical digital subscriber lines (SDSL) DSL lines that have the same upload and download speeds. 123

Synthesis Constructing a larger entity out of constituent parts, as a way of producing information; contrasts with *analysis.* 508

System A group of components that interact to achieve some purpose. 6

System definition phase The first phase in the SDLC, in which developers, with the help of eventual users, define the new system's goals and scope, assess its feasibility, form a project team, and plan the project. 240

System conversion The process of *converting* business activity from the old system to the new. 246

Systems analysis and design The process of creating and maintaining information systems. It is sometimes called systems development. 234

Systems analysts IS professionals who understand both business and technology. They are active throughout the systems development process and play a key role in moving the project from conception to conversion and, ultimately, maintenance. Systems analysts integrate the work of the programmers, testers, and users. 241

Systems development The process of creating and maintaining information systems. It is sometimes called *systems analysis and design.* 234

Systems development life cycle (SDLC) The classical process used to develop information systems. These basic tasks of systems development are combined into the following phases: system definition, requirements analysis, component design, implementation, and system maintenance (fix or enhance). 238

Table Also called a *file*, a group of similar rows or records in a database. 96

Tag In markup languages such as HTML and XML, notation used to define a data element for display or other purposes. 456

Tangible benefit A benefit of an IS that can be measured as a dollar value. 264

TCP/IP–OSI architecture A protocol architecture having five layers that evolved as a hybrid of the TCP/IP and the OSI architecture. This architecture is used on the Internet and on most internets. 397

Team portal A Web site that publishes information about the team's activities. 318

Technical feasibility One of four dimensions of feasibility. 240

Technical safeguards Safeguards that involve the hardware and software components of an information system. 279

Terabyte (TB) 1,024GB. 73

Test plan Groups of sequences of actions that users will take when using the new system. 246

Text mining Data-mining technique that searches large bodies of documents for keywords and keyword patterns; commonly used in counterterrorism intelligence. 513

Thick client A software application that requires programs other than just the browser on a user's computer—that is, that requires code on both a client and server computers. 80

Thick-client e-commerce Interorganizational processing in which software, in addition to the browser, be installed on the client computer; sometimes such software poses a security risk. 185

Thin client A software application that requires nothing more than a browser and can be run on only the user's computer. 80

Thin-client e-commerce Interorganizational processing in which the client computer needs only a browser to participate. 185

Three-tier architecture Architecture used by most e-commerce server applications. The tiers refer to three different classes of computers. The user tier consists of users' computers that have browsers that request and process Web pages. The server tier consists of computers that run Web servers and in the process generate Web pages and other data in response to requests from browsers. Web servers also process application programs. The third tier is the database tier, which runs the DBMS that processes the database. 458

Time The duration from start to finish to develop an IS; one of the critical drivers in large-scale IS development, which typically involves trade-offs with cost and requirements. 530

Time value of money The idea that money received today is not the same as money received at some time in the future because of the interest rate the sum could be earning if invested today. 574

Timely information Information that is produced in time for its intended use. 25

Top-level domain (TLD) The last letters in any domain name. For example, in the domain name www.icann.org the top-level domain is *.org*. Similarly, in the domain name www.ibm.com, *.com* is the top-level domain. For non-U.S. domain names, the top-level domain is often a two-letter abbreviation for the country in which the service resides. 407

Total cost of ownership (TCO) A technique used to evaluate the cost of an IS, measured as the sum of all the costs of the system, for the life of the system. 572

Trade-off A decision that must be made to favor one thing over another; in project development, a company might choose a trade-off of cost over scope. 530

Transaction processing system (TPS) An information system that supports operational decision making. 329

Transmission Control Program (TCP) TCP operates at Layer 4 of the TCP/IP–OSI architecture. TCP is used in two ways: as the name of a Layer 4 *protocol* and as part of the name of the TCP/IP–OSI protocol architecture. The architecture gets its name because it usually includes the TCP protocol. TCP receives messages from Layer-5 protocols (like http) and breaks those messages up into segments that it sends to a Layer-3 protocol (like IP).   398

Transport Layer Security (TLS)   A protocol, using both asymmetric and symmetric encryption, that works between Levels 4 (transport) and 5 (application) of the TCP–OSI protocol architecture. TLS is the new name for a later version of SSL.   128, 585

Treasury management information systems   Accounting information systems that help manage retained earnings, dividend payments, and long-term financing.   430

Trojan horse   Virus that masquerades as a useful program or file. The name refers to the gigantic mock-up of a horse that was filled with soldiers and moved into Troy during the Peloponnesian Wars. A typical Trojan horse appears to be a computer game, an MP3 music file, or some other useful, innocuous program.   84, 185

True party   The authentic sender of a digital message, which digital signatures and digital certificates seek to verify.   588

Tuning   Adjusting information systems from time to time to changes in the workload.   260

Tunnel   A virtual, private pathway over a public or shared network from the VPN client to the VPN server.   130

Uncertainty   Those things we don't know that we don't know.   575, 581

Unified Modeling Language (UML)   A series of diagramming techniques that facilitates OOP development. UML has dozens of different diagrams for all phases of system development. UML does not require or promote any particular development process.   361, 550

Unified process (UP)   A methodology designed for use with the Unified Modeling Language (UML) that uses use cases that describe the application of a new system.   550

Uniform resource locator (URL)   A document's address on the Web. URLs begin on the right with a top level domain, and, moving left, include a domain name and then are followed by optional data that locates a document within that domain.   407

Unix   An operating system developed at Bell Labs in the 1970s. It has been the workhorse of the scientific and engineering communities since then.   78

Unshielded twisted pair (UTP) cable   A type of cable used to connect the computers, printers, switches, and other devices on a LAN. A UTP cable has four pairs of twisted wire. A device called an RJ-45 connector is used to connect the UTP cable into NIC devices.   117

Unstructured decision   A type of decision for which there is no agreed-on decision-making method.   330

Unstructured decision process   A decision process that evolves as each step in the decision process is taken.   509

Unsupervised data mining   A form of data mining whereby the analysts do not create a model or hypothesis before running the analysis. Instead, they apply the data-mining technique to the data and observe the results. With this method, analysts create hypotheses after the analysis to explain the patterns found.   206

Upgrade   A license offered by software vendors in the initial purchase of a product that allows users to obtain an updated version of the product for far less than the price of a new copy.   352

Use case   A description of an application of a new system that is used with the Unified Modeling Language (UML) and the Unified Process (UP).   550

User tier   In the three-tier architecture, the tier that consists of computers that have browsers that request and process Web pages.   458

Usurpation   Occurs when unauthorized programs invade a computer system and replace legitimate programs. Such unauthorized programs typically shut down the legitimate system and substitute their own processing.   277

Value chain   A network of value-creating activities.   40

Version management   Use of software to control configuration of documents, designs, and other electronic versions of products.   322

Vertical-market application   Software that serves the needs of a specific industry. Examples of such programs are those used by dental offices to schedule appointments and bill patients, those used by auto mechanics to keep track of customer data and customers' automobile repairs, and those used by parts warehouses to track inventory, purchases, and sales.   79

Video conferencing   Technology that combines a conference call with video cameras.   320

Virtual organization   An organization that exists by means of electronic networks and service agreements, but that does not exist in a three-dimensional, bricks-and-mortar form.   188

Virtual private network (VPN)   A WAN connection alternative that uses the Internet or a private internet to create the appearance of private point-to-point connections. In the IT world, the term *virtual* means something that appears to exist that does not exist in fact. Here, a VPN uses the public Internet to create the appearance of a private connection.   130

Virtual team   A team in which the team members work in different geographic locations but collaborate by means of information systems that support communication.   321

Visual development tools   Tools used in RAD projects to improve developer productivity. An example is Microsoft's Visual Studio.Net.   549

Voice-over IP (VOIP)   A technology that provides telephone communication over the Internet.   319

Volatile memory   Data that will be lost when the computer or device is not powered.   74

Vulnerability   An opening or a weakness in a security system. Some vulnerabilities exist because there are no safeguards or because the existing safeguards are ineffective.   581

Waterfall   The fiction that one phase of the SDLC can be completed in its entirety and the project can progress, without any backtracking, to the next phase of the SDLC. Projects seldom are that simple; backtracking is normally required.   249

Web farm   A facility that runs multiple Web servers. Work is distributed among the computers in a Web farm so as to maximize throughput.   458

Web pages   Documents encoded in HTML that are created, transmitted, and consumed using the World Wide Web.   456

Web server   A program that processes the HTTP protocol and transmits Web pages on demand. Web servers also process application programs.   457

Web storefront   In e-commerce, a Web-based application that enables customers to enter and manage their orders.   451

Webcast   A broadcast over the Internet of the proceedings of, typically, a large conference or meeting, such as a company's annual meeting of stockholders.   320

WebEx   A moderated conference call in which attendees dial in for audio on a conference-call line and point their browsers to a Web site controlled by the moderator; all can then see the same screen display.   320

Web-log   See *Blog*.   3

Wide area network (WANs)   A network that connects computers located at different geographic locations.   116

Wiki   A common-knowledge base maintained by its users; processed on Web sites that allow users to add, remove, and edit content.   318

Windows   An operating system designed and sold by Microsoft. It is the most widely used operating system.   77

Wired Equivalent Privacy (WEP)   A wireless security standard developed by the IEEE 802.11 committee that was insufficiently tested before it was deployed in communications equipment. It has serious flaws.   416, 590

Wireless NIC (WNIC)   Devices that enable wireless networks by communicating with wireless access points. Such devices can be cards that slide into the PCMA slot or they

can be built-in, onboard devices. WNICs operate according to the 802.11 protocol.   119

Work breakdown structure (WBS)   A hierarchy of the tasks required to complete a project; for a large project, it might involve hundreds or thousands of tasks.   534

Workflow control   Use of software and IS to monitor the execution of a work team's processes; ensures that actions are taken at appropriate times and prohibits the skipping of steps or tasks.   323

World Wide Web Consortium (W3C)   A body that sponsors the development and dissemination of Web standards.   476–477

Worm   A virus that propagates itself using the Internet or some other computer network. Worm code is written specifically to infect another computer as quickly as possible.   84

Worth-its-cost information   When an appropriate relationship exists between the cost of information and its value.   26

Wi-Fi Protected Access (WPA and WPA2)   An improved wireless security standard developed by the IEEE 802.11 committee to fix the flaws of the Wired Equivalent Privacy (WEP) standard. Only newer wireless hardware uses this technique.   416, 590

WPA2   An improved version of WPA.   590

XML schema   An XML document that specifies the structure of other XML documents. An XML schema is metadata for other XML documents. For example, a SalesOrder XML schema specifies the structure of SalesOrder documents.   477

XML Web services   Sometimes called *Web services*; a set of standards that facilitate distributed computing using Internet technology. The goal of Web services is to provide a standardized way for programs to access one another remotely, without the need to develop proprietary solutions.   479

INDEX

Page numbers followed by f denote figures.